Early Praise for *Quantum Computing*

You'll remember shaking your head when someone tries to win a metaphysical argument with recourse to quantum physics. I call it the "countdown to quantum." While you won't win those arguments with this book, you'll learn about what quantum computing really consists of and that it's not the infinite speed classical computer of popular opinion. I know nothing of the technical challenges of building quantum hardware, but there will be a corresponding challenge finding programmers competent in these skills. This book excels at teaching the necessary concepts.

➤ **Nigel Lowry**
Director, Lemmata

Truly scintillating. Professor Mehta's *Quantum Computing* opened my eyes to a beautiful new world of practical probabilistic programming.

➤ **Ross Henderson**
CEO, CAREM, a geospatial epidemiology company

Quantum computing has a reputation for being tricky and often tangled up in complex maths; even its basic building blocks can run counter to our everyday understanding of the world. This book takes a different approach to describing quantum phenomena that's much easier to initially grasp and then goes into how we can use it to build programs, giving us an abstraction that is actually useful back in the real world. Starting from the basics of quantum states and working up to building real programs using quantum computers, this book covers it all. It's even got some maths if you miss that.

➤ **Tim Nugent**
Owner, Lonely.Coffee

No other book teaches the fundamentals so clearly. I can't imagine beginning quantum programming without this book.

➤ **Nick Watts**
Software Engineer, CAS, a division of the American Chemical Society

Quantum Computing

Program Next-Gen Computers for Hard, Real-World Applications

Nihal Mehta, Ph.D.

The Pragmatic Bookshelf

Raleigh, North Carolina

Many of the designations used by manufacturers and sellers to distinguish their products are claimed as trademarks. Where those designations appear in this book, and The Pragmatic Programmers, LLC was aware of a trademark claim, the designations have been printed in initial capital letters or in all capitals. The Pragmatic Starter Kit, The Pragmatic Programmer, Pragmatic Programming, Pragmatic Bookshelf, PragProg and the linking *g* device are trademarks of The Pragmatic Programmers, LLC.

Every precaution was taken in the preparation of this book. However, the publisher assumes no responsibility for errors or omissions, or for damages that may result from the use of information (including program listings) contained herein.

Our Pragmatic books, screencasts, and audio books can help you and your team create better software and have more fun. Visit us at *https://pragprog.com*.

The team that produced this book includes:

Publisher: Andy Hunt
VP of Operations: Janet Furlow
Executive Editor: Dave Rankin
Development Editor: Brian MacDonald
Copy Editor: L. Sakhi MacMillan
Indexing: Potomac Indexing, LLC
Layout: Gilson Graphics

For sales, volume licensing, and support, please contact *support@pragprog.com*.

For international rights, please contact *rights@pragprog.com*.

ISBN-13: 978-1-68050-720-1
Book version: P1.0—August 2020

Contents

Preface

Richard Feynman, a Nobel Laureate, first postulated[1] a computer rooted in the laws of quantum mechanics that govern the behavior of subatomic particles such as muons, gluons, quarks, and bosons. It's a theory that strains credulity at every turn—its bizarre concepts jar against everyday experience. A long line of distinguished quantum physicists from Niels Bohr to Albert Einstein and Richard Feynman have been exasperated by the very theory they helped create. Yet, surprisingly, the theory has correctly predicted every phenomenon that physicists have thrown at it. These same principles now have their sights trained on digital computing. For the first time since Eniac, the modern computer built at the University of Pennsylvania in 1946, the underlying fabric of computing is threatened: bits, with their rigid 0 and 1 states, are replaced with *fluid* units that seemingly exist in both states simultaneously, giving us unprecedented ways to tackle challenging computational tasks. Quantum mechanics is the most spectacular theory ever put forth, and we are going to latch onto its coattails to learn about quantum computing and how it's challenging the notions of conventional computing.

I first got interested in quantum computing years ago when I was exploring ways to squeeze better performance from the mathematical-based computer models that I was tasked with building for some of the world's largest organizations. Time and again, though the computer models would return acceptable solutions, I couldn't get them to do even better. It's like the models hit a wall. Quantum mechanical concepts such as tunneling seemed to offer a way to punch through the barrier. But quantum mechanics is strange, and it was far from clear how to model computational tasks using subatomic particles. I created "paper" models to help make sense of the counter-intuitive quantum mechanics concepts. But, with no real quantum hardware to validate the models, they remained untested ideas that I filed away.

---

1. https://link.springer.com/article/10.1007/BF02650179

Over the years, there's been much research[2] on testing out small pieces of quantum machinery, but there was no integrated computer on which one could write any meaningful code. All this changed in 2017 when IBM released a quantum computer which, incredibly, was freely available to one and all—quantum computing was no longer the sole province of high-octane research laboratories. Armed with an internet connection, anyone could get their hands on some über-cool computer technology. I was finally able to test and refine my "paper" models on an actual quantum computer.

But writing a book on quantum computing poses a singular challenge of weaving a coherent tale from two distinct threads: its origins in quantum mechanics and its relationship with computer science. As a result, the tools of one are used to explain the other—which, for computer science, boils down to treating the inherent random nature of quantum computing as a branch of probability theory. Neither of these approaches is satisfactory. It takes a fair amount of effort, for example, to build the intuition for probabilistic algorithms, and at the same time, quantum mechanics is alien to many computer professionals.

I, however, believe that there's a third aspect that's overlooked: a conceptual bridge that straddles both quantum mechanics and computer science. I introduce a way to model quantum phenomena based on quantum mechanical principles that intersects computer science precepts and gives a way to master the big ideas of quantum computing. This will help you better appreciate why it's garnering attention and why computer scientists and corporations think it's the next big bet and are willing to spend big dollars. Mathematics underpins much of quantum mechanics and is essential in any investigation of quantum computing. But, with this model, I promise to not use mathematics as a refuge to get to the bottom of thorny topics. I'll factor the fundamental concepts of quantum mechanics on the computer science base layer in a natural and intuitive way that neatly brings in the quantum mechanical concepts without baffling you. You'll begin to see these models from Chapter 2, Goodbye Mr. Bits—From Classical to Quantum Bits, on page 19 onward.

Is This Book for Me?

This book is for developers new to quantum programming as well as those who may have read and heard about this technology and are looking for a quick way to get started. This book will also be helpful to students who are studying quantum computing at university. They'll find that the topics covered in this book complement their classroom lectures.

---

2.   https://en.wikipedia.org/wiki/Timeline_of_quantum_computing

I don't expect you to have any background or previous exposure to quantum mechanics or quantum programming. I'll introduce you to the relevant concepts and help you gain the necessary dexterity. But I do expect that you know how to program using any one of the multitude of high-level languages available today, such as C#, Java, JavaScript, Objective-C, Python, and so on. Although you don't need to know assembly language programming, you should at least be familiar with the notion of Boolean gates and logical operations, and the fundamentals of complex numbers, basic trigonometry, and vector and matrix operations, such as multiplying them and finding their inverses. (See Appendix 1, Mathematical Review, on page 391, to brush up on these subjects.) You'll need to know these topics to apply advanced quantum effects in your programs from Chapter 6, Designer Genes—Custom Quantum States, on page 141, onward.

After reading this book, you'll learn the following:

Introducing quantum effects in your programs
> You'll understand the value that quantum mechanics can bring to solving computational tasks over that of classical machines. You'll learn a new mindset to manipulate bits using quantum principles.

Apply quantum computing to real world problems
> You'll design quantum algorithms to solve real world problems. One of the major themes of this book is to develop your intuition so that you properly apply quantum concepts for your own challenging computational tasks.

Discern which problems are suitable for quantum computers
> Not all applications are suited for quantum computers. You'll learn to identify the problems that are best suited for quantum computers and which ones are better solved using conventional computers.

Interface with a quantum computer from within your application
> By invoking a quantum computer from within your own program, you can execute the heavy-lifting portion of your code on a quantum computer and transparently return results back to your application.

How Will This Book Give Me What I Want?

Quantum mechanics can be an imposing hurdle to get over before becoming proficient in quantum computing. Yet a systematic exploration of the fundamental ideas can make this subject engaging. We take a hands-on-first approach in this book by emphasizing writing programs on an actual quantum computer so that you get a concrete handle on the quantum mechanical concepts.

I've organized the material using familiar ideas from classical computers in *Goodbye Mr. Bits—From Classical to Quantum Bits* through *Beam Me Up, Scotty—Quantum Tagging and Entangling*. You'll go to the heart of quantum programming and get a taste for how quantum effects are reshaping computing. In subsequent chapters, you'll learn to tailor quantum phenomena in your own quantum programs.

- We begin in Chapter 1, Hello Quantum, on page 1, by demonstrating how quantum computing is trespassing on the traditional turf of conventional computing. Learning quantum programming without using a motivating application is like trying to explore a new city by riding in the subway. The subway, like programming syntax, can take you from one stop to another, but you have to step out to experience the city's sights and culture. Thus, you'll set up and run a quantum program on a standard scheduling problem and see for yourself how a quantum computer solves it.

- The traditional way of analyzing computers with 0 and 1 bits seems to not apply with quantum computing. In Chapter 2, Goodbye Mr. Bits—From Classical to Quantum Bits, on page 19, you'll be introduced to a way to think about quantum computing using the standard tools of classical computing. You'll learn about quantum bits and compare and contrast them with the binary bits of conventional computing. You'll see that quantum bits exist in a blended state of the two binary bits. You'll also learn the *Qubelets Model*, a new way to think about quantum programming that computer professionals will find familiar. Much like Google's Street View that lets you explore a city from your desk, the model you'll get to work with rapidly gets to the heart of quantum computing using intuitive concepts. These ideas animate the subsequent quantum mechanical principles used for computation in the later chapters.

- In Chapter 3, Elementary, My Dear Watson—Quantum Logic, on page 41, you'll work with quantum gates that are largely similar to their classical counterparts. These gates build the scaffolding for the parts where the quantum mechanical effects take place in your program. By themselves, the quantum logic gates don't offer any inherent advantages over their classical counterparts. You can build quantum programs with these gates, but your code won't perform better than that designed to work on classical computers.

- In Chapter 4, All Together Now—Quantum Superposition, on page 77, and Chapter 5, Beam Me Up, Scotty—Quantum Tagging and Entangling, on page 107, you'll learn why quantum computing has the potential to corner the market for solving hard computational problems. These quantum mechanical concepts constitute the core of quantum computing applications. You'll learn about quantum gates that allow you to nudge quantum bits around in ways you can't with classical computers.

Quantum computing isn't fantasy but is solidly grounded in reality. To this end, we'll show that the Qubelets Model explains the quantum mechanical nature of a well-known set of physics experiments and illustrate its connections with quantum programming. You'll be introduced to the Mega-Qubit on page 91—a framework that'll help you understand and work with quantum superposition, a quantum phenomenon that manages all possible solutions at once.

- In Chapter 6, Designer Genes—Custom Quantum States, on page 141, Chapter 7, Small Step for Man—Single Qubit Programs, on page 173, and Chapter 8, Giant Leap for Mankind—Multi-Qubit Programs, on page 227, you'll learn to design quantum algorithms where you can precisely control quantum bits to suit your purpose. Understanding these concepts is crucial to writing quantum programs that work reliably.

  There's a handy list of gates, which groups the different ways to introduce quantum effects when designing your quantum algorithms for your own problems.

- In Chapter 9, Alice in Quantumland—Quantum Cryptography, on page 279, and Chapter 10, Quantum Search, on page 295, you'll learn how the core quantum concepts of *entanglement* and *superposition* are used in real-world applications. You'll learn how quantum computing encrypts virtually break-proof messages and also about algorithms that sweep through the potential solutions of hard-to-solve computational tasks rapidly.

- While learning quantum computing, it's easy to forget its origin in quantum mechanics and the oddball principles that govern the natural world around us. So if you're interested to know more about how quantum computing is strongly intertwined with quantum mechanics, see Appendix 3, Quantum Mechanics with Qubelets, on page 415, to get a peek at the deep relationship between them.

Most chapters have programming exercises and problems that reinforce concepts you've learned in the chapter and help you become familiar with this new technology. All exercises and problems have solutions. So you'll find them instructive even if you glance through them.

If You Want Just the Basics

If you'd like to learn just the basic ideas of quantum computing, largely avoiding complex numbers and trigonometry, read the following:

- Chapter 1, Hello Quantum, on page 1, through Chapter 5, Beam Me Up, Scotty—Quantum Tagging and Entangling, on page 107.

- Quantum States and Probabilities, on page 142, in Chapter 6, Designer Genes—Custom Quantum States, on page 141.

- Quantum States as Vectors, on page 174, Quantum Gates as Matrices, on page 175, and Sequence of Gates as Matrix Multiplication, on page 219, in Chapter 7, Small Step for Man—Single Qubit Programs, on page 173.

- Chapter 8, Giant Leap for Mankind—Multi-Qubit Programs, on page 227, onward.

If You're Impatient

If you're in a hurry to learn about quantum effects, you can jump ahead to Chapter 4, All Together Now—Quantum Superposition, on page 77, and see how quantum computers handle all possible states of a computational problem.

If You're Really, Really Impatient

If quantum computing is gnawing at you and you're already somewhat familiar with quantum mechanics, dive straight to Chapter 6, Designer Genes—Custom Quantum States, on page 141. When using quantum computers to solve hard problems modeled with multiple qubits, you'll see that the concepts introduced in Qubelets Model, on page 20, are an alternative to using the standard Bloch sphere. You'll learn that qubelets let you visualize how qubits interact with each other and figure out where to introduce quantum effects. You'll learn how to precisely create tailor-made quantum states in your programs and then carefully fine-tune them to solve your computational problem.

What's Unique in This Book?

If you're new to quantum computing, you'll find that the material in this book is quite different from what you'll see in others. In fact, it's only in Chapter 6, Designer Genes—Custom Quantum States, on page 141, that you'll begin to see parallels with the literature.

If you're already familiar with quantum computing, you'll find a new, and hopefully more intuitive, take on standard concepts. In my mind, the following sections, in particular, stand out most:

Modeling Quantum Bits with the Qubelets Model, on page 20: Describes a way to think about quantum states as components similar to, say, analyzing a block on an inclined plane in classical physics. Specifically, we introduce the *qubelets* to model quantum states.

Multi-Qubit Superposition: The Mega-Qubit, on page 91: Getting a handle on quantum superposition using the conceptual device of the *mega-qubit.*

Intuition Behind Entanglement, on page 120: Making sense of *quantum entanglement* with qubelets and the mega-qubit.

Rotating Qubelets Through Any Angle, on page 150: Relating the standard Bloch sphere prevalent in quantum computing with the qubelets introduced in this book.

Classifying Quantum Gates, on page 202: New way to categorize quantum gates, based on how they directly affect qubits rather than on abstract rotations around the Bloch sphere.

Teleporting Mega-Qubit, on page 263: Seeing the teleporting states as a concrete concept rather than as esoteric calculations.

Tell-Your-Boss Version: The "Key" Idea, on page 281: Thinking of quantum cryptography as a way to send many messages on the same channel at the same time to confuse anyone illegally listening in.

Canceling Circuit, on page 304: Explains how to control the odds of a quantum program returning the correct result.

Online Resources

All source code for the examples in this book can be downloaded from the book's page on the Pragmatic Bookshelf's website at https://pragprog.com/book/nmquantum/quantum-computing. You'll also find an errata page at https://pragprog.com/book/nmquantum/errata.

Acknowledgments

I'm grateful that the Pragmatic Bookshelf agreed to publish this book. The current technical-books landscape is teeming with so many books that it's hard to discern any publisher's unique imprint. But, from their very earliest books, I've been struck by the winsome style of Pragmatic books. Although the credit for producing such well-written books lies with the respective authors, there seemed to be something else at play too—a secret style guide of some sort that makes every Pragmatic book a delight to read. I wanted my book to have that same secret sauce.

I struck gold with Brian MacDonald as the Development Editor. Right from the start, Brian understood the challenges of making this particular topic presentable. His comments and guidance were crucial to ensuring that I wrote the material in a way that the reader would find useful, without devolving into minutiae that is so easy to fall into with technical content. It was also Brian's suggestion to start the book with a practical example that immediately demonstrates quantum computing instead of subjecting the reader to abstract theory and relying on the reader's patience to plow through before seeing something useful. I believe that you'll enjoy the book much more as a result of this approach.

I deeply appreciate the efforts of Susan Conant, L. Sakhi MacMillan, and all the other editors at Pragmatic Bookshelf for helping shape this book. They always reviewed the manuscript promptly, and their advice raised the quality of the presentation.

I want to thank Meghan Blanchette, who was the first editor on this book. Meghan gave me, a first-time author, advice on tightening up my writing that is reflected on every page.

I also want to thank the technical reviewers and all the readers that submitted errata. Their detailed comments and feedback encouraged me that I was on the right track. The technical reviewers for this book were: Craig Castelaz, Ashish Dixit, Jan Goyvaerts, Nigel Lowry, Nick McGinness, Tim Nugent, Kim Shrier, Tibor Simic, Gianluigi Spagnuolo, Charley Stran, Stefan Turalski, Nick Watts, Boris Vasile, Mitchell Volk, and Stephen Wolff. Two readers in particular, Kaoru Hosokawa and Michael Blake, identified several errata throughout the beta release cycle.

The impetus for writing this book came when it finally dawned on me in the summer of 2018 that my daughter, Mira, would be going away to the University of Chicago in the fall and I would need something to combat the loneliness that would set in.

Come, let's shine a beam of photons on the world of computer programming and see it in a new light.

Nihal Mehta
September 2019

If you think you understand quantum mechanics, you don't understand quantum mechanics.

> *Richard P. Feynman, jointly awarded the Nobel Prize in Physics 1965 for "fundamental work in quantum electrodynamics, with deep-ploughing consequences for the physics of elementary particles"*

CHAPTER 1

Hello Quantum

Quantum computers inhabit the microscopic world of neutrinos and mesons and muons and electrons buzzing about protons and neutrons—a smorsgasbord of subatomic particles bringing with them a cornucopia of strange concepts. Literally from the tiniest aspects of computing to the way we design algorithms, quantum computing introduces a new paradigm for programming computers for mainstream applications that demand heavy number crunching, such as:

- Optimizing scanning of magnetic resonance images (MRI) in radiology.[1]
- Understanding complex molecular structures for building life-saving drugs.[2]
- Hyper-large-scale logistics and transportation-routing problems.[3]
- Auto companies[4] are betting that quantum computers will help build better batteries, route autonomous vehicles (self-driving cars), and optimize assembly lines.

The promise that quantum computing is blazing a new way to solve super-hard problems is palpable. In 2017 and 2018, at least \$450 million[5] was poured into quantum technology companies, more than four times the amount of the previous two years. Google announced [6] the results of a quantum program that blasted through calculations to produce certifiable random numbers in three minutes, twenty seconds, a task which they estimate would have taken 100,000 classical computers running the fastest known algorithms

---

1. https://blogs.microsoft.com/blog/2018/05/18/microsoft-quantum-helps-case-western-reserve-university-advance-mri-research/

2. https://www.ibm.com/blogs/research/2017/09/quantum-molecule/

3. https://blog.daimler.com/en/2018/11/07/quantum-computers-future-daimler-google-ibm-technology/

4. https://www.axios.com/quantum-computing-cars-vw-mercedes-ford-3223a464-c65a-4163-b92b-6b7761116384.html

5. https://www.nature.com/articles/d41586-019-02935-4

6. https://www.nature.com/articles/s41586-019-1666-5

roughly 10,000 years to complete. Google expects that this capability can be used in optimization applications, machine learning, and designing new materials, among others, and is currently planning on demonstrating cryptographic protocols.[7] But the true significance of this milestone is proving that quantum effects can be controlled and programmatically introduced at sufficient scales to perform computations even though it may not have any immediate utility. (You'll understand how Google made these computations in How Did Google Show Superiority of Quantum Computers over Classical Computers?, on page 352.)

Governments around the world, too, are catching on to the power of quantum computers:

- In December 2018, the United States Congress unanimously passed the National Quantum Initiative Act,[8] which has been signed into law. This law is a ten-year commitment by the United States to "accelerate the development of quantum information science and technology applications" through partnerships with universities, startups, and corporations. Further, the United States (and China) considers quantum computing a national security priority.

- China is investing $400 million to build the world's largest quantum research center, the National Laboratory for Quantum Information Science, which they claim will have the calculating power of "one million times all existing computers around the world combined."[9]

- India[10] is pouring $1.12 billion over five years into quantum technologies.

- The European Union, Australia, Japan, Switzerland, and several others[11] are investing in quantum computing.

- Russia[12] will plow $790 million over the next five years into "basic and applied quantum research."

As this technology, which *The New York Times* calls the "jazziest and most mysterious concepts in modern science,"[13] ramps up, it's a good time to clock in.

---

7.   https://www.nytimes.com/2019/10/30/opinion/google-quantum-computer-sycamore.html

8.   https://www.congress.gov/bill/115th-congress/house-bill/6227

9.   https://www.scmp.com/news/china/society/article/2110563/china-building-worlds-biggest-quantum-research-facility

10. https://www.nature.com/articles/d41586-020-00288-x

11. https://www.economist.com/technology-quarterly/2019/02/18/quantum-technology-is-beginning-to-come-into-its-own

12. https://www.nature.com/articles/d41586-019-03855-z

13. https://www.nytimes.com/2019/10/21/science/quantum-computer-physics-qubits.html

But quantum computing can be hard to learn. Even a program with a few lines can stymie experienced programmers. For example, look at these lines:

```
u3(pi/3,pi/2,-pi/2) q[0];
u3(pi/3,pi/4,-pi/2) q[0];
```

These statements look familiar, if somewhat puzzling. Although these lines look vague, they trigger quantum effects in the program. So the challenge with quantum programming stems not from mastering a new syntax but from grasping a whole different set of concepts than those in classical computing.

So it's fair to ask, Why are quantum phenomena important? How do they help solve hard computational problems? And, is it worth spending time and effort to learn this technology today?

In this book, I intend to show you how and why quantum mechanics offers a promising alternative to classical computing for hard problems and that it's not as hard to work with as you may think. To convince you that the technology is already upon us, you'll be learning quantum computing by running your programs on a real quantum computer.

But, to master quantum computing, you'll need to come up to speed with new ways of thinking of about traditional computational tasks. So, in this chapter, we'll review a scheduling problem that's typical of the kinds where quantum computing can make a big difference. We'll work with a variant whose solution is easy to verify yet allows you to see real quantum phenomena in action. You'll also get a chance to try your hand at an actual quantum program.

In the rest of the chapters, I'll introduce you to quantum phenomena useful to computing and how to trigger them in your programs. Each chapter builds on ideas described in the earlier ones. Learning different quantum effects can feel like isolated piecemeal techniques that leave you wondering about their utility. So as you learn new quantum concepts, we'll use the scheduling problem to bring these topics together in a meaningful way.

Types of Quantum Computers

A quantum computer isn't something you download off the internet or buy at a store. Quantum computers are big hulking beasts that require careful and delicate installation. They have to be cooled to temperatures close to absolute zero—that's just a few bone-chilling degrees above -273°C, if you want to be precise. Your refrigerator, by comparison, is a sauna where your quantum computer may go after a hard day at work.

Quantum Computers Are Huge and Fragile

It's not our intention to give you a rundown of the blueprints of how quantum computers are built. It's instructive, however, to get a sense of what it takes to build them.

Quantum computer hardware isn't built from sturdy silicon material that can be handled by human hands or robotic arms. Rather, it's built[14] from atoms, which are a million times thinner than human hair. In the case of the CNOT gate, a device used in quantum computers, which we talk about in Controlled NOT (CNOT) Gate, on page 47, a single Beryllium atom is first stripped of an electron to form a positive ion. This ion is then laser cooled to extremely low temperatures (much cooler than what you'd experience in Antarctica) so as to arrest its naturally swaying movement. Then, a finely tuned pulse of light plays with the remaining electrons in the Beryllium ion to cause the Controlled NOT operations. This apparatus requires precision engineering and is housed in carefully monitored facilities. It's not something that can be rigged up, say, in portable devices.

All this just so that less than a handful of atoms can be used for some of the toughest computational tasks.

Currently, there are two main types of quantum computers:

Quantum Circuit Computers
These computers are built from a network of quantum gates that take an initial guess of a solution to a computational task and transform it using quantum principles to one that solves the problem.

Adiabatic Quantum Computers
In these computers, the computational task is represented as the energy of a configuration of subatomic particles. The energy is then *annealed*, or gradually lowered, to arrive at the solution.

Neither one has computational advantage over the other. Recent research[15] shows that quantum algorithms designed for one type of hardware can be transformed to execute on the other in comparable time.

---

14. https://journals.aps.org/prl/abstract/10.1103/PhysRevLett.75.4714

15. https://physicsworld.com/a/quantum-adiabatic-and-quantum-circuit-algorithms-are-equivalent-say-physicists/

Lately, IBM has made it a cinch for the general public to get access to a quantum circuit computer with minimal set up. So, in this book, we will learn to write quantum programs for these quantum computers. As it turns out, I believe that for someone just starting out, the quantum circuit computer is easier to grasp. You will see that many concepts are a distant cousin of conventional computers and, thus, easier to digest.

Quantum Computing in Thirty Seconds

Quantum computing can seem mysterious and foreboding. But, at its core, quantum computing is driven by a few fundamental tenets. Having this bird's-eye view may give you a better sense of what's going on:

- In quantum computing the application's variables or information units are represented as subatomic particles, just as the 0 and 1 states of conventional computing. Think of these states as the two faces of a coin.

- Quantum mechanics theorizes that subatomic particles spin like tossed coins.

- Just as coins land on either the head or the tail face, the spinning subatomic particles when brought to rest also settle into one of the two, 0 or 1, states.

- Crucially, quantum computing differs from classical computing in the following aspects:

    - All the action happens when the coins are *in the air*. That is, while in the air, you influence how they spin so that they land on the faces associated with the optimal solution.

      In classical computing using probabilistic techniques, on the other hand, all the action happens *after* the coin lands.

    - You have the means to invoke quantum mechanical phenomena to *coordinate* all the tosses simultaneously. By intertwining the actions, you can influence the way they spin as a group that can't be reproduced had you operated on them individually.

      For example, with three coins, a quantum computer would simultaneously consider all eight cases shown in the figure on page 6.

In classical computing, even with parallel computers, only one bit at a time is worked on. Moreover, what you do on one bit doesn't simultaneously affect the state of another.

- It's this ability to intricately orchestrate *all* the coins in mid-flight that drives the "being in all states at once" portrayal of quantum computing and gives rise to new ways to solve complex problems.

We'll sketch this out in more detail starting from Modeling Quantum Bits with the Qubelets Model, on page 20.

Your First Quantum Program

The way to program quantum computers differs from what you would do for traditional computers. Although the quantum programming syntax borrows from today's computer languages, such as JavaScript, C#, or Python, the underlying concepts are widely divergent. Objects such as JavaScript Promises help us write organized and efficient code. But, under the hood, the machine language instructions are pretty much the same as those, say, for FORTRAN or BASIC. Quantum programming is different. The underlying hardware has fundamentally changed. So, to write code that works on these machines, we need to rethink the way we write computer programs.

Rather than introduce quantum computing on a "Hello World" program or some other contrived example, we'll jump right in and run a practical computational task on a quantum computer. This exercise will immediately show you that this technology is real.

A Scheduling Problem

We'll use a quantum computer to come up with a schedule for Las Vegas shows. This scheduling task is a simpler version of a problem discussed in Knuth's *The Art of Computer Programming [Knu11]*, Section 7.1.1. In our version, we deal with contemporary performers but have retained the timeless Las Vegas hotels.

Joe asks:
What Makes a Problem Hard?

Since the quantum equivalents of the binary bits and gates work differently in the quantum world, not every application is suitable for quantum computers. For example, quantum computers aren't used to verify whether an email address is correctly filled out in an HTML form or for transactional applications, such as putting information into a database or streaming video to a browser. Rather, quantum computers are ideally suited where a computer has to crunch through a large number of possible solutions of computational tasks.

Such a problem will allow you to see quantum effects in play and will drive home the point that quantum phenomena can fruitfully be put to use in common computational applications and not merely reserved for esoteric and highly idealized cases. The scheduling problem has several candidate solutions, as well as features that allow you to exercise many quantum principles, yet is simple enough to understand the solution space without getting overwhelmed with details.

Our job is to schedule three talk show hosts for a comedy festival over two days at three hotels. We have to slot the shows based on the hotels that each artist can perform at:

- Jimmy Kimmel performs only at Aladdin and Bellagio.
- Bill Maher performs only at Bellagio and Caesars.
- Trevor Noah performs only at Caesars and Aladdin.

For these kinds of problems, whether you write a program for a conventional computer or a quantum one, you must first express them with logical constraints. Only then can you write a program to hunt for a valid solution.

For a vast range of applications, including these types of scheduling problems, this form boils down to searching for a feasible solution to a system of Boolean logic expressions. This way of modeling applications is referred to as the *Boolean Satisfiability (SAT)*[16] problem in computer science. Following Knuth, we go through this analysis in the next section.

Modeling Boolean Logic Expressions

 Setting up the Boolean logic expressions for computational problems is more art than science. For many problems, there are several acceptable ways to model them. Knuth's book is a great resource to get an overall flavor on this way of modeling.

---

16. https://en.wikipedia.org/wiki/Boolean_satisfiability_problem

Writing a System of Boolean Logic Expressions

To write a quantum program for this scheduling problem, we model it using a system of Boolean logic expressions. Start by defining three Boolean variables k,m,n as follows:

- k means that Jimmy Kimmel does Bellagio on Day 1 and Aladdin on Day 2; k-bar or $\overline{k}$ means that Kimmel does them in opposite order: Aladdin on Day 1 and Bellagio on Day 2.

- m means that Bill Maher does Bellagio on Day 1 and Caesars on Day 2; m-bar or $\overline{m}$ means that Maher does them in opposite order: Caesars on Day 1 and Bellagio on Day 2.

- n means that Trevor Noah does Aladdin on Day 1 and Caesars on Day 2; n-bar or $\overline{n}$ means that Noah does them in opposite order: Caesars on Day 1 and Aladdin on Day 2.

Next, we set up Boolean logic expressions that ensure that no two artists are slated at the same hotel on the same day—the *conflict constraints*. For example, on Day 1 at Aladdin, Kimmel and Noah cannot perform at the same time. This restriction results in the following logic expression:

- Aladdin on Day 1: $\neg\,(\overline{k} \wedge n) = k \vee \overline{n}$

The symbol $\wedge$ stands for the *Logical AND*, $\vee$ for *Logical OR*, and $\neg$ is *Logical NOT*.

Thus, the left-hand side of the first relation, for example, states that Kimmel performing at Aladdin on Day 1 ($\overline{k}$), *and* Noah at Aladdin on Day 1 (n), expressed as $(\overline{k} \wedge n)$, cannot be true at the same time: $\neg\,(\overline{k} \wedge n)$. That is, both can't perform at Aladdin on the same day. The right-hand side is its simplification via De Morgan's rule (see Boolean Logic Expressions, on page 393).

Similarly, we can define the logic expressions for the other slots:

- Aladdin on Day 2: $\neg\,(k \wedge \overline{n}) = \overline{k} \vee n$
- Bellagio on Day 1: $\neg\,(k \wedge m) = \overline{k} \vee \overline{m}$
- Bellagio on Day 2: $\neg\,(\overline{k} \wedge \overline{m}) = k \vee m$
- Caesars on Day 1: $\neg\,(\overline{m} \wedge \overline{n}) = m \vee n$
- Caesars on Day 2: $\neg\,(m \wedge n) = \overline{m} \vee \overline{n}$

For a valid schedule, all these logic expressions must be true. That is,

$$(k \lor \overline{n}) \land (\overline{k} \lor n) \land (\overline{k} \lor \overline{m}) \land (k \lor m) \land (m \lor n) \land (\overline{m} \lor \overline{n}) = 1$$

In general, unless there are specialized techniques for a specific class of Boolean logic expressions, the only way to find a valid set of Boolean variables is go through each combination one at a time.

Single Letter Variables

 Although you'll prefer using more suggestive variable names in your programs, I'll use single-letter variables so that they're easier to relate back to the Boolean logic expressions.

In subsequent chapters, you'll learn how quantum mechanical principles come together to get a feasible schedule for the performers at the Vegas hotels by only scanning a fraction of the combinations.

In the next section, you'll get a rapid-fire overview of how this search is done on a quantum computer. We'll explain in detail in subsequent chapters.

Running on a Quantum Computer

I selected the IBM Q Experience,[17] a cloud service to run quantum computers, for all the code examples in this book because it requires minimal setup, making it ideal to learn this new technology—there are no installation or connectivity battles to overcome before you can use a quantum computer. All you need is a web browser and an internet connection. You can also use the material in this book with Microsoft's or Amazon's quantum computer—it's much the same as what you'll see here. We're just using the IBM computer because we have to pick one.

To write and run your programs on the IBM Q Experience, which we'll also refer to as the IBM Quantum Computer, you'll need to first set up an account. You can sign up in one of two ways:

- Get a free IBMid account from https://quantum-computing.ibm.com/login.
- Use your Google, Twitter, LinkedIn, or GitHub account.

Later, in Chapter 11, Where to Go from Here, on page 339, you'll see how to invoke the IBM Quantum Computer from within your own applications using an API Token.

---

17. https://www.research.ibm.com/ibm-q/technology/experience

The examples for the IBM Q Experience are written in the *Open Quantum Assembly Language.*[18,19,20] These programs use a .qasm file extension. We'll learn this language along the way.

You'll Write Most Programs Using Drag-and-Drop

Although .qasm looks like assembly language, you'll learn quantum computing concepts by dragging and dropping quantum devices on a graphical interface. This visual form of your program translates into .qasm code. You can also upload the source code in this book, which then produces the visual representation.

Once you understand how to design algorithms with quantum effects, programming them in a conventional language becomes routine. In Programming with Qiskit, on page 353, you'll learn to program quantum concepts using conventional languages such as Python. With these languages, though, you don't get the immediate interactivity that drag-and-drop brings when learning about quantum phenomena.

In addition to IBM's Qiskit, you can use the principles and techniques in this book to program quantum computers in languages from other vendors, such as Amazon's Braket, on page 381, Google's Cirq, on page 381, and Microsoft's Q#, on page 384.

Although we'll work with the IBM Quantum Computer, our examples are universal and easily modified to run on other quantum circuit computers.

Now that we've settled on a quantum computer and signed into our account, let's take a walk-through of the interface before we run the quantum program to find a feasible schedule for the talk show hosts.

On quantum circuit computers, a quantum program is also called a *circuit*, which is a visual representation of the sequence of quantum instructions. Thus, to start writing a quantum program, log in to the IBM Quantum Computer and click the Circuit Composer icon on the left margin, as shown in the figure on page 11.

---

18. https://arxiv.org/abs/1707.03429
19. https://github.com/Qiskit/openqasm
20. https://github.com/Qiskit/openqasm/blob/master/spec/qasm2.rst

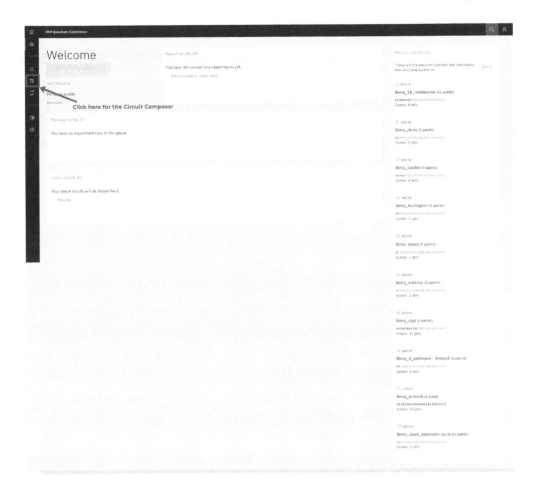

This takes you to a page that lists your quantum programs. To create a new program, click the New Circuit button, shown in the following figure:

This action will open up the following interface:

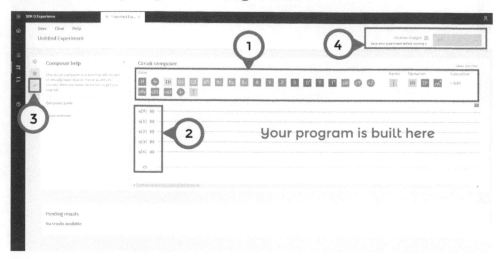

This interface is called the Composer. Its key elements are as follows:

1. In a quantum circuit computer, the quantum instructions are called *gates*. To write a program, you drag and drop these gates on the main area labeled Your Program Is Built Here.

2. The variables of your computational problem are stored in arrays that are the subatomic particles in the computer. The "quantum" stuff happens here.

3. To see the code corresponding to the visual drag-and-dropping of the gates, click this tab to open the Circuit editor.

4. To Save and Run, click the respective buttons in this area.

Over the subsequent chapters, you'll learn to write quantum programs from scratch. For now, though, you'll run a complete program and see for yourself how it solves the *Hotel Scheduling Problem*. You can get the program from the book's official page.[21]

Simple Scheduling Problem

The quantum program you'll run is actually a simpler version of the Hotel Scheduling Problem formulated in Writing a System of Boolean Logic Expressions, on page 8, as its solution is easier to verify.

---

21. https://pragprog.com/book/nmquantum/quantum-computing

Simple Scheduling Problem

In the simpler version, we'll work with just one hotel, Bellagio, and the two hosts, Kimmel and Maher. The solution to this problem is then that each of them performs on a different day—we can't have both perform on the same day or have a day when neither performs.

The first few lines of the program are listed here:

Bellagio_Hotel_Scheduling_Problem_Final.qasm
```
OPENQASM 2.0;
include "qelib1.inc";

// Initialize Quantum and Classical Registers
qreg q[7];
creg c[2];

// Generate All Combinations
h q[0];
h q[1];
h q[2];
h q[3];

//// ITERATION 1
// Constraints (to tag optimal solution)
x q[4];
x q[5];
cx q[0],q[1];
cx q[2],q[3];
x q[0];
x q[1];
x q[3];
x q[1];
x q[3];
ccx q[1],q[3],q[4];
x q[1];
x q[2];
x q[3];
ccx q[0],q[2],q[5];
x q[0];
x q[2];
ccx q[4],q[5],q[6];
x q[0];
x q[2];
z q[6];
```

The first line specifies the version of the Open Quantum Assembly Language (OpenQASM) for our programs. On the second line, we pull in an include file containing the specifications for commonly used functions in a quantum program. These two lines form the header in every program we write for IBM's Quantum Computer. We will cover the remaining lines in subsequent chapters.

Quantum Programming Language Versus Conventional Languages

Although the statements in a quantum program resemble those of digital computers, they are instructions to invoke quantum phenomena to solve computationally intensive problems. They're not a direct replacement for those used in conventional computer languages. They're based on a fundamentally new template with its own set of concepts and schemes, which you'll learn about in subsequent chapters.

To import this program, click the Circuit Composer tab on the bar on the left edge of the browser to go to the page that lists your programs. On the top of this list, click the Import QASM File button and select the program you just created from your desktop:

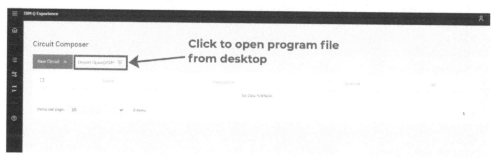

Once the program has been loaded, you'll see it in the list. Click it to open the program in the Composer. You'll see the following visual representation of the code you just imported:

To see the code listing, click the Circuit Editor tab on the left edge of the Composer.

We'll explain how the code works in subsequent chapters. For now, though, Save the code and click the Run button on the top right.

On the next screen, you have a choice of quantum computers, the *backend*, available along with a simulator in the drop down on the left:

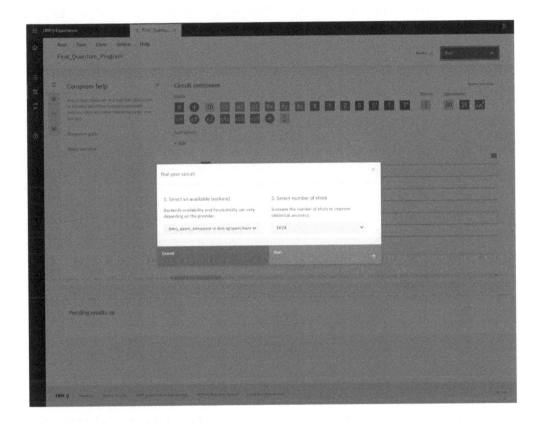

If you choose to run the program on a real quantum computer, your program will be placed in queue. Depending on the workload of the specific quantum computer selected, my programs have taken anywhere from fifteen minutes up to a day to get back the results. Of course, the actual runtime of your code on the computer is very quick. Using the simulator, on the other hand, will give you results almost immediately.

Use the default in the second drop-down, Number of Shots. We will explain later when to change this value.

Quantum Computer Simulators

Quantum computers rely on marshalling the quantum mechanical nature of subatomic particles to get them to perform computations for super-hard applications. These quantum features include *superposition* and *entanglement*, concepts we'll study later, and need special-purpose hardware from the ground up. These phenomena can't be reproduced on classical machines. Consequently, although simulators mimic these characteristics on digital computers, they can't tap into their inherent potential power. Hence, simulators are good for only small applications.

Examining the Output

The link to the Results of your program, whether it's still waiting to be executed or is complete, appear below the Composer. Scroll the page to get to it and click the link when it's available to view the results. (Every time you execute a program, a new Results link is created.)

On the Results page, scroll down to the Result section, where you'll see a graphical output similar to the following figure:

Result

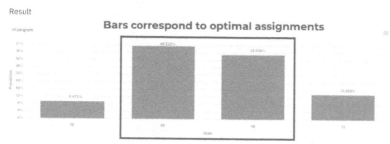

We'll go over interpreting the output of the program in the next chapter. For now, I just want to point out a few salient points about how the program reports the results of an execution.

Quantum computers work with the quantum equivalents of binary bits. So, while they go about computing a solution differently from classical machines, we'll still deal with the 0 and 1 binary concepts in our programs.

In the Hotel Scheduling program, we defined the quantum equivalents of the classical bits representing the various options for the talk show hosts to perform. Thus, the program returns values for these options as strings of 0s and 1s, which you'll see at the bottom of each bar.

For reasons that'll become clear in subsequent chapters, the taller middle two bars correspond to feasible schedules. The binary strings at the base of these bars are 01 and 10. These are the ones that correctly solve the Boolean logic expressions for the simpler version. The others are discarded. I realize you may not understand the how and why of selecting this particular string of 0s and 1s gives the optimal solution nor how it relates to the problem variables. But it'll soon start making sense. Although we'll go over this example in detail in Searching for an Optimal Schedule, on page 324, the point I want to make now is that quantum programs return valid results for real world problems—they're not just laboratory experiments.

This string of 0s and 1s corresponds to the following solutions:

$k = 0 \mapsto$ Jimmy Kimmel performs at Alladin on Day 1 and at Bellagio on Day 2
$m = 1 \mapsto$ Bill Maher performs at Bellagio on Day 1 and at Caesars on Day 2

and

$k = 1 \mapsto$ Jimmy Kimmel performs at Bellagio on Day 1 and at Aladdin on Day 2
$m = 0 \mapsto$ Bill Maher performs at Caesars on Day 1 and at Bellagio on Day 2

In other words, limiting our attention to just the assignments for Bellagio, the solutions represent two valid schedules:

	Solution 1	Solution 2
Day 1	Maher	Kimmel
Day 2	Kimmel	Maher

This, then, is a typical way quantum programs are used in practice in the industry: create a system of binary logic expressions, model the task as a Boolean Satisfiability problem, and then set up those expressions in a program. The more variables you use, the more complex the expressions—in this case, as the number of talk show hosts, days, and hotels increase, the number of possible solutions increases exponentially. In other words, the problem grows astronomical quickly. Traditional methods quickly reach their limit with such problems, which means that developers settle for imperfect solutions, which leaves money on the table. As you'll soon understand, a quantum computer solves such problems in a heartbeat.

Even though this problem can be solved using a custom-built technique, as explained in *Knuth [Knu11]*, a quantum program is still more efficient in the sense that it's both easier to set up and it returns a solution quickly.

Quantum Computers Are Still in Their Infancy

 The number of bits that a quantum computer can handle, their stability, and the speed of computations are improving continually. So, although quantum computers haven't quite achieved the *quantum advantage*, the point at which quantum computers are faster than classical ones, the gap between them is closing—dare I say—daily.

Bottom Line

Quantum computing is real—it's no longer just theory and wishful thinking, nor do you need pots of money to use one. It has literally come to a theater near you.

Unlike other kinds of computer technology, quantum computing works on a totally different set of principles and needs specialized hardware. As a result, classical code won't work on them. You have to rewrite your programs from the ground up.

Although I glossed over several aspects of running the Hotel Scheduling Problem on a quantum computer, I wanted to drive home the point that quantum programs are:

- Not isolated statements that do nothing useful other than demonstrate esoteric concepts; they can do useful computations for standard applications.

- Like conventional programs in the sense that you use standard interfaces to program and get your code to execute on them—you're not working in lab coats in sterile environments on particle accelerators.

- Programmable using standard statements. While these types of computers are based on quantum mechanics, the programming statements are mundane—no arcane constructs—and use familiar programming instructions.

In the next chapter, we'll learn about quantum mechanics principles in a way that emphasizes its connection with computer science and makes the quantum aspects more concrete.

If quantum mechanics hasn't profoundly shocked you, you haven't understood it yet.

> Niels Bohr, awarded the Nobel Prize in Physics 1922 for
> "his services in the investigation of the structure of atoms
> and of the radiation emanating from them"

## CHAPTER 2

Goodbye Mr. Bits—From Classical to Quantum Bits

The program that solved the Hotel Scheduling Problem in the previous chapter, as well as the output, were in a form similar to what we would see in classical computing. Yet the machinery on which the program ran lies squarely in the crosshairs of quantum mechanics. The binary bits of classical computers are replaced by bits whose behavior is governed by particle physics, which opens ways of computing that have the potential to dramatically boost performance over that of classical computers. In this chapter, we peek behind the curtain and get a glimpse of *qubits*, the quantum replacement of classical binary bits.

Learning quantum programming isn't like a JavaScript ninja wanting to pick up Objective-C, where the syntax and grammar may differ but the basic ideas remain the same. Quantum programming is different, from the unique ways in which quantum computers represent information to how they're cranked to get a result. To understand quantum programming, we'll start with the familiar so that we'll be better able to see the jump-off point.

Comparing Classical to Quantum Computing

When you write a computer program to implement an algorithm on a conventional computer, you'd use a high-level language such as C#, Java, Python, or a myriad others in vogue today. Your program would include statements such as:

- Branching statements (if-then blocks).
- for-loops to execute a chunk of code multiple times.
- Variable assignments.

The computer's compiler then encodes your program's statements as low-level instructions that get executed on your computer's operating system. These low-level instructions replace what you wrote with operations on binary (1 and 0) bits that are held in *registers* or storage locations accessible by a computer's central processing unit (CPU):

- Moving bits in and out of registers.
- Incrementing or decrementing the value in registers.
- Comparing the value in a register with that of another register.
- Jumping to different parts of the code based on the state of registers.
- Performing Boolean operations on bits using Boolean logic gates.

Thus, computer programs are just a sequence of bit-level operations.

Classical computers are built from Boolean logic gates and bits driven by the technology of electronic transistors housed in integrated circuits or chips. Quantum computers work with logic gates but are based on quantum mechanical principles. The difference in the underlying physics between quantum and classic computers offers new ways to write computer programs; the tools of classical bits and gates are supplemented by quantum gates, which resemble the standard gates but manipulate *quantum bits* or *qubits* instead of standard binary bits. Unlike standard bits, which at any time are always in one of the two binary states, quantum bits appear as if hovering between these two states, such as a tossed coin before it lands. When it's spinning in the air, it still has two distinct states even though it appears to be both heads and tails at the same time. Standard programming statements can't capture this ability of qubits to be in a suspension of states and yet perform computational tasks.

Quantum computing forces us to rethink how we design algorithms and write programs for quantum computers. To master the jargon of quantum programming, we'll first review *quantum bits*, the quantum replacements of classical bits. This will introduce us to the terminology used in quantum programming, the so-called *quantum speak*.

Modeling Quantum Bits with the Qubelets Model

Quantum bits or *qubits* are the workhorses of quantum programming. They're governed by quantum mechanical principles that make it seem as if they're oscillating between the two binary states. As a result, we can make the qubits interact with each other in ways that let us, for example, formulate decision-making logic circuits that boost their runtime performance or encrypt data in virtually unbreakable ways. Thus, to become proficient at writing quantum programs, we need to first understand how to control these qubits.

Classical bits are binary; you'll only find them in one of two well-defined states, 1 or 0. Quantum bits, or qubits, also have two well-defined states corresponding to the classical binary states 0 and 1. Unlike classical binary bits, though, qubits can be in a *blended* state that is a combination of these two states, such as the coin toss alluded to earlier. This state isn't an average like 0.5. Rather, it's a concept of both states existing at the same time.

To remind us that qubits exist in a blended state, they're decorated with extra symbols to distinguish them from standard binary bits. In particular, we'll label the idealized states as $|0\rangle$ and $|1\rangle$, respectively.

Bra-Ket Notation

 The notation to denote quantum states was devised by Paul Dirac, one of the founders of quantum mechanics. In this chapter, we use the *ket*, $|q\rangle$, to represent the quantum bit q.

We'll introduce its partner, the *bra*, $\langle 0|$, in Can the Quantum Gate Matrix Be Anything?, on page 187.

You'll hear words such as "blended," "combination," and "superposition" used to describe this state, but they're not to be taken literally. The English language doesn't have good terms for quantum concepts, so we have to resort to approximations.

Readers familiar with quantum mechanics will recognize that the blended states are just another version of Schrödinger's cat, a famous thought experiment illustrating being in two states at the same time. You can learn more about this concept here.[1]

To bring quantum computing into sharper focus and help us recognize its potential to solve some of the most complex computational tasks of today, we first upgrade the coin-toss analogy to a more nuanced model. In this model, we reinterpret qubits and their quantum states as a collection of imaginary particles that we call *qubelets*. These qubelets are not physical subatomic particles and can't be isolated from a qubit. They're merely a figment of our imagination that gives us something concrete to hold onto when talking about nebulous quantum concepts. Over the subsequent chapters, we'll work with this model to get to the core of quantum computing concepts and intuitively understand them. With this foundation, you'll learn to harness quantum

---

1. https://gizmodo.com/breakthrough-quantum-cat-experiment-captured-on-camera-1786923180

principles to design quantum programs for your own applications instead of blindly running well-known algorithms in the literature.

The Qubelets Model Is Unique to This Book

Quantum mechanics is shrouded under dense mathematics that even experts find challenging. As a result, it's hard to develop an intuition for the central concepts related to quantum computing and how they come into play for solving computational problems. To this end, I developed the *Qubelets Model* as a way to bring home the quantum ideas in a form that computer professionals would find familiar.

The Qubelets Model, though, is not just a superficial knock-off of quantum mechanics that loses steam as we get deeper into the subject. We'll ride this model to the crux of quantum computing and explore real-life quantum phenomena with actual programs. This will help build your intuition so that you can design quantum algorithms for your own complex applications. In later chapters, we'll tie this model with the mathematical theory of quantum mechanics and establish that this model is a valid way to think about quantum computing.

In Chapter 3, Elementary, My Dear Watson—Quantum Logic, on page 41, through Chapter 5, Beam Me Up, Scotty—Quantum Tagging and Entangling, on page 107, I'll introduce quantum concepts by extending familiar constructs from classical computing. You'll learn the statements to initiate quantum effects in your programs and do basic but meaningful computational work, with a minimal amount of mathematics, that you can't reproduce on classical computers.

To push quantum computers to take on more complex computational problems, such as those described in Chapter 9, Alice in Quantumland—Quantum Cryptography, on page 279, and Chapter 10, Quantum Search, on page 295, you'll learn new ways to manipulate quantum bits in Chapter 6, Designer Genes—Custom Quantum States, on page 141, and Chapter 7, Small Step for Man—Single Qubit Programs, on page 173. Alhough these chapters rely on the mathematics that underpins quantum mechanics, I'll relate them back to the no-mathematics concepts introduced earlier so that their motivation is clearer.

Specifically, imagine a qubit as the brew in a witch's cauldron whose constituents are just two ingredients, pentagons and triangles, that don't dissolve or mix with each other, as shown in the following figure:

Call these pentagon and triangle shapes *qubelets* or baby qubits:

- The pentagon qubelet is a baby $|0\rangle$ qubit.
- The triangle qubelet is a baby $|1\rangle$ qubit.

For example, the $|1\rangle$ qubit is a "brew" containing only one ingredient, triangle $|1\rangle$ qubelets:

Going forward, we'll dispense with the cauldron and draw the quantum state as a rectangular box. Thus, the $|0\rangle$ qubit will only consist of pentagon $|0\rangle$ qubelets as shown in the following figure:

Similarly, the $|1\rangle$ qubit is a bundle of triangle qubelets:

Qubits in Blended States

A qubit in a blended state of $|0\rangle$ and $|1\rangle$ is shown as follows:

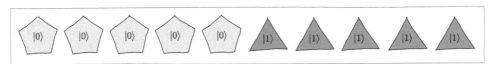

Here, there are an equal number of pentagon and triangle qubelets, indicating that the qubit is equally likely to collapse to 1 or 0.

We could also show the pentagon and triangle qubelets alternating:

In this case, you can think of the subatomic particle whirling through the $|1\rangle$ and $|0\rangle$ states like the faces of a spinning coin. Feel free to use whichever format you prefer. The key principle to bear in mind is that it's only the relative number of pentagon and triangle qubelets that's important, not their order or how they're arranged.

Qubelets and Polarized Light

Another way to think about qubelets and blended states is a beam of light made up of two polarized waves—one traveling in the horizontal plane and the other in the vertical plane:

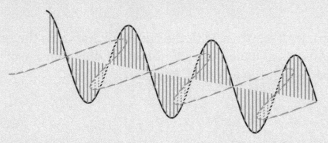

The vertical wave is made up of triangle $|1\rangle$ qubelets, and the horizontal wave corresponds to pentagon $|0\rangle$ qubelets.

In each polarized wave of light, we may associate the maximum amplitude of a wave with the corresponding number of qubelets: the more qubelets of a particular type, the greater the amplitude. For example, a quantum state that has fewer pentagon $|0\rangle$ qubelets than triangle $|1\rangle$ qubelets would have the following polarized waves in the beam of light:

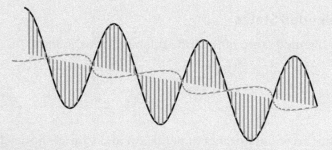

The smaller amplitude of the horizontal polarized wave is a result of there being fewer pentagon $|0\rangle$ qubelets than triangle $|1\rangle$ qubelets in the quantum state.

This view of quantum states, though, fails to explain many of the quantum phenomena that we'll need in quantum computing. But it's a good stand-in till you get comfortable working with qubelets.

Equivalent Qubits

Since it's only the ratio of the number of pentagon |0⟩ to triangle |1⟩ qubelets that matters, the qubit on the left is equivalent to the qubit on the right in the following diagram:

In each of the left and right bundles of qubelets, the number of pentagons and triangles is the same. Thus, the left and right qubit each will collapse to either 1 or 0 with equal probability.

Only the Relative Number of Qubelets Is Important

It's only the proportion of pentagon |0⟩ to triangle |1⟩ qubelets that governs the collapse of the qubit to a classical state—the actual number of pentagon and triangle qubelets doesn't count.

Biased Qubits

The qubits we've seen so far have symmetric quantum states: either all states contain pentagon |0⟩ qubelets, or they have all triangle |1⟩ qubelets, or they have an equal number of pentagon |0⟩ and triangle |1⟩ qubelets. Quantum states, however, can be unbalanced, or *biased*, in which there are more of one type of qubelets than the other. For example, the qubit shown in the following diagram has more pentagon |0⟩ qubelets than triangle |1⟩ qubelets:

So when we talk about qubits, we're actually talking about their quantum states.

Qubelets Model the Coin in the Air

Going back to the coin-toss analogy, the qubelets model the coin as it's spinning in the air and thus, as you'll see, give a way to influence how it lands.

Classical Versus Quantum Bits

Contrasting classical bits with quantum bits is like imagining a world atlas to be like Google Maps—although the paper almanac differs in fundamental ways from the browser version, you can still make meaningful comparisons that highlight their differences by assuming they work more or less the same. With this in mind, you can think of a 0 classical bit as containing only a single pentagon $|0\rangle$ qubelet, as shown in the following figure:

0 Bit

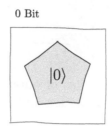

Likewise, a 1 classical bit has just a triangle $|1\rangle$ qubelet:

1 Bit

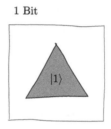

A quantum bit, as we've just seen, can have both pentagon $|0\rangle$ and triangle $|1\rangle$ qubelets as shown next:

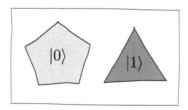

Or it can even be one where the number of pentagon $|0\rangle$ qubelets differs from that of the triangle $|1\rangle$ qubelets:

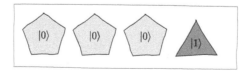

Moreover, over the course of a program, the number of pentagon $|0\rangle$ and triangle $|1\rangle$ qubelets in a qubit can change—it's not fixed as in classical bits. Simply put, a quantum bit, like Google Maps, is far more versatile than a classical bit, which is more akin to a paper map. We'll see that this added flexibility is largely responsible for giving quantum computers an edge over conventional computers.

Collapsing Qubits

When we want to inspect the state of a classical bit while a program is being executed in a conventional computer program, we simply write out the variable that holds the bit. The act of looking at the bit doesn't affect its state.

In quantum computing, on the other hand, we can never directly observe the quantum state of a qubit: we can't peer into the cauldron to check out a qubit's quantum state—the brew is opaque. The only way to examine the quantum state is to reach into the cauldron and randomly pull out a qubelet. At that point, two things happen:

1. The remaining qubelets in the cauldron fade away, as they are no longer of any use—the laws of quantum mechanics dictate that you can't select another qubelet.

2. The selected qubelet, either a pentagon $|0\rangle$ or a triangle $|1\rangle$, is anointed the state of the qubit and we say that the qubit has *collapsed*. The cauldron is effectively "reset" so that it only contains the selected qubelet.

For example, if a pentagon $|0\rangle$ qubelet is selected, the qubit collapses to the *idealized* quantum state $|0\rangle$ and all the other pentagon $|0\rangle$ and triangle $|1\rangle$ qubelets vanish from the state. And if a triangle $|1\rangle$ qubelet is picked from the cauldron, the qubit collapses to the *idealized* quantum state $|1\rangle$ and the pentagon $|0\rangle$ and other triangle $|1\rangle$ qubelets disappear.

In general, though, we can't conclusively predict which of the two idealized states the quantum state collapses to: sometimes it collapses to $|0\rangle$ and at other times to $|1\rangle$. To put it another way, finding a qubit in a specific state after collapsing it doesn't tell us anything about the relative number of pentagon $|0\rangle$ and triangle $|1\rangle$ qubelets in the quantum state before it collapsed. In particular, if we were to start again from a qubit in an identical quantum state and collapse it, there's no guarantee that the qubit will collapse to the same classical state as the previous selection.

Thus, in quantum computing, as we'll learn in subsequent chapters, all the computational work is done on qubits whose quantum states have not collapsed.

Only after we're convinced that all the qubits hold the optimal or desired states that your program is tasked with finding, do we then collapse them.

What Are Quantum Programs?

A quantum program is a sequence of instructions, or actions, that guides qubits from one quantum state to another such that each qubit arrives at a state that corresponds to the optimal solution.

For example, a quantum instruction changes the quantum state of a qubit, as shown in the following figure:

In this case, the quantum instruction, shown as a box, takes a qubit whose quantum state is shown on the left with two pentagon $|0\rangle$ qubelets and three triangle $|1\rangle$ qubelets to another one shown on the right with five pentagon $|0\rangle$ qubelets and two triangle $|1\rangle$ qubelets. Chaining these quantum instructions together results in a series of steps that varies a qubit's quantum state.

In a quantum program, we apply these instructions to several qubits and modify their quantum states. In subsequent chapters, we'll learn to write the proper sequence of various instructions so as to get the qubits to collapse to the desired binary states.

This graphical depiction of a quantum programming instruction underscores the crucial role that subatomic physics plays in contending with challenging computational problems. In classical computing, each statement acts on binary bits that hold only one value at a time. In contrast, because a qubit in effect has many qubelets, or tiny bits, a quantum instruction juggles with all of them at once. Thus, quantum computing has two features that together offer a powerful break from classical computing:

- A quantum instruction works on all the qubelets in a qubit's quantum state simultaneously.

- As the quantum state of the qubits is altered, the number of pentagon $|0\rangle$ and triangle $|1\rangle$ qubelets in the quantum state can grow or shrink as necessary and isn't limited by any physical constraint.

As a result, because the qubits can hold an exponentially large number of qubelets, or tiny states, even a quantum program with a reasonably small set of qubits can solve extremely large problems. We'll expand on this theme from Chapter 4, All Together Now—Quantum Superposition, on page 77, onward.

Pentagon and Triangle Shapes Are Visuals for the Idealized Quantum States

 The pentagon and triangle shapes have no quantum significance. They are just visuals for the idealized quantum states $|0\rangle$ and $|1\rangle$, respectively, and give a way to pictorially explain the mathematics describing quantum phenomena.

Measuring Qubits

Having settled on an understanding of qubits and quantum states, we're ready for the next step in our journey. To get anything useful out of qubits, we control them with quantum gates, the quantum equivalent of classical gates.

To get a feel for quantum programs steering quantum states to the correct solution, imagine a magic trick where your selected card appears at the top of the deck. It may look random, but the shuffling of the deck is actually a controlled reordering of the cards to force the selected card to the top of the deck. Likewise, even though the quantum bits collapse randomly to one of the two idealized states, the quantum program applies the quantum gates in a way that forces the qubits to collapse to the desired state.

Because quantum gates guide qubits to reliably transition from one quantum state to another, they work differently from the classical gates. You can't simply take the code you wrote for a conventional computer and run it on a quantum computer. In fact, because of the unique way that quantum gates work, you'll need to redesign your *logic circuit*, the interconnection of classical logic gates to perform a computational task, and, thus, your program, so that you get the qubits to simultaneously collapse to binary states that correspond to an optimal solution, as we saw in A Scheduling Problem, on page 6. In quantum computing, the interconnection of quantum gates is called a *quantum circuit*.

Quantum Circuits Are Wireless

 Even though we draw quantum logic circuits with wires connecting the quantum gates, you shouldn't think that qubits flow through them as electrons would. The wires in a quantum circuit aren't physical as they are in electronic circuits. Rather, you should think of the wires as a conveyor belt that brings the quantum gates in the order drawn in the circuit to act on the qubit.

Before we string quantum gates together to build a complete program, you must first learn how quantum gates behave individually so that you understand how to rework your application's logic circuit. We'll start with the Measure gate. Every quantum program you write needs these.

Measure Gate

In the previous section we saw that since quantum states can't be directly observed, the only thing that a quantum program can disclose is the collapsed states of qubits. So although we'll write programs that intelligently vary the quantum states of qubits to arrive at states that correspond to an optimal solution, we have to eventually collapse the qubits to obtain the associated binary states. Hence, before studying other gates and quantum statements, we must first know how to read the result of a quantum computation that changes a qubit's quantum state. That is, we need a way to collapse a qubit's quantum state in code.

The Measure gate is a quantum instruction that collapses a qubit: it randomly selects a qubelet from the qubit and returns the state of the selected qubelet. The returned state is a classical binary state. Conceptually, the Measure gate is shown in the following circuit:

The left qubit has two pentagon $|0\rangle$ qubelets and three triangle $|1\rangle$ qubelets. The Measure gate randomly selects a qubelet, for example, a pentagon $|0\rangle$ qubelet, from the left qubit. The left qubit is collapsed to $|0\rangle$ and the returned classical state is 0. This act of collapsing a qubit is called *measuring* or *examining* the qubit.

Under the hood, the process works a little differently. So let's fix the figure above. After collapsing the qubit, the Measure—the binary value corresponding to the idealized quantum state—is recorded in a register. By convention, this recording action is depicted as shown in the circuit on page 31.

The down arrow is the Measure gate writing to a standard classical register on the bottom horizontal line.

A Measure gate records the binary state of the collapsed qubit, which forms the output of your quantum program. Thus, you can think of the Measure gate as your program's return statement.

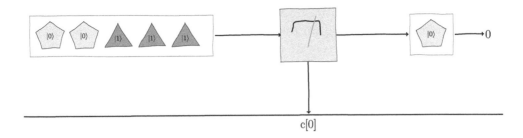

Selecting a Qubelet Is Measuring a Qubit

The process of randomly selecting a qubelet, collapsing the qubit by getting rid of the other qubelets in the quantum state, and recording the state of the selected qubelet as a binary bit is called *measuring* a qubit.

For example, when we say that the Measure gate collapses the qubit to 0, it's shorthand for the Measure gate selecting a pentagon $|0\rangle$ qubelet, throwing away the other qubelets, and logging 0, the corresponding binary state associated with the selected pentagon $|0\rangle$ qubelet, in the classical register. Thus, collapsing a qubit is effectively measuring it.

It shouldn't escape your attention, though, that unless you're writing a random number generator, collapsing the qubit on the left with two pentagon $|0\rangle$ qubelets and three triangle $|1\rangle$ qubelets is premature: sometimes you'll end up with a 0 and at other times a 1 in the classical register. The challenge in quantum computing is to coax qubits to quantum states that have an extremely high likelihood of collapsing to the optimal binary states so that you don't end up logging random states when you measure the qubits. Before seeing how to work with qubits in a program, we'll start by covering how to use a Measure gate in code.

Writing the Quantum Program

To declare a Measure gate in a quantum program, we'll build the following circuit:

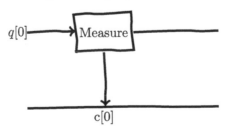

This circuit has a single qubit held in the quantum register q[0], and a single classical register, c[0], where the Measure gate records the binary bit associated with the collapsed quantum state of the qubit.

To write a program for this circuit, go to the IBM Quantum Computer and click the Create a circuit button. This opens the Circuit Composer, where you can connect the gates for the circuit as shown in the following figure:

The Circuit Composer initializes five quantum registers and five classical registers. Our circuit, though, only has a single qubit and a single classical register. To remove the extra qubits and classical registers, go to the Composer Home panel on the left and click the Circuit editor tab. In the Circuit editor panel, you'll see the following initial code:

```
❶ OPENQASM 2.0;
❷ include "qelib1.inc";

❸ qreg q[5];
❹ creg c[5];
```

Every quantum program begins with the headers shown on the first two lines followed by the code that specifies the quantum circuit:

❶ Specify the version of the *Quantum Assembly Language* used for the quantum program.

❷ Reference the include file that contains pre-built functions for the quantum instructions.

❸ The keyword qreg declares the 0-based quantum register array that holds the qubits. The default name for this array is q, but you can change it to another label if you'd like. The length of the array is the number of qubits you'll use in your program. All qubits are initialized to |0⟩. Later, we'll learn how to initialize it to |1⟩ and other blended states.

❹ The keyword creg declares the 0-based classical register array that holds the binary values of the collapsed qubits. The default name for this array is c, but you can change it to another label if you'd like. The length of this array is the number of collapsed qubits you want your program to return.

To get rid of the extra qubits and classical registers, set their lengths to 1:

```
qreg q[1];
creg c[1];
```

To connect the Measure gate to the qubit in q[0], *drag* it from the palette to the top line, representing the qubit register:

When you release the mouse, the Measure gate is dropped onto the line for the quantum register, q[0], and its downward arrow points to the line for the classical register, c[0], as shown in the following figure:

You can also directly declare a Measure gate in code by first specifying the gate, followed by the action the gate does on the qubit. In this case the Measure gate collapses the qubit in q[0] and logs the associated binary state to the classical register, c[0].

```
measure q[0] -> c[0];
```

This completes the quantum circuit for the Measure gate writing to a classical register. Here's complete code listing:

```
Measure_Gate.qasm
OPENQASM 2.0;
include "qelib1.inc";
qreg q[1];
creg c[1];

measure q[0] -> c[0];
```

Since the qubit in the quantum register q[0] is initialized to $|0\rangle$, the quantum circuit effectively looks like the following figure:

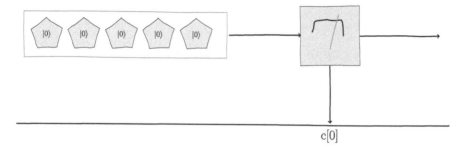

$$c[0]$$

The qubelets in the box on the left simply indicate the quantum state of $|0\rangle$—they're not related to the length of the quantum register array.

When the Measure gate acts on the q[0] qubit, it selects a random qubelet from its quantum state, collapses it, and writes the state of the selected qubit to the classical register, c[0], as a binary bit. Since the q[0] qubit is initialized to $|0\rangle$, its quantum state only has pentagon $|0\rangle$ qubelets, as shown in the previous figure. Thus, the Measure gate always selects a pentagon $|0\rangle$ qubelet and writes a 0 to the classical register, c[0].

Don't Add Gates After a Measure Gate

 Do not attach any gates to a qubit after you've measured its value with a Measure gate. Although the qubit is still active, its quantum state before you measured it is forever lost. In particular, don't use them to debug your program, as you'll get inconsistent or meaningless results.

Running the Quantum Program

To run this quantum program, click the Run button on the top right of the window. (If the button is grayed out, Save your program first.) The dialog window shown on page 35 opens.

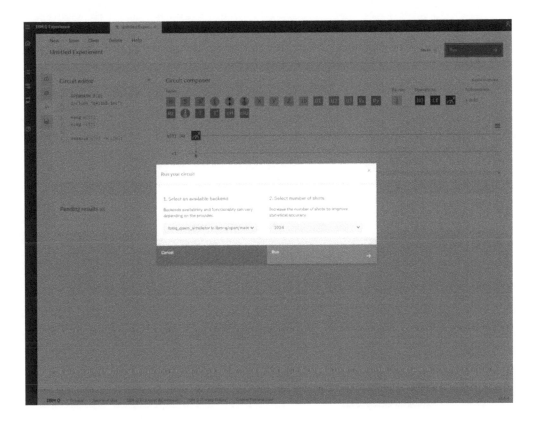

Before running the program, you need to specify the following:

- Select the quantum computer (the backend) you'd like to run your program on. The drop-down lists the available quantum computers that IBM offers, as well as a simulator.

  The simulator will run your code immediately. The actual quantum computers run in the cloud—executing your code on one of them depends on the number of other programs in queue, so your program's execution may be delayed.

- As we discussed in Measure Gate, on page 30, because the Measure gate randomly picks a qubelet from the quantum state of the qubit it's acting on, all quantum programs are run multiple times. Each run is a *shot*. The goal of quantum computing, then, is to design algorithms that tilt the odds so that the optimal solution is returned in the vast majority of shots.

The results of your program's execution will appear as a link in the Result section below the Composer. When you click the link, you will see the following Results page:

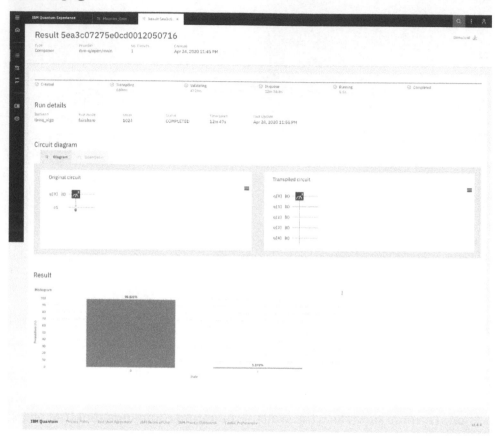

At the top of the page, the runtime metrics are listed. Next, you'll see the following sections:

Original Circuit: This is the circuit you built on the Composer.

Transpiled Circuit: The circuit diagram you entered on the Composer is compiled, or transpiled, in which some gates are substituted with equivalent ones before your code is executed. We'll see examples of these replacements in later chapters. For the most part, though, you don't need to worry about this circuit.

Result: The results of your program's execution appear in this section. A quantum program logs the results of its execution differently from how classical programs would. In a classical program, you have a wide variety of ways of documenting the results of a run, such as printing the values of your program's variables when your code terminates. In quantum programming, the results of an execution are recorded in the classical registers as binary bits corresponding to the collapsed states of qubits. In other words, when your quantum program terminates, each classical register will hold a binary bit: 0 or 1. In particular, because a quantum program is run multiple times, the number of times each binary bit is seen in a register is shown as a percentage.

Running on a Simulator

If you elected to run your code on the simulator, the results of your run will be shown as follows:

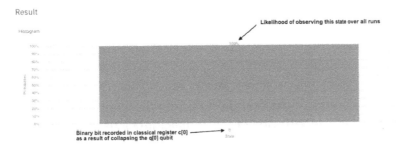

The value recorded in the classical register, c[0], is shown at the base of the big blue bar. The height of the big blue bar is the confidence or probability of observing the value shown at the base of the bar. In the case of a $|0\rangle$ qubit, the computer's confidence that it collapses to $|0\rangle$, corresponding to the binary state 0, is 100%; in other words, the probability that c[0] = 0 is 1, an unequivocal certainty.

Running on a Real Quantum Computer

If, instead, you ran your program on a real quantum computer, your output will be similar to the following figure:

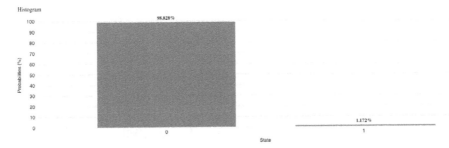

On a real quantum computer, in most shots the Measure gate collapses the qubit to $|0\rangle$ as expected. But in a small percentage of shots, the qubit collapses to $|1\rangle$. So we see two bars in the this figure: the taller bar is the higher percentage for the classical register, c[0], holding the corresponding binary bit, 0, and the shorter one for the classical register logging 1.

The reason why we see a tiny fraction of shots in which the Measure gate collapses the $|0\rangle$ qubit yet writes the binary bit 1 to the classical register lies with the way real qubits exist in nature.

Artificial qubits used in a simulator are "pure." That is, a $|0\rangle$ qubit will have only pentagon $|0\rangle$ qubelets. Real qubits, on the other hand, are not always precisely aligned within the magnetic fields of the quantum computer's hardware. Conceptually, we model a real $|0\rangle$ qubit as follows:

The vast majority of qubelets in the real $|0\rangle$ qubit are the pentagon baby $|0\rangle$ qubelets. But there's also a smattering of $|1\rangle$ triangle qubelets.

Likewise, a "real" $|1\rangle$ qubit is shown as follows:

So when we're working with real qubits, our quantum circuit looks like the following figure:

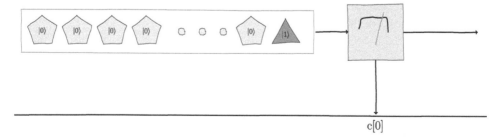

c[0]

When the Measure gate collapses the real $|0\rangle$ qubit on the left, there's a small chance that a triangle $|1\rangle$ gets selected. Thus, a binary 1 bit is written in the classical registers on those seldom occasions. Consequently, every now and then, you'll see this errant behavior show up as tiny bars on the output graph.

As the engineering of quantum computers improves, the effect of noise will reduce. So we won't worry about the difference between real and artificial qubits in our quantum programs. But when interpreting the outputs of your programs, you'll sometimes see them collapsing the qubits incorrectly. Discard these states as noise.

Bottom Line

Qubits are the central computing components of quantum computers. Compared to classical binary bits that are always in one of two states, 0 or 1, qubits exist in states that are a combination of two idealized quantum states, $|0\rangle$ and $|1\rangle$. The quantum states are not a solid monolithic state as are the binary states. Rather, you can think of the quantum states as an aggregate of tiny states called qubelets. This model implies that quantum bits have a fluidity or elasticity to them that differentiates them from their classical counterparts, as reviewed in Qubits in Blended States, on page 23.

The other marquee feature of quantum programming is the instructions represented as quantum gates, the quantum equivalent of classical logic gates. These gates alter the quantum states of qubits.

Since qubits don't reveal their states until you inspect them, the only way to get anything out of a quantum program is to destroy the qubit's quantum state using the Measure gate, as shown in Measure Gate, on page 30. The qubit then collapses to one of the two idealized quantum states, and the corresponding binary state is returned as in a standard computer.

In the next chapter, we'll learn about quantum gates that juggle qubits before they're measured. These gates allow us to model the familiar and, or, as well as more sophisticated programming constructs such as if-then statements.

Try Your Hand

Many chapters in this book have a section where you'll find exercises that test and reinforce your understanding of the concepts we've covered. Working through them will enhance your mastery of the topics.

Solutions to these exercises are given in Quantum Bits Solutions, on page 425.

1. Consider the qubit with the quantum state containing six pentagon $|0\rangle$ and two triangle $|1\rangle$ qubelets, as shown in the figure on page 40.

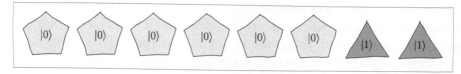

a. Simplify this qubit. That is, draw an equivalent qubit with fewer qubelets.

b. Decide whether the following statements are True or False:

   i. When this qubit is measured, since the pentagon $|0\rangle$ qubelets outnumber the triangle $|1\rangle$ qubelets, it'll always collapse to the idealized quantum state $|0\rangle$.

   ii. When this qubit is measured over multiple shots, the relative frequencies of recording the binary state 0 to 1 is 3:1.

   iii. When measuring this qubit, a triangle $|1\rangle$ qubelet is selected. The number of remaining triangle $|1\rangle$ qubelets in the quantum state is reduced by 1.

   iv. If this qubit is measured again immediately in the same program, it could collapse to a different idealized state.

2. You find a qubit collapsed to the $|1\rangle$ state. What can you say about its state before it collapsed?

3. How is $|0\rangle$ different from 0?

4. A qubit's state is $|1\rangle$. If a Measure gate inspects it, what value will it record?

5. When a Measure gate inspects a qubit, does it record all states that the qubit can collapse to?

Crime is common. Logic is rare. Therefore it is upon the logic rather than upon the crime that you should dwell.

> *Sir Arthur Conan Doyle, "The Adventure of the Copper Beeches"*

CHAPTER 3

Elementary, My Dear Watson—Quantum Logic

In the previous chapter, we covered how to work with the Measure gate and tip qubits to binary states. We continue building up our toolkit with quantum gates that coax qubits to collapse in controlled ways, for it's only through precision that qubits can take on our application's tasks.

In this chapter, you'll learn about gates that perform logic operations, the bread and butter of computer programs, but on qubits instead of standard binary bits. These gates are like the fuel injectors in your car—by themselves they don't grab our attention but are crucial for regulating the fuel flow to the engine. Likewise, these gates have no particular computational advantage over their classical brethren: they shuttle qubits around the quantum circuit where more complex, and useful, operations are done. Getting how these logic gates work with qubits down pat will let us write programs from Chapter 4, All Together Now—Quantum Superposition, on page 77, onward, where we can explore gates that are rooted in quantum mechanics rather than talking about them in the abstract.

Quantum Logic Operations Aren't Assembly Language

 Fundamentally, digital computers hinge on Boolean logic operations, such as AND, OR, and NOT, on 0 and 1 bits. Every program you write on a classical computer, even if it doesn't explicitly use Boolean logic, ultimately gets compiled into machine code where Boolean operations are applied. On the other hand, even though you're working with bits and logical operations for the large class of Boolean Satisfiability problems, such as the Hotel Scheduling Problem, where you search through the many combinations of 0s

Quantum Logic Operations Aren't Assembly Language

and 1s to find one that works, you'd program in, say, Python, rather than assembly language.

The quantum logic operations you'll see in this chapter play the same role as their classical Boolean counterparts for solving Boolean Satisfiability problems although they go about it in a different way. In this sense, just because quantum computing uses qubits and quantum logical gates, you shouldn't equate quantum programming with assembly language. Boolean logic is the nature of the computational problem, not the programming language.

Quantum computers don't have explicit equivalents of the standard classical logic gates, such as the AND and OR gates. Instead, the following quantum gates let us apply standard logic operations in quantum programs:

1. *NOT (X) Gate*
2. *Controlled NOT (CNOT) Gate*
3. *Controlled Controlled NOT (CCNOT) Gate*

The Controlled Controlled NOT name is unusual. Just like the "spam, spam, spam, egg, and spam" breakfast item in the Monty Python episode, these gates also come in flavors such as Controlled Controlled Controlled NOT. The basic operation of these variations, however, is fundamentally the same. So, we'll only cover Controlled Controlled NOT.

NOT (X) Gate

Formally, the NOT gate belongs to the Pauli family of quantum gates and is also called the Pauli-X gate. Hence, the gate is often labeled with an X. (In Universal Quantum Gates, on page 158, we'll see why the Pauli-X or X gate is fittingly called the NOT gate.) The other gates in this family are the Pauli-Y and the Pauli-Z gates, which we'll discuss in Chapter 7, Small Step for Man—Single Qubit Programs, on page 173. For more information, see Section 2.4.1.1 in *Explorations in Quantum Computing [Wil11]*.

Think of the NOT gate as a *switcher*—its sole purpose is to replace the state on the qubit from one to the other. Although this seems simple, this gate plays a large role in quantum programs.

In a binary system, if, for instance, a bit is "NOT 1," it has to be 0. Thus, we can talk about the NOT gate in terms of the $|0\rangle$ and $|1\rangle$ qubits that it acts on. When a classical NOT or X gate gets a 0, it returns a 1, and vice versa.

Working with Idealized or Pure Qubits

Since these gates perform logic operations on qubits instead of binary bits, we'll study them using the idealized or pure quantum bits $|0\rangle$ and $|1\rangle$. That is, the $|0\rangle$ qubit is basically a single pentagon $|0\rangle$ qubelet, as shown here:

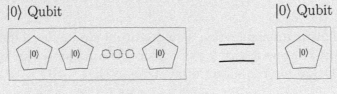

And the $|1\rangle$ qubit is a single triangle $|1\rangle$ qubelet:

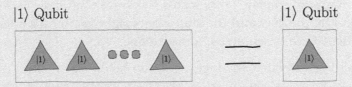

Once we understand how these gates operate with idealized qubits, we'll apply these concepts in the next chapter, Chapter 4, All Together Now—Quantum Superposition, on page 77, to qubits with blended states.

Likewise, the quantum counterpart of the NOT gate will return a $|1\rangle$ if presented with a $|0\rangle$, as the following figure shows:

And when it acts on a $|1\rangle$ qubit, it switches the qubit's state to $|0\rangle$:

Algebraic Logic of NOT Gate

The quantum NOT gate's truth table is:

Input	Output
$|1\rangle$	$|0\rangle$
$|0\rangle$	$|1\rangle$

When formulating an application as a quantum circuit, we'll frequently find it useful to first express it with logic or algebraic equations. The logic equation for a NOT gate that acts on a quantum state $|a\rangle$ is:

$$|a\rangle \mapsto 1 \oplus |a\rangle$$

where the mapping symbol $\mapsto$ indicates the state that is on its left is before the operation by the gate and the state on its right is after it's operated on by the gate. The $\oplus$ is the exclusive-OR operation.

You can readily verify that the logic equation holds when $|a\rangle$ is $|1\rangle$ or $|0\rangle$. (See Boolean Logic Expressions, on page 393.) Remarkably, though, this equation also works when $|a\rangle$ is a blended state. (We'll show this in Chapter 4, All Together Now—Quantum Superposition, on page 77.)

Using the NOT Gate in Code

Let's build a quantum circuit with a NOT or X gate. Like all diligent programmers, we'll first draw the quantum circuit on paper before writing code.

As you may have guessed, the circuit is pretty much just a NOT gate. Since this circuit will become actual working code, we need to initialize the input to some state, otherwise nothing will happen when you run the program. We'll initialize with a $|0\rangle$ qubit.

You may be tempted to think we're done. But, if you want to see whether the NOT gate is working as it's supposed to, there's still one more crucial step before we can say we have a fully working circuit. Quantum mechanics will give us ample opportunities to contemplate weighty matters such as "If a cat is in a box, is it dead or alive?" But this isn't one of those times. For our program to return a result, we need to make an *explicit measurement* of the output. Thus, we add a Measure gate that measures the qubit at the output of the X gate and writes it to a classical register, as shown in the figure on page 45.

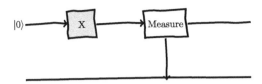

For the quantum circuit shown here, we need just a one-dimensional array for the quantum register with a single qubit, and a single-bit classical register to record the binary value associated with the collapsed qubit.

We can now build this circuit and run it on a quantum computer. Go to the IBM site and create a new circuit. You can use the default names for the quantum and classical registers.

Next, from the palette, select the X gate and drag and drop it on the top line, which represents the qubit in q[0]:

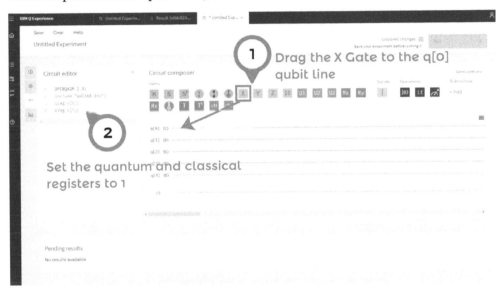

Then, set the quantum and classical registers to 1:

```
qreg q[1];
creg c[1];
```

The q[0] qubit is automatically initialized to |0⟩. This results in the circuit shown in the following schematic:

The code to specify the NOT (X) gate is straightforward:

```
x q[0];
```

The NOT gate is specified with an x followed by the qubit that is its input, the q[0].

Finally, add a Measure gate to inspect the output of the NOT gate. Make sure to record the measurement to the single classical register, c[0], as shown schematically in the following figure:

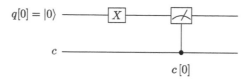

The complete code listing is as follows:

```
NOT_Gate.qasm
OPENQASM 2.0;
include "qelib1.inc";
qreg q[1];
creg c[1];
x q[0];
measure q[0] -> c[0];
```

Before running this program, let's review what will take place:

- The gates fire from left to right. That is, gates to the left will execute before those on the right.

- The qubit in q[0], which is initialized to $|0\rangle$, is fed to the NOT (X) gate.

- The NOT gate operates on the qubit, switching its state to $|1\rangle$.

- The Measure gate examines the qubit in q[0] and collapses it to the idealized $|1\rangle$ state.

- The associated classical 1 state is recorded in the classical register, c[0]. That is, c[0] will hold the value 1.

To put it succinctly, the following actions have taken place in the quantum program:

$$|0\rangle \mapsto |1\rangle \mapsto 1 \mapsto c[0]$$

Now, run this program by clicking the Run button and select whether you want to run on a real quantum computer or the simulator. After a few seconds, depending on the load on the system, the output of this program will look like this:

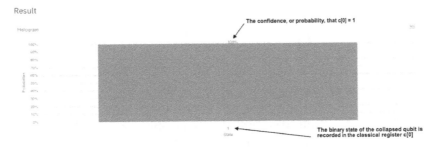

This output is from executing on a simulator. If you run on a real computer, you'll get a similar result, though you may also see that in a tiny fraction of shots the real qubit incorrectly collapsed to |0⟩.

Let's go over this output step-by-step:

1. The value in c[0], which records the measurement of the qubit, is at the base of the blue bar. In this case the value recorded in c[0] will be 1.

2. The big blue bar in the center is not the 1 state: its height is the confidence or probability of observing the value at the base of the blue bar, which will be 1, an unequivocal certainty, at least in the make-believe world of the simulator. (Due to noise, on a real quantum computer you'll sometimes see the 0 state, albeit infrequently.)

The NOT gate may not seem like it does much, but it plays a vital role when setting up Boolean logic expressions in a quantum program. The NOT gate, though, isn't "smart": it blindly switches states, no questions asked. In the next section, you'll see how to limit switching of the states to only under certain conditions with the Controlled NOT (CNOT) gate.

Controlled NOT (CNOT) Gate

While the NOT gate switches the states of single qubits, the CNOT gate juggles two qubits simultaneously—an atom-sized expansion of the capability of quantum gates but a gigantic breakthrough for computing. Since quantum programming doesn't have the direct equivalents of if-then statements, the CNOT gate fills that gap. Moreover, learning to deal with two qubits opens the path for handling even more qubits, which is important if we want to use quantum computing for complex computational tasks.

The two qubits that the CNOT gate operates on are labeled as control and target, respectively. The CNOT gate is drawn as shown on page 48.

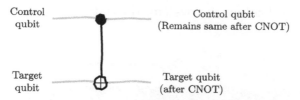

The top gray line represents the control qubit and the bottom gray line represents the target qubit. The black vertical line, the filled circle on the control qubit line, and the circle with the plus, $\oplus$, on the target line represent the CNOT gate. The vertical line indicates that the two qubits are coupled, in the sense that the CNOT gate acts on both qubits simultaneously. The gray lines on the left of the CNOT gate show the values of the two qubits before they're acted upon by the CNOT gate, while the gray lines on the right show the values of the qubits after they're operated on by the CNOT gate.

CNOT Gate Is Also Called the Feynman Gate

The CNOT gate is called the Feynman gate in honor of Richard Feynman, who first mused about building computers that exploit quantum mechanics.[a][b] These were not idle thoughts. Feynman was awarded the 1965 Nobel Prize in Physics for his research on quantum electrodynamics and its consequences for the physics of elementary particles. The Feynman diagrams, which arose from this work, grace the pages of every recent-day textbook on quantum mechanics. He knew full well what he was unleashing when he broached the possibility of quantum computers.

a. https://link.springer.com/article/10.1007/BF02650179
b. https://link.springer.com/article/10.1007/BF01886518

The CNOT gate switches the target qubit's state if the control qubit is $|1\rangle$ and leaves the target qubit's state alone if the control qubit is $|0\rangle$. Simply put, when the control qubit is $|1\rangle$, the target acts like a NOT gate.

Let's write all this down explicitly. When the control qubit is $|1\rangle$ and the target qubit is $|0\rangle$, the CNOT gate will switch the target qubit to $|1\rangle$:

$$\begin{array}{ccc} \text{Control} \ |1\rangle & \overset{CNOT}{\longmapsto} & |1\rangle \\ \text{Target} \ |0\rangle & & |1\rangle \end{array}$$

And if the target qubit is $|1\rangle$, the CNOT gate will switch the target qubit to $|0\rangle$:

$$\begin{array}{ccc} \text{Control} \ |1\rangle & \overset{CNOT}{\longmapsto} & |1\rangle \\ \text{Target} \ |1\rangle & & |0\rangle \end{array}$$

When the control qubit is $|0\rangle$, the target qubit $|0\rangle$ is unscathed:

$$\begin{array}{lll} Control & |0\rangle & \overset{CNOT}{\mapsto} & |0\rangle \\ Target & |0\rangle & & |0\rangle \end{array}$$

And if the target qubit is $|1\rangle$, it's also not touched:

$$\begin{array}{lll} Control & |0\rangle & \overset{CNOT}{\mapsto} & |0\rangle \\ Target & |1\rangle & & |1\rangle \end{array}$$

When dealing with multiple qubits that are being acted upon as a group by a gate, such as the control and target, we'll find it more convenient to concatenate the qubits before and after the gate's operation, as shown here:

$$|a\rangle \, |b\rangle \mapsto |a'\rangle \, |b'\rangle$$

The variables a, b are the control and target qubits, respectively, before passing them to the CNOT gate. And the variables a', b' are the values of the control and target qubits after the operation of the gate. In fact, we can further clean up the notation and get rid of the intermediate symbols like this:

$$|ab\rangle \mapsto |a'b'\rangle$$

Thus, when the control qubit is $|1\rangle$ and the target qubit is $|0\rangle$, the operation of the CNOT gate is shown as:

$$|10\rangle \mapsto |11\rangle$$

Here, the left qubit on both sides of the mapping represents the control bit. And since it's $|1\rangle$, the target qubit, the right bit, is switched from $|0\rangle$ to $|1\rangle$.

The following figure summarizes the operation of the CNOT gate:

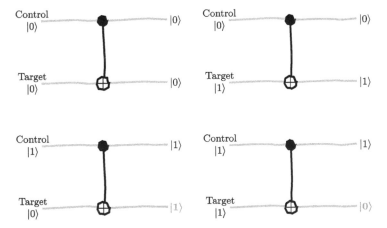

The target qubits in the two bottom circuits highlight that they've been switched because the control qubit is $|1\rangle$.

Algebraic Logic of CNOT Gate

We can also write a truth table for the CNOT gate as shown here:

Control$_0$	Target$_0$	Control$_1$	Target$_1$
$|0\rangle$	$|0\rangle$	$|0\rangle$	$|0\rangle$
$|0\rangle$	$|1\rangle$	$|0\rangle$	$|1\rangle$
$|1\rangle$	$|0\rangle$	$|1\rangle$	$|1\rangle$
$|1\rangle$	$|1\rangle$	$|1\rangle$	$|0\rangle$

Control$_0$ and Target$_0$ are the two qubit values before the application of the CNOT gate, and Control$_1$ and Target$_1$ are the values after. Note that the control qubit's value after the CNOT operation will be the same as it was before the operation.

In this table, if you hide the third column, the one labeled with Control$_1$, and relabel the fourth column as Output, you get the following truth table:

Control$_0$	Target$_0$	Output
$|0\rangle$	$|0\rangle$	$|0\rangle$
$|0\rangle$	$|1\rangle$	$|1\rangle$
$|1\rangle$	$|0\rangle$	$|1\rangle$
$|1\rangle$	$|1\rangle$	$|0\rangle$

This truth table is identical to that of an XOR or Exclusive OR gate, $\oplus$, used in classical computing, that returns a 1 if and only if one of its inputs is 1. If both inputs are 0 or both are 1, the XOR gate returns a 0. That is, the target gate after the application of the CNOT gate is equivalent to an XOR operation, as shown in this figure:

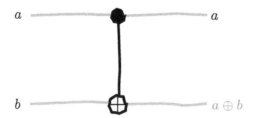

As a result, the operation of the CNOT gate can be expressed by the following logic equation:

$$\begin{pmatrix} |a\rangle \\ |b\rangle \end{pmatrix} \mapsto \begin{pmatrix} |a\rangle \\ |a\rangle \oplus |b\rangle \end{pmatrix}$$

where the qubit on top is the control and the qubit on the bottom is the target.

Common Uses of the CNOT Gate

Although the CNOT gate is the quantum double of the classical XOR gate, in quantum programming we'll find it more convenient to think of and use it as a gate in which the state of one qubit, the control, affects the other, the target. Despite the apparent simplicity of the CNOT gate, it still manages to hide a few tricks up its sleeve—shhh, the CNOT gate engages in exotic practices such as teleporting. We won't, however, instantaneously send anyone or anything halfway across the earth. Our interests in the CNOT gate include doing practical things with qubits such as copying or swapping them.

FAN-OUT Gate

In quantum computing, you can't simply copy a qubit from one register to another by making a statement like q[0] = q[1]. But we can configure a CNOT gate so that a qubit in one register "picks up" the state of a qubit in another register like this:

$$q[0] = |a\rangle \quad \underline{\quad\bullet\quad} \quad |a\rangle$$

$$q[1] - |0\rangle \quad \underline{\quad\oplus\quad} \quad |a\rangle$$

This configuration is similar to the XOR gate, except that here the target qubit is always $|0\rangle$. The qubit to be copied, $|a\rangle$, is the control qubit in register q[0]. The target qubit is clamped at $|0\rangle$. After the operation of the CNOT gate, the target qubit will also be $|a\rangle$.

To see that this arrangement works, let's first suppose that $|a\rangle$, the control qubit in register q[0], is $|0\rangle$. The target qubit, in register q[1], will be unaffected and will continue to be $|0\rangle$.

When the control qubit, $|a\rangle$, in register q[0], is $|1\rangle$, then the target qubit in q[1] is switched from $|0\rangle$ to $|1\rangle$.

We summarize this operation in the following truth table:

Control Qubit $q[0]$ - Before	Target Qubit $q[1]$ - Before	Control Qubit $q[0]$ - After	Target Qubit $q[1]$ - After
$|0\rangle$	$|0\rangle$	$|0\rangle$	$|0\rangle$
$|1\rangle$	$|0\rangle$	$|1\rangle$	$|1\rangle$

So in both cases, we see that the qubit in q[1], the target, has the same quantum state as the qubit in q[0], the control.

Although it's more descriptive to refer to this way of configuring the CNOT gate as a COPY gate, in digital electronics it's traditionally been labeled a FAN-OUT gate because a single bit feeds the inputs of several gates.

SWAP Gate

To swap the values of two registers, you can't use assignment operators like you would in classical computing. Instead, as with the FAN-OUT gate, you can use three CNOT gates, as shown here:

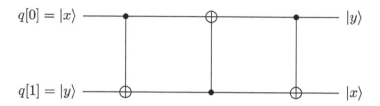

In this circuit, the state of the qubit in register q[0] is swapped with the state of the qubit in register q[1] after all three CNOT gates have acted on them. You can verify the swap by setting the $|x\rangle$ and $|y\rangle$ qubits to either of the $|1\rangle$ and $|0\rangle$ states, respectively, and then tracing how the states transition along both the upper and lower rails.

SWAP Gate Is Also Available Out-of-the-Box

On the IBM Quantum Computer, the SWAP gate is available out-of-the-box. You can drag it from the palette onto your circuit in the Composer.

The SWAP gate is shown within the dotted box:

$$q[0] = |x\rangle \quad\quad |y\rangle$$
$$q[1] = |y\rangle \quad\quad |x\rangle$$

To swap the qubits in, say, the q[0] and q[1] qubits, you'd declare it as follows:

```
swap q[0],q[1];
```

Using the CNOT Gate in Code

To see how to represent a CNOT gate in a quantum program, let's build the following circuit:

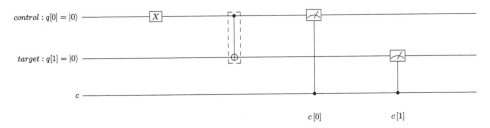

In this diagram, the two quantum bits are in the one-dimensional quantum register q: the control bit is in q[0] and the target bit is in q[1]. The top horizontal line represents the control qubit in register q[0]. The middle horizontal line is the target qubit in q[1]. The CNOT gate is within the dotted box. (Note that going forward, when the context is clear, we'll omit the dotted box to reduce clutter in our circuits). After the CNOT gate operates on the control and target qubits, the two Measure gates knock them down and record the corresponding binary states in the one-dimensional classical register c.

In this circuit, we've placed a NOT gate on the control qubit's line. The reason is that we want to see the target qubit switch states. (If we simply fed the $|0\rangle$ qubit to the CNOT gate, then nothing would happen—the target qubit would be unaffected by the CNOT gate.)

To build this circuit on the IBM quantum computer, follow these steps:

1. Create a new circuit and give it a name.

2. The Composer initializes with five quantum registers and five classical registers. Since we only need two of each, click the Circuit editor tab in the Composer Help panel and set the size of the quantum and classical registers to 2:

   ```
   qreg q[2];
   creg c[2];
   ```

3. On the Composer window, drag and drop the NOT gate, also labeled as the X gate, on the top line for the control qubit.

4. Select the CNOT gate, shown with a plus sign in a blue circle, representing the target, and drag and drop it onto the second qubit line that represents the target qubit, as shown here:

When you release the gate, you'll see a vertical line going up to the control qubit on the first line.

5. Add the two Measure gates to record the binary values corresponding to the collapsed qubits. The control qubit in the quantum register q[0] is recorded in the classical register c[0], and the target qubit in q[1] is logged in the classical register c[1]. At this point, your circuit should look like the following:

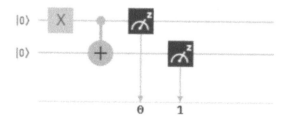

The classical registers only record the collapsed state of the qubits. Hence, they're shown on a single line even though, technically, each should be on a separate one. This shortcut keeps the diagrams from getting unwieldy when your program has more classical registers.

The code listing for this circuit is as follows:

CNOT_Gate_Circuit.qasm
```
Line 1  OPENQASM 2.0;
     2  include "qelib1.inc";
```

```
3  qreg q[2];
4  creg c[2];
5
6  x q[0];
7  cx q[0],q[1];
8
9  measure q[0] -> c[0];
10 measure q[1] -> c[1];
```

The first two lines are the standard header lines. These are followed by the declarations for the one-dimensional quantum and classical arrays, respectively. The qubits are implied to be initialized to $|0\rangle$.

On line 6, we specify the NOT gate, labeled as x, operating on the $|0\rangle$ qubit in q[0]. The NOT gate, specified on line 6, switches it to $|1\rangle$ before passing it as the control bit for the CNOT gate. The crux of this program is the CNOT gate declaration on line 7, shown again here:

```
cx q[0],q[1];
```

The CNOT gate is declared with the cx keyword followed by the quantum registers holding the control and target qubits, respectively.

Lastly, on lines 9 and 10, we measure the control and target qubits using Measure gates that record the corresponding binary states the qubits collapse to in the respective classical registers.

When we execute this program, the q[0] qubit is switched by the NOT gate to $|1\rangle$ and fed as the control qubit to the CNOT gate. The CNOT gate, in turn, switches the target qubit to $|1\rangle$. Finally, the control qubit, which is $|1\rangle$, is collapsed to a triangle $|1\rangle$ qubelet and the corresponding binary bit, 1, is recorded in c[0]. The target qubit, which is $|1\rangle$, is also collapsed to a triangle $|1\rangle$ qubelet and the corresponding binary bit, 1, is written to c[1]. Thus, both classical registers record a 1, which is shown in the following figure:

Result

The state at the bottom of the blue bar is the concatenated value of c[1] and c[0], which in this case is 11. Since this state will always be the output for this program, the height of the bar is 1 or 100%.

Using the IBM Computer: Multi-Bit Classical Register

A *multi-bit register* is a one-dimensional array containing many elements. It's used to record the binary values corresponding to multiple collapsed qubits. Programmatically, a classical register c that records the binary values of, say, 5 collapsed qubits, is declared with the creg keyword:

```
creg c[5];
```

This array records the final result of the computational task performed by your program.

Visually, the one-dimensional array, c, of n elements is shown:

$$\boxed{c[n-1]}\ \boxed{c[n-2]}\ \boxed{c[n-3]}\quad \circ\circ\circ\quad \boxed{c[2]}\quad \boxed{c[1]}\quad \boxed{c[0]}$$

The value in the last element in the 0-based array, c[n-1], is shown on the left, and the value of the first element, c[0], is on the right. We'll represent the values in each element of the classical register using a shorthand notation by concatenating all the values, c[0], c[1], ..., c[n-2], c[n-1] in reverse order as a single string: c[n-1]c[n-2]...c[2]c[1]c[0]. For example, suppose that at the conclusion of the program, the n elements in the classical register are:

$$
\begin{aligned}
c[0] &= 1 \\
c[1] &= 0 \\
c[2] &= 0 \\
&\ \vdots \\
c[n-2] &= 1 \\
c[n-1] &= 1
\end{aligned}
$$

Then we'll write all the values in the register in reverse order as 11...001, where the classical state in c[n-1] is the first position in the string and the state in c[0] is in the last. Since each element records either a 0 or 1, the total number of distinct strings of 0s and 1s is $2 \times 2 \times \cdots 2$ (n times), or 2^n.

It may seem more expedient to also write the quantum states in reverse order to match those of the classical register. But, as you'll see in Chapter 8, Giant Leap for Mankind—Multi-Qubit Programs, on page 227, it's more natural to continue to write the quantum bits as $|\,q[0]q[1] \cdots q[n-1]\,\rangle$ and not in the reverse order.

The CNOT gate gives you a single control bit that determines when to switch a qubit's state. But, as in classical programs where you can use if statements with multiple conditions or clauses, in the next section, you'll learn to use multiple control bits to determine when to switch states with the Controlled Controlled NOT (CCNOT) gate.

Controlled Controlled NOT (CCNOT) Gate

The CCNOT gate, called a *Toffoli* gate, is a CNOT gate with an additional control qubit, as shown in the following figure:

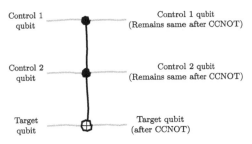

For the CCNOT gate, both control qubits need to be $|1\rangle$ for the target qubit to switch states. If either control qubit is $|0\rangle$, the target qubit isn't affected. So, as in the CNOT gate case, the CCNOT gate behaves like a NOT gate when both control bits are $|1\rangle$:

$$|110\rangle \longrightarrow |111\rangle$$
$$|111\rangle \longrightarrow |110\rangle$$

Here, in each group of concatenated qubits, the two control qubits are on the left and middle, and the target qubit is on the right.

Algebraic Logic of CCNOT Gate

We can express the operation of the CCNOT gate on the control and target qubits with the following logic equation:

$$\begin{pmatrix} |a\rangle \\ |b\rangle \\ |c\rangle \end{pmatrix} \mapsto \begin{pmatrix} |a\rangle \\ |b\rangle \\ |c\rangle \oplus (|a\rangle \wedge |b\rangle) \end{pmatrix}$$

where $|a\rangle$ and $|b\rangle$ are the two control qubits, respectively, and $|c\rangle$ is the target qubit. The term in parenthesis evaluates to $|1\rangle$ when both control qubits, $|a\rangle$ and $|b\rangle$, are $|1\rangle$. We can label the inputs and outputs of the CCNOT gate as in the following figure:

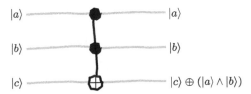

The additional control qubit gives a greater layer of flexibility when formulating the circuits for a wide array of applications. As a result, CCNOT gates are heavily used in quantum programs. Because the classical logic gates such as AND and OR have no quantum equivalents, we can use the CCNOT gates to reproduce their functionality, which we describe next.

Common Uses of the CCNOT Gates

Quantum mechanics imposes rigid requirements on the behavior of quantum gates that may seem odd. One such constraint is *reversibility*: given the states of qubits after they've been acted upon by a gate, we should be able to unambiguously deduce their states before the gate operated upon them. (We'll have more to say about this restriction in Chapter 7, Small Step for Man—Single Qubit Programs, on page 173.) This means that, at a minimum, quantum gates always have the same number of input and output qubits.

Because AND and OR gates have multiple inputs but only a single output, the reversibility condition implies they have no native quantum equivalents. But we can reproduce the behavior of classical gates.

If you're not familiar with logic gates in classical computing, you can find resources online that will get you up to speed.[1,2]

AND Gate

To build the quantum equivalent of an AND gate, we can use the CCNOT gate, as shown here:

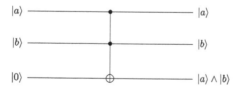

The AND gate resembles a CCNOT gate, except that the target qubit is set to $|0\rangle$. Thus, the target qubit after the application of the CCNOT gate is:

$$|0\rangle \longrightarrow |0\rangle \oplus (|a\rangle \wedge |b\rangle)$$

Referring to Boolean Logic Expressions, on page 393, we can manipulate this expression and bring it to a recognizable form. Starting with the formula to convert an exclusive-OR operation in terms of the basic NOT and OR operations, the operation on the target qubit can be written as:

$$|0\rangle \cdot (\neg(|a\rangle \wedge |b\rangle)) \vee (|1\rangle \cdot (|a\rangle \wedge |b\rangle))$$

1. https://en.wikipedia.org/wiki/Boolean_algebra
2. https://en.wikipedia.org/wiki/Logic_gate

This simplifies to:

$$|0\rangle \ \vee \ (\ |1\rangle \ \wedge \ (\ |a\rangle \ \wedge \ |b\rangle \ ))$$

Or:

$$|1\rangle \ \wedge \ (\ |a\rangle \ \wedge \ |b\rangle \ )$$

Finally, we can write the value of the target qubit as:

$$|a\rangle \ \wedge \ |b\rangle$$

Hence, by initializing the target qubit to $|0\rangle$ before the application of the CCNOT gate, the state of the target qubit after the application will be identical to an AND operation on the two control qubits $|a\rangle$ and $|b\rangle$.

OR Gate

Likewise, to build the quantum equivalent of an OR gate, you can use the CCNOT gate as shown here:

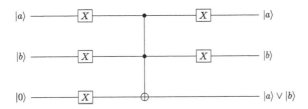

To understand why this configuration works as a quantum OR gate, it's easier to analyze the case when both $|a\rangle$ and $|b\rangle$ input qubits are $|0\rangle$. To switch the CCNOT gate target qubit state, we first have to apply a NOT gate on the input qubits. This switches their states from $|0\rangle$ to $|1\rangle$. The CCNOT gate is activated and the target qubit's state is switched. Since the target must be switched to $|0\rangle$, we feed a $|1\rangle$ qubit to the CCNOT's target.

In all other cases, when at least one of the input qubits is $|1\rangle$, the application of the NOT gates would mean that at least one of the CCNOT's control qubits is $|0\rangle$. So the target qubit will be unaffected and will continue to be $|1\rangle$, as required by the OR operation.

Finally, after the CCNOT gate operates, switch the $|a\rangle$ and $|b\rangle$ qubits back to their original states by applying the NOT gate to each qubit. In quantum programming, we always take care to return qubits back to their initial states to prevent them from inadvertently getting *entangled.* We'll see in Entangling Qubits, on page 120, that unintended interactions of qubits prevent them from freely participating in quantum operations later in your program.

Because of the versatility of the CCNOT gate to mimic classical logic gates, you can think of it as the Swiss Army knife of quantum gates.

Using the CCNOT Gate in Code

To see how to declare a CCNOT gate in a quantum program, let's use the following circuit:

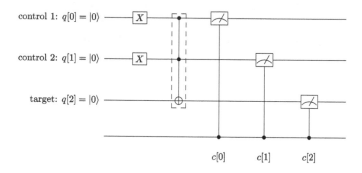

Similar to the quantum program for the CNOT gate, we'll apply a NOT gate to each of the control qubits of the CCNOT gate. This way, we can explicitly switch the target qubit's state.

To build this circuit on the IBM Quantum Computer, we'll use three qubits and three classical registers to record the value of the collapsed qubits. Go to the Circuit editor and update the quantum and classical register lengths to 3 from the default 5:

```
qreg q[3];
creg c[3];
```

Then drag and drop the NOT and Measure gates as before. The CCNOT gate is shown as a purple circle with a plus sign in the palette:

This time, drag the ccX gate to the target qubit, which is the third line corresponding to q[2]. Since there are only two other qubits in the circuit, the system will correctly wire up the CCNOT gate.

The complete code for this circuit is as follows:

```
CCNOT_Gate_Circuit.qasm
OPENQASM 2.0;
include "qelib1.inc";

qreg q[3];
creg c[3];

x q[0];
x q[1];
ccx q[0],q[1],q[2];
measure q[0] -> c[0];
measure q[1] -> c[1];
measure q[2] -> c[2];
```

The initialization of the quantum and classical registers, switching the q[0] and q[1] qubits' states using NOT or X gates, and measuring the control and target qubits after applying the CCNOT gate are declared as explained earlier. The CCNOT gate itself looks like this:

```
ccx q[0],q[1],q[2];
```

The declaration follows the familiar pattern of first specifying the gate, in this case ccX, and then the two control qubits, in q[0] and q[1], and the target qubit in q[2].

When we run this program, the two control qubits in q[0] and q[1] are |1⟩. Thus, the target qubit switches from |0⟩ to |1⟩. The output of this program on a simulator will look like the figure shown on page 62.

Result

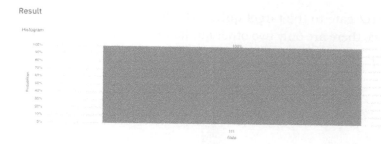

The state at the bottom of the blue bar is the concatenated c[2]c[1]c[0] value, which will be 111. Since this state will always be the output for this program, the height of the blue bar is 1 or 100%. (On a real computer, the 111 state will be seen most frequently. That is, it'll be the bar with the highest height.)

Summary of Quantum Logic Gates

The following table summarizes the NOT, CNOT, and CCNOT quantum gates:

Gate	Algebraic Expression	Common Uses
NOT	$\|a\rangle \mapsto \|1\rangle \oplus \|a\rangle$	Switching a qubit's state
CNOT	$\begin{pmatrix} \|a\rangle \\ \|b\rangle \end{pmatrix} \mapsto \begin{pmatrix} \|a\rangle \\ \|a\rangle \oplus \|b\rangle \end{pmatrix}$	FAN-OUT Gate, SWAP Gate
CCNOT	$\begin{pmatrix} \|a\rangle \\ \|b\rangle \\ \|c\rangle \end{pmatrix} \mapsto \begin{pmatrix} \|a\rangle \\ \|b\rangle \\ \|c\rangle \oplus (\|a\rangle \wedge \|b\rangle) \end{pmatrix}$	AND Gate, OR Gate

Logic Expressions to Quantum Circuit

So far, we've talked about quantum gates operating one at a time for the most part. Now, we're ready to put our knowledge of them to use by seeing how quantum gates can represent logic equations, a crucial first step to ultimately searching for a valid solution to them.

To keep things simple, we'll work with just the logic equations for slotting the talk show hosts, Kimmel and Maher, at the Bellagio, described in Writing a System of Boolean Logic Expressions, on page 8. Since we'll be using quantum bits to model the binary variables, we use $|k\rangle$ and $|m\rangle$, instead of k and m, to express the logic expression, namely:

$$\text{Bellagio on Day 1: } |\overline{k}\rangle \vee |\overline{m}\rangle$$

and

$$\text{Bellagio on Day 2: } |k\rangle \vee |m\rangle$$

For the Bellagio to have an artist perform on each day of the festival, both of these must evaluate to true, or $|1\rangle$:

$$\left(\,|\overline{k}\rangle \ \vee \ |\overline{m}\rangle\,\right) \wedge \left(\,|k\rangle \ \vee \ |m\rangle\,\right) = |1\rangle\,.$$

We'll call this logic expression the *Bellagio Constraints*.

Conceptually, the left-hand side of this logical expression can be drawn like the following:

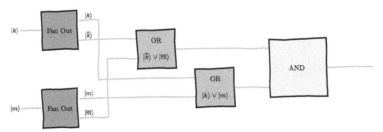

The only wrinkle in an otherwise straightforward logical expression of two OR clauses joined with an AND clause is the matter of simultaneously handling $|k\rangle$, $|m\rangle$, and their complements, $|\overline{k}\rangle$, $|\overline{m}\rangle$, in quantum circuits. It's not just applying a NOT operation to $|k\rangle$ and $|m\rangle$. Such an operation only affects a single qubit; $|k\rangle$ becomes $|\overline{k}\rangle$, for example, and then we no longer have $|k\rangle$. Rather, we need both $|k\rangle$ and $|\overline{k}\rangle$ to exist at the same time in the quantum circuit. Simply put, we need a way for a quantum state in a quantum register, say q[0], to force the quantum state in *another* quantum register, q[1], for instance, to be its complement.

In quantum computing, as we saw in FAN-OUT Gate, on page 51, we can synchronize two quantum states by using the quantum registers holding the control and target qubits of a CNOT gate, as shown here:

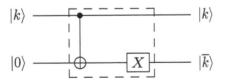

If $|k\rangle$ is $|0\rangle$, then the control and target qubits after the CNOT operation remain $|0\rangle$, but the NOT gate on the target qubit switches it to $|1\rangle$.

Likewise, if $|k\rangle$ is $|1\rangle$, then the control and target qubits after the CNOT operation are $|1\rangle$, and after the NOT operation on the target qubit, that qubit is $|0\rangle$. Thus, in both instances, we see that the two quantum registers holding the control and target qubits have complementary values.

This kind of configuration, without the NOT gate operating on the target qubit of the CNOT gate, is called a FAN-OUT gate. In the exercises, you'll have an opportunity to set one up and experiment with it.

We now have all the ingredients to translate the conceptual circuit to a real quantum circuit. The two FAN-OUT gates are realized with CNOT gates, and the OR and AND gates with CCNOT gates, as shown here:

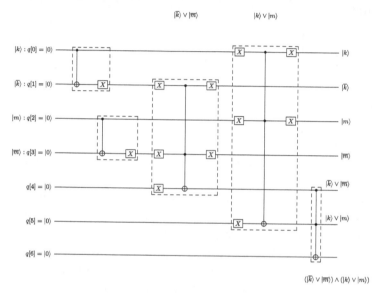

This circuit has 7 quantum registers, q[0]–q[6], specified as follows:

- Quantum registers q[0] and q[1] house the $|k\rangle$ and $|\bar{k}\rangle$ qubits, respectively.

- Quantum registers q[2] and q[3] house the $|m\rangle$ and $|\bar{m}\rangle$ qubits, respectively.

- Quantum registers q[4]–q[6] are the target qubits for the three CCNOT gates respectively.

The FAN-OUT gate for $|k\rangle$ and $|\bar{k}\rangle$ includes a CNOT gate followed by a NOT gate, as shown in the following figure:

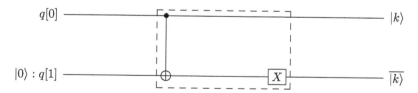

The code for these gates is the following:

```
cx q[0],q[1];
x q[1];
```

The quantum register q[0] represents the qubit for the quantum variable $|k\rangle$. The target qubit, q[1], is operated on by the NOT gate and represents the complement of $|k\rangle$, $|\bar{k}\rangle$.

Similarly, the FAN-OUT gate for $|m\rangle$ and $|\bar{m}\rangle$ is shown in the following figure:

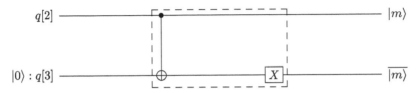

Here's the associated code:

```
cx q[2],q[3];
x q[3];
```

Next, the circuit for the OR clause, $|\bar{k}\rangle \vee |\bar{m}\rangle$, is specified with a CCNOT gate surrounded by NOT gates, as shown in the following figure:

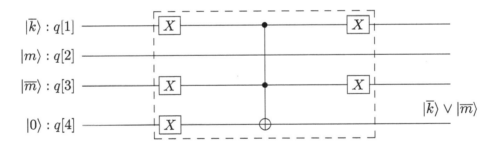

The code for this circuit is the following:

```
x q[1];
x q[3];
x q[4];
ccx q[1],q[3],q[4];
x q[1];
x q[3];
```

The controls are the qubits in the quantum registers q[1] and q[3], representing $|\bar{k}\rangle$ and $|\bar{m}\rangle$, respectively. The target is the qubit in the q[5] quantum register and represents the OR clause $|\bar{k}\rangle \vee |\bar{m}\rangle$.

Similarly, the OR clause $|k\rangle \vee |m\rangle$ is set up like this:

```
x q[0];
x q[2];
x q[5];
ccx q[0],q[2],q[5];
x q[0];
x q[2];
```

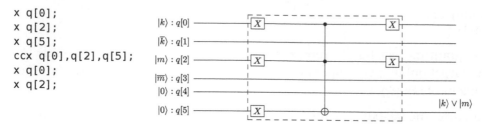

In this case, the controls are the qubits in the quantum registers q[0] and q[2], representing $|k\rangle$ and $|m\rangle$, respectively. The target is the qubit in the q[5] quantum register and represents the OR clause $|k\rangle \vee |m\rangle$.

Finally, these two OR clauses are joined with an AND operator using the CCNOT gate:

```
ccx q[4],q[5],q[6];
```

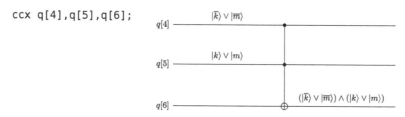

This completes the setup of the quantum circuit for the Bellagio Constraints.

If you'd like to run this circuit, you'll need to initialize the $|k\rangle$ and $|m\rangle$ qubits and then insert the Measure gates to read their collapsed states. For example, to execute the program with $|k\rangle = |1\rangle$ and $|m\rangle = |0\rangle$, we'd set up the following quantum circuit:

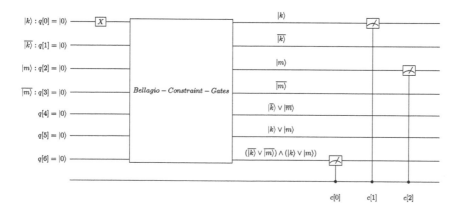

The box labeled Bellagio-Constraints-Gates encapsulates the gates modeling the Bellagio Constraints. A NOT gate is applied to the quantum register q[0] representing $|k\rangle$:

```
x q[0];
```

Note that the quantum register q[2] representing $|m\rangle$ is initialized by default to $|0\rangle$, so we don't have to do anything further here.

Finally, Measure gates are inserted to record the binary values associated with collapsing the following qubits:

- The Bellagio Constraints, which is the target qubit of the CCNOT gate in quantum register q[6], is recorded in the classical register c[0]:

  ```
  measure q[6] -> c[0];
  ```

- Qubit $|k\rangle$ in quantum register q[0], representing the artist Jimmy Kimmel's schedule, is recorded in the classical register c[1]:

  ```
  measure q[0] -> c[1];
  ```

- Qubit $|m\rangle$ in quantum register q[2], representing the artist Bill Maher's schedule, is recorded in the classical register c[2]:

  ```
  measure q[2] -> c[2];
  ```

Putting all this together, we get the following complete code listing for this circuit:

```
Bellagio_Constraints_k_1_m_0.qasm
// Initialize Quantum and Classical Registers
qreg q[7];
creg c[3];

// q[0]: |k> (Kimmel)
// q[1]: NOT |k> (NOT Kimmel)
// q[2]: |m> (Maher)
// q[3]: NOT |m> (NOT Maher)

// Initialize |k> to |1>
x q[0];

// Fan Out for |k> and NOT |k>
❶ cx q[0],q[1];
x q[1];

// Fan Out for |m> and NOT |m>
❷ cx q[2],q[3];
x q[3];
```

```
// (NOT |k>) OR (NOT |m>)
③ x q[1];
x q[3];
x q[4];
ccx q[1],q[3],q[4];
x q[1];
x q[3];

// |k> OR |m>
④ x q[0];
x q[2];
x q[5];
ccx q[0],q[2],q[5];
x q[0];
x q[2];

// ( (NOT |k>) OR (NOT |m>) ) AND (|k> OR |m>)
⑤ ccx q[4],q[5],q[6];

// Measure whether all constraints are met. Yes:1, No:0
⑥ measure q[6] -> c[0];

// Measure |k>
measure q[0] -> c[1];

// Measure |m>
measure q[2] -> c[2];
```

❶ FAN-OUT for $|k\rangle$ and $|\bar{k}\rangle$.

❷ FAN-OUT for $|m\rangle$ and $|\bar{m}\rangle$.

❸ OR gate for $|\bar{k}\rangle \vee |\bar{m}\rangle$.

❹ OR gate for $|k\rangle \vee |m\rangle$.

❺ AND gate to test whether both $|\bar{k}\rangle \vee |\bar{m}\rangle$ and $|k\rangle \vee |m\rangle$ are satisfied.

❻ The Measure gates for recording whether the qubit q[6], representing the constraint $(|k\rangle \vee |\bar{m}\rangle) \wedge (|k\rangle \vee |m\rangle)$, is satisfied and those for recording the qubits q[0] for Kimmel and q[2] for Maher, respectively.

If you run this circuit, the values recorded in the classical registers will be these:

$$c[0] = 1$$
$$c[1] = 1$$
$$c[2] = 0$$

This output corresponds to a valid schedule (since the Bellagio Constraints evaluates to 1 at termination). In the above circuit, we explicitly set the initial states for $|k\rangle$ and $|m\rangle$ and got lucky when they turned out to be a valid schedule. Our eventual goal, though, is to write a quantum program that automatically finds a valid schedule without having to iteratively try different combinations till we hit upon one that satisfies the constraints.

In the exercises at the end of this chapter, you'll have a chance to experiment with other values for $|k\rangle$ and $|m\rangle$. Specifically, you'll see that when a valid schedule can't be formed, the Bellagio Constraints is 0.

Now that the logical expressions representing the computation problem have been set up in the quantum program, we can begin introducing quantum effects in the program. In the next chapter, you'll first see how qubits can hold all solutions at once, an aspect that has no parallels in classical computing. In subsequent chapters, you'll then learn to apply more quantum effects to identify the correct solution.

Bottom Line

Functionally, quantum logic gates are similar to the classical equivalents but operate on quantum bits instead of binary bits. Although quantum programming doesn't have replicas of the binary logic gates such as AND and OR gates, their logic is replicated by suitably configuring the quantum Controlled NOT (CNOT) Gate, on page 47, and Controlled Controlled NOT (CCNOT) Gate, on page 57. But by themselves, the quantum logic gates offer no inherent advantage over the classical logic gates. In fact, even the quantum circuit on page 62 won't work any better than one designed with classical gates—you'll still need to iterate through all possible combinations to find the optimal solution.

Nonetheless, quantum logic gates play a crucial role in quantum computing: because they work with quantum bits, they can model a computational problem's constraints in a quantum program, like we did with the Bellagio Constraints. Classical binary gates can't be plugged in because they don't work on quantum hardware.

In the quantum programs in this chapter, we worked with the idealized, or pure, quantum bits, $|0\rangle$ and $|1\rangle$. In the next chapter, you'll learn to apply the Qubelets Model on page 20 on gates that act on blended qubits. We'll start with quantum gates that create blended quantum states. Once we know how to put qubits in states that have pentagon $|0\rangle$ and triangle $|1\rangle$ qubelets, we'll hook them up with the quantum logic gates that take us on an arc toward obtaining solutions in a fraction of the time of classical computing's check-each-one approach.

Try Your Hand

Solutions to these exercises are given in Quantum Logic Gates Solutions, on page 426.

For any code listing in the exercises, assume the following header lines:

```
OPENQASM 2.0;
include "qelib1.inc";
```

If you want to run any exercise, you must include them in the code you'd like to execute.

1. Write the code for the following circuit:

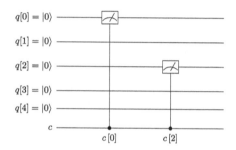

   a. Write the binary states recorded by the Measure gates. Write your answer as a concatenated string of the elements in the classical register.

   b. Run your code on a simulator.

   c. Run your code on a real quantum computer. Did you get the output you expected?

2. Consider the quantum circuit shown here:

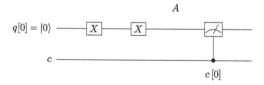

   a. Write a quantum program for this circuit.
   b. Is the state at point A blended?
   c. Write the state at point A.
   d. Can you observe the state at point A?
   e. What is the value recorded by the Measure gate?

f. Which of the following figures matches the output for the quantum circuit?

Figure 1—Output A

Figure 2—Output B

3. Draw the circuit for the following code:

```
NOT_Measure_NOT.qasm
qreg q[1];
creg c[1];

x q[0];
measure q[0] -> c[0];
x q[0];
```

4. Draw the circuit diagram and write the code for initializing a qubit in the quantum register q[0] to |1⟩.

5. Write the code for the circuit shown here:

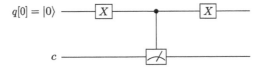

6. In the standard configuration of the CNOT gate, the target qubit's state is switched only when the control qubit is $|1\rangle$.

    a. Draw a quantum circuit to show how to control the switching of the target qubit's state when the control qubit is $|0\rangle$. (To test your circuit, set the target qubit to $|1\rangle$ and declare Measure gates to record the results.)

    b. Write the quantum program for the circuit you designed.

    c. Write down the values in each of the classical registers when the program terminates.

7. Consider the following quantum circuit:

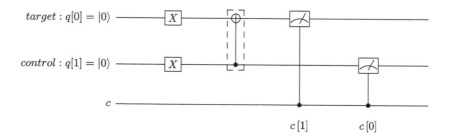

    a. Write a quantum program for this circuit.
    b. At termination, what are the values in the classical registers?

8. The following quantum circuit made up of three CNOT gates is used to SWAP qubits from one quantum register to another:

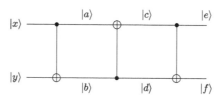

    a. Work out the quantum states $|a\rangle$, $|b\rangle$, $|c\rangle$, $|d\rangle$, $|e\rangle$, and $|f\rangle$ for the following values of $|x\rangle$ and $|y\rangle$:

        i. $|x\rangle$ is $|0\rangle$ and $|y\rangle$ is $|0\rangle$.
        ii. $|x\rangle$ is $|0\rangle$ and $|y\rangle$ is $|1\rangle$.
        iii. $|x\rangle$ is $|1\rangle$ and $|y\rangle$ is $|0\rangle$.
        iv. $|x\rangle$ is $|1\rangle$ and $|y\rangle$ is $|1\rangle$.

b. Write a quantum program to implement the SWAP gate when $|x\rangle$ is $|1\rangle$ and $|y\rangle$ is $|0\rangle$. Measure the value of the top qubit in the first cell of the classical register and the bottom qubit in the second cell.

   i. Write the classical register as a concatenated string when the program terminates.

9. The following circuit represents a FAN-OUT gate that makes a copy of a qubit:

$$q[0] = |a\rangle \quad\quad\quad |a\rangle$$
$$q[1] = |0\rangle \quad\quad\quad |a\rangle$$

a. Using this gate, design a quantum circuit that copies a $|1\rangle$ qubit, that is, $|a\rangle = |1\rangle$. Add Measure gates as appropriate to confirm that the qubit has been copied.

b. Write a quantum program for your circuit.

10. You'll need to become proficient in manipulating Boolean logic expressions if you want to design your own quantum programs. This exercise will give you an opportunity to sharpen your skills.

In OR Gate, on page 59, we argued that the CCNOT configuration on page 59 mimics an OR gate. Using Boolean algebra, explain why this is so. (Refer to Boolean Logic Expressions, on page 393, to brush up on frequently used expressions.)

11. In Writing a System of Boolean Logic Expressions, on page 8, the restrictions on the days each artist can perform at the hotels is listed. In this problem, you'll work with the following subset of the constraints related to the artists, Kimmel and Maher, performing at the Bellagio:

- Bellagio on Day 1: $|\bar{k}\rangle \vee |\bar{m}\rangle$
- Bellagio on Day 2: $|k\rangle \vee |m\rangle$

The qubits $|k\rangle$ and $|m\rangle$ stand for the artists Kimmel and Maher, respectively.

a. Draw a quantum circuit for the Bellagio Constraints with the following initial states:

$$|k\rangle = |1\rangle$$
$$|m\rangle = |1\rangle$$

b. Write a quantum program for the circuit you created.

c. Execute your program and measure the values of the $|\bar{k}\rangle$ and $|\bar{m}\rangle$ qubits as well as the Bellagio Constraints.

d. What can you say about this set of initial conditions?

12. In Writing a System of Boolean Logic Expressions, on page 8, the restrictions on the days each artist can perform at the hotels is listed. In this problem, you'll work with the following subset of the constraints related to the artists, Kimmel and Noah, performing at the Aladdin:

- Aladdin on Day 1: $|k\rangle \vee |\bar{n}\rangle$
- Aladdin on Day 2: $|\bar{k}\rangle \vee |n\rangle$

The qubits $|k\rangle$ and $|n\rangle$ stand for the artists Kimmel and Noah, respectively.

a. Write the logic expression that prevents scheduling conflicts for the artists performing at Aladdin, the *Aladdin Constraints*.

b. Draw a quantum circuit for the performance schedule for Jimmy Kimmel and Trevor Noah at Aladdin. The circuit should include the following:

- Initialize the quantum variables for Kimmel and Noah to $|1\rangle$ and $|1\rangle$, respectively.

- Insert a Measure gate to record the truth value of the constraint that determines whether the schedule is valid.

- Insert Measure gates to record the states for the variables representing Kimmel and Noah.

c. Write a quantum program for your circuit.

d. Does this initial set of quantum variables correspond to a valid schedule? If so, what days do Kimmel and Noah perform at Aladdin.

13. In Writing a System of Boolean Logic Expressions, on page 8, the restrictions on the days each artist can perform at the hotels is listed. In this problem, you'll work with the following subset of the constraints related to the artists Maher and Noah performing at Caesars:

- Caesars on Day 1: $|m\rangle \vee |n\rangle$
- Caesars on Day 2: $|\bar{m}\rangle \vee |\bar{n}\rangle$

The qubits $|m\rangle$ and $|n\rangle$ stand for the artists Maher and Noah, respectively.

a. Write the logic expression that prevents scheduling conflicts for the artists performing at Caesars, the *Caesars Constraints*.

b. Draw a quantum circuit for the performance schedule for Maher and Noah at Caesars. The circuit should include the following:

   - Initialize the quantum variables for Maher and Noah to $|1\rangle$ and $|1\rangle$, respectively.

   - Insert a Measure gate to record the truth value of the constraint that determines whether the schedule is valid.

   - Insert Measure gates to record the states for the variables representing Maher and Noah.

c. Write a quantum program for your circuit.

d. Does this initial set of quantum variables correspond to a valid schedule?

e. By experimenting with different quantum states for the variables for Maher and Noah, determine a feasible schedule for them.

CHAPTER 4

All Together Now—Quantum Superposition

In the previous chapter, we covered how to prod qubits from one idealized state, such as $|1\rangle$ and $|0\rangle$, to another idealized state by applying logic operations on them. In this chapter, we investigate gates that capitalize on quantum effects to poke qubits into states that are a combination, or *superposition*, of the $|1\rangle$ and $|0\rangle$ quantum states. In other words, we'll extend the Qubelets Model on page 20 to study ways to jab qubits and, more importantly for our purposes, push them into other quantum states until we're ready to collapse them. Since these quantum superposition gates have no classical equivalents, their behavior can't be natively reproduced on classical computers. We'll see that this singular characteristic is one of the major drivers of designing quantum algorithms that give us the ability to deal with the entire solution space as a single unit. In later chapters, you'll see that superposition forms the basis for quantum programs that rapidly home in on the optimal solution of computational problems with X-ray-vision–like precision.

We've seen how to perform logical operations with qubits. So we begin the next phase of our study of quantum computing by covering how to put qubits in a blended state that is a superposition of $|0\rangle$ and $|1\rangle$. Putting qubits in superposition, as well as performing logic operations on them, is needed to solve Boolean expressions.

By the end of this chapter, you'll learn how to use superposition and the central role it plays in dealing with "all solutions at once," which makes quantum computing appealing. You'll also see that the collapse of qubits from arbitrary quantum states is controllable, a key aspect for making quantum computing reliable and practical.

Operating on Qubelets

The quantum computing literature is replete with a litany of the same smattering of algorithms expounded over and over again in the language of mathematics. Mathematics simplifies the tale but sometimes interferes with developing an intuitive feel for the topic. So if you want to mature into an accomplished quantum programmer and develop your own algorithms instead of recycling canned routines, it's worth spending time to strengthen your grasp of quantum superposition.

We'll work with the Qubelets Model on page 20 to help you visualize how quantum gates operate on qubits and handle multiple quantum states simultaneously. Building on this understanding of quantum computing, you'll get an intuitive feel for designing quantum algorithms for your own computational tasks.

With this model of qubits as a bundle of pentagon and triangle qubelets, we can now talk about the different things that can happen to qubelets when a qubit is acted on by quantum gates. The qubelets are, of course, imaginary. So the actions on them by the gates aren't real physical processes but fictional mechanisms that nonetheless accurately predict how they act on qubits. I know it may not be clear what these operations do; stick with me. Their purpose will become apparent shortly.

Basic Operations

Specifically, the ways that quantum gates operate on a qubit's qubelets include:

- *Switching*: A quantum gate can switch a qubelet of one type with another. For example, in the $|0\rangle$ qubit, the pentagon $|0\rangle$ qubelet is replaced with a triangle $|1\rangle$ qubelet, resulting in a $|1\rangle$ qubit, as shown in the following figure:

This operation is a NOT operation but done on qubelets.

- *Splitting* or *Replacing*: A quantum gate can split or replace qubelets. For example, a pentagon $|0\rangle$ qubelet can be split into two qubelets: a pentagon $|0\rangle$ qubelet and a triangle $|1\rangle$ qubelet, as shown in the figure on page 79.

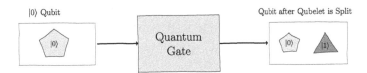

The quantum gate acts on the $|0\rangle$ qubit, containing a single pentagon $|0\rangle$ qubelet, and modifies it to a qubelet containing a single pentagon $|0\rangle$ and a single triangle $|1\rangle$ qubelet.

- *Inverting*: A quantum gate can invert qubelets of the same type. For instance, the pentagon $|0\rangle$ qubelet on the left is turned upside-down, as shown here:

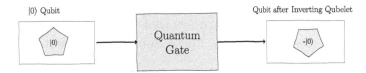

Comparing it to a coin, this operation on a qubelet is akin to rotating the coin face.

To show that a qubelet has been inverted, we'll use a negative sign. Thus, $-|0\rangle$ is an inverted pentagon qubelet. If you measure this qubit, it'll still collapse to the 0 classical state.

- *Operating on Inverted Qubelets*: When a quantum gate operates on inverted qubelets, the affected qubelets are given another half turn. For example, consider a quantum gate that inverts triangle $|1\rangle$ qubelets:

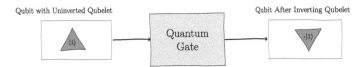

If a quantum gate acts on this inverted triangle $|1\rangle$ qubelet, the qubelet will be given a half turn, shown as follows:

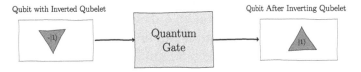

After the quantum gate operates on the inverted qubelet, the qubelet is put into the original non-inverted orientation.

- *Affecting only one type*: It's not necessary that a quantum gate operates on the entire bundle of qubelets. It can modify only one type of qubelet, for example, the pentagon $|0\rangle$ qubelets, and leave the other type, the triangle $|1\rangle$ qubelets, unaffected:

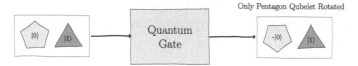

The pentagon $|0\rangle$ qubelet is inverted, while the triangle $|1\rangle$ qubelet isn't touched.

- *Canceling Qubelets*: It's possible that we can end up with a qubit in which some qubelets of one type are inverted while others of the same type are not. In this case, the inverted and non-inverted qubelets *interfere*—cancel or erase each other out.

Interference

 In quantum mechanics, the term *interference* is used to describe phenomena where the intensities of particles such as photons and electrons are neutralized, similar to the interference pattern of colliding waves.[1]

In the following figure, the qubit on the left has two non-inverted pentagon $|0\rangle$ qubelets, one non-inverted triangle $|1\rangle$ qubelet, and one inverted triangle $|1\rangle$ qubelet:

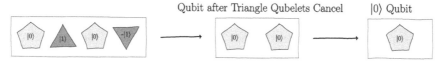

The inverted and non-inverted triangle $|1\rangle$ qubelets cancel each other out, leaving only the two pentagon $|0\rangle$ qubelets, as shown in the middle qubit. Further, since the middle qubit can only collapse to $|0\rangle$, it's equivalent to a qubit with a single pentagon $|0\rangle$ qubelet, as shown in the right qubit.

---

1.   https://en.wikipedia.org/wiki/Double-slit_experiment#Interference_of_individual_particles.

Canceling Qubelets and Polarized Light

Polarization isn't directly involved in quantum computing, but it illustrates *canceling*, a central concept in quantum computing. Canceling isn't setting a bit to 0. It's removing the bit completely from the computer, a notion that is alien to classical computing—one can't just get rid of registers. In quantum computing, however, since a qubit holds multiple states, canceling or removing states is common. Nonetheless, canceling is "unnatural" in computing, so a physical analogy may make it credible.

Canceling qubelets seems contrived: when thinking of a quantum state as a spinning coin, what does it mean when we say that the tails face is canceled?

But this notion isn't as far-fetched as it appears. Consider, for example, a beam of light that's made up of two polarized waves:

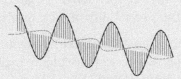

Think of this wave as made up of pentagon $|0\rangle$ qubelets and triangle $|1\rangle$ qubelets, where the triangles outnumber the pentagons.

Now add the following vertically polarized wave that is shifted by half a wavelength from that of the vertical polarized wave in the previous figure:

This wave is made up entirely of triangle $|1\rangle$ qubelets that are inverted.

The resulting combined beam of light would look like this:

The two vertical polarized waves now are directly opposite each other and, hence, cancel each other out, leaving only the horizontal polarized wave:

The non-inverted triangle $|1\rangle$ qubelets from the first beam of light cancel with the inverted triangle $|1\rangle$ qubelets from the second beam, giving a horizontally polarized beam that's effectively a quantum state made up of pentagon $|0\rangle$ qubelets.

Compound Operations

In general, a particular quantum gate applies a specific combination of these operations. So, for example, you could have a quantum gate that switches and inverts qubelets as shown in the following figure:

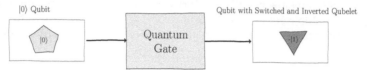

This quantum gate replaces the pentagon $|0\rangle$ qubelet with a triangle $|1\rangle$ qubelet and inverts it, as shown on the right in the previous figure. (If you measure the right qubit, it would still collapse to the $|1\rangle$ idealized quantum state. The inversion doesn't affect the probability of picking the triangle $|1\rangle$ qubelet.)

This odd behavior of qubits isn't invented by scientists. It's apparently how nature works—we've simply discovered the rules to explain quantum mechanical phenomena and harness them to build the next generation of computers.

Quantum gates can apply other operations on qubelets—the rotations don't always have to be a half turn. We'll get precise with these operations in Chapter 6, Designer Genes—Custom Quantum States, on page 141. But for now, we're ready to see how quantum computers act on a qubit's bundle of qubelets to put the qubits in superposition.

Putting Qubits in Blended States

The Hadamard (H) gate puts qubits in blended states of $|0\rangle$ and $|1\rangle$. It's the signature gate of quantum computing and forms the bedrock of quantum programs. For me, it was one of the two quantum gates that brought home the terrific potential of quantum computing. (The other is the Pauli-Z gate, which we'll cover in Chapter 5, Beam Me Up, Scotty—Quantum Tagging and Entangling, on page 107.)

The H gate is fundamentally a *qubelet splitter*, which is the basic mechanism to create blended qubits. For example, it takes a $|0\rangle$ qubit, which is essentially a pentagon $|0\rangle$ qubelet, and splits it into another pentagon $|0\rangle$ and triangle $|1\rangle$ qubelet, as shown in the following figure:

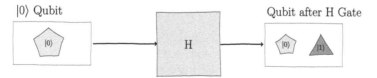

If you measure the blended qubit on the right, it'll collapse to $|0\rangle$ roughly 50% of the time and will flop to $|1\rangle$ the other times. You'll never actually see the qubit in a blended state.

The H gate is often the first quantum gate you declare in quantum programs. It puts qubits in superposition so that other quantum gates can act on them to modify their quantum states.

\// **Joe asks:**
ใ๊

Why Is It Called the Hadamard Gate?

The oddly named gate is a tribute to the French mathematician Jacques Hadamard, who along with the German mathematician Issai Schur, is credited with formulating the tensor product of matrices,[a] a specialized matrix multiplication technique that's central to analyzing the superposition states in quantum circuits. We'll get to see how this works in Chapter 8, Giant Leap for Mankind—Multi-Qubit Programs, on page 227.

---

a.   https://en.wikipedia.org/wiki/Hadamard_product_(matrices)

H Gate on $|0\rangle$ Qubit

To see this gate in action, let's build the following quantum circuit:

This circuit has only a single quantum register, q[0] initialized with a $|0\rangle$ qubit, and a single-bit classical register, c[0]. The Measure gate collapses the quantum state after the H gate acts on the qubit, and it records the corresponding binary value that the qubit settles down to in the classical register c[0].

On the IBM Quantum Computer, you can simply drag the H gate from the palette and place it on the wire representing q[0]. Then, drag the Measure gate and record the value of the collapsed qubit in c[0].

The code listing, excluding the header, for this circuit is as follows:

H_Gate.qasm
```
qreg q[1];
creg c[1];

// Put q[0] in superposition
h q[0];
measure q[0] -> c[0];
```

Declare the H gate, as shown on the highlighted line: the type of gate, in this case, h, followed by the qubit, q[0], that it acts on.

When we execute this program, the q[0] qubit is put into a superposition by the H gate. That is, it's now a bundle of pentagon |0⟩ and triangle |1⟩ qubelets. Thus, when this qubit is measured, it'll randomly collapse to the |0⟩ or |1⟩ idealized states, which correspond to the 0 or 1 binary states, with equal probability, as shown in the following output:

Result

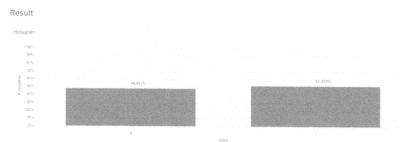

The output shows that the qubit, after its been operated on by the H gate, collapses roughly half the time to |0⟩ and about half the time to |1⟩, which are, in turn, recorded as 0 and 1 in the classical registers.

But what does the assertion "qubit collapses to |1⟩ half the time" really mean? To see what's behind this claim, let's rerun this program a little differently than a standard execution.

When a quantum program is typically invoked, it's rarely just run once. More likely, the program is run repeatedly. For each run, or shot, the following steps are executed:

- The qubits in the quantum register are operated upon by the quantum gates as specified in the quantum program.

- The Measure gates inspect the qubits and record the corresponding binary states in the classical register.

- The system keeps a running tally of the 1 and 0 values observed in the classical register after each shot. At the end of the specified number of runs, the system shows the number of times, as a percentage, a 1 or 0 was observed in each classical register element.

Let's make this a little less abstract by investigating what happens when we force our program to execute just once. To specify the number of times, or shots, you want to execute your program, click the Run button and on the dialog window that opens, specify the number of shots in the second drop-down list as shown on page 85.

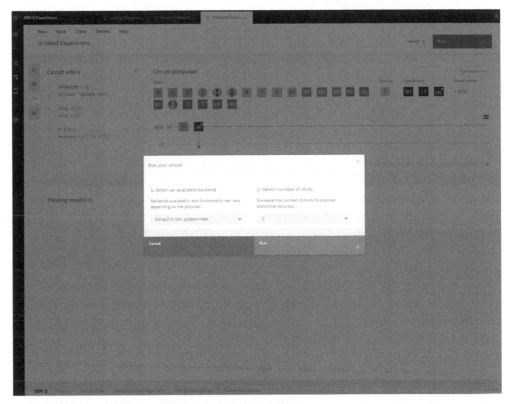

Then run your code. The solitary qubit in this circuit can only collapse once in a single run. So, you'll only find it in *either* a 0 or 1 binary state in the classical register at termination. Put another way, one of these two possibilities will occur with 100% probability. In my case, the qubit collapsed to |1⟩ with the corresponding binary state 1, as shown in the following figure:

This single shot run confirms that the qubit still only collapses to one of the two idealized quantum states—there's no bizarre two-headed bit created. In our subsequent quantum programs, we'll always execute them several times and keep count of the number of times each qubit collapses to |0⟩ or |1⟩ in each run.

H Gate on $|1\rangle$ Qubit

The H gate acts almost identically on the $|1\rangle$ qubit:

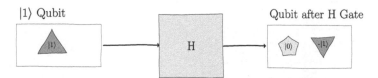

The blended qubit on the right still has an equal number of pentagon $|0\rangle$ qubelets and triangle $|1\rangle$ qubelets. But the triangle $|1\rangle$ qubelets are inverted from those on the qubelets bundle after the H gate acted on a $|0\rangle$ qubit. We label the quantum state on an inverted qubit with a negative sign. Thus, the operation of the H gate on a $|1\rangle$ qubit is expressed as:

$$|1\rangle \mapsto |0\rangle \text{ and } - |1\rangle$$

When the qubit with the bundle of inverted triangle $|1\rangle$ qubelets is inspected, a pentagon $|0\rangle$ or $|1\rangle$ qubelet will still be randomly picked with equal probability; in other words, examining a $|1\rangle$ qubit immediately after it's operated on by the H gate will still be statistically equivalent had the H gate acted on a $|0\rangle$ qubit.

It seems that the behavior of the H gate is the same whether we feed it a $|0\rangle$ or a $|1\rangle$ qubit—the probabilities of recording a 0 or 1 in the classical register are identical. But in quantum programming, we write quantum instructions that modify the quantum states of qubits. That is, the program works with qubelets, and it's not till the end that we collapse the qubits and record the corresponding binary states. So even though the H gate collapses the $|0\rangle$ and $|1\rangle$ qubits identically, it affects the pentagon $|0\rangle$ qubelets and the triangle $|1\rangle$ qubelets differently. (This state of affairs is akin to what John Wanamaker, a pioneering U.S. retailer, famously quipped: "Half the money I spend on advertising is wasted; the trouble is I don't know which half.") We'll have more to say about these types of collapses in Chapter 6, Designer Genes—Custom Quantum States, on page 141.

H Gate on $|1\rangle$ Qubit with an Inverted $|1\rangle$ Qubelet

The H gate can also act on a $|1\rangle$ qubit in which the triangle $|1\rangle$ qubelet is inverted on the left qubit:

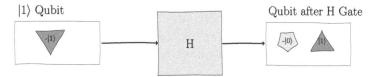

As we saw earlier, when the H gate acts on a |1⟩ qubit, an equal number of pentagon |0⟩ and triangle |1⟩ qubelets are created, but the triangle qubelets are inverted. But when a |1⟩ qubit in which the triangle |1⟩ qubelets are initially inverted is acted on by the H gate, the H gate splits the qubelets: the pentagon |0⟩ qubelets stay in their initial orientation (inverted), but the triangle |1⟩ qubelets are inverted from their initial orientation.

The chances of picking either a pentagon or triangle qubit is still roughly half, and so the qubit will still collapse to either |0⟩ or |1⟩ with approximately equal probability.

H Gate on |0⟩ Qubit with Inverted |0⟩ Qubelet

And, of course, a |0⟩ qubit could be an inverted pentagon |0⟩ qubelet, as shown in the following figure:

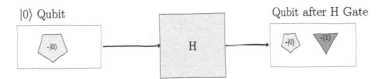

Here again, when the H gate operates on the inverted pentagon |0⟩ qubelet, the qubelet is split into another pentagon |0⟩ qubelet and triangle |1⟩ qubelet, but they're inverted.

Summary of Basic H Gate Operations

At first, the operation of the H gate may seem confusing. But you only need to keep in mind the following:

- The H gate is a qubelet splitter.

- When a triangle |1⟩ qubelet is split, the resulting triangle |1⟩ qubelet is inverted while the pentagon |0⟩ qubelet is not inverted.

- When an inverted qubelet is fed to the H gate, the operation of the H gate is inverted—a non-inverted qubelet is inverted and an inverted qubelet is non-inverted.

All this inverting and non-inverting of qubelets has no impact on the probability of which classical state is ultimately recorded in the classical register. This randomness, though, isn't yet helpful and, in practice, we don't collapse the qubit right away. In the next section, we'll see that inverted qubelets give a path to control the collapse of qubits and not have them flop about randomly. You'll learn to continue operating on the bundle of pentagon |0⟩ and triangle

$|1\rangle$ qubelets till they cough up something useful—essentially, we'll tilt the odds to favor specific classical states when the qubits collapse. First we need to heighten our understanding of the superposition gates.

Back-to-Back H Gates: The First Hint of Taming Randomness

In the previous section, we saw the H gate operating on $|0\rangle$ and $|1\rangle$ qubits. When we measure a qubit that's just been fed to an H gate, though, all we ever get is one of the two classical states. We never see inverted qubelets. We can, however, indirectly confirm the existence of inverted qubelets in a qubit by not inspecting it immediately but by passing it to other gates before collapsing it.

So the next quantum circuit we'll look at is hooking up two consecutive H gates, as shown in the following figure:

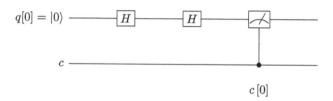

Note that the second H gate acts on a blended qubit that's been put in a superposition of $|1\rangle$ and $|0\rangle$ by the first H gate.

Here's the corresponding quantum program, excluding the header:

```
H_H_Measure.qasm
qreg q[1];
creg c[1];

// Back-to-back H gates
h q[0];
h q[0];

measure q[0] -> c[0];
```

We might be tempted to think that two coin tosses are just as random as a single toss—the coin still lands heads or tails with equal probability—so the collapse of the qubit after being operated on twice by the H gate should also collapse to 1 with roughly the same likelihood as 0. But that isn't the case. The state of the collapsed qubit is shown in the figure on page 89.

Result

In every shot, the qubit consistently collapses to 0. We get the same behavior whether we run one shot, 1,024, or a million. In each case, the second toss counters the first and arrests the randomness so that, in effect, the coin always lands showing the same face. This circuit is the first clue that the collapse of a blended qubit isn't always random but can be controlled.

You'll see similar results on a real quantum computer, as shown in the following figure:

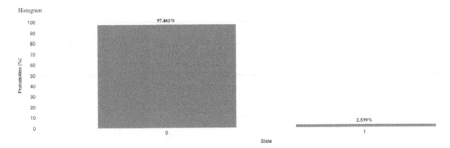

In almost every case, the qubit returns to the original state of $|0\rangle$. Because you're running on a real quantum computer, expect tiny disturbances so that in a small number of instances the qubit doesn't get back to $|0\rangle$.

Why Back-to-Back H Gates are Neutralizers

Analyzing this quantum circuit with the Qubelets Model gives us a clearer picture of what's going on with the qubit when it's consecutively operated on by two H gates. The quantum circuit is initialized with a $|0\rangle$ qubit, which is basically just a single pentagon $|0\rangle$ qubelet, as shown in the left qubit in this figure:

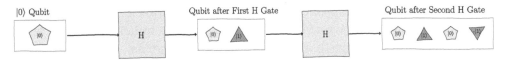

The middle qubit is the result of the first H gate on the left acting on the $|0\rangle$ qubit. The H gate splits the pentagon $|0\rangle$ qubelet in the $|0\rangle$ qubit on the left into another pentagon |0⟩ qubelet and a triangle |1⟩ qubelet, as shown in the middle qubit in the same figure.

This blended qubit in the middle is then operated on by the second H gate on the right. This H gate splits the qubelets in the middle qubit as follows:

- The pentagon |0⟩ qubelet is split into another pentagon |0⟩ qubelet and a triangle |1⟩ qubelet.

- The triangle |1⟩ qubelet is split into a pentagon |0⟩ qubelet and an *inverted* triangle |1⟩ qubelet.

The two triangle |1⟩ qubelets, one inverted and the other non-inverted, in the right qubit in the figure cancel each other out, leaving two pentagon |0⟩ qubelets, as shown in the middle qubit here:

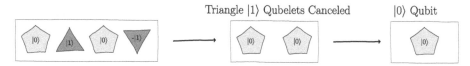

And such a qubit is equivalent to one with a single pentagon |0⟩ qubelet, as shown on the right. In other words, a |0⟩ qubit acted on by two back-to-back H gates just returns to being a |0⟩ qubit again. (In the exercises at the end of this chapter, you'll see that back-to-back H gates work identically on a |1⟩ qubit.)

The sequence of steps outlined on the right qubit take place instantaneously. There's no time lag. And, more importantly, even though we've drawn these transformations as happening after the gates, they really take place as the gate is operating on the qubit.

So, although a single H gate acts like a coin toss, back-to-back H gates never behave randomly. This decidedly oddball characteristic is a direct result of selectively inverting only the triangle qubelets. In fact, if the H gate was just like a fair coin toss, it wouldn't be terribly interesting from an algorithmic standpoint.

Back-to-back H gates by themselves, though, aren't very useful—you end up right where you started from. But, you learned how to analyze quantum circuits with the Qubelets Model. And it did demonstrate that randomness is controllable: the "selective negation" which wipes out qubelets gives us levers to collapse qubits in ways that solve Boolean logic expressions without having to sequentially test every possibility. We'll cover these techniques in Chapter 10, Quantum Search, on page 295, after we've investigated other ways to handle qubits.

Parallels with Quantum Mechanics

Thus far, we've talked about quantum mechanics concepts in the abstract and have not talked about how it came about and its motivations. So as to make quantum computing less science fiction and to give you confidence in the Qubelets Model, we've described experiments in Appendix 3, Quantum Mechanics with Qubelets, on page 415, whose behavior you can analyze with qubelets. You'll also see that the H gate is a direct derivative of these phenomena.

Multi-Qubit Superposition: The Mega-Qubit

Controlling randomness is, without doubt, an essential ingredient for quantum computing. But quantum computing offers an even more compelling case for reinventing computing. It gives us a way to deal with the entire solution space as a single unit. This may sound intimidating, but we'll learn that to think about the entire solution space at once, we must focus on the characteristics a solution obeys rather than on the individual solutions themselves. So, before designing quantum algorithms that find a solution to a system of Boolean expressions, we need to first get comfortable with this shift in mindset.

Parallel H Gates

For our next exercise, we'll deal with two qubits and learn how to grapple with all-solutions-at-once. We'll start with the following circuit with two qubits:

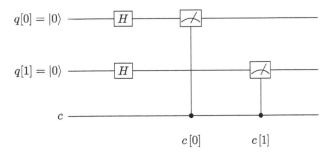

Here's the code, excluding the header, for this circuit:

```
Parallel_H_Gates.qasm
qreg q[2];
creg c[2];

// Put qubits in superposition
h q[0];
h q[1];

measure q[0] -> c[0];
measure q[1] -> c[1];
```

Each qubit is initialized to $|0\rangle$ and acted on by the H gate. This puts each qubit in a superposition, as shown here:

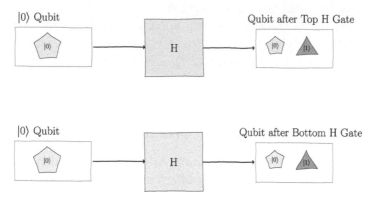

If we feed these qubits to other gates, then those other gates will operate on blended qubits. To put it another way, those gates will operate on the various combinations formed by the qubelets in the top and bottom qubits. We represent these combinations of qubelets as a *mega-qubit*, as shown in the following figure:

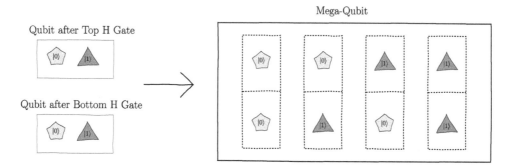

In each combination, or column, of qubelets in the mega-qubit on the right, the top qubelet is from the top qubit, and the bottom qubelet from the bottom qubit. The qubelets on the top represent the quantum state of the top qubit, and those on the bottom represent the bottom qubit. Thus, each column is a possible state of the qubits. In this case, the mega-qubit has four states: $|00\rangle$, $|01\rangle$, $|10\rangle$, and $|11\rangle$, where the first digit is the top qubit and the second one is the bottom qubit.

Mega-Qubit Is the Quantum State of System

The mega-qubit models the quantum state of the system. It's an aggregate of the entire set of qubelet columns, each of which represents a possible value of the qubits in the circuit.

The mega-qubits used to analyze the behavior of qubits, however, are a mental device to help us analyze quantum circuits and write programs that properly harness quantum behavior. They're not real, at least not in the traditional sense. No one really knows what happens at the quantum level. So the mega-qubit serves as a stand-in for subatomic phenomena that helps us arrive at results that can be verified.

Even though we've drawn the mega-qubit holding four distinct combinations or columns of qubelets, in reality they are *all* presented simultaneously to the subsequent gates as blended qubits. The mega-qubit, in fact, represents the *state of the entire system* and is the key to how quantum computers solve problems. Thus, you may think of a quantum computer as a massively parallel processor running on jet fuel.

When we run this circuit, after passing the top and bottom qubits to the H gate, we measure them, thereby collapsing them. Measuring the qubits is equivalent to first selecting a qubelet combination, or column, at random from the mega-qubit and then recording the corresponding binary bits. So we'll see each of the four cases—00, 01, 10, and 11—roughly 25% of the time, as shown here:

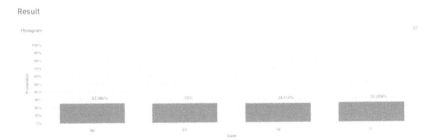

Note that as per the quantum circuit, we're recording the collapsed state of q[0] in c[0] of the classical register and that of q[1] in c[1]. Thus, in each string of qubits at the bottom of the bars in the output, the left character corresponds to the classical state that the qubit in q[1] collapses to, and the right character is the binary state of the collapsed qubit in q[0].

Operating on Mega-Qubits

To see how a quantum computer deals with a mega-qubit, consider the following quantum circuit:

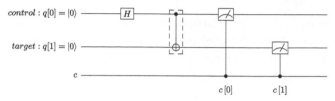

The code for this circuit is the following:

CNOT_with_H_on_Control.qasm

```
qreg q[2];
creg c[2];

h q[0];
cx q[0],q[1];
measure q[0] -> c[0];
measure q[1] -> c[1];
```

After the top qubit is operated on by the H gate, the qubits will be in the quantum states shown here:

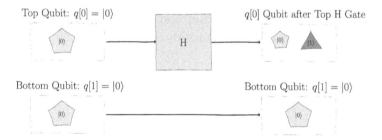

This blended qubit is put into a superposition with the bottom $|0\rangle$ qubit: each qubelet in the top qubit pairs up with the single pentagon $|0\rangle$ qubelet in the bottom qubit to form the following mega-qubit:

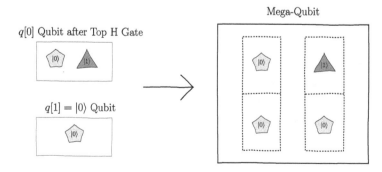

The top qubelets in each column are associated with the q[0] qubit, and the bottom qubelets are associated with the q[1] qubit.

When this mega-qubit is operated on by the CNOT gate, all the qubelet combinations are simultaneously operated on by the CNOT gate. Even though all the qubelet combinations are acted on all at once, to work out what the new mega-qubit would look like, we apply the CNOT gate individually on each qubelet combination. As we saw in Controlled NOT (CNOT) Gate, on page 47, the CNOT gate leaves $|00\rangle$ as is but changes $|10\rangle$ to $|11\rangle$. Thus, the mega-qubit after applying the CNOT gate is shown here:

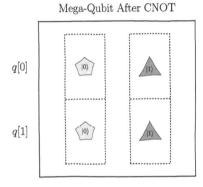

Mega-Qubit After CNOT

If we now measure the control and target qubits, one of the two qubelet combinations in the mega-qubit would be randomly selected with equal probability. Thus, we would see the states 00 or 11 roughly equally. Specifically, the output of the program is shown in the following figure:

Taming the Mega-Qubit Explosion: A Sneak Peek

While the mega-qubit model gives us a way to think about quantum superposition, it introduces a significant challenge: with two qubits, we get four pairs of qubelet combinations or columns; with three qubits, we get eight combinations; and with n qubits we get 2^n combinations. For large problems, this situation rapidly becomes unmanageable when designing quantum programs.

The hardware won't break a sweat, but writing and thinking about code in the classical way becomes impractical.

Quantum programming takes a different approach. Instead of focusing on writing software that steers each combination through the program individually, in quantum programming our objective will be to identify the characteristics of a solution and then configure gates to cull the quantum states that don't play a role in solving the computational task. We won't know what the optimal solution is to a computational task when we write the code, we will know that the Boolean constraints have to be met. Specifically, we'll see how the Z gate, which we study in Chapter 5, Beam Me Up, Scotty—Quantum Tagging and Entangling, on page 107, inverts qubelets to cancel out the unwanted states. We'll get into the details later, but I wanted to give you at least a glimpse of the path forward. Next we'll review how to put the qubits in a quantum circuit into superposition.

Triggering Superposition in Practical Quantum Circuits

In practical quantum circuits such as those for solving a system of Boolean equations, we have qubits that represent the system's variables, the *primary* or independent qubits, and those that are the "working," or *secondary* qubits. For example, in the quantum circuit that represents the schedule of performers in the Bellagio Constraints, only qubits q[0] and q[2] represent the performer's schedule; the others are working or intermediate qubits required to correctly model the constraints in the quantum circuit, as shown here:

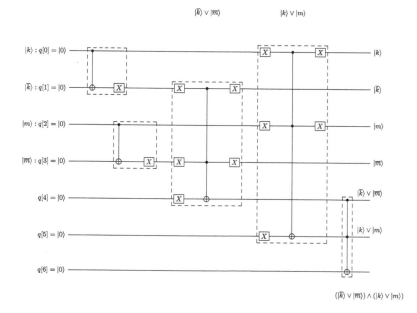

Thus, we only need to place the primary qubits q[0] and q[2] into blended states. The others, the secondary or dependent qubits, get driven into blended states by the gates that operate on them. The modified circuit showing the H gates acting on the q[0] and q[2] qubits is shown in the following figure:

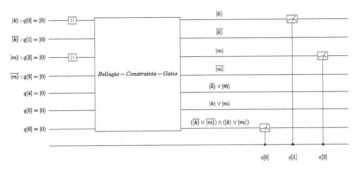

The pentagon $|0\rangle$ and triangle $|1\rangle$ qubelets from each primary qubit join together to form the qubelet combinations in the mega-qubit. Since there are only two primary qubits, q[0] and q[2], there'll be 2^2 or 4 independent qubelet combinations in the mega-qubit. Each qubelet combination will hold a possible quantum state of all the qubits. In particular, the mega-qubit after q[0] and q[2] have been operated on by the H gates looks like this:

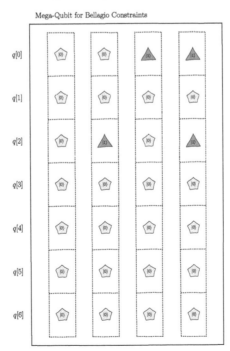

Mega-Qubit for Bellagio Constraints

Each column of qubelets corresponds to a possible combination of qubits. The qubelet in the top cell is in q[0], the qubelet in the second from top cell is in q[1], and so on to the qubelet in the bottom cell in q[6]. So, the second column, for example, is the quantum state $|0010000\rangle$.

After the qubelet combinations in the mega-qubit are operated on by the gates that model the Bellagio Constraints, but before the qubit q[6] is measured, is shown here:

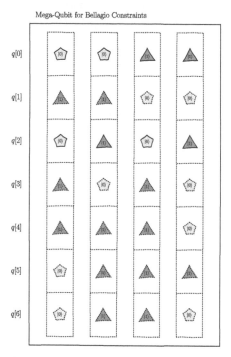

In each column of qubelets, the primary qubelets are in the first and third cells representing q[0] and q[2], respectively. The qubelets in the other cells of each column are determined by the gates operating on the various qubits. The qubelets corresponding to the primary qubits, q[0] and q[2], are shown in solid outlines on the first and third rows, respectively, while the others are dotted. Note that although we only applied the H gate to the qubits in q[0] and q[2], all the qubits are forced into blended states.

For example, the gates in the top left of the Bellagio Constraints circuit perform a FAN-OUT operation on the q[0] and q[1] qubits, representing the quantum states $|k\rangle$ and $|k\rangle$, respectively. Thus, when the top cell of column 1, the left-most, holds a pentagon $|0\rangle$ qubelet, the qubelet in the second cell of the same column will be a triangle $|1\rangle$. And, since its state is based on the qubelet in the top cell, the triangle is dotted. Likewise, the qubelets in the other cells are determined by tracing how the quantum gates affect them, as listed in this table:

	Qubit	Column 1	Column 2	Column 3	Column 4
$\overline{\lvert k\rangle}$	q[0]	$\lvert 0\rangle$	$\lvert 0\rangle$	$\lvert 1\rangle$	$\lvert 1\rangle$
$\lvert k\rangle$	q[1]	$\lvert 1\rangle$	$\lvert 1\rangle$	$\lvert 0\rangle$	$\lvert 0\rangle$
$\lvert m\rangle$	q[2]	$\lvert 0\rangle$	$\lvert 1\rangle$	$\lvert 0\rangle$	$\lvert 1\rangle$
$\overline{\lvert m\rangle}$	q[3]	$\lvert 1\rangle$	$\lvert 0\rangle$	$\lvert 1\rangle$	$\lvert 0\rangle$
$\lvert k\rangle \vee \overline{\lvert m\rangle}$	q[4]	$\lvert 1\rangle$	$\lvert 1\rangle$	$\lvert 1\rangle$	$\lvert 0\rangle$
$\overline{\lvert k\rangle} \vee \lvert m\rangle$	q[5]	$\lvert 0\rangle$	$\lvert 1\rangle$	$\lvert 1\rangle$	$\lvert 1\rangle$
$(\lvert k\rangle \vee \overline{\lvert m\rangle}) \wedge (\overline{\lvert k\rangle} \vee \lvert m\rangle)$	q[6]	$\lvert 0\rangle$	$\lvert 1\rangle$	$\lvert 1\rangle$	$\lvert 0\rangle$

Note that the quantum states $\lvert 0\rangle$ and $\lvert 1\rangle$ shown in this table represent the pentagon and triangle qubelets and not the quantum states of the qubits themselves. The quantum state of a qubit is obtained by reading across a row in the table or the mega-qubit shown in the previous figure. So, the quantum state of the q[0] qubit, representing the $\lvert k\rangle$ variable, is obtained by reading across the first row: $\lvert 0011\rangle$.

If you run this circuit over multiple shots, the qubits won't collapse to a single quantum state like they did in Chapter 3, Elementary, My Dear Watson—Quantum Logic, on page 41. Since we're measuring blended qubits, the mega-qubit resolves to one of the columns at random, and the qubits that have the Measure gates, q[0], q[2], and q[6], are collapsed. For each selected column, the classical registers will record the binary states corresponding to the qubelets in rows 1, 3, and 7 corresponding to qubits q[0], q[2], and q[6], of the mega-qubit. These collapsed states are listed in this table:

Classical Register	Column 1	Column 2	Column 3	Column 4
$q[0] \mapsto c[1]$	0	0	1	1
$q[2] \mapsto c[2]$	0	1	0	1
$q[6] \mapsto c[0]$	0	1	1	0

Since each classical state is reported as a concatenated string c[2]c[1]c[0], when you run this program, you'll see four bars in the output corresponding to the four columns in the mega-qubit. By reading from bottom to top for each column in the above table, you'll get the four states: 000, 110, 101, and 011, all appearing with equal probability, as shown in the figure on page 100.

Without having to explicitly write for-loops, we got our quantum program to cycle through all combinations for the system of Boolean expressions. We're ultimately only interested in those states in which c[0] is 1 since those

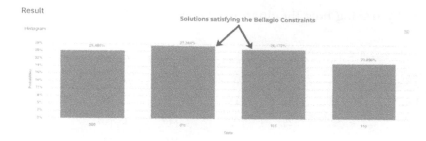

correspond to solutions when the Bellagio Constraints are satisfied—that is, the states 011 and 101. At the moment, the combinations that correctly solve the system of Boolean expressions, however, are indistinguishable from the others.

In the next chapter, Chapter 5, Beam Me Up, Scotty—Quantum Tagging and Entangling, on page 107, we turn our attention to the matter of plucking the optimal solution while discarding the unwanted ones. Specifically, you'll learn about gates that identify the states that satisfy the Boolean expressions and knock out states that give incorrect solutions. We'll see in Chapter 10, Quantum Search, on page 295, that the mega-qubits don't adversely impact runtime performance, especially as the number of variables increases.

Bottom Line

Dealing with the entire gamut of possible solutions to a system of Boolean expressions simultaneously in quantum computers has no parallel in conventional processors. The ability of quantum computers to pull off this feat hinges on qubits holding blended quantum states, which we model with pentagon $|0\rangle$ and triangle $|1\rangle$ qubelets.

Although the qubelets are imaginary subatomic particles, they give us a familiar way to accurately account for the quantum mechanical principles and correctly predict the outcome of quantum instructions or gates on quantum bits. Specifically, the operations on page 78 that modify the qubelets in a qubit's quantum state by a quantum gate include:

- *Switching* qubelets from one type to another as in from, say, pentagon $|0\rangle$ to triangle $|1\rangle$ qubelets.

- *Splitting* or *Replacing* qubelets into another set of qubelets. For example, a pentagon $|0\rangle$ qubelet is replaced by a set consisting of a pentagon $|0\rangle$ and a triangle $|1\rangle$ qubelet:

- – The splitting operation done by the H Gate on page 82 is fundamental to quantum computing, it's key to triggering qubits holding multiple states.

- *Inverting* qubelets by giving them a half turn:

  - – Inverted qubelets play a grand role in quantum computing since they can pair up with non-inverted qubelets of the same type and cancel each other out. That is, the canceled pair of qubelets is removed from the quantum state.

The terrific potential of quantum computers manifests not with individual qubits holding multiple qubelets but when all the qubits come together to form the mega-qubit, as we saw in Mega-Qubit on page 91. The qubelets from different qubits pair up within the quantum hardware to form columns of qubelets that represent all possible solutions to the computational problem. The mega-qubit is then fed as a single monolithic unit to the subsequent gates in the quantum circuit. The quantum gates don't cycle through these combinations one by one but act on all the states in the mega-qubit at once—a characteristic that can't be replicated on classical computers.

As we saw with the quantum program for the Bellagio Constraints on page 96, even though the mega-qubit contains the optimal solution, it's indistinguishable from the other solutions that don't satisfy the Boolean constraints. In the next chapter, you'll learn about quantum gates that identify the optimal state. We'll also study *entanglement*, which is another quantum phenomenon that forms the bedrock of quantum cryptography and other applications.

Try Your Hand

Solutions to these exercises are given in Quantum Superposition Solutions, on page 434.

These exercises demonstrate that by judiciously wiring up quantum gates, it's possible to orchestrate the collapse of qubits and that they don't just gyrate uncontrollably.

For any code listing in the exercises, assume the following header lines:

```
OPENQASM 2.0;
include "qelib1.inc";
```

1. The NOT gate operates on a $|0\rangle$ qubit as shown in this quantum circuit:

$$|0\rangle \;\rule{1cm}{0.4pt}\; \boxed{X} \;\rule{1cm}{0.4pt}\; |1\rangle$$

Show the operation of the NOT gate in terms of qubelets.

2. An inverted triangle $|1\rangle$ qubelet is operated on by a NOT gate:

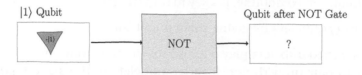

a. How is this qubelet affected by the NOT gate?

b. If you measure the qubit after it's operated on by the NOT gate, what binary state would be logged in the classical register?

3. a. Draw the qubelets for the $|0\rangle$ qubit after it's been operated on by the H and X gates, as shown in the following quantum circuit:

b. Compare the qubelets against the following quantum circuit:

c. If you measure the qubit after it's been operated on by both gates in the previous circuits, would you notice any statistical difference in the output?

4. Simplify the following qubits.

a.

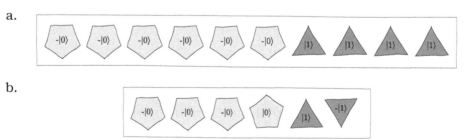

b.

5. Consider the following quantum state of a qubit:

Compare the likelihoods of the qubit collapsing to $|0\rangle$ versus $|1\rangle$.

6. Describe the quantum operations, if any, you can apply to convert the quantum state of the qubit on the left to the quantum state on the right in the following figure:

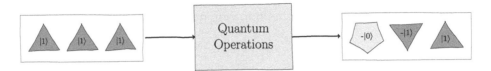

Hint: Consider the quantum operations such as switching and inverting qubelets listed in Basic Operations, on page 78. (In Quantum Circuit Synthesis, or Guess the Gate, on page 246, you'll learn to design the quantum circuit that implements the quantum operations taking the quantum state on the left qubit to the one on the right.)

7. a. Draw a quantum circuit and write the quantum program that simulates a coin toss on the real IBM computer.

   b. How many shots would you specify for this program?

8. In the following circuit, back-to-back H gates are applied to a $|1\rangle$ qubit. Using qubelet diagrams, what is the quantum state of the qubit after it's operated on by both H gates?

9. Consider the following quantum circuit with three back-to-back H gates, shown as follows:

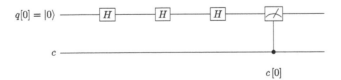

   a. Draw the qubelets in the qubit after it's been acted upon by all three gates.

   b. Write the quantum program for this circuit.

   c. Execute this program and examine the output. What strikes you?

10. When writing quantum programs, it's crucial that you understand how to transform quantum states to ones that increase the likelihood of collapsing to states that solve your computational task. For example, what quantum gates should be performed on the qubit on the left to take it to the state on the right in the following quantum circuit:

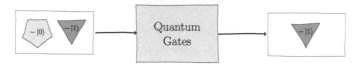

That is, the quantum gates should remove the inverted pentagon $|0\rangle$ qubelet from the quantum state.

11. Consider a gate that operates as follows:

- Doesn't affect the pentagon $|0\rangle$ qubelets.
- Inverts the triangle $|1\rangle$ qubelets.

How will this gate transform the following qubit:

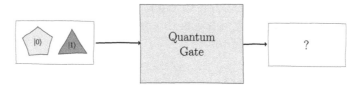

12. The following mega-qubit is the result of being operated on by quantum gates. If you measure the qubits making up the mega-qubit, which classical state is it most likely to be recorded as in the classical register?

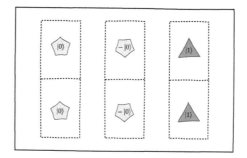

13. Draw the mega-qubit for the following quantum circuit shown on page 105.

14. Consider the following quantum circuit:

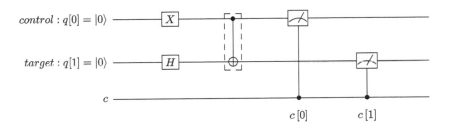

a. Draw the mega-qubit before it's fed to the CNOT gate.

b. Draw the mega-qubit after it's operated on by the CNOT gate.

c. List the states, and their probabilities, that are recorded in the classical register when the mega-qubit collapses.

d. If you just measure the bottom qubit and it happens to be 0, what can you say about the top qubit?

e. Write a quantum program for this circuit and compare the output with the mega-qubit you drew earlier.

15. Consider the quantum circuit that models the Aladdin Constraints as outlined in Logic Expressions to Quantum Circuit, on page 62.

a. Where would you place the H gates?

b. Run the quantum program. What can you say about the states shown in the output?

16. Draw the quantum circuit corresponding to the code listing shown here:

```
h q[1];
h q[0];
x q[0];
ccx q[0],q[1],q[2];
```

CHAPTER 5

Beam Me Up, Scotty—Quantum Tagging and Entangling

The ability of quantum gates to act on the entire solution space at once offers a spectacular way to tackle some of today's most complex problems. But for quantum computing to live up to its billing, we need a way to tease out the optimal solution efficiently, as opposed to grinding through all the possible solutions as a classical computer would do.

In this chapter, you'll see that the mega-qubit isn't just a nifty bookkeeping device to track how gates affect all possible states at the same time. It underpins a central tenet of quantum mechanics that makes a quantum computer not just another hyper-fast computer but one that solves problems in ways that can't be duplicated on classical computers. With the mega-qubit, you'll learn new ways to cancel qubelets and command qubits to quantum states in a controlled and disciplined manner. We'll also see that the underlying quantum physics requires us to design our quantum circuits in a specific way, otherwise the qubits get "locked" in suboptimal quantum states and can't be freely manipulated. By the end of this chapter, you'll understand the core premise of quantum computing and glimpse the levers that collapse qubits to the optimal solution.

Tagging the Optimal Solution

To pull out an optimal solution we must first learn to identify it even though we may not yet know what it is. This stipulation isn't as strange as it sounds—we already know a few things about an optimal solution:

- It satisfies the Boolean expressions, or the *constraints*, that represent your computational task.

- The mega-qubit holds all the qubelet combinations, including the one corresponding to an optimal solution.

We can use these facts to understand how to recognize an optimal solution in the mega-qubit. Consider again the Bellagio Constraints from Logic Expressions to Quantum Circuit, on page 62, as shown here:

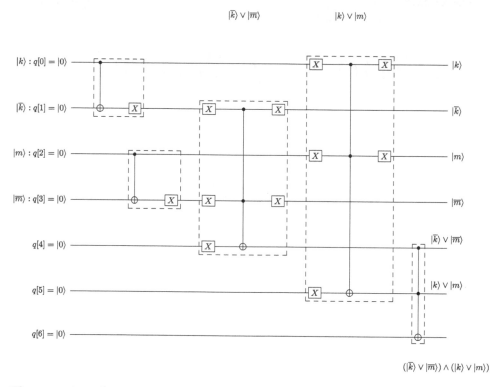

The quantum logic gates shown in the figure model the Boolean expressions for a workable schedule, one in which the talk show hosts slotted at the Bellagio won't violate any of the performers' requirements for the days they can perform. For example, consider the CCNOT gate that straddles the qubits in quantum registers q[0], q[2], and q[5] that's enclosed by the dotted box second from the right. This gate models the constraint $k \vee m$. Recall from Writing a System of Boolean Logic Expressions, on page 8, that this Boolean expression enforces the restriction that either Kimmel or Maher perform at the Bellagio on Day 1. Likewise, the CCNOT gate in the middle requires either one of them to appear at the Bellagio on Day 2.

If the quantum states at the controls of these CCNOT gates meet the constraints, then their respective target bits are $|1\rangle$, indicating that the corresponding constraint is met. These targets then form the control bits of the final CCNOT gate shown on the extreme right. If both its controls are $|1\rangle$, indicating that both the constraints for the performers on both days are met, then its target in q[6] is $|1\rangle$. Thus, a qubelet combination representing a valid lineup drives the qubelet in the quantum register q[6] to a $|1\rangle$.

This setup immediately points the way toward an approach: we need a gate that detects those qubelet combinations where there's a triangle $|1\rangle$ qubelet in the cell representing q[6], the qubit that signals whether all constraints are met. We study such a gate next.

Pauli-Z (Z) Gate

In quantum computing, the Pauli-Z, or Z, gate operates like this:

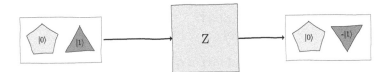

As seen in the figure, the triangle $|1\rangle$ qubelet is inverted but the pentagon $|0\rangle$ qubelets aren't affected. On the other hand, if the triangle $|1\rangle$ qubelet is inverted, the Z gate would put it in a non-inverted orientation, as shown here:

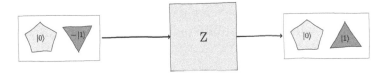

In both cases, the triangle $|1\rangle$ qubelet is inverted from its original orientation, while the pentagon $|0\rangle$ qubelet is left alone.

Unlike the X and H gates, which operate on both the pentagon $|0\rangle$ and triangle $|1\rangle$ qubelets, the Z gate operates on the triangle $|1\rangle$ qubelets only. This ability to act on only one type of qubelet gives an additional degree of precision to pare non-optimal solutions from the quantum states held in superposition by the qubits.

Controlled Z (CZ) Gate

Just as the CNOT gate applied the NOT operation on the target qubit if the control qubit is $|1\rangle$, the Controlled Z or CZ gate inverts the triangle $|1\rangle$ qubelet on the target qubit when the control qubit is $|1\rangle$, as shown in the figure on page 110.

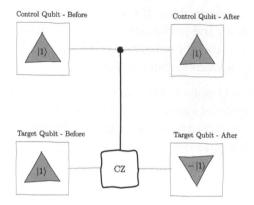

We can write this operation as follows:

$$\begin{array}{lcl} \textit{Control} \ |1\rangle & \overset{CZ}{\mapsto} & |1\rangle \\ \textit{Target} \ |1\rangle & & -|1\rangle \end{array}$$

By concatenating the control and target qubits, you can express this mapping more succinctly:

$$|11\rangle \ \mapsto \ -\ |11\rangle$$

Even though only the qubelet on the target qubit has been inverted by the CZ gate, the negative sign on the right of the mapping doesn't indicate which qubit's qubelets are inverted. The reason we don't need to know which qubelet is inverted is that when these qubits pair up to form a mega-qubit, we look at the combination as a unit.

On the other hand, if the target qubit is $|0\rangle$ with a pentagon $|0\rangle$ qubelet, the CZ gate doesn't do anything, as shown here:

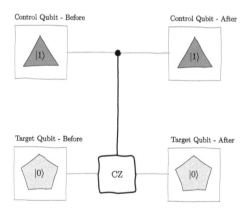

In this case, although the control qubit is $|1\rangle$, the CZ gate doesn't affect the target qubit, which continues to be $|0\rangle$. That is, when the control bit is $|1\rangle$, the CZ gate acts like a Z gate.

As with the CNOT and CCNOT gates, when the control qubit is $|0\rangle$, the CZ also doesn't affect the target qubit.

Algebraic Logic of CZ Gate

Like we did with the CNOT and CCNOT gates, we can write a truth table for the CZ gate as follows:

Control$_0$	Target$_0$	Control$_1$	Target$_1$
$|0\rangle$	$|0\rangle$	$|0\rangle$	$|0\rangle$
$|0\rangle$	$|1\rangle$	$|0\rangle$	$|1\rangle$
$|1\rangle$	$|0\rangle$	$|1\rangle$	$|0\rangle$
$|1\rangle$	$|1\rangle$	$|1\rangle$	$-|1\rangle$

Control$_0$ and Target$_0$ are the two qubit values before the application of the CZ gate, and Control$_1$ and Target$_1$ are the values after. So it's only in the single case, when both the control and target qubits are $|1\rangle$, that the CZ gate modifies the target qubit.

Later, in Using the Controlled Z Gate in Practice, on page 117, we'll see how this basic operation of the CZ gate extends to mega-qubits that are a superposition of multiple qubits.

Realizing a Controlled Z Gate

The Controlled Z (CZ) gate plays a marquee role in quantum programs. Although it's on the palette and you can drag and drop it on the Composer, it's instructive to see how it's built up from CNOT and H gates. You'll see that even though the H gate splits qubelets, they neatly cancel out so that only the triangle $|1\rangle$ qubelet is inverted when the control qubit is $|1\rangle$.

The CZ gate is a composite gate constructed from the CNOT and H gates, as shown in the following figure:

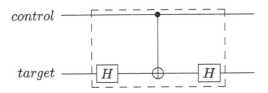

It's not immediately apparent why placing an H gate on the target qubit before and after the CNOT gate operates on the qubit would result in a gate that inverts only the $|1\rangle$ qubit on the target when there's a $|1\rangle$ on the control qubit, while leaving every other combination of $|1\rangle$ and $|0\rangle$ alone. So we'll walk through this circuit in a fair amount of detail to see how it reproduces the behavior of a Controlled Z gate. This analysis will reinforce how quantum gates work with qubits in superposition. With a bit of practice, you'll find that many of the steps will become second nature and you'll do them in your head. In Chapter 7, Small Step for Man—Single Qubit Programs, on page 173, we'll cover techniques to perform this analysis rapidly. But, it's instructive to see how the qubits, and their qubelets, are progressively modified as different gates act upon them. This helps remove the magic and mystery when we apply the mathematical techniques later.

Control and Target Qubits Are $|1\rangle$

We'll first analyze the case when both the control and target qubits are $|1\rangle$, as shown in this circuit:

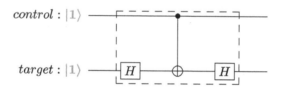

(In practice, to obtain a $|1\rangle$ qubit, you would apply a NOT or X gate to a $|0\rangle$ qubit. We'll assume that's been done in the following analysis.)

We start by evaluating the portion of the quantum circuit shown within the dotted box in the figure:

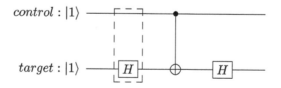

As discussed in Putting Qubits in Blended States, on page 82, the H gate splits the bottom $|1\rangle$ qubit, the target, into a pentagon $|0\rangle$ qubelet and an inverted triangle $|1\rangle$ qubelet, while the control qubit on top, q[0], is unaffected, as shown in the figure on page 113.

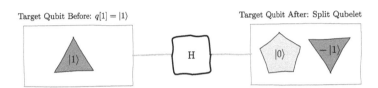

Next, the single triangle $|1\rangle$ qubelet on the top qubit pairs up with the pentagon $|0\rangle$ and the inverted triangle $|1\rangle$ qubelets of the bottom qubit, forming a mega-qubit. Since the mega-qubit forms instantaneously on actual quantum hardware, we combine the steps and directly draw the mega-qubit as shown in the following figure:

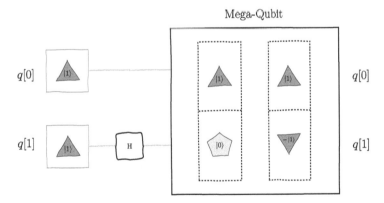

We now evaluate the CNOT gate, shown within the dotted box:

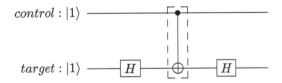

The CNOT gate operates on each qubelet combination simultaneously in the mega-qubit on the left to form the one on the right, as shown in the figure on page 114.

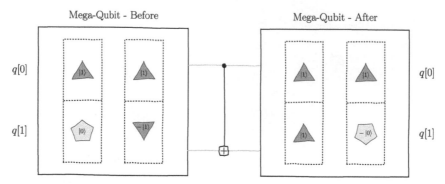

Since the top qubelet in each qubelet column on the left mega-qubit is a triangle $|1\rangle$ qubelet, the bottom qubelets are switched by the CNOT gate. That is, a pentagon $|0\rangle$ qubelet is replaced with a triangle $|1\rangle$ qubelet, and vice versa.

Finally, we look at the quantum circuit with the H gate within the dotted box:

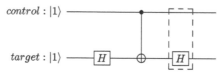

The bottom qubelets in the mega-qubit after they're operated on by the CNOT gate, shown in the previous figure, are fed to an H gate. This H gate splits the bottom qubelets, as shown here:

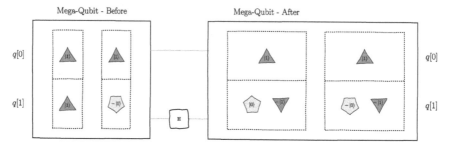

Recall from Putting Qubits in Blended States, on page 82, that the H gate splits a triangle $|1\rangle$ qubelet into a pentagon $|0\rangle$ qubelet and an inverted triangle $|1\rangle$ qubelet. And it splits an inverted pentagon $|0\rangle$ qubelet into an inverted pentagon $|0\rangle$ and an inverted triangle $|1\rangle$ qubelet. That is, a $|0\rangle$ qubelet is split without any inversions.

Next, in each qubelets column, the top two qubelets team up with the bottom two qubelets to form four qubelet combinations or columns in the right mega-qubit, as shown in the figure on page 115.

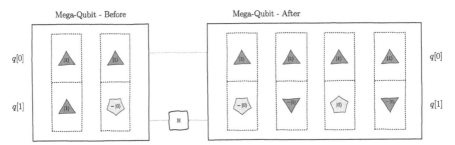

We'll write the quantum state of each pair as a concatenated string of the qubelet in q[0], the top qubit, followed by the qubelet in q[1], the bottom qubit. The qubelet pair in the first column on the mega-qubit on the right, $- |10\rangle$, cancels with the qubelet pair in the third column, $|10\rangle$, leaving only the qubelet pairs in the second and fourth columns, as shown here:

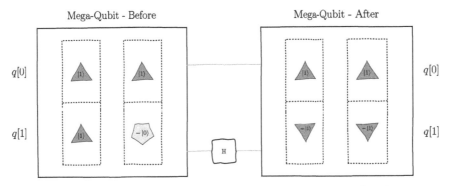

Since these two qubelet pairs are identical, the probability of picking any pair is the same as having just a single pair of qubelets. That is, the mega-qubit will only hold this combination, $- |11\rangle$, as shown in the next figure:

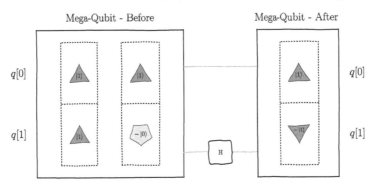

Putting the entire sequence of qubelets and mega-qubits together, we see that the target $|1\rangle$ qubit is inverted when the control and target qubits are each $|1\rangle$:

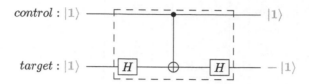

Although we end up with a single qubelet combination, each application of the H gate doubles the number of qubelet combinations in the mega-qubit. Classical computers would buckle under such an onslaught of bits. But, quantum computers can handle this strain. Moreover, the inversions of qubelets leads to combinations that cancel out, a concept that doesn't exist in classical computers.

Control Qubit Is $|0\rangle$

When the control qubit is $|0\rangle$, the CNOT gate doesn't modify the qubits. Thus, the circuit is effectively as shown here:

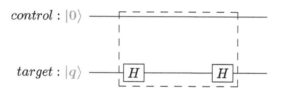

The target qubit is acted upon by two back-to-back H gates. As we saw in Back-to-Back H Gates: The First Hint of Taming Randomness, on page 88, a sequence of two H gates leaves the qubit in its original state. Thus, when the control qubit is $|0\rangle$, the target qubit $|q\rangle$ remains as is. So, qubit pair $|00\rangle$ will still be $|00\rangle$ after being operated on by this quantum circuit. Likewise, the qubit pair $|01\rangle$ will also continue to be $|01\rangle$.

The remaining case, when the control qubit is $|1\rangle$ and the target qubit is $|0\rangle$, can be analyzed in a similar manner. You'll see that the CZ gate doesn't modify the target qubit. That is, $|10\rangle$ continues to be $|10\rangle$ after operation by this gate.

For all the cases, then, this circuit correctly reproduces the behavior of the CZ gate. Thus, a Controlled Z gate can be realized by placing an H gate on the target qubit before and after the CNOT gate.

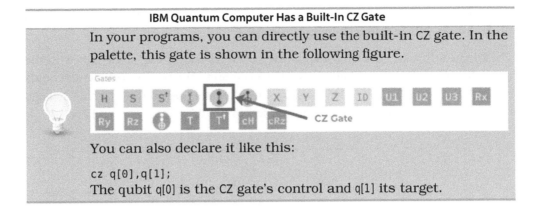

IBM Quantum Computer Has a Built-In CZ Gate

In your programs, you can directly use the built-in CZ gate. In the palette, this gate is shown in the following figure.

CZ Gate

You can also declare it like this:

```
cz q[0],q[1];
```

The qubit q[0] is the CZ gate's control and q[1] its target.

Using the Controlled Z Gate in Practice

To see how the CZ gate is used in practice, we'll again work with the quantum circuit that models the Bellagio Constraints. As in Triggering Superposition in Practical Quantum Circuits, on page 96, we first have the H gates operate on the q[0] and q[2] qubits to put them in blended states, as shown here:

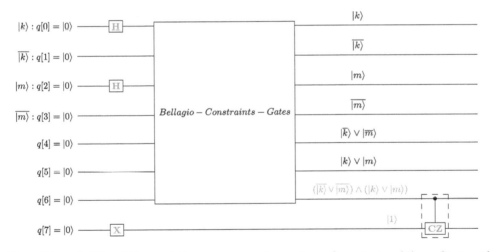

The q[0] and q[2] qubits each have an equal number of pentagon $|0\rangle$ and triangle $|1\rangle$ qubelets. So, the mega-qubit fed to the Bellagio Constraints will be a superposition of quantum states that holds all possible combinations of the quantum states, $|k\rangle$ and $|m\rangle$, representing the schedules of Kimmel and Maher, including the optimal state.

In addition, we've declared another qubit, q[7] at the bottom of the quantum circuit. This qubit is the target qubit of the CZ gate, shown within the dotted box in the bottom right of the circuit. Its control is the q[6] qubit, which is $|1\rangle$ if all the Bellagio Constraints are met. Its target, the q[7] qubit, is clamped at

$|1\rangle$ by first connecting it to a NOT or X gate. The reason for fixing the CZ gate's target to $|1\rangle$ will become clear in a moment.

The mega-qubit for this circuit will have columns containing eight cells with the top cell containing the qubelet for q[0], and so on to the bottom cell, which holds the qubelet for q[7]. Thus, the mega-qubit, after it's operated on by the Bellagio Constraints but before the q[7] qubit is fed to the CZ gate, is shown here:

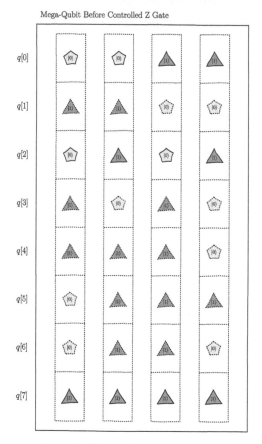

Mega-Qubit Before Controlled Z Gate

The top six cells in each qubelet column are identical to those shown in Triggering Superposition in Practical Quantum Circuits, on page 96. The additional qubelet cell in each column at the bottom corresponds to q[7]. Since q[7] hasn't been acted upon by any gate other than the X gate, the bottom cell in every column will be a triangle $|1\rangle$ qubelet. (Because the q[7] qubit isn't affected by the gates for the Bellagio Constraints, the qubelets don't have a dotted outline like the secondary qubelets.)

When q[7] is fed to the CZ gate, the CZ gate inverts the triangle $|1\rangle$ qubelet in the q[7] qubit's cell when the qubelet in the cell associated with q[6], its control, is a triangle $|1\rangle$ qubelet, as shown here:

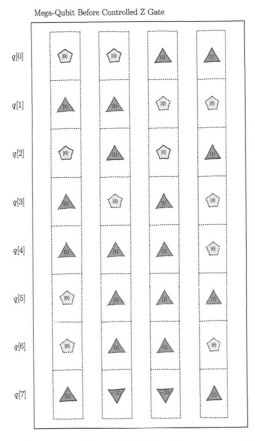

Mega-Qubit Before Controlled Z Gate

The bottom cells in the second and third columns are inverted triangle $|1\rangle$ qubelets as these columns have a triangle $|1\rangle$ qubelet in the cell in the second to last row, corresponding to the q[6] qubit. These columns with inverted triangle $|1\rangle$ qubelets indicate that these quantum states meet the Bellagio Constraints. So, we've identified the qubelet combinations that satisfy the Boolean constraints.

Even though we've tagged those columns that represent quantum states that fit the Bellagio Constraints, we haven't yet tipped the scales to favor those columns. So, if you run this quantum program and measure the states of q[0], q[2], the variables that represent the schedule of the two performers modeled in this circuit, as well as the qubit in q[6] that indicates whether the schedule is valid, the output will show all four quantum states in the mega-qubit occurring with the same probability.

By using the CZ gate, we've *tagged* or marked those quantum states that satisfy the Boolean expressions represented by the quantum circuit. But before seeing how to collapse the mega-qubit to these tagged states, we have to take care of some side effects peculiar to quantum computing.

Entangling Qubits

When programming with traditional languages, you can safely ignore the underlying digital electronics. But with quantum computing, the quantum mechanical principles are always lurking around. In fact, quantum superposition comes with its own unique by-products that *entangle* or force qubits to depend on each other. Qubit states are, of course, coordinated by the quantum gates that operate on them. That is, their states are determined by the sequence of gates that act on them, just as in classical computers. But, entanglement ties the qubits in a deeper way that has more to do with quantum mechanics than Boolean logic. If these bindings aren't properly accounted for in our programs, this oddity can interfere with collapsing the mega-qubit into the tagged states that solve the computational problem. In this section, we'll learn techniques to counter these effects.

Entanglement plays a central role in quantum mechanics as well as in several applications in quantum computing. We'll study this topic by going through detailed and complete steps so you gain a solid intuitive feel for this concept.

Intuition Behind Entanglement

To understand this uniquely quantum mechanical phenomenon, let's work with the following quantum circuit:

$$q[0] = |0\rangle \quad \boxed{H} \quad \bullet$$
$$q[1] = |0\rangle \quad \oplus$$

Here's the code for this circuit:

```
h q[0];
cx q[0],q[1];
```

Before running this circuit on the IBM Quantum Computer, we'll first analyze it in our minds. We'll follow the same approach we've been doing but mentally reason out many of the steps that reorganize and tweak the qubelets. The exercise will help boost our intuition for working with quantum circuits.

Both the top and bottom qubits, q[0] and q[1], are $|0\rangle$. So each essentially contains a pentagon $|0\rangle$ qubelet. The H gate splits the pentagon $|0\rangle$ qubelet in the top qubit so that it now has a pentagon $|0\rangle$ qubelet and a triangle $|1\rangle$ qubelet. These pair up with the pentagon $|0\rangle$ qubelet in the bottom qubit to form a mega-qubit with two qubelet pairs, as shown on the left mega-qubit in the figure:

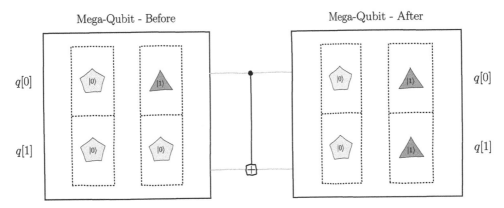

Writing each pair as a concatenated string as before, the qubelet combination in the left column in the mega-qubit on the left is $|00\rangle$ and the right column is $|10\rangle$.

Next, the CNOT gate operates on each pair of qubelets in the left mega-qubit. The top qubelet in each pair is fed to the CNOT gate's control and the bottom qubelet is passed to its target. Since the left pair has a pentagon $|0\rangle$ on the top, it won't be affected by the CNOT gate. The right pair, however, has a triangle $|1\rangle$ qubelet. Thus, the CNOT gate will switch its bottom qubelet from a pentagon $|0\rangle$ qubelet to a triangle $|1\rangle$ qubelet. As a result, the mega-qubit on the right, after the CNOT gate has operated on it, will have two pairs: one will be in the state $|00\rangle$ and the other will be $|11\rangle$, as shown on the right mega-qubit in the previous figure. We can write this operation of the entire circuit as:

$$|00\rangle \;\mapsto\; \begin{cases} |00\rangle \\ |11\rangle \end{cases}$$

Continuing this train of thought, we can figure out the quantum states when other combinations of $|1\rangle$s and $|0\rangle$s are applied to the q[0] and q[1] qubits of this quantum circuit. Specifically,

q[0] = $|0\rangle$ **and** q[1] = $|1\rangle$

When q[0] is $|0\rangle$ and q[1] is $|1\rangle$, the top $|0\rangle$ qubit is split by the H gate into a pentagon $|0\rangle$ qubelet and a triangle $|1\rangle$ qubelet. These pair up with the $|1\rangle$ qubit's triangle $|1\rangle$ qubelet on the bottom to form the mega-qubit shown on the left in the figure on page 122.

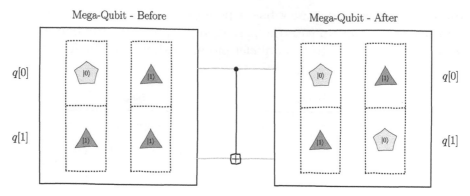

The mega-qubit after the CNOT gate is shown on the right. The first column in the right mega-qubit is $|01\rangle$ and the second is $|10\rangle$.

The operation of this circuit is expressed as:

$$|01\rangle \mapsto \begin{cases} |01\rangle \\ |10\rangle \end{cases}$$

$q[0] = |1\rangle$ **and** $q[1] = |0\rangle$

When q[0] is $|1\rangle$ and q[1] is $|0\rangle$, the top $|1\rangle$ qubit is split by the H gate into a pentagon $|0\rangle$ qubelet and an inverted triangle $|1\rangle$ qubelet. These pair up with the $|0\rangle$ qubit's pentagon $|0\rangle$ qubelet on the bottom to form the mega-qubit as shown on the left in the figure:

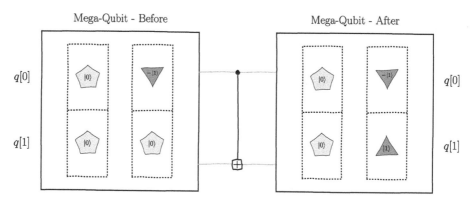

The mega-qubit after the CNOT gate is shown on the right. The first column on the right mega-qubit is $|00\rangle$ and the second is $- |11\rangle$. The negative sign on the second pair is due to the inverted triangle $|1\rangle$ qubelet in the top cell.

The operation of this circuit is expressed as:

$$|10\rangle \mapsto \begin{cases} |00\rangle \\ - |11\rangle \end{cases}$$

$q[0] = |1\rangle$ **and** $q[1] = |1\rangle$

When q[0] is $|1\rangle$ and q[1] is $|1\rangle$, the top qubit is split by the H gate into a pentagon $|0\rangle$ qubelet and an inverted triangle $|1\rangle$ qubelet. These pair up with the $|1\rangle$ qubit's triangle $|1\rangle$ qubelet on the bottom to form the mega-qubit as shown on the left in the following figure:

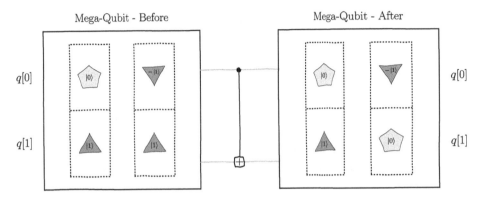

The mega-qubit after the CNOT gate is shown on the right. The first column on the right mega-qubit is $|01\rangle$ and the second is $-|10\rangle$. The negative sign on the second pair is due to the inverted triangle $|1\rangle$ qubelet in the top cell.

The operation of this circuit is expressed as:

$$|11\rangle \mapsto \begin{cases} |01\rangle \\ -|10\rangle \end{cases}$$

While we can't directly inspect the mega-qubits, we can plug in Measure gates and record which states are written to the classical register, as shown:

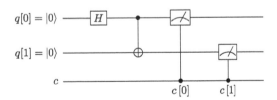

The code for this circuit is the following:

```
h q[0];
cx q[0],q[1];
measure q[0] -> c[0];
measure q[1] -> c[1];
```

The two Measure gates are shown on the highlighted lines.

In each case, when we measure the q[0] and q[1] qubits, we're first selecting one of the qubit pairs in the corresponding mega-qubit and then collapsing it, as summarized in the following table:

Initial q[0]	Initial q[1]	Mega-Qubit Pairs	Classical State
$|0\rangle$	$|0\rangle$	$|00\rangle$ and $|11\rangle$	00 or 11
$|0\rangle$	$|1\rangle$	$|01\rangle$ and $|10\rangle$	01 or 10
$|1\rangle$	$|0\rangle$	$|00\rangle$ and $-|11\rangle$	00 or 11
$|1\rangle$	$|1\rangle$	$|01\rangle$ and $-|10\rangle$	01 or 10

For example, in the third case, when the initial state of q[0] is $|1\rangle$ and q[1] is $|0\rangle$, one of the qubit pairs in the mega-qubit, $|00\rangle$ or $-|11\rangle$, is selected at random. Thus, the classical register will record either 00 or 11. (The negative sign indicates an inverted qubelet but doesn't affect the classical state the qubit collapses to.)

If we peek into c[0] and see that it's a 0, we're guaranteed that c[1] will have logged a 0. On the other hand, if c[0] is 1, then c[1] is 1. You can verify that this *forcing* behavior holds for the other cases in the table.

To put it another way, when you know the classical state in any one of the two classical register elements, you can always correctly infer the Boolean state in the other classical register element. Consequently, we only need one Measure gate in this circuit, for example, the one measuring the q[0] qubit:

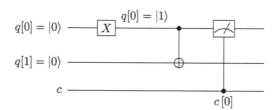

(Of course, we could also have measured just the q[1] qubit and deduced the state that the q[0] qubit collapses to.)

It's not reducing the Measure gates that's the focus in this circuit, though. Something fundamental is at play here. To see this, consider the circuit from, say, the q[1] quantum register's perspective. In particular, let's again work with the third row in the table where q[0] is $|1\rangle$ and q[1] is $|0\rangle$. The portion of the mega-qubit that's visible to q[1] is shown by hiding the qubelets associated with q[0], as in the figure on page 125.

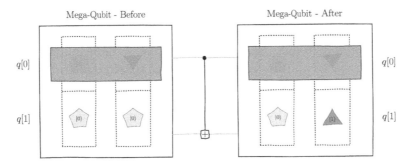

Look at the mega-qubit on the right after the CNOT gate operates on the qubits. As far as the q[1] quantum register is concerned, it holds a pentagon $|0\rangle$ qubelet and a triangle $|1\rangle$ qubelet, as shown in the lower part of the right mega-qubit. In other words, the quantum state held by the q[1] register is:

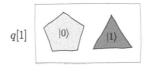

Thus, regardless of how the q[0] qubit collapses, it's reasonable for you to expect that the q[1] qubit would collapse roughly half the time to 0 and the other times to 1. After all, how would the q[1] quantum register know about the qubelets in q[0]? But, as our analysis of measuring mega-qubits showed, the classical state that the q[1] qubit collapses to is *forced* by the collapsed classical state of the q[0] qubit. That is, the q[1] qubit is *entangled* with the q[0] qubit—the state of one completely determines the state of the other, no matter if it collapses right away or much later.

Quantum Mechanics Is Bizarre

If entanglement baffles you, you're in good company. Physicists from Neils Bohr to Richard Feynman simply accept this facet of quantum mechanics and instead worry about wielding the rules of quantum mechanics to explain the world around us.[1] Quantum mechanics, in this sense, is bizarre: we can get quantum computers to solve complex problems without fully understanding quantum mechanical phenomenon.

The Qubelets Model and mega-qubits help drive home these quantum mechanical principles so we can correctly design quantum algorithms even though no one truly understands entanglement.

---

1. https://www.nytimes.com/2019/09/07/opinion/sunday/quantum-physics.html

To convince yourself that this oddball behavior actually occurs, let's write a quantum program in which the initial states are again as listed in the third row of the previous table. This time, to make a more clinching case for entanglement, we'll run the program on a real IBM quantum computer and entangle real qubits as opposed to the phony ones in the simulator. The code looks like this:

Entanglement_1_0_Real_Computer.qasm
```
qreg q[2];
creg c[2];

// Set q[0] to |1>
x q[0];

// Entangle Qubits
h q[0];
cx q[0],q[1];

measure q[0] -> c[0];
measure q[1] -> c[1];
```

When you run this program, you'll get an output similar to the following:

Result

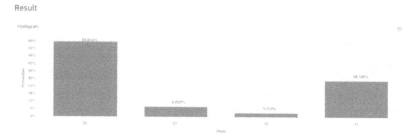

This output was generated with 8,192 shots. You can use fewer shots if you'd like—the general pattern will be similar. (Because you're running on a real computer, you may get slightly different results.)

You should still see that the two states written to the classical register by far most often are 00 and 11. These correspond to the following classical states:

c[0]	c[1]
0	0
1	1

The other two states, 10 and 01 are rarely seen and happen only when the qubits mistakenly collapse. Thus, this program confirms that entanglement is real; the qubits are in lockstep, so the collapse of one forever decides the fate of the other.

Even though we only reviewed the case when the initial states of the qubits were $|1\rangle$ and $|0\rangle$, respectively, you'll get similar results for the other three cases—in each case the qubits will only collapse to two of the four possible states.

Although we've only discussed entangling two qubits, several qubits can be intertwined. In fact, given the ease with which qubits can be entangled, this phenomenon occurs quite frequently in quantum computing.

Entanglement in Quantum Mechanics

Remarkably, qubits remain entangled even when you send one of the qubits millions of miles away in interstellar space. The moment you collapse one, say, the one in outer space, the one on earth is now guraranteed to collapse into a complementary state no matter how far away the one in space has traveled. This state of affairs seems to violate the laws of physics—if one qubit collapses, how does its twin instantaneously get word of the state it collapses to across the vast expanse of space? This question has tormented physicists who have disdainfully called it "spooky action at a distance." To explain this discrepancy, physicists have had to extend their current theories so that these types of quantum effects are governed by other mechanisms.

But for all its vexing and idiosyncratic characteristics, entanglement is as real as a block of concrete and underpins some exotic applications. For example, entanglement has recently been used to create quantum telescopes that can take images of starlight from faint stars.[a] More recently, scientists are exploring ways to peer inside black holes from where even light can't escape. By entangling a pair of qubits and then letting one of them be captured by a black hole, physicists are hoping to study the other one for clues for what goes on inside a black hole.[b] Entangled qubits are also being used to build low-power radar applications for use in the military and for medical devices.[c] Since an entangled qubit only affects its dual, you don't need to employ high-powered beams. And entanglement is central to teleporting, where quantum states can be transferred from one point in space to somewhere else. You'll learn about this phenomenon in Design a Teleporting Circuit, on page 256.

a. https://arxiv.org/abs/1809.03396
b. https://phys.org/news/2019-03-ion-aces-quantum-scrambling.html
c. https://arxiv.org/pdf/1908.03058.pdf

Entanglement in Quantum Computing

In quantum computing, the interplay of quantum superposition and entanglement gives rise to a diverse spectrum of algorithms that have no classical analogs. At one end, we have algorithms that go straight to the heart of entanglement to encrypt tamper-proof messages. (We'll review this method in Chapter 9, Alice in Quantumland—Quantum Cryptography, on page 279.)

On the other end, in quantum search, where our chief concern is canceling qubelet combinations in the mega-qubit, entanglement couples quantum states, causing them to gyrate in unintended ways, rendering the superposition-of-all-states-at-once ineffective. So, in the next section, we investigate how to modify our quantum programs to unravel these states.

Basic Idea

We've seen that all it takes to entangle qubits is a couple of gates, for example, the H and CNOT gates. And, as these gates are regularly used in quantum circuits, entangled qubits are more the rule than the exception in our programs.

Once qubits are locked into entangled states, it's impossible to then transform them to other states that cancel out. Simply put, entangled qubits interfere with the controlled cancellation of quantum states. Specifically, in the Hotel Scheduling Problem introduced in A Scheduling Problem, on page 6, the gates representing the *schedule* constraints entangle the qubits representing the performers with the *working* qubits, which are the targets of the CNOT gates. So, we snap qubits out of their entangled states by setting them back to their original states. We can then continue to operate on the disentangled qubits and remove unwanted states that don't meet the constraints.

Qubits can be restored back to their original states by recognizing the following operations:

- Back-to-back H gates
- Back-to-back CCNOT gates

We reviewed the first case in Back-to-Back H Gates: The First Hint of Taming Randomness, on page 88. For the second case, consider the following circuit:

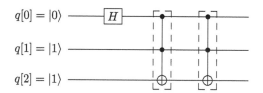

In particular, let's see whether the two back-to-back CCNOT gates restore qubits to their original quantum states after they act on them. That is, we want to investigate whether the quantum state after the H gate acts on the q[0] qubit, which together with q[1] and q[2] we'll call the *left* quantum state, is recovered after the CCNOT gates acts on them.

This *left* quantum state is the mega-qubit formed by the qubelets of the q[0] qubit after it's split by the H gate *and* combined with the qubelets of the qubits in q[1] and q[2]. To strengthen our dexterity with analyzing quantum circuits, we'll construct this mega-qubit mentally: the $|0\rangle$ qubit in q[0] consists of a pentagon $|0\rangle$ qubelet that's split by the H gate into a pentagon $|0\rangle$ qubelet and a triangle $|1\rangle$ qubelet. Next, each of these qubelets links up with the triangle $|1\rangle$ qubelets associated with the $|1\rangle$ qubits in q[1] and q[2], respectively. Thus, we end up with a mega-qubit consisting of two qubelet columns or combinations, as shown in the left mega-qubit in the figure:

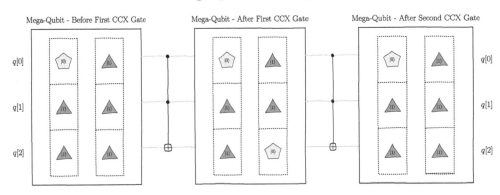

Recall from Controlled Controlled NOT (CCNOT) Gate, on page 57, that only when both control bits are $|1\rangle$, the CCNOT gate inverts the target qubit. In the first qubelet combination, the top cell is a pentagon $|0\rangle$ qubelet. So this qubelet combination isn't affected by the CCNOT gate and remains as is as shown in the first column in the center mega-qubit. The second qubelet combination on the left, though, has a triangle $|1\rangle$ qubelet on both its control bits. Thus, the first CCNOT gate switches the triangle $|1\rangle$ qubit in the bottom cell, associated with the q[2] qubit, its target. This operation is shown in the second column of qubelets in the center mega-qubit. The center mega-qubit, then, is the quantum state after the first CCNOT gates on the qubits.

In a similar way, the second CCNOT gate acts on the two qubelet combinations in the center mega-qubit, resulting in the qubelet combinations in the right mega-qubit. This right mega-qubit has identical qubelet columns to the one on the left. That is, the quantum state on the left mega-qubit is the same as that on the right, indicating that back-to-back CCNOT gates recover the original *left* quantum state.

Thus, both back-to-back H gates and back-to-back CCNOT gates are their own *inverses*. Wherever we see these gates acting on qubits, we can reset those qubits by immediately using those gates again on those qubits.

Disentangling Qubits

To get a feel for disentangling qubits, consider the following circuit:

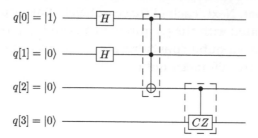

In this circuit, q[0] is $|1\rangle$ and the others, q[1]–q[3] are each $|0\rangle$. This will be the original quantum state that we'll recover.

Although we can use the qubelets model to study how this circuit modifies the qubits, this time we'll directly run the quantum program listed here:

Basic_Idea_Entangling_Qubits.qasm

```
Line 1  // Header
        qreg q[4];
        creg c[4];

     5  // Set q[0] to |1>
        x q[0];

        // Put qubits in superposition
        h q[0];
    10  h q[1];

        // Entangle them
        ccx q[0],q[1],q[2];

    15  cz q[2],q[3];

        measure q[0] -> c[0];
        measure q[1] -> c[1];
        measure q[2] -> c[2];
    20  measure q[3] -> c[3];
```

On line 6, we declare a NOT gate to initialize the q[0] qubit to $|1\rangle$. The Measure gates are declared on lines 17–20. On line 15 we declare a CZ gate. This CZ gate is the IBM Quantum Computer's built-in gate and is realized identically to what we studied in Realizing a Controlled Z Gate, on page 111.

If you run this program, you'll get an output similar to the output shown on page 131.

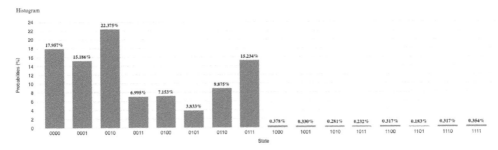

This program ran on a 5-qubit real quantum computer using 8192 shots.

The classical register shows multiple states, indicating that the qubits collapse to several states. In other words, the gates have put the qubits in a mega-qubit holding many qubelet combinations—that is, in a superposition of quantum states.

If we simply disentangle the qubits by reversing the action of all gates, including the CZ gate acting on the q[3] qubit, we'll just get back to where we started and won't have made any headway toward finding an optimal solution.

Recognizing that the CZ gate is used to tag optimal states in the mega-qubit while non-optimal states are left alone, as described in Using the Controlled Z Gate in Practice, on page 117, we won't undo its operation. We'll only reverse the action of the gates to the left of the CZ gate. As a result, qubelet combinations that are not optimal get disentagled so that subsequent gates can remove them.

Disentanging Qubits Implies Disentagling Qubelets

 When you disentangle qubits, you should think in terms of disentangling qubelets in the various qubelet combinations or columns in the mega-qubit.

To overturn the operations of the gates to the left of the CZ gate, hook up gates to the right of the CZ gate so that these new gates mirror those on the left, as shown within the box with the solid border in the figure:

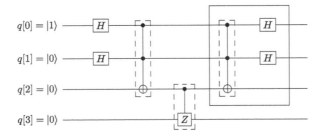

The code listing for disentangling the qubits is shown on page 132.

Basic_Idea_Disentangling_Qubits.qasm
```
qreg q[4];
creg c[4];

x q[0];

// Put qubits in superposition
h q[0];
h q[1];


ccx q[0],q[1],q[2];
cz q[2],q[3];

// Disentangling Qubits
➤ ccx q[0],q[1],q[2];
➤ h q[0];
➤ h q[1];

// Measure Gates
measure q[0] -> c[0];
measure q[1] -> c[1];
measure q[2] -> c[2];
measure q[3] -> c[3];
```

The "mirror image" gates are flagged; you declare them in the reverse order of those before the CZ gate.

When you run this circuit, you'll see that the original state is recovered, as shown in the following output:

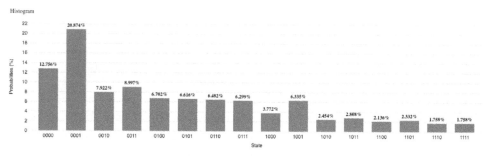

This program ran on a 5-qubit real quantum computer using 8192 shots.

The binary state that's most often seen is 0001. Recall that the classical states are labeled as a concatenated string with c[4] on the left and c[0] on the right. Thus, 0001 corresponds to the classical state with c[0] holding 1 and c[1]–c[3] equal to 0. This classical state is obtained when the q[0] qubit collapses to $\pm |1\rangle$ and the q[1]–q[3] qubits each to $\pm |0\rangle$. So, in quantum computing, because we can never directly examine the quantum state of a qubit, all we can ever say is that we have recovered the original quantum state, perhaps with a different orientation.

Disentangling the Bellagio Constraints

In a quantum program, not all qubits have to be disentangled. So that you know which qubits are slated for disentangling, consider again the quantum circuit for the Bellagio Constraints but this time with the H and CZ gates hooked up as described in Using the Controlled Z Gate in Practice, on page 117:

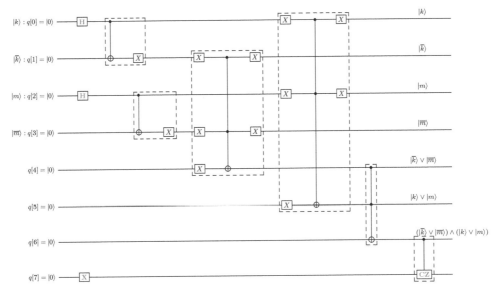

The mega-qubit after the Controlled Z gate on the right is shown in the figure on page 134.

The bottom cell of each column in the mega-qubit shows the qubelet in the q[7] qubit after the Controlled Z gate. The second and third columns have inverted triangle $|1\rangle$ qubelets, indicating that the qubelets in the corresponding columns give a solution that satisfies the Boolean expression—they are a valid schedule. The first and fourth columns give bookings that violate the constraints. You'll learn to get rid of these columns in the mega-qubit in Chapter 10, Quantum Search, on page 295.

First, though, before applying those techniques, the qubits need to be disentangled, otherwise they'll forever be stubbornly locked in their current states and you won't be able to cancel them out. If you disentangle all the qubits, you're back where you started. Since you want solutions corresponding to a valid schedule, you want to keep the columns that are tagged as workable. That is, you want to retain the qubelets in the bottom cell of each column in the mega-qubit. In other words, you only need to disentangle the qubits in q[0]–q[6].

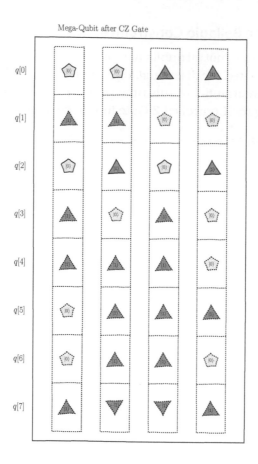

Mega-Qubit after CZ Gate

To disentangle the qubits in q[0]–q[6], you reverse the operations of the logic gates so that they form a mirror image around an imaginary vertical line passing through the Controlled Z gate, as shown here:

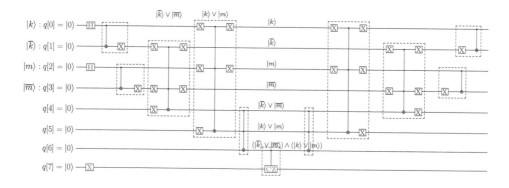

Notice that only a small part of this circuit relies on quantum effects—the H gates on the left and the Controlled Z gate on the right. The rest of the circuit deals with the standard logic operations, albeit for quantum hardware.

You'll also see that several qubits are acted on by back-to-back X gates. These effectively don't affect the quantum state and can be removed. We'll leave them in the circuit, however, so that you see the pattern. Later, after you've verified the program works, you can remove these redundant gates.

We'll leave this circuit here and turn our attention to look at ways that precisely guide qubits from one quantum state to another. We'll pick up the tale again in *Quantum Search*, where we'll apply these techniques to eliminate the unwanted columns in the mega-qubit.

Using Entanglement in Applications

 Entanglement is a "pure" quantum phenomenon that you'll never encounter in classical computing. Before you can fully leverage this effect, you need to learn a few more concepts in Chapter 6, Designer Genes—Custom Quantum States, on page 141, and Chapter 7, Small Step for Man—Single Qubit Programs, on page 173. With this background, you'll see how it's used in real-world applications in Chapter 9, Alice in Quantumland—Quantum Cryptography, on page 279.

Bottom Line

We've seen that by triggering a quantum circuit with judiciously connected H gates, we can get the mega-qubit to hold qubelet combinations representing all possible states of the qubits in a quantum circuit. In this chapter, we learned to further manipulate the mega-qubit of quantum states in ways that have no counterpart in classical computing. In Pauli-Z (Z) Gate, on page 109, we saw that the Z gate inverts triangle $|1\rangle$ qubelets while leaving the pentagon $|0\rangle$ qubelets alone. As a result, its complementary gate, the Controlled Z gate, described in Controlled Z (CZ) Gate, on page 109, presents a mechanism to tag or flag specific qubelet combinations in the mega-qubit that correspond to solutions that solve a Boolean system of equations. Specifically, this gate inverts a triangle $|1\rangle$ qubelet in those qubelet columns of a mega-qubit that represents optimal solutions, as illustrated in Using the Controlled Z Gate in Practice, on page 117.

Next, we saw that quantum hardware is intimately tied to the unique behavior of particles in the subatomic realm. In particular, in ways that have nothing to do with the theory of digital computing, qubits are susceptible to getting shackled or *entangled* with each other and fiercely resist any attempt to manipulate them. As we'll see in Chapter 9, Alice in Quantumland—Quantum Cryptography, on page 279, we can exploit this phenonmenon to encrypt and decrypt messages that are impervious to getting hacked using today's technologies. But in quantum search, qubits in lock-step are a hindrance. In Disentangling Qubits, on page 130, we saw that by hooking up gates symmetrically, we can restore quantum states so that subsequent gates can sweep away unwanted quantum states.

We're at a point in our tale where we understand enough about quantum computing to glimpse how quantum programs diverge conceptually from traditional ones. Quantum programs aren't a line-by-line conversion of classical programs to make them run on quantum devices. Rather, quantum computing gives us new ways to manipulate the information bits of our computational problems—putting them in superposition, entangling and disentangling them, and inverting their qubelets to wipe out suboptimal states.

We're now ready to formalize our intuitive discussion of quantum computing in the next chapter. You'll also learn techniques that speed up your analysis of quantum circuits. These methods will help ensure that your quantum algorithms converge to the optimal quantum states.

Try Your Hand

Solutions to these exercises are given in Quantum Tagging and Entangling Solutions, on page 442.

For any code listing in the exercises, assume the following header lines:

```
OPENQASM 2.0;
include "qelib1.inc";
```

1. The Z gate inverts triangle $|1\rangle$ qubelets but leaves the pentagon $|0\rangle$ qubelets alone.

    a. Design a circuit that mimics the Z gate for the pentagon $|0\rangle$ qubelets. That is, your circuit should leave triangle $|1\rangle$ qubelets alone but invert $|0\rangle$ pentagon qubelets:

    $$|0\rangle \mapsto -|0\rangle$$
    $$|1\rangle \mapsto |1\rangle$$

    b. Confirm the behavior of your circuit by drawing the qubelets at various stages for the following cases:

        i. Circuit initialized with a $|0\rangle$ qubit.
        ii. Circuit initialized with a $|1\rangle$ qubit.

2. Consider the quantum circuit shown in the following figure:

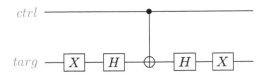

a. Write a quantum program for this circuit.
b. Describe the behavior of this circuit.

3. In Controlled Controlled NOT (CCNOT) Gate, on page 57, we learned about modeling an AND gate operating on two qubits. For many real-life problems, we need to apply an AND operation on several qubits. One way to model an AND gate with four *input* qubits is by *cascading* CCNOT gates, as shown in the following quantum circuit:

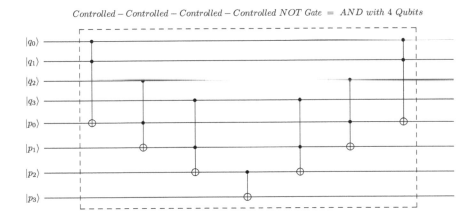

Controlled – Controlled – Controlled – Controlled NOT Gate = AND with 4 Qubits

The four input qubits are q[0]–q[3]. Note how the target of the first CCNOT gate on the left is used as a control, together with the q[2] qubit for the second CCNOT gate. The second CCNOT gate's target will be $|1\rangle$ only when $|q_0\rangle$, $|q_1\rangle$, $|q_3\rangle$, and $|q_4\rangle$ qubits are each $|1\rangle$. This way, we can continue to handle additional qubits so that they all have to be $|1\rangle$ for the target qubit, $|p_3\rangle$, of the CNOT gate at the very bottom to be $|1\rangle$. Hence, this circuit is an AND gate that operates on four qubits. The result of the operation will be $|p_3\rangle$.

Moreover, since this circuit will be part of a larger program, the gates on the right of the CNOT gate at the bottom are a mirror image of those on the right for disentangling the qubits.

a. Write a quantum program for this circuit.

b. Initialize your program so that qubits $|q_0\rangle$–$|q_3\rangle$ are initialized to $|1\rangle$. Declare Meaure gates so that you can confirm your program works correctly.

4. Consider the following quantum circuit:

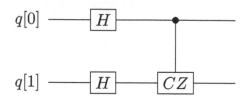

The mega-qubits before and after the CZ gate—that is, each qubit has been operated on by the H gate, respectively—look like this:

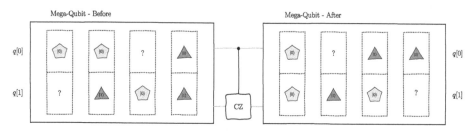

a. Determine the missing qubelets in the mega-qubits shown in the figure.
b. Are the qubits entangled? Justify your answer.

5. Consider the following quantum circuit:

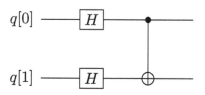

a. Draw the mega-qubit after the H and CNOT gates have operated on the qubits.

b. Are the two qubits entangled? Justify your answer.

c. Write a quantum program and confirm whether your answer to the previous question matches your program's output.

6. In the following circuit, shown on page 139, the gates modeling the Bellagio Constraints are shown within the dotted box.

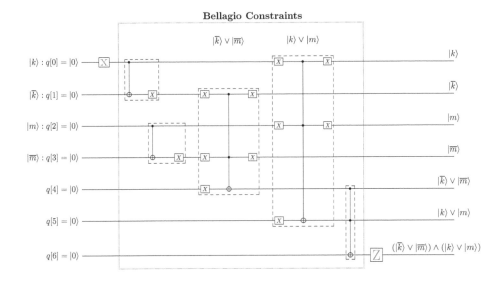

The X gate on the $|k\rangle$ qubit sets it to $|1\rangle$. And a Z gate is placed on the qubit in q[6] on the bottom right.

(Notice that this circuit is equivalent to the one described in Disentangling the Bellagio Constraints, on page 133, but uses one less qubit. We'll use this form in Chapter 10, Quantum Search, on page 295.)

a. Draw the mega-qubit after all the gates have acted on these qubits.

b. Write a quantum program for this circuit. In your program, add a Measure gate to qubits q[0], q[2], and q[6].

c. Run your program on the IBM Quantum Computer Simulator. Explain your output.

d. Add the quantum logic gates to *disentangle* the qubits to your program. Insert these gates before the Measure gates. (Only reverse the operation of the gates that model the Bellagio Constraints. Don't reverse the Z gate.)

e. Run your program on the IBM Quantum Computer Simulator. Again, explain your output. What can you say about the qubelet in the quantum register q[6] before the Measure gate collapses it?

CHAPTER **6**

Designer Genes—Custom Quantum States

The core of quantum computing lies in the distinctive way that qubelets cancel out, leading to quantum states that rapidly collapse to the optimal solution or that entangle qubits so that they're in lockstep. These phenomena have no analog in classical computing.

Entangled qubits, in particular, offer more ways to boost performance of hard-to-crack problems, such as earth-to-satellite communications. Here information is sent across noisy channels over large distances, and the challenge is to compress the signal to increase the rate of transmission with minimal loss of data. In these cases, we typically do the following:

- Create two sets of entangled qubits.

- Keep one set on earth and send the other group with the satellite when it's launched into orbit.

- Perform operations on the home qubits to put them into some state.

- Transmit only the sequence of operations to the entangled qubits on the satellite.

- The system on the satellite applies the sequence of operations on its set of entangled qubits and recovers the intended state of the qubits operated on earth.

The size of the message is highly compressed since you're only sending the sequence of operations and not the final state of the home qubits. Moreover, the message is secure since any eavesdropper wouldn't have the original entangled qubits to decipher the message.

For these types of quantum algorithms to work, we need a rich repertoire of gates that nudge qubits into quantum states with exactitude—merely splitting and inverting qubelets doesn't give the fine-grained resolution demanded by these applications. So, our emphasis in this chapter is to build the scaffolding that bridges the visual qubelet model with the kinds of mathematics used in quantum computing. Once we understand how to meticulously fine-tune quantum states, we can then explore these applications in Chapter 9, Alice in Quantumland—Quantum Cryptography, on page 279.

We start by covering how qubelets and quantum states are denoted mathematically. Then we'll expand our notion of how the pentagon $|0\rangle$ and triangle $|1\rangle$ qubelets give rise to an infinite range of quantum states. This generalized view of qubelets motivates a new class of quantum states that precisely warp a qubit into any quantum state we desire. Instead of simply splitting qubelets symmetrically like the H gate, we'll learn to shape the quantum state so that they heavily skew toward one or the other types of qubelets. Unlike a fair coin toss, these qubits strongly favor one classical state over the other.

 Joe asks:
Why Do We Need the Math?

Our main aim with quantum computers is to write programs for problems that resist solutions by traditional mathematical methods. It seems paradoxical, then, to undertake a mathematical study, especially since, due to their large sizes, we never explicitly program these techniques. So it's natural to question what mathematics buys us.

Learning the mathematics behind quantum computing is important for several reasons:

- It introduces us to the rich family of other types of quantum gates: these give us additional ways to manipulate qubits in applications such as quantum cryptography and superdense coding.

- You'll need the mathematics to analyze portions of your programs and motivate patterns for wiring quantum gates; in other words, the mathematical analysis will guide you in designing quantum algorithms for industrial-scale applications.

- It gives a way to see what's going on in our quantum circuits: unlike classical programs, you can't put breakpoints in your code, expecting to probe intermediate quantum states—the qubits will immediately collapse.

Our interest, then, in the mathematics of quantum mechanics is strictly practical.

Quantum States and Probabilities

To understand how quantum gates precisely calibrate the quantum states of qubits in programs, we need a systematic way to represent blended states.

To model such states in code, let's start with a qubit containing seven pentagon $|0\rangle$ qubelets and three inverted triangle $|1\rangle$ qubelets, shown here:

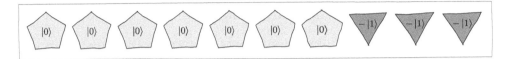

Looking at this qubit, we can deduce the following:

- When measured, the pentagon $|0\rangle$ qubelets have a greater chance of being selected than the triangle $|1\rangle$ qubelets; in other words, the qubit is skewed toward collapsing to the $|0\rangle$ idealized state than the $|1\rangle$ idealized state.

- Qubelets can be inverted, such as the triangle ones in the figure.

We express these observations for the quantum state $|\psi\rangle$ of the qubit with the following equation:

$$|\psi\rangle = \omega_0 |0\rangle + \omega_1 |1\rangle$$

The magnitudes of the coefficients ω_0 and ω_1 relate to the probabilities of the qubit collapsing to the idealized states $|0\rangle$ and $|1\rangle$, respectively; for example, the greater the value of ω_0 *relative* to ω_1, the greater the chance the qubit collapses to $|0\rangle$ when measured. A negative coefficient merely indicates whether the corresponding qubelets are inverted in the qubit but doesn't affect the probabilities.

Adding Pentagon $|0\rangle$ and Triangle $|1\rangle$ Qubelets

The equation for the quantum state of a qubit isn't addition in the usual sense. Instead, think of the pentagon $|0\rangle$ qubelets as, say, apples, and the triangle $|1\rangle$ qubelets as oranges. Then the addition is akin to stating:

It makes no sense to say that this adds up to 10: it remains forever as 7 apples and 3 oranges. The equation for the quantum state of a qubit is a similar addition. The benefit, though, of writing it as an "addition" of the idealized quantum states (the apples and oranges) is to get a better handle on manipulating quantum states in code.

To head off the contradiction where probabilities are positive and inversions are negative, ω_0 and ω_1 don't directly represent probabilities of the two states. Instead, we let the square of these coefficients, ω_0^2 and ω_1^2, represent the probabilities. This way, the coefficients for inverted qubelets can be negative, yet their squares, representing probabilities, are always positive.

Formally, ω_0 and ω_1 are called *amplitudes* and their squares are the probabilities:

$$\text{Probability of collapsing to } |0\rangle = \omega_0^2$$

$$\text{Probability of collapsing to } |1\rangle = \omega_1^2$$

Amplitudes and probabilities are concepts that arise out of quantum wave mechanics. For a light-hearted yet serious introduction to this topic, see Chapter 4: Wave Mechanics in *What is Quantum Mechanics? A Physics Adventure [Col09]*.

Since the qubit can only collapse to two states, $|0\rangle$ and $|1\rangle$, the probabilities ω_0^2 and ω_1^2 must add up to 1:

$$\omega_0^2 + \omega_1^2 = 1$$

Further, this equation implies that each coefficient is less than or equal to 1:

$$\omega_0 \leq 1$$

$$\omega_1 \leq 1$$

Thus, we can indicate inversions of the pentagon or triangle qubelets and at the same time express the probabilities of selecting these qubelets, respectively. Moreover, since the probabilities are the squares of the amplitudes, the inversion of a specific type of qubelet doesn't affect the chances of the qubit collapsing to the corresponding idealized state.

Normalizing Qubelets

To relate the pentagon $|0\rangle$ and triangle $|1\rangle$ qubelets in a qubit with the likelihoods of their collapsing to the idealized states, $|0\rangle$ and $|1\rangle$, respectively, their numbers must first be *normalized*. That is, normalization is a way to ensure that their respective probabilities add up to 1, which in turn limits the values for the amplitudes.

In general, let a and b be the amplitudes of $|0\rangle$ and $|1\rangle$, respectively, of a quantum state, as stated here:

$$a\,|0\rangle + b\,|1\rangle$$

If $a^2 + b^2 \neq 1$, then the square of the amplitudes doesn't give valid probabilities. Thus, for the quantum state to be legal, these amplitudes must be normalized as follows:

$$\frac{a}{\sqrt{a^2 + b^2}}\,|0\rangle + \frac{b}{\sqrt{a^2 + b^2}}\,|1\rangle$$

The corrected amplitudes ω_0 and ω_1 are:

$$\omega_0 = \frac{a}{\sqrt{a^2 + b^2}}$$

$$\omega_1 = \frac{b}{\sqrt{a^2 + b^2}}$$

When we square these amplitudes and sum them up, we get:

$$\left(\frac{a}{\sqrt{a^2 + b^2}}\right)^2 + \left(\frac{b}{\sqrt{a^2 + b^2}}\right)^2 = \frac{a^2}{a^2 + b^2} + \frac{b^2}{a^2 + b^2} = 1$$

Since $|0\rangle$ and $|1\rangle$ are the only two states that the qubit can collapse to, the square of the amplitudes, the probabilities ω_0^2 and ω_1^2, correctly add up to 1.

Number of Qubelets Define the Amplitudes

This definition of amplitudes gives new meaning to the notion of qubelets:

Absolute Value of the Amplitudes

The number of pentagon $|0\rangle$ and triangle $|1\rangle$ qubelets in the qubit is related to the absolute values of the amplitudes, $|\omega_0|$ and $|\omega_1|$, respectively, as follows:

$$|\omega_0| = \frac{\text{Number of pentagon } |0\rangle \text{ qubelets}}{\sqrt{\text{Number of pentagon } |0\rangle \text{ qubelets}^2 + \text{Number of triangle } |1\rangle \text{ qubelets}^2}}$$

$$|\omega_1| = \frac{\text{Number of triangle } |1\rangle \text{ qubelets}}{\sqrt{\text{Number of pentagon } |0\rangle \text{ qubelets}^2 + \text{Number of triangle } |1\rangle \text{ qubelets}^2}}$$

We can also express the number of pentagon $|0\rangle$ qubelets to the number of triangle $|1\rangle$ qubelets as the following ratio:

$$|\omega_0| : |\omega_1| = \text{Number of pentagon } |0\rangle \text{ qubelets} : \text{Number of triangle } |1\rangle \text{ qubelets}$$

Sign of the Amplitudes

The sign of the amplitudes indicates whether those qubelets are inverted: a positive sign implies that the corresponding qubelets are not inverted while a negative sign denotes that they are.

For instance, in the previous figure at the beginning of this section, there are seven pentagon $|0\rangle$ qubelets and three inverted triangle $|1\rangle$ qubelets in the qubit. The amplitudes ω_0 and ω_1 are:

$$\omega_0 = \frac{7}{\sqrt{7^2 + 3^2}} = 0.9191$$

$$\omega_1 = -\frac{3}{\sqrt{7^2 + 3^2}} = -0.3939$$

The negative sign for ω_1 indicates the inverted triangle qubelets in the qubit. Hence, the quantum state shown in the previous figure is:

$$\frac{7}{\sqrt{7^2 + 3^2}} \,|0\rangle \; - \; \frac{3}{\sqrt{7^2 + 3^2}} \,|1\rangle \; = 0.9191 \,|0\rangle \; - 0.3939 \,|1\rangle$$

The probability that this qubit collapses to $|0\rangle$, ω_0^2, and the probability that it collapses to $|1\rangle$, ω_1^2, are calculated as follows:

$$\omega_0^2 \;=\; \left(\frac{7}{\sqrt{7^2 + 3^2}} \right)^2 \;=\; 0.8448$$

$$\omega_1^2 \;=\; \left(\frac{-3}{\sqrt{7^2 + 3^2}} \right)^2 \;=\; 0.1552$$

These probabilities correctly sum to 1:

$$\omega_0^2 + \omega_1^2 = \left(\frac{7}{\sqrt{7^2 + 3^2}} \right)^2 + \left(\frac{3}{\sqrt{7^2 + 3^2}} \right)^2 = 1$$

Qubelets Visualize the Ratio of Amplitudes

When we represent a quantum state with pentagon $|0\rangle$ and triangle $|1\rangle$ qubelets, we're actually visualizing the ratio of the number of pentagon $|0\rangle$ qubelets to those of the triangle $|1\rangle$ qubelets.

Moreover, their orientation—whether the qubelets are inverted—indicates the sign of the corresponding amplitude.

Quantum Gates and Amplitudes

The restriction that the squares of the amplitudes add up to 1 for a valid quantum state must also hold throughout the circuit; in other words, when quantum gates operate on qubits and modify their quantum states, the squares of the amplitudes of each new new state must also sum up to 1. Consider, for example, an H gate acting on a $|0\rangle$ qubit:

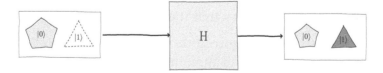

The $|0\rangle$ qubit has only a pentagon $|0\rangle$ qubelet, but to remind us, in general, that a quantum state can have both types of qubelets, albeit with varying amplitudes or probabilities, we draw the $|0\rangle$ qubit on the left, in which the triangle $|1\rangle$ qubelet has a dotted outline indicating it's not active in this qubit.

As described in Putting Qubits in Blended States, on page 82, the H gate splits the pentagon $|0\rangle$ qubelet into a pentagon $|0\rangle$ qubelet and a triangle $|1\rangle$ qubelet, as shown in the right qubit.

In the language of amplitudes, the H gate splits the amplitudes:

$$|0\rangle \mapsto a\,|0\rangle + a\,|1\rangle$$

Because both the pentagon $|0\rangle$ and triangle $|1\rangle$ qubelet are in equal numbers, the amplitudes a are the same for $|0\rangle$ and $|1\rangle$ on the right-hand side.

For this qubit's quantum state to be valid, the squares of the amplitudes must add up to 1:

$$a^2 + a^2 = 1$$

Or

$$
\begin{aligned}
2a^2 &= 1 \\
a^2 &= \frac{1}{2} \\
|a| &= \frac{1}{\sqrt{2}}
\end{aligned}
$$

Both types of qubelets aren't inverted. So, the quantum state after the H gate acts on the qubit is:

$$|0\rangle \mapsto \frac{1}{\sqrt{2}}\,|0\rangle + \frac{1}{\sqrt{2}}\,|1\rangle$$

Probabilities and the Output of Quantum Programs

With this formal definition of a quantum state in terms of amplitudes and probabilities, let's relate them to the output of the following quantum circuit:

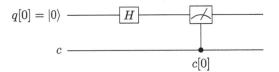

This is the associated quantum program:

```
qreg q[1];
creg c[1];

h q[0];
measure q[0] -> c[0];
```

In this circuit, we simply have an H gate operate on the $|0\rangle$ qubit and then measure the qubit. When you run this program, the Measure gate will collapse the q[0] qubit on the right so that about half the time a 0 is written to the classical register and the other times a 1 is recorded, like this:

Result

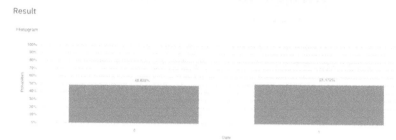

That is, the probabilities of collapsing to $|0\rangle$ and $|1\rangle$ are:

$$\text{Probability of collapsing to } |0\rangle \;=\; \omega_0^2 \;=\; \frac{1}{2}$$

$$\text{Probability of collapsing to } |1\rangle \;=\; \omega_1^2 \;=\; \frac{1}{2}$$

We can take square roots of ω_0^2 and ω_1^2, respectively, but we won't, in general, know whether the pentagon $|0\rangle$ and triangle $|1\rangle$ qubelets are inverted. So, the best we can say about the quantum state of the qubit before it was measured is:

$$\pm \frac{1}{\sqrt{2}}\,|0\rangle \;\pm\; \frac{1}{\sqrt{2}}\,|1\rangle$$

This circuit exemplifies the inherent tension in quantum computing: you work with qubelets and amplitudes whose values you can only surmise but never with probabilities whose values you can accurately measure.

Focus on Amplitudes, Not Probabilities

 Although probabilities determine the final output of quantum programs, you'll focus on manipulating amplitudes, not probabilities, when you're designing quantum algorithms.

The stipulation that the probabilities—the squares of the amplitudes—add up to 1 regulates how the qubelets can be finessed into various configurations. Quantum gates can't willy-nilly jerk them around. In the rest of this chapter, we'll learn that all quantum gates, including the ones we've worked with so far, such as NOT, H, and Z, are specified based on how they affect the amplitudes of the qubits they act on.

Try Your Hand

In this chapter, we include the exercises as part of the main text, as the concepts tightly build up on the content of previous sections. This lets you strengthen your grasp of the material before moving on to the next section.

Solutions to these exercises are given in Quantum States, Amplitudes, and Probabilities Solutions, on page 450.

For any code listing in the exercises, assume the following header lines:

```
OPENQASM 2.0;
include "qelib1.inc";
```

1. Consider the qubit shown here:

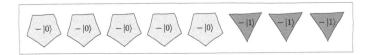

    a. Write the mathematical expression representing the quantum state of the qubit above.

    b. What are the probabilities of the qubit collapsing to $|0\rangle$ and $|1\rangle$, respectively?

2. Consider a qubit that is in the following quantum state $|\psi\rangle$:

$$|\psi\rangle = -\frac{0.35}{N}|0\rangle + \frac{0.28}{N}|1\rangle$$

    a. Calculate N so that $|\psi\rangle$ is a valid quantum state.
    b. Draw the qubit represented by the quantum state $|\psi\rangle$.

3. Does the following equation represent a valid quantum state?

$$0.2523|0\rangle - 0.7517|1\rangle$$

4. Consider the following expression:

$$-0.4472|0\rangle + \omega_1|1\rangle$$

    a. What should ω_1 be so that it's a valid quantum state? (Assume ω_1 is positive.)

    b. Draw the qubelets for this quantum state.

5. Consider the following quantum state for the qubit:

$$\omega_0 |0\rangle + \omega_1 |1\rangle$$

The amplitudes ω_0 and ω_1 have their usual meanings. If the qubit has no triangle qubelets, what are the values of these amplitudes?

6. Consider the following quantum circuit:

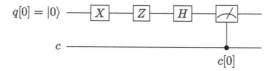

a. Draw the qubelets after each gate operates on the qubit.

b. Write the quantum states after each quantum gate operates on the qubit.

c. What are the probabilities of the qubit collapsing to $|0\rangle$ and $|1\rangle$, respectively, when collapsed by the Measure gate?

d. Write a quantum program for this circuit.

e. Run your program and compare its output with the probabilities you computed earlier.

Rotating Qubelets Through Any Angle

In the qubits we've considered so far, the pentagon $|0\rangle$ and triangle $|1\rangle$ qubelets have either been non-inverted or inverted. But qubelets are more versatile: they can be rotated through arbitrary angles. Understanding how to work with arbitrarily rotated qubelets in your quantum programs can turbo charge them. New quantum gates that use fractionally rotated qubelets make data transmission using entangled qubits over large distances[1] possible (among other things). Having this expanded range of quantum gates in your toolkit can give your programs a burst of power. Lots of it, in fact.

Consider a qubit where the pentagon $|0\rangle$ qubelets are rotated through, say, 20° clockwise and the triangle $|1\rangle$ qubelets through 30° anticlockwise:

---

1.   https://science.sciencemag.org/content/356/6343/1140.

The combined effect of rotating the pentagon $|0\rangle$ and triangle $|1\rangle$ qubelets swivels the qubit in 3D space—that is, the quantum state of a qubit dictates how it's warped in the real world. So, even though we'll draw the qubelets in 2D, their rotations govern how the qubit spins in 3D.

The math you're about to see here to depict these warped qubits is more complex than we've used to this point. You're going to need to remember things like polar coordinates and complex numbers. That's because, ultimately, quantum computing has some pretty complex math behind it, and you'll need to understand these topics at least at the basic level to be able to design circuits that use these more complex gates. I'll show you the equations first, and their relationship to the pentagon $|0\rangle$ and triangle $|1\rangle$ qubelets, and then how to apply them. You can take it on faith that the equations work, or you can see the complete derivation in Appendix 2, From Qubelets to the Bloch Sphere, on page 399.

Qubelets and the Bloch Sphere

Although we'll not rely on the Bloch sphere when designing algorithms, it's been a staple of quantum computing as it provides a way to visualize quantum states. Qubelets are another way to represent the same information and, more importantly from my view, are easier to generalize when designing multi-qubit programs: you don't have to spin Bloch spheres in your mind to figure out where the qubits end up. So it's instructive to see that they're related and are, in fact, one and the same thing but with different perspectives.

In Classifying Quantum Gates, on page 202, you'll learn new ways to apply operations on qubelets. In Chapter 8, Giant Leap for Mankind—Multi-Qubit Programs, on page 227, you'll use these techniques to work with multi-qubit programs without resorting to juggling Bloch spheres.

We represent the warping of the qubit as a point on the surface of a *Bloch sphere* which is a sphere whose radius is 1 as shown in the image on page 152.

(Even though the pentagon $|0\rangle$ and triangle $|1\rangle$ qubelets making up the quantum state are a point on the surface of the Bloch sphere, we've drawn it as a patch to better illustrate how it's associated with the qubelets.)

The angle that the state leans away from the vertical or the Z-axis is θ. And the angle swept out in the plane of the equator, the XY-plane is φ. Both angles are measured in radians.

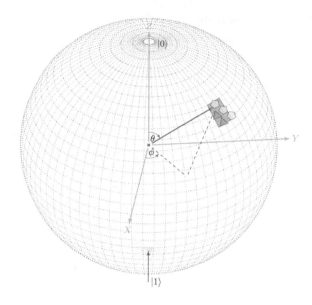

Radians Versus Degrees

Mathematically, we use radians to measure angles instead of degrees. So, 180° is π radians. Although when the context is clear, we may say cos 180° instead of the technically correct cos π to help us make a point. But we'll always use $e^{i\pi}$ instead of e^{i180}. See https://en.wikipedia.org/wiki/Radian for more information.

Moreover, in mathematics, anticlockwise angles are positive and clockwise angles are negative.

Mathematically, we express this point, or the quantum state $|\psi\rangle$, by the following equation:

$$|\psi\rangle = \cos\frac{\theta}{2}|0\rangle + e^{i\varphi}\sin\frac{\theta}{2}|1\rangle$$

Thus, cos $(\theta/2)$ is the amplitude of $|0\rangle$, and $e^{i\varphi}\sin(\theta/2)$ is the amplitude of $|1\rangle$. Note that $i = \sqrt{-1}$ is the *imaginary* or *complex* number.

If you want to understand why this equation represents the quantum state of a qubit as well as how the complex number i is involved, see Appendix 2, From Qubelets to the Bloch Sphere, on page 399.

Note a few points about the Bloch sphere:

- The latitudes are measured from the north pole toward the equator unlike those on a globe. So, the north pole is at the 0° latitude. These latitudes are associated with the angle θ that measures how much the quantum state swings away from the Z-axis.

- All of the quantum states on a given latitude differ only by $e^{i\varphi}$. Since $|e^{i\varphi}|^2 = e^{i\varphi}e^{-i\varphi} = 1$, the probabilities of all quantum states on the same latitude collapsing to $|0\rangle$ or $|1\rangle$ are the same. In other words, you can move the quantum state along the same latitude, or about the north-south axis, without affecting their probabilities of collapsing to the idealized states.

- The longitudes measure the angle φ that is swept by the quantum state in the plane of the equator.

The equation for the quantum state written in the previous equation is related to the qubelets as follows:

- The angle φ is the difference between the rotations of the triangle $|1\rangle$ qubelets and the the pentagon $|0\rangle$ qubelets, measured in radians. Thus, for the qubit shown in the beginning of this section, the angle φ is:

$$\varphi = \frac{(30 - (-20))\pi}{180} = \frac{5\pi}{18} \text{ radians}$$

- The normalized value of the pentagon $|0\rangle$ qubelets is $\cos \theta/2$. Relating this to the amplitudes in Normalizing Qubelets, on page 144, for the quantum state expressed as $a|0\rangle + b|1\rangle$, yields the following equation:

$$\cos \frac{\theta}{2} = \frac{3}{\sqrt{3^2 + 2^2}}$$
$$\frac{\theta}{2} = \cos^{-1} \frac{3}{\sqrt{13}}$$
$$\theta = 1.176 \text{ radians}$$

Or, θ is 67.38°.

Inverse Trigonometric Functions

To obtain the angle θ, use the *inverse* trigonometric functions[2] *arccosine* and *arcsine* to get the angles (in radians) that correspond to the amplitudes.

For example, consider the following quantum state:

$$\frac{1}{\sqrt{2}} |0\rangle + \frac{1}{\sqrt{2}} |1\rangle = \cos\frac{\theta}{2} |0\rangle + \sin\frac{\theta}{2} |1\rangle$$

---

2.   https://en.wikipedia.org/wiki/Inverse_trigonometric_functions

Inverse Trigonometric Functions

The amplitude for $|0\rangle$ is related to the angle θ as follows:

$$\frac{1}{\sqrt{2}} = \cos\frac{\theta}{2}$$

$$\frac{\theta}{2} = \cos^{-1}\frac{1}{\sqrt{2}}$$

$$\frac{\theta}{2} = \frac{\pi}{4}$$

$$\theta = \frac{\pi}{2}$$

The function $\cos^{-1}$ used here is the arccosine and is available on scientific calculators.

Once you know $\cos(\theta/2)$, $\sin(\theta/2)$ is calculated as follows:

$$\sin^2\frac{\theta}{2} = 1 - \cos^2\frac{\theta}{2}$$

$$= 1 - \left(\frac{3}{\sqrt{13}}\right)^2$$

$$= 1 - \frac{9}{13}$$

$$= \frac{4}{13}$$

$$\sin\frac{\theta}{2} = \sqrt{\frac{4}{13}}$$

$$= \frac{2}{\sqrt{13}}$$

Hence, the quantum state $|\psi\rangle$ of the qubit having 3 pentagon $|0\rangle$ qubelets rotated 20° clockwise and 2 triangle qubelets rotated 30° anticlockwise is:

$$\frac{3}{\sqrt{13}}|0\rangle + e^{i\frac{5\pi}{18}}\frac{2}{\sqrt{13}}|1\rangle$$

Now that you know how to calculate the quantum state of qubits with an arbitrary number of pentagon $|0\rangle$ and triangle $|1\rangle$ qubelets rotated through any angle, you can precisely put a qubit into any specific quantum state. All you do is vary the following:

- *Relative* number, or ratio, of the pentagon $|0\rangle$ and triangle $|1\rangle$ qubelets.
- *Relative* difference between the rotations of the pentagon $|0\rangle$ and triangle $|1\rangle$ qubelets.

In the next section, we'll look at special-purpose quantum gates that meticulously put qubits into these tailor-made states.

Joe asks:

How to Remember the Equation for the Quantum State?

Despite the formidable looking equation for the quantum state, you can quickly work out the general equation of the quantum state by bearing in mind the following:

1. Recall from H Gate on $|1\rangle$ Qubit, on page 86, that the H gate splits the $|1\rangle$ qubit into a pentagon $|0\rangle$ qubelet and an inverted triangle $|1\rangle$ qubelet:

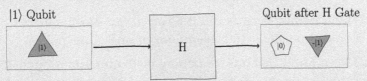

As we discussed in Number of Qubelets Define the Amplitudes, on page 145, the quantum state for the right qubit is:

$$\frac{1}{\sqrt{2}}\,|0\rangle \; - \frac{1}{\sqrt{2}}\,|1\rangle$$

2. The following cosines:

    a. The cosine of 45° or $\pi/4$:

    $$\cos\frac{\pi}{4} = \frac{1}{\sqrt{2}}$$

    b. The cosine of 180° or π:

    $$\cos\pi = -1$$

3. The angle φ starts with the same sound as that for *floor*. Thus, φ sweeps out an angle on the "floor," or the plane, of the equator. The other angle, θ, measures the latitude or the tilt from the vertical axis.

With these basic facts, we can quickly reason our way to the equation for the quantum state:

1. The qubit split by the H gate has an equal likelihood of collapsing to 0 or 1. Thus, it lies on the equator of the Bloch sphere, which is on the 90° latitude. This angle is double that of an angle whose cosine would be $1/\sqrt{2}$.

2. The difference in rotations between the inverted triangle $|1\rangle$ qubelet and non-inverted pentagon $|0\rangle$ qubelet is 180° or π radians. So, $e^{i\pi} = \cos\pi + i\sin\pi = -1$.

3. We can, thus, put these facts together to deduce that the equation for the quantum state is:

$$\cos\frac{\theta}{2}\,|0\rangle \; + e^{i\varphi}\sin\frac{\theta}{2}\,|1\rangle$$

Try Your Hand

Solutions to these exercises are given in Rotating Qubelets Through Any Angle Solutions, on page 453.

1. Consider a qubit with the quantum state shown here:

    a. Which hemisphere would it lie on in the Bloch sphere?
    b. Would it be closer to the equator or one of the poles?

2. Consider a qubit that has 18 pentagon $|0\rangle$ qubelets rotated 45° anticlockwise and 19 triangle $|1\rangle$ qubelets rotated 25° clockwise as shown:

    Which of the locations, A, B, or C, would this state correspond to on the Bloch sphere shown here:

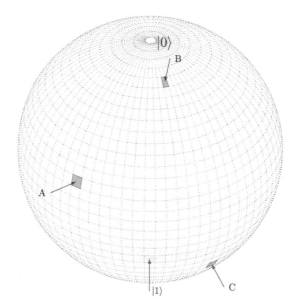

3. Which of the following qubits best matches the quantum state represented by the shaded patch labeled *A* on the Bloch sphere shown here:

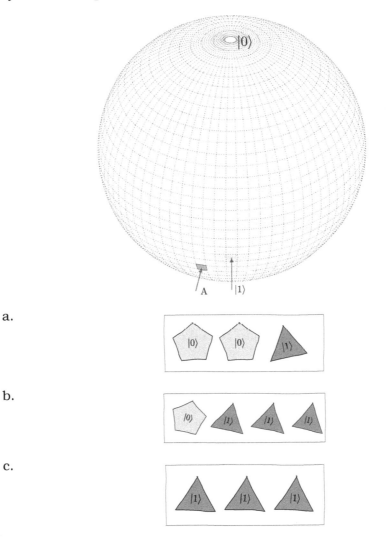

a.

b.

c.

4. Consider a qubit with a single pentagon $|0\rangle$ qubelet rotated 90° anticlockwise and a single triangle $|1\rangle$ qubelet rotated 90° clockwise:

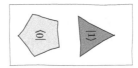

a. Write the equation for its quantum state.
b. How does this qubit compare to a $|1\rangle$ qubit operated on by a H gate?
c. Suppose the pentagon $|0\rangle$ qubelets are rotated 45° and the triangle $|1\rangle$ qubelets are rotated 225°. What can you say about its quantum state?

Universal Quantum Gates

Now that we know how to specify made-to-order quantum states, in this section you'll study quantum gates that put qubits in these custom states.

In general, every quantum gate, including the NOT, H, Z, and the quantum logic gates, operates on quantum states defined with complex numbers. Recall from Rotating Qubelets Through Any Angle, on page 150, the quantum state $|\psi\rangle$ is written as follows:

$$|\psi\rangle = \cos\frac{\theta}{2}|0\rangle + e^{i\varphi}\sin\frac{\theta}{2}|1\rangle$$

Consider a quantum state defined by $|\psi_a\rangle$, as follows:

$$|\psi_a\rangle = \cos\frac{\theta_a}{2}|0\rangle + e^{i\varphi_a}\sin\frac{\theta_a}{2}|1\rangle$$

When a quantum acts on this state, it'll take it to another state, $|\psi_b\rangle$, defined as follows:

$$|\psi_b\rangle = \cos\frac{\theta_b}{2}|0\rangle + e^{i\varphi_b}\sin\frac{\theta_b}{2}|1\rangle$$

In other words, all quantum gates take a qubit in one quantum state specified with complex numbers, $|\psi_a\rangle$, to another state, $|\psi_b\rangle$, also defined with complex numbers, as follows:

$$|\psi_a\rangle \mapsto |\psi_b\rangle$$

Substituting for $|\psi_a\rangle$ and $|\psi_b\rangle$, we get:

$$\cos\frac{\theta_a}{2}|0\rangle + e^{i\varphi_a}\sin\frac{\theta_a}{2}|1\rangle \mapsto \cos\frac{\theta_b}{2}|0\rangle + e^{i\varphi_b}\sin\frac{\theta_b}{2}|1\rangle$$

Because quantum states are specified by the number and orientation of the pentagon $|0\rangle$ and triangle $|1\rangle$ qubelets, you can define a quantum gate by how it acts on the $|0\rangle$ and $|1\rangle$ quantum states, respectively. Then, when the gate operates on a blended state, its actions on the pentagon $|0\rangle$ and triangle $|1\rangle$ qubelets are combined to give the resulting quantum state.

Action of Quantum Gate on $|0\rangle$

In particular, every quantum gate takes a $|0\rangle$ state and puts it in the following quantum state, $|\psi_0\rangle$:

$$|\psi_0\rangle = \cos\frac{\theta}{2}|0\rangle + e^{i\varphi}\sin\frac{\theta}{2}|1\rangle$$

For example, the NOT gate discussed in NOT (X) Gate, on page 42, takes a qubit in the $|0\rangle$ state and switches it to the $|1\rangle$ state. Because $\cos\frac{\pi}{2} = 0$ and $\sin\frac{\pi}{2} = 1$, we can write this operation on the quantum states as:

$$\text{NOT:}\ |0\rangle \mapsto \cos\frac{\pi}{2}|0\rangle + e^{0}\sin\frac{\pi}{2}|1\rangle = |1\rangle$$

Action of Quantum Gate on $|1\rangle$

Since the $|1\rangle$ state is directly opposite the $|0\rangle$ state on the Bloch sphere, the action of a quantum gate on a qubit in the $|1\rangle$ state puts it opposite to that of what it did with the $|0\rangle$ state.

So, replace θ by $\pi - \theta$ and φ by $\pi + \varphi$. (See Sphere Leads to Two Parameters, on page 406, for more details on these substitutions.) Then simplify the resulting equations:

$$
\begin{aligned}
|\psi_1\rangle &= \cos\frac{\pi - \theta}{2}|0\rangle + e^{i(\pi+\varphi)}\sin\frac{\pi - \theta}{2}|1\rangle \\
&= \cos\left(\frac{\pi}{2} - \frac{\theta}{2}\right)|0\rangle - e^{i\varphi}\sin\left(\frac{\pi}{2} - \frac{\theta}{2}\right)|1\rangle \\
&= \sin\frac{\theta}{2}|0\rangle - e^{i\varphi}\cos\frac{\theta}{2}|1\rangle
\end{aligned}
$$

We simplified these equations using the Trigonometric Identities.[3]

States Have Two, but Gates Have Three Parameters

For reasons that we'll explain in Can the Quantum Gate Matrix Be Anything?, on page 187, we tweak the quantum state $|\psi_1\rangle$ by multiplying the right hand side by $-e^{i\lambda}$:

$$|\psi_1\rangle = -e^{i\lambda}\sin\frac{\theta}{2}|0\rangle + e^{i(\lambda+\varphi)}\cos\frac{\theta}{2}|1\rangle$$

This change doesn't affect the probabilities of the quantum state collapsing to $|0\rangle$ or $|1\rangle$.

The new parameter, λ, gives an additional degree of freedom to calibrate quantum states: we can fine-tune the quantum state along a latitude by

---

3.   https://en.wikipedia.org/wiki/List_of_trigonometric_identities#Reflections

adjusting the relative orientations of the pentagon $|0\rangle$ and triangle $|1\rangle$ qubelets but without modifying the probabilities of the qubit collapsing to $|0\rangle$ or $|1\rangle$. This allows the qubit to interact differently with other qubits in the mega-qubit, depending on where the quantum state falls on the latitude. Simply put, without violating the laws of physics that call for the probabilities of a qubit collapsing to $|0\rangle$ or $|1\rangle$ adding up to 1, we can influence how qubits interact with each other in the mega-qubit and thereby govern how the program executes.

This general-purpose way of using three parameters to describe the operation on a qubit is referred to as the *Universal (U)* or U3 gate. We write it as follows:

$$U3\,(\theta,\,\varphi,\,\lambda):\ |0\rangle\ \mapsto\ \cos\frac{\theta}{2}\,|0\rangle\,+\,e^{i\varphi}\sin\frac{\theta}{2}\,|1\rangle$$

$$U3\,(\theta,\,\varphi,\,\lambda):\ |1\rangle\ \mapsto\ -e^{i\lambda}\sin\frac{\theta}{2}\,|0\rangle\,+\,e^{i(\lambda+\varphi)}\cos\frac{\theta}{2}\,|1\rangle$$

U2 and U1 Gates

The Universal (U) gate comes in two other flavors, defined using two parameters and one parameter, respectively:

U2 Gate

The U2 gate is just the U3 gate in which θ is set to $\frac{\pi}{2}$.

$$U2\,(\varphi,\,\lambda)=U3\left(\frac{\pi}{2},\,\varphi,\,\lambda\right)$$

U1 Gate

The U1 gate is just the U3 gate with $\theta=0$ and $\varphi=0$.

$$U1\,(\lambda)=U3\,(0,\,0,\,\lambda)$$

Thus, the U2 and U1 gates are just versions of the U3 gate in which one or two parameters, respectively, are predefined. In the next section, you'll see that different values for θ, φ, and λ let you define arbitrary quantum states.

Using the Universal Gates in Code

You can use the three Universal gates in your code—they're not just theoretical concepts. With these gates, you can create precise quantum states.

So far in our quantum programs, we've only used single-qubit gates that put qubits in states that collapse as follows:

- Always collapses to $|0\rangle$.
- Always collapses to $|1\rangle$.
- Collapses to $|0\rangle$ or $|1\rangle$ with equal probability.

But with the U3 gate, we can collapse the qubit so that it predictably favors one or the other idealized state. For example, to put a $|0\rangle$ qubit in a quantum state so that it falls frequently to $|0\rangle$ but also collapses to $|1\rangle$ a significant number of times that's more than just noise, we maneuver it to a state that is in the upper hemisphere:

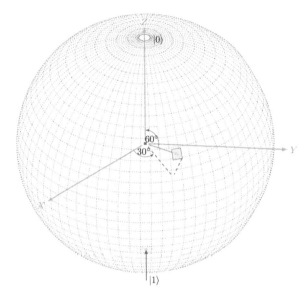

(The tiny square at the tip of the arrow is just to indicate that the tip is on the surface of the sphere.)

In this state, the angle θ that the state makes with the vertical is 60° or $\pi/3$ radians, and the angle φ is 30° or $\pi/6$ radians.

To put the $|0\rangle$ qubit in this state, we set the parameters of the U3 gate as follows:

$$U3\left(\frac{\pi}{3}, \frac{\pi}{6}, 0\right): |0\rangle \mapsto \cos\frac{\frac{\pi}{3}}{2}|0\rangle + e^{i\frac{\pi}{6}}\sin\frac{\frac{\pi}{3}}{2}|1\rangle$$

$$= \cos\frac{\pi}{6}|0\rangle + \left(\cos\frac{\pi}{6} + i\sin\frac{\pi}{6}\right)\sin\frac{\pi}{6}|1\rangle = \frac{\sqrt{3}}{2}|0\rangle + \left(\frac{\sqrt{3}}{2} + i\frac{1}{2}\right)\frac{1}{2}|1\rangle$$

$$= \frac{\sqrt{3}}{2}|0\rangle + \left(\frac{\sqrt{3}}{4} + i\frac{1}{4}\right)|1\rangle$$

The probability of this state collapsing to $|0\rangle$ is the square of the amplitude for $|0\rangle$:

$$\text{Probability of collapsing to } |0\rangle = \left(\frac{\sqrt{3}}{2}\right)^2 = \frac{3}{4}$$

Since the amplitude of the $|1\rangle$ is a complex quantity, the probability of this state collapsing to $|1\rangle$ is calculated by multiplying with its conjugate complex:

$$\text{Probability of collapsing to } |1\rangle \;=\; \left(\frac{\sqrt{3}}{4} + i\frac{1}{4}\right)\left(\frac{\sqrt{3}}{4} - i\frac{1}{4}\right)$$

$$= \frac{3}{16} - i^2\frac{1}{16}$$

$$= \frac{3}{16} + \frac{1}{16}$$

$$= \frac{1}{4}$$

Thus, the sum of the probabilities adds up to 1, as required for a valid quantum state.

To put a $|0\rangle$ qubit in this quantum state, we'll build a circuit using a U3 gate where $\theta = \pi/3$ radians, $\varphi = \pi/6$ radians, and $\lambda = 0$:

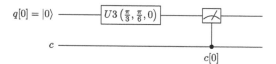

Actually, we only need the U3 gate, but since we can't directly observe a quantum state, we'll connect the Measure gate and confirm that it collapses the qubit to 0 and 1, respectively, with the probabilities calculated.

To run this circuit on the IBM Quantum Computer, start by programming a New Circuit. Set the number of quantum and classical registers to 1 each by directly modifying the code:

```
qreg q[1];
creg c[1];
```

Next, drag a U3 gate from the gates palette onto the wire for $q[0]$. You can set its parameters by clicking on the gate in the Circuit Composer and then clicking the tiny pencil icon, shown in this figure:

On the panel that slides into view, set the three parameters: theta for the angle θ, phi for the angle φ, and lambda for λ. All parameters must be specified in radians. You can use pi for π if you'd like.

To specify the U3 gate, you declare it with its parameters in parenthesis followed by the qubit it acts on:

```
u3(pi/3,pi/6,0) q[0];
```

Finally, drag the Measure gate and record the collapse of the $q[0]$ qubit in the classical register $c[0]$:

```
measure q[0] -> c[0];
```

The complete code listing for this program, excluding the header, is as follows:

```
U3_Theta_60_Phi_30.qasm
qreg q[1];
creg c[1];
u3(pi/3,pi/6,0) q[0];
measure q[0] -> c[0];
```

When you run this quantum program, you'll get an output that looks similar to the following results:

Result

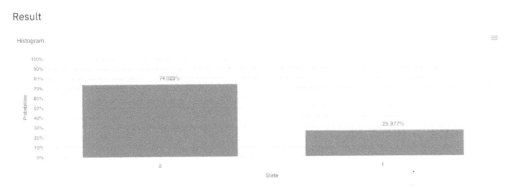

This output confirms that the $|0\rangle$ qubit has been put into a quantum state where the theoretical probability of it collapsing to $|0\rangle$ or $|1\rangle$ approximately matches the frequency of the 0 and 1 states observed in the classical register.

This circuit is interesting in its own right, as it demonstrates how to reliably collapse a qubit to either the $|0\rangle$ or $|1\rangle$ idealized states in quantum programs according to predetermined odds. But what does this control really buy us when designing quantum algorithms? What's the value of creating quantum states that have a robust chance of collapsing to the "wrong" classical state? It turns out that nonzero probabilities play a central role in quantum algorithms but in a way that's different than in classical algorithms. In the next section, we'll explore the real role of probability in quantum programming and how to think about it when designing algorithms based on quantum phenomena.

Standard Gates Are Universal Gates Too

Before showing you how to use the Universal gates in your programs to create arbitrary quantum states, we'll review the parameters to reproduce the NOT, Z, and H gates we've studied so far.

Universal Gate as a NOT Gate

To get the Universal gate to mimic the NOT gate reviewed in NOT (X) Gate, on page 42, set $\theta = \pi$, $\varphi = 0$, and $\lambda = \pi$:

$$U3\,(\pi, 0, \pi) : |0\rangle \;\mapsto\; \cos\frac{\pi}{2}|0\rangle + e^{0}\sin\frac{\pi}{2}|1\rangle$$
$$= \;|1\rangle$$

(The previous equation is simplified by recognizing that $\cos \pi/2 = 0$, $\sin \pi/2 = 1$, and $e^{i\pi} = \cos \pi + i\sin \pi = -1$.)

Thus, the $U3(\pi, 0, \pi)$ gate switches a $|0\rangle$ qubit to a $|1\rangle$ qubit. Similarly, we compute how the U3 gate acts on the $|1\rangle$ qubit:

$$U3\,(\pi, 0, \pi) : |1\rangle \;\mapsto\; -e^{i\pi}\sin\frac{\pi}{2}|0\rangle + e^{i\pi}\cos\frac{\pi}{2}|1\rangle$$
$$= \;|0\rangle$$

That is, the $U3\,(\pi, 0, \pi)$ gate switches a $|1\rangle$ qubit to $|0\rangle$. Thus, with this set of parameters, the U3 gate switches a $|0\rangle$ qubit to the $|1\rangle$ state, and vice versa.

The Not Gate Called the Pauli-X Gate

If you chart the way the NOT gate acts on the $|0\rangle$ qubit on the Bloch sphere, the arrow pointing vertically upward to the $|0\rangle$ quantum state at the north pole gets rotated so that it points straight down to the $|1\rangle$ state at the south pole:

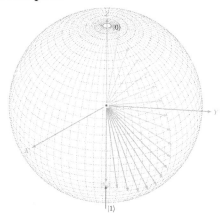

In this diagram we've relabeled the U-axis to the more familiar X-axis.

The arrow representing the quantum state is in effect rotated about the X-axis. Hence, the NOT gate is also called the Pauli-X gate.

Universal Gates as Z and H Gates

For the Universal (U) gate to behave like the Z gate (reviewed in Pauli-Z (Z) Gate, on page 109) and H gate (Summary of Basic H Gate Operations, on page 87), respectively, the corresponding values for the three parameters, θ, φ, and λ, for the Z and H gates are as follows:

$$Z \text{ gate:} \quad = \quad U3 \left(0, \pi, 0\right)$$
$$H \text{ gate:} \quad = \quad U3 \left(\frac{\pi}{2}, 0, \pi\right)$$

Since θ for the U3 gate mimicking the H gate is $\pi/2$, we can also use the U2 gate as an H gate with the following parameters:

$$H \text{ gate:} \quad = \quad U3 \left(\frac{\pi}{2}, 0, \pi\right)$$
$$= \quad U2 \left(0, \pi\right)$$

The Universal (U) gates reproduce the behavior of every quantum gate, so you could, if you'd like, write your programs using just them. The gates such as NOT, Z, and H, though, are special versions of the Universal gate that make writing (and reading) programs more convenient.

Heads I Win, Tails You Lose, or How to Prevail with Qubelets

Probabilistic algorithms provide the key to hard-to-solve problems, such as those in machine learning and artificial intelligence. Although these algorithms use probability in widely different ways, they all have the same motivation: use randomness to redirect the search.

Quantum states have probabilities written all over them. You might think, therefore, that using probability is a magic solution to quantum problems. Although this is true in a strictly mathematical sense, it's not easy to create a valid solution path by chaining together probabilities. So, in this section, we'll show that working with qubelets and amplitudes offers an alternative way to design algorithms.

To illustrate, build the following circuit on the IBM Quantum Computer:

The complete code listing, excluding the header, is as follows:

```
U3_Theta_60_Phi_30_H_Measure.qasm
qreg q[1];
creg c[1];

u3(pi/3,pi/6,0) q[0];
h q[0];
measure q[0] -> c[0];
```

❶ Specify the lengths of the quantum and classical registers.

❷ Declare the U3 gate and set θ to $\pi/3$ radians or 60°, φ to $\pi/6$ radians or 30°, and λ to 0.

❸ Split the qubit with an H gate.

❹ Collapse the qubit and record the classical state it falls to by inspecting it with the Measure gate.

When you run this program, the $|1\rangle$ qubelets are effectively removed and you'll get an output similar to the following:

Result

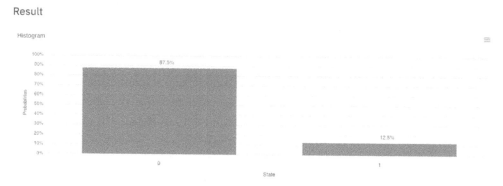

By introducing the H gate before measuring the qubit, we've halved the likelihood of the qubit collapsing to $|1\rangle$ compared to the program without the H gate. It's instructive to work out why this happens, as it also shows you how to analyze quantum programs.

Although probabilities are the only things we can concretely measure in quantum programs, the real action in quantum programs happens before the qubit collapses. We get a clearer picture of how a quantum circuit works if we work with amplitudes and qubelets instead of dealing with probabilities.

The quantum state of the qubit $q[0]$ after the U3 gate acts on it is:

$$U3\left(\frac{\pi}{3}, \frac{\pi}{6}, 0\right): |0\rangle \mapsto \frac{\sqrt{3}}{2}|0\rangle + \left(\frac{\sqrt{3}}{4} + i\frac{1}{4}\right)|1\rangle$$

Recall from Number of Qubelets Define the Amplitudes, on page 145, the ratio of the amplitude magnitudes is the ratio of the number of pentagon $|0\rangle$ qubelets to that of the triangle $|1\rangle$ qubelets:

Number of pentagon $|0\rangle$ qubelets : Number of triangle $|1\rangle$ qubelets $= \left| \frac{\sqrt{3}}{2} \right| : \left| \frac{\sqrt{3}}{4} + i\frac{1}{4} \right|$

To obtain the magnitude of the complex number on the right-hand side, use its complex conjugate as follows:

$$\left| \frac{\sqrt{3}}{4} + i\frac{1}{4} \right| = \sqrt{\left(\frac{\sqrt{3}}{4} + i\frac{1}{4} \right)\left(\frac{\sqrt{3}}{4} - i\frac{1}{4} \right)}$$

$$= \sqrt{\left(\frac{\sqrt{3}}{4} \right)^2 - i^2 \left(\frac{1}{4} \right)^2}$$

$$= \sqrt{\frac{3}{16} + \frac{1}{16}}$$

$$= \frac{1}{2}$$

Measuring Magnitudes of Complex Numbers

The square of a number is often used to measure the "raw strength" of a number. For example, -5 may be less than 3, but in terms of their magnitudes, $(-5)^2 = 25$ is greater than $3^2 = 9$.

When it comes to complex numbers such as $a + i\,b$, squaring gives another complex number:

$$(a + i\,b)^2 = a^2 + 2iab + b^2$$

$$= (a^2 + b^2) + i\,2ab$$

$$= c + i\,d$$

The real part of this complex number, c, is $a^2 + b^2$ and its imaginary part, d, is $2ab$. In other words, squaring just replaces one complex number with another.

On the other hand, multiplying $a + i\,b$ with its complex conjugate $a - i\,b$ gives:

$$(a + i\,b)(a - i\,b) = a^2 - i^2 b^2 = a^2 + b^2$$

(Note that $i^2 = (\sqrt{-1})^2 = -1$.) The number in the previous equation has no imaginary part. Moreover, since it's the sum of two squares, it's non-negative. Hence, it makes a good metric to gauge the magnitudes of complex numbers.

Thus, the ratio of the amplitude magnitudes is the ratio of the number of pentagon $|0\rangle$ qubelets to that of the triangle $|1\rangle$ qubelets:

Number of pentagon $|0\rangle$ qubelets : Number of triangle $|1\rangle$ qubelets $= \frac{\sqrt{3}}{2} : \frac{1}{2}$

This ratio is simplified to $\sqrt{3} : 1$ or $1.7321 : 1$. If you like to deal with qubelets in whole numbers, you could multiply the ratio by 10,000 to get $17,321 : 10,000$. The qubit would have 17,321 pentagon $|0\rangle$ qubelets and 10,000 triangle $|1\rangle$ qubelets. But since the analysis is conceptual, you could equally well work with fractional qubelets. In fact, we'll go one step further: we'll analyze this circuit without drawing any qubelets.

After the U3 Gate:

The U3 gate puts the $|0\rangle$ qubit into a quantum state that has the following qubelets:

- $\sqrt{3}$ pentagon $|0\rangle$ qubelets.
- 1 triangle $|1\rangle$ qubelet.

After the H Gate:

The H gate splits qubelets as follows:

Splitting the $|0\rangle$ Qubelets

The H gate splits a $|0\rangle$ qubit into a pentagon $|0\rangle$ qubelet a triangle $|1\rangle$ qubelet (see H Gate on $|0\rangle$ Qubit, on page 83):

Thus, the $\sqrt{3}$ pentagon qubelets are split into:

- $\sqrt{3}$ pentagon $|0\rangle$ qubelets that have the same orientation as those after the U3 gate.

- $\sqrt{3}$ triangle $|1\rangle$ qubelets that have the same orientation as those after the U3 gate.

Splitting the $|1\rangle$ Qubelet

The H gate splits a $|1\rangle$ qubit into a pentagon $|0\rangle$ qubelet a triangle $|1\rangle$ qubelet (see H Gate on $|1\rangle$ Qubit, on page 86):

Thus, the single triangle qubelets is split into:

- 1 pentagon $|0\rangle$ qubelet that has the same orientation as those after the U3 gate.

- 1 *inverted* triangle $|1\rangle$ qubelet that is oriented exactly opposite to that after the U3 gate.

The *inverted* triangle $|1\rangle$ qubelet will cancel out with one of the non-inverted ones. Thus, after both the U3 and H gates act on the $|0\rangle$ qubit, we'll end up with a quantum state containing the following qubelets:

- $\sqrt{3} + 1$ pentagon $|0\rangle$ qubelets.
- $\sqrt{3} - 1$ triangle $|1\rangle$ qubelets.

To calculate probabilities, normalize the number of qubelets as follows:

$$\text{Probability of qubit collapsing to } |0\rangle = \left(\frac{\sqrt{3}+1}{\sqrt{(\sqrt{3}+1)^2+(\sqrt{3}-1)^2}}\right)^2$$

$$= 0.9331$$

Similarly,

$$\text{Probability of qubit collapsing to } |1\rangle = \left(\frac{\sqrt{3}-1}{\sqrt{(\sqrt{3}+1)^2+(\sqrt{3}-1)^2}}\right)^2$$

$$= 0.067$$

These probabilities roughly match the corresponding values from the execution of the quantum program as shown in the figure at the beginning of this section. Importantly, although we used probabilities, it was only at the end. To analyze the intermediate steps, we split and canceled qubelets by capitalizing on the quantum nature of the gates in the program. More importantly, we got a sense of writing quantum programs that are guaranteed to arrive at an optimal solution in a single, or at most a few, shots or runs.

This circuit analysis suggests that when synthesizing or designing quantum algorithms, you can take an approach that does away with the traditional role of probability and instead focus on canceling qubelets. Begin with a sea of pentagon $|0\rangle$ and triangle $|1\rangle$ qubelets and then introduce quantum gates to whittle them down so that the quantum state is forced to collapse to the classical state that solves the computational task.

This notion of splitting qubelets to create more qubelets that, ironically, have greater chances of canceling them out is central to quantum computing: the quantum state that initially favored one over the other idealized state now gets even more biased toward that state. This effect is called *amplification* and forms the core of designing quantum algorithms used to search for optimal solutions in Chapter 10, Quantum Search, on page 295.

Try Your Hand

Solutions to these exercises are given in Universal Gates Solutions, on page 455.

For any code listing in the exercises, assume the following header lines:

```
OPENQASM 2.0;
include "qelib1.inc";
```

1. In Back-to-Back H Gates: The First Hint of Taming Randomness, on page 88, we saw that two H gates connected in sequence effectively leave a qubit unchanged. To demonstrate that a Universal gate simulates an H gate, build

the following circuit on the IBM Quantum Computer, where one of the H gates has been replaced with a $U2\,(0,\,\pi)$ gate:

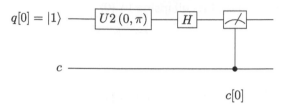

a. Write a program for this circuit.

b. Run your program and determine the state that's recorded in the classical register when the qubit $q[0]$ collapses when the program terminates.

c. Set the φ parameter on the U2 gate to $\pi/2$:

```
u2(pi/2,pi) q[0];
```

Run the program and compare the output with what you got earlier. Why do you think the output is different?

2. a. In Heads I Win, Tails You Lose, or How to Prevail with Qubelets, on page 165, we saw that by using an H gate to further split qubelets after the qubit's operated on by the $U3\,(\pi/3,\,\pi/6,\,0)$ gate, more $|1\rangle$ qubelets are forced to cancel out, thereby increasing the likelihood of the qubit collapsing to $|0\rangle$. So, would adding one more H gate, as shown here, cause even more $|1\rangle$ qubelets to cancel out?

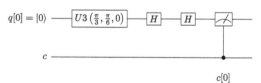

b. This hunch of continuing to split qubelets to produce more $|1\rangle$ qubelets so that they cancel out is correct. But you need to add a gate such as a $U3(\pi/3,\,0,\,0)$ in between the two H gates, as shown in the following figure:

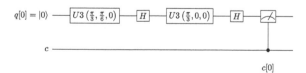

i. Write a program for this circuit.

ii. Run your program and examine its output. Does the probability of the qubit collapsing to $|0\rangle$ improve when compared to the circuit in Heads I Win, Tails You Lose, or How to Prevail with Qubelets?

In the next chapter, we'll explore why sandwiching a gate such as a $U3(\pi/3, 0, 0)$ between two back-to-back H gates increases the odds of the qubit collapsing to $|0\rangle$. Intuitively, though, the sandwiched gate perturbs the orientation of the $|0\rangle$ qubelets so that they are slightly misaligned and the neutralizing effect of the H gates doesn't occur.

3. Consider a quantum circuit in which a gate acts on a $|0\rangle$ qubit and puts it into the state shown on the right in the following figure:

The right qubit has one pentagon $|0\rangle$ qubelet and two triangle $|1\rangle$ qubelets. The triangle $|1\rangle$ qubelets are rotated 30° anticlockwise.

a. Calculate the quantum state for the right qubit.

b. Which hemisphere would this quantum state fall on the Bloch sphere?

c. What are the probabilities of this state collapsing to $|0\rangle$ and $|1\rangle$, respectively?

d. What gate would you use that takes the $|0\rangle$ qubit and puts it into the state you calculated previously?

e. Write a quantum program for this quantum circuit. Add a Measure gate to collapse the qubit and record the classical state it collapses to.

f. Run your program and examine its output. Do the probabilities of collapsing to the classical states match your calculations?

Bottom Line

The promise of quantum computing to offer super-fast solutions to optimization problems or virtually foolproof ways to safely send messages depends on twisting qubits, and by association, rotating their qubelets through arbitrary angles.

Although the Bloch sphere is traditionally used to depict the gradual blending of quantum states from a pure $|0\rangle$ state at the north pole to a pure $|1\rangle$ state at the south pole, its 3D shape makes it hard to visualize the actions of quantum gates. The model described in Modeling Quantum Bits with the Qubelets Model, on page 20, takes this single shape and breaks it into two shapes, pentagons and triangles, that you can rotate independently in 2D space without having to do any mental calisthenics. More importantly, fundamental quantum concepts like canceling and entangling become transparent without being couched in abstract mathematics. In other words, the Qubelets Model accurately represents the Bloch Model but in an actionable form particularly suited for quantum computing.

Qubelets are teased to precise quantum states using devices called Universal gates. In this chapter, you learned to work with these gates in quantum programs. To specify Universal gates in code, we declare them using parameters related to a quantum state that are, in turn, defined by the relative number, or ratio, of pentagon $|0\rangle$ and triangle $|1\rangle$ qubelets and the relative difference between their rotations. To this end, we covered how to mathematically express quantum states in terms of amplitudes and probabilities in Quantum States and Probabilities, on page 142, and to plot the states on a unit sphere called the Bloch sphere in Rotating Qubelets Through Any Angle, on page 150. With this mapping, Universal gates act on qubits and regulate their states with full control. In later chapters, we'll need these high-fidelity gates when designing algorithms that tackle complex applications in unprecedented ways.

Even though probabilities govern how qubits land on $|0\rangle$ and $|1\rangle$, as you saw in Heads I Win, Tails You Lose, or How to Prevail with Qubelets, on page 165, when designing algorithms, your mindset should be on figuring out how to orient qubelets to remove states that won't lead to optimal solutions. Universal gates give you the means to rotate the appropriate set of qubelets so that they are directly opposed to others and cancel out.

In the next chapter, we'll analyze circuits where you'll learn about other quantum gates that twist qubelets in a variety of ways.

CHAPTER 7

Small Step for Man—Single Qubit Programs

In the previous chapter, Chapter 6, Designer Genes—Custom Quantum States, on page 141, you saw how to precisely specify any quantum states. In this chapter, you'll learn ways to manipulate qubits to any arbitrary quantum state.

The quantum programs you've seen so far have been somewhat limited. You've learned to invoke quantum phenomena in programs, got them to work predictably, and used the Qubelets Model on page 20, to analyze them. But to hook up more gates and deal with more qubits to solve big problems, you need to learn techniques that'll let you handle larger circuits. In particular, because we need to consider the all-states-at-once nature of quantum computing, the bookkeeping gets more intricate. You'll ratchet up your toolkit with techniques that show you how to keep track of the quantum states of qubits through a program's circuitry without going through the one-bit-at-a-time way of individually tracing the qubelets in each qubit and tabulating where they end up.

In this chapter, you'll work with single-qubit programs. Although single-qubit programs aren't terribly exciting from an applications standpoint, the ideas and techniques you'll learn here extend directly to multi-qubit programs in the next chapter. Moreover, the techniques described here will help you figure out which gates to use and how to connect them in your quantum circuit so that the mega-qubit and its quantum states end up where you want them to. This will help you design quantum algorithms for your own applications.

Quantum States as Vectors

In Quantum States and Probabilities, on page 142, we saw that a quantum state can be expressed as a combination of the $|0\rangle$ and $|1\rangle$ states as follows:

$$\omega_0 |0\rangle + \omega_1 |1\rangle$$

The parameters ω_0 and ω_1 are the amplitudes whose squares are the probabilities of collapsing to 0 or 1, respectively.

We can express the quantum state more compactly. Since a qubit is a blended state of just the two quantum states, $|0\rangle$ and $|1\rangle$, we can represent it as a 2×1 vector of two rows and one column (see Working with Matrices and Vectors, on page 394):

$$\begin{pmatrix} \omega_0 \\ \omega_1 \end{pmatrix}$$

In this vector, the top element represents the amplitude for the pentagon $|0\rangle$ qubelets, and the bottom represents the amplitude for the triangle $|1\rangle$ qubelets in the qubit.

The vector for the idealized quantum state $|0\rangle$ will have $\omega_0 = 1$ and $\omega_1 = 0$:

$$|0\rangle \equiv \begin{pmatrix} 1 \\ 0 \end{pmatrix}$$

Pictorially, this vector represents the following qubelets in the qubit:

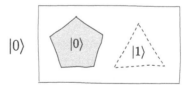

The triangle $|1\rangle$ qubelet is drawn with a dotted outline as it's not active in this qubit.

Likewise, the vector for the idealized quantum state $|1\rangle$ will have $\omega_0 = 0$ and $\omega_1 = 1$:

$$|1\rangle \equiv \begin{pmatrix} 0 \\ 1 \end{pmatrix}$$

In this case, this vector corresponds to the following qubelets in the qubit shown on page 175.

The pentagon $|0\rangle$ qubelet is drawn with a dotted outline since it's not active in the $|1\rangle$ qubit.

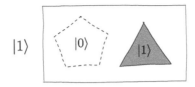

Consider a qubit with seven pentagon $|0\rangle$ qubelets and three inverted triangle $|1\rangle$ qubelets, shown in the following figure:

You can calculate its quantum state as described in *Quantum States and Probabilities* to get:

$$0.9191 \, |0\rangle \ - 0.3939 \, |1\rangle$$

Rewrite this equation as a vector:

$$\begin{pmatrix} 0.9191 \\ -0.3939 \end{pmatrix}$$

Sometimes, you'll find it convenient to write the previous vector in terms of the vectors for the idealized quantum states $|0\rangle$ and $|1\rangle$, as shown here:

$$\begin{pmatrix} 0.9191 \\ -0.3939 \end{pmatrix} = 0.9191 \begin{pmatrix} 1 \\ 0 \end{pmatrix} - 0.3939 \begin{pmatrix} 0 \\ 1 \end{pmatrix}$$

In general, the quantum state of a single qubit in terms of vectors is:

$$\omega_0 \, |0\rangle \ + \omega_1 \, |1\rangle \ \equiv \begin{pmatrix} \omega_0 \\ \omega_1 \end{pmatrix} \equiv \omega_0 \begin{pmatrix} 1 \\ 0 \end{pmatrix} + \omega_1 \begin{pmatrix} 0 \\ 1 \end{pmatrix}$$

The squares of the amplitudes ω_0 and ω_1 still add up to 1 for the vector to be a valid representation of a quantum state:

$$\omega_0^2 + \omega_1^2 = 1$$

Quantum Gates as Matrices

The go-to visual for orthogonal vectors is unit lengths directed along the coordinate axes. This picture, though appealing, quickly breaks down. With two qubits, we'll have vectors with 2^2 or 4 elements, making them hard to visualize in 3D space. As explained in From Sphere to Hemisphere: The True Space, on page 408, in the weird geometry of quantum mechanics, the vector for $|0\rangle$ points upward while that for $|1\rangle$ is downward and not perpendicular to the vector for $|0\rangle$.

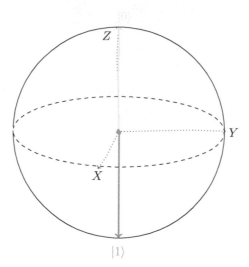

When quantum computers become practical to unleash on large scale problems, we'll be dealing with several qubits. So we'll get more mileage thinking about vectors, as mathematicians would, as opposed to another picture. In this interpretation, we treat the elements of a vector as selectors of the corresponding column of a matrix. For instance, consider the following $N \times 1$ vector x of N elements:

$$x = \begin{pmatrix} x_1 \\ x_2 \\ \vdots \\ x_N \end{pmatrix}$$

Multiplying an $M \times N$ matrix A with the $N \times 1$ vector x, we get:

$$Ax = \begin{bmatrix} a_{11} & a_{12} & \cdots & a_{1N} \\ a_{21} & a_{22} & \cdots & a_{2N} \\ \vdots & & & \vdots \\ a_{M1} & a_{M2} & \cdots & a_{MN} \end{bmatrix} \begin{pmatrix} x_1 \\ x_2 \\ \vdots \\ x_N \end{pmatrix} = \begin{pmatrix} a_{11} \\ a_{21} \\ \vdots \\ a_{M1} \end{pmatrix} x_1 + \begin{pmatrix} a_{12} \\ a_{22} \\ \vdots \\ a_{M2} \end{pmatrix} x_2 + \cdots + \begin{pmatrix} a_{1N} \\ a_{2N} \\ \vdots \\ a_{MN} \end{pmatrix} x_N$$

Each column of the matrix is multiplied by the corresponding element of the vector x. (If you'd like more details on how we get this result, see Working with Matrices and Vectors, on page 394.)

From Vectors to Matrices

A vector whose first element is 1 and whose other elements are 0 pulls the first column of a matrix, and a vector whose second element is 1 (and 0 elsewhere) selects the second column, and so on. This suggests a way to model quantum gates with matrices.

For example, consider a quantum gate that operates on the $|0\rangle$ qubit and modifies its quantum state to $\alpha_0 |0\rangle + \alpha_1 |1\rangle$. We write this operation in vector form as:

$$\begin{pmatrix} 1 \\ 0 \end{pmatrix} \mapsto \begin{pmatrix} \alpha_0 \\ \alpha_1 \end{pmatrix}$$

This transformation can be expressed with a matrix A: the right-hand side of the previous equation is the first column of matrix A so that it's selected when A is multiplied by the vector for the $|0\rangle$ qubit. That is,

$$A\begin{pmatrix} 1 \\ 0 \end{pmatrix} = \begin{bmatrix} \alpha_0 & * \\ \alpha_1 & * \end{bmatrix}\begin{pmatrix} 1 \\ 0 \end{pmatrix} = \begin{pmatrix} \alpha_0 \\ \alpha_1 \end{pmatrix}$$

We don't yet know the second column, hence, we indicate our lack of knowledge with asterisks.

Likewise, if $\beta_0 |0\rangle + \beta_1 |1\rangle$ is the quantum state after the gate acts on $|1\rangle$, then these amplitudes form the second column of the matrix A. That is, when the matrix A is multiplied by the $|1\rangle$ qubit vector, we get a vector whose elements are the amplitudes β_0 and β_1, respectively. That is:

$$A\begin{pmatrix} 0 \\ 1 \end{pmatrix} = \begin{bmatrix} * & \beta_0 \\ * & \beta_1 \end{bmatrix}\begin{pmatrix} 0 \\ 1 \end{pmatrix} = \begin{pmatrix} \beta_0 \\ \beta_1 \end{pmatrix}$$

Putting these two matrices together, we get the complete matrix A for the gate, as follows:

$$A = \begin{bmatrix} \alpha_0 & \beta_0 \\ \alpha_1 & \beta_1 \end{bmatrix}$$

The first column of the A matrix is the quantum state when the gate operates on the $|0\rangle$ qubit, and the second column is when the gate operates on the $|1\rangle$ qubit.

Quantum Gate Matrices Are Square

Quantum gates are always square matrices. That is, the matrices have the same number of rows and columns.

The reason for this property stems from the way that vectors are column selectors of matrices. When a matrix is multiplied by a vector, an element of a vector selects the corresponding column of the matrix. This forces the number of columns of the matrix to be the same as the number of elements of the vector.

Second, since each element selects a column, the final result of this multiplication will be a vector. This vector represents the quantum state of the qubit after it's acted on by the quantum gate. For a single qubit, its quantum state can only collapse to one of two classical states. Thus, the vector, a column of the matrix, can have only two elements. Hence, the matrix for single-qubit quantum gates has exactly two rows and two columns.

Later, when we analyze quantum gates that operate on multiple qubits, we'll see that this property continues to hold.

Next, we apply this recipe to compute the A_H matrix for the H gate.

H Gate Matrix

To compute the matrix A_H for the H gate, we'll work out the vectors when the H gate operates on the $|0\rangle$ qubit for the first column and then the $|1\rangle$ qubit for the second column.

First Column of the H Gate Matrix

As described in Putting Qubits in Blended States, on page 82, the H gate splits a $|0\rangle$ qubit into one with a pentagon $|0\rangle$ qubelet and a triangle $|1\rangle$ qubelet, as shown in the following figure:

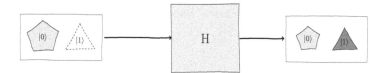

The vector for the $|0\rangle$ qubit on the left has only a pentagon $|0\rangle$ qubelet. So its vector is:

$$\begin{pmatrix} 1 \\ 0 \end{pmatrix}$$

The H splits the $|0\rangle$ qubit on the left to one with a pentagon $|0\rangle$ qubelet and a triangle $|1\rangle$ qubelet. Its quantum state is:

$$\frac{1}{\sqrt{1^2 + 1^2}} \, |0\rangle \; + \; \frac{1}{\sqrt{1^2 + 1^2}} \, |1\rangle$$

Both amplitudes are positive as the pentagon and triangle qubelets aren't inverted. Hence, the vector for the right qubit is:

$$\begin{pmatrix} \dfrac{1}{\sqrt{2}} \\ \dfrac{1}{\sqrt{2}} \end{pmatrix}$$

We can express the previous operation as:

$$A_H \begin{pmatrix} 1 \\ 0 \end{pmatrix} = \begin{pmatrix} \dfrac{1}{\sqrt{2}} \\ \dfrac{1}{\sqrt{2}} \end{pmatrix}$$

The top element of the vector on the left-hand side will select the first column of the matrix A_H. Thus, the first column is the right-hand side in the previous equation:

$$A_H = \begin{bmatrix} \dfrac{1}{\sqrt{2}} & * \\ \dfrac{1}{\sqrt{2}} & * \end{bmatrix}$$

Second Column of the H Gate Matrix

To determine the second column of the matrix A_H, we split a $|1\rangle$ qubit by the H gate, as shown in the following figure:

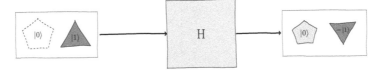

The H gate splits the $|1\rangle$ qubit to one with a pentagon $|0\rangle$ qubelet and an *inverted* triangle $|1\rangle$ qubelet, as shown in the right qubit in this figure.

The vector for the $|1\rangle$ qubit on the left only has a triangle $|1\rangle$ qubelet. Thus, its vector is:

$$\begin{pmatrix} 0 \\ 1 \end{pmatrix}$$

The vector for the right qubit is:

$$\begin{pmatrix} \dfrac{1}{\sqrt{2}} \\ -\dfrac{1}{\sqrt{2}} \end{pmatrix}$$

Thus, applying the matrix A_H to the vector for the left qubit, we get the vector for the right qubit:

$$A_H \begin{pmatrix} 0 \\ 1 \end{pmatrix} = \begin{pmatrix} \dfrac{1}{\sqrt{2}} \\ -\dfrac{1}{\sqrt{2}} \end{pmatrix}$$

The bottom element of the vector on the left-hand side will pull the second column of the matrix A_H. Thus, the second column is the right-hand side in the previous equation:

$$A_H = \begin{bmatrix} * & \dfrac{1}{\sqrt{2}} \\ * & -\dfrac{1}{\sqrt{2}} \end{bmatrix}$$

Complete H Gate Matrix

The complete matrix A_H for the H gate is:

$$A_H = \begin{bmatrix} \dfrac{1}{\sqrt{2}} & \dfrac{1}{\sqrt{2}} \\ \dfrac{1}{\sqrt{2}} & -\dfrac{1}{\sqrt{2}} \end{bmatrix} = \dfrac{1}{\sqrt{2}} \begin{bmatrix} 1 & 1 \\ 1 & -1 \end{bmatrix}$$

Following an analogous calculation, the matrix, A_{NOT}, for the NOT gate works out as:

$$A_{NOT} = \begin{bmatrix} 0 & 1 \\ 1 & 0 \end{bmatrix}$$

Likewise, the matrix, A_Z, for the Z gate is:

$$A_Z = \begin{bmatrix} 1 & 0 \\ 0 & -1 \end{bmatrix}$$

And the matrix that leaves a qubit alone is:

$$A_{ID} = \begin{bmatrix} 1 & 0 \\ 0 & 1 \end{bmatrix}$$

This is simply the *identity* matrix. Both the pentagon $|0\rangle$ and triangle $|1\rangle$ qubelets are unaffected by this gate. (You can find this gate, ID, on the IBM Quantum Computer's palette, but it'll have no practical value in your programs.)

Matrix and Vector Multiplication Are Reversed from How They Appear in the Circuit

When the 2×2 A matrix is applied to compute how the gate affects a qubit's quantum state, the A matrix is written before the vector for the quantum state: Ax, where x is the 2×1 vector for the quantum state.

This multiplication order is the opposite of how it's represented in the circuit: the qubit is first shown followed by the gate that acts on it. This reversal is typical of matrix equations where the operation that's applied last is actually written first. That is, we'll never write the action of the gate on the qubit as xA, the order in which the qubit and gate appear in the circuit. This form is mathematically meaningless: you can't multiply a 2×1 vector with a 2×2 matrix.

Applying the Gate Matrix on Blended Qubits

Although we computed the A matrix for a single qubit quantum gate by seeing how the gate affects the $|0\rangle$ and $|1\rangle$ qubits, the same matrix can be used to figure out how the gate affects blended qubits that contain both pentagon $|0\rangle$ and triangle $|1\rangle$ qubelets.

We'll illustrate applying a gate's matrix on a blended qubit by having the H gate act on the following blended qubit:

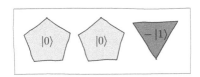

This qubit has two pentagon $|0\rangle$ qubelets and one inverted triangle $|1\rangle$ qubelet.

Before applying the A_H matrix for the H gate on this qubit, we'll first work out how this qubit is modified by working with individual qubelets. We'll then compare the final state of this qubit with that obtained with the A_H matrix.

Working Out the Final State by Individually Splitting Qubelets

As we learned in Putting Qubits in Blended States, on page 82, when the H gate acts on this blended qubit, each qubelet is split as follows:

- Each pentagon $|0\rangle$ qubelet is split into a pentagon $|0\rangle$ and a triangle $|1\rangle$ qubelet. Thus, the two pentagon $|0\rangle$ qubelets will be split into two pentagon $|0\rangle$ qubelets and two triangle $|1\rangle$ qubelets.

- The single inverted triangle $|1\rangle$ qubelet will split into an inverted pentagon $|0\rangle$ qubelet and a triangle $|1\rangle$ qubelet.

Putting all this together, we have the following:

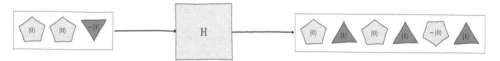

One of the non-inverted pentagon $|0\rangle$ qubelets cancels with an inverted pentagon $|0\rangle$ qubelet. Thus, we end up with a qubit containing one pentagon $|0\rangle$ qubelet and three triangle $|1\rangle$ qubelets, as shown in the following figure:

Working Out the Final State by Applying the A_H Matrix

Now, that we've seen how the H gate acts on this blended qubit, let's work this operation out by applying the A_H matrix.

We need to first determine the quantum state of the qubit before we pass it to the H gate. This qubit contains two pentagon $|0\rangle$ qubelets and a single inverted triangle $|1\rangle$ qubelet. Its quantum state is:

$$\frac{2}{\sqrt{2^2+1^2}}\,|0\rangle - \frac{1}{\sqrt{2^2+1^2}}\,|1\rangle = \frac{2}{\sqrt{5}}\,|0\rangle - \frac{1}{\sqrt{5}}\,|1\rangle$$

Or, writing as a vector:

$$\begin{pmatrix} \dfrac{2}{\sqrt{5}} \\[2ex] -\dfrac{1}{\sqrt{5}} \end{pmatrix} = \frac{1}{\sqrt{5}} \begin{pmatrix} 2 \\ -1 \end{pmatrix} = \begin{pmatrix} 0.8944 \\ -0.4472 \end{pmatrix}$$

To figure out the state of the blended qubit after its been acted on by the H gate, we apply the A_H matrix to this quantum state:

$$A_H \frac{1}{\sqrt{5}} \begin{pmatrix} 2 \\ -1 \end{pmatrix} = \frac{1}{\sqrt{2}} \begin{bmatrix} 1 & 1 \\ 1 & -1 \end{bmatrix} \times \frac{1}{\sqrt{5}} \begin{pmatrix} 2 \\ -1 \end{pmatrix} = \frac{2}{\sqrt{10}} \begin{pmatrix} 1 \\ 1 \end{pmatrix} - \frac{1}{\sqrt{10}} \begin{pmatrix} 1 \\ -1 \end{pmatrix} = \frac{1}{\sqrt{10}} \begin{pmatrix} 1 \\ 3 \end{pmatrix}$$

The quantum state on the right-hand side corresponds to a qubit with a single pentagon $|0\rangle$ qubelet and three triangle $|1\rangle$ qubelets, as we showed earlier.

Even though we tested the A_H matrix on a single quantum state, in general, it'll correctly predict the quantum state after the H gate operates on any blended state.

The operations of a quantum gate on any quantum state are, thus, represented compactly as a matrix. In general, an A matrix for a single qubit quantum gate is defined as:

$$\begin{bmatrix} \alpha_0 & \beta_0 \\ \alpha_1 & \beta_1 \end{bmatrix}$$

To determine how this matrix modifies a qubit, multiply it with the vector for the quantum state as follows:

$$\begin{bmatrix} \alpha_0 & \beta_0 \\ \alpha_1 & \beta_1 \end{bmatrix} \begin{pmatrix} \omega_0 \\ \omega_1 \end{pmatrix}$$

The elements ω_0 and ω_1 in the vector are the amplitudes for $|0\rangle$ and $|1\rangle$, respectively, in the qubit.

Simply put, the A matrix then completely defines a quantum gate: like DNA, it contains the blueprint for how the quantum gate affects a qubit in any quantum state.

Try Your Hand

Solutions to these exercises are given in Quantum Gates as Matrices Solutions, on page 460.

In this section's exercises, I encourage you to work out any matrix calculations using the method described in Multiplying Matrices, on page 396. In later sections, you may find Using a Computer Algebra System for Multiplying, on page 397, more convenient, but for now the manual calculations will help solidify interpreting the columns of the gate matrix as its actions on the idealized quantum states.

For any code listing in the exercises, assume the following header lines:

```
OPENQASM 2.0;
include "qelib1.inc";
```

1. Determine whether the following vectors represent valid quantum states:

   a.
   $$\begin{pmatrix} 0.7071 \\ -0.2929 \end{pmatrix}$$

   b.
   $$\begin{pmatrix} -0.8062 \\ -0.5916 \end{pmatrix}$$

2. Consider the following quantum circuit:

   a. Draw the qubelets before and after the Z gate. (Note that the the qubit has been initialized to $|1\rangle$.)

   b. Write the quantum state in vector form both before and after the Z gate acts on the $|1\rangle$ qubit.

3. Consider the following quantum circuit:

   a. Draw the qubelets before and after the H gate. (Note that the the qubit has been initialized to $|1\rangle$.)

   b. Write the quantum state in vector form both before and after the H gate acts on the $|1\rangle$ qubit.

4. In this exercise, you'll work out the matrix, A_{NOT}, for the NOT gate.

   a. When a NOT gate acts on a $|0\rangle$ qubit, it switches the pentagon $|0\rangle$ qubelet to a triangle $|1\rangle$ qubelet, as shown in the following figure:

   (The dotted triangle $|1\rangle$ qubelet on the left qubit indicates it's not active. Thus, its amplitude and the probability of its being selected is 0.)

     i. Write this operation as a multiplication of the A_{NOT} matrix with a vector.

     ii. Specify the first column of the A_{NOT} matrix.

   b. When a NOT gate acts on a $|1\rangle$ qubit, it switches the triangle $|1\rangle$ qubelet to a pentagon $|0\rangle$ qubelet, as shown in the following figure:

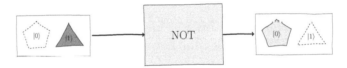

     i. Write this operation as a multiplication of the A_{NOT} matrix with a vector.

     ii. Specify the second column of the A_{NOT} matrix and, then, write the complete matrix.

   c. Consider the blended qubit shown in the following figure:

     i. Write its normalized quantum state as a vector.

     ii. Analyzing the operation of the NOT gate on qubelets, write the quantum state as a vector of the qubit after the NOT gate acts on it.

     What are the probabilities of this qubit collapsing to 0 and 1, respectively.

iii. Apply the A_{NOT} matrix to calculate the quantum state of this qubit after the NOT gate acts on it. How does this state compare with the results you obtained in the previous part of this exercise?

What are the probabilities of this qubit collapsing to 0 and 1, respectively.

5. In this exercise, you'll work out the matrix, A_Z, for the Z gate.

a. As shown in Pauli-Z (Z) Gate, on page 109, the Z gate leaves a $|0\rangle$ qubit alone, as shown in the following figure:

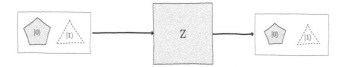

i. Write this operation as a multiplication of the A_Z matrix with a vector.

ii. Specify the first column of the A_Z matrix.

b. When a Z gate acts on a $|1\rangle$ qubit, it inverts the triangle $|1\rangle$ qubelet, as shown in the following figure:

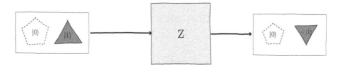

i. Write this operation as a multiplication of the A_Z matrix with vector.

ii. Specify the second column of the A_Z matrix and, then, write the complete matrix.

c. Consider the blended qubit shown in the following figure:

i. Write the normalized quantum state as a vector of this blended qubit.

ii. Using qubelets, work out the operation of the Z gate on this qubit. Write the quantum state as a vector of the qubit after the Z gate acts on it.

iii. Apply the A_Z matrix to calculate the quantum state of this qubit after the Z gate acts on it. How does this state compare with the results you obtained in the previous part of this exercise?

Can the Quantum Gate Matrix Be Anything?

Armed with Universal Quantum Gates, on page 158, and knowing that the A matrix has the entire "genetic code" of a quantum gate, you might be tempted to think that its elements can be arbitrarily set. But like the amplitudes on the state vector, the A matrix is similarly restricted.

This section establishes a key result that underlies a large swath of quantum computing. The development involves linear algebra and complex numbers. Knowing this material will guide you in designing quantum circuits tuned for your own applications.

We saw in Rotating Qubelets Through Any Angle, on page 150, that quantum states are made up of complex numbers. When dealing with complex numbers, we first need to update what we mean when we "square the amplitudes to get the probabilities" of the qubit collapsing to $|0\rangle$ and $|1\rangle$, respectively.

When dealing with complex numbers, instead of squaring them, multiply them with their complex conjugates, as outlined in Measuring Magnitudes of Complex Numbers, on page 167.

The probabilities of the qubit collapsing to $|0\rangle$ and $|1\rangle$ are:

$$\text{Probability of qubit collapsing to } |0\rangle = \omega_0^* \omega_0$$
$$\text{Probability of qubit collapsing to } |1\rangle = \omega_1^* \omega_1$$

Since, in general, the amplitudes can be complex numbers, each is multiplied by its complex conjugate, ω_0^* and ω_1^*, respectively.

As before, these probabilities must add up to 1:

$$\omega_0^* \omega_0 + \omega_1^* \omega_1 = 1$$

In quantum computing, the complex conjugates, ω_0^* and ω_1^*, form a row vector called a *bra* and written as $\langle \psi^\dagger |$—pronounced "bra-ψ-dagger":

$$\langle \psi^\dagger | = \begin{pmatrix} \omega_0^* & \omega_1^* \end{pmatrix}$$

The *bra* row vector, $\langle \psi^\dagger |$, together with its dual, the *ket* column vector, $| \psi \rangle$, make up the *bra-ket*[1] notation for expressing quantum states in quantum mechanics.

The inner product[2] of the *bra*, $\langle \psi^\dagger |$, and *ket*, $| \psi \rangle$, is:

$$\left\langle \psi^\dagger \right| \left| \psi \right\rangle = \begin{pmatrix} \omega_0^* & \omega_1^* \end{pmatrix} \begin{pmatrix} \omega_0 \\ \omega_1 \end{pmatrix} = \omega_0^* \omega_0 + \omega_1^* \omega_1$$

This expression sums to 1, as we just saw previously.

Next, consider a qubit with a quantum state ψ defined by the amplitudes ω_0 and ω_1 for the idealized states. Write this state as a vector:

$$\psi = \begin{pmatrix} \omega_0 \\ \omega_1 \end{pmatrix}$$

Let ψ' be the quantum state of this qubit after it's acted on by a quantum gate defined by the A_G matrix, as shown in the following figure:

$$| \psi \rangle \quad\rule[0.5ex]{1.5cm}{0.4pt}\boxed{G}\rule[0.5ex]{1.5cm}{0.4pt}\quad | \psi' \rangle$$

The amplitudes of the idealized states $|0\rangle$ and $|1\rangle$ are ω_0' and ω_1', respectively:

$$\psi' = \begin{pmatrix} \omega_0' \\ \omega_1' \end{pmatrix}$$

Using the A_G matrix, we can express this operation with the following equation:

$$A_G | \psi \rangle = | \psi' \rangle = A_G \begin{pmatrix} \omega_0 \\ \omega_1 \end{pmatrix} = \begin{pmatrix} \omega_0' \\ \omega_1' \end{pmatrix}$$

To compute the sum of the probabilities of this transformed qubit collapsing to $|0\rangle$ and $|1\rangle$, respectively, compute the inner product of this qubit's quantum state, *bra*, $\langle \psi^{\dagger\prime} |$, and its *ket*, $| \psi' \rangle$:

$$\langle \psi^{\dagger\prime} | \cdot | \psi' \rangle$$

The *ket*, $| \psi' \rangle$, is as shown earlier:

$$A_G | \psi \rangle = | \psi' \rangle$$

---

1.   https://en.wikipedia.org/wiki/Bra%E2%80%93ket_notation
2.   https://en.wikipedia.org/wiki/Dot_product

Non-Inverted and Inverted Qubelets Have Real Conjugates

Recall from Rotating Qubelets Through Any Angle, on page 150, that the general equation for a quantum state $|\psi\rangle$ is:

$$|\psi\rangle = \cos\frac{\theta}{2}|0\rangle + e^{i\varphi}\sin\frac{\theta}{2}|1\rangle$$

In vector form:

$$|\psi\rangle = \begin{pmatrix} \cos\dfrac{\theta}{2} \\ e^{i\varphi}\sin\dfrac{\theta}{2} \end{pmatrix} = \begin{pmatrix} \cos\dfrac{\theta}{2} \\ (\cos\varphi + i\sin\varphi)\sin\dfrac{\theta}{2} \end{pmatrix}$$

Here, the angle φ is the relative difference in orientations between the pentagon $|0\rangle$ and triangle $|1\rangle$ qubelets.

When both the pentagon $|0\rangle$ and triangle $|1\rangle$ qubelets are non-inverted or both are inverted, the relative difference in their orientations, φ, is 0. Thus, $\sin 0 = 0$ and $\cos 0 = 1$ and the quantum state vector $|\psi_{same}\rangle$ is:

$$|\psi_{same}\rangle = \begin{pmatrix} \cos\dfrac{\theta}{2} \\ (\cos 0 + i\sin 0)\sin\dfrac{\theta}{2} \end{pmatrix} = \begin{pmatrix} \cos\dfrac{\theta}{2} \\ \sin\dfrac{\theta}{2} \end{pmatrix}$$

Both elements in this vector are real. So its complex conjugate, $\langle\psi_{same}^\dagger|$, will be a row vector of real numbers too:

$$\langle\psi_{same}^\dagger| = \begin{pmatrix} \cos\dfrac{\theta}{2} & \sin\dfrac{\theta}{2} \end{pmatrix}$$

The transpose of this row vector is identical to that for $|\psi_{same}\rangle$.

Likewise, if either of the pentagon $|0\rangle$ qubelets or the triangle $|1\rangle$ qubelets are inverted and the other type is not, then the relative difference in their orientations, φ, is 180° or π radians. Thus, $\sin\pi = 0$ and $\cos\pi = -1$ and the quantum state vector ψ_{opp} is:

$$|\psi_{opp}\rangle = \begin{pmatrix} \cos\dfrac{\theta}{2} \\ (\cos\pi + i\sin\pi)\sin\dfrac{\theta}{2} \end{pmatrix} = \begin{pmatrix} \cos\dfrac{\theta}{2} \\ -\sin\dfrac{\theta}{2} \end{pmatrix}$$

Both elements in this vector are real too. Its complex conjugate, $\langle\psi_{opp}|$, will also be a row vector of real numbers:

$$\langle\psi_{opp}^\dagger| = \begin{pmatrix} \cos\dfrac{\theta}{2} & -\sin\dfrac{\theta}{2} \end{pmatrix}$$

The transpose of this row vector is the same as that for $|\psi_{opp}\rangle$.

Thus, for both these cases, the complex conjugates for the vectors of the quantum states have only real elements, and everything we talked about in Quantum States and Probabilities, on page 142, still holds.

The *bra*, $\langle\psi^{\dagger\prime}|$, is obtained by taking the conjugate transpose[3] of the previous equation:

$$\langle\psi^{\dagger}|\,A_G^* = \langle\psi^{\dagger\prime}|$$

Rewriting the inner product using the previous equation, we get the following:

$$\langle\psi^{\dagger\prime}|\,|\psi^{\prime}\rangle = \langle\psi^{\dagger}|\,A_G^{\dagger}A_G|\psi\rangle$$

Writing the Conjugate Transpose of a Matrix

The conjugate transform, $A^{\dagger}$, of a matrix, A, is also called the *Hermitian* matrix. To compute the conjugate transform of a matrix, do the following two steps:

1. Write its transpose A^T—the rows become the columns and the columns become rows.

2. Replace each element in the transposed matrix with its complex conjugate.

For example, to write the conjugate transform of the following matrix:

$$A = \begin{bmatrix} 1 & 1 \\ 0 & i \end{bmatrix}$$

The transposed matrix, A^T, is:

$$A^T = \begin{bmatrix} 1 & 0 \\ 1 & i \end{bmatrix}$$

Next, replace each element with its complex conjugate. In this matrix, the only complex number is the one in the bottom right, i. Reverse the sign of the imaginary part to get the complex conjugate, $-i$. Thus, the complex conjugate matrix, $A^{\dagger}$, is:

$$A^{\dagger} = \begin{bmatrix} 1 & 0 \\ 1 & -i \end{bmatrix}$$

Most Important Step in Quantum Computing

Now comes one of the most important steps in quantum computing: if $A_G^{\dagger}A_G$ works out to the identity matrix, I, then the previous inner product, or sum of the probabilities is:

---

3.   https://en.wikipedia.org/wiki/Conjugate_transpose

$$\langle \psi^{\dagger \prime} | \; | \psi^\prime \rangle = \langle \psi^\dagger | \, A_G^\dagger A_G | \psi \rangle$$
$$= \langle \psi^\dagger | \, I | \psi \rangle$$
$$= \langle \psi^\dagger | \; | \psi \rangle$$

The last term on the right-hand side is the sum of the probabilities of the qubit collapsing to $|0\rangle$ and $|1\rangle$ *before* the gate acts on it. We saw earlier that this sum is 1. Thus, the inner product of the *bra* and *ket* of the quantum state after the gate acts on it is 1. That is, the sum of the probabilities *after* the gate acts on the qubit adds up to 1, confirming that the transformed state is a valid quantum state.

In other words, for the transformed quantum state to be a valid quantum state, the following must be true:

$$A_G^\dagger A_G = I$$

Or, equivalently, the conjugate transpose, $A_G^\dagger$, is the inverse of A_G. Such matrices are called *unitary* matrices and have the special property that their inverses are the conjugate transforms.

Unitary Matrices Make Reversible Gates

Unitary matrices aren't just a theoretical nice-to-know type of result. They directly limit how quantum gates are built. To see why, consider again the equation that relates the matrix A_G for a quantum gate G with the Hermitian or unitary matrix $A_G^\dagger$:

$$A_G^\dagger A_G = I$$

Post-multiply both sides by A_G^{-1}:

$$A_G^\dagger A_G A_G^{-1} = I A_G^{-1}$$
$$A_G^\dagger = A_G^{-1}$$

That is, the quantum gate $G^\dagger$ defined by the *dagger* matrix, $A_G^\dagger$, is the inverse of the matrix for the quantum gate G.

Likewise, pre-multiply both sides of the equation that relates the two matrices by $(A_G^\dagger)^{-1}$:

$$(A_G^\dagger)^{-1} A_G^\dagger A_G = (A_G^\dagger)^{-1} I$$
$$A_G = (A_G^\dagger)^{-1}$$

That is, the inverse of the *dagger* matrix is the matrix of the quantum gate G. This condition that forces the matrix of one gate to be an inverse of the other means that the action of any quantum gate on a qubit is *reversed* by the *dagger* gate. It's for this reason back-to-back H gates, in which $H^\dagger = H$, don't change the quantum state of the qubit they act on, as described in Back-to-Back H Gates: The First Hint of Taming Randomness, on page 88.

Unitary matrices are a defining feature of quantum gates. This is a startling requirement and puts a brake on arbitrarily defined matrices for quantum gates—their matrices have to be unitary.

Quantum Gates Have the Same Number of Inputs and Outputs

For a gate to *reverse* the actions on a qubit of another gate means that every quantum gate must have the same number of input bits as output bits, otherwise the reverse action won't work. It's for this reason that quantum computing doesn't have the direct equivalents of the classical AND and OR gates. These classical logical functions had to be reproduced using the CNOT gates, as shown in Chapter 3, Elementary, My Dear Watson—Quantum Logic, on page 41.

At first blush reversibility seems like a relatively innocuous action on a qubit. In quantum computing, though, because of the unique ability of qubits to hold multiple quantum states, you'll learn to put back a subset of qubelets to their original states and only work with those that lead to the optimal solution. This feature gives you even more ways to control qubits. In Chapter 10, Quantum Search, on page 295, you'll see the central role that reversibility plays in turbo-charging search algorithms. To put it another way, you've seen *how* quantum computing works with the Qubelets Model on page 20. Unitary matrices give you *why* quantum computing can be a game changer.

The mathematical perspective is important to know. But in practice, you'll often find it more convenient to quickly work out how a gate affects a qubit qualitatively. Once you're convinced that the gate modifies the quantum state the way you want, you can then resort to the mathematics to confirm your instincts. In the next section, I'll guide you through such an exercise to sharpen your intuition for quantum computing.

Try Your Hand

Solutions to these exercises are given in Gate Matrix Restrictions Solutions, on page 464.

For any code listing in the exercises, assume the following header lines:

```
OPENQASM 2.0;
include "qelib1.inc";
```

1. Consider a quantum gate G defined by the matrix, A_G, as follows:

$$A_G = \begin{bmatrix} 1 & -1 \\ i & -i \end{bmatrix}$$

  a. Write its Hermitian matrix, $A_G^\dagger$, or its conjugate transpose.
  b. Is A_G a valid matrix for the quantum gate?

2. Consider a quantum gate $S^\dagger$ defined by the matrix, $A_{S^\dagger}$, as follows:

$$A_{S^\dagger} = \begin{bmatrix} 1 & 0 \\ 0 & -i \end{bmatrix}$$

  a. Write its Hermitian matrix or its conjugate transpose.
  b. Is $A_{S^\dagger}$ a valid matrix for the gate?

3. Consider the A_H matrix for the H gate that we saw in H Gate Matrix, on page 178:

$$\begin{bmatrix} \dfrac{1}{\sqrt{2}} & \dfrac{1}{\sqrt{2}} \\ \dfrac{1}{\sqrt{2}} & -\dfrac{1}{\sqrt{2}} \end{bmatrix}$$

  a. Write its Hermitian matrix, $A_H^\dagger$, or its conjugate transpose.
  b. Is A_H a valid matrix for the gate?

4. The matrix, A_U, for the Universal gate, $U3(\theta, \varphi, \lambda)$, is:[4]

$$A_U = \begin{bmatrix} \cos\dfrac{\theta}{2} & -e^{i\lambda}\sin\dfrac{\theta}{2} \\ e^{i\varphi}\sin\dfrac{\theta}{2} & e^{i(\lambda+\varphi)}\cos\dfrac{\theta}{2} \end{bmatrix}$$

  a. Write the matrix A_U for $U3(\pi/3, \pi/2, -\pi/2)$.

  b. Write its Hermitian matrix, $A_U^\dagger$.

  c. Is the matrix A_U unitary?

---

4. https://quantum-computing.ibm.com/support/guides/introduction-to-quantum-circuits#other-single-qubit-gates

d. Define the parameters for a $U3^\dagger(\theta, \varphi, \lambda)$ gate that implements the Hermitian matrix, $A_U^\dagger$.

e. Consider the following quantum circuit:

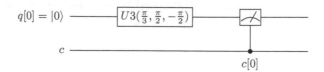

i. Compute the quantum state when the $U3(\pi/3, \pi/2, -\pi/2)$ acts on the $|0\rangle$ qubit.

ii. What are the calculated or theoretical probabilities of the qubit collapsing to the idealized states $|0\rangle$ and $|1\rangle$, respectively?

iii. Write a quantum program for this circuit.

iv. Run your program and check whether its output matches the probabilities of the q[0] qubit collapsing to the idealized states you calculated in the previous part.

f. Introduce another $U3(\theta, \varphi, \lambda)$ gate, using the parameters you calculated earlier, between the $U3(\pi/3, \pi/2, -\pi/2)$ and Measure gates, as shown in the following figure:

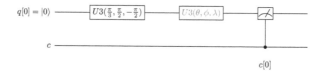

i. Write a quantum program for this circuit with back-to-back Universal gates.

ii. Run your program and explain its output.

g. Replace the $U3(\theta, \varphi, \lambda)$ gate in the previous circuit with a $U3(\pi/3, \pi/4, -\pi/2)$, as shown in the following circuit:

Note that the second U3 gate differs from the first in only the value for the second parameter, φ.

   i.   Write a quantum program for this circuit.

   ii. Run this program and compare its output with the circuit in the previous part.

5. In most of the exercises you've seen so far, you worked with a given quantum state and had to find the new state after it's been acted on by a gate. When designing your own algorithms, you'll often want a qubit to be in a specific state. Thus, you'll need to work out what gates must operate on the qubit to bring it to the desired quantum state. In this exercise, you'll work on a simpler version: you'll figure out the original quantum state of the qubit when given the gate that acts on it and the final quantum state.

The quantum state vector of a qubit after it's acted on by the $S^\dagger$ gate is:

$$\begin{pmatrix} \dfrac{1}{\sqrt{2}} \\[2mm] -\dfrac{1}{\sqrt{2}}\, i \end{pmatrix}$$

What was the quantum state *before* it was acted on by the $S^\dagger$ gate? Use the following matrices, A_S and $A_{S^\dagger}$, related to the S and $S^\dagger$ gates, respectively:

$$S \text{ Gate} \ : \ A_S \ = \ \begin{bmatrix} 1 & 0 \\ 0 & i \end{bmatrix}$$

$$S^\dagger \text{ Gate} \ : \ A_{S^\dagger} \ = \ \begin{bmatrix} 1 & 0 \\ 0 & -i \end{bmatrix}$$

Intuitively Analyzing the Quantum Gate Matrix

By this point, you've topped up your toolkit with the equation for the quantum state, the Bloch sphere, Universal gates, and quantum gate matrices. Given any quantum gate, you can work out how it'll modify any arbitrary quantum state. But before reaching into your arsenal, it is always worth trying to see if you can intuitively reason out how the gate acts on the qubit. This will come in handy when you're designing your own quantum algorithms and want to quickly determine if the gate modifies the qubelets as you want, without getting distracted by the mathematics.

To demonstrate this way of thinking, we'll work with the S gate defined by the following matrix:

$$A_S = \begin{bmatrix} 1 & 0 \\ 0 & i \end{bmatrix}$$

We want to see how this gate affects the following qubit:

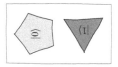

Both types of qubelets are rotated from their non-inverted orientations: the pentagon $|0\rangle$ qubelet is rotated 90° anticlockwise and the triangle $|1\rangle$ qubelet is inverted upside down 180°. The relative difference in their orientations, φ, is $90° - 180° = -90°$. We can compute the equation for its quantum state, but we'll hold off for a bit.

Angles Are Measured Anticlockwise

In mathematics, positive angles are measured by going in the anticlockwise direction. Thus, an angle of 270° means rotating three-quarters of a complete rotation anticlockwise. This angle is equivalent to −90°, a quarter-circle rotation in the *clockwise* direction.

Before working out how the S gate affects these qubelets, let's first see how the gate modifies each idealized state.

S Gate on the $|0\rangle$ Qubit

When this gate acts on the $|0\rangle$ qubit having a pentagon $|0\rangle$ qubelet, the first column of the A_S matrix defines how it changes the qubit's state:

$$A_S \begin{pmatrix} 1 \\ 0 \end{pmatrix} = \begin{bmatrix} 1 & 0 \\ 0 & i \end{bmatrix} \begin{pmatrix} 1 \\ 0 \end{pmatrix} = \begin{pmatrix} 1 \\ 0 \end{pmatrix}$$

In other words, this gate leaves the pentagon $|0\rangle$ qubelets alone.

S Gate on the $|1\rangle$ Qubit

When a $|1\rangle$ qubit holding a triangle $|1\rangle$ qubelet is fed to this gate, the second column of the A_S matrix governs how it changes the qubit's quantum state:

$$A_S\begin{pmatrix} 0 \\ 1 \end{pmatrix} = \begin{bmatrix} 1 & 0 \\ 0 & i \end{bmatrix}\begin{pmatrix} 0 \\ 1 \end{pmatrix} = \begin{pmatrix} 0 \\ i \end{pmatrix}$$

The modified quantum state only has a triangle $|1\rangle$ qubelet. But the presence of the complex number i hints that something else is going on with the triangle $|1\rangle$ qubelet.

Deciphering the Presence of the Complex Number

Recall from Rotating Qubelets Through Any Angle, on page 150, the vector for a general quantum state and equate it with the vector obtained previously. That is:

$$\begin{pmatrix} 0 \\ i \end{pmatrix} = \begin{pmatrix} \cos\dfrac{\theta}{2} \\ e^{i\varphi}\sin\dfrac{\theta}{2} \end{pmatrix}$$

The angle φ is the relative difference in orientations between the pentagon $|0\rangle$ and triangle $|1\rangle$ qubelets, the quantity that we're most concerned with.

In keeping with our "down-home" analysis, let's restate the general quantum state vector as:

$$\begin{pmatrix} 0 \\ i \end{pmatrix} = \begin{pmatrix} \text{something} \\ e^{i\varphi} \times \text{something else} \end{pmatrix}$$

Here, the "something" terms indicate values we're not interested in at the moment. In fact, we can go one step further: since the top term of the vector is 0, we can express the right-hand side of the previous equation as:

$$\begin{pmatrix} 0 \\ i \end{pmatrix} = \begin{pmatrix} 0 \\ e^{i\varphi} \times \text{something else} \end{pmatrix}$$

Using Euler's formula,[5] expand $e^{i\varphi}$:

$$e^{i\varphi} = \cos\varphi + i\sin\varphi$$

---

5.   https://en.wikipedia.org/wiki/Euler%27s_formula#Applications_in_complex_number_theory

The expanded form of the vector for the quantum state is:

$$\begin{pmatrix} 0 \\ i \end{pmatrix} = \begin{pmatrix} 0 \\ (\cos \varphi + i \sin \varphi) \times \text{ something else} \end{pmatrix}$$

Since the bottom term of the vector is a "pure" complex number, namely, i, *experiment* with values that force $\cos \varphi$ to 0. In fact, it's easy to see that if $\varphi = \pi/2$ or 90°, $\cos \pi/2 = 0$. Moreover, $\sin \varphi = \sin \pi/2 = 1$.

In other words, the S gate rotates the triangle $|1\rangle$ qubelet by 90° anticlockwise:

(Note that since there are no pentagon $|0\rangle$ qubelets in the idealized $|1\rangle$ qubit, the relative angle φ is computed from the position of the triangle $|1\rangle$ before the S gate acts on the qubit.)

Now, we can put together the action of the S gate on the original blended qubit:

- The pentagon $|0\rangle$ qubelets are left alone.
- The triangle $|1\rangle$ qubelets are rotated 90° anticlockwise.

Pictorially, the action of the S gate on the blended qubit is shown in the following figure:

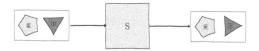

Since only the relative difference between the orientations of the pentagon $|0\rangle$ and triangle $|1\rangle$ qubelets determine the angle φ, you could just as well first rotate both qubelets by 90° clockwise so that the pentagon $|0\rangle$ qubelet is non-inverted, and then apply the S gate, as shown in the following figure:

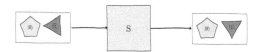

If this action of the S gate meets your needs, then proceed to quantitatively verify the operation and confirm your hunch.

Precisely Calculating the S Gate Action

To apply the S gate matrix to the blended qubit, you need to compute its quantum state vector. Again, we'll do this quickly:

Calculating the Qubelet Amplitudes

Since the qubit has one pentagon $|0\rangle$ and one triangle $|1\rangle$ qubelet, the probability of it collapsing to either one of these is half. Take the square root to get the amplitudes and write the state as follows:

$$\frac{1}{\sqrt{2}}|0\rangle + e^{i\varphi}\frac{1}{\sqrt{2}}|1\rangle$$

Or, writing as a vector:

$$\begin{pmatrix} \dfrac{1}{\sqrt{2}} \\ e^{i\varphi}\dfrac{1}{\sqrt{2}} \end{pmatrix}$$

Note the $e^{i\varphi}$ term on the bottom element associated with the triangle $|1\rangle$ qubelet. At this point, we just know the probabilities of choosing a pentagon $|0\rangle$ or triangle $|1\rangle$ qubelet from the blended qubit. We still don't know how they're oriented.

Calculating the Qubelet Orientations

Since φ measures the relative difference in rotations, it helps to rotate both types of qubelets by 90° clockwise so that the pentagon $|0\rangle$ qubelet is non-inverted:

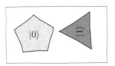

In this quantum state, the relative difference φ between the rotations of the pentagon $|0\rangle$ and triangle $|1\rangle$ qubelets is still 90° or $\pi/2$. Thus, the term $e^{i\varphi}$:

$$e^{i\varphi} = \cos\frac{\pi}{2} + i\sin\frac{\pi}{2}$$
$$= i$$

And this qubit's quantum state expressed as a vector is:

$$\begin{pmatrix} \dfrac{1}{\sqrt{2}} \\ i\dfrac{1}{\sqrt{2}} \end{pmatrix} = \frac{1}{\sqrt{2}}\begin{pmatrix} 1 \\ i \end{pmatrix}$$

Now that we have the quantum state as a vector, multiply it by the S gate's matrix A_S to get the resultant state:

$$A_S \frac{1}{\sqrt{2}} \begin{pmatrix} 1 \\ i \end{pmatrix} = \frac{1}{\sqrt{2}} \begin{bmatrix} 1 & 0 \\ 0 & i \end{bmatrix} \begin{pmatrix} 1 \\ i \end{pmatrix} = \frac{1}{\sqrt{2}} \begin{pmatrix} 1 \\ -i^2 \end{pmatrix} = \frac{1}{\sqrt{2}} \begin{pmatrix} 1 \\ -1 \end{pmatrix}$$

The negative sign in the bottom term comes from $e^{i\varphi}$ with $\varphi = \pi$. That is,

$$\begin{aligned} e^{i\pi} &= \cos \pi + i \sin \pi \\ &= -1 \end{aligned}$$

This vector corresponds to a quantum state in which the pentagon $|0\rangle$ qubelet is non-inverted and the triangle $|1\rangle$ qubelet is inverted upside down, as shown in the following figure:

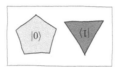

This state is identical to the one we informally calculated earlier.

This exercise was, of course, a simple one, and it may have been easier to use the S gate matrix. In general, though, the qubelets could be arbitrarily rotated, and you may need to apply a sequence of gates to get them to the desired state. In these cases, you may often find it easier to work with pictures and identify which rotations of the qubelets you need to apply before validating the operations with precise mathematical calculations.

Before learning to use these matrices when the qubit is acted on by several gates in sequence, it's helpful to have a handy cheat sheet listing the pertinent details for gates you'll see in practice.

Try Your Hand

Solutions to these exercises are given in Analyzing Quantum Gate Matrices Solutions, on page 474.

For any code listing in the exercises, assume the following header lines:

```
OPENQASM 2.0;
include "qelib1.inc";
```

1. In problems and programming exercises so far, you've approached them using qubelets. When you're working as part of a team, however, the

other members may not be familiar with this model.[6] So in this exercise, you'll work through the example in the previous section, but stated using the language and terms you'll encounter in the workplace.

a. Specify a Universal gate, $U3(\theta, \varphi, \lambda)$, that puts a $|0\rangle$ qubit into a quantum state, ψ, defined by the following vector:

$$\psi = \frac{1}{\sqrt{2}}\begin{pmatrix} 1 \\ i \end{pmatrix}$$

b. Write a program using this gate and confirm that the quantum state collapses to $|0\rangle$ and $|1\rangle$ as you'd expect.

c. Using the parameters for the $U3(\theta, \varphi, \lambda)$ gate you calculated previously, write a program that implements the following quantum circuit:

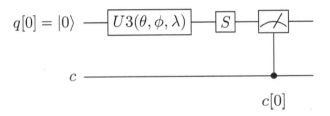

Use the following statement to declare the S gate:

s q[0];

d. By looking at the output of your program, can you confirm that the pentagon $|1\rangle$ qubelets are rotated as you calculated?

2. Which gate would you use to rotate the pentagon $|0\rangle$ qubelets by 90° clockwise while leaving the triangle $|1\rangle$ qubelets alone, as shown in the following circuit:

Intuitively reason out the type of gate you'd use in this circuit.

---

6. You could, of course, recommend this book to them.

Classifying Quantum Gates

In previous sections and chapters, you've seen that quantum computing handles qubits, the information units of your problems, differently than classical computers. You've learned about a few quantum gates that manipulate a qubit's quantum state. But, as you develop quantum algorithms to solve your own challenging problems, you'll want even more ways of changing a qubit's quantum state. So it's important to build an intuitive feel for how they nudge quantum states. Specifically, you'll learn to tie the rotation of the qubelets to a gate's matrix. To put it another way, you'll learn that the gate matrices are an X-ray into how gates affect quantum states.

Classification Based on How Gates Modify Qubelets

 Although there are several ways to introduce quantum effects in programs, you'll see that they can be classified into a few basic types. Thinking of them in terms of these groups organizes the gates in your mind and, more importantly, helps you determine which ones to apply when you're developing your own quantum algorithms for your specific problem.

This section, in particular, shows how a gate's matrix is intimately related to rotating qubelets and is a crucial step in building your intuition for writing quantum programs.

For most gates, their operation on a qubit is defined by how they rotate just the triangle |1⟩ qubelets. The reason is that in quantum computing, it's only the *relative* difference between the pentagon |0⟩ and triangle |1⟩ qubelets that influences the computation. Thus, you can always hold the pentagon |0⟩ qubelet in the non-inverted position and rotate the triangle |1⟩ qubelet to make them do any calculation you want.

I've classified the gates by how they function from a practical standpoint rather than by how they rotate qubelets around the coordinate axes on the Bloch sphere. So a few gates that normally appear in the same group in the literature will show up in different categories here.

The categories for the quantum gates that operate on single qubits are:

- *Universal Gates*
- *Gates That Switch Qubelets*
- *Gates That Rotate the Triangle Qubelets*

- *Gates That Split Qubelets*
- *Identity (ID) Gate*

Although you've not seen many of the gates listed in this section earlier in the book, they're just special cases of those you've learned about.

Some Gates Have Confusing Names

Some gates have names based on the three coordinate axes. These names come from how they move a quantum state on the Bloch sphere. That is, when you carefully plot how a quantum state changes on the Bloch sphere when acted on by the gate, it'll seem like the gate rotates the quantum state around the corresponding axis. Although technically correct, I find these descriptions hard to picture. Moreover, from a practical standpoint, when multiple gates act on the qubit or when dealing with multiple qubits, these visualizations quickly get confusing. So instead of classifying the gates based on rotations on the Bloch sphere, I'll explain how the gates operate on the pentagon $|0\rangle$ and triangle $|1\rangle$ qubelets. When designing your own algorithms, you'll find it easier to work with these descriptions rather than as rotations on the Bloch sphere.

Universal Gates

These gates let you arbitrarily change the quantum state of a qubit. There are three types of Universal gates:

- *U3 Gate*
- *U2 Gate*
- *U1 Gate*

Complex Numbers in Gate Matrices Indicate Rotation of Triangle $|1\rangle$ Qubelets

Complex numbers in a gate matrix can only come from the exponent terms. These terms are associated with the angle φ, the relative difference between the pentagon $|0\rangle$ and triangle $|1\rangle$ qubelets.

Thus, when you see complex numbers in a gate matrix, the qubelets are rotated.

U3 Gate

The $U3(\theta, \varphi, \lambda)$ gate is a general quantum gate that forms the basis for all gates.

The matrix, A_{U3}, for the $U3(\theta, \varphi, \lambda)$ gate is:

$$A_{U3} = \begin{bmatrix} \cos\dfrac{\theta}{2} & -e^{i\lambda}\sin\dfrac{\theta}{2} \\ e^{i\varphi}\sin\dfrac{\theta}{2} & e^{i(\lambda+\varphi)}\cos\dfrac{\theta}{2} \end{bmatrix}$$

U2 Gate

The $U2(\varphi, \lambda)$ gate is a Universal gate but has the θ parameter fixed to $\pi/2$.

The matrix, A_{U2}, for the $U2(\varphi, \lambda)$ gate is:

$$A_{U2} = \frac{1}{\sqrt{2}} \begin{bmatrix} 1 & e^{-i\lambda} \\ e^{i\varphi} & e^{i(\lambda+\varphi)} \end{bmatrix}$$

The $U2(\varphi, \lambda)$ gate is equivalent to the $U3(\pi/2, \varphi, \lambda)$ gate in which θ is preset to $\pi/2$.

U1 Gate

The U1 gate is a variant of the U3 gate in which two of the three parameters, θ and φ, are predefined.

The matrix, A_{U1}, for the $U1(\lambda)$ gate is:

$$A_{U1} = \begin{bmatrix} 1 & 0 \\ 0 & e^{i\lambda} \end{bmatrix}$$

The $U1(\lambda)$ gate is equivalent to the $U3(0, 0, \lambda)$ gate.

Declaring the Universal Gates in Code

Declare these gates in your program as listed below:

U3 Gate

To use, say, a $U3(\pi/3, \pi/4, \pi/2)$ gate on the q[0] qubit, declare it as follows:

```
u3(pi/3,pi/4,pi/2) q[0];
```

U2 Gate

To use, for example, a $U2(\pi/2, \pi/3)$ gate on the q[0] qubit, declare it like this:

```
u2(pi/2,pi/3) q[0];
```

U1 Gate

To use, for instance, a $U1(\pi/2)$ gate on the q[0] qubit, declare it in this way:

```
u1(pi/2) q[0];
```

Gates That Switch Qubelets

These gates switch pentagon $|0\rangle$ qubelets to triangle $|1\rangle$ qubelets, and triangle $|1\rangle$ qubelets to pentagon $|0\rangle$ qubelets. The gates in this section differ by how they rotate the qubelets when switching them.

These gates are commonly used for logic operations.

The following gates are in this group:

- *NOT (X) Gate*
- *Y Gate*

NOT (X) Gate

The NOT (X) gate switches a pentagon $|0\rangle$ qubelet to a triangle $|1\rangle$ qubelet, and a triangle $|1\rangle$ qubelet to a pentagon $|0\rangle$ qubelet, as shown in the following figure:

After the NOT (X) gate is applied, orientation of the qubelets is also switched. The pentagon $|0\rangle$ qubelet takes on the original orientation of the triangle $|1\rangle$ qubelet. Likewise, the orientation of the triangle $|1\rangle$ qubelet after the NOT (X) gate is that of the original pentagon $|0\rangle$ qubelet.

On the right qubit, the faded qubelets behind the pentagon $|0\rangle$ and triangle $|1\rangle$ qubelets in the foreground indicate what type each qubelet was originally.

The matrix, A_χ, for the NOT (X) gate is:

$$A_\chi = \begin{bmatrix} 0 & 1 \\ 1 & 0 \end{bmatrix}$$

The NOT (X) gate is equivalent to the $U3(\pi, \pi, 0,)$ gate.

The NOT gate belongs to the *Pauli* family of gates and is also called the Pauli-X gate. When the NOT gate acts on a qubit, it modifies the qubit's quantum state so that it seems that it's rotated about the X-axis on the Bloch sphere.

Y Gate

The Y gate is like the NOT (X) gate, but after switching the qubelets, it rotates the pentagon $|0\rangle$ a quarter turn clockwise and the triangle $|1\rangle$ qubelets a quarter turn anticlockwise, as shown in the figure on page 206.

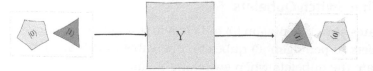

(Look at the labels on the qubelets to track the rotations.)

On the right qubit, the faded qubelets behind the qubelets in the foreground indicate their original position.

The matrix, A_Y, for the Y gate is:

$$A_Y = \begin{bmatrix} 0 & -i \\ i & 0 \end{bmatrix}$$

The Y gate is equivalent to the $U3(\pi, \pi/2, \pi/2)$ gate.

The Y gate belongs to the *Pauli* family of gates and is also called the Pauli-Y gate. When the Y gate acts on a qubit, it modifies the qubit's quantum state so that it seems that it's rotated about the *Y*-axis on the Bloch sphere.

Declaring the Gates That Switch Qubelets in Code

Declare these gates in your program as listed below:

NOT (X) Gate

To use a NOT (X) gate on, for instance, the q[0] qubit, declare it like this:

```
x q[0];
```

Y Gate

To use a Y gate on, say, the q[0] qubit, declare it as follows:

```
y q[0];
```

Gates That Rotate the Triangle Qubelets

These gates rotate the triangle $|1\rangle$ qubelets through different angles while leaving the pentagon $|0\rangle$ qubelets alone. The gates in this section differ by how much they rotate the triangle $|1\rangle$ qubelets. They're also referred to as *Phase* gates because only the φ parameter, the relative difference between the angles of the pentagon $|0\rangle$ and triangle $|1\rangle$ qubelets, is varied.

Situations where you would use these gates include:

- To "tag" certain qubelets without affecting the probabilities of how they collapse to the idealized states, $|0\rangle$ and $|1\rangle$.

- To "twist" certain qubelets so that they can either cancel out or be prevented from doing so. For example, by rotating some qubelets a specific amount, you can misalign them so they can't be removed from the mega-qubit.

The following gates are in this group:

- *Z Gate*
- *S Gate*
- *S-Dagger Gate*
- *T Gate*
- *T-Dagger Gate*
- *Rz Gate*

Z Gate

The Z gate leaves the pentagon $|0\rangle$ qubelets alone but rotates the triangle $|1\rangle$ qubelets by 180°, as shown in the following figure:

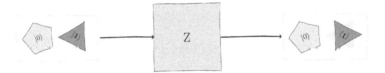

On the right qubit, the faded triangle $|1\rangle$ qubelet behind the triangle $|1\rangle$ qubelet in the foreground indicates its original position.

The matrix, A_Z, for the Z gate is:

$$A_Z = \begin{bmatrix} 1 & 0 \\ 0 & -1 \end{bmatrix}$$

The Z gate is equivalent to the $U3(0, \pi, 0)$ gate.

Since the Z gate rotates the triangle $|1\rangle$ qubelets a half turn, applying it twice on a qubit will bring the qubit back to the orientation before the Z gate was applied. Thus, Z gate's matrix is its own inverse:

$$A_Z = A_Z^{-1}$$

The Z gate belongs to the *Pauli* family of gates and is also called the Pauli-Z gate. When the Z gate acts on a qubit, it modifies the qubit's quantum state so that it seems that it's rotated about the *Z*-axis on the Bloch sphere.

S Gate

The S gate leaves the pentagon $|0\rangle$ qubelets alone but rotates the triangle $|1\rangle$ qubelets 90°, or a quarter turn anticlockwise, as shown in the following figure:

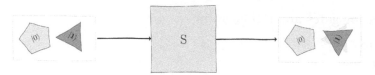

On the right qubit, the faded triangle $|1\rangle$ qubelet behind the triangle $|1\rangle$ qubelet in the foreground indicates its original position.

The matrix, A_S for the S gate is:

$$A_S = \begin{bmatrix} 1 & 0 \\ 0 & i \end{bmatrix}$$

The S gate is equivalent to the $U3(0, \pi/2, 0)$ gate.

The S gate matrix, A_S, is related to the Z gate matrix, A_Z: $A_S^2 = A_Z$. That is:

$$\begin{bmatrix} 1 & 0 \\ 0 & i \end{bmatrix}\begin{bmatrix} 1 & 0 \\ 0 & i \end{bmatrix} = \begin{bmatrix} 1 & 0 \\ 0 & -1 \end{bmatrix}$$

In other words, the S gate matrix, A_S, is a "square root" of the Z gate matrix, A_Z. From the qubelets' perspective, applying the S gate twice will rotate the triangle $|1\rangle$ qubelets by two quarter turns anticlockwise, which is equivalent to a half turn or by 180°, the same as if the Z gate was applied instead.

You can think of the "s" in "square root" as a mnemonic for the S gate.

Since the S gate rotates the triangle $|1\rangle$ qubelets by half the amount of the Z gate, the quantum state is also rotated about the Z-axis.

S-Dagger Gate

The $S^\dagger$ gate—pronounced "S-dagger"—leaves the pentagon $|0\rangle$ qubelets alone but rotates the triangle $|1\rangle$ qubelets –90°, or a quarter turn clockwise, as shown in the following figure:

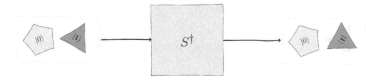

On the right qubit, the faded triangle $|1\rangle$ qubelet behind the triangle $|1\rangle$ qubelet in the foreground indicates its original position.

The matrix, $A_{S^\dagger}$, for the $S^\dagger$ gate is:

$$A_{S^\dagger} = \begin{bmatrix} 1 & 0 \\ 0 & -i \end{bmatrix}$$

The $S^\dagger$ gate is equivalent to the $U3(0, -\pi/2, 0)$ gate.

Since the $S^\dagger$ gate rotates the triangle $|1\rangle$ qubelet a quarter turn clockwise, a quarter turn *anticlockwise* will bring the qubit back to the orientation before the $S^\dagger$ was applied. That is, the S gate reverses the action of the $S^\dagger$ gate. In terms of matrices, the two are related as follows:

$$A_S = A_{S^\dagger}^*$$

Or,

$$A_{S^\dagger} = A_S^*$$

The $S^\dagger$ gate matrix, $A_{S^\dagger}$, is related to the Z gate matrix, A_Z: $A_{S\dagger}^2 = A_Z$. That is:

$$\begin{bmatrix} 1 & 0 \\ 0 & -i \end{bmatrix}\begin{bmatrix} 1 & 0 \\ 0 & -i \end{bmatrix} = \begin{bmatrix} 1 & 0 \\ 0 & -1 \end{bmatrix}$$

In other words, the $S^\dagger$ gate matrix, $A_{S^\dagger}$, is also a "square root" of the Z gate matrix, A_Z. From the qubelets' perspective, applying the $S^\dagger$ gate twice will rotate the triangle $|1\rangle$ qubelets by two quarter turns clockwise which is equivalent to a half turn or by 180°, the same as if the Z gate was applied instead.

Since the $S^\dagger$ gate rotates the triangle $|1\rangle$ qubelets by half the amount of the Z gate, albeit in a different direction, the quantum state is also rotated about the Z-axis.

T Gate

The T gate leaves the pentagon $|0\rangle$ qubelets alone but rotates the triangle $|1\rangle$ qubelets 45°, or a one-eighth turn anticlockwise, as shown in the following figure:

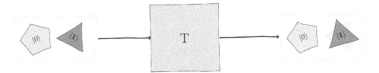

On the right qubit, the faded triangle $|1\rangle$ qubelet behind the triangle $|1\rangle$ qubelet in the foreground indicates its original position.

The matrix, A_T, for the T gate is:

$$A_T = \begin{bmatrix} 1 & 0 \\ 0 & e^{i\frac{\pi}{4}} \end{bmatrix}$$

The T gate is equivalent to the $U3(0, \pi/4, 0)$ gate.

The T gate matrix, A_T, is related to the S gate matrix, A_S: $A_T^2 = A_S$. That is:

$$\begin{bmatrix} 1 & 0 \\ 0 & e^{i\frac{\pi}{4}} \end{bmatrix}\begin{bmatrix} 1 & 0 \\ 0 & e^{i\frac{\pi}{4}} \end{bmatrix} = \begin{bmatrix} 1 & 0 \\ 0 & e^{i\frac{\pi}{2}} \end{bmatrix} = \begin{bmatrix} 1 & 0 \\ 0 & i \end{bmatrix}$$

In other words, the T gate matrix, A_T, is a "square root" of the S gate matrix, A_S. From the qubelets' perspective, applying the T gate twice will rotate the triangle $|1\rangle$ qubelets by two one-eighth turns anticlockwise, which is equivalent to an anticlockwise quarter turn or by 90°, the same as if the S gate was applied instead.

Since the T gate rotates the triangle $|1\rangle$ qubelets by half the amount of the S gate, or a quarter of the Z gate rotation, the quantum state is also rotated about the Z-axis.

T-Dagger Gate

The $T^\dagger$ gate—pronounced "T-dagger"—leaves the pentagon $|0\rangle$ qubelets alone but rotates the triangle $|1\rangle$ qubelets –45°, or a one-eighth turn clockwise, as shown in the following figure:

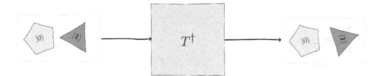

On the right qubit, the faded triangle $|1\rangle$ qubelet behind the triangle $|1\rangle$ qubelet in the foreground indicates its original position.

The matrix, $A_{T^\dagger}$, for the $T^\dagger$ gate is:

$$A_{T^\dagger} = \begin{bmatrix} 1 & 0 \\ 0 & e^{-i\frac{\pi}{4}} \end{bmatrix}$$

The $T^\dagger$ gate is equivalent to the $U3(0, -\pi/4, 0)$ gate.

Since the $T^\dagger$ gate rotates the triangle $|1\rangle$ qubelets a one-eighth turn clockwise, a one-eighth turn *anticlockwise* will bring back the qubit to the orientation before the $T^\dagger$ was applied. In terms of matrices, the two are related as follows:

$$A_T = A^*_{T^\dagger}$$

Or,

$$A_{T^\dagger} = A^*_T$$

The $T^\dagger$ gate matrix, $A_{T^\dagger}$, is related to the $S^\dagger$ gate matrix, $A_{S^\dagger}$: $A^2_{T\dagger} = A^\dagger_S$. That is:

$$\begin{bmatrix} 1 & 0 \\ 0 & e^{-i\frac{\pi}{4}} \end{bmatrix} \begin{bmatrix} 1 & 0 \\ 0 & e^{-i\frac{\pi}{4}} \end{bmatrix} = \begin{bmatrix} 1 & 0 \\ 0 & e^{-i\frac{\pi}{2}} \end{bmatrix} = \begin{bmatrix} 1 & 0 \\ 0 & -i \end{bmatrix}$$

In other words, the $T^\dagger$ gate matrix, $A_{T^\dagger}$, is also a "square root" of the $S^\dagger$ gate matrix, $A_{S^\dagger}$. From the qubelets' perspective, applying the $T^\dagger$ gate twice will rotate the triangle $|1\rangle$ qubelets by two one-eighth turns clockwise, which is equivalent to a clockwise half turn or by $-90°$, the same as if the $S^\dagger$ gate was applied instead.

Since the $T^\dagger$ gate rotates the triangle $|1\rangle$ qubelets by half the amount of the $S^\dagger$ gate, or a quarter of the Z gate rotation, the quantum state is also rotated about the Z-axis.

Rz Gate

The $R_z(\theta)$ gate is a generalization of the other gates in this class in that it rotates the the triangle $|1\rangle$ qubelet through an arbitrary angle while leaving the pentagon $|0\rangle$ qubelets alone, as shown in the following figure:

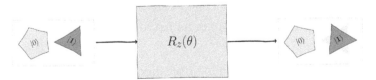

On the right qubit, the faded triangle $|1\rangle$ qubelet behind the triangle $|1\rangle$ qubelet in the foreground indicates its original position. The triangle $|1\rangle$ qubelet is rotated by $55°$ anticlockwise from its original position on the left qubit.

The matrix, $A_{R_z}(\theta)$, for the $R_z(\theta)$ gate is:

$$A_{R_z}(\theta) = \begin{bmatrix} 1 & 0 \\ 0 & e^{i\theta} \end{bmatrix}$$

θ Is Related to the Amplitudes

 The parameter θ is strongly associated with angles in general. In fact, as shown in Rotating Qubelets Through Any Angle, on page 150, θ refers to the tilt from the vertical when the quantum state is plotted on the Bloch sphere. So it may not be obvious that θ actually measures the number of pentagon $|0\rangle$ and triangle $|1\rangle$ qubelets in the quantum state. Then, θ can be related to the Number of Qubelets on page 145.

The $R_z(\theta)$ gate is equivalent to the $U3(0, \theta, 0)$ gate.

The A_{R_z} gate is part of the *Rotation* family of gates since it effectively rotates the quantum state of a qubit around the Z-axis.

You may sometimes see the $A_{R_z}(\theta)$ matrix written as:

$$\begin{bmatrix} e^{-i\frac{\theta}{2}} & 0 \\ 0 & e^{i\frac{\theta}{2}} \end{bmatrix}$$

This matrix represents a clockwise rotation of the pentagon $|0\rangle$ qubelets by $\theta/2$ and an anticlockwise rotation of the triangle $|1\rangle$ qubelets by $\theta/2$. But, by rotating both qubelets by $\theta/2$ anticlockwise, we can set the pentagon $|0\rangle$ qubelet with no rotation and rotate the triangle $|1\rangle$ qubelet by θ as shown in the A_{R_z} matrix.

Declaring the Gates That Rotate the Triangle Qubelets in Code

Declare these gates in your program as listed here:

Z Gate

To use a Z gate on, say, the q[0] qubit, declare it as follows:

```
z q[0];
```

S Gate

To use an S gate on, for example, the q[0] qubit, declare it like this:

```
s q[0];
```

S-Dagger Gate

> To use an $S^\dagger$ gate on, say, the q[0] qubit, declare it as follows:

> `sdg q[0];`

T Gate

> To use a T gate on, for instance, the q[0] qubit, declare it as shown here:

> `t q[0];`

T-Dagger Gate

> To use a $T^\dagger$ gate on, for example, the q[0] qubit, declare it as follows:

> `tdg q[0];`

Rz Gate

> To use, say, a $R_z(\pi/3)$ gate on the q[0] qubit, declare it as shown here:

> `rz(pi/3) q[0];`

Gates That Split Qubelets

Next we'll look at gates that split qubelets. For example, a pentagon $|0\rangle$ may be split into other pentagon $|0\rangle$ and triangle $|1\rangle$ qubelets. The gates in this group differ from each other based on the number and rotations of the qubelets created. They're also referred to as the *superposition* gates since they turn an idealized quantum state into a blended one.

These gates are used to put qubits in blended states.

This group includes the following gates:

- *Hadamard (H) Gate*
- *Rx Gate*
- *Ry Gate*

Hadamard (H) Gate

The Hadamard (H) gate splits qubelets. That is, it splits a pentagon $|0\rangle$ qubelet into a pentagon $|0\rangle$ qubelet and a triangle $|1\rangle$ qubelet, as shown in the following figure:

And it splits a triangle $|1\rangle$ qubelet into a pentagon $|0\rangle$ qubelet and an *inverted* triangle $|1\rangle$ qubelet, as shown in the following figure:

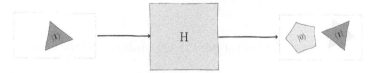

On the right qubit, the faded triangle $|1\rangle$ qubelet behind the triangle $|1\rangle$ qubelet in the foreground indicates its original position.

Notice that unlike the previous figures, the inverted triangle $|1\rangle$ qubelet on the right doesn't have a negative sign. Now that qubelets can be arbitrarily rotated, it's more accurate to let $e^{i\varphi}$ determine the signs. In particular, note that for an inverted qubelet, $\varphi = \pi$ and $e^{i\pi} = \cos \pi + i \sin \pi = -1$. So, the negative sign comes in naturally for inverted qubelets.

The matrix, A_H, for the H gate is:

$$A_H = \frac{1}{\sqrt{2}} \begin{bmatrix} 1 & 1 \\ 1 & -1 \end{bmatrix}$$

The Hadamard (H) gate is equivalent to the $U3(\pi/2, 0, \pi)$ gate or the $U2(0, \pi)$ gate.

Rx Gate

Unlike the H gate, in which a qubelet is split into an equal number of pentagon $|0\rangle$ and triangle $|1\rangle$ qubelets, the $R_x(\theta)$ gate shifts the "balance" so that the qubit has more of one type of qubelets than the other. For example, when the $R_x(\theta)$ gate acts on the $|0\rangle$ qubit, it may split it as shown in the following figure:

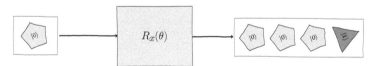

The number of pentagon $|0\rangle$ and triangle $|1\rangle$ qubelets created depends on the parameter θ. Additionally, the R_x gate rotates the triangle $|1\rangle$ qubelets by a quarter turn clockwise, or $-90°$, from the position of the pentagon $|0\rangle$ qubelets.

Likewise, the R_x gate splits the triangle $|1\rangle$ qubelets in a similar manner. The exact number of pentagon $|0\rangle$ and triangle $|1\rangle$ qubelets created is best calculated from the gate matrix, A_{R_x}, shown in the next section.

The matrix, A_{R_x}, for the $R_x(\theta)$ gate is:

$$A_{R_x}(\theta) = \begin{bmatrix} \cos\dfrac{\theta}{2} & -i\sin\dfrac{\theta}{2} \\ -i\sin\dfrac{\theta}{2} & \cos\dfrac{\theta}{2} \end{bmatrix}$$

The $R_x(\theta)$ gate is equivalent to the $U3(\theta, -\pi/2, \pi/2)$ gate.

The A_{R_x} gate is part of the *Rotation* family of gates since it effectively rotates the quantum state of a qubit around the X-axis.

Ry Gate

Like the $R_x(\theta)$ gate, the $R_y(\theta)$ gate splits a qubelet so that the qubit ends up with an unequal number of pentagon $|0\rangle$ and triangle $|1\rangle$ qubelets. The main difference between the two is that the $R_y(\theta)$ gate doesn't rotate any qubelets like the $R_x(\theta)$ gate. For example, when the $R_y(\theta)$ gate acts on the $|0\rangle$ qubit, it may split it as shown in the following figure:

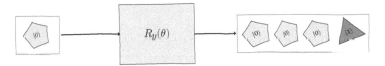

As with the $R_x(\theta)$ gate, the number of pentagon $|0\rangle$ and triangle $|1\rangle$ qubelets created by the R_y gate depends on the parameter θ and is best calculated from the gate matrix, A_{R_y}, as we see next.

The matrix, A_{R_y}, for the $R_y(\theta)$ gate is:

$$A_{R_y}(\theta) = \begin{bmatrix} \cos\dfrac{\theta}{2} & -\sin\dfrac{\theta}{2} \\ \sin\dfrac{\theta}{2} & \cos\dfrac{\theta}{2} \end{bmatrix}$$

The $R_y(\theta)$ gate is equivalent to the $U3(\theta, 0, 0)$ gate.

The A_{R_y} gate is part of the *Rotation* family of gates since it effectively rotates the quantum state of a qubit around the Y-axis.

Declaring the Gates That Split Qubelets in Code

Declare these gates in your program as listed:

Hadamard (H) Gate

To use an H gate on, say, the q[0] qubit, declare it as follows:

```
h q[0];
```

Rx Gate

To use, for instance, a $R_x(\pi/3)$ gate on the q[0] qubit, declare it like this:

```
rx(pi/3) q[0];
```

Ry Gate

To use, say, a $R_y(\pi/3)$ gate on the q[0] qubit, declare it as follows:

```
ry(pi/3) q[0];
```

Identity (ID) Gate

The Identity gate leaves all qubelets alone. That is, when it acts on a qubit, it leaves all the qubelets in their original states:

The matrix, A_{ID}, for the ID gate is:

$$A_{ID} = \begin{bmatrix} 1 & 0 \\ 0 & 1 \end{bmatrix}$$

This is also the *identity* matrix.

The ID gate is equivalent to the $U3(0, 0, 0)$ gate.

The Identity gate is primarily of theoretical interest. You sometimes use it for aesthetic reasons to line up gates in your circuits, but it doesn't affect the computation.

To use an ID gate on, say, the q[0] qubit, declare it as follows:

```
id q[0];
```

Try Your Hand

Solutions to these exercises are given in Solutions: Quantum Gates and How to Use Them, on page 479.

For any code listing in the exercises, assume the following header lines:

```
OPENQASM 2.0;
include "qelib1.inc";
```

1. When building your own quantum circuits, you may work with qubelets to figure out how to get your programs to return the correct solution for your computational tasks. Eventually, though, you'll need to translate the actions on the qubelets to quantum gates you can declare in your programs. This exercise tests your understanding of gates and how they affect qubelets.

    Decide whether the following statements are True or False:

    a. The Y gate puts a $|1\rangle$ qubit in a blended state.

    b. An $S^\dagger$ gate followed by a T gate has the same effect on a $|0\rangle$ qubit as it does on a $|1\rangle$ qubit.

    c. The action of an S gate on a $|1\rangle$ qubit can be reversed by two $T^\dagger$ gates.

    d. An S gate followed by a T gate rotates the triangle qubelets by $135°$ anticlockwise.

    e. You can use an $R_x(\theta)$ gate to put a qubit in a blended state.

2. A Y gate operates on a non-inverted $|0\rangle$ qubit.

    a. Draw the quantum state after the Y gate acts on the $|0\rangle$ qubit.

    b. What would be the state had a NOT (X) gate acted on the $|0\rangle$ qubit instead of the Y gate?

    c. If you measure the state on the right, would you notice any difference had you used a NOT (X) gate instead?

3. Consider the circuit shown in the following figure:

    $$q[0] = |0\rangle \quad \boxed{X} \quad \boxed{T} \quad \boxed{X}$$

    Which qubelets would be rotated in the q[0] qubit after all three gates act on it? Explain your reasoning.

4. Consider the following quantum circuit:

a. Write a program for this circuit.

b. Run this program and look at its output. Why do you think the $S^\dagger$ gate prevents the second H gate from reversing the actions of the first H gate?

c. Next, insert an S gate after the $S^\dagger$ gate and before the second H gate, as shown in the following figure:

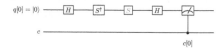

Write a quantum program for this circuit and compare its output with that of the previous part.

5. Consider the following circuit:

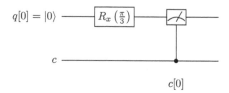

a. Write a program for this circuit.

b. Use the following A_{R_x} matrix to compute the state $|\psi\rangle$ of the $|0\rangle$ qubit after it has been acted on by the $R_x(\pi/3)$ gate:

$$A_{R_x}(\theta) = \begin{bmatrix} \cos\dfrac{\theta}{2} & -i\sin\dfrac{\theta}{2} \\ -i\sin\dfrac{\theta}{2} & \cos\dfrac{\theta}{2} \end{bmatrix}$$

c. What's the ratio of pentagon $|0\rangle$ to triangle $|1\rangle$ qubelets in $|\psi\rangle$?

d. What are the angles of rotations of the pentagon $|0\rangle$ and triangle $|1\rangle$ qubelets in $|\psi\rangle$?

e. Compute the probabilities of the $|\psi\rangle$ state collapsing to the idealized states, $|0\rangle$ and $|1\rangle$.

f. Run the program and compare its output with the probabilities you computed in the previous part.

Sequence of Gates as Matrix Multiplication

When writing quantum programs for your applications, knowing how the qubelets end up helps you decide when and where to inject quantum effects so that your program returns the optimal solution with a high likelihood. So having a way to succinctly describe how a quantum gate acts on any quantum state of a qubit is useful. The real value, though, of holding a gate's "genomic code" is figuring out how a sequence of gates modifies a qubit's quantum state. For example, consider the quantum circuit shown in the following figure:

$$|0\rangle \;-\boxed{H}-\boxed{S^\dagger}-\boxed{R_x(\tfrac{\pi}{6})}-\boxed{T}-\boxed{R_x(\tfrac{\pi}{2})}-$$

Working out the cumulative effect of these gates on the $|0\rangle$ qubit is cumbersome. If you write a program for this circuit and run it, you'll only get the collapsed state of the qubit, as you won't know the rotation of qubelets before you measure it. But, the gate matrices reveal how the qubits end up without collapsing the qubelets.

To see how to compute the action of these gates on the $|0\rangle$ qubit, start with the first gate, H. The quantum state $|\psi_H\rangle$ after the H gate acts on the $|0\rangle$ qubit is:

$$|\psi_H\rangle = A_H |0\rangle$$

Vectors Versus Kets—Notational Convenience

When using gate matrices to figure out how a gate acts on a quantum state, you multiply the matrix with the vector for the quantum state. For example, when a quantum state $|\psi\rangle$ with amplitudes ω_0 and ω_1 is fed to a gate G, whose matrix is A_G, it changes the quantum state $|\psi\rangle$ to $|\psi_G\rangle$, according to the following equation:

$$|\psi_G\rangle = A_G \begin{pmatrix} \omega_0 \\ \omega_1 \end{pmatrix}$$

We'll frequently find it convenient to drop the vector for $|\psi\rangle$ and instead write the previous equation as:

$$|\psi_G\rangle = A_G |\psi\rangle$$

Because this form emphasizes the qubit over its amplitudes, it's sometimes easier to see the actions of the gates in context.

So that you can pictorially see the $|0\rangle$ qubit being modified by the gates, label the quantum circuit with this state, as shown in the following figure:

$$|0\rangle \quad \boxed{H} \quad \overset{|\psi_H\rangle = A_H|0\rangle}{} \quad \boxed{S^\dagger} \quad \boxed{R_x(\tfrac{\pi}{6})} \quad \boxed{T} \quad \boxed{R_x(\tfrac{\pi}{2})}$$

The next gate that acts on this qubit is the $S^\dagger$ gate, which takes it to the state $|\psi_{S^\dagger}\rangle$:

$$|\psi_{S^\dagger}\rangle = A_{S^\dagger}|\psi_H\rangle$$

Now comes the *key* step: replace the quantum state $|\psi_H\rangle$ in terms of the gate matrix A_H for the H gate, as stated earlier:

$$|\psi_{S^\dagger}\rangle = A_{S^\dagger}A_H|0\rangle$$

To see the progression of quantum states pictorially, label the quantum state after the $S^\dagger$ gate acts on the qubit, as shown in the following figure:

$$|0\rangle \quad \boxed{H} \quad \overset{|\psi_H\rangle = A_H|0\rangle}{} \quad \boxed{S^\dagger} \quad \overset{|\psi_{S^\dagger}\rangle = A_{S^\dagger}A_H|0\rangle}{} \quad \boxed{R_x(\tfrac{\pi}{6})} \quad \boxed{T} \quad \boxed{R_x(\tfrac{\pi}{2})}$$

Continuing in a similar manner, the quantum state $|\psi_{R_x(\pi/6)}\rangle$ after the $R_x(\pi/6)$ gate is:

$$|\psi_{R_x(\pi/6)}\rangle = A_{R_x(\pi/6)}A_{S^\dagger}A_H|0\rangle$$

Likewise, after the T gate, the quantum state $|\psi_T\rangle$ is:

$$|\psi_T\rangle = A_T A_{R_x(\pi/6)}A_{S^\dagger}A_H|0\rangle$$

And, after the $R_x(\pi/2)$ gate acts on the qubit, the quantum state $|\psi_{R_x(\pi/2)}\rangle$ is:

$$|\psi_{R_x(\pi/2)}\rangle = A_{R_x(\pi/2)}A_T A_{R_x(\pi/6)}A_{S^\dagger}A_H|0\rangle$$

In other words, a chain of quantum gates is equivalent to one whose matrix is obtained by multiplying the matrices of the gates in the chain in *reverse* order.

Gate Matrices Are Multiplied in the Reverse Order in Which Gates Are Applied

 Consider a qubit acted on by two gates, G1 and G2, respectively, as shown in the following figure:

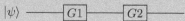

Gate Matrices Are Multiplied in the Reverse Order in Which Gates Are Applied

In terms of matrices, the action of the gates on the qubits are written in the *reverse* order in which the gates are applied. Thus, if A_{G1} and A_{G2} are matrices for the two gates, G1 and G2, respectively, the quantum state $|\psi\rangle$ on the $|0\rangle$ qubit is calculated as follows:

$$|\psi\rangle = A_{G2}A_{G1}|0\rangle$$

Even though you draw the gates operating on the qubit from left to right, the matrices are written from *right to left* in the order that they operate on the qubit.

Thus, in the previous circuit, the final quantum state $|\psi\rangle$ that the $|0\rangle$ qubit ends up in after the H, $S^{\dagger}$, $R_x(\pi/6)$, T, and $R_x(\pi/2)$ gates act on it is:

$$|\psi\rangle = A_{R_x(\pi/2)}A_T A_{R_x(\pi/6)}A_{S^{\dagger}}A_H |0\rangle$$

$$= \begin{bmatrix} \cos\dfrac{\pi}{4} & -i\sin\dfrac{\pi}{4} \\ -i\sin\dfrac{\pi}{4} & \cos\dfrac{\pi}{4} \end{bmatrix} \begin{bmatrix} 1 & 0 \\ 0 & e^{i\frac{\pi}{4}} \end{bmatrix} \begin{bmatrix} \cos\dfrac{\pi}{12} & -i\sin\dfrac{\pi}{12} \\ -i\sin\dfrac{\pi}{12} & \cos\dfrac{\pi}{12} \end{bmatrix} \begin{bmatrix} 1 & 0 \\ 0 & -i \end{bmatrix} \begin{bmatrix} \dfrac{1}{\sqrt{2}} & \dfrac{1}{\sqrt{2}} \\ \dfrac{1}{\sqrt{2}} & -\dfrac{1}{\sqrt{2}} \end{bmatrix} \begin{pmatrix} 1 \\ 0 \end{pmatrix}$$

$$= \begin{pmatrix} -0.0794593112989455 - i\,0.433012701892219 \\ 0.433012701892219 - i\,0.786566092485493 \end{pmatrix}$$

Each matrix is associated with a gate. For example, the first matrix corresponds to the $R_x(\pi/2)$ gate.

Thus, this sequence of gates takes the $|0\rangle$ qubit and puts it in the following state:

$$\begin{pmatrix} 1 \\ 0 \end{pmatrix} \mapsto \begin{pmatrix} -0.0794593112989455 - i\,0.433012701892219 \\ 0.433012701892219 - i\,0.786566092485493 \end{pmatrix}$$

Use a Computer Algebra System for Matrix Multiplications

Instead of multiplying matrices by hand, use a computer algebra system to do the heavy lifting for you. See Using a Computer Algebra System for Multiplying, on page 397, for one such system that you can use for free on the internet.

You'll also find this calculated state in the *Visualizations* panel of the Composer. Click the Bar Graph icon on the left tabs, as shown in the figure on page 222.

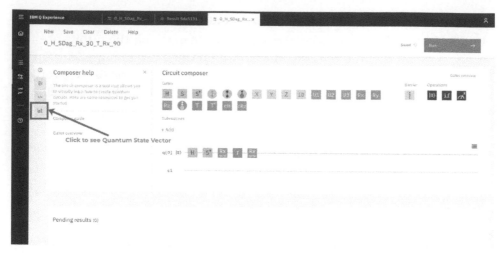

The quantum state is reported under the State Vector drop-down list, as in the following figure:

Note: the quantum state vector shown in the previous figure uses j for the complex number instead of i. Both forms are valid and used interchangeably. Also, the state is written as a row vector.

This quantum state is a theoretical result obtained by multiplying gate matrices. If you run this circuit on an actual quantum computer, though, and measure the state at the end, you'll find that the $|0\rangle$ qubit collapses to the idealized states roughly in accordance with this quantum state.

Matrix multiplication simplifies the action of a sequence of gates on a qubit—the final quantum state of a qubit falls out directly. But we lose the rationale of why the calculations work. In this sense, the Qubelets Model on page 20 provides the insight behind the math.

In the next chapter, we'll expand the idea of gate matrices to analyze circuits with multiple qubits.

Try Your Hand

Solutions to these exercises are given in Sequence of Gates as Matrix Multiplication Solutions, on page 484.

For any code listing in the exercises, assume the following header lines:

```
OPENQASM 2.0;
include "qelib1.inc";
```

1. As you start building larger quantum circuits, you'll come across several gates in sequence. In these situations, you can frequently replace them with a another gate, thereby reducing the number of gates in your program. In this problem, you're asked to work out whether such replacements are possible.

    In each of the following quantum circuits, determine whether the quantum state after the $|0\rangle$ qubit is acted on by the gates can be estimated from the corresponding multiplication of the respective gate matrices shown below each circuit:

    a.

    $$|0\rangle \quad \boxed{H} \quad \boxed{S^\dagger} \quad |\psi\rangle$$

    $$|\psi\rangle = A_H A_{S^\dagger} |0\rangle$$

    b.

    $$|0\rangle \quad \boxed{H} \quad \boxed{T^\dagger} \quad \boxed{T} \quad \boxed{Y} \quad |\psi\rangle$$

    $$|\psi\rangle = A_Y A_H |0\rangle$$

    c.

    $$|0\rangle \quad \boxed{H} \quad \boxed{S} \quad |\psi\rangle$$

    $$|\psi\rangle = A_{S^\dagger}^\dagger A_H |0\rangle$$

    d.

    $$|0\rangle \quad \boxed{H} \quad \boxed{S} \quad \boxed{T^\dagger} \quad |\psi\rangle$$

    $$|\psi\rangle = A_T A_H |0\rangle$$

    e.

    $$|0\rangle \quad \boxed{H} \quad \boxed{Z} \quad \boxed{H} \quad |\psi\rangle$$

    $$|\psi\rangle = A_X |0\rangle$$

2. Consider again the quantum circuit in the previous section:

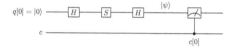

a. Can you execute this circuit on a quantum computer? If not, what do you need to do to get it running on a quantum computer?

b. Write a quantum program for your circuit in the previous part.

c. Using the quantum state vector in the previous section, compute the probabilities of the qubit collapsing to the idealized states $|0\rangle$ and $|1\rangle$, respectively.

d. Run your program and compare its output with the probabilities you calculated in the previous part.

3. Consider the following quantum circuit:

a. Express the quantum state $|\psi\rangle$ in terms of the gate matrices.

b. Compare the quantum state vector you calculated in the previous part with that shown in the Visualizations tab on the IBM Quantum Computer.

c. What are the probabilities for the qubit q[0] to collapse to the idealized states?

d. Write a program for this circuit.

e. Run your program and compare its output with the probabilities you calculated in an earlier part.

Bottom Line

Although quantum gates are at the center of quantum computing and form the bulk of the statements in any quantum program, they just do three things:

- Switch Qubelets on page 205
- Rotate Qubelets on page 206
- Split Qubelets on page 213

Unlike classical computing, which has a wide range of ways to manipulate data, quantum computing crunches out a solution to hugely complex problems merely by tinkering with qubelets. Looking back at the coin-toss analogy in

Quantum Computing in Thirty Seconds, on page 5, it's as if you're tweaking the spinning coins so that they land on the faces corresponding to the correct solution.

Like a fingerprint, each gate has its own distinct matrix, which completely codifies how a quantum state is modified. These matrices essentially document how the gate modifies the number of pentagon $|0\rangle$ and triangle $|1\rangle$ qubelets as well as how the relative difference in their rotations is changed. Or, if you prefer to limit the number of things you're juggling in your head, you can equivalently think in terms of how the triangle $|1\rangle$ qubelets are rotated, as described in Intuitively Analyzing the Quantum Gate Matrix, on page 195.

The various gates in quantum programming give a range of preset ways in which to switch, split, and rotate qubelets. These simplify declaring these gates in your quantum programs. But if you need to introduce quantum effects with finer control, you can use the Universal Gates, on page 203, which give you complete freedom in how you want to mold the qubelets.

Using matrices to represent the quantum gates also leads to a handy way to work out how a chain of quantum gates affects a qubit: multiplying the gate matrices written in the reverse order of when they act on the qubit gives the final state of the qubit. Ironically, even though matrix multiplication mirrors how qubits change, don't think of your quantum program as one big matrix multiplication. The reason is that as the number of qubits increases, matrix multiplication quickly gets unwieldy on classical computers, as we'll see in the next chapter. The true value of matrices is that they help in building patterns that can then be extrapolated to larger problems, as you'll learn in Chapter 10, Quantum Search, on page 295.

But, first, in the next chapter, you'll extend the matrix technique to circuits with multiple qubits. Specifically, you'll develop matrices for multi-qubit gates, such as the CNOT on page 47 and CCNOT on page 57 gates and also see how these gates are paired up with single qubit gates.

## CHAPTER 8

Giant Leap for Mankind—Multi-Qubit Programs

If you step back and think about it, it's actually quite remarkable that a 2×2 matrix is all it takes to tell you how it transforms any of the infinite quantum states of a single qubit: regardless of the number of pentagon $|0\rangle$ and triangle $|1\rangle$ qubelets, or their relative rotations, the gate matrix correctly expresses how the gate affects the qubit.

In this chapter, you'll learn to generalize the matrix concept for gates that handle multiple qubits. As with single-qubit gate matrices, once you know how to represent multi-qubit gates, you can then hook up any configuration of gates and reliably predict how the qubits will collapse. But, as I pointed out at the end of the previous chapter, matrices aren't an end to themselves, especially when dealing with many qubits. So it's imperative to think about them intuitively and how they form the basis for patterns that can be applied to circuits and programs that use several qubits.

We'll start by generalizing the notion of idealized states when working with multiple qubits. Then we'll look at the single-qubit gate matrices, but from the perspective of deducing how the gate modifies the qubelets rather than as signatures for a specific gate. This viewpoint lets us formulate matrices for multi-qubit gates. Finally, you'll learn to apply these methods to introduce quantum effects customized for your application. You'll design a teleporting circuit by breaking it up into smaller and more manageable parts, a paradigm that'll guide you when developing your quantum programs.

Idealized States Redux—Multi-Qubit Version

Before learning to precisely manipulate multiple qubits in quantum circuits, like you did with single qubits in Chapter 6, Designer Genes—Custom Quantum States, on page 141, and Chapter 7, Small Step for Man—Single Qubit Programs, on page 173, you need to augment your understanding of idealized states.

Idealized States for One Qubit

The idealized states for single qubits are the two ways that it can collapse. Consider, for example, a qubit having five pentagon $|0\rangle$ and two triangle $|1\rangle$ qubelets (both rotated), as shown in the following figure:

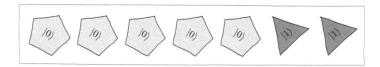

Regardless of how the pentagon $|0\rangle$ and triangle $|1\rangle$ qubelets are rotated, this qubit collapses in one of the following two ways:

Collapses to $|0\rangle$

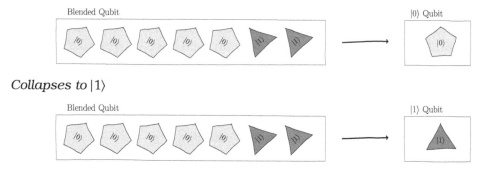

Collapses to $|1\rangle$

Of course, the qubit would collapse more frequently to $|0\rangle$ than $|1\rangle$ because the qubit has a greater number of pentagon $|0\rangle$ qubelets than triangle $|1\rangle$ qubelets. But it would always collapse to one of these two types.

Thus, as in Quantum States and Probabilities, on page 142, any quantum state $|\psi_1\rangle$ can be expressed in terms of the idealized states $|0\rangle$ and $|1\rangle$, as follows:

$$|\psi_1\rangle = \omega_0 |0\rangle + \omega_1 |1\rangle$$

The parameters ω_0 and ω_1 are the amplitudes associated with the idealized states. By setting different values for the amplitudes ω_0 and ω_1, you can specify any quantum state. And the subscript on the quantum state $|\psi_1\rangle$ indicates that it's a quantum state for a single qubit.

In terms of vectors, as shown in Quantum States as Vectors, on page 174, the quantum state $|\psi_1\rangle$ can also be written as:

$$|\psi_1\rangle = \begin{pmatrix} \omega_0 \\ \omega_1 \end{pmatrix} = \omega_0 \begin{pmatrix} 1 \\ 0 \end{pmatrix} + \omega_1 \begin{pmatrix} 0 \\ 1 \end{pmatrix}$$

Idealized States for Two Qubits

When dealing with two qubits, the situation is similar: each qubit collapses to either $|0\rangle$ or $|1\rangle$. Thus, we can write the ways that two qubits collapse as follows:

Qubit 1	Qubit 2
$|0\rangle$	$|0\rangle$
$|0\rangle$	$|1\rangle$
$|1\rangle$	$|0\rangle$
$|1\rangle$	$|1\rangle$

Thus, the idealized states of the two qubits are as follows:

$$|00\rangle, \ |01\rangle, \ |10\rangle, \ |11\rangle$$

These, then, are the 2^2, or 4, idealized states for two qubits, and any two-qubit quantum state can be expressed in terms of these four idealized states. Specifically, if the quantum state of the first qubit is $|\psi_1\rangle$ and that of the second is $|\psi_2\rangle$, then the quantum state of the two-qubit system is written as $|\psi_1\psi_2\rangle$.

$$|\psi_1\psi_2\rangle = \omega_{00} |00\rangle + \omega_{01} |01\rangle + \omega_{10} |10\rangle + \omega_{11} |11\rangle$$

The coefficients ω_{00}, ω_{01}, ω_{10}, and ω_{11} are the amplitudes of the idealized states $|00\rangle$, $|01\rangle$, $|10\rangle$, and $|11\rangle$, respectively.

Since the two qubits can only collapse to these four idealized states, the probabilities of collapsing to them, the "squares" of the amplitudes—an amplitude multiplied by its conjugate—sum up to 1:

$$\omega_{00} \omega_{00}^* + \omega_{01} \omega_{01}^* + \omega_{10} \omega_{10}^* + \omega_{11} \omega_{11}^* = 1$$

The quantum state of a two-qubit system is completely defined by these four amplitudes. It's also expressed by the vector shown.

$$|\psi_1\psi_2\rangle = \begin{pmatrix} \omega_{00} \\ \omega_{01} \\ \omega_{10} \\ \omega_{11} \end{pmatrix}$$

This vector, in turn, can be written in terms of the four idealized states:

$$|\psi_1\psi_2\rangle = \begin{pmatrix} \omega_{00} \\ \omega_{01} \\ \omega_{10} \\ \omega_{11} \end{pmatrix} = \omega_{00}\begin{pmatrix} 1 \\ 0 \\ 0 \\ 0 \end{pmatrix} + \omega_{01}\begin{pmatrix} 0 \\ 1 \\ 0 \\ 0 \end{pmatrix} + \omega_{10}\begin{pmatrix} 0 \\ 0 \\ 1 \\ 0 \end{pmatrix} + \omega_{11}\begin{pmatrix} 0 \\ 0 \\ 0 \\ 1 \end{pmatrix}$$

Since there are four idealized states, the quantum state of a two-qubit system will be a 4×1 vector. Specifically, the vectors for the four idealized states are:

$$|00\rangle = \begin{pmatrix} 1 \\ 0 \\ 0 \\ 0 \end{pmatrix}, \quad |01\rangle = \begin{pmatrix} 0 \\ 1 \\ 0 \\ 0 \end{pmatrix}, \quad |10\rangle = \begin{pmatrix} 0 \\ 0 \\ 1 \\ 0 \end{pmatrix}, \quad |11\rangle = \begin{pmatrix} 0 \\ 0 \\ 0 \\ 1 \end{pmatrix}$$

Each element in the vector corresponds to an idealized state. So, the first element is associated with $|00\rangle$, the second with $|01\rangle$, and so on, till the last with $|11\rangle$.

These idealized states aren't just theoretical concepts. They underpin all quantum programs, as shown in the next section.

Idealized States and Quantum Programs

Idealized states are closely intertwined with quantum programs—they're the outputs. Consider, for example, the two-qubit quantum circuit shown in the following figure:

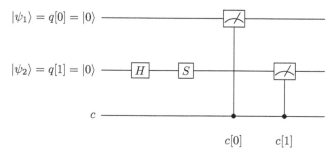

Analyze this circuit by first looking at each qubit individually:

Qubit q[0]

No gates act on the q[0] qubit:

$$|\psi_1\rangle = |0\rangle$$

Qubit q[1]

The H gate splits the $|0\rangle$ qubit in q[0] to a pentagon $|0\rangle$ qubelet and a triangle $|1\rangle$ qubelet. The S gate then rotates the triangle $|1\rangle$ qubelet 90°, or a quarter turn clockwise, as shown in the following figure:

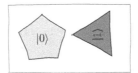

Alternatively, you can also use the gate matrices (see Classifying Quantum Gates, on page 202) and the vector for the idealized state $|0\rangle$, as follows:

$$|\psi_2\rangle = A_S A_H |0\rangle$$

$$= \begin{bmatrix} 1 & 0 \\ 0 & i \end{bmatrix} \begin{bmatrix} \frac{1}{\sqrt{2}} & \frac{1}{\sqrt{2}} \\ \frac{1}{\sqrt{2}} & \frac{-1}{\sqrt{2}} \end{bmatrix} \begin{pmatrix} 1 \\ 0 \end{pmatrix}$$

$$= \frac{1}{\sqrt{2}} \begin{bmatrix} 1 & 1 \\ i & -i \end{bmatrix} \begin{pmatrix} 1 \\ 0 \end{pmatrix}$$

$$= \frac{1}{\sqrt{2}} \begin{pmatrix} 1 \\ i \end{pmatrix}$$

This vector indicates that the quantum state $|\psi_2\rangle$ is made up of a pentagon $|0\rangle$ qubelet and a triangle $|1\rangle$ qubelet rotated 90° anticlockwise.

But, because this is a quantum circuit, there's an additional step that has no classical equivalent: the formation of the mega-qubit, as described in Multi-Qubit Superposition: The Mega-Qubit, on page 91, to get the quantum state $|\psi_1 \psi_2\rangle$ of the two-qubit circuit.

The pentagon $|0\rangle$ qubelet in the top qubit q[0] pairs up with the qubelets in the bottom qubit q[1] to give the mega-qubit shown in the figure on page 232.

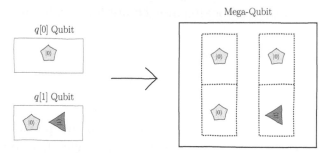

This mega-qubit can collapse to either of the two qubelet combinations with equal probability. To get the quantum state of the mega-qubit, normalize the chances of picking a qubelet combination by following the procedure similar to that described in Normalizing Qubelets, on page 144, but apply it for qubelet combinations instead of qubelets:

$$|\psi_1 \psi_2\rangle = \frac{1}{\sqrt{1^2 + 1^2}} |00\rangle + \frac{i}{\sqrt{1^2 + 1^2}} |01\rangle$$
$$= \frac{1}{\sqrt{2}} |00\rangle + \frac{i}{\sqrt{2}} |01\rangle$$

The triangle $|1\rangle$ qubelet at the bottom of the second qubelet combination is rotated a quarter turn anticlockwise. As a result you see the complex number i associated with the second term.

Since this qubit has two qubelet combinations, it collapses in one of the following two ways:

Collapses to $|00\rangle$

When this mega-qubit is measured, the qubelet combination on the left is selected roughly 50% of the time and collapses to $|00\rangle$, as shown here:

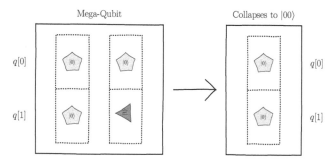

This corresponds to the following vector:

$$\begin{pmatrix} 1 \\ 0 \\ 0 \\ 0 \end{pmatrix}$$

Collapses to $|01\rangle$

When this mega-qubit is measured, the qubelet combination on the right is selected roughly 50% of the time and collapses to $|01\rangle$, as shown in the following figure:

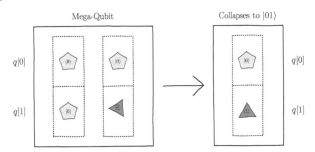

Although rotated qubelets play a pivotal role in quantum effects such as entangling and canceling qubelets, when a qubit collapses, qubelets are reset to their non-rotated orientations. Thus, the rotated triangle $|1\rangle$ qubelet snaps back to the non-rotated position.

The collapsed qubelet combination corresponds to the following vector:

$$\begin{pmatrix} 0 \\ 1 \\ 0 \\ 0 \end{pmatrix}$$

You can verify that this circuit does indeed work as the analysis just described by running it on the IBM Quantum Computer. The code listing for this circuit is as follows:

```
0_Measure_1_H_S_Measure.qasm
Line 1  qreg q[2];
2  creg c[2];
3
4  h q[1];
5  s q[1];
6  measure q[0] -> c[0];
7  measure q[1] -> c[1];
```

The H and S gates acting on the q[1] qubit are declared on lines 4 and 5, respectively, followed by the Measure gates.

The output of this program running on a real quantum computer is shown in the following figure:

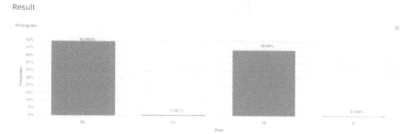

This program collapses to the two binary states 00 and 10 roughly half the time. The other two states are just noise when using a real quantum computer. Because of the way that IBM's classical register is structured (see Using the IBM Computer: Multi-Bit Classical Register, on page 56), the highest numbered classical bit, in this case c[1], is written first. Thus, the 10 state corresponds to c[1]c[0], which, in turn, records the qubits q[1]q[0]. Hence, the measured classical states 00 and 01 correspond to $|00\rangle$ and $|01\rangle$, respectively. In other words, the measured classical states reflect the idealized states.

Idealized States for Three or More Qubits

Determining the idealized states for three or more qubits is analogous: document the ways that the qubits collapse. For example, a three-qubit quantum state $|\psi_1\psi_2\psi_3\rangle$ collapses to the following 8×1 vectors:

$$|000\rangle = \begin{vmatrix} 1 \\ 0 \\ 0 \\ 0 \\ 0 \\ 0 \\ 0 \\ 0 \end{vmatrix}, \quad |001\rangle = \begin{vmatrix} 0 \\ 1 \\ 0 \\ 0 \\ 0 \\ 0 \\ 0 \\ 0 \end{vmatrix}, \quad |010\rangle = \begin{vmatrix} 0 \\ 0 \\ 1 \\ 0 \\ 0 \\ 0 \\ 0 \\ 0 \end{vmatrix}, \quad |011\rangle = \begin{vmatrix} 0 \\ 0 \\ 0 \\ 1 \\ 0 \\ 0 \\ 0 \\ 0 \end{vmatrix}$$

$$|100\rangle = \begin{vmatrix} 0 \\ 0 \\ 0 \\ 0 \\ 1 \\ 0 \\ 0 \\ 0 \end{vmatrix}, \quad |101\rangle = \begin{vmatrix} 0 \\ 0 \\ 0 \\ 0 \\ 0 \\ 1 \\ 0 \\ 0 \end{vmatrix}, \quad |110\rangle = \begin{vmatrix} 0 \\ 0 \\ 0 \\ 0 \\ 0 \\ 0 \\ 1 \\ 0 \end{vmatrix}, \quad |111\rangle = \begin{vmatrix} 0 \\ 0 \\ 0 \\ 0 \\ 0 \\ 0 \\ 0 \\ 1 \end{vmatrix}$$

The idealized states for n qubits follow a similar pattern: you'll end up with 2^n states. As n—the number of qubits in your program—grows, the number of idealized states grows exponentially and become impossible to write down. But the mega-qubit is able to handle all these states simultaneously. So, whereas it's difficult for a classical computer to work with them, a quantum computer merely needs n qubits, a far smaller number, to work with.

In the next section, you'll see how the idealized states are intimately tied to the gate matrix.

Speed Reading a Gate's Operation from Its Matrix

In Classifying Quantum Gates, on page 202, you saw that single-qubit quantum gates can be classified by how they affect qubelets. In this section, you'll learn to infer a gate's matrix and understand how it affects the qubelets. We'll not be concerned with whether the given matrix is unitary on page 191. Our interest is merely to figure out how the gate acts on the pentagon $|0\rangle$ and triangle $|1\rangle$ qubelets. Thus, we'll assume valid gate matrices.

Single-Qubit Gate Matrices

To fix these ideas in your mind, consider the following 2×2 matrix:

$$\begin{bmatrix} a & c \\ b & d \end{bmatrix}$$

The letters a, b, c, and d denote complex numbers. Their complex conjugates are a^*, b^*, c^*, and d^*, respectively. So, if a is $0.5 + i0.5$, then $a^* = 0.5 - i0.5$. Equivalently, in polar coordinates using Euler's formula:

$$a = \frac{1}{\sqrt{2}}e^{i\frac{\pi}{4}}$$

$$a^* = \frac{1}{\sqrt{2}}e^{-i\frac{\pi}{4}}$$

Even though this matrix encodes how any quantum state, including blended ones, are modified by the corresponding gate, we'll determine how the gate affects the qubelets by focusing on how the matrix affects the idealized states $|0\rangle$ and $|1\rangle$, respectively.

To this end, as described in Quantum Gates as Matrices, on page 175, the first column lists the amplitudes of the quantum state obtained when the gate operates on $|0\rangle$.

In other words, when the gate corresponding to this matrix acts on $|0\rangle$, the gate puts the qubelet in the quantum state defined by the first column, as shown here:

$$|0\rangle \mapsto a|0\rangle + b|1\rangle = \begin{pmatrix} a \\ b \end{pmatrix}$$

Similarly, when the gate acts on the $|1\rangle$ qubelet, the gate puts the qubelet in the quantum state defined by the second column, as follows:

$$|1\rangle \mapsto c|0\rangle + d|1\rangle = \begin{pmatrix} c \\ d \end{pmatrix}$$

Let's now cover how to look at the entries of the gate matrix and reason out the following ways that the gate changes the qubelets:

- *Leave Qubelets Alone*
- *Switch Qubelets*
- *Split Qubelets*
- *Rotate Qubelets*
- *Compound Operations on Qubelets*

Leave Qubelets Alone

When a gate acts on the pentagon $|0\rangle$ qubelets only and doesn't affect the triangle $|1\rangle$ qubelets, the element corresponding to the amplitude of $|1\rangle$ in the first column is zero. That is, the second element in the first column is zero:

$$\begin{bmatrix} a & c \\ 0 & d \end{bmatrix}$$

If the gate acts on the triangle $|1\rangle$ qubelets only and leaves the pentagon $|0\rangle$ qubelets alone, then the amplitude for $|0\rangle$ is zero. That is, the first element in the second column is zero:

$$\begin{bmatrix} a & 0 \\ b & d \end{bmatrix}$$

Switch Qubelets

When a gate switches a qubelet, it "changes" it to the other type. For example, a pentagon $|0\rangle$ qubelet is switched to a triangle $|1\rangle$ qubelet. The entry for the amplitude of $|0\rangle$ becomes zero and the one for the amplitude of $|1\rangle$ is nonzero:

$$\begin{bmatrix} 0 & c \\ b & d \end{bmatrix}$$

In the same way, when a triangle $|1\rangle$ qubelet is switched to a pentagon $|0\rangle$ qubelet, the second element in the second column is zero:

$$\begin{bmatrix} a & c \\ b & 0 \end{bmatrix}$$

For instance, the NOT gate, which switches a pentagon $|0\rangle$ qubelet with a triangle $|1\rangle$ qubelet, and a a triangle $|1\rangle$ qubelet with a pentagon $|0\rangle$ qubelet, has the following matrix:

$$\begin{bmatrix} 0 & 1 \\ 1 & 0 \end{bmatrix}$$

Split Qubelets

When a gate splits either a pentagon $|0\rangle$ or a triangle $|1\rangle$ qubelet, it creates qubelets of both types. For example, splitting a pentagon $|0\rangle$ qubelet creates both a pentagon $|0\rangle$ and a triangle $|1\rangle$ qubelet. In other words, both entries in the respective column are nonzero.

If a gate splits both pentagon $|0\rangle$ and triangle $|1\rangle$ qubelets, then the matrix has all nonzero entries like the H gate:

$$\begin{bmatrix} \dfrac{1}{\sqrt{2}} & \dfrac{1}{\sqrt{2}} \\ \dfrac{1}{\sqrt{2}} & \dfrac{-1}{\sqrt{2}} \end{bmatrix}$$

Rotate Qubelets

When a gate rotates a qubelet, it shows up as a complex number in the entry associated with that qubelet. For example, when a gate acts on a triangle $|1\rangle$ qubelet and rotates it by, say, $\pi/4$ radians or $45°$ anticlockwise (and leaves the pentagon $|0\rangle$ qubelet alone), the quantum state is expressed as:

$$|1\rangle \mapsto e^{i\frac{\pi}{4}} |1\rangle$$

Using Euler's formula, write the previous equation as:

$$|1\rangle \;\mapsto\; \left(\cos\frac{\pi}{4} + i\sin\frac{\pi}{4}\right)|1\rangle$$

$$= \left(\frac{1}{\sqrt{2}} + i\frac{1}{\sqrt{2}}\right)|1\rangle$$

Write this operation in the bottom right element of the matrix:

$$\begin{bmatrix} 1 & 0 \\ 0 & \left(\frac{1}{\sqrt{2}} + i\frac{1}{\sqrt{2}}\right) \end{bmatrix}$$

Thus, any time you see a complex number as an entry in the gate matrix, it means the corresponding qubelet is rotated.

Compound Operations on Qubelets

Knowing how to recognize the basic operations we've listed will let you infer when a gate combines them when modifying the qubelets. For example, consider the gate matrix associated with the Y Gate, on page 205, as follows:

$$\begin{bmatrix} 0 & -i \\ i & 0 \end{bmatrix}$$

Looking at the first column associated with the gate acting on the $|0\rangle$ qubit, the complex number i in the bottom element indicates that the pentagon $|0\rangle$ qubelet is switched to the triangle $|1\rangle$ qubelet *and* is rotated.

You can calculate the exact angle of rotation by noticing that i can be expressed as follows, again using Euler's formula:

$$i = \cos\frac{\pi}{2} + i\sin\frac{\pi}{2}$$

Thus, the triangle $|1\rangle$ qubelet is rotated $\pi/2$ radians, or a quarter turn anti-clockwise.

You can reason out the action on the $|1\rangle$ qubit in a similar way by looking at the second column.

Two-Qubit Gate Matrices

Just as the columns of a single-qubit gate matrix correspond to the idealized states, the columns of a matrix representing a two-qubit gate, such as the Controlled NOT (CNOT) Gate, on page 47, correspond to the four idealized states—$|00\rangle$, $|01\rangle$, $|10\rangle$, and $|11\rangle$— for two qubits:

$$\begin{bmatrix} a & e & i & m \\ b & f & j & n \\ c & g & k & o \\ d & h & l & p \end{bmatrix}$$

The letters $a - p$ are complex numbers with the usual conjugates $a^* - p^*$.

Each column is the action of the gate on the idealized state associated with that column. For example, look at the *Controlled NOT (CNOT) Gate* gate in which the control qubit is set to $|1\rangle$ and its target to $|0\rangle$, as shown in the following figure:

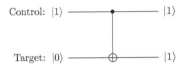

Because the control is $|1\rangle$, the target qubit is switched to $|1\rangle$.

Or, the $|10\rangle$ state is changed by the CNOT gate to the $|11\rangle$ state. To express this operation as a matrix column, write the latter as a vector:

$$|10\rangle \mapsto \begin{pmatrix} 0 \\ 0 \\ 0 \\ 1 \end{pmatrix}$$

Thus, the third column of the matrix A_{CNOT} for the CNOT gate is:

$$\begin{bmatrix} * & * & 0 & * \\ * & * & 0 & * \\ * & * & 0 & * \\ * & * & 1 & * \end{bmatrix}$$

Similarly, you can fill the other columns:

CNOT acts on $|00\rangle$

When the control qubit is $|0\rangle$, the target qubit continues to be $|0\rangle$. Thus, $|00\rangle \mapsto |00\rangle$ or:

$$|00\rangle \mapsto \begin{pmatrix} 1 \\ 0 \\ 0 \\ 0 \end{pmatrix}$$

CNOT acts on $|01\rangle$

Since the control qubit is $|0\rangle$, the target qubit is unaffected and continues to $|1\rangle$. Thus, $|01\rangle \mapsto |01\rangle$ or:

$$|01\rangle \mapsto \begin{pmatrix} 0 \\ 1 \\ 0 \\ 0 \end{pmatrix}$$

CNOT acts on $|11\rangle$

In this case, the control qubit is $|1\rangle$. So, the target qubit switches from $|1\rangle$ to $|0\rangle$. Thus, $|11\rangle \mapsto |10\rangle$ or:

$$|11\rangle \mapsto \begin{pmatrix} 0 \\ 0 \\ 1 \\ 0 \end{pmatrix}$$

Putting these vectors as the appropriate columns in the previous matrix, we'll get the CNOT gate's matrix A_{CNOT}:

$$A_{CNOT} = \begin{bmatrix} 1 & 0 & 0 & 0 \\ 0 & 1 & 0 & 0 \\ 0 & 0 & 0 & 1 \\ 0 & 0 & 1 & 0 \end{bmatrix}$$

Notice that we've suppressed the column labels, but you should still associate each column with the corresponding idealized states.

Following the same line of reasoning, you can derive the gate matrix A_{CZ} for the Controlled Z (CZ) Gate, on page 109. The CZ gate only rotates the triangle $|1\rangle$ qubelet on the target qubit when the control bit is $|1\rangle$, as shown in the following figure:

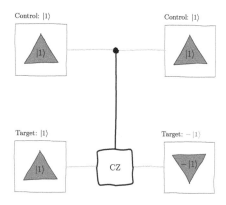

That is, the state $|11\rangle$ becomes $-|11\rangle$. Writing the latter as a vector:

$$|11\rangle \mapsto \begin{pmatrix} 0 \\ 0 \\ 0 \\ -1 \end{pmatrix}$$

The CZ gate leaves the other idealized states alone. Or, in terms of vectors:

$$|00\rangle \mapsto \begin{pmatrix} 1 \\ 0 \\ 0 \\ 0 \end{pmatrix}, \quad |01\rangle \mapsto \begin{pmatrix} 0 \\ 1 \\ 0 \\ 0 \end{pmatrix}, \quad |10\rangle \mapsto \begin{pmatrix} 0 \\ 0 \\ 1 \\ 0 \end{pmatrix}$$

In the first two instances, the control qubit is $|0\rangle$. Thus, the target qubit is unchanged. In the last case, even though the control qubit is $|1\rangle$, the target qubit is $|0\rangle$ and not affected by the CZ gate.

These vectors form the rest of the columns of the CZ gate's matrix A_{CZ}:

$$A_{CZ} = \begin{bmatrix} 1 & 0 & 0 & 0 \\ 0 & 1 & 0 & 0 \\ 0 & 0 & 1 & 0 \\ 0 & 0 & 0 & -1 \end{bmatrix}$$

With matrices for two-qubit gates, you can follow the procedure in Sequence of Gates as Matrix Multiplication, on page 219, to work out how circuits with two-qubit gates modify quantum states. For example, see the following circuit:

Obtain the two-qubit quantum state $|\psi_1\psi_2\rangle$ as follows:

$$|\psi_1\psi_2\rangle = A_Z A_{CNOT} |10\rangle$$

$$= \begin{bmatrix} 1 & 0 & 0 & 0 \\ 0 & 1 & 0 & 0 \\ 0 & 0 & 1 & 0 \\ 0 & 0 & 0 & -1 \end{bmatrix} \begin{bmatrix} 1 & 0 & 0 & 0 \\ 0 & 1 & 0 & 0 \\ 0 & 0 & 0 & 1 \\ 0 & 0 & 1 & 0 \end{bmatrix} \begin{pmatrix} 0 \\ 0 \\ 1 \\ 0 \end{pmatrix}$$

$$= \begin{pmatrix} 0 \\ 0 \\ 0 \\ -1 \end{pmatrix}$$

Notice the order of the multiplication of the A_Z and A_{CNOT} matrices is reverse that of the order in which the corresponding gates are applied to the input state $|10\rangle$ in the quantum circuit. Also, in the previous equation, the input state $|10\rangle$ is replaced with a vector which has a 1 in the third element, corresponding to $|10\rangle$.

The result of this multiplication is a vector whose last element is -1. The bottom element is associated with the quantum state $|11\rangle$. So, a -1 value indicates that this sequence of gates changes the quantum state as follows:

$$|10\rangle \mapsto - |11\rangle$$

For this circuit, you can verify this result by manually working out the action of the gates on the qubits: the control qubit is 1, the CNOT gate switches the bottom qubit to $|1\rangle$, which the CZ gate then inverts to $- |1\rangle$. This corresponds to the quantum state $- |11\rangle$, as found earlier using matrices and vectors. As the number of gates increases, this sort of analysis becomes tedious and error-prone. But the matrix approach always works.

Matrix and Vector Multiplication Isn't a Replacement for Quantum Computing

You may get the idea that multiplying gate matrices with the vector for a quantum state is really all that it takes to do quantum computations. In fact, this principle drives many simulators in various computer languages. But as the number of qubits increases, classical computers would grind to a halt as they run out of resources trying to do matrix math. Quantum computers, on the other hand, are impervious to this excessive workload, as they work with the mega-qubit using quantum mechanical principles instead of using classical means.

Still, the matrix method is important to learn since it gives you a way to analyze small portions of a circuit and see how the qubelets are affected. If you try to use Measure gates instead, you won't get a complete picture of how the rotations of the qubelets of different qubits interact.

You can apply this technique of multiplying quantum state vectors with gate matrices as long as your quantum circuit only has two-qubit gates. In the next section, you'll learn to include single-qubit gates that switch, split, and rotate qubelets on one or both qubits in your quantum circuits.

Circuits with Single- and Two-Qubit Gates

When designing your own quantum programs you'll frequently want to apply a single-qubit gate on one or both qubits in addition to the two-qubit gates. For example, consider the following circuit:

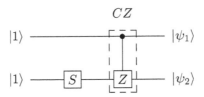

A single-qubit S gate is applied on the bottom qubit before it's fed to the target of the CZ gate. So, this circuit contains the single-qubit S gate coupled with the two-qubit CZ gate. In other words, you end up with a situation where you have to deal with the 2×2 matrix for the S gate as well as the 4×4 matrix for the CZ gate.

To apply the matrix method to calculate the quantum states of the qubits in this circuit, the matrices need to be *compatible* so that they can be multiplied. For square matrices, this means that the matrices must have the same dimensions.

Thus, the single-qubit S gate is "made" into a two-qubit gate by appending the second qubit, the top one in this case, as a *pass-through*, as shown in the following figure:[1,2]

Next, use the single-qubit S gate's 2×2 matrix as a guide to calculate the matrix for the two-qubit S gate. For reference, the matrix A_S for the S Gate, on page 208, is:

$$A_S = \begin{bmatrix} 1 & 0 \\ 0 & i \end{bmatrix}$$

Notice that this matrix implies that the pentagon $|0\rangle$ qubelets are unaffected, while the triangle $|1\rangle$ qubelets are rotated by $\pi/2$ radians, or 90° anticlockwise:

1. https://docs.microsoft.com/en-us/quantum/concepts/multiple-qubits
2. http://www.cs.bham.ac.uk/internal/courses/intro-mqc/current/lecture05_handout.pdf

$$i = \cos\frac{\pi}{2} + i\sin\frac{\pi}{2}$$

$$= e^{i\frac{\pi}{2}}$$

$$= e^{i\varphi} \text{ where } \varphi = \frac{\pi}{2}$$

The angle $\varphi = \pi/2$ indicates the relative difference between the pentagon $|0\rangle$ and triangle $|1\rangle$ qubelets.

As we did for the CNOT gate earlier in this section, work out the columns of the 4×4 matrix by seeing what this circuit does to each of the four idealized states, $|00\rangle$, $|01\rangle$, $|10\rangle$, and $|11\rangle$:

$|00\rangle$ *Idealized State:*

The top qubit, $|q_1\rangle = |0\rangle$, is a pass-through. So it's unchanged by the gate.

The bottom qubit, $|q_2\rangle = |0\rangle$, is fed to the S gate. From this gate's matrix, A_S, the bottom $|0\rangle$ qubit, is also unaffected.

Thus, $|00\rangle \mapsto |00\rangle$. Write the latter state as a vector:

$$|00\rangle \mapsto \begin{pmatrix} 1 \\ 0 \\ 0 \\ 0 \end{pmatrix}$$

Note that the first element of this vector is associated with $|00\rangle$.

$|01\rangle$ *Idealized State:*

The top qubit, $|q_1\rangle = |0\rangle$, is a pass-through. So, it's unchanged by the gate.

The bottom qubit, $|q_2\rangle = |1\rangle$, becomes $i|1\rangle$ when acted on by the S gate in accordance with the gate matrix A_S. Thus, $|01\rangle \mapsto i|01\rangle$. Write the latter state as a vector:

$$|01\rangle \mapsto \begin{pmatrix} 0 \\ i \\ 0 \\ 0 \end{pmatrix}$$

The second element, associated with $|01\rangle$, is i.

$|10\rangle$ *Idealized State:*

The top qubit, $|q_1\rangle = |1\rangle$, is a pass-through. So it's unchanged by the gate.

The bottom qubit, $|q_2\rangle = |0\rangle$, is fed to the S gate and is unchanged in accordance with the gate matrix A_S. Thus, $|10\rangle \mapsto |10\rangle$. Write the latter state as a vector:

$$|10\rangle \mapsto \begin{pmatrix} 0 \\ 0 \\ 1 \\ 0 \end{pmatrix}$$

The third element is associated with $|10\rangle$.

$|11\rangle$ *Idealized State:*

The top qubit, $|q_1\rangle = |1\rangle$, is a pass-through. So it's unchanged by the gate.

The bottom qubit, $|q_2\rangle = |1\rangle$, becomes $i|1\rangle$ when acted on by the S gate in accordance with the gate matrix A_S. Thus, $|11\rangle \mapsto i|11\rangle$. Write the latter state as a vector:

$$|11\rangle \mapsto \begin{pmatrix} 0 \\ 0 \\ 0 \\ i \end{pmatrix}$$

These vectors then form the columns of the 4×4 matrix for the pass-through two-qubit S gate:

$$\begin{bmatrix} 1 & 0 & 0 & 0 \\ 0 & i & 0 & 0 \\ 0 & 0 & 1 & 0 \\ 0 & 0 & 0 & i \end{bmatrix}$$

Now, the matrices for both the pass-through S gate and the CZ gate are the same size. Thus, you can multiply their matrices to get how these gates act on $|11\rangle$:

$$|\psi_1\psi_2\rangle = A_Z A_S|11\rangle$$

$$= \begin{bmatrix} 1 & 0 & 0 & 0 \\ 0 & 1 & 0 & 0 \\ 0 & 0 & 1 & 0 \\ 0 & 0 & 0 & -1 \end{bmatrix} \begin{bmatrix} 1 & 0 & 0 & 0 \\ 0 & i & 0 & 0 \\ 0 & 0 & 1 & 0 \\ 0 & 0 & 0 & i \end{bmatrix} \begin{pmatrix} 0 \\ 0 \\ 0 \\ 1 \end{pmatrix}$$

$$= \begin{pmatrix} 0 \\ 0 \\ 0 \\ -i \end{pmatrix}$$

Notice that the order of multiplying the matrices A_Z and A_S is opposite to the order in which the corresponding gates are applied to the input state $|11\rangle$. Also, the input state $|11\rangle$ is replaced with its vector in the previous equation.

Quantum Circuit Synthesis, or Guess the Gate

The gate matrix technique is a useful tool to analyze how gates modify quantum states. But they can also guide you to select gates that transform a given quantum state to another. For example, suppose you want to take a state that has a triangle $|1\rangle$ qubelet to one that has an inverted pentagon $|0\rangle$ qubelet, as shown in the following figure:

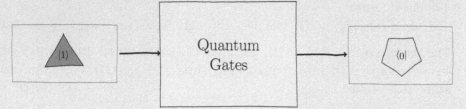

The vector for the quantum state with the single triangle $|1\rangle$ qubelet is:

$$\begin{pmatrix} 0 \\ 1 \end{pmatrix}$$

And, the vector for the quantum state after the quantum operations is:

$$\begin{pmatrix} -1 \\ 0 \end{pmatrix}$$

Thus, you can represent this change of state by the following equation:

$$A_0 \begin{pmatrix} 0 \\ 1 \end{pmatrix} = \begin{pmatrix} -1 \\ 0 \end{pmatrix}$$

The matrix A_0 represents a sequence of quantum operations implemented by hooking up quantum gates. To determine the gate matrices that underpin these quantum operations, apply matrix operations to tease apart A_0 to reveal the gates.

Since a triangle $|1\rangle$ qubelet on the left is switched to a pentagon $|0\rangle$ qubelet on the right, albeit inverted, it seems reasonable that a NOT gate will be a part of this sequence of gates. So, modify the A_0 matrix by "pulling" the matrix for the NOT gate out, as follows:

$$A_0 = A_{NOT} A_1$$

$$= \begin{bmatrix} 0 & 1 \\ 1 & 0 \end{bmatrix} A_1$$

Substituting for A_0 in the previous equation:

$$\begin{bmatrix} 0 & 1 \\ 1 & 0 \end{bmatrix} A_1 \begin{pmatrix} 0 \\ 1 \end{pmatrix} = \begin{pmatrix} -1 \\ 0 \end{pmatrix}$$

As A_1 still needs to be determined, simplify the left hand side by multiplying both sides by the Hermitian transpose of A_{NOT}:

$$\begin{bmatrix} 0 & 1 \\ 1 & 0 \end{bmatrix}\begin{bmatrix} 0 & 1 \\ 1 & 0 \end{bmatrix}A_1\begin{pmatrix} 0 \\ 1 \end{pmatrix} = \begin{bmatrix} 0 & 1 \\ 1 & 0 \end{bmatrix}\begin{pmatrix} -1 \\ 0 \end{pmatrix}$$

$$A_1\begin{pmatrix} 0 \\ 1 \end{pmatrix} = \begin{pmatrix} 0 \\ -1 \end{pmatrix}$$

Thus, A_1 represents a gate that leaves the pentagon $|0\rangle$ qubelets alone but inverts the triangle $|1\rangle$ qubelets. That is, A_1 represents a Z gate.

In other words, the triangle $|1\rangle$ qubelet can be made into an inverted pentagon $|0\rangle$ qubelet by first applying the NOT gate, followed by the Z gate. This operation is expressed as follows:

$$A_Z A_{NOT}\begin{pmatrix} 0 \\ 1 \end{pmatrix} = \begin{pmatrix} -1 \\ 0 \end{pmatrix}$$

Notice that the gate matrices are written in the order opposite in which they're applied to the qubit.

We're making the assumption that the NOT gate is applied last. If it turns out that we hit a dead end and are unable to get the quantum state we want, we try other placements of the NOT gate's matrix A_{NOT}.

The multiplication of the matrices with the vector for $|11\rangle$ results in the quantum state $-i|11\rangle$:

$$|11\rangle \mapsto i|11\rangle$$

Once again, to convince yourself that the matrix procedure gives the correct result, you can reason this circuit out manually: the S gate on the bottom qubit, $|1\rangle$, rotates its triangle $|1\rangle$ qubelet by $\pi/2$ radians, or a quarter turn anticlockwise. Since, the control qubit to the CZ gate is $|1\rangle$, the CZ gate will rotate the triangle $|1\rangle$ qubelet on the target qubit on the bottom by a half turn. So, the triangle $|1\rangle$ qubelet will end up rotated a quarter turn clockwise, or $-\pi/2$ radians, as shown in the figure on page 248.

Analyzing existing circuit designs is useful to pick up ways to work with qubits. But eventually you'll want to twist qubelets in ways unique to your application. So in the next section, you'll learn how matrices also help to identify the gates you'll need in your own designs.

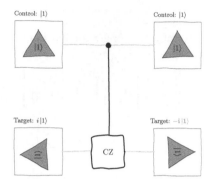

The circuits in this section were initialized with idealized states. In the next section, you'll learn to work with circuits seeded with blended states obtained as a result of a previous computation.

Working with Blended States: Mega-Qubit as a Tensor

As you start working with larger quantum circuits, you'll analyze chunks of it at a time. Consequently, you'll need to consider blended states that are the result of previous parts of your circuit. Consider the following circuit, where the bottom qubit is in a blended state:

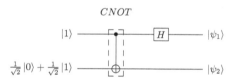

Specifically, the bottom qubit has a single pentagon $|0\rangle$ qubelet and a single triangle $|1\rangle$ qubelet, as shown in the following figure.

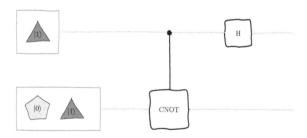

When working with quantum computers, you shouldn't consider qubits as individual units as you would when working with classical bits in conventional computers. Rather, you should think about them as forming a "super" qubit, as described in Multi-Qubit Superposition: The Mega-Qubit, on page 91, made up of all combinations of qubelets from both qubits. An example is shown in the following figure.

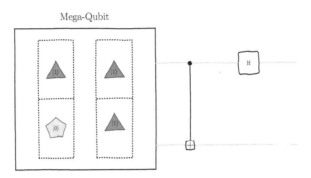

The single triangle $|1\rangle$ qubelet in the top qubit combines with the two qubelets in the bottom qubit to form the two qubelet combinations, $|10\rangle$ and $|11\rangle$, in the mega-qubit shown on the left in the previous figure.

Quantum physicists write these combinations using the *tensor* operator, $\otimes$, as follows:

$$|1\rangle \otimes \left(\frac{1}{\sqrt{2}} |0\rangle + \frac{1}{\sqrt{2}} |1\rangle \right) = \frac{1}{\sqrt{2}} |1\rangle \, |0\rangle + \frac{1}{\sqrt{2}} |1\rangle \, |1\rangle$$

$$= \frac{1}{\sqrt{2}} |10\rangle + \frac{1}{\sqrt{2}} |11\rangle$$

In other words, the tensor operator couples each qubelet on the left of it to each qubelet on its right. Thus, the quantum state of the mega-qubit in terms of a vector is:

$$|1\rangle \otimes \left(\frac{1}{\sqrt{2}} |0\rangle + \frac{1}{\sqrt{2}} |1\rangle \right) = \begin{pmatrix} 0 \\ 0 \\ \frac{1}{\sqrt{2}} \\ \frac{1}{\sqrt{2}} \end{pmatrix} = \frac{1}{\sqrt{2}} \begin{pmatrix} 0 \\ 0 \\ 1 \\ 1 \end{pmatrix}$$

Now that we've represented the blended-state inputs to this quantum circuit, we can analyze how the circuit will modify them by using the gate matrix multiplication technique described in Two-Qubit Gate Matrices, on page 238.

Joe asks:

What Are Tensors?

Perhaps due to their origins in Einstein's general theory of relativity, a topic that rivals quantum mechanics in terms of mastering the underlying mathematics, tensors can seem pretty daunting if you're seeing them for the first time. But, in quantum computing, they describe the mega-qubit.

The *tensor* operator, $\otimes$, is used to enumerate qubelet combinations in a mega-qubit. For example, consider two quantum states, $|\psi_1\rangle$ and $|\psi_2\rangle$, as follows:

$$|\psi_1\rangle = a|0\rangle + b|1\rangle$$
$$|\psi_2\rangle = c|0\rangle + d|1\rangle$$

The tensor product of the two states, $|\psi_1\rangle \otimes |\psi_2\rangle$, is similar to multiplying polynomials:

$$|\psi_1\rangle \otimes |\psi_2\rangle = (a|0\rangle + b|1\rangle) \otimes (c|0\rangle + d|1\rangle)$$
$$= ac|0\rangle|0\rangle + ad|0\rangle|1\rangle + bc|1\rangle|0\rangle + bd|1\rangle|1\rangle$$
$$= ac|00\rangle + ad|01\rangle + bc|10\rangle + bd|11\rangle$$

Note that in the above equation, states of the form $|\psi_1\rangle|\psi_2\rangle$ are combined under a single *ket*: $|\psi_1\psi_2\rangle$. Also, maintain the order of the $|0\rangle$s and $|1\rangle$s and don't switch them around. That is, don't write, say, the second terms as $ad|10\rangle$ where the first and second qubits are swapped—it's not the same as $ad|01\rangle$.

Thus, the mega-qubit formed by these two quantum states will contain the qubelet combinations stated above. The coefficients ac, ad, bc, and bd determine the number of times each of the combinations, $|00\rangle$, $|01\rangle$, $|10\rangle$, and $|11\rangle$, appear in the mega-qubit, respectively. In other words, tensors are just a way of organizing the qubelet combinations succinctly.

Once you've represented the mega-qubit formed by individual qubits using tensors, you can then do gate operations directly on the states by modifying the appropriate qubit. For example, if the first qubit is fed to the control of a CNOT gate and the second to the target, the resulting operation can be done by inspection:

$$ac|00\rangle + ad|01\rangle + bc|10\rangle + bd|11\rangle \overset{CNOT}{\mapsto} ac|00\rangle + ad|01\rangle + bc|11\rangle + bd|10\rangle$$

In accordance with the operation of the CNOT gate, only the second qubits in the last two terms are switched.

The tensor operator can also be applied to the vectors for the quantum states:

$$\begin{pmatrix} a \\ b \end{pmatrix} \otimes \begin{pmatrix} c \\ d \end{pmatrix} = \begin{pmatrix} a\begin{pmatrix} c \\ d \end{pmatrix} \\ b\begin{pmatrix} c \\ d \end{pmatrix} \end{pmatrix} = \begin{pmatrix} ac \\ ad \\ bc \\ bd \end{pmatrix}$$

Unlike when multiplying vectors, tensors can be applied even if the dimensions of the vectors are *incompatible*. For instance, you can apply a tensor operator to a single-qubit quantum state and a two-qubit quantum state, an operation that would be illegal if you were multiplying them:

$$\begin{pmatrix} \omega_0 \\ \omega_1 \end{pmatrix} \otimes \begin{pmatrix} \omega_{00} \\ \omega_{01} \\ \omega_{10} \\ \omega_{11} \end{pmatrix} = \begin{vmatrix} \omega_0 \begin{pmatrix} \omega_{00} \\ \omega_{01} \\ \omega_{10} \\ \omega_{11} \end{pmatrix} \\ \omega_1 \begin{pmatrix} \omega_{00} \\ \omega_{01} \\ \omega_{10} \\ \omega_{11} \end{pmatrix} \end{vmatrix} = \begin{vmatrix} \omega_0 \omega_{00} \\ \omega_0 \omega_{01} \\ \omega_0 \omega_{10} \\ \omega_0 \omega_{11} \\ \omega_1 \omega_{00} \\ \omega_1 \omega_{01} \\ \omega_1 \omega_{10} \\ \omega_1 \omega_{11} \end{vmatrix}$$

The coefficients ω_0 and ω_1 are the amplitudes of the single-qubit quantum state. And the coefficients ω_{00}, ω_{01}, ω_{10}, and ω_{11} are the amplitudes of the idealized states for the two-qubit quantum state.

The flexibility of tensors extends to gate matrices too.[a] Our preferred method in this book, though, is to limit the use of tensors to specify the mega-qubit.

---

a.   https://docs.microsoft.com/en-us/quantum/concepts/vectors-and-matrices

To apply this technique, the single-qubit H gate must be made into a two-qubit gate by appending the bottom qubit as a pass-through, as shown in the following figure:

Work out the 4×4 matrix for this pass-through two-qubit gate using the following A_H matrix. For reference, the matrix A_H for the Hadamard (H) Gate, on page 213, is:

$$A_H = \frac{1}{\sqrt{2}} \begin{bmatrix} 1 & 1 \\ 1 & -1 \end{bmatrix}$$

Each column of the gate matrix corresponds to using the four idealized states as inputs:

$|00\rangle$ *Idealized State*

For the idealized state $|00\rangle$, the top qubit is $|0\rangle$ and the bottom qubit is $|0\rangle$. The top $|0\rangle$ qubit is split by the H gate as follows:

$$|0\rangle \mapsto \frac{1}{\sqrt{2}}|0\rangle + \frac{1}{\sqrt{2}}|1\rangle$$

The bottom $|0\rangle$ qubit is a pass-through so remains at $|0\rangle$. Thus, the quantum state after the pass-through H gate is the following mega-qubit:

$$\left(\frac{1}{\sqrt{2}}|0\rangle + \frac{1}{\sqrt{2}}|1\rangle\right) \otimes |0\rangle = \frac{1}{\sqrt{2}}|00\rangle + \frac{1}{\sqrt{2}}|10\rangle$$

Or, in terms of a vector:

$$|00\rangle \mapsto \frac{1}{\sqrt{2}}\begin{pmatrix} 1 \\ 0 \\ 1 \\ 0 \end{pmatrix}$$

$|01\rangle$ *Idealized State*

For the idealized state $|01\rangle$, the top qubit is $|0\rangle$ and the bottom is $|1\rangle$. The top $|0\rangle$ qubit is split by the H gate as follows:

$$|0\rangle \mapsto \frac{1}{\sqrt{2}}|0\rangle + \frac{1}{\sqrt{2}}|1\rangle$$

The bottom $|1\rangle$ qubit is a pass-through so remains at $|1\rangle$. Thus, the quantum state after the pass-through H gate is the following mega-qubit:

$$\left(\frac{1}{\sqrt{2}}|0\rangle + \frac{1}{\sqrt{2}}|1\rangle\right) \otimes |1\rangle = \frac{1}{\sqrt{2}}|01\rangle + \frac{1}{\sqrt{2}}|11\rangle$$

Or, in terms of a vector:

$$|01\rangle \mapsto \frac{1}{\sqrt{2}}\begin{pmatrix} 0 \\ 1 \\ 0 \\ 1 \end{pmatrix}$$

$|10\rangle$ *Idealized State*

For the idealized state $|10\rangle$, the top qubit is $|1\rangle$ and the bottom qubit is $|0\rangle$. The top $|1\rangle$ qubit is split by the H gate as follows:

$$|1\rangle \mapsto \frac{1}{\sqrt{2}}|0\rangle - \frac{1}{\sqrt{2}}|1\rangle$$

The bottom $|0\rangle$ qubit is a pass-through so remains at $|0\rangle$. Thus, the quantum state after the pass-through H gate is the following mega-qubit:

$$\left(\frac{1}{\sqrt{2}}|0\rangle - \frac{1}{\sqrt{2}}|1\rangle\right) \otimes |0\rangle = \frac{1}{\sqrt{2}}|00\rangle - \frac{1}{\sqrt{2}}|10\rangle$$

Or, in terms of a vector:

$$|10\rangle \mapsto \frac{1}{\sqrt{2}}\begin{pmatrix} 1 \\ 0 \\ -1 \\ 0 \end{pmatrix}$$

$|11\rangle$ *Idealized State*

For the $|11\rangle$ idealized state, the top qubit is $|1\rangle$ and the bottom qubit is $|0\rangle$. The top $|1\rangle$ qubit is split by the H gate as follows:

$$|11\rangle \mapsto \frac{1}{\sqrt{2}}|0\rangle - \frac{1}{\sqrt{2}}|1\rangle$$

The bottom $|1\rangle$ qubit is a pass-through so remains at $|1\rangle$. Thus, the quantum state after the pass-through H gate is the following mega-qubit:

$$\left(\frac{1}{\sqrt{2}}|0\rangle - \frac{1}{\sqrt{2}}|1\rangle\right) \otimes |1\rangle = \frac{1}{\sqrt{2}}|01\rangle - \frac{1}{\sqrt{2}}|11\rangle$$

Or, in terms of a vector:

$$|11\rangle \mapsto \frac{1}{\sqrt{2}}\begin{pmatrix} 0 \\ 1 \\ 0 \\ -1 \end{pmatrix}$$

To get the 4×4 matrix for this pass-through two-qubit H gate, arrange these four vectors as the columns of a matrix A_{H_2}:

$$A_{H_2} = \frac{1}{\sqrt{2}}\begin{bmatrix} 1 & 0 & 1 & 0 \\ 0 & 1 & 0 & 1 \\ 1 & 0 & -1 & 0 \\ 0 & 1 & 0 & -1 \end{bmatrix}$$

Now both the gates in the circuit are identical 4×4 matrices. So we can multiply them with the 4×1 quantum state vector for the input mega-qubit and get the output mega-qubit $|\psi_1\psi_2\rangle$:

$$|\psi_1\psi_2\rangle = A_{H_2} A_{CNOT} \frac{1}{\sqrt{2}} \begin{pmatrix} 0 \\ 0 \\ 1 \\ 1 \end{pmatrix}$$

$$= \frac{1}{\sqrt{2}} \frac{1}{\sqrt{2}} \begin{bmatrix} 1 & 0 & 1 & 0 \\ 0 & 1 & 0 & 1 \\ 1 & 0 & -1 & 0 \\ 0 & 1 & 0 & -1 \end{bmatrix} \begin{bmatrix} 1 & 0 & 0 & 0 \\ 0 & 1 & 0 & 0 \\ 0 & 0 & 0 & 1 \\ 0 & 0 & 1 & 0 \end{bmatrix} \begin{pmatrix} 0 \\ 0 \\ 1 \\ 1 \end{pmatrix}$$

$$= \frac{1}{2} \begin{bmatrix} 1 & 0 & 0 & 1 \\ 0 & 1 & 1 & 0 \\ 1 & 0 & 0 & -1 \\ 0 & 1 & -1 & 0 \end{bmatrix} \begin{pmatrix} 0 \\ 0 \\ 1 \\ 1 \end{pmatrix}$$

$$= \frac{1}{2} \begin{pmatrix} 1 \\ 1 \\ -1 \\ -1 \end{pmatrix}$$

Note that the the gate matrices are multiplied in the reverse order in which they act on the two qubits.

The $|\psi_1\psi_2\rangle$ mega-qubit corresponds to:

$$|\psi_1\psi_2\rangle = \frac{1}{2}|00\rangle + \frac{1}{2}|01\rangle - \frac{1}{2}|10\rangle - \frac{1}{2}|11\rangle$$

Notice that the negative signs are associated with the idealized states and not with individual qubits.

The qubelet columns in the mega-qubit are a reflection of the idealized states in the quantum state. In essence, it encapsulates the quantum state in a graphical way. The mega-qubit representation of the quantum state, however, reveals a subtlety not readily apparent from writing it out as an equation. In the next section, we explore how the mega-qubit manages to keep this trick up its sleeve.

Rotating Qubelets in the Mega-Qubit

To illustrate the curious property of a mega-qubit, consider the quantum state $|\psi_1\psi_2\rangle$ stated earlier:

$$|\psi_1\psi_2\rangle = \frac{1}{2}|00\rangle + \frac{1}{2}|01\rangle - \frac{1}{2}|10\rangle - \frac{1}{2}|11\rangle$$

The mega-qubit corresponding to this quantum state is shown in the figure on page 255.

Mega-Qubit for $|\psi_1\psi_2\rangle$

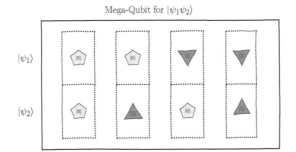

The triangle $|1\rangle$ qubelets in the top cell of the third and fourth qubelet combinations are inverted. This gives the negative signs associated with these qubelet combinations in the quantum state equation.

But, you could also straighten these triangle $|1\rangle$ qubelets in the top cell and instead invert the qubelets in the third and fourth columns, as shown in the following figure:

Equivalent Mega-Qubit for $|\psi_1\psi_2\rangle$ After Rotating Qubelets

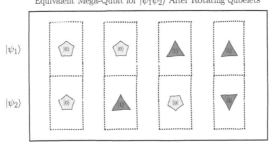

Because of the inverted qubelets in the bottom cell of the third and fourth qubelet combinations, these will still have a negative sign in the equation for the quantum state. In other words, it makes no difference which qubelet is rotated in a qubelet combination, they all result in the same quantum state.

In the next section, you'll see the outsized role this curious property of the mega-qubit plays in some of the more exotic quantum algorithms.

Recap

In general, the method to analyze two-qubit circuits boils down to these steps:

- Use tensors to work out the input mega-qubit vector.

- Obtain 2×2 matrices for all gates in the circuit. If necessary, change single-qubit gates to two-qubit gates by appending suitable pass-through qubits.

- Multiply the gate matrices in reverse of the order in which they act on the mega-qubit with the input mega-qubit vector.

In the next section, we demonstrate how the method to analyze two-qubit circuits can be used to design a three-qubit quintessential quantum computing circuit, but using only two-qubit circuits as building blocks.

Design a Teleporting Circuit

As the number of qubits in your circuit increases, these analytic methods using gate matrices or tensors break down. Instead, the idea is to identify patterns that guide your design of quantum algorithms. You'll learn about this more in Chapter 10, Quantum Search, on page 295. In addition to dealing with the growing size of your circuits, another equally important consideration is figuring out how to properly harness quantum effects and designing your algorithms with them in mind. In this section, we'll use the methods introduced in this chapter and analyze a *teleporting* quantum circuit.[3] This circuit shares many characteristics for down-to-earth applications such as encrypting messages using quantum theory, described in Chapter 9, Alice in Quantumland—Quantum Cryptography, on page 279.

Our goal as budding quantum computer scientists is to design a quantum program for teleporting.

Although your own applications will vary in their intent and objectives, when designing quantum algorithms, a few broad strokes are common:

- Identify relevant quantum effects that are the most suitable for the problem.
- Implement the quantum effects.
- Refine the design to properly use the chosen quantum effects.

Admittedly, these are fairly high level. Nonetheless, they're important to explicitly state since quantum effects rarely come in tidy packages that solve your problem cleanly. More likely, as you'll see shortly, your program will need to account for the different ways that the qubelets collapse before you can complete your design. You'll see these steps play out when designing the circuit for teleporting, as well as when you build a scheme to securely send messages in Chapter 9, Alice in Quantumland—Quantum Cryptography, on page 279.

Identify Quantum Effects

Throughout the course of this book, you've seen several ways of introducing quantum effects in programs such as switching on page 205, rotating on page 206, and splitting on page 213 qubelets. But these effects are *local* in the sense

---

3. https://docs.microsoft.com/en-us/quantum/techniques/putting-it-all-together

\|/ **Joe asks:**
ʒ̊ʒ   # What is Teleporting?

In science fiction, teleporting is when you disappear in one place and magically reappear on the far side of the universe instantly. In the real-life version, we have to contend with a few more details.

In practice, the objects to teleport are few and tiny—roughly the size of qubits. And what's teleported aren't bulky objects but wispy quantum states. The distances, too, are nowhere near cosmic scales. But by far, the most important difference is that, unlike science fiction, qubits don't just materialize out of thin air while teleporting. For teleporting to work, a qubit is first sent to the other place together with a user-guide. The idea is that this qubit becomes the "vessel" which sports the quantum state that will later be teleported.

You also have the engineering aspect of physically getting a qubit from one place to the other to act as the "vessel." For our purposes of designing quantum programs, it'll suffice to lump the operational details into a *quantum channel*. The quantum channel is an abstraction that lets us gloss over the mechanical blueprints—don't think of it as something that you can pick up at your neighborhood hardware store. Our purpose isn't to actually build a teleporting machine but to understand design principles that you can use in practical problems.

that they affect only the qubit that is being acted on. Quantum phenomena can be *nonlocal*, too, where actions on one qubit are intertwined with another qubit, as described in Entangling Qubits, on page 120.

For teleporting, a promising quantum effect to consider is entangling qubits. The basic premise is to keep one and send its entangled twin over a *quantum channel* to the other place. This way, anything you do to one would instantly affect the other—a feature of teleporting. So our initial quantum circuit design looks like the following figure:

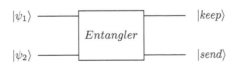

The entangled qubits, $|keep\rangle$ and $|send\rangle$, are called the *carrier* qubits. They form the means by which we teleport the quantum state $|\psi_0\rangle$. The $|keep\rangle$ qubit remains with us and we transfer the $|send\rangle$ qubit to the place we want to teleport a quantum state $|\psi_0\rangle$.

Next, we need a way to "load" the quantum state $|\psi_0\rangle$ we want to teleport to the $|keep\rangle$ qubit, the one we retain. The motivation for loading is that once the quantum state $|\psi_0\rangle$ is tied with the $|keep\rangle$ qubit, it's automatically linked with its entangled twin, the $|send\rangle$ qubit, which was previously sent to the place where the quantum state $|\psi_0\rangle$ The quantum state to load the quantum state $|\psi_0\rangle$ onto the $|keep\rangle$ qubit is shown in the following schematic:

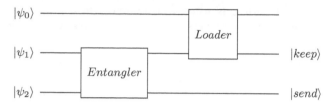

Entangle the $|keep\rangle$ and $|send\rangle$ qubits first before loading the quantum state $|\psi_0\rangle$ to be teleported with the $|keep\rangle$ qubit. Then, at some later point, when you load the quantum state $|\psi_0\rangle$ onto the $|keep\rangle$ qubit, it'll be instantaneously transmitted to the $|send\rangle$ qubit. Otherwise, if the quantum state $|\psi_0\rangle$ was first loaded onto the $|keep\rangle$ qubit and then the $|keep\rangle$ qubit was entangled with the $|send\rangle$ qubit, the $|send\rangle$ qubit would, in effect, be physically transporting the state to the other place, as it would do in classical communication.

We end up with a three-qubit circuit. In the next section, we break up the three-qubit circuit into two-qubit sections and then combine the results to get the overall design.

Implement Quantum Effects

One way to continue with the design is to generalize the matrix multiplication technique to three-qubit circuits. Although this can be done, we'll get unwieldy 8×8 matrices and 8×1 vectors. Instead, we'll design each block individually as a two-qubit circuit.

Design Entangler Block

In this part of the circuit, the $|keep\rangle$ and $|send\rangle$ qubits are entangled using the following circuit:

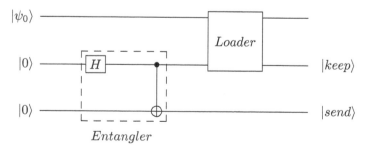

The gates in the dotted box entangle the $|keep\rangle$ and $|send\rangle$ qubits. In Intuition Behind Entanglement, on page 120, we used mega-qubits to demonstrate that the two qubits are entangled. Here we'll do the same, but using the gate matrices.

The single-qubit H gate is first "converted" to a two-qubit pass-through H gate. As shown in the previous section, it's matrix A_{H_2} is:

$$A_{H_2} = \frac{1}{\sqrt{2}} \begin{bmatrix} 1 & 0 & 1 & 0 \\ 0 & 1 & 0 & 1 \\ 1 & 0 & -1 & 0 \\ 0 & 1 & 0 & -1 \end{bmatrix}$$

And for the CNOT gate, its matrix A_{CNOT} is:

$$A_{CNOT} = \begin{bmatrix} 1 & 0 & 0 & 0 \\ 0 & 1 & 0 & 0 \\ 0 & 0 & 0 & 1 \\ 0 & 0 & 1 & 0 \end{bmatrix}$$

Thus, the matrix for the entanglement $A_{Entangler}$ is:

$$A_{Entangler} = A_{CNOT} A_{H_2}$$

$$= \frac{1}{\sqrt{2}} \begin{bmatrix} 1 & 0 & 0 & 0 \\ 0 & 1 & 0 & 0 \\ 0 & 0 & 0 & 1 \\ 0 & 0 & 1 & 0 \end{bmatrix} \begin{bmatrix} 1 & 0 & 1 & 0 \\ 0 & 1 & 0 & 1 \\ 1 & 0 & -1 & 0 \\ 0 & 1 & 0 & -1 \end{bmatrix}$$

$$= \frac{1}{\sqrt{2}} \begin{bmatrix} 1 & 0 & 1 & 0 \\ 0 & 1 & 0 & 1 \\ 0 & 1 & 0 & -1 \\ 1 & 0 & -1 & 0 \end{bmatrix}$$

Since the $|keep\rangle$ and $|send\rangle$ qubits are initialized to $|0\rangle$, their entangled state $|keep\ send\rangle$ is given by the first column of the previous matrix:

$$|keep\ send\rangle = \frac{1}{\sqrt{2}} \begin{pmatrix} 1 \\ 0 \\ 0 \\ 1 \end{pmatrix}$$

This corresponds to the following state for $|keep\ send\rangle$:

$$|keep\ send\rangle = \frac{1}{\sqrt{2}} |00\rangle + \frac{1}{\sqrt{2}} |11\rangle$$

Even though the $|keep\rangle$ and $|send\rangle$ qubits are part of the same circuit, they'll ultimately be separated. To remind us of their distinct existence, we'll write them as follows:

$$|keep\ send\rangle = |keep\rangle\ |send\rangle$$

Thus, we'll also write their state as:

$$|keep\rangle\ |send\rangle = \frac{1}{\sqrt{2}}|0\rangle\ |0\rangle + \frac{1}{\sqrt{2}}|1\rangle\ |1\rangle$$

You can confirm that this state is entangled by imagining collapsing, say, the first qubit. Since this quantum state has only two qubelet combinations, $|00\rangle$ and $|11\rangle$, if you see a $|0\rangle$, the $|keep\ send\rangle$ quantum state has collapsed to $|00\rangle$. Thus, the second qubit is guaranteed to be $|0\rangle$. Likewise, if the first qubit collapsed to $|1\rangle$, the $|keep\rangle\ |send\rangle$ quantum state collapses to $|11\rangle$, forcing the second qubit to $|1\rangle$. A similar argument holds if you instead measured the second qubit.

So no matter which qubit you measure, the other's fate is automatically determined.

Now that we've established that the $|keep\rangle\ |send\rangle$ state is entangled, don't collapse it, but *load* the quantum state $|\psi_0\rangle$ onto the $|keep\rangle$ qubit.

Design Loader Block

Loading the quantum state $|\psi_0\rangle$ onto the $|keep\rangle$ qubit doesn't mean that the latter somehow physically "carries" the former. Rather, quantum mechanics gives you the ability to create a "joint" state—a mega-qubit—in which the quantum state $|\psi_0\rangle$ is combined with that of $|keep\rangle$.

We'd like to create the "joint" state in such a way that no matter which way $|keep\rangle$ collapses, the quantum state $|\psi_0\rangle$ is recoverable. One way to create such a mega-qubit is to use the following *loader* circuit:

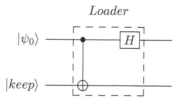

Loader

To see how this circuit creates a mega-qubit where the quantum state $|\psi_0\rangle$ is tied with $|keep\rangle$, start by writing $|\psi_0\rangle$ in terms of the idealized states:

$$|\psi_0\rangle = \omega_0|0\rangle + \omega_1|1\rangle$$

The coefficients ω_0 and ω_1 are the amplitudes associated with $|0\rangle$ and $|1\rangle$, respectively.

$|\psi_0\rangle$ then interacts with $|keep\rangle$ to form the following mega-qubit:

$$|\psi_0\rangle \otimes |keep\rangle = (\omega_0 |0\rangle + \omega_1 |1\rangle) \otimes |keep\rangle$$
$$= \omega_0 |0\ keep\rangle + \omega_1 |1\ keep\rangle$$

Notice that for this circuit, we've not separated the qubits. That is, we've written $|0\ keep\rangle$ instead of $|0\rangle |keep\rangle$. The reason is that both the $|\psi_0\rangle$ and $|keep\rangle$ qubits remain together, not separated from each other like the $|send\rangle$ qubit.

The first qubit in each term is fed to the control of the CNOT gate and the $|keep\rangle$ qubit to its target.

It'll be easier to see how this circuit works if we work with the $|keep\rangle$ qubit in the abstract without writing it in terms of the idealized states. Since we then won't have the coefficients of the idealized states, we can't write the state as a vector and won't be able to use the matrix method. So we'll analyze the circuit by inspection.

The mega-qubit consists of two terms: $\omega_0 |0\ keep\rangle$ and $\omega_1 |1\ keep\rangle$. We'll analyze how the loader circuit affects each term separately.

$\omega_0 |0\ keep\rangle$ Term

When the control is $\omega_0 |0\rangle$, the target is left alone. Thus, $\omega_0 |0\ keep\rangle$ is unaffected by the CNOT gate.

The H gate splits the first qubit, $|0\rangle$:

$$\omega_0 |0\ keep\rangle \mapsto \omega_0 \left(\frac{1}{\sqrt{2}} |0\rangle + \frac{1}{\sqrt{2}} |1\rangle\right) |keep\rangle$$
$$= \frac{\omega_0}{\sqrt{2}} |0\ keep\rangle + \frac{\omega_0}{\sqrt{2}} |1\ keep\rangle$$

$\omega_1 |1\ keep\rangle$ Term

When the control is $\omega_1 |1\rangle$, the target is switched. Thus, $|1\ keep\rangle$ is modified by the CNOT gate as follows:

$$\omega_1 |1\ keep\rangle \mapsto \omega_1 |1\ KEEP\rangle$$

Here $|KEEP\rangle$ is the complement of $|keep\rangle$. That is,

$$|KEEP\rangle = |1\rangle - |keep\rangle$$

In other words, $|KEEP\rangle$ is the same as $NOT(|keep\rangle)$ or $|\overline{keep}\rangle$. We use capitals since it's less clutter and makes the equations easier to read.

The H gate splits the first qubit, $|1\rangle$:

$$\omega_1 |1\ KEEP\rangle \ \mapsto\ \omega_1\left(\frac{1}{\sqrt{2}}|0\rangle - \frac{1}{\sqrt{2}}|1\rangle\right)|KEEP\rangle$$

$$= \frac{\omega_1}{\sqrt{2}}|0\ KEEP\rangle - \frac{\omega_1}{\sqrt{2}}|1\ KEEP\rangle$$

Thus, the quantum state after the loader circuit acts on the qubits is:

$$\omega_0 |0\ keep\rangle + \omega_1 |1\ keep\rangle \mapsto \frac{\omega_0}{\sqrt{2}}|0\ keep\rangle + \frac{\omega_0}{\sqrt{2}}|1\ keep\rangle + \frac{\omega_1}{\sqrt{2}}|0\ KEEP\rangle - \frac{\omega_1}{\sqrt{2}}|1\ KEEP\rangle$$

Rearrange the terms so that the $|0\rangle$ states are grouped together; the same goes for the $|1\rangle$ states:

$$\omega_0 |0\ keep\rangle + \omega_1 |1\ keep\rangle \mapsto |0\rangle\left(\frac{\omega_0}{\sqrt{2}}|keep\rangle + \frac{\omega_1}{\sqrt{2}}|KEEP\rangle\right) + |1\rangle\left(\frac{\omega_0}{\sqrt{2}}|keep\rangle - \frac{\omega_1}{\sqrt{2}}|KEEP\rangle\right)$$

In the quantum state on the right-hand side, the amplitudes ω_0 and ω_1 that defined the quantum state $|\psi_0\rangle$ are now associated with the $|keep\rangle$ qubit. In other words, the loader circuit takes the amplitudes for the state to be teleported, $|\psi_0\rangle$, and transfers them to the $|keep\rangle$ qubit.

At this point, we have a chain of quantum effects: the $|keep\rangle$ is entangled with $|send\rangle$, and the quantum state $|\psi_0\rangle$ is linked with $|keep\rangle$. In the meantime, the $|send\rangle$ qubit could be millions of miles away beyond the heliosphere and in intergalactic space. So in the next section, we'll see how the quantum state $|\psi_0\rangle$ becomes associated with the $|send\rangle$ qubit too.

Evaluating the Teleporting Circuit

To illustrate teleporting, we'll use the qubit in the following figure:

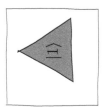

This qubit has a single triangle $|1\rangle$ qubelet rotated a quarter turn clockwise. It's quantum state $|\psi_0\rangle$ is:

$$|\psi_0\rangle = i|1\rangle$$

We'll teleport this rotated triangle $|1\rangle$ qubelet. That is, we'll show that the teleporting circuit relays the information that defines the quantum state $|\psi_0\rangle$ through the $|keep\rangle$ qubit to its entangled partner, the $|send\rangle$ qubit. The teleporting circuit is shown in figure on page 263.

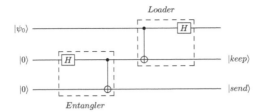

Next, we'll work out the *teleporting* mega-qubit associated with this circuit.

Teleporting Mega-Qubit

The $|keep\rangle$ and $|send\rangle$ qubits are first entangled as described in the previous section. This results in the following mega-qubit:

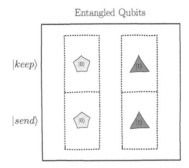

This mega-qubit has two qubelet combinations: $|00\rangle$ and $|11\rangle$.

To remind us that the $|send\rangle$ qubit is physically separated from the $|keep\rangle$ qubit, we'll draw the qubelet combinations so that the qubelets associated with the $|send\rangle$ qubit, the bottom qubelets in each column, are detached, as shown in the following figure:

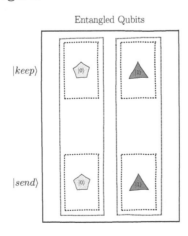

Even when disconnected, however, the two qubits are still entangled and act as a unit, shown within the outer dotted box of each qubelet combination—one of the bizarre characteristics of quantum mechanics.

The single 90° rotated triangle $|1\rangle$ qubelet of $|\psi_0\rangle$ then joins with the qubelet combinations of those of the $|keep\rangle$ and $|send\rangle$ qubits forming the complete mega-qubit having two qubelet combinations for this three-qubit circuit, as shown in the following figure:

Teleporting Mega-Qubit

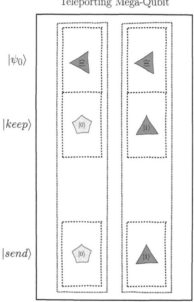

Since this mega-qubit can collapse to either of these qubelet combinations with equal probability, normalize the chances of picking each qubelet combination to get the mega-qubit's quantum state following the procedure similar to that described in Normalizing Qubelets, on page 144, but for qubelet combinations instead of qubelets:

$$|\psi_0\rangle = \frac{i}{\sqrt{1^2 + 1^2}}|10\rangle\ |0\rangle\ +\ \frac{i}{\sqrt{1^2 + 1^2}}|11\rangle\ |1\rangle$$
$$= \frac{i}{\sqrt{2}}|10\rangle\ |0\rangle\ +\ \frac{i}{\sqrt{2}}|11\rangle\ |1\rangle$$

To continue to emphasize that the qubelets for the $|send\rangle$ qubit are physically separate from those of the rest of the circuit, we've pulled the third qubelet in each of the terms of the previous equation out and show it detached from the rest of the quantum state. Thus, you'll see, for example, $i\,|10\rangle\ |0\rangle$, instead of $i\,|100\rangle$.

You can also derive this mega-qubit using the following tensor product:

$$i|1\rangle \otimes \frac{1}{\sqrt{2}}(|0\rangle\, |0\rangle + |1\rangle\, |1\rangle\,) = \frac{i}{\sqrt{2}}\,|10\rangle\, |0\rangle + \frac{i}{\sqrt{2}}\,|11\rangle\, |1\rangle$$

This mega-qubit is then acted on by the *loader* circuit described next.

Loader Circuit on Teleporting Mega-Qubit

We'll use the gate matrix technique to work out how the *loader* circuit modifies the qubelet combinations in the mega-qubit. Visually, we'll confirm that the 90° rotated triangle $|1\rangle$ qubelet gets automatically transferred by quantum effects to the physically distant $|send\rangle$ qubit without you having to do any further programming.

Since the *loader* circuit only affects the first two qubits, we can use the two-qubit gate matrices to analyze how the teleporting mega-qubit is affected by it.

The matrix for the loading circuit, A_{Loader}, is:

$$A_{Loader} = A_{H_2}A_{CNOT}$$

$$= \frac{1}{\sqrt{2}}\begin{bmatrix} 1 & 0 & 1 & 0 \\ 0 & 1 & 0 & 1 \\ 1 & 0 & -1 & 0 \\ 0 & 1 & 0 & -1 \end{bmatrix}\begin{bmatrix} 1 & 0 & 0 & 0 \\ 0 & 1 & 0 & 0 \\ 0 & 0 & 0 & 1 \\ 0 & 0 & 1 & 0 \end{bmatrix}$$

$$= \frac{1}{\sqrt{2}}\begin{bmatrix} 1 & 0 & 0 & 1 \\ 0 & 1 & 1 & 0 \\ 1 & 0 & 0 & -1 \\ 0 & 1 & -1 & 0 \end{bmatrix}$$

You'll use this matrix to work out how it affects each of the qubelet combinations.

When depicting qubelet combinations in the mega-qubit, retain the complex part of the amplitudes. These relate to the relative difference in rotations between the qubelets in each combination. The real part of the amplitudes is associated with the likelihoods of selecting a qubelet combination. In the mega-qubit, they translate to the number of qubelet combinations.

Next, analyze each qubelet combination individually and then aggregate them to get the final complete mega-qubit.

$\frac{i}{\sqrt{2}}\,|10\rangle\, |0\rangle$ *Qubelet Combination*

The first two qubelets, $i|10\rangle$, in this combination are from the $|\psi_0\rangle$ and the $|keep\rangle$ qubits. Thus, the vector for the "partial" quantum state that's applied to the *loader* circuit is:

$$\frac{i}{\sqrt{2}}\begin{pmatrix} 0 \\ 0 \\ 1 \\ 0 \end{pmatrix}$$

The *loader* circuit modifies this partial state as follows:

$$A_{Loader}\frac{i}{\sqrt{2}}\begin{pmatrix} 0 \\ 0 \\ 1 \\ 0 \end{pmatrix} = \frac{1}{\sqrt{2}}\begin{bmatrix} 1 & 0 & 0 & 1 \\ 0 & 1 & 1 & 0 \\ 1 & 0 & 0 & -1 \\ 0 & 1 & -1 & 0 \end{bmatrix}\frac{i}{\sqrt{2}}\begin{pmatrix} 0 \\ 0 \\ 1 \\ 0 \end{pmatrix}$$

$$= \frac{i}{2}\begin{pmatrix} 0 \\ 1 \\ 0 \\ -1 \end{pmatrix}$$

This vector corresponds to the following qubelet combination:

$$\frac{i}{2}\begin{pmatrix} 0 \\ 1 \\ 0 \\ -1 \end{pmatrix} = \frac{i}{2}(\,|01\rangle - |11\rangle\,) = \frac{i}{2}|01\rangle - \frac{i}{2}|11\rangle$$

To get the full qubelet combination, append the third qubelet from the |*send*⟩ qubit:

$$\left(\frac{i}{2}|01\rangle - \frac{i}{2}|11\rangle\right)|0\rangle = \frac{i}{2}|01\rangle\,|0\rangle - \frac{i}{2}|11\rangle\,|0\rangle$$

The corresponding qubelet combination is shown in the figure on page 267.

Notice that the qubelets of the $|\psi_0\rangle$ quantum state in the top cell of each qubelet combination are rotated by quarter turns as dictated by their respective amplitudes in the previous equation.

$\frac{i}{\sqrt{2}}|11\rangle\,|1\rangle$ *Qubelet Combination*

The first two qubelets, $i|11\rangle$, in this qubelet combination are from the $|\psi_0\rangle$ and |*keep*⟩ qubits. Thus, the vector for the "partial" quantum state that's applied to the *loader* circuit is:

$$\frac{i}{\sqrt{2}}\begin{pmatrix} 0 \\ 0 \\ 0 \\ 1 \end{pmatrix}$$

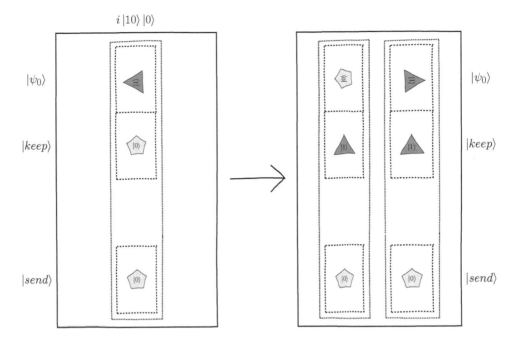

The *loader* circuit modifies this partial state as follows:

$$
A_{Loader} \frac{i}{\sqrt{2}} \begin{pmatrix} 0 \\ 0 \\ 0 \\ 1 \end{pmatrix} = \frac{1}{\sqrt{2}} \begin{bmatrix} 1 & 0 & 0 & 1 \\ 0 & 1 & 1 & 0 \\ 1 & 0 & 0 & -1 \\ 0 & 1 & -1 & 0 \end{bmatrix} \frac{i}{\sqrt{2}} \begin{pmatrix} 0 \\ 0 \\ 0 \\ 1 \end{pmatrix}
$$

$$
= \frac{i}{2} \begin{pmatrix} 1 \\ 0 \\ -1 \\ 0 \end{pmatrix}
$$

This vector corresponds to the following qubelet combination:

$$
\frac{i}{2} \begin{pmatrix} 1 \\ 0 \\ -1 \\ 0 \end{pmatrix} = \frac{i}{2}(\,|00\rangle \, - \, |10\rangle \,) = \frac{i}{2} |00\rangle \, - \frac{i}{2} |10\rangle
$$

To get the full qubelet combination, append the third qubelet from the |*send*⟩ qubit:

$$
\left(\frac{i}{2} |00\rangle \, - \frac{i}{2} |10\rangle \right) |1\rangle \, = \frac{i}{2} |00\rangle \, |1\rangle \, - \frac{i}{2} |10\rangle \, |1\rangle
$$

The corresponding qubelet combination is shown in the following figure:

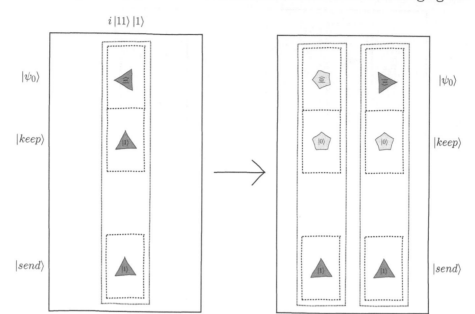

Notice, as in the previous qubelet combination, the qubelets of the $|\psi_0\rangle$ are rotated by quarter turns as required by their respective amplitudes in the previous equation.

These four qubelet combinations then form the complete mega-qubit, as shown in the figure on page 269.

This mega-qubit is the quantum state after the $|keep\rangle$ and $|send\rangle$ qubits have been entangled and the $|\psi_0\rangle$ qubit loaded onto $|keep\rangle$. In other words, the single anticlockwise rotated triangle $|1\rangle$ qubelet should be transferred, or teleported, to the $|send\rangle$ qubit.

Looking at the mega-qubit, however, you don't see a rotated triangle $|1\rangle$ qubelet in any bottom cell for the $|send\rangle$ qubit. To see that the $|send\rangle$ qubit does indeed carry the rotated triangle $|1\rangle$ qubelet, we'll massage the mega-qubit in the next section to reveal the qubelet in the desired orientation.

Refining the Design for Desired Behavior

As we stated at the beginning of this section, rarely will you get a one-to-one match between a quantum effect and the problem you're solving. The idea of using quantum entangling for teleporting seems fitting. But by itself, you won't automatically see the state you want to teleport magically show up on the $|send\rangle$ qubit. So you'll need to add some post-processing to get what you're

Final Teleporting Mega-Qubit

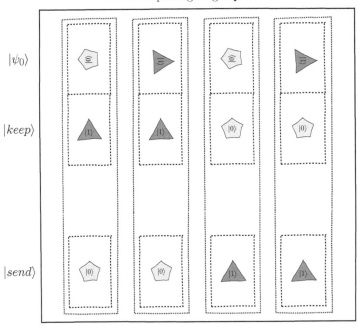

looking for, much like you'd refine a program in a traditional programming language that wasn't performing as designed. So, in this section, you'll see the kinds of steps you'll need to take to shape the end result of the quantum effect to something that actually solves your problem. In Chapter 9, Alice in Quantumland—Quantum Cryptography, on page 279, you'll see a tighter way in which quantum effects and the post quantum processing go hand in hand when designing quantum algorithms.

As a first step, it's a good idea to try rotating qubelets to see if the result pops out. Since it's only the relative difference in rotations between the qubelets that defines quantum states, turning qubelets while retaining the relative difference in their orientations may reveal desired states without affecting the mega-qubit.

Looking at the third qubelet combination, you can get the state you want to teleport by rotating the triangle $|1\rangle$ qubelet in the bottom cell a quarter turn anticlockwise. To keep the state of the entire qubelet combination unchanged, twist an already rotated qubelet a corresponding turn the other way. In this case, rotate the top pentagon $|0\rangle$ qubelet a quarter turn clockwise.

Likewise, rotate the qubelets in the other qubelet combinations so that the top qubelets in each cell go back to their original non-oriented states, while simultaneously rotating the bottom qubelet in each combination an equal amount the other way. As shown in Rotating Qubelets in the Mega-Qubit, on page 254, these rotations don't affect the state of the mega-qubit. These rotations result in the following mega-qubit:

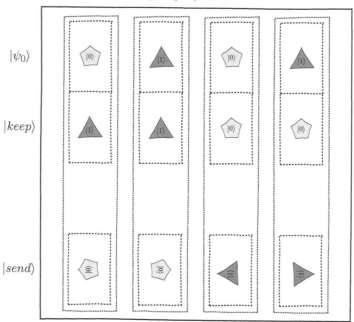

Final Teleporting Mega-Qubit After Rotations

Only the bottom qubelet in the third combination has a triangle $|1\rangle$ qubelet correctly rotated a quarter turn anticlockwise. None of the other qubelet combinations mirror the exact state being teleported. But with a set of deterministic operations, these qubelets can be brought to the required state.

Operations Are Not yet Available in Current Quantum Computers

 The operations you're about to see aren't yet implemented by today's quantum computers. They're part of the theory of quantum computing, though, and you'll see gates that implement them in the future.

Specifically, apply the following operations:

If $|\psi_0\ keep\rangle\ =\ |00\rangle$
   This case corresponds to the third qubelet combination. Its bottom qubelet associated with the $|send\rangle$ qubit correctly reflects the state to be transported. Do nothing.

If $|\psi_0 \, keep\rangle = |01\rangle$

This case corresponds to the first qubelet combination. Its bottom qubelet associated with the $|send\rangle$ qubit is a pentagon $|0\rangle$ qubelet that's rotated a quarter turn clockwise.

To get this qubelet in the proper state, switch it to a triangle $|1\rangle$ qubelet by using a NOT gate. The NOT gate will preserve the quarter turn clockwise rotation.

If $|\psi_0 \, keep\rangle = |10\rangle$

This case corresponds to the fourth qubelet combination. Its bottom qubelet associated with the $|send\rangle$ qubit is a triangle $|1\rangle$ qubelet, but rotated a quarter turn clockwise.

To get this qubelet in the proper orientation, apply a Z gate which inverts or rotates triangle $|1\rangle$ qubelets by a half turn.

If $|\psi_0 \, keep\rangle = |11\rangle$

This case corresponds to the second qubelet combination. Its bottom qubelet associated with the $|send\rangle$ qubit is a pentagon $|0\rangle$ qubelet rotated a quarter turn clockwise.

To get this qubelet in the proper orientation, apply a NOT gate to switch the pentagon $|0\rangle$ qubelet to a triangle $|1\rangle$ qubelet. Then, apply a Z gate to rotate the triangle $|1\rangle$ qubelet by a half turn to bring it to the proper orientation.

With these "post–quantum-processing" steps defined, the teleportation program is complete. If you now collapse the $|\psi_0\rangle$ and $|keep\rangle$ qubits and apply the corresponding operation as listed above, the $|send\rangle$ qubit will reflect the state of $|\psi_0\rangle$.

We have one final loose end to tie up. We worked out the post–quantum-processing steps for a single specific state: a triangle $|1\rangle$ qubit rotated a quarter turn anticlockwise. That is,

$$|\psi_0\rangle = i|1\rangle$$

It just so happens that the same post-processing steps we just worked out also hold when teleporting a general state:

$$|\psi_0\rangle = \omega_0|0\rangle + \omega_1|1\rangle$$

When designing your own algorithms, you can start with a specific state like we did, work out the post–quantum-processing steps for that state and then fine-tune them, if necessary, for the general state. Or you could directly analyze the general state. In the latter case, you'll work with gate matrices on quantum state vectors defined symbolically. The resulting analysis becomes more algebraic than graphical.

Although the teleporting circuit may not be immediately practical, it illustrates a couple of key design principles for quantum algorithms:

- By judiciously breaking up the design into salient blocks involving fewer qubits, we were able to design an algorithm using smaller 4×4 matrices instead of dealing with 8×8 gate matrices for three-qubit circuits.

- Post–quantum-processing steps are an important facet of the algorithmic design, enabling you to correctly harness the power of quantum effects for your problem.

In the next chapter, Chapter 9, Alice in Quantumland—Quantum Cryptography, on page 279, you'll learn how these principles lead to a protocol for highly secure communication.

Bottom Line

With multi-qubit programs, you're finally in a position to introduce quantum effects that give new ways to solve your computational problems. The unique way in which qubelets of multiple qubits pair up with each other results in an exponential number of states that a quantum computer simultaneously deals with.

Although quantum computing affords you this unprecedented capability of juggling the equivalent of many states, getting them to perform a useful computational task is another matter. Representing gates as matrices and then matrix math gives you the means to work with all these states at once. But as the number of qubits increases, matrices become large and unwieldy and won't provide the insight you need to design algorithms. Nonetheless, by breaking up your design into smaller blocks, as you saw with the teleporting circuit, you can design programs that work with more qubits.

A crucial aspect of designing quantum algorithms for your problems is identifying which quantum effect would work best. Even though entangling is a shoo-in for teleporting, in general you won't find such an obvious quantum effect for your problem. As you'll see in the next chapter, you'll use a general quantum phenomenon and then build additional logic around it to solve a particular computational task.

Try Your Hand

Solutions to these exercises are given in Multi-Qubit Programs Solutions, on page 488.

For any code listing in the exercises, assume the following header lines:

```
OPENQASM 2.0;
include "qelib1.inc";
```

1. In each of the following cases, identify the coefficient for the stated idealized state.

    a. What's the amplitude, ω_{01}, for $|01\rangle$ in the following vector?

    $$\begin{pmatrix} 0 \\ \dfrac{1}{\sqrt{2}} \\ 0 \\ i\dfrac{1}{\sqrt{2}} \end{pmatrix}$$

    b. What's the amplitude, ω_{00}, for $|00\rangle$ in the following vector?

    $$\begin{pmatrix} \dfrac{-i}{2} \\ \dfrac{1}{2} \\ \dfrac{1}{2} \\ \dfrac{1}{2} \end{pmatrix}$$

2. Can a 3×3 matrix represent a quantum gate? Explain your answer.

3. Consider a qubit with the following quantum state:

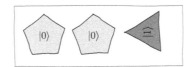

Which of the following is the correct way to write its quantum state?

a. $i|001\rangle$

b.

$$\begin{pmatrix} \dfrac{1}{\sqrt{5}} \\[6pt] \dfrac{1}{\sqrt{5}} \\[6pt] -\dfrac{1}{\sqrt{5}} \end{pmatrix}$$

c. $\dfrac{2}{\sqrt{5}}|0\rangle + \dfrac{i}{\sqrt{5}}|1\rangle$

4. In classical computing, you're encouraged to use print or write statements to look at the values of your program's variables during debugging. In this problem, you'll see the pitfall of placing Measure gates in your quantum programs to examine their states for debugging.

   Consider the following quantum state $|\psi\rangle$:

   $$|\psi\rangle = \frac{2}{5}|00\rangle + \frac{4i}{5}|01\rangle - \frac{i}{5}|10\rangle + \frac{2}{5}|11\rangle$$

   a. Calculate the probabilities of collapsing to each of the four idealized states.

   b. If you measure the second qubit, what is the probability of recording a 1?

   c. If a 1 is logged in the classical register, does the quantum state of the system change? If so, what is the new quantum state?

5. Consider the following 4×4 matrix:

   $$\begin{bmatrix} 1 & 0 & 0 & 0 \\ 0 & 1 & 0 & 0 \\ 0 & 0 & 1 & 0 \\ 0 & 0 & 0 & -i \end{bmatrix}$$

   What type of gate does it describe?

6. In SWAP Gate, on page 52, you saw a quantum gate that swapped the quantum states of two qubits with each other. In a Controlled SWAP Gate, also called a Fredkin gate, the two quantum states $|\psi_1\rangle$ and $|\psi_2\rangle$ are swapped only if the control qubit is $|1\rangle$, as depicted in the figure on page 275.

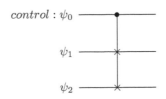

a. What are the dimensions of this gate's matrix?

b. Write out its gate matrix.

7. Determine the matrix for the following quantum circuits:

a.

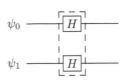

b.

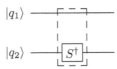

In this case, though, obtain the gate matrix by inspection using the gate matrix of the pass-through S gate computed in Circuits with Single- and Two-Qubit Gates, on page 243, as a reference:

$$A_S = \begin{bmatrix} 1 & 0 & 0 & 0 \\ 0 & i & 0 & 0 \\ 0 & 0 & 1 & 0 \\ 0 & 0 & 0 & i \end{bmatrix}$$

8. For each circuit shown, calculate its matrix:

a.

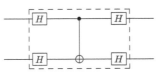

b.

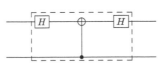

9. When working out the gates to correctly rotate the qubelets in your programs, it's important to bear in mind that you can reorient qubelets without affecting the quantum state of the qubelet combinations. In this exercise, you're asked to identify rotations that maintain the same quantum state.

For each of the qubelet combinations, determine the rotations of the qubelets that make the quantum state of the combination on the right identical to that on the left:

a.

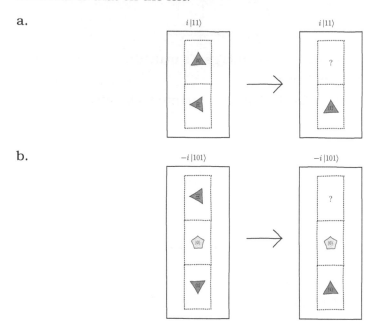

b.

10. As you start writing quantum programs with more qubits, you'll find it useful to easily go back and forth between the tensor product of quantum states and its mega-qubit so that you can see how the gate affects the quantum state. Thus, in the next few problems, you'll test your understanding of tensors and how they relate to the mega-qubit.

Write the quantum state vector and draw the mega-qubit for the following tensor operations:

a. $$|1\rangle \otimes |0\rangle \otimes |1\rangle \otimes |1\rangle \otimes |0\rangle$$

b. $$\frac{1}{\sqrt{2}}(|0\rangle + i|1\rangle) \otimes |0\rangle$$

c. $$\frac{1}{\sqrt{2}}(|0\rangle - i|1\rangle) \otimes \frac{1}{\sqrt{2}}(|0\rangle + i|1\rangle)$$

d. $$|1\rangle \otimes X|1\rangle \otimes H|0\rangle$$

$X|1\rangle$ is the operation of the NOT gate on $|1\rangle$ and $H|0\rangle$ is the operation of the H gate on $|0\rangle$.

11. The ability to factor a quantum state as a tensor product of qubits indicates whether the qubits are entangled. If it's not possible to write the

quantum state as a tensor product of individual qubits, then the qubits can't exist independently of each other and are entangled. In this problem, you'll try factoring quantum states to determine whether the qubits are entangled.

Write the following quantum states as tensor products, if possible, and determine whether the qubits are entangled.

a.
$$|\psi\rangle = \frac{3}{10}|00\rangle + \frac{1}{10}|01\rangle - \frac{9}{10}|10\rangle - \frac{3}{10}|11\rangle$$

b.
$$|\psi\rangle = \frac{1}{\sqrt{2}}|01\rangle + \frac{1}{\sqrt{2}}|10\rangle$$

12. Consider the following tensor product:

$$\frac{1}{\sqrt{2}}(|0\rangle + i|1\rangle) \otimes \frac{1}{\sqrt{2}}(|0\rangle + |1\rangle) \otimes \frac{1}{\sqrt{2}}(|0\rangle - |1\rangle)$$

Its associated mega-qubit is:

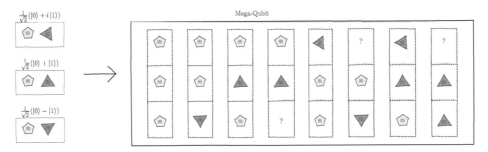

Identify the type and rotation of the three missing qubelets.

13. In quantum computing, the ability to rotate qubelets underpins all quantum effects such as canceling and entangling quantum states. So in this problem, you'll work with a mega-qubit and figure out the quantum circuit that created it.

Look at the following mega-qubit on page 278.

a. Enumerate the ways that this mega-qubit can collapse. For each way, estimate the corresponding probability of the mega-qubit collapsing to it, as well as the state that's logged in a classical register.

b. Write the quantum state for this mega-qubit.

c. Write the quantum state as a tensor product.

d. From the tensor product you found in the previous part, work out a quantum circuit that produces the given mega-qubit.

Mega-Qubit Quantum State $|\psi\rangle = |\psi_0\psi_1\rangle$

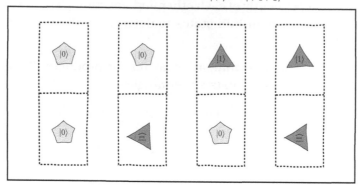

14. Suppose you'd like to teleport two quantum states, $|\psi_1\rangle$ and $|\psi_2\rangle$. Can you use the teleporting circuit described in Design a Teleporting Circuit, on page 256, to teleport the two states one after the other—that is, teleport $|\psi_1\rangle$ and then teleport $|\psi_2\rangle$?

15. Consider the teleporting circuit discussed in Design a Teleporting Circuit, on page 256. Suppose the $|\psi_0\rangle$ and $|keep\rangle$ collapse so that the quantum states for all three qubits are as follows:

$$|\psi_0\rangle \;\mapsto\; |1\rangle$$
$$|keep\rangle \;\mapsto\; |0\rangle$$
$$|send\rangle \;\mapsto\; \frac{1}{\sqrt{2}}|0\rangle - \frac{i}{\sqrt{2}}|1\rangle$$

Refer to Refining the Design for Desired Behavior, on page 268, to determine the quantum state that's teleported.

16. Can the following circuit teleport a quantum state?

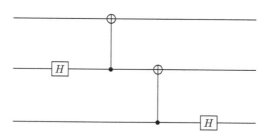

If so, identify the Entangler and Loader parts, and label the $|keep\rangle$, $|send\rangle$, and the qubit holding the quantum state, $|\psi_0\rangle$, to be teleported.

"Curiouser and curiouser!" cried Alice (she was so much surprised, that for the moment she quite forgot how to speak good English).

> — *Lewis Carroll, author of Alice in Wonderland*

## CHAPTER 9

Alice in Quantumland—Quantum Cryptography

Quantum computing has the potential to rapidly factor large numbers. That's a problem for standard cryptography, which relies on classical computers being unable to handle that level of computation.[1,2] When that happens, almost all transactions—financial, medical, business—will be rendered moot, as there would be no reliable way to secretly share information. The situation is so dire that there's a tremendous urgency to find an adequate replacement when quantum computers become commonplace.

In this chapter, you'll learn the main ideas behind quantum cryptographic methods and why quantum mechanics makes such methods inherently safe from eavesdropping and other attempts to break them. To help you build your own intuition when designing quantum algorithms, as in the previous discussion on building a teleporting circuit, we'll identify a suitable quantum effect coupled with additional logic to build a secure protocol for communicating between different parties.

Just as in classical cryptography, any exchange of information entails the use of *keys*. These are binary strings which encrypt and decrypt the message to be sent. The primary challenge in cryptography is the distribution of the keys between the sender and receiver before any message is sent. After reviewing how keys are used to encrypt messages, you'll see how quantum computing provides unique ways to share keys between the parties

---

1. https://www.scottaaronson.com/blog/?p=208
2. https://en.wikipedia.org/wiki/Shor%27s_algorithm

communicating. These methods, with their signature quantum effects, have no classical analogs.

Quantum Channels, Not Mainstream

In quantum cryptography, we'll be sending qubits from one location to another, as we did in Design a Teleporting Circuit, on page 256. Moving qubits takes place over what is loosely called a *quantum channel*—you can't move them over classical transmission cables, such as copper wires. Engineering work is still needed before such quantum channels become commercially viable. In the meantime, we'll continue to use these channels in our analysis as if they're readily available. But you should be aware that a large part of the technology undergirding quantum cryptography isn't yet ready for prime time, although scientists and engineers have made substantial progress, as we'll review in How Real Is BB84?, on page 290.

Encrypting with Symmetric Keys

In cryptography, messages are encrypted using *keys*, which are strings to make the original message gobbledygook. Broadly speaking, the keys are of two types:

- *Symmetric* key algorithms where both the sender and receiver use the same key to encrypt and decrypt messages. In classical cryptography, the *Advanced Encryption Standard (AES)*[3] is a widely used symmetric key algorithm.

- *Asymmetric Key* algorithms use different keys for encrypting and decrypting messages. These algorithms, such as RSA,[4] are also called *public/private key* algorithms since one of the keys is publicly known. Using the public key, anyone can encrypt a message, but only the intended receiver can decrypt it based on the private key. These algorithms are used, for instance, to send encrypted information, such as credit card transactions, over the web. With asymmetric cryptography, the key distribution is moot since the public key is well known and doesn't have to be kept secret.

Both types of algorithms are secure. Though with symmetric key algorithms, you have the additional burden of ensuring that the secret key is first securely communicated to the receiver. But, as we'll see, with quantum computing, safely delivering keys is assured.

---

3.   https://en.wikipedia.org/wiki/Advanced_Encryption_Standard

4.   https://en.wikipedia.org/wiki/RSA_(cryptosystem)

Once a secret key is generated, the message can be encrypted by adding the secret key to the message doing modulo-2 addition, for example, on each bit. In modulo-2 addition, you add each bit of the message with the corresponding bit of the secret key but throw out the carry over. Thus,

$$
\begin{aligned}
0 + 0 &= 0 \\
0 + 1 &= 1 \\
1 + 0 &= 1 \\
1 + 1 &= 0
\end{aligned}
$$

So if your message is 0110101001 and the secret key is 0101010101, then the encrypted message is:

$$
\begin{array}{r}
0\ 1\ 1\ 0\ 1\ 0\ 1\ 0\ 0\ 1 \\
+\ 0\ 1\ 0\ 1\ 0\ 1\ 0\ 1\ 0\ 1 \\
\hline
=\ 0\ 0\ 1\ 1\ 1\ 1\ 1\ 1\ 0\ 0
\end{array}
$$

The encrypted message 0011111100 is sent to the receiver, who then decrypts it by subtracting the secret key to recover the original message:

$$
\begin{array}{r}
0\ 0\ 1\ 1\ 1\ 1\ 1\ 1\ 0\ 0 \\
-\ 0\ 1\ 0\ 1\ 0\ 1\ 0\ 1\ 0\ 1 \\
\hline
=\ 0\ 1\ 1\ 0\ 1\ 0\ 1\ 0\ 0\ 1
\end{array}
$$

Despite the simplicity of symmetric key methods, if the key is used just once, it's highly resistant to attacks.

The concepts of quantum cryptography are, at first sight, strange. So that you don't get lost in the minutiae, we next outline the main ideas that'll help frame the subsequent discussion. We'll call it the Tell-Your-Boss version, as it's a quick way to get across the key concepts without going into details.

Tell-Your-Boss Version: The "Key" Idea

Quantum cryptography is a topic where it's easy to lose the plot with all the exchange of information taking place to transmit a single message. So before getting into the nitty-gritty details, you'll look at the key insight that undergirds all of quantum cryptography. The intent is to get you to appreciate the quantum effects at play rather than making sure that all the auxiliary logic is properly connected up.

The central problem in cryptography is making sure that the sender and receiver have the necessary encryption and decryption keys before any message is communicated. With the keys in place, the sender encrypts the message and transmits it over a public channel, confident that only the receiver can decrypt it. Thus, we'll focus on getting the keys across to the receiver: the *Quantum Key Distribution (QKD)* problem.

In classical cryptography, information is encrypted with a key and then sent along a public channel to the receiver. In quantum cryptography, information is also encrypted with a key, but what's sent is a mega-qubit. To put it another way, instead of sending a single encrypted string, the mega-qubit contains, in effect, several encrypted strings. The following figure shows a mega-qubit carrying two such strings:

Should the mega-qubit fall into the wrong hands, the thieves wouldn't count themselves among the lucky few. Despite the mega-qubit carrying the encrypted strings, it's virtually impossible to extract them. Because the strings are in a superposition in the mega-qubit, the only way to get anything out of a mega-qubit is to collapse its qubits. But this is easier said than done. In the mega-qubit shown in the previous figure, the first qubit can collapse to $|0\rangle$ or $|1\rangle$, the second to $|1\rangle$, the third to $|0\rangle$ or $|1\rangle$, and so on. Thus, for this example, the mega-qubit could collapse to $|0111001011\rangle$, or even $|1111011111\rangle$ or $|0100000101\rangle$ or any of the $2^8 - 3 = 253$ other combinations. As the number of bits in the binary string gets larger in any real-life transaction, the chances that a random collapsing of the mega-qubit results in the actual encryption key is virtually nil. In other words, the quantum nature of the mega-qubit means that the secret encryption key is safe from any attempt to pry it out.

Yet, the receiver needs to pull out the correct encryption key from the mega-qubit. Quantum cryptographic algorithms are a way for the sender and receiver to legitimately get around the inherent tamper-proof seal of the mega-qubit. They're a carefully choreographed sequence of actions taken by both the sender and receiver so that the latter can recover the correct key, despite eavesdroppers on the public channels over which the sender and receiver communicate. In the next section, we'll describe one such mechanism.

The BB84 Key Exchange Mechanism

The most commonly cited quantum key exchange mechanism is *BB84*,[5] named after Charles Bennet and Gilles Brassard, who devised this scheme and presented it at the International Conference on Computers, Systems and Signal

---

5.　https://www.sciencedirect.com/science/article/pii/S0304397514004241

Processing in 1984. Over the years, this mechanism has been shown to be highly secure.[6] [7]

In quantum cryptography, both quantum and classical information is exchanged: a quantum channel carries quantum traffic—the mega-qubit—and a classical channel for non-quantum or classical information.

The underlying quantum effect for the BB84 mechanism is based on Back-to-Back H Gates: The First Hint of Taming Randomness, on page 88. The first H gate takes the qubits and puts them in a blended state. The second H gate then puts the qubits back to their original states. In quantum cryptography, this concept is divvied up between the sender and receiver: the sender puts the qubit in a blended state by applying a H gate to the qubit. The receiver then applies another H gate on the blended qubits to recover the original states that the sender wants to convey. The complete state of the mega-qubit—the "content," if you will—isn't relevant to the security of the channel.

Of course, if eavesdroppers get hold of the blended qubits during their transmission from the sender to the receiver, then they too could simply apply the H gate to reveal the original message. Thus, to thwart any attempt by eavesdroppers to steal the message, the message is transmitted in two phases:

1. Establish trust between the sender and receiver.
2. Only after the security of the channel is assured, create a single-use key to encrypt and decrypt the message.

Notice that in every transmission, a secure channel between the sender and receiver is first assured before a single-use key is generated. Besides the mega-qubit itself being a cagey player, as was hinted at in the previous section and which we'll explore in depth here, this two-step handshake between the sender and receiver virtually guarantees that the message is fully protected.

Next, we'll describe the role of quantum computing in these two phases.

Establish Trust

In this phase, the sender and receiver confirm that they're able to communicate securely without any malicious middlemen snooping around. The actual message to be transmitted isn't used in this determination. The only publicly known information is that both parties use H gates for their work.

---

6. https://arxiv.org/abs/quant-ph/0003004
7. https://www.nature.com/articles/srep16200

The trust is established by both the sender and receiver taking independent steps and then comparing their results, as follows:

Sender Creates a Random Quantum State

Sender creates a quantum state that's a long random string of $|0\rangle$ and $|1\rangle$ qubits.

To illustrate the steps, we'll use the following five-qubit quantum state expressed as a tensor product:

$$|01101\rangle = |0\rangle \otimes |1\rangle \otimes |1\rangle \otimes |0\rangle \otimes |1\rangle$$

The resulting mega-qubit has a single qubelet combination.

The $|1\rangle$ qubits are created by having a NOT gate operate on a $|0\rangle$ qubit, as shown in the following circuit:

$|0\rangle$ ——————— $|0\rangle$

$|0\rangle$ ——$\boxed{X}$—— $|1\rangle$

$|0\rangle$ ——$\boxed{X}$—— $|1\rangle$

$|0\rangle$ ——————— $|0\rangle$

$|0\rangle$ ——$\boxed{X}$—— $|1\rangle$

Sender Applies H Gate on Random Qubits

Next, the sender randomly selects some qubits and applies the H gate on them creating a mega-qubit with several qubelet combinations.

For example, if the H gate is applied to just the first, second, and last qubits, the quantum circuit is modified as shown in the following figure:

$|0\rangle$ ——————$\boxed{H}$—— $|\psi_0\rangle = \frac{1}{\sqrt{2}}(|0\rangle + |1\rangle)$

$|0\rangle$ ——$\boxed{X}$——$\boxed{H}$—— $|\psi_1\rangle = \frac{1}{\sqrt{2}}(|0\rangle - |1\rangle)$

$|0\rangle$ ——$\boxed{X}$——————— $|\psi_2\rangle = |1\rangle$

$|0\rangle$ ——————————— $|\psi_3\rangle = |0\rangle$

$|0\rangle$ ——$\boxed{X}$——$\boxed{H}$—— $|\psi_4\rangle = \frac{1}{\sqrt{2}}(|0\rangle - |1\rangle)$

The quantum state created by this circuit is expressed as the following tensor product:

$$|\psi_0\psi_1\psi_2\psi_3\psi_4\rangle = H|0\rangle \otimes H|1\rangle \otimes |1\rangle \otimes |0\rangle \otimes H|1\rangle$$

$H|0\rangle$ and $H|1\rangle$ are the actions of the H gate on the $|0\rangle$ and $|1\rangle$ qubits, as stated here:

$$H|0\rangle = \frac{1}{\sqrt{2}}(|0\rangle + |1\rangle)$$
$$H|1\rangle = \frac{1}{\sqrt{2}}(|0\rangle - |1\rangle)$$

Thus, by expanding the tensor product, the mega-qubit, $|\psi_0\psi_1\psi_2\psi_3\psi_4\rangle$, is:

$$
\begin{aligned}
|\psi_0\psi_1\psi_2\psi_3\psi_4\rangle &= H|0\rangle \otimes H|1\rangle \otimes |1\rangle \otimes |0\rangle \otimes H|1\rangle\\
&= \frac{1}{\sqrt{2}}(|0\rangle + |1\rangle) \otimes \frac{1}{\sqrt{2}}(|0\rangle - |1\rangle) \otimes |1\rangle \otimes |0\rangle \otimes \frac{1}{\sqrt{2}}(|0\rangle - |1\rangle)\\
&= \frac{1}{2}(|00\rangle - |01\rangle + |10\rangle - |11\rangle) \otimes |1\rangle \otimes |0\rangle \otimes \frac{1}{\sqrt{2}}(|0\rangle - |1\rangle)\\
&= \frac{1}{2}(|001\rangle - |011\rangle + |101\rangle - |111\rangle) \otimes |0\rangle \otimes \frac{1}{\sqrt{2}}(|0\rangle - |1\rangle)\\
&= \frac{1}{2}(|0010\rangle - |0110\rangle + |1010\rangle - |1110\rangle) \otimes \frac{1}{\sqrt{2}}(|0\rangle - |1\rangle)\\
&= \frac{1}{2\sqrt{2}}(|00100\rangle - |01100\rangle + |10100\rangle - |11100\rangle - |00101\rangle + |01101\rangle - |10101\rangle + |11101\rangle)
\end{aligned}
$$

This mega-qubit has eight qubelet combinations, with each combination having five qubelets, as shown below:

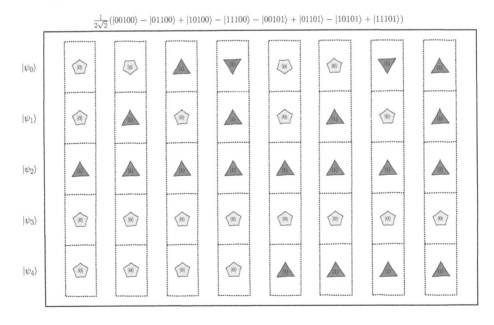

$$\frac{1}{2\sqrt{2}}(|00100\rangle - |01100\rangle + |10100\rangle - |11100\rangle - |00101\rangle + |01101\rangle - |10101\rangle + |11101\rangle)$$

Mega-Qubit Sent Across Quantum Channel

The sender transmits the mega-qubit over the quantum channel to the receiver.

Picture this mega-qubit as a superposition of its qubelet combinations, drawn using familiar 0/1 bits to emphasize the idea that what's being transmitted is actually a superposition of several binary strings as opposed to a single string in classical cryptography, as shown in this figure:

The negative qubelet combinations in the mega-qubit are drawn upside-down.

Receiver Applies H Gate on Random Qubits

The receiver gets the mega-qubit from the quantum channel and randomly selects qubits and applies the H gate.

Suppose the receiver selects the first, third, and last qubits and applies the H gate, as shown in the figure below:

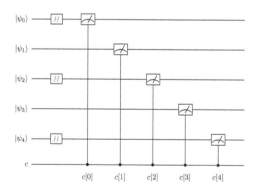

By sheer chance, some qubits will have back-to-back H gates applied to them, while others won't. In fact, if you put the sender's and receiver's circuits side by side, you'll get the *overall* circuit as shown in the figure on page 287.

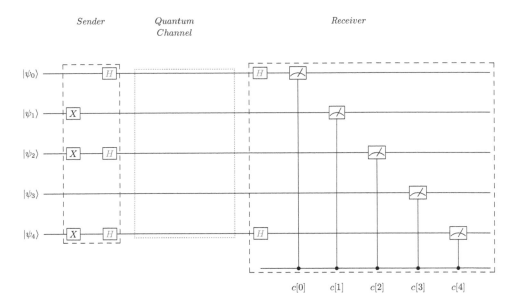

Only the first and last qubits have back-to-back H gates. Thus, when measured, these qubits will hold the original state set by the sender. Thus, c[0] records a 0 and c[4] logs a 1, matching those of the sender.

There's no guarantee that the other qubits will match, although some may by chance. (For example, because of the random nature of how the blended quantum state of the third qubit collapses, c[2] will have roughly a 50% chance of matching the original state set by the sender.)

Overall Circuit Is Not a Single Program

Although we've drawn the *overall* circuit in a single diagram, it doesn't result in a single quantum program. It's actually implemented as three separate parts: the sender's circuit, the receiver's circuit, and the quantum channel that transmits the qubits from sender to receiver.

Both Parties Compare Which Qubits Have Back-to-Back H Gates

Over an assumed "leaky" classical channel, where eavesdroppers can freely listen in, both the sender and receiver announce which qubits they applied H gates to. Thus, both the sender and receiver, as well as any eavesdroppers, will know which qubits match. Tellingly, though, the actual values of the qubits aren't shared—just whether they were acted on by back-to-back H gates. So while the sender and receiver would know the values, eavesdroppers wouldn't.

Given that both the sender and the receiver independently select the qubits to apply the H gate to, statistically we expect that about 50% of the time their choices will match. Thus, in practice, the sender starts by choosing a sufficiently long string of qubits so that the matched qubits are still adequate to make a secret key.

Optional Step for an Enhanced Seal of Trust

If you still need additional evidence that the quantum channel is free from eavesdroppers and middlemen with nefarious intent, the sender selects a subset of the matching qubits and declares their actual original quantum states over the leaky classical channel. Only if these states are identical to those measured by the receiver is the communication deemed safe and private.

 Joe asks:

What Makes BB84 Tamper-Proof?

Quantum cryptography not only makes it hard to illegally tap messages but provides incontrovertible proof when tampered. The certificate of tamper-free messages comes directly from the principles of quantum mechanics. In classical cryptography, on the other hand, no one is the wiser when a hacker stealthily listens in.

In quantum cryptography, the odds stack up against evil-doers quickly:

- Firstly, there's the mega-qubit itself. Even if someone managed to snatch it, they can't simply read it like a classical string. They have to collapse the qubits. And since at least half of the qubits are in a blended state, the likelihood is tiny that every qubit would collapse to the original state at the same time.

- Secondly, the mega-qubit doesn't contain the complete information. Even if you had full knowledge of the original quantum states, you still wouldn't know the secret key. The actions of the receiver have to be factored in.

- If establishing an enhanced level of trust, the presence of an eavesdropper is easily detected. The moment an eavesdropper probes a qubit to inspect its state, the overall quantum state of the system is immediately altered so that there's a mismatch when the sender and receiver compare their qubits.

Thus, the security of the quantum channel hinges on whether a match occurs when the H gate is applied to roughly half the qubits selected by both the sender and receiver. Remarkably, it's only the total number that is relevant—not the quantum states of the qubits themselves nor which qubits are selected. In other words, trust is established by sharing minimal information, which in itself makes it more secure, since it reduces the attack surface, or the amount of content that can fall into wrong hands.

Create the Secret Key

Now that the sender and receiver have established a secure quantum channel, they each independently determine the secret key based on the matching qubits. The secret key itself is never sent across any channel, as it would be in classical cryptography.

Specifically, the secret key is derived as follows:

- Discard the qubits used for establishing the enhanced level of trust.

- Consider those qubits to which both the sender and receiver apply H gates:

  - Since sender generates the random string to initiate the negotiation, sender knows the quantum state of the matching qubits.

  - Receiver obtains the quantum state of the matching qubits from the value recorded in the classical register.

- Form the secret key by both sender and receiver concatenating the values of the matching qubits:

  - If the length of the key is shorter than the message to be sent, the key is repeated as many times as necessary.

  - Other schemes, such as reversing the bits in each repetition, could be used if both parties agree to them.

In the example, the sender and receiver apply H gates to the first and last qubits. The secret key is, thus, $|01\rangle$, assuming that the optional step isn't needed in this transmission. The sender then encrypts the message using this key. And the receiver decrypts the message using the same key, even though the actual key is never sent across the channel.

The BB84 mechanism's strength is, thus, multifold:

- Using mega-qubits to establish trust of the communication channel makes it foolproof—virtually impossible for any hacker to operate successfully. Moreover, any attempt to crack it is easily detectable, and no message is communicated till the channel is clear.

- The secret key itself is derived independently by both the sender and receiver and is never actually sent across the channel.

- Each new transmission uses a new secret key—the same key is never used again.

BB84 Using Entangled Qubits

 In the BB84 mechanism, each qubit is first operated on by the sender and then the receiver. Using entangled qubits, however, such as those described in Design a Teleporting Circuit, on page 256, the sender operates on one and the receiver works on the other entangled qubit.[8] This way, if any entangled qubit is illegitimately intercepted, the sender immediately knows and can stop the communication.

How Real Is BB84?

Quite real.

Scientists and engineers in several countries have racked up a growing list of experiments demonstrating that BB84 is a feasible and secure method of communication. Many of these implementations are based on optical quantum computing using light, or photons, as qubits to transmit information. So although the quantum computers are different than the IBM Quantum Computer, the underlying principles and quantum circuits described in this chapter are the same.

Here's a partial list of these demonstrations:

- In 2002–2007, the DARPA Quantum Network,[9] [10] a joint effort by Harvard and Boston Universities and BBN Technologies, was the world's first QKD experiment. It used "polarization-entangled photon pairs"[11] and operated continuously for three years in the Cambridge, Massachusetts, and Boston area. At its peak, it interconnected ten sites. Keys created by this mechanism were used in standard internet security protocols.

  In collaboration with MIT, this setup was also used to test a proof-of-concept version of a quantum eavesdropper.

- In 2006, Los Alamos National Laboratory (LANL) together with the National Institute for Standards and Technology (NIST) in the United States, using a severely throttled pulsed laser beam, produced photons

---

8. https://journals.aps.org/prl/abstract/10.1103/PhysRevLett.67.661
9. https://iopscience.iop.org/article/10.1088/1367-2630/4/1/346
10. https://en.wikipedia.org/wiki/DARPA_Quantum_Network
11. https://arxiv.org/abs/quant-ph/0503058

that mimicked individual qubits and proved that QKD works over long distances.[12] These distances are comparable to the spans in today's fiber networks.

- In 2008, forty-one research and industrial organizations from the European Union, Switzerland, and Russia tested a QKD network using eight sites around Vienna.[13] The system used a variety of systems, including entangled photons, to demonstrate that they could be successfully interconnected.

See here[14] for other experiments around the world.

Bottom Line

In quantum cryptography, the deterministic and the inherent probabilistic nature of quantum mechanics come together to secure communications between two parties. The back-to-back nature of connecting H gates provides a reliable mechanism for the parties to lock in a secret key. At the same time, should the mega-qubit fall into the wrong hands during transit, the random way in which qubits collapse makes it virtually impossible for the interloper to glean anything of value. It's like sending a booby-trapped package. Quantum computing has the potential to seriously crimp the hacking industry.

Although you can't yet build and deploy quantum cryptographic algorithms like you would for other types of applications, the principles you have learned in this chapter will apply when commercially viable hardware becomes commonplace. That is, the security schemes to establish trust between communicating parties and the quantum circuits will still be valid, although they will be implemented differently than the programs you have been working with so far.

In the next chapter, you'll see how quantum computing provides new ways to slash the time searching for solutions to hard problems in many diverse industries.

Try Your Hand

Solutions to these exercises are given in Quantum Cryptography Solutions, on page 504.

---

12. https://iopscience.iop.org/article/10.1088/1367-2630/8/9/193

13. https://iopscience.iop.org/article/10.1088/1367-2630/11/7/075001

14. https://en.wikipedia.org/wiki/Quantum_key_distribution#Commercial

1. Alice wants to send a message to Bob and they agree to use the BB84 mechanism to set up a secret key to encrypt and decrypt her message.

   Suppose Alice sets up her circuit as shown in the following figure:

   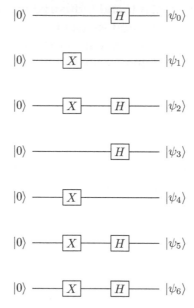

   a. Decide whether the following statements are True or False:

      i. The random key is 000000.

      ii. The secret key is 0110111.

      iii. The random key is:

      $$H|0\rangle \otimes |1\rangle \otimes H|1\rangle \otimes H|0\rangle \otimes |1\rangle \otimes H|1\rangle \otimes H|1\rangle$$

      iv. The random key is 0110111.

      v. Assuming that the first and last qubits are used for establishing an enhanced level of trust, the secret key is:

      $$|1\rangle \otimes H|1\rangle \otimes H|0\rangle \otimes |1\rangle \otimes H|1\rangle$$

   b. When Bob receives the qubits, he applies the H gate on the second, third, fourth, sixth, and seventh qubits. Draw his circuit.

   c. Alice and Bob want an enhanced level of trust before Alice sends a message to Bob. They agree to use the seventh qubit to test. What do they do next?

   d. What is the secret key? Who sets it up?

2. Imagine it's 2025 and the internet has a parallel network of optical routers and switches using pulsed lasers alongside the classical world wide web. These devices send single photons, effectively acting as single qubits. In other words, the world wide web has gone quantum.

   In this new world, you'd like to buy a book from the Pragmatic Bookshelf, the number one site for computer professionals. As in the classical way to buy a book, you first select your book, add it to the cart, enter your address and payment information, and click Buy.

   Now, before your browser on your desktop or smart device sends your information to the bookstore, it first initiates a "handshake" or negotiation with the Pragmatic Bookshelf site to generate a secret key using the BB84 mechanism. This secret key will then be used to encrypt your personal details.

   Suppose your machine generates the following quantum program for the "handshake":

   ```
   x q[0];
   x q[2];
   x q[4];
   x q[6];
   x q[7];
   x q[8];
   h q[0];
   h q[1];
   h q[3];
   h q[4];
   h q[6];
   h q[8];
   ```

   a. Draw the quantum circuit associated with this program. On the classical channel, what qubits does your machine declare that it applies the H gates on?

   b. What random string did your smart device come up with?

   c. Your machine sends the qubits to the Pragmatic Bookshelf site. On a classical channel, the site declares it has applied H gates on qubits 1, 2, 4, 6, 7, and 9. Assuming that 2 and 9 are used to establish an enhanced level of trust, what is the secret key derived by your machine?

3. In the experimental setups in How Real Is BB84?, on page 290, to test the feasibility of using the BB84 mechanism to generate secret keys and communicate securely, researchers used predominantly optical devices. Assume that for some reason, these devices are only able to rotate photons, and hence, qubits, by a quarter turn.

What type of gates would the sender and receiver need to use to negotiate a secret key using the BB84 mechanism?

4. In this exercise, you'll see that intercepting a mega-qubit isn't particularly useful. To this end, consider the following mega-qubit:

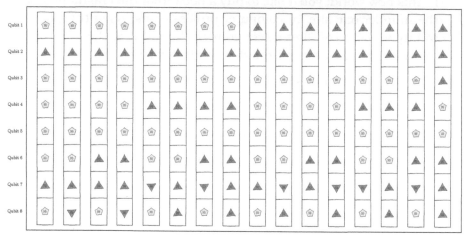

a. An interceptor gets hold of this mega-qubit and collapses it. Which of the following states may be logged in the classical registers?

    i.   10100010

    ii. 01000101

    iii. 11100111

    iv. 11001111

b. After recording the collapsed state, the interceptor sends the collapsed mega-qubit—the one you identified in the previous part—to the intended receiver. The receiver then applies the H gate on qubits 1, 2, 4, and 6. What are the possible states that the receiver can observe?

c. On the classical channel, the sender and receiver each declare that they applied the H gates on qubits 1, 2, 4, and 6.

    i.   If qubit 1 is used to establish an enhanced level of trust, what is the probability that the interceptor is detected?

    ii. If qubits 1 and 2 are used to establish an enhanced level of trust, what is the probability that the interceptor is detected?

    iii. If qubits 1, 2, and 4 are used to establish an enhanced level of trust, what is the probability that the interceptor is detected?

## CHAPTER 10

Quantum Search

In Chapter 9, Alice in Quantumland—Quantum Cryptography, on page 279, you saw how a circuit that essentially duplicates back-to-back quantum gates collapses qubits to their original states thereby permitting recovery of a secret message. Quantum effects get even more tantalizing when applied to applications such as the optimal routing of airliners, detecting the presence of cancer cells in medical images, or even simply making you rent another movie or buy another book. In each of these cases, classical computer algorithms churn through millions of possibilities to come up with a flight schedule, correctly diagnose diseases, or offer up movie or book choices that nudge you to another click-to-buy. But quantum computers hold the promise of simultaneously evaluating all these millions of combinations and identifying the correct one in just a handful of steps. The techniques you'll see here are impossible to conduct with classical computers.

Harnessing these quantum effects, however, gets more intricate than the applications you worked with earlier. In Design a Teleporting Circuit, on page 256, although you could potentially teleport hundreds of qubits, the quantum entanglement effects are localized in groups of a few qubits. As with teleporting, in Chapter 9, Alice in Quantumland—Quantum Cryptography, on page 279, the mechanism to share cryptographic keys that can't be meddled with, again, relies on quantum effects restricted to groups of a couple of qubits. In searching for solutions across a large number of possibilities, the quantum effects are intertwined across the entire gamut of all possible quantum states—you can't break up the problem and apply quantum effects in smaller chunks.

To design quantum-based search algorithms, you need to shed the "classical" ways of thinking and develop a new mindset. In this chapter, you'll begin that transformation.

Working with Simple Applications

To better illustrate the quantum effects in search problems, we'll work with simple applications. This will help build your intuition instead of getting caught in mathematical minutiae. But you should bear in mind that the concepts you'll learn can be extended to larger problems.

Also, although the quantum technology and hardware is evolving rapidly, we're limited, when compared to classical machines, by the number of qubits we can program with. Working with smaller problems for which you can develop quantum circuits will let you see how quantum effects are introduced for yourself—a far more satisfying approach than just a theoretical exposition.

So rather than just showing you how to hook up S gates and $T^{\dagger}$ gates that demonstrate arbitrary quantum behavior and leaving this chapter out of the book entirely, I wanted to at least give you a taste for how quantum computing can be brought to bear on applications that search through a vast number of permutations. This way, you'll ready to solve industrial scale problems when larger quantum computers become available.

Grover's Algorithm

Giving developers a way to simultaneously hold all solutions to a problem is like taking kids to a candy store but then having them first figure out the combination of the lock to the store before they can eat all the sweets they want. Likewise, quantum computers exploit the natural ability of subatomic particles to remain suspended so that each can collapse to one of two states —a collection of n quantum particles effectively holds all 2^{n} states. But the challenge is to figure out how to collapse the qubits so that they land on the correct solution of the problem.

When the constraints of the problem are well defined, we can use *Grover's algorithm*,[1][2] a technique that identifies the optimal solution from the mega-qubit by eliminating the non-optimal ones. (Also see *Quantum Computer Science [Mer07]*.) To use this algorithm, your application's constraints must be set up with Boolean logic expressions, using the quantum logic gates as shown in Logic Expressions to Quantum Circuit, on page 62. Think of these gates as a referee: given a potential solution of $|0\rangle$ and $|1\rangle$ qubits, they'll say whether the

1.   https://arxiv.org/abs/quant-ph/9605043
2.   https://arxiv.org/abs/quant-ph/0109116

qubits satisfy the Boolean logic expressions. For those qubit values that meet the constraints, their qubelets are rotated, or *tagged*, to distinguish them from those that aren't feasible. The quantum logic gates don't actually produce a valid set of qubit values that satisfy the Boolean logic expressions.

The quantum logic gates model the Boolean logic expressions we set up when we defined the problem. The solution we're looking for is one that satisfies those expressions. A classical computer would test each solution in turn. The quantum circuit considers all the possible solutions in the mega-qubit at the same time, and the logic gates are used to eliminate all the solutions except for the correct ones. These steps are shown schematically in the following figure:

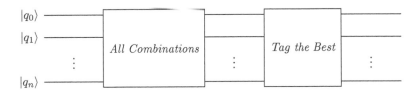

The high-level steps in Grover's algorithm are shown by the following figure:

Tagging and Canceling Are Referenced Differently in the Literature

In the literature, the tagging phase is called the *oracle*—a function that decrees whether a given state of 0s and 1s qualifies as a solution for the Boolean logic expressions.

The canceling phase is called *reflection and amplification*. The mathematics of the Canceling Circuit can also be interpreted as reflecting the amplitudes along a suitable axis, which has the effect of reducing the non-optimal amplitudes and simultaneously magnifying those that satisfy the constraints.

Before showing you how Grover's algorithm can be used for larger problems, you'll first get a close-up view of the basic building blocks on a two-qubit circuit[3] so that you can better see the quantum effects working. In Fundamental Circuit Pattern for Searching, on page 314, we'll describe a pattern to apply these quantum effects to larger applications with more qubits.

---

3. https://quantum-computing.ibm.com/support/guides/user-guide?page=5ddb0f995d640300671cc61b

Quantum Effects in Grover's Algorithm

Grover's algorithm is a sequence of the following quantum effects:

- Superposition to generate all 2^n combinations of n qubits.
- Rotate qubelets to achieve the following:
  - Tag optimal qubelet combinations in the mega-qubit.
  - Cancel, or eliminate, non-optimal qubelet combinations from the mega-qubit.

Because of the nature of quantum mechanics, the qubelet combinations within the mega-qubit are acted on simultaneously by the quantum gates. Thus, you can think of Grover's algorithm as a massively parallel computation.

Qubelets Versus Bloch Sphere

So far, for the most part, you've worked with circuits that illustrate how quantum gates work, but other than in a few cases, such as the Design a Teleporting Circuit, on page 256, you've not had to chain gates in tandem to achieve a specific goal.

The material in this section reaffirms the validity of analyzing quantum programs with mega-qubits—pentagon $|0\rangle$ and triangle $|1\rangle$ qubelets and their rotations. This framework gives a way to work with multiple qubits and correctly models how quantum gates act on qubits. On the other hand, to get it right by visualizing simultaneous rotations of multiple qubits using multiple Bloch spheres in 3D space and figuring out how they interact and remove non-optimal states is a daunting prospect.

Generating All Combinations

To generate all possible quantum states of n qubits, apply an H gate on each qubit. For two qubits, the circuit shown in the following figure generated all four quantum states:

All Combinations

$$|0\rangle \quad \boxed{H}$$
$$|0\rangle \quad \boxed{H}$$

The top and bottom H gates each split the $|0\rangle$ qubit as follows:

$$|0\rangle \mapsto \frac{1}{\sqrt{2}}(|0\rangle + |1\rangle)$$

Thus, the mega-qubit after each qubit is acted on by the respective H gate is:

$$\frac{1}{\sqrt{2}}(\,|0\rangle\,+\,|1\rangle\,)\otimes\frac{1}{\sqrt{2}}(\,|0\rangle\,+\,|1\rangle\,)=\frac{1}{2}\,|00\rangle\,+\frac{1}{2}\,|01\rangle\,+\frac{1}{2}\,|10\rangle\,+\frac{1}{2}\,|11\rangle$$

This mega-qubit has four qubelet combinations, as shown in the following figure:

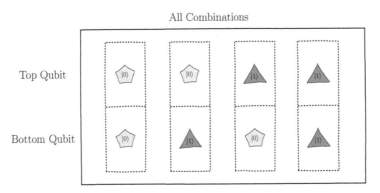

Each qubelet combination corresponds to one of the four possible states of two qubits: $|00\rangle$, $|01\rangle$, $|10\rangle$, or $|11\rangle$.

Tagging the Best

After applying the H gates to the qubits, the mega-qubit holds all possible solutions to the application problem, including the optimal qubelet combination. The challenge in designing a quantum algorithm, then, is to remove the non-optimal quantum states. Grover's algorithm is a way to retain a specific qubelet combination in the mega-qubit while removing the others. To illustrate how Grover's algorithm goes about eliminating non-optimal quantum states, we'll initially assume that we know which qubelet combination in the mega-qubit is optimal. Of course, in a real application, you'd like your program to find the optimal solution. So in Tagging When You Don't Know the Optimal Solution, on page 325, you'll learn to design a quantum circuit that doesn't require you to identify up front the optimal quantum state.

For now, though, suppose we want to retain the fourth qubelet combination, $|11\rangle$. We can achieve this by applying a Controlled Z (CZ) gate, described in Controlled Z (CZ) Gate, on page 109, as shown in the following circuit:

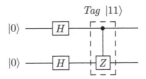

The CZ gate only affects the $|11\rangle$ qubelet combination:

$$|11\rangle \overset{CZ}{\longmapsto} -\ |11\rangle$$

The other states' qubelet combinations are left alone. The mega-qubit after applying the CZ gate is as shown in the following figure:

Tag $|11\rangle$

The inverted qubelet on the fourth qubelet combination, corresponding to $|11\rangle$, is, thus, tagged to differentiate it from the others.

Qubelet Inversions Are Tied to the Equation for a Quantum State

Recall from Rotating Qubelets Through Any Angle, on page 150, the quantum state $|\psi\rangle$ is:

$$|\psi\rangle = \cos\frac{\theta}{2}\,|0\rangle + e^{i\varphi}\sin\frac{\theta}{2}\,|1\rangle$$

The terms $\cos\theta/2$ and $\sin\theta/2$ are the amplitudes for $|0\rangle$ and $|1\rangle$, respectively, and determine the probabilities of the qubit collapsing to those states. And φ is the relative difference in orientations between the pentagon $|0\rangle$ and triangle $|1\rangle$ qubelets.

So when one of them, say, the pentagon $|0\rangle$ qubelet, is not inverted while the other, the triangle $|1\rangle$, is, the relative difference between their orientation, φ, is 180° or π radians. Thus,

$$e^{i\varphi} = e^{i\pi}$$
$$= \cos\pi + i\sin\pi$$

Noting that $\cos\pi = -1$ and $\sin\pi = 0$, the $e^{i\varphi}$ term in the quantum state is –1. Thus, when the relative difference in orientations between the pentagon $|0\rangle$ and triangle $|1\rangle$ qubelets is 180°—one is inverted while the other isn't—a negative sign is associated with that qubelet combination.

The quantum state, $|\psi_{tag}\rangle$, of this mega-qubit is:

$$|\psi_{tag}\rangle = \frac{1}{2}(\,|00\rangle + |01\rangle + |10\rangle - |11\rangle\,)$$

Or, in vector form:

$$|\psi_{tag}\rangle = \frac{1}{2}\begin{pmatrix} 1 \\ 1 \\ 1 \\ -1 \end{pmatrix}$$

The amplitude of the $|11\rangle$ qubelet combination is negative; the others are positive.

You can also confirm this on the IBM Quantum Computer by looking at the Statevector—a graphical view of the quantum state vector in which the amplitudes are shown as bars whose heights are their magnitudes and whose colors correspond to the complex component (relative orientation between the qubelets)—as shown in the following figure:

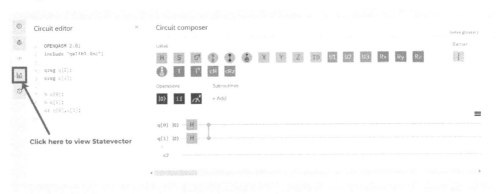

You'll see a graphical view of the quantum vector, as shown in the following figure:

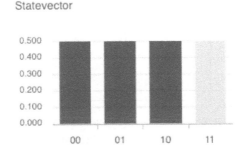

The four idealized states are shown as bars whose heights are the amplitudes. The color of the bar indicates the sign of the amplitude. The lighter colored bar on the extreme right, corresponding to $|11\rangle$, indicates its amplitude is negative.

You can reason similarly to tag another state, for instance, $|10\rangle$, where q[0]=1 and q[1]=0. When we tagged $|11\rangle$, we applied a CZ gate so that the bottom triangle $|1\rangle$ qubelet could be inverted. Thus, to tag $|10\rangle$, where the second qubit, q[1], is $|0\rangle$, you need to first switch it to $|1\rangle$. To this end, consider the following circuit:

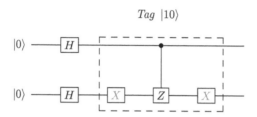

Tag $|10\rangle$

Even though you can analyze this circuit with matrices and confirm that the amplitude of the $|10\rangle$ qubelet combination is negative, you should be able to reason this out in your mind as follows:

- To tag $|10\rangle$ where the bottom qubit is $|0\rangle$, the bottom qubit must first be switched to $|1\rangle$ before being fed to the target of the CZ gate.

  The mega-qubit after the first set of H gates on the left and the first X gate on the bottom qubit, before the target of the CZ gate, is as shown in the following figure:

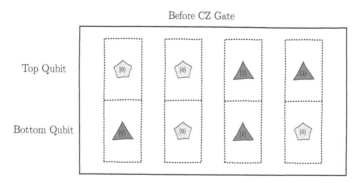

Before CZ Gate

- The CZ gate only affects the $|11\rangle$ qubelet combination, the third column in the previous figure, and inverts the bottom triangle $|1\rangle$ qubelet as shown in the figure on page 303.

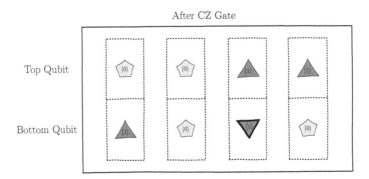

After CZ Gate

Thus, the qubelet combination $|11\rangle$ will have a negative sign.

- Finally, to switch $-|11\rangle$ to $-|10\rangle$, apply an X gate to the bottom qubit again. The X gate toggles the bottom qubelets in all qubelet combinations, as shown in the following figure:

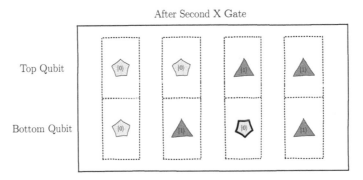

After Second X Gate

The bottom qubelet in the third column is switched to a pentagon $|0\rangle$ qubelet and the others are restored to their original qubelet types before the first X gate was applied to both qubits.

As a result of these operations, the mega-qubit $|\psi_{tag}\rangle$ is:

$$|\psi_{tag}\rangle = \frac{1}{2}(|00\rangle + |01\rangle - |10\rangle + |11\rangle)$$

Or, in vector form:

$$|\psi_{tag}\rangle = \frac{1}{2}\begin{pmatrix} 1 \\ 1 \\ -1 \\ 1 \end{pmatrix}$$

The amplitude of the $|10\rangle$ qubelet combination is negative and the others are positive. The $|10\rangle$ qubelet combination is, thus, tagged.

You can check the Statevector on the IBM Quantum Computer's console. This time, it'll be as shown in the following figure.

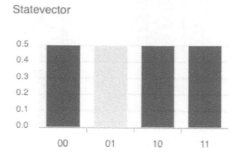

Statevector

The lighter colored bar, indicating a negative amplitude, is associated with 01. But, in the discussion above, we wrote the state as $|q_0 q_1\rangle$, which is the reverse of the way that the IBM Quantum Computer console writes it. Thus, 01 on the console actually corresponds to the tagged state $|10\rangle$.

Using Drag-and-Drop to Build the Circuit Gives You Insight

 Dragging and dropping gates from the palette while keeping the Statevector tab active lets you see how the circuit modifies the quantum states as you add gates. You'll notice that some gates barely affect the states, but other placements introduce large scale changes in the quantum state.

In summary, then, to tag a particular qubelet combination, its amplitude has a different sign, achieved by inverting one of its qubelets, than the other combinations or idealized states. If you measured the qubits at this stage, however, then despite the amplitude of the tagged qubelet combination being negative, the mega-qubit formed by the two qubits would collapse to all four quantum states with roughly equal probability. That is, there seems to be no preference yet to tagging the optimal qubelet combinations. In the next section, you'll see how the untagged qubelet combinations are removed from the mega-qubit.

Canceling Circuit

To identify the tagged qubelet combinations representing the optimal solutions for your application, you need to remove the others from the mega-qubit. We'll call this part of the program that eliminates the non-tagged qubelet combinations the Canceling Circuit.

The design of the Canceling Circuit illustrates why designing quantum circuits is vexing and puts a spotlight on a crucial aspect: when analyzing quantum

\\// **Joe asks:**
ʔⱴ # Why the Second X Gate?

The Tagging Circuit for $|10\rangle$ illustrates a trademark feature of quantum computing: gates that reverse the action of those applied earlier, such as the X gate after the CZ gate. In conventional programming, after writing a statement that, for example, increments a variable, it would be unusual to decrement it later if there was no computational logic dictating it. Yet this quirky way of programming is a hallmark of quantum computing.

The reason for this seemingly redundant way of hooking up gates in quantum computers is because you're working with many states at the same time. When you applied the first X gate on the bottom qubit, it switched the bottom qubelets for all the qubelet combinations, not just the one that had to be tagged. So after you're done dealing with the tagged qubelet combination by applying the CZ gate, you need to reverse the action of the first X gate and restore the other qubelet combinations back to their original states. This way, you can focus the quantum effects on specific qubelet combinations even though the quantum computer deals with all of them at the same time.

circuits, even though your attention is on one set of states, always bear in mind that this set is just one of the many qubelet combinations in the mega-qubit associated with the circuit. What gates you apply to one state are simultaneously applied to the other combinations. It's imperative that you keep the other states on your radar. Consequently, designing an algorithm is a combination of pattern extrapolation—a quantum effect for two qubits is extended to more qubits—applying matrices to portions of a circuit to precisely work out how gates modify quantum states and a healthy dose of guesswork or trial-and-error to calibrate the quantum effects. You'll get lost in minutiae if you try to be absolutely precise. Rather, you'll see how by using intuition and heuristic arguments, you can turn general ideas of quantum effects into workable code. By the end of this chapter, you'll have a pattern that you can use to solve larger applications with more qubits.

In the Canceling Circuit, in particular, you have to eliminate several non-tagged states. What you do to remove one state impacts the others too. So you can't just focus on one non-tagged state at a time. You have to think broadly first before zeroing in on specific gates.

Begin, then, by identifying at a high level the quantum effects you'll need to use, as we'll describe next.

Tagging Quantum States

With so many non-tagged and tagged states, it seems reasonable to expect that some form tagging will be used. Ironically, you'll be *tagging* non-tagged states, as those are the ones that need to be eliminated.

Whatever states you end up deciding to tag, it'll likely be when certain conditions are met. Thus, you'll use a Controlled Z or CZ gate here, as shown in the following figure:

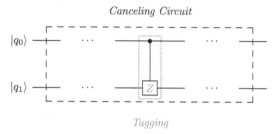

Tagging

For most gates, you want to add a second one to reverse its effects (known as "backing out"). This time, you won't do that because you want to retain the tagged solution—it's the main purpose of this section of your program.

The matrix A_{CZ} for this CZ gate is:

$$A_{CZ} = \begin{bmatrix} 1 & 0 & 0 & 0 \\ 0 & 1 & 0 & 0 \\ 0 & 0 & 1 & 0 \\ 0 & 0 & 0 & -1 \end{bmatrix}$$

Splitting Qubits

No amount of rotating the qubelets in the non-tagged qubelet combinations will get rid of them: operations you apply on one will also be applied to the others, so there's no net effect. Thus, paradoxically, to remove the non-tagged quantum states or qubelet combinations from the mega-qubit, you need to introduce additional qubelet combinations in the mix to provide opportunities for qubelet combinations to cancel.

Specifically, begin by applying an H gate to each qubit, as shown in the following figure:

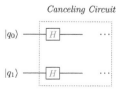

The dots indicate that other gates will be added later to this circuit.

Following the procedure in Two-Qubit Gate Matrices, on page 238, the matrix A_{H_2} defining these stacked H gates is:

$$A_{H_2} = \frac{1}{2}\begin{bmatrix} 1 & 1 & 1 & 1 \\ 1 & -1 & 1 & -1 \\ 1 & 1 & -1 & -1 \\ 1 & -1 & -1 & 1 \end{bmatrix}$$

Before moving on to the next step in the design, back out these gates as you saw in Why the Second X Gate?, on page 305, so that whichever qubelet combinations you don't want to affect get restored back to their original states, as shown in the following figure:

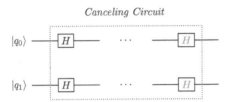

Canceling Circuit

The dots indicate that you'll have other gates before the H gates are backed out.

Finding Asymmetry

Thus far, despite creating more qubelet combinations by splitting qubits, the overall mega-qubit is still somewhat symmetric in the sense that there are an equal number of each type of qubelet combination in the mega-qubit. To tilt the odds toward the optimal solution, you need to introduce asymmetry to favor some qubelet combinations over others. Moreover, whatever you do must work regardless of the quantum state that's tagged. That is, just as we needed to introduce H gates to add more qubelet combinations to increase opportunities to cancel, we'll need to first find symmetries.

Look again at the A_{H_2} matrix shown previously. Each column spells out how the gates modify the idealized state corresponding to that column. Specifically, each element in the column will tell you how the gate affects each of the idealized states when they act on the qubelet combination corresponding to that column. For example, the third column stipulates that the $|10\rangle$ qubelet combination in the mega-qubit is modified as follows:

$$|10\rangle \mapsto \begin{pmatrix} 1 \\ 1 \\ -1 \\ -1 \end{pmatrix}$$

$$= \frac{1}{2}|00\rangle + \frac{1}{2}|01\rangle - \frac{1}{2}|10\rangle - \frac{1}{2}|11\rangle$$

Likewise, the second column tells you how the $|01\rangle$ qubelet combination is affected:

$$|01\rangle \mapsto \begin{pmatrix} 1 \\ -1 \\ 1 \\ -1 \end{pmatrix}$$

$$= \frac{1}{2}|00\rangle - \frac{1}{2}|01\rangle + \frac{1}{2}|10\rangle - \frac{1}{2}|11\rangle$$

Compare the two quantum states: you'll see that, for instance, the $|01\rangle$ qubelet combination has a positive sign from the gates acting on $|10\rangle$ and a negative sign when they act on $|01\rangle$.

In fact, by evaluating how all other idealized states are modified by the circuit, you'll notice that $|00\rangle$ is the only qubelet combination that always retains the same sign for any idealized state. (You can also see that the first row of A_{H_2} is the only one in which every element has the same sign.)

This, then, is the lever we're looking for. $|00\rangle$ is the only qubelet combination that will consistently appear in the mega-qubit after the H gates, regardless of which quantum state is tagged by the Tagging Circuit.

Tagging $|00\rangle$

To tag $|00\rangle$, using the same logic outlined for tagging $|10\rangle$ in Tagging the Best, on page 299, place X gates as shown in the following figure:

Canceling Circuit

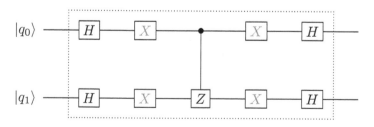

These X gates need to be backed out since they're only used as an intermediate step so that the non-tagged qubelet combinations are consistently tagged.

The matrix A_{X_2} for these stacked X gates is:

$$A_{X_2} = \begin{bmatrix} 0 & 0 & 0 & 1 \\ 0 & 0 & 1 & 0 \\ 0 & 1 & 0 & 0 \\ 1 & 0 & 0 & 0 \end{bmatrix}$$

The CZ gate tags the $|00\rangle$ qubelet combination so that it's not restored by the "backing-out" gates as the other combinations are. But, and this is a very important point, keeping these combinations in the mega-qubit regardless of which state is tagged *forces* some other qubelet combinations to cancel out so that the overall probability of the mega-qubit collapsing to some state continues to be 1.

At this point you have a design that breaks the symmetry in the mega-qubit. So it's worthwhile now to precisely see how these non-optimal qubelet combinations are canceled out. To this end, break up the circuit into parts, as shown in the following circuit:

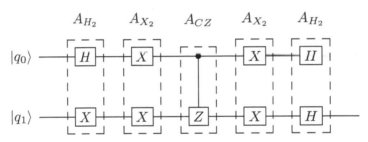

The label above each part is the matrix describing the operation of that part. For example, A_{H_2} is the matrix that shows how a two-qubit quantum state is changed when each qubit is acted on by an H gate.

The matrix $A_{Canceling}$ for the Canceling Circuit is the following product of these matrices:

$$A_{Canceling} = A_{H_2} \times A_{X_2} \times A_{CZ} \times A_{X_2} \times A_{H_2}$$

$$= \frac{1}{2}\begin{bmatrix} 1 & 1 & 1 & 1 \\ 1 & -1 & 1 & -1 \\ 1 & 1 & -1 & -1 \\ 1 & -1 & -1 & 1 \end{bmatrix} \times \begin{bmatrix} 0 & 0 & 0 & 1 \\ 0 & 0 & 1 & 0 \\ 0 & 1 & 0 & 0 \\ 1 & 0 & 0 & 0 \end{bmatrix} \times \begin{bmatrix} 1 & 0 & 0 & 0 \\ 0 & 1 & 0 & 0 \\ 0 & 0 & 1 & 0 \\ 0 & 0 & 0 & -1 \end{bmatrix} \times \begin{bmatrix} 0 & 0 & 0 & 1 \\ 0 & 0 & 1 & 0 \\ 0 & 1 & 0 & 0 \\ 1 & 0 & 0 & 0 \end{bmatrix} \times \frac{1}{2}\begin{bmatrix} 1 & 1 & 1 & 1 \\ 1 & -1 & 1 & -1 \\ 1 & 1 & -1 & -1 \\ -1 & -1 & -1 & 1 \end{bmatrix}$$

$$= \frac{1}{2}\begin{bmatrix} 1 & -1 & -1 & -1 \\ -1 & 1 & -1 & -1 \\ -1 & -1 & 1 & -1 \\ -1 & -1 & -1 & 1 \end{bmatrix}$$

Remember that the order of multiplying matrices is opposite to that in which the corresponding parts of the circuit they describe appear.

This matrix has both positive and negative terms in each column. In particular, the positive terms appear on the diagonal of the matrix and the negatives on the non-diagonal terms. These negative terms will be instrumental in wiping out the non-optimal states.

To see how the Canceling Circuit removes the non-tagged qubelet combinations, multiply its matrix $A_{Canceling}$ with the vector $|\psi_{tag}\rangle$ for the $|10\rangle$ tagged state:

$$A_{Canceling} \times |\psi_{tag}\rangle = \frac{1}{2}\begin{bmatrix} 1 & -1 & -1 & -1 \\ -1 & 1 & -1 & -1 \\ -1 & -1 & 1 & -1 \\ -1 & -1 & -1 & 1 \end{bmatrix} \times \frac{1}{2}\begin{pmatrix} 1 \\ 1 \\ -1 \\ 1 \end{pmatrix}$$

$$= \frac{1}{4}\begin{pmatrix} 1 \\ -1 \\ -1 \\ -1 \end{pmatrix} + \frac{1}{4}\begin{pmatrix} -1 \\ 1 \\ -1 \\ -1 \end{pmatrix} - \frac{1}{4}\begin{pmatrix} -1 \\ -1 \\ 1 \\ -1 \end{pmatrix} + \frac{1}{4}\begin{pmatrix} -1 \\ -1 \\ -1 \\ 1 \end{pmatrix}$$

$$= \frac{1}{4}\begin{pmatrix} 1-1+1-1 \\ -1+1+1-1 \\ -1-1-1-1 \\ -1-1+1+1 \end{pmatrix}$$

$$= \begin{pmatrix} 0 \\ 0 \\ -1 \\ 0 \end{pmatrix}$$

In other words,

$$A_{Canceling} \times |\psi_{tag}\rangle = -|10\rangle$$

Even though the last remaining state, $|10\rangle$, after all the others have been eliminated, has a negative sign, when it collapses, 10 will still be recorded in the classical register.

Notice the way the terms in the previous equation cancel out: the negative terms pair up with the positive terms in each element of the quantum state vector, except for the element that will remain. That is, the non-tagged qubelet combinations, $|00\rangle$, $|01\rangle$, and $|11\rangle$, are removed from the mega-qubit.

Unscrambling Quantum States and Matrices

Multiplying matrices to get the matrix for the Canceling Circuit, $A_{Canceling}$, looks formidable. But, since A_{X_2} and A_{H_2} are their own inverses, the multiplication for $A_{Canceling}$ can be rewritten as:

$$A_{Canceling} = A_{H_2} A_{X_2} A_{CZ} A_{X_2} A_{H_2}$$

$$= A_{H_2} A_{X_2} A_{CZ} A_{X_2}^{-1} A_{H_2}^{-1}$$

$$= \left(A_{H_2} A_{X_2}\right) A_{CZ} \left(A_{H_2} A_{X_2}\right)^{-1}$$

The last equation is obtained by noting that $X^{-1} Y^{-1} = (YX)^{-1}$.

In this form, the matrix equation is the conjugate found in group theory:[a]

$$A B A^{-1}$$

Here, A and B are generic matrices, or transformations, that describe how the state of a system changes by these two transformations, respectively. The conjugate is an "almost-inverse" in that it restores most of the qubelets back to their original states, except the ones that have to be retained.

Don't confuse this conjugate with complex conjugates discussed earlier. The group theory conjugates have a rich connection with quantum mechanics. (See *Group Theory and its Application to the Quantum Mechanics of Atomic Spectra* [WG59] for more information. The author was awarded the Nobel Prize in Physics in 1963[b] for introducing group theory in quantum mechanics. Another classic is *The Theory of Groups and Quantum Mechanics [WR14]*. Warning: these books are highly theoretical and not needed for quantum computing. I've mentioned them here to emphasize the deep connection between the matrix method for analyzing circuits and the group theoretic formulation of quantum mechanics.)

---

a. https://en.wikipedia.org/wiki/Conjugacy_class
b. https://www.nobelprize.org/prizes/physics/1963/summary/

We didn't explicitly work out the Canceling Circuit by analyzing how the pentagon $|0\rangle$ and triangle $|1\rangle$ qubelets form qubelet combinations that are transformed by the circuit. Doing so would have been painfully tedious and error-prone—and not particularly enlightening. With the stack of H gates at the beginning and end of the Canceling Circuit acting on blended states to begin with, you end up with too many split qubelets to keep organized. Rather, thinking holistically but still in terms of rotating and toggling qubelets, and how these operations in turn affect qubelet combinations, will guide you better as you design your own algorithms.

It may, though, seem that we somehow got lucky with the way we designed the Canceling Circuit to get the non-tagged states to cancel out. In fact, when dealing with larger numbers of qubits, the chances of getting all the non-tagged to cancel out are unlikely. But, as you'll see in the next section, you can apply the concept multiple times to whittle away at the non-tagged states in each iteration by reducing the probabilities of the qubits collapsing to these non-tagged qubelet combinations at each iteration.

Canceling by Any Other Name Is ... Amplification

In the literature, the Canceling Circuit is described as *reflection* about the "average value of all the amplitudes" followed by "amplification" of the tagged state. See, for example, Grover himself explaining it here.[4] This characterization makes for some nice graphics of bars turning upside down and contracting. But I find this way of thinking hard to connect back to what's happening in the quantum machine and, more importantly, extracting design principles from it to develop algorithms for other types of applications.

Multiple Iterations

In the case in the previous section, the negative terms in each column of the matrix neatly lined up so that the non-optimal qubelet combinations got eliminated. When your application has to deal with many qubits, the math may not always work out so neatly. In fact, you'll have to iterate the Tagging and Canceling circuits a few times to remove the non-optimal qubelet combinations.

In general, the number of iterations depends on the number, n, of qubits in your circuit:

$$\text{Number of Iterations} = O(\sqrt{n})$$

The symbol O is the Big-O function that indicates the complexity of the algorithm (loosely speaking, the number of iterations) in terms of the number of variables. We expect that the number of iterations will increase as your problem size increases. But you want to strive to design algorithms where the growth in iterations isn't exponential, making them impossible to implement on actual machines.

Thus, the overall structure of Grover's algorithm is as shown in the figure on page 313.

---

4.   https://cryptome.org/qc-grover.htm

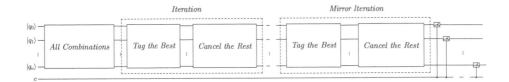

Putting the Quantum Effects Together

Going back to the two-qubit circuits that implement the quantum effects, connect them up in sequence, as shown in the following diagram:

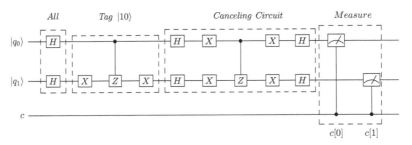

The quantum program describing this circuit is shown below:

Putting_Quantum_Effects_Together_Grovers_Algorithm.qasm

```
// Initialize Quantum and Classical Registers
qreg q[2];
creg c[2];

// Generate All Combinations
h q[0];
h q[1];

// Tag |10> Quantum State
x q[1];
cz q[0],q[1];
id q[0]; // Dummy gate for visually lining up circuit
x q[1];

// Canceling Circuit
h q[0];
h q[1];
x q[0];
x q[1];
cz q[0],q[1];
x q[0];
x q[1];
h q[0];
h q[1];

// Collapse Qubits
measure q[0] -> c[0];
measure q[1] -> c[1];
```

Executing this circuit cancels out all the qubelet combinations except for the tagged one, $|10\rangle$. The output of this program is shown in the following figure:

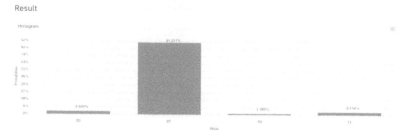

This output was obtained by running on a real quantum computer. The 01 state has highest probability of being observed in the classical register. Because the IBM Quantum Computer labels the bars opposite of our convention, the 01 state actually corresponds to 10. This indicates that the two qubits collapsed to $|10\rangle$, the tagged state. (The other states are the result of noise when running on a real quantum computer.)

Optimizing Your Quantum Programs

 As you hook up the tagging and canceling blocks, you'll frequently see back-to-back H or back-to-back X gates. Since these gates restore the qubit to the state before these gates were applied, you can remove them when they occur in your code.

Now that you've seen how these quantum effects come together to eliminate non-tagged quantum states, in the next section, you'll begin to put these effects together to hunt for optimal solutions for realistic applications.

Fundamental Circuit Pattern for Searching

Although the circuit in the previous section eliminated non-tagged quantum states, it can't directly be used to search for solutions for your applications for the following reasons:

- The qubits aren't handled symmetrically: the control qubit of the CNOT gate is $|q_0\rangle$ and its target is $|q_1\rangle$. So for a problem in which the optimal solution isn't known beforehand, it's tricky knowing how to place gates so that the optimal solution is properly tagged.

- The circuit to tag a state assumed you knew which state to tag. For example, the circuit to tag $|11\rangle$ is different than that to tag $|10\rangle$. For your applications, you won't know the state to tag when you're designing your program—that's the state you actually want the quantum program to find.

Thus, in this section, you'll see a circuit that symmetrically handles the qubits representing your problem's variables. This pattern, derived from Grover's algorithm, which we'll call the Fundamental Pattern, can then be more readily extended to actual applications.

As in the previous section, we'll first discuss the Fundamental Tagging Pattern followed by the Fundamental Canceling Pattern. These two together give the Fundamental Pattern for Searching for Optimal Solutions.

Fundamental Tagging Pattern

To this end, consider the circuit to tag, for example, $|011\rangle$, shown within the dashed box in the following figure:

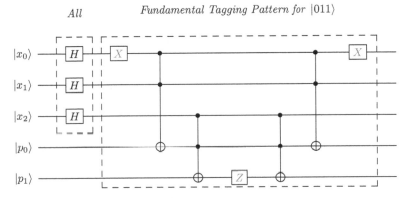

Fundamental Tagging Pattern for $|011\rangle$

The variables for the application problem are $|x_0\rangle$, $|x_1\rangle$, and $|x_2\rangle$. Hence, the H gates are only applied to these three qubits, as shown within the dashed box on the left. Qubits $|p_0\rangle$ and $|p_1\rangle$ represent the constraints that bind the variables, $|x_0\rangle$, $|x_1\rangle$, and $|x_2\rangle$, to specific states.

This circuit has 5 qubits, so it has 2^5 or 32 idealized states. Thus, its 32×32 matrix is quite unmanageable. But you can confirm that $|011\rangle$ is tagged by wiring up this circuit and checking out Statevector on the IBM Quantum Computer's Console, which is as shown in the figure on page 316.

The labels below the bars may be hard to read. Helpfully, on the Console, you'll also find the individual quantum states listed as a row vector. The important point, though, is that the label 00110, second from right, is lighter than the others indicating its amplitude is negative.

Bear in mind that the IBM Quantum Computer labels states opposite to the way we're writing them, even though it doesn't matter in this case. So, 00110 corresponds to $|p_1 p_0 q_2 q_1 q_0\rangle$. Keeping only the qubits corresponding to the application's variables, $|x_0\rangle$, $|x_1\rangle$, and $|x_2\rangle$, and ignoring the other two, the

Statevector

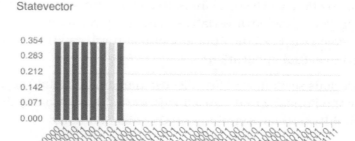

state for the lighter bar corresponds to $|x_0\rangle = |0\rangle, |x_1\rangle = |1\rangle$, and $|x_2\rangle = |1\rangle$, or $-|011\rangle$.

Since only the first three qubits, $|x_0\rangle$, $|x_1\rangle$, and $|x_2\rangle$, are proxies for the application's variables, there will be 2^3, or 8, primary or independent states. Thus, the quantum state is:

$$0.354(|000\rangle + |001\rangle + |010\rangle - |011\rangle + |100\rangle + |101\rangle + |110\rangle + |111\rangle)$$

Each of the eight idealized states has the same amplitude, 0.354, which is $1/\sqrt{8}$, indicating that the mega-qubit has a $1/8$ probability of collapsing to each of these states even though the amplitude of $|011\rangle$ is negative.

In this form, the tagged state is $-|011\rangle$.

Although confirming the tagged state by checking the Statevector on the IBM Quantum Computer is a good idea, it's useful to know how to work with CCNOT gates by inspection.

Analyzing the CCNOT Gate

First focus on just the two CCNOT gates within the dashed box, as shown in the following figure:

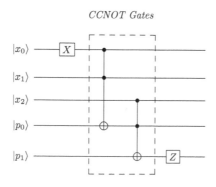

CCNOT Gates

Consider first the CCNOT gate on the left. Only when both its control qubits, $|x_0\rangle$ and $|x_1\rangle$, are $|1\rangle$ will its target qubit, $|p_0\rangle$, be $|1\rangle$. For any other combination of its control qubits, the target, $|p_0\rangle$, is $|0\rangle$.

For the second CCNOT gate, its control qubits are $|x_2\rangle$, the third application variable, and $|p_0\rangle$, the qubit representing the constraint that both $|x_0\rangle$ and $|x_1\rangle$ are $|1\rangle$. Thus, if $|x_2\rangle$ and $|p_0\rangle$ are each $|1\rangle$, then the target $|p_1\rangle$ switches to $|1\rangle$.

To put it another way, all three variable qubits, $|x_0\rangle$, $|x_1\rangle$, and $|x_2\rangle$, have to be $|1\rangle$ for $|p_1\rangle$, the qubit fed to the Z gate, to be $|1\rangle$. In this case, the Z gate inverts the triangle $|1\rangle$ qubelet by a half turn. That is, the state $|111\rangle$ is tagged.

Thus, by placing an X gate on $|x_0\rangle$, one of the controls of the first CCNOT gate, a $|0\rangle$ state on $|x_0\rangle$ will get switched to $|1\rangle$ so that both CCNOT gates' control qubits are $|1\rangle$. As a result, the Z gate will still invert $|p_1\rangle$'s triangle $|1\rangle$ qubelet. In other words, the original state $|011\rangle$ is tagged.

By changing the placement of the X gates, you can tag other states. For example, to tag $|010\rangle$, use the following circuit:

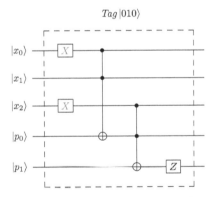

$Tag\,|010\rangle$

In this case, X gates are placed on $|x_0\rangle$ and $|x_2\rangle$. Thus, when these qubits are set to $|0\rangle$, the respective controls associated with these qubits are $|1\rangle$. Consequently, a state of $|010\rangle$ puts $|p_1\rangle$ to $|1\rangle$. And the Z gate, in turn, rotates its triangle $|1\rangle$ qubelet by a half turn. That is, the state $|010\rangle$ is tagged.

Finally, as part of Grover's algorithm, the Tagging Circuit is actually fed a mega-qubit containing all possible combinations of the application's independent or primary variables. So, these X and CCNOT gates act on all states and not just on the state to be tagged. Thus, as described in Why the Second X Gate?, on page 305, you need to add the gates to back out the changes to the other other states that aren't to be tagged. In this way, the desired state is tagged while the rest return to their original non-inverted states. The complete circuit to tag $|010\rangle$ is shown in the following figure:

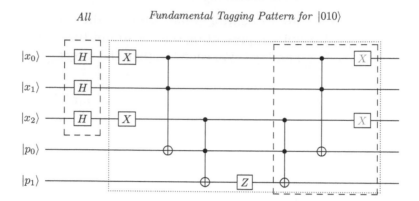

The gates within the dashed box to the right of the Z gate back out the changes made by the X and CCNOT gates to the left of the Z gate.

Next, we'll design a generic Fundamental Canceling Circuit that can be applied to practical applications.

Fundamental Canceling Pattern

To derive the Fundamental Canceling Pattern, redraw the Canceling Circuit, on page 304, in terms of its functional components as shown in the following figure:

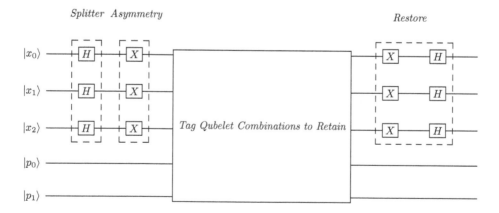

Replace the Tagging Qubelet Combinations to Retain block with CCNOT gates so that the Z gate on the bottom qubit, $|p_1\rangle$ is fired, as shown in the following figure:

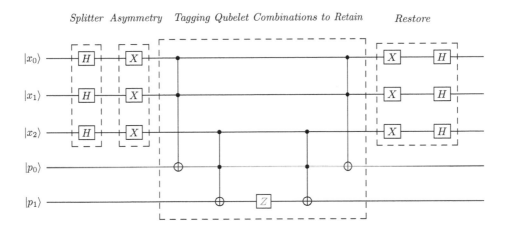

Hook up theses circuits together to get the Fundamental Pattern for Search, as shown in the following figure:

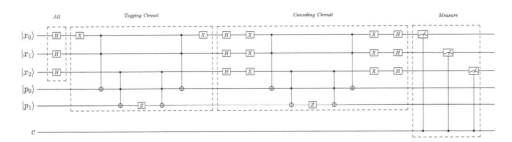

The quantum program associated with the above circuit is written as follows:

```
Grover_Fundamental_Pattern_for_Search.qasm
// Initialize Quantum and Classical Registers
qreg xvar[3]; // Qubits for the variables
qreg p[2]; // Qubits for the constraints
creg c[3]; // Classical Register

// Generate All Combinations
h xvar[0];
h xvar[1];
h xvar[2];

// Tag |011> Quantum State
x xvar[0];
ccx xvar[0],xvar[1],p[0];
ccx xvar[2],p[0],p[1];
```

```
z p[1];
ccx xvar[2],p[0],p[1];
ccx xvar[0],xvar[1],p[0];
x xvar[0];

// Fundamental Canceling Circuit
id xvar[1]; // Dummy gate to visually line up other gates
id xvar[2]; // Dummy gate to visually line up other gates
h xvar[0];
h xvar[1];
h xvar[2];
x xvar[0];
x xvar[1];
x xvar[2];
ccx xvar[0],xvar[1],p[0];
ccx xvar[2],p[0],p[1];
z p[1];
ccx xvar[2],p[0],p[1];
ccx xvar[0],xvar[1],p[0];
x xvar[0];
x xvar[1];
x xvar[2];
h xvar[0];
h xvar[1];
h xvar[2];

// Collapse Qubits
measure xvar[0] -> c[0];
measure xvar[1] -> c[1];
measure xvar[2] -> c[2];
```

In this code, instead of using a single array, q, for the qubits, we've declared two arrays: xvar for the application's variables qubits and p for the qubits representing the application's constraints. (To prevent any confusion with the X gate, in the code, we've used xvar to represent the variable qubits.)

The output of running this code on a simulator is shown in the following figure:

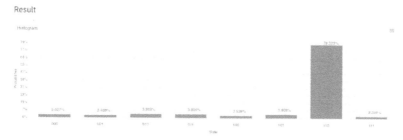

The highest bar is the one labeled 110. Bearing in mind that the IBM Quantum Computer reports the quantum states in the reverse order of how we've written them, the 110 bar corresponds to the $|x_0 x_1 x_2\rangle = |011\rangle$ quantum state. This, of course, is the tagged quantum state, while the likelihood of finding other non-tagged states is substantially lower.

Running on an Actual Quantum Computer

 If you try and execute programs with more than a few qubits on an actual quantum program, your results may not match those of the simulator. The reason is that the current state-of-the-art quantum computers are still highly susceptible to noise. As a result, qubits don't behave as expected and frequently get into incorrect states.

Quantum computing is still in its infancy, so our goal is to cover the principles so that we're ready when the engineering of these machines improves.

Can We Do Better?

Although the Fundamental Circuit for Search does a pretty cool job of retaining the tagged quantum state, $|110\rangle$, while at the same time severely suppressing non-tagged quantum states from surviving, it's possible to boost the odds for observing the tagged quantum state. In this section, you'll see how to improve the chances of collapsing the qubits to $|110\rangle$ increase from around to 78% to over 90%.

According to Grover's algorithm, the number of iterations is $O(\sqrt{n})$, where n is the number of independent qubits. In the circuit in the previous section, there are 3 qubits. So the theoretical number of iterations is $\sqrt{3} = 1.732$, which is rounded off to 2 cycles. So, let's add another round of the Tagging and Canceling circuits. The code for this revised program is listed below:

Grover_Fundamental_Pattern_for_Search_2_Iterations.qasm

```
// Initialize Quantum and Classical Registers
qreg xvar[3]; // Qubits for the variables
qreg p[2]; // Qubits for the constraints

creg c[3]; // Classical Register

// Generate All Combinations
h xvar[0];
h xvar[1];
h xvar[2];

//// ITERATION 1 ////
// Iteration 1: Tagging Circuit
x xvar[0];
ccx xvar[0],xvar[1],p[0];
ccx xvar[2],p[0],p[1];
```

```
z p[1];
ccx xvar[2],p[0],p[1];
ccx xvar[0],xvar[1],p[0];
x xvar[0];

// Iteration 1: Canceling Circuit
id xvar[1];
id xvar[2];
h xvar[0];
h xvar[1];
h xvar[2];
x xvar[0];
x xvar[1];
x xvar[2];
ccx xvar[0],xvar[1],p[0];
ccx xvar[2],p[0],p[1];
z p[1];
ccx xvar[2],p[0],p[1];
ccx xvar[0],xvar[1],p[0];
x xvar[0];
x xvar[1];
x xvar[2];
h xvar[0];
h xvar[1];
h xvar[2];

//// END OF ITERATION 1 /////

//// ITERATION 2 ////
// Iteration 2: Tagging Circuit
x xvar[0];
ccx xvar[0],xvar[1],p[0];
ccx xvar[2],p[0],p[1];
z p[1];
ccx xvar[2],p[0],p[1];
ccx xvar[0],xvar[1],p[0];
x xvar[0];

// Iteration 2: Canceling Circuit
id xvar[1];
id xvar[2];
h xvar[0];
h xvar[1];
h xvar[2];
x xvar[0];
x xvar[1];
x xvar[2];
ccx xvar[0],xvar[1],p[0];
ccx xvar[2],p[0],p[1];
z p[1];
ccx xvar[2],p[0],p[1];
ccx xvar[0],xvar[1],p[0];
```

```
x xvar[0];
x xvar[1];
x xvar[2];
h xvar[0];
h xvar[1];
h xvar[2];

//// END OF ITERATION 2 ////

// Collapse Qubits
measure xvar[0] -> c[0];
measure xvar[1] -> c[1];
measure xvar[2] -> c[2];
```

I simply copied and pasted the Tagging and Canceling circuits' code blocks before the statements for the Measure gates for the second iteration. The resulting circuit on the IBM Quantum Computer is shown in the following figure:

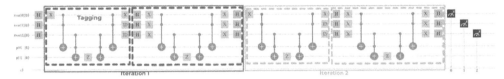

This time when you run this program, you'll get an output that's similar to the following figure:

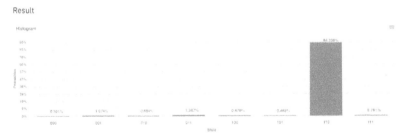

The probability of recording 110 in the classical register, corresponding to the tagged quantum state $|110\rangle$, has shot up to around 94% using two iterations from around 78% with one iteration.

Thus, by using asymmetry and rotating the qubelets of the quantum state we want to retain, we're forcing the non-tagged states to cancel out when the "restoring" gates are applied.

In the next section, we'll use this generic pattern to find an assignment of performers at the Bellagio, introduced in A Scheduling Problem, on page 6.

Searching for an Optimal Schedule

In all the circuits you've seen so far in this chapter, the tagged quantum state was specified up front. In this section, you'll learn to design circuits that tag the optimal solutions for actual application problems even though you don't know about them when you're setting up your code.

To illustrate this way of designing circuits, we'll develop a quantum algorithm to find a valid schedule for Kimmel and Maher performing at the Bellagio. The constraints governing when these stand-up hosts do their acts are listed in A Scheduling Problem, on page 6, and stated here:

- Bellagio on Day 1: $|\overline{k}\rangle \vee |\overline{m}\rangle$
- Bellagio on Day 2: $|k\rangle \vee |m\rangle$

The qubits $|k\rangle$ and $|m\rangle$ stand for the comedians Kimmel and Maher, respectively.

The quantum circuit that models these constraints is explained in Logic Expressions to Quantum Circuit, on page 62, and shown in the following figure:

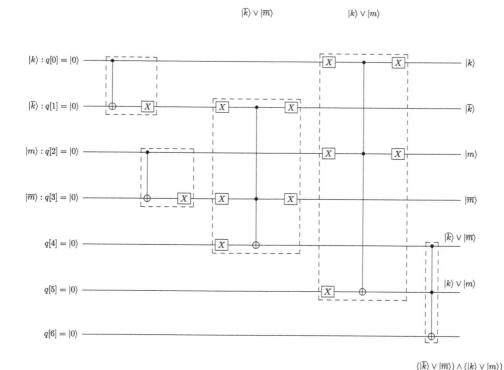

$$((\overline{k}\rangle \vee |\overline{m}\rangle)) \wedge (|k\rangle \vee |m\rangle))$$

You'll use this set of gates in several places in your program. So we'll refer to it as Bellagio-Constraint-Gates.

Tagging When You Don't Know the Optimal Solution

Among the many ways that classical computers differ from quantum computers, one of the most fundamental is the ability of quantum computers to simultaneously hold *all* possible solutions for the application problem. Whereas in classical computing, the algorithms start with an initial guess and then work up to an optimal solution, Grover's algorithm takes the reverse tack—starting from all solutions, it whittles away at the mega-qubit to remove non-optimal solutions.

So that the algorithm removes qubelet combinations from the mega-qubit that are non-optimal, you need to differentiate between optimal qubelet combinations—those that satisfy the system of Boolean logic expressions—from non-optimal, those that don't.

Before the quantum program can get rid of the non-optimal qubelet combinations, you need to first generate all possible qubelet combinations by placing H gates on the variable qubits, as described in Tagging the Optimal Solution, on page 107, as shown in the following circuit:

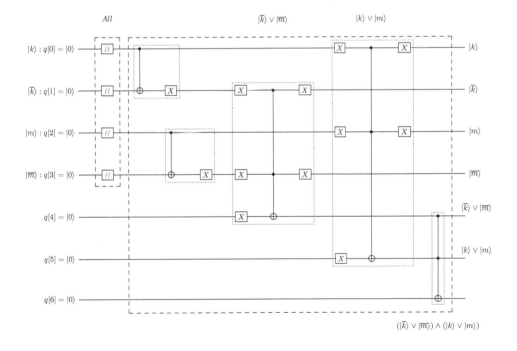

The first four qubits, q[0]–q[3], are the variables $|k\rangle$, $|\overline{k}\rangle$, $|m\rangle$, and $|\overline{m}\rangle$, respectively. The H gates are, thus, applied to these four, as shown in the dashed box on the left in the previous circuit.

Since the H gate splits each of these four qubits into a pentagon $|0\rangle$ and a triangle $|1\rangle$ qubelet, the mega-qubit now contains all 2^4, or 16, qubelet combinations, each representing a possible set of $|0\rangle$ and $|1\rangle$ states that satisfies the Boolean logic expressions.

Qubits q[4] and q[5] represent the contraints for the assignments at the Bellagio on Days 1 and 2, respectively. These form the control qubits for the CCNOT gate at the bottom right in the previous circuit. When a qubelet combination satisfies these constraints, these controls are $|1\rangle$, which, in turn, makes its target, qubit q[6], switch from $|0\rangle$ to $|1\rangle$.

These qubelet combinations—those that make q[6] $|1\rangle$—are the ones that should be tagged. For the others, at least one of the constraints will not be met. That is, one of q[4] or q[5] is $|0\rangle$. For these non-optimal qubelet combinations, the target qubit, q[6], will remain $|0\rangle$. Thus, by applying a Z gate to q[6], as shown in the following figure, only those qubelet combinations corresponding to states that satisfy the Boolean logic expressions will have an inverted triangle $|1\rangle$ qubelet in q[6]:

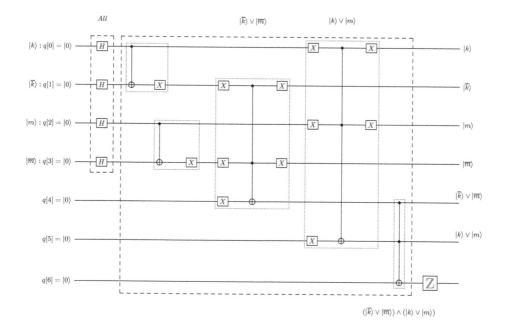

$$(\,(|\overline{k}\rangle \vee |\overline{m}\rangle) \wedge (|k\rangle \vee |m\rangle)\,)$$

To complete the Tagging Circuit, following the explanation in Why the Second X Gate?, on page 305, and Disentangling the Bellagio Constraints, on page 133, you need to hook up quantum gates that mirror the Bellagio Constraints, as shown in the following circuit:

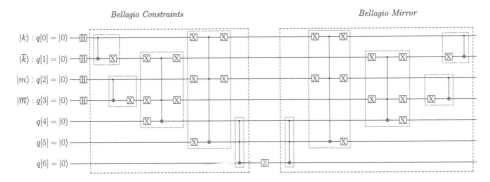

The group of gates in the large dashed box on the left model the Bellagio Constraints. The gates in the large dashed box on the right mirror those in the left and are labeled Bellagio Mirror.

So that the circuit diagrams illustrate the essential structure of Grover's algorithm, from now on we'll replace these two groups by blocks, as shown in the following circuit:

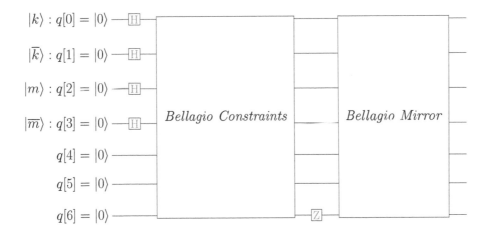

Thus, without knowing what states or qubelet combinations satisfy the Boolean logic expressions, the circuit shown in the previous figure will tag the correct qubelet combinations in the mega-qubit. Next, you'll design the circuit that removes the non-tagged qubelet combinations—the ones that don't lead to a valid schedule—from the mega-qubit.

Gates Are Easy to Misplace

In quantum computing you have to be extra careful when placing gates in your circuit. Unlike classical programs, quantum programs have several blocks of code that are similar, making it easy to overlook or misplace a gate. Moreover, since the quantum program deals with multiple qubelet combinations, inserting Measure gates as watch points isn't helpful. Incorrectly placed gates won't result in compile-time errors, so debugging gets unnecessarily tedious.

One way to mitigate the issue with multiple qubelet combinations in the mega-qubit is to not generate all combinations with the H gate at the beginning. This lets you start with a single state, letting you more easily trace how it changes as it passes through the circuit.

Completing the Program with the Canceling Circuit

To complete the quantum program, you need to add the Canceling Circuit to the circuit we designed in the previous section. According to the Fundamental Canceling Pattern, on page 318, the Canceling Circuit is just the Tagging Circuit surrounded by H and X gates, as shown in the following figure:

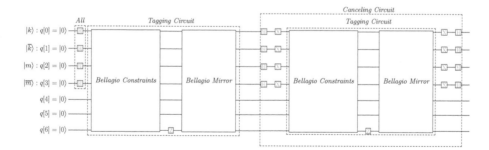

Before writing a program for this circuit to obtain the assignment of the talk show hosts, Kimmel and Maher, to the days they perform at the Bellagio, first determine the number of iterations of the Tagging and Canceling circuits needed. Since there are four primary application variables in q[0]–q[3], then as stated in Multiple Iterations, on page 312, the number of iterations, n, is given by:

$$\text{Number of Iterations} \approx O(\sqrt{n})$$
$$= O(\sqrt{4})$$
$$= 2$$

Thus, your final circuit will require another set of the Tagging Circuit followed by the Canceling Circuit. That is, the quantum program will have the following structure:

- H gates on the independent variables to generate all combinations.
- Tagging Circuit for Iteration 1.
- Canceling Circuit for Iteration 1.
- Tagging Circuit for Iteration 2.
- Canceling Circuit for Iteration 2.

The first few lines of the code with two such iterations is listed as follows:

Bellagio_Hotel_Scheduling_Problem_Final.qasm

```
// Initialize Quantum and Classical Registers
qreg q[7];
creg c[2];

// Generate All Combinations
h q[0];
h q[1];
h q[2];
h q[3];

//// ITERATION 1
// Constraints (to tag optimal solution)
x q[4];
x q[5];
cx q[0],q[1];
cx q[2],q[3];
x q[0];
x q[1];
x q[3];
x q[1];
x q[3];
ccx q[1],q[3],q[4];
x q[1];
x q[2];
x q[3];
ccx q[0],q[2],q[5];
x q[0];
x q[2];
ccx q[4],q[5],q[6];
x q[0];
x q[2];
z q[6];
```

(You can get the complete code listing from the book's page on the Pragmatic Bookshelf's website at https://pragprog.com/book/nmquantum/quantum-computing.)

The code includes the Measure gates for q[0] and q[2] only, the variables for Kimmel and Maher, respectively. Measure gates aren't needed for q[1] and q[3], as these are the complements of the ones being measured.

The complete circuit for this code on the IBM Quantum Computer console is shown in the following figure:

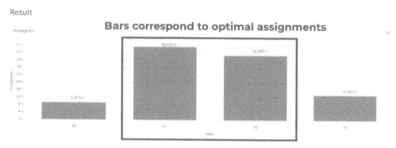

The solid vertical line roughly in the center of the figure demarks the two iterations. Each iteration contains the Tagging and Canceling circuits.

When you run this program on the IBM Quantum Computer simulator, you'll get an output that's similar to the following chart:

Result

Bars correspond to optimal assignments

This program collapses to the quantum states associated with the two taller middle bars most frequently—around 75%, or roughly three out of four shots. The labels at the bottom of these bars are 01 on the left bar and 10 on the right bar.

As the states reported by the IBM Quantum Computer are in the reverse order of the way we denote them, the left bit on each state represents the collapse of the $|k\rangle$ qubit, and the right bit logs that of the $|m\rangle$ qubit.

Thus, the taller left bar labeled 01 corresponds to the following solution:

$k = 0 \mapsto$ Jimmy Kimmel performs at Alladin on Day 1 and at Bellagio on Day 2
$m = 1 \mapsto$ Bill Maher performs at Bellagio on Day 1 and at Caesars on Day 2

(See Writing a System of Boolean Logic Expressions, on page 8, where these variables have been defined.)

Likewise, the taller right bar labeled 10 correponds to the following solution:

$k = 1 \mapsto$ Jimmy Kimmel performs at Bellagio on Day 1 and at Aladdin on Day 2

$m = 0 \mapsto$ Bill Maher performs at Caesars on Day 1 and at Bellagio on Day 2

Limiting our attention to just the Bellagio, these states translate to the following assignments, respectively:

	01 Solution	10 Solution
Day 1	Maher	Kimmel
Day 2	Kimmel	Maher

Preparing Your Program for Running on a Real Quantum Computer

Before running your program on a real quantum computer, you can do a few things to reduce the effect of noise when computing with real qubits. Specifically, consider the following ways to improve performance:

Remove Back-to-Back Gates
Back-to-back gates leave the state of a qubit unchanged. So removing them has no effect on the final result.

Use Large Rotations of Qubelets
Where possible, rotate qubelets by half turns instead of quarter turns when introducing quantum effects in your code. Larger rotations are less susceptible to noise than rotating qubclets through smaller angles.

Test for Optimality
Despite all your efforts, when you run your quantum program on a real computer, it's quite likely that the qubits will collapse to incorrect states. Thus, to make it easier to identify which states correspond to optimal solutions and those that don't, run your states through the quantum gates that model the application's constraints. That is, before the Measure gates that collapse the qubits, insert the block of gates representing the constraints. Finally, put a Measure gate on the qubit that indicates whether all constraints are met. (For the Bellagio problem, this would be the q[6] qubit.)

Then, on the output, consider as candidates for optimality only the states that have logged a 1 in the corresponding bit. Confirm that they are indeed optimal by plugging their states into constraints set up on a classical computer.

Bottom Line

Generating all possible quantum states or rotating qubelets is well and good, but eliminating qubelet combinations from the mega-qubit ups the ante on figuring the correct quantum effects to apply. Even though applications in quantum cryptography deal with several qubits, the BB84 protocol is designed around quantum effects applied to single qubits. The quantum effects in search applications, though, are necessarily intertwined across multiple qubits simultaneously. You need to tease out symmetries with combinations of gates that may appear overly complicated but will become clear when you look at gate matrices.

Our analysis of Grover's algorithm continues a theme you saw in Design a Teleporting Circuit, on page 256, where we used circuits of fewer qubits as building blocks for larger circuits. Here, by studying quantum effects in smaller circuits, we then generalized them for circuits with many more qubits. Specifically, the Fundamental Circuit Pattern for Searching, on page 314, forms a template that can be extended to search applications modeled as Boolean logic expressions. As explained in Searching for an Optimal Schedule, on page 324, by integrating the gates that model the logical constraints of the application, you end up with a design that triggers quantum effects to get an optimal solution.

A not-as-much-touted perk, but one that heightens the appeal of Grover's algorithm, is that you can use generic quantum principles—no customized techniques specifically tuned for a particular application—to get optimal solutions. For the Hotel Scheduling Problem, *The Art of Computer Programming [Knu11]* describes a specialized technique. This technique, though, may not work as well in other kinds of applications modeled as Boolean logic expressions. Grover's algorithm, on the other hand, is general purpose and can be applied in the same way on many other types of applications modeled as Boolean logic expressions.

In the next chapter, we'll talk about how you can continue to expand your learning of quantum computing.

Try Your Hand

Solutions to these exercises are given in Quantum Search Solutions, on page 510.

For any code listing in the exercises, assume the following header lines:

```
OPENQASM 2.0;
include "qelib1.inc";
```

If you want to run any exercise, you must include them in the code you'd like to execute.

1. As you start designing your own quantum algorithms, you'll need to figure out what gates to use and where to place them in your circuit. To this end, understanding how gates manipulate quantum states is crucial. To strengthen your intuition when handling quantum gates, fluently rotating the pentagon $|0\rangle$ and triangle $|1\rangle$ qubelets is helpful. The following exercises relate mega-qubits with rotated qubelets and their corresponding quantum states.

    Write each of the following mega-qubits in terms of the idealized states. In each case, identify the tagged qubelet combination, if any, and its corresponding quantum state:

    a.

    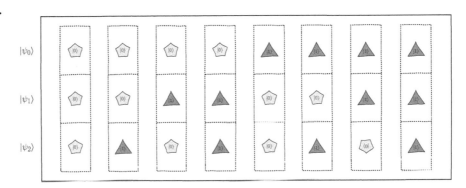

    b.

    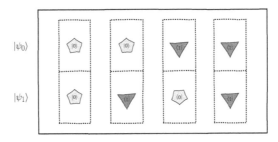

    c.

    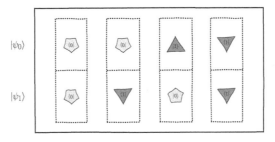

d.

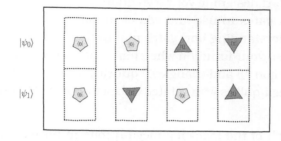

2. In this problem, you'll see the perils of rushing to conclusions. Rotating and toggling qubelets do matter. A gate that rotates the triangle $|1\rangle$ qubelets by a quarter turn instead of switching it with the other type can affect the behavior of a circuit even if the other gates in the circuit are unchanged.

To illustrate the importance of carefully working out the precise quantum effects you need to incorporate in your quantum program, you'll analyze a circuit to identify the missing quantum gate to tag the $|01\rangle$ quantum state.

To this end, look at the following circuit:

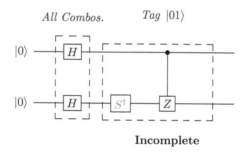

The mega-qubit after each qubit is acted on by the H gate is shown in the following figure:

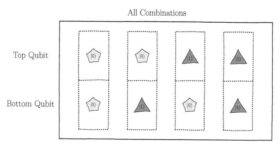

a. What's the difference between the X, S, and $S^{\dagger}$ gates?

b. Draw the mega-qubit after the $S^\dagger$ gate acts on the bottom qubit. Write the mega-qubit's quantum state in terms of the idealized states.

c. Draw the mega-qubit after the CZ gate acts on the qubits. Write the mega-qubit's quantum state in terms of the idealized states.

d. What operations must be applied to the qubelets so that the $|01\rangle$ quantum state is tagged?

e. Using the Canceling Circuit, on page 304, write a quantum program using your design in the previous part to eliminate the non-tagged quantum states. Examine the output to confirm that your program works correctly.

f. Alluding back to the introduction to this exercise, what are two morals you can draw?

3. As you saw in Finding Asymmetry, on page 307, finding a column in the A_{H_2} matrix for two stacked gates was crucial to building the Canceling Circuit when working with two qubits. With three qubits and three stacked H gates, as shown in the following circuit, what column in this circuit's matrix, A_{H_3}, is symmetric?

$$|q_0\rangle \quad \text{---} \boxed{H} \text{---}$$

$$|q_1\rangle \quad \text{---} \boxed{H} \text{---}$$

$$|q_2\rangle \quad \text{---} \boxed{H} \text{---}$$

4. In this exercise, you'll start with the following Tagging Circuit:

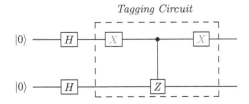

Tagging Circuit

a. Which quantum state is tagged? Confirm your answer by looking at the Statevector on the IBM Quantum Computer.

b. Write the tagged state as a vector.

c. Feed your quantum state obtained in the previous part to the Canceling Circuit, on page 304. Using its matrix $A_{Canceling}$, show that the non-tagged states are eliminated. For your reference, $A_{Canceling}$ is:

$$A_{Canceling} = \frac{1}{2}\begin{bmatrix} 1 & -1 & -1 & -1 \\ -1 & 1 & -1 & -1 \\ -1 & -1 & 1 & -1 \\ -1 & -1 & -1 & 1 \end{bmatrix}$$

   d. Append the Canceling Circuit, on page 304, to this Tagging Circuit and write a program for the whole circuit. Remember to include Measure gates to collapse the qubits and record their states in the classical register.

   e. Run your program and confirm that only the tagged state is recorded in the classical registers.

5. Explain what's wrong with each of the following circuit block's depiction of Grover's algorithm:

   a.

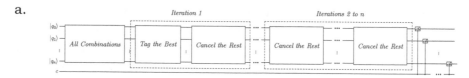

   b.

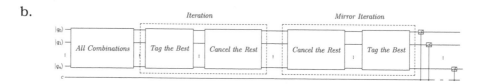

   c.

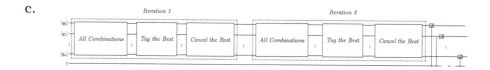

6. Following the Fundamental Circuit Pattern for Searching, on page 314, the circuit shown in the following figure tags two qubits:

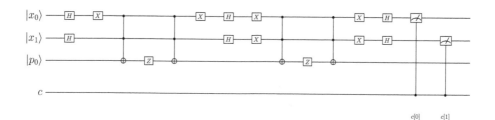

    a. Identify the All Combinations, Tagging Circuit, and Canceling Circuit sections of the circuit.

    b. Which state is tagged?

    c. Write a program for this circuit.

    d. Run your program and confirm that the state recorded in the final register matches the one you identified as being tagged. (Since this program has several qubits and gates, run your code on a simulator, as you may find that running on today's real quantum computers leads to incorrect results.)

7. Consider the following circuit that's modeled after the Fundamental Circuit Pattern for Searching, on page 314:

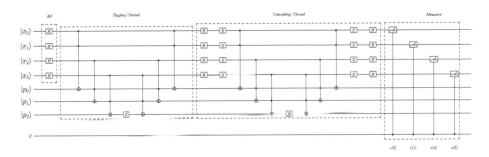

    a. Identify where you need to insert X gates so that this circuit tags $|1011\rangle$ and eliminates the other states.

    b. Write a program for your modified circuit.

    c. Run your program on the IBM Quantum Computer simulator and confirm that only the tagged state $|1011\rangle$ survives and the others are eliminated.

    d. What can you do to improve the odds of getting the qubits to collapse to the tagged state?

    e. Revise your program accordingly.

    f. Run your revised program on the IBM Quantum Computer simulator and see whether your suggestion does indeed improve the odds of retaining the $|1011\rangle$ tagged state.

Now this is not the end. It is not even the beginning of the end. But it is, perhaps, the end of the beginning.

➤ *Sir Winston Churchill, at a 1942 speech at London's Mansion House*

CHAPTER 11

Where to Go from Here

We've obsessively focused on building your intuition for applying quantum effects in code and designing practical quantum programs for your applications. Moreover, every time you were introduced to a new quantum effect, I wanted to get you to see how it works in a quantum program—getting dazzled by the strange ways that qubits behave takes a back seat to actually learning how to capitalize on these phenomena. Quantum mechanics forces a wholly different way of approaching problems than those of classical programming. Topping your toolbox with the latest gizmo isn't useful if you don't know how to use it. Thus, a major thrust of this book was to show you how to think "quantum" so that you can develop your own algorithms.

In the rest of this chapter, we touch upon topics to continue your learning of quantum computing. Think of this chapter as opening doors just enough to glimpse what's inside and whet your appetite.

Well-Known Algorithms

Although we have focused on ways that let you use quantum algorithms in practical applications, you may find some other quantum algorithms interesting:

- Deutsch-Jozsa algorithm
- Bernstein-Vazirani algorithm
- Simon's algorithm
- Quantum Fourier transforms

The first three demonstrate that for a specialized class of problems, quantum computing does indeed offer computational advantages over that of classical computing. These are primarily of historical and theoretical interest. The fourth one, Quantum Fourier transforms, is the basis for Shor's algorithm to factor large numbers, thereby threatening modern-day cryptography.

We'll only go through the fundamentals of the Deutsch-Jozsa algorithm, as it gives another opportunity to see how to jump start an analysis of a quantum circuit using qubelets. You can find more information on the others in many textbooks on quantum computing.

Deutsch-Jozsa Algorithm

The Deutsch-Jozsa algorithm[1][2] illustrates that for a special class of functions, quantum computing identifies the function's nature from a single measurement rather than sampling it multiple times, as you'd have to do with a classical approach. To demonstrate this feat, Deutsch-Jozsa restricted this function F to be one of the following two types:

Constant: A constant function, F_C, is one in which the output will always be the same no matter what the input is. For two qubits, a constant function could be, for example:

$$F_C(|q_0\rangle, |q_1\rangle) = |0\rangle$$

It always returns a $|0\rangle$ no matter what the states of the input qubits are. In other words, the function F_C is:

$|q_0\rangle$	$|q_1\rangle$	$F_C(|q_0\rangle, |q_1\rangle)$
$|0\rangle$	$|0\rangle$	$|0\rangle$
$|0\rangle$	$|1\rangle$	$|0\rangle$
$|1\rangle$	$|0\rangle$	$|0\rangle$
$|1\rangle$	$|1\rangle$	$|0\rangle$

Alternatively, F_C could also be defined as:

$$F_C(|q_0\rangle, |q_1\rangle) = |1\rangle$$

In this case, the function F_C returns $|1\rangle$ for any combination of the input qubits $|q_0\rangle$ and $|q_1\rangle$.

Balanced: A balanced function, F_B, is one where half the input combinations return a $|0\rangle$ and the other half return a $|1\rangle$. For example, one such function F_B is shown in the table on page 341.

---

1.   https://www.jstor.org/stable/52182?seq=1
2.   https://en.wikipedia.org/wiki/Deutsch%E2%80%93Jozsa_algorithm

$\lvert q_0 \rangle$	$\lvert q_1 \rangle$	$F_B(\lvert q_0 \rangle, \lvert q_1 \rangle)$
$\lvert 0 \rangle$	$\lvert 0 \rangle$	$\lvert 0 \rangle$
$\lvert 0 \rangle$	$\lvert 1 \rangle$	$\lvert 1 \rangle$
$\lvert 1 \rangle$	$\lvert 0 \rangle$	$\lvert 1 \rangle$
$\lvert 1 \rangle$	$\lvert 1 \rangle$	$\lvert 0 \rangle$

The first and last input combinations return a $\lvert 0 \rangle$ while the second and third return a $\lvert 1 \rangle$.

The Deustsch-Jozsa algorithm is merely concerned with figuring out whether the function F is constant or balanced—not the precise form of the function. That is, it's not concerned if the function F returns, say, a $\lvert 0 \rangle$ or $\lvert 1 \rangle$ for a particular set of inputs, but only whether it's a constant or a balanced function.

The problem, then, is:

Given: For any combination of inputs, you're told what the function returns (but not the function F itself).

Determine: Whether the function F is constant or balanced.

Solving on a Classical Computer

If you use a classical computer to establish the type of function, you'd need to sample a significant number of input combinations.

Consider, again, the two-qubit example stated previously. Suppose you start with $\lvert q_0 \rangle = \lvert 0 \rangle$ and $\lvert q_1 \rangle = \lvert 0 \rangle$; you'll observe $\lvert 0 \rangle$. Since both the constant and balanced functions defined earlier return $\lvert 0 \rangle$ for this set of inputs, you need to check another set. Say you pick $\lvert q_0 \rangle = \lvert 1 \rangle$ and $\lvert q_1 \rangle = \lvert 1 \rangle$. This time, again, you'll observe $\lvert 0 \rangle$ and won't be able to say which type of function is producing these values. Next, you pick $\lvert q_0 \rangle = \lvert 0 \rangle$ and $\lvert q_1 \rangle = \lvert 1 \rangle$. Again, the output is $\lvert 1 \rangle$. If the function was constant, you'd have seen $\lvert 0 \rangle$ matching the earlier outputs. Now you can conclude that the function is balanced.

Of course, you could get lucky by choosing $\lvert q_0 \rangle = \lvert 0 \rangle$ and $\lvert q_1 \rangle = \lvert 0 \rangle$ as your first choice and $\lvert q_0 \rangle = \lvert 0 \rangle$ and $\lvert q_1 \rangle = \lvert 1 \rangle$ as your second choice. In this case, since the outputs of each set are different, you'd conclude that the function is not constant and, therefore, must be balanced. In the worst case, though, you'll need half the number of total combinations plus one more to establish the nature of the function.

A quantum computer, on the other hand, can tell you the type of function, constant or balanced, from just one measurement. In the next section, you'll see how quantum computers can pull this off.

Solving on a Quantum Computer

The Deutsch-Jozsa algorithm prescribes how to get the type of function from just one sample. This algorithm has two things going for it that gives it an edge over classical computers:

- By putting qubits in superposition, quantum computers can implicitly go through all cases simultaneously.
- Back-to-back H gates restore the mega-qubit to its original state.

To see how these two quantum effects are put to use, we'll work with a simpler case put forth by Deutsch.[3]

Deutsch's Algorithm

In this simpler version, the function F works on only a single qubit:

Function F is Constant:
> A constant function returns the same value for both states of the qubit. For example, the following is a function $F(|x\rangle)$ that always returns a $|0\rangle$:

$$F(|0\rangle) = |0\rangle$$
$$F(|1\rangle) = |0\rangle$$

Function F is Balanced:
> A balanced function $F(|x\rangle)$ will return $|0\rangle$ for one state and $|1\rangle$ for the other. For example,

$$F(|0\rangle) = |0\rangle$$
$$F(|1\rangle) = |1\rangle$$

Deutsch's algorithm has three parts:

- *Incorporate* the function F.
- *Embed* the function F in a quantum circuit.
- *Collapse and measure* the top qubit only. A 0 indicates a constant function and a 1 points to a balanced function.

We'll see how these parts work to identify whether the function is constant or balanced.

---

3. https://arxiv.org/abs/quant-ph/9708016

First, Deutsch assumed that the function F could be *incorporated* in a quantum circuit as follows:

$$|x\rangle \xrightarrow{\quad} \boxed{U_F} \xrightarrow{\quad} |x\rangle$$
$$|y\rangle \xrightarrow{\quad} \qquad \xrightarrow{\quad} |y\rangle \oplus F(|x\rangle)$$

The $|x\rangle$ and $|y\rangle$ qubits on the left are the inputs to the block U_F. The top qubit on the right of the block U_F is unchanged by the block. The bottom qubit, on the other hand, has its state changed to $|y\rangle \oplus F(|x\rangle)$, as depicted. (The symbol $\oplus$ is the Exclusive-OR operator.)

So, if F is the constant function, $F(|x\rangle) = |0\rangle$, defined earlier, then the truth table—which relates inputs and outputs—for the U_F block works out as follows for the following set of inputs for $|x\rangle$ and $|y\rangle$:

$|x\rangle$	$|y\rangle$	$F(|x\rangle)$	$|y\rangle \oplus F(|x\rangle)$
$|0\rangle$	$|0\rangle$	$|0\rangle$	$|0\rangle$
$|0\rangle$	$|1\rangle$	$|0\rangle$	$|1\rangle$
$|1\rangle$	$|0\rangle$	$|0\rangle$	$|0\rangle$
$|1\rangle$	$|1\rangle$	$|0\rangle$	$|1\rangle$

To figure out the gates for U_F corresponding to this truth table, first work out its matrix for these inputs:

Input: $|x\rangle = |0\rangle \ |y\rangle = |0\rangle$

For this input combination, the outputs $|x\rangle$ and $|y\rangle \oplus F(|x\rangle)$ written as a two-qubit quantum state is:

$$|00\rangle \mapsto |00\rangle$$

Writing this state as a vector:

$$\begin{pmatrix} 1 \\ 0 \\ 0 \\ 0 \end{pmatrix}$$

This vector becomes the first column of the matrix for U_F.

Input: $|x\rangle = |0\rangle \ |y\rangle = |1\rangle$

For this input combination, the outputs $|x\rangle$ and $|y\rangle \oplus F(|x\rangle)$ written as a two-qubit quantum state is:

$$|01\rangle \mapsto |01\rangle$$

Writing this state as a vector:

$$\begin{pmatrix} 0 \\ 1 \\ 0 \\ 0 \end{pmatrix}$$

This vector becomes the second column of the matrix for U_F.

Input: $|x\rangle = |1\rangle\,|y\rangle = |0\rangle$

For this input combination, the outputs $|x\rangle$ and $|y\rangle \oplus F(|x\rangle)$, written as a two-qubit quantum state, is:

$$|10\rangle \mapsto |10\rangle$$

Writing this state as a vector:

$$\begin{pmatrix} 0 \\ 0 \\ 1 \\ 0 \end{pmatrix}$$

This vector becomes the third column of the matrix for U_F.

Input: $|x\rangle = |1\rangle\,|y\rangle = |1\rangle$

For this input combination, the outputs $|x\rangle$ and $|y\rangle \oplus F(|x\rangle)$ written as a two-qubit quantum state is:

$$|11\rangle \mapsto |11\rangle$$

Writing this state as a vector:

$$\begin{pmatrix} 0 \\ 0 \\ 0 \\ 1 \end{pmatrix}$$

This vector becomes the fourth and last column of the matrix for U_F.

Thus, the matrix A_{U_F} for the U_F block is:

$$A_{U_F} = \begin{bmatrix} 1 & 0 & 0 & 0 \\ 0 & 1 & 0 & 0 \\ 0 & 0 & 1 & 0 \\ 0 & 0 & 0 & 1 \end{bmatrix}$$

This matrix is just the identity matrix. In other words, the block U_F doesn't affect the states passed to it, as shown in the following circuit:

$$U_F$$

$$|x\rangle \quad\quad\quad |x\rangle$$

$$|y\rangle \quad\quad\quad |y\rangle \oplus F(|x\rangle)$$

If the function F is a balanced function as defined previously, $F(|0\rangle) = |0\rangle$ and $F(|1\rangle) = |1\rangle$, the truth table for U_F is:

$|x\rangle$	$|y\rangle$	$F(|x\rangle)$	$|y\rangle \oplus F(|x\rangle)$
$|0\rangle$	$|0\rangle$	$|0\rangle$	$|0\rangle$
$|0\rangle$	$|1\rangle$	$|0\rangle$	$|1\rangle$
$|1\rangle$	$|0\rangle$	$|1\rangle$	$|1\rangle$
$|1\rangle$	$|1\rangle$	$|1\rangle$	$|0\rangle$

Following the steps to calculate the matrix for the constant function, you'll get the matrix corresponding to the preceding truth table for the balanced function:

$$A_{U_F} = \begin{bmatrix} 1 & 0 & 0 & 0 \\ 0 & 1 & 0 & 0 \\ 0 & 0 & 0 & 1 \\ 0 & 0 & 1 & 0 \end{bmatrix}$$

The first two columns are the identity columns. That is, when the top qubit, $|x\rangle$, is $|0\rangle$, the output qubits, $|x\rangle$ and $|y\rangle \oplus F(|x\rangle)$, are unchanged. On the other hand, from the third and fourth columns, when the top qubit is $|1\rangle$, the bottom qubit's state is switched from what it was passed. In other words, this matrix is that of the Controlled NOT (CNOT) Gate, on page 47, as shown in the following circuit:

$$U_F$$

$$|x\rangle \quad\quad\quad |x\rangle$$

$$|y\rangle \quad\quad\quad |y\rangle \oplus F(|x\rangle)$$

Having worked out the circuit block U_F for different types of constant and balanced functions, Deutsch then *embedded* it, as shown in the following circuit:

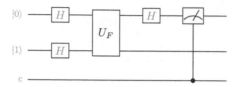

Only the top qubit is measured. As you'll see shortly, you only need to measure it to determine the nature of the function.

Now although we won't know what the function F is, what we want to study here is the response of this circuit—that is, what would the outputs look like if the function F is constant versus balanced.

The two H gates on the left put the qubits in superposition by splitting the qubits and creating a mega-qubit with all possible states:

$$
\begin{aligned}
H|0\rangle \otimes H|1\rangle &= \frac{1}{\sqrt{2}}(|0\rangle + |1\rangle) \otimes \frac{1}{\sqrt{2}}(|0\rangle - |1\rangle) \\
&= \frac{1}{2}|0\rangle(|0\rangle - |1\rangle) + |1\rangle(|0\rangle - |1\rangle) \\
&= \frac{1}{2}(|00\rangle - |01\rangle + |10\rangle - |11\rangle)
\end{aligned}
$$

The corresponding mega-qubit that is then fed to the CNOT gate is shown in the following figure:

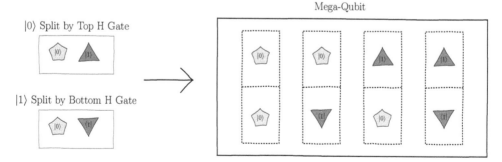

The top H gate splits the $|0\rangle$ qubit into a pentagon $|0\rangle$ qubelet and a triangle $|1\rangle$ qubelet. The bottom H gate splits the $|1\rangle$ qubit into a pentagon $|0\rangle$ qubelet and an *inverted* triangle $|1\rangle$ qubelet. These qubelets then form the mega-qubit shown on the right, where the bottom triangle $|1\rangle$ qubelets in the second and fourth columns are inverted, or rotated by half a turn.

If the F is the constant function defined previously, $F(|x\rangle) = |0\rangle$, then as explained earlier, Deutsch's circuit boils down to the following figure:

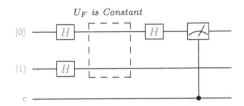

The U_F block is essentially a pass-through—it doesn't affect the states of the qubits. Thus, the back-to-back H gates operating on the top qubit restore it back to its original state $|0\rangle$.

If the F is the balanced function defined previously, then Deutsch's circuit for this function is shown in the following figure:

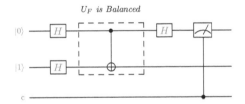

In this case, as you saw earlier, the U_F block works out to a CNOT gate.

The mega-qubit formed by the H gate splitting the $|0\rangle$ and $|1\rangle$ qubits shown earlier is fed to the CNOT gate, as shown in the following figure:

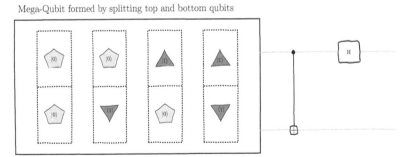

The top qubelets are fed to the control qubit of the CNOT gate and the bottom qubelets to its target qubit. The CNOT gate toggles its target qubit only when its control is a triangle $|1\rangle$ qubelet for that combination. Thus, the mega-qubit after the CNOT gate acts on it is shown in the figure on page 348.

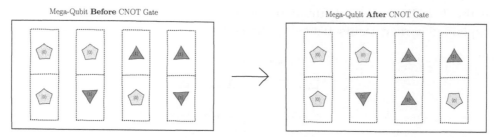

Mega-Qubit **Before** CNOT Gate

Mega-Qubit **After** CNOT Gate

The bottom qubelets in the third and the fourth qubelet combinations have switched to a triangle $|1\rangle$ qubelet and an inverted pentagon $|0\rangle$ qubelet, respectively. The corresponding quantum state is:

$$\frac{1}{2}(\,|00\rangle \,-\, |01\rangle \,-\, |10\rangle \,+\, |11\rangle\,)$$

The H gate on the right of the CNOT gate splits the top qubelets in each combination stated previously. The bottom qubelets aren't affected.

You can continue the analysis by splitting the top qubelets and working out the new mega-qubit. Alternatively, you can also write the matrix for the section of the circuit after the CNOT gate and then apply this quantum state to it. But before going down any of these paths, see if you can rewrite the quantum state in a way that suggests how the H gate modifies this state. Since the second qubit is unaffected, write the quantum state by grouping the combinations based on the second qubit. That is, the first and third terms are grouped together, and the second and fourth, as shown here:

$$\begin{aligned}\frac{1}{2}(\,|00\rangle \,-\, |01\rangle \,-\, |10\rangle \,+\, |11\rangle\,) &= \frac{1}{2}(\,|0\rangle \,-\, |1\rangle\,)\,|0\rangle \,-\, \frac{1}{2}(\,|0\rangle \,-\, |1\rangle\,)\,|1\rangle \\ &= \frac{1}{\sqrt{2}}\frac{|0\rangle \,-\, |1\rangle}{\sqrt{2}}\,|0\rangle \,-\, \frac{1}{\sqrt{2}}\frac{|0\rangle \,-\, |1\rangle}{\sqrt{2}}\,|1\rangle\end{aligned}$$

The first, or the top, qubit in both terms is:

$$\frac{|0\rangle \,-\, |1\rangle}{\sqrt{2}}$$

This quantum state is what you would have got by splitting a $|1\rangle$ qubit with an H gate. Thus, if this top qubit is split again by the H gate, then it's as if back-to-back H gates are applied to a $|1\rangle$ qubit. To put it another way, if the quantum state after the CNOT gate has its top qubit split by an H gate, then the algebra will work out to:

$$\frac{1}{\sqrt{2}}\,|1\rangle\,|0\rangle \,-\, \frac{1}{\sqrt{2}}\,|1\rangle\,|1\rangle$$

So if you now measure the top qubit, you'll find that it always collapses to $|1\rangle$ and records 1 in the classical register.

In other words, measuring the top qubit in Deutsch's circuit gives a different result for a constant versus a balanced function. In particular, when the top qubit is measured:

- A $|0\rangle$ indicates the function F is constant.
- A $|1\rangle$ indicates the function F is balanced.

So regardless of what the function $|F\rangle$ is, a single measurement of the top qubit will tell you its type.

Know How the H Gate Splits $|0\rangle$ and $|1\rangle$ Qubits

In quantum computing, it's a good idea to keep in mind the asymmetric way the H splits $|0\rangle$ and $|1\rangle$ qubits:

$$H|0\rangle = \frac{1}{\sqrt{2}}|0\rangle + \frac{1}{\sqrt{2}}|1\rangle$$

$$H|1\rangle = \frac{1}{\sqrt{2}}|0\rangle - \frac{1}{\sqrt{2}}|1\rangle$$

The triangle $|1\rangle$ qubelet when the H gates splits a $|1\rangle$ qubit is inverted, or rotated by a half turn.

You'll find many occasions where knowing how the H gate works algebraically greatly simplifies your analysis. And with a little practice, you'll find that you'll be able to do the analysis shown here in your head.

For a single qubit function, Deutsch's algorithm shows how to *embed* the function within a circuit that lets you determine the type of function from just one measurement. The Deutsch-Jozsa algorithm extends this idea to functions of many qubits.

For example, for a five-qubit function $F\big(|q_0\rangle, |q_1\rangle, |q_2\rangle, |q_3\rangle, |q_4\rangle\big)$, the possibilities are:

- The function is constant and returns a $|0\rangle$ for all 2^5, or 32, states.
- The function is constant and returns a $|1\rangle$ for all 2^5, or 32, states.
- The function is balanced and returns a $|0\rangle$ for half the states and $|1\rangle$ for the other half.

For this function, using a classical computer, in the worst case, you would need $16 + 1 = 17$ samples to establish its type—constant or balanced. But, with the Deutsch-Jozsa circuit, you'll just need one measurement.

In general, for an n-qubit function F, the Deutsch-Jozsa circuit is shown in the following figure:

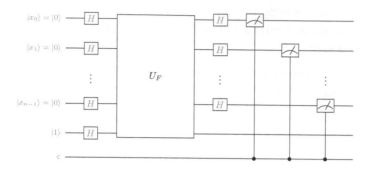

As in the Deutsch circuit, the n qubits are initialized to $|0\rangle$ and split by an H gate. The bottom qubit is initialized to $|1\rangle$. These $(n+1)$ qubits are then passed to the U_F block. Finally, the top n qubits are split again by H gates and then measured.

In this case, if the top n collapsed qubits each record a 0 in the classical register, then the function F is constant, otherwise it's balanced. So, here again, a single measurement, albeit of n qubits, is all that's needed to establish the type of function.

Repeating the Same Assignment of Gates

You'll frequently find that the splitting of the top n qubits by the stacked H gates is written as:

$$H|0\rangle \otimes H|0\rangle \otimes \cdots \otimes H|0\rangle = H^{\otimes n}|0\rangle$$

This shortcut carries over to drawing quantum circuits too. For example, the Deutsch-Jozsa circuit with $(n+1)$ qubits can be redrawn as follows:

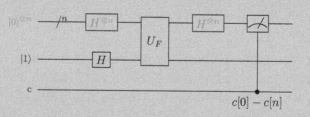

The *slash-n* on the top line indicates that it actually represents n qubits, all getting split by the H gate.

Even though you only needed one measurement for both Deutsch's circuit for a single-qubit function and the Deutsch-Jozsa circuit for a multi-qubit function, you didn't just sample the function directly. The circuits were made up of several gates. But the number of gates increases in linear proportion to the number of qubits, while the number of cases to sample in a classical algorithm increases exponentially. So the computational complexity of the Deutsch-Jozsa circuit dramatically improved from that of classical algorithms.

Other Algorithms

We went through the Deutsch algorithm in a fair amount of detail, as I wanted to give you a taste of the types of analysis that researchers historically undertook to establish that quantum computing is a high-powered alternative to classical computing. The problem that Deutsch and Deutsch-Jozsa considered may not be immediately applicable, but as we've seen in this book, the ideas embodied in these algorithms are used to solve practical applications.

The Bernstein-Vazirani and Simon algorithms are in a similar vein—using highly specialized functions, they demonstrate that quantum computing offers faster ways to implement them than classical computing.

Another class of quantum algorithm is the Quantum Fourier transforms. These are the quantum analogs of the classical Fourier transforms and are concerned with finding periods, or repetitions, in a function. Shor's algorithm, which is based on Quantum Fourier transforms, took on heightened significance since it could factor—essentially repetitions—large numbers. And since the current cryptographic standards rely on the difficulty of factoring large numbers using classical techniques, quantum computing makes these cryptographic methods breakable. Ironically, though, as important as Shor's algorithm is, unless you have a need to factor large numbers, it's value is more as a *deterrent*—the fact that you can factor large numbers and break current cryptographic methods forces cryptography to be based on different methods, as described in Chapter 9, Alice in Quantumland—Quantum Cryptography, on page 279.

If you're interested to learn more about these algorithms, several descriptions, which you can find to suit the level of rigor you want, are freely available on the internet.

> ⑊⑊
> ⨜
>
> ### Joe asks:
> # How Did Google Show Superiority of Quantum Computers over Classical Computers?

Google demonstrated a computation on a quantum computer[a] [b] that took three minutes, twenty seconds, which they estimate would take 10,000 years on a classical supercomputer.

How did they do it?

Google generated a quantum circuit whose gates, such as Controlled Z, S, and T, are prescribed according to a randomized algorithm—one that randomly selects the type of gates. Unlike a well-know algorithm such as the Deutsch-Jozsa circuit that solves a highly contrived problem, the Google circuit isn't aimed at any particular problem. It's just a pseudo-random quantum circuit. Consequently, the quantum states of the qubits at the end of the program can be estimated in one of two ways:

1. By a classical computer using the matrix techniques you've seen in earlier chapters.

2. Running the circuit on a quantum computer and measuring the quantum states.

The Google team compared the results from the two computations—classical matrix calculations versus executing on quantum hardware—and ensured that the quantum machine was producing the right results. Then the team amped up the circuit beyond the computational limits of classical computers. Since quantum computers handle multiple states simultaneously, their circuit ran for less than three and a half minutes.

Because of the way that qubits encode a quantum state, storing them using 64-bit floating point numbers rapidly jacks up the memory requirements on classical hardware. To get a sense for how quickly the memory escalates, recall from Rotating Qubelets Through Any Angle, on page 150, that a quantum $|\psi\rangle$ is specified as:

$$|\psi\rangle = \cos\frac{\theta}{2}|0\rangle + e^{i\varphi}\sin\frac{\theta}{2}|1\rangle$$

Thus, you need two quantities to define a state: the angle θ, which relates to the ratio of pentagon $|0\rangle$ and triangle $|1\rangle$ qubelets in the quantum state; and φ, which is the difference in rotations between the triangle $|1\rangle$ qubelet and the pentagon $|0\rangle$ qubelet. In terms of the Bloch sphere, these angles are the "longitudes" and "latitudes," respectively, of the state on the sphere.

Assuming that each angle is stored as a floating point number of 8 bytes or 64 bits,[c] the total number of bytes per quantum state is:

$$\text{number of bytes} = 2 \text{ angles per quantum state} \times 8 \text{ bytes per sngle}$$
$$= 2 \text{ angles per quantum state} \times 2^3 \text{ bytes per angle}$$
$$= 2^4 \text{ bytes per quantum state}$$

For a quantum circuit of n qubits, there will be 2^n quantum states. That is, the vector to hold the idealized states will have 2^n elements. Thus, the number of bytes to hold these 2^n states in memory is:

$$\text{number of bytes for n-qubit circuit} = 2^n \text{ quantum states} \times 2^4 \text{ bytes per quantum state}$$
$$= 2^{n+4} \text{ bytes}$$

Google's circuit used 53 qubits. Thus, for a classical computer to reproduce the calculations of the quantum circuit, it would require the following amount of memory:

$$\text{number of bytes on a classical computer} = 2^{53+4}$$
$$\approx 1.44 \times 10^{17} \text{ bytes}$$
$$\approx 144 \text{ petabytes}$$

(1 petabyte is 10^{15} bytes)

This is just the memory to hold the idealized states. The gate matrices will need to be stored too. And even though these are sparse—few nonzero entries—with such large dimensions, they add up pretty quickly too.

By comparison, the Summit Supercomputer,[d] among the world's fastest, at the U.S. Department of Energy's Oak Ridge National Laboratory (ORNL), holds about 250 PB. To put it another way, a puny 53-qubit quantum computer rivals one of the fastest supercomputers in operation today. And just a slightly larger quantum circuit, using less than, say, 100 qubits, will be beyond the reach of any classical computer.

Thus, despite the arbitrariness of Google's quantum circuit, I believe that their experiment is encouraging. (And, in fact, there are even some real-life applications for it.[e]) Quantum computing is still a relatively young field and this result is akin to the first powered flight of the airplane by Orville and Wilbur Wright, a distance that is less than the walk on the jetbridge to board a modern jetliner. It bristles with the promise of quantum feats still to come.

---

a. https://ai.googleblog.com/2019/10/quantum-supremacy-using-programmable.html
b. https://www.nature.com/articles/s41586-019-1666-5
c. https://en.wikipedia.org/wiki/IEEE_754
d. https://www.olcf.ornl.gov/summit/
e. https://www.nytimes.com/2019/10/30/opinion/google-quantum-computer-sycamore.html

Programming with Qiskit

Although we've used the QASM language to program our quantum circuits on the IBM Quantum Computer, the primary way we coded the circuits was by dragging and dropping gates from the gates palette onto the Composer.

This drag-and-drop process results in the circuits being programmed in the QASM language.

But QASM is a low-level assembly language that we can't integrate with other systems, such as a database to pull in data to build circuits. Dragging and dropping gates lets us learn about quantum concepts without getting distracted by classical language-specific constructs. In practice, though, you'll want to invoke quantum phenomena in conventional programming languages. In this section, you'll learn to incorporate quantum effects in classical languages. You'll still design quantum algorithms using the techniques you've learned in this book, but you'll use classical languages to program and execute them on real quantum computers.

Quantum Information Science Kit, or Qiskit (pronounced kiss-kit), is a Python framework that IBM has contributed to the open source community. Using Qiskit,[4] you can use all the quantum effects you've learned in this book but program them in Python, although the code is executed on the IBM Quantum Computer or a simulator. While the drag-and-drop way of programming quantum computers is good when learning about quantum concepts, Qiskit comes packed with goodies that let you write industrial-grade quantum code. I'll first introduce you to the basics of using Qiskit and then show you things you can do only with it.

Quantum Programming Is Not Python Specific

With Qiskit, you'll program quantum effects using Python, but quantum computing isn't Python specific. Quantum concepts are independent of any language. You'll still design quantum algorithms using the techniques you've learned in this book—Qiskit is an alternative way to trigger them on IBM's quantum hardware, using Python instead of the QASM assembly language. Later in this section, you'll see that these same quantum effects can be triggered on quantum hardware of other vendors, such as Amazon, Google, and Microsoft.

To use the programs in this section, you should, nonetheless, know Python,[5] [6] including working with arrays and complex numbers and opening and navigating your way in Jupyter Notebooks[7] on your local machine.

---

4.   https://qiskit.org/
5.   https://pragprog.com/book/gwpy3/practical-programming-third-edition
6.   https://pragprog.com/book/dzpyds/data-science-essentials-in-python
7.   https://jupyter.org/try

You can use Qiskit in one of two ways:

- On the IBM Quantum Experience website, using Jupyter Notebooks.
- Locally on your machine by writing Python programs or coding in Jupyter Notebooks.

We'll briefly go over getting started with both ways. Then you can choose whichever mode you prefer to program with Qiskit.

Using the IBM Quantum Experience

To use Qiskit on the IBM Quantum Experience, you can click the Qiskit Notebook icon on the left margin, as shown in the following figure:

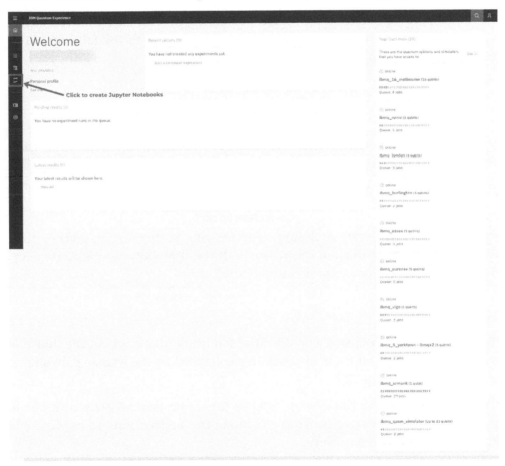

You'll be taken to a page where you can create a new Jupyter Notebook or open one that you created previously.

On the IBM Quantum Experience, new notebooks have the statements to import the Qiskit libraries as well as configure the notebook to access the methods to run on a real quantum computer. For now, you can delete these lines. I'll show you what you need to import to run the programs in this section. (If you choose to leave them in, then make sure you include any specific ones I highlight in the programs.)

Working Locally

To work in Jupyter Notebooks locally, first install Qiskit on your computer, from here,[8] [9] and follow the instructions for your operating system. Note that to run Qiskit, Python 3 is required.

To make sure you've installed Qiskit correctly, you can check its version by opening a new Python 3 Jupyter Notebook and typing in the following lines in a code cell. Then hit Shift-Enter to execute them:

```
import qiskit
from qiskit import *

qiskit.__qiskit_version__
```

You'll see a list of the various components that make up Qiskit and their respective versions.

Now you're ready to write your first quantum program with Qiskit.

Jupyter Notebooks

 We'll use Python 3 Jupyter Notebooks in this section so they can be used interchangeably on both the IBM Quantum Experience and on your local machine.

Hello Qiskit

To get started with Qiskit, consider the following quantum circuit that has just a single qubit which is immediately collapsed by the Measure gate shown in the figure on page 357.

The Python code for this circuit follows the same general structure of the programs written earlier but also includes the instructions to execute the circuit on quantum hardware:

---

8.   https://developer.ibm.com/technologies/quantum-computing/videos/programming-on-quantum-computers-pt-2/

9.   https://qiskit.org/documentation/install.html

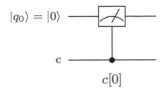

$$|q_0\rangle = |0\rangle$$

$$c$$

$$c[0]$$

- Declare quantum and classical registers to hold the qubits and their collapsed states, respectively.

- Declare the quantum gates that act on the qubits.

- Collapse the qubits using the Measure gates, and log their states in the classical register.

- Specify how many shots, or the number of times you want to run the circuit.

- Run the circuit.

- View the results.

These general steps translate to the following Python code:

①
```python
import numpy as np
import math
from qiskit import(
QuantumCircuit,
QuantumRegister,
ClassicalRegister,
execute,
Aer)
from qiskit.visualization import plot_histogram
```

②
```python
circuit = QuantumCircuit()
```

③
```python
q = QuantumRegister(1,'qreg')
circuit.add_register( q )
```

④
```python
c = ClassicalRegister(1,'creg')
circuit.add_register(c)
```

⑤
```python
circuit.measure(0,0)
```

⑥
```python
circuit.draw(output='mpl')
```

⑦
```python
backend = Aer.get_backend('qasm_simulator')
```

⑧
```python
job = execute( circuit, backend, shots=1024 )
```

⑨
```python
hist = job.result().get_counts()
plot_histogram( hist )
```

❶ The NumPy library will let you handle arrays of qubits in your applications. The math library lets you use mathematical functions in your programs. To use Qiskit, you need to import the Qiskit libraries. The other libraries are related to the Qiskit objects you'll use in your programs. As you get more familiar with Qiskit, you'll understand which ones you'll need. For now, you can just copy and paste these.

❷ Define a circuit object to which gates will be added.

❸ Declare and add the quantum register to hold the qubits in the circuit.

The first argument is the length of the register and the second is its label. In this case, there's only a single qubit in the circuit. All qubits are initialized to |0⟩.

❹ Declare and add the classical register to record the collapsed states of the qubits in the circuit.

The first argument is the length of the register and the second is its label. In this case, there's only a cell to record the solitary qubit in the circuit.

❺ Declare the Measure gate. The first argument is the index of the qubit in the quantum register you want to collapse; the second is the index in the classical register where you want to log the state. For this circuit, the collapsed state of q[0] is recorded in c[0].

❻ This command draws the quantum circuit. When working in Jupyter Notebooks, you may want to periodically draw the circuit as you're building it to make sure it's correct.

The argument refers to the style of the circuit layout. The mpl option uses Python's Matplotlib visualization library to draw the circuit that closely resembles the circuits on the Composer. Leaving this argument blank uses the default library on the machine where your notebook is executing. On the IBM Quantum Experience, the default option is mpl. So you can invoke the draw method with no arguments.

❼ Identify the quantum machine, or backend you want this code to run on. In this case, we're using the qasm_simulator, which isdefined in the Aer object, to run the circuit.

Aer[10] is Qiskit's simulator framework that lets you simulate the noisy behavior of real quantum devices. In addition, using the statevector_simulator,

---

10. https://qiskit.org/aer/

it calculates the Statevector of the circuit and, with the unitary_backend, the matrix for the complete circuit.

❽ Run the code on the selected backend or quantum machine. You pass the quantum circuit in the first argument, specify the backend in the second, and the number of shots in the third.

❾ Tally up the number of times each quantum state the qubits collapse to and plot as a histogram.

Pasting Code in Jupyter Notebooks

Before pasting code into Jupyter Notebooks, make sure you've imported the Qiskit and relevant Python libraries, such as NumPy and math:

```
from qiskit import(
QuantumCircuit,
QuantumRegister,
ClassicalRegister,
execute,
Aer)
from qiskit.visualization import plot_histogram
```

You can directly copy and paste the code you'll see in this chapter into Python 3 Jupyter Notebooks. You can paste into a single code cell or split it across as many cells as you'd like. To run the code in a code cell, click Shift-Enter.

Be aware that the code you enter is cumulative. That is, any new gates you declare are added to the circuit previously defined. Thus, you may end up with a circuit that you didn't intend.

You'll follow this basic structure to declare and run other quantum circuits on quantum computers—you'll just have more gates.

Quantum Gates in Qiskit

In Qiskit, each gate is a method of the circuit object. Thus, to declare a gate, you'd invoke the appropriate method followed by the qubits it operates on as arguments for the method. The following is a partial list to show you the general pattern for declaring gates in your circuit:

H Gate:

To use an H gate acting on the qubit in register q[0], declare it as follows:

```
circuit.h( q[0] )
```

S Gate:

To use an S gate acting on, for example, the qubit in register q[1], declare it as follows:

```
circuit.s(q[1])
```

$T^\dagger$ *Gate*

To use a $T^\dagger$ gate acting on, for instance, the qubit in register q[2], declare it as follows:

```
circuit.tdg(q[2])
```

Notice how the "dagger" symbol is abbreviated to "dg" when declaring these types of gates.

CNOT Gate

To use a CNOT gate whose control bit is, for example, the qubit in register q[3] and whose target qubit is in register q[4], declare is as follows:

```
circuit.cnot(q[3],q[4])
```

U3 Gate

To use a U3 gate that's defined using three parameters, θ, φ, and λ, which operates on, say, the qubit in q[3], declare it as follows:

```
circuit.u3(0,math.pi,0,q[3])
```

Here, the U3 gate's parameters are set to $\theta = 0$, $\varphi = \pi$, and $\lambda = 0$. (Recall from U3 Gate, on page 203, that these parameters only affect the triangle $|1\rangle$ qubelet by inverting it, or rotating it by half a turn.)

Measure Gate

To measure, for instance, the qubit in register q[0] and record its state in classical register c[0], declare it as follows:

```
circuit.measure(q[0],c[0])
```

The first argument refers to the qubit, and its collapsed state is logged in the classical register in the second argument.

To use these gates, you should have previously declared the circuit object as, for example, circuit = QuantumCircuit() and also the qubits as q = QuantumRegister(5,'qreg'), a quantum register holding five qubits, followed by circuit.add_register(q) to add the qubits to the circuit.

Consider, again, the Qiskit program for the quantum circuit in Intuition Behind Entanglement, on page 120, shown in the figure on page 361.

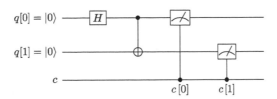

The Qiskit program is listed here:

```
Line 1  # Header lines - import libraries
     -  import numpy as np
     -  import math
     -  from qiskit import(
     5  QuantumCircuit,
     -  QuantumRegister,
     -  ClassicalRegister,
     -  execute,
     -  Aer)
    10  from qiskit.visualization import plot_histogram
     -
     -  # Define circuit
     -  circuit = QuantumCircuit()
     -
    15  # Declare and add quantum and classical registers
     -  q = QuantumRegister(2,'qreg') # 2 Qubits Register
     -  circuit.add_register( q )
     -
     -  c = ClassicalRegister(2,'creg') # 2 Bits Classical Register
    20  circuit.add_register(c)
     -
     -  # Declare the H Gate
     -  circuit.h(q[0])
     -
    25  # Declare the CNOT Gate
     -  circuit.cnot(q[0],q[1])
     -
     -  # Collapse Qubits
     -  circuit.measure(q[0],c[0])
    30  circuit.measure(q[1],c[1])
     -
     -  # Draw the circuit
     -  circuit.draw(output='mpl')
     -
    35  # Use simulator to run the circuit
     -  backend = Aer.get_backend('qasm_simulator')
     -
     -  # Define the run parameters and execute
     -  job = execute( circuit, backend, shots=1024 )
    40
     -  # Tally the results
     -  hist = job.result().get_counts()
     -
```

```
   # Plot the histogram of quantum states
45 plot_histogram( hist )
```

The H, CNOT, and the two Measure gates are declared on lines 23–30. The rest of the program is similar to that listed previously.

When you run this program, you'll see the output states, $|00\rangle$ and $|11\rangle$, appear with roughly equal probabilities. (These states are entangled because once you observe one, the other's state is known even if the other qubit isn't measured.)

Qiskit Shortcuts

If you're not picky about labeling your quantum and classical registers and can work with a single register of each, you can declare quantum circuits and the gates as follows:

Declaring Circuit and Quantum Register

You can declare the QuantumCircuit object and the quantum register by passing in the length of register, or the number of qubits in the circuit, as an argument to the QuantumCircuit object as follows:

```
circuit1 = QuantumCircuit(5)
```

This statement declares a circuit with five qubits.

Declaring Circuit with Both Quantum and Classical Registers

To set up a circuit with both quantum and classical registers, pass the length of both registers, respectively, as follows:

```
circuit2 = QuantumCircuit(3,2)
```

The first argument is the number of qubits in the circuit, and the second is the number of bits in the classical register. In this case, the circuit has three qubits and two bits in the classical register.

Declaring Gates

To declare gates and the qubits they act on, you can specify just the index of the qubit in the quantum register. For example, to declare an H gate that operates on, say, the qubit in q[2], declare it as follows:

```
circuit1.h(2)
```

Arrays as Arguments

Qiskit also lets you pass in arrays as arguments for the gates to create multiple gates. To create an H gate on all four qubits of circuit2 defined earlier, pass the array of qubits, using Python's built-in range function, for instance, as follows:

```
circuit2.h(range(3))
```

You can even pass in arrays as arguments for the Measure gate. For example, you can declare Measure gates on qubits q[0] and q[2] that log their states in the classical register cells c[0] and c[1], as follows:

```
circuit2.measure([0,2],[0,1])
```

The previous two statements set up the following quantum circuit:

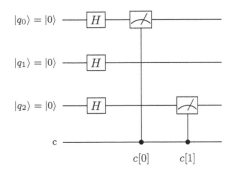

Running on an Actual Quantum Computer

Running your programs on an actual quantum computer follows the same basic steps as that of using the simulator, except for a few minor differences, which I'll discuss in this section:

API Token: Include the API token in your code, which lets you execute your programs on an actual quantum computer.

Backend to Run Code: Replace the code to run on the simulator with one of the actual quantum computers.

Viewing the Results: Because running code on a quantum computer doesn't take place immediately, due to other programs ahead of yours, you have to break up your program into two parts: one to set up the quantum circuit and invoke the quantum computer and the second to view the results of your run later.

Saving the API Token for Working Locally

If you'd like to run your Qiskit programs on a real quantum computer but trigger it locally, you need to first save an API token on your local machine.[11] (When running Jupyter Notebooks from your account on the IBM Quantum

---

11. https://qiskit.org/documentation/install.html#access-ibm-quantum-systems

Experience, you don't need to save it. You only need to include it, as shown in the following description.)

The API token is listed under your account information on the home page of the IBM Quantum Experience. To get the API token, go to your user profile by either clicking the See more link or the user icon on the top right, as shown in the following figure:

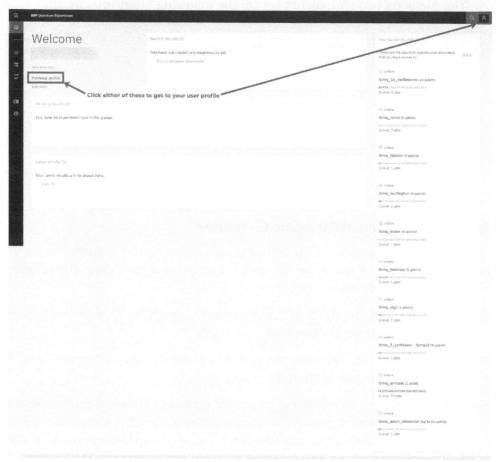

Then, click the Copy token link as shown in the figure on page 365.

Next, on your local machine, open a new Jupyter Notebook, type in the following lines, and paste the API token as shown:

```
from qiskit import IBMQ
IBMQ.save_account('«API Token»')
```

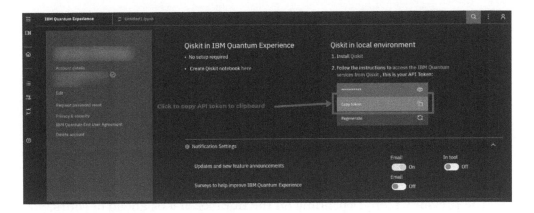

To save the API token to your machine, execute the cell by pressing `Shift-Enter`. You only need to save it once.

If you have an API token from a version of Qiskit older than 0.11, update your token as follows:

```
IBMQ.update_account()
```

Backend to Run Code

To set up your quantum circuit to run on a real quantum computer, you follow the same steps to define your quantum circuit. But instead of selecting the simulator, pick one of the real quantum computers, as shown here:

```
from qiskit import(
QuantumCircuit,
QuantumRegister,
ClassicalRegister,
execute,
Aer,
❶ IBMQ)
❷ from qiskit.providers.ibmq import least_busy
from qiskit.visualization import plot_histogram

❸ provider = IBMQ.load_account()

«Set up Quantum Circuit»

❹ real_devices = provider.backends(simulator=False, operational=True)
backend = least_busy(real_devices)

❺ job = execute( circuit, backend, shots=1024 )
```

❶ Import Qiskit, including the IBMQ library, to access the methods to run on a real quantum computer. Also, import the least_busy library to identify the real quantum computer with the lightest load.

❷ To run your code on the quantum computer that has the fewest jobs in queue, select the least busy backend.

❸ Define a provider object by loading it with the saved API token. You'll need this when running Jupyter Notebooks on the IBM Quantum Experience or locally.

❹ Filter the list of available backends to those that are real quantum computers and currently operational. From this list, select the one that has the fewest number of jobs.

❺ Just as with the simulator, run your program with the backend selected in the previous step. Depending on the number of jobs ahead of yours, you may have to come back later to view the results.

To run your program on a specific quantum computer, get the list of available backends:

```
provider.backends()
```

Then, use the get_backend() method on the provider object and pass in the name of the quantum computer, as follows:

```
backend = provider.get_backend('ibmq_16_melbourne')
```

In this case, we've selected the 16-qubit quantum computer in Melbourne. Execute your circuit on this backend.

To learn about other things you can do with the provider object, go here.[12]

Viewing the Results

To view the results of running your program on a real quantum computer, get the Job ID of the execution from the IBM Quantum Experience website, as shown in the figure on page 367.

Copy the Job ID onto the clipboard.

Unless you've left your notebook running, open a new notebook, import the standard Qiskit libraries, and define a provider object with your API token. Then, specify the backend on which you ran your code and paste the Job ID, as shown next:

```
provider = IBMQ.load_account()
backend = provider.get_backend('«Backend»')
job = backend.retrieve_job('«Job ID»')
```

---

12. https://quantum-computing.ibm.com/jupyter/tutorial/fundamentals/3_the_ibmq_account.ipynb (You'll need to log in to the IBM Quantum Experience.)

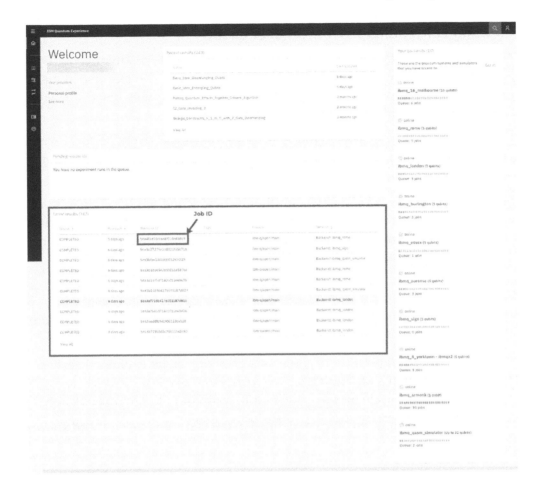

This gets the job object, just as when you ran a quantum program on the simulator. Access the results and tally them up by how many times each state is logged. Finally, plot the counts as a histogram chart, shown as follows:

```
hist = job.result().get_counts()
plot_histogram( hist )
```

Now that you've seen how to build and run your quantum programs on a simulator as well as on real quantum hardware—including using shortcuts to declare mulitple gates in a single statement—in the rest of this section, you'll see a few features that you can only use with Qiskit and not in the drag-and-drop programs created with the IBM Quantum Experience.

Creating Larger Circuits from Smaller Circuits

As your programs get larger, you'll find it helpful to write modular code. That is, you'll want to define chunks or groups of gates that you can use in many places in your circuit as a unit without having to individually insert the gates that make up the block. You can do this two ways:

User-Defined Gates: Create groups of gates that collectively perform some operation such as swapping the quantum states of two qubits, or the Boolean logic operations such as OR.

Partial Circuits: Create partial circuits that you can then hook up to make a larger circuit. For example, you make a partial circuit that generates all combinations of quantum states. You can then plug this circuit into another one that, say, implements Boolean logic expressions.

User-Defined Gates

Qiskit lets you group gates and then refer to them as a single unit in your circuit. To specify these user-defined gates,[13] follow these steps:

- Define the configuration of gates as a circuit object, as explained earlier.
- Make these gates an instruction.
- To use it in your circuit as a single unit, Append it to the main circuit object.

Consider, for example, an OR gate, defined in OR Gate, on page 59, and shown in the figure below:

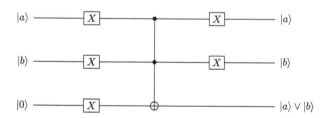

To define this configuration of the CCNOT gate and the associated NOT (X) gates as an or_gate gate in your Python code, start by setting up these gates as an or_gate_circuit object:

```
Line 1  or_gate_circuit = QuantumCircuit(3, name=' OR ')
    2  or_gate_circuit.x(range(3))
    3  or_gate_circuit.ccx(0,1,2)
    4  or_gate_circuit.x(range(2))
    5  or_gate = or_gate_circuit.to_instruction()
```

---

13. https://qiskit.org/documentation/tutorials/circuits_advanced/1_advanced_circuits.html#Composite-Gates

Declare the circuit object for the OR gate with three qubits, as shown on line 1. The name parameter is the label for this group of gates when the circuit is displayed. Notice how we've padded the label with a space on either side of the text. This puts some margin on either side of the label in the box for the gate when it's shown in the circuit.

If you don't plan on viewing the circuit, you can leave it blank; the system will assign a generic label.

Declare the gates that make up the OR gate on lines 2–4. Notice how the X gates are declared by passing in the appropriate array as the argument. For example, to create the two NOT (X) gates on the right, the argument for the NOT (X) gate on line 4 is an array formed by range(2).

The way we've set up the OR gate implies that the input qubits are in q[0] and q[1] and the result of the logical OR operation is reflected in the qubit in q[3]. The order of the qubits—q[0], q[1], and q[2]—define the arguments for this group of gates.

Finally, on line 5, convert this group of gates to an Instruction so that it can be inserted in the main circuit as just another gate.

For example, look at a circuit in which the OR gate is hooked up as follows:

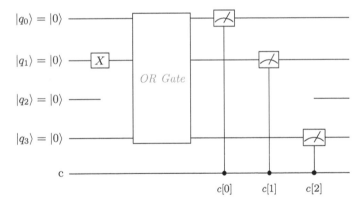

The OR gate operates on the qubits in q[0] and q[1] and puts the results of the operation in the qubit in q[3]. Since the qubit in q[1] is first acted on by the NOT (X) gate, its state is changed to $|1\rangle$.

The Qiskit code for this circuit is as follows:

```
Line 1  main_circuit = QuantumCircuit(4,3)
     2  main_circuit.x(1)
     3  main_circuit.append(or_gate, [0,1,3])
     4  main_circuit.measure([0,1,3],[0,1,2])
```

On line 1, declare the main_circuit using four qubits and three classical registers. On line 2, set the qubit in q[1] to |1⟩ with an NOT (X) gate. On line 3, add the OR gate you configured previously to the main_circuit. The first argument is the circuit object for the group of gates for the OR gate. The qubits in q[0] and q[1] are the inputs, and the qubit in q[3] holds the result of the logical OR operations. This set of qubits is passed in as an array as the second argument of the append() method. Lastly, on line 4 declare the Measure gates. The qubits being measured, q[0], q[1], and q[3], are passed in as array in the first argument. And the classical registers that log their collapsed states are also passed in as an array in the second argument to the Measure gate's method.

If you'd like to see the OR Gate block replaced with the actual gates that make it up, use the decompose() method of the circuit object, as follows:

```
decomposed_circuit = main_circuit.decompose()
```

You'll see the following circuit:

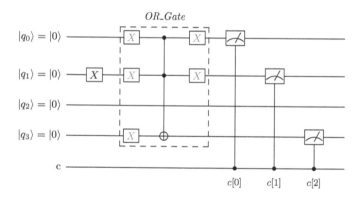

The dashed box is only to illustrate to you the new gates shown. It's not drawn by Qiskit. Notice that even though the target qubit of the CNOT gate was specified right below its second control qubit, in the actual circuit it's two qubits below, as was defined in the second argument of the append().

Partial Circuits

Qiskit lets you break up your circuits into functional units and build each separately. Then, you can simply hook them up one after another by "adding" them. The circuits should have the same number of qubits.

For example, consider the following circuit that generates all combinations of three qubit states:

$$|q_0\rangle \quad —\boxed{H}—$$

$$|q_1\rangle \quad —\boxed{H}—$$

$$|q_2\rangle \quad —\boxed{H}—$$

You can set these gates in an all_combinations_circuit as follows:

```
all_combinations_circuit = QuantumCircuit(3)
all_combinations_circuit.h(range(3))
```

Likewise, you can set up a measure_circuit that has the same number of qubits but only two classical registers:

```
measure_circuit = QuantumCircuit(3,2)
```

And you can define the Measure gates to record the states of qubits in q[0] and q[2] as follows:

```
measure_circuit.measure([0,2],[0,1])
```

The quantum state of the qubit in q[0] is logged to c[0] and that of the qubit in q[2] to c[1].

Now, "add" the two circuits, stated as follows:

```
new_circuit = all_combinations_circuit + measure_circuit
```

This creates the following circuit:

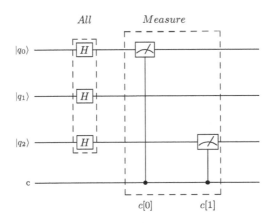

Output States as an Array

In all the quantum programs you've seen in this book, the output is reported as a histogram of quantum states. When writing applications for real world problems, though, you may want the results in a form that you can do some further processing on.

After executing the circuit, the metrics for that run are held in the Result object. Use the get_counts() to pull out the tallies of each of the idealized states as an array, shown as follows:

```
≪Import Qiskt, other libraries≫
≪Set up Quantum Circuit≫

# Use simulator to run the circuit
backend = Aer.get_backend('qasm_simulator')

# Define the run parameters and execute
job = execute( circuit, backend, shots=1024 )

# Tally the results
collapsed_states_array = job.result().get_counts()
print(collapsed_states_array)
```

The system will return a dictionary of name-value pairs, as shown here:

```
{'01': 520, '10': 504}
```

Each name-value entry corresponds to an idealized state. The name is the state and the value is the number of times that state was seen in the execution. In this example, the 01 state appeared 520 times out of 1,024 shots.

You can now extract these states and their counts from the array and use them in your application.

Displaying the Statevector

To display the Statevector, the quantum state vector, you have to use the statevector_simulator backend, shown as follows:

```
≪Import Qiskt, other libraries≫
≪Set up Quantum Circuit≫

backend = Aer.get_backend('statevector_simulator')
job = execute(circuit, backend)
result = job.result()
statevector = result.get_statevector(decimals=3)
print(statevector)
```

Then, as highlighted in the code, use the get_statevector() method on the result object to get the quantum state as a Python array.

For example, consider the quantum state $|\varphi_0\rangle$:

$$|\varphi_0\rangle = \frac{1}{\sqrt{2}}|01\rangle + \frac{1}{\sqrt{2}}|10\rangle$$

The corresponding vector is:

$$|\varphi_0\rangle = \begin{pmatrix} 0 \\ \dfrac{1}{\sqrt{2}} \\ \dfrac{1}{\sqrt{2}} \\ 0 \end{pmatrix}$$

Qiskit would return this vector as the following Python array where each entry is written up to three decimal places:

```
[0.    +0.j 0.707+0.j 0.707+0.j 0.    +0.j]
```

Each element is stated as a complex number using j instead of i (both are mathematically equivalent).

Circuit Matrices

Qiskit also gives you the matrix for your quantum circuit. To get this matrix, you have to run your circuit on the unitary_simulator backend, as the following shows:

```
«Import Qiskt, other libraries»
«Set up Quantum Circuit»

# Run the quantum circuit on a unitary simulator backend
backend = Aer.get_backend('unitary_simulator')
job = execute(circuit, backend)
result = job.result()

# Show the results
print(result.get_unitary(circuit, decimals=3))
```

Then, as highlighted in the code, use the get_unitary() method on the result object to get the matrix of the circuit as an "array of arrays."

Setting Up Arbitrary Quantum States

In all the circuits you've seen so far, the qubits are initialized to $|0\rangle$. Qiskit gives you a mechanism to initialize the amplitudes[14] of the idealized states to any value provided the respective probabilites—square of the amplitudes—add up to 1.

---

14. https://qiskit.org/documentation/tutorials/circuits/3_summary_of_quantum_operations.html#Arbitrary-initialization

For example, suppose you want to set the initial quantum state $|\varphi_0\rangle$ of a two-qubit system to:

$$|\varphi_0\rangle = \frac{\sqrt{3}}{2}|10\rangle + +\frac{1}{2}|11\rangle$$

Writing $|\varphi_0\rangle$ as a vector:

$$|\varphi_0\rangle = \begin{vmatrix} 0 \\ \frac{\sqrt{3}}{2} \\ 0 \\ \frac{1}{2} \end{vmatrix}$$

Remember that when programming the IBM Quantum Computer, the right-most bit refers to $|q_0\rangle$. Thus, the $|10\rangle$ quantum state is actually the $|01\rangle$ state for the IBM Quantum Computer. Hence, the second element is $\sqrt{3}/2$ in the quantum state vector stated above. The first and third elements are 0 as they correspond to states that are not present in the initial quantum state.

Set up this vector in Python as an array labeled input_quantum_state:

```
《Import Qiskt, math, NumPy libraries》
```

```
# Define the input quantum state
input_quantum_state = [0,
                math.sqrt(3)/2*complex(1,0),
                0,
                1/2 * complex(1,0)]
```

The array has the four elements corresponding to the vector $|\varphi_0\rangle$.

Next, initialize the quantum circuit with this quantum state, as follows:

```
Line 1  # Initialize circuit
    2   q = QuantumRegister(2)
    3   c = ClassicalRegister(2)
    4   circuit = QuantumCircuit(q,c)
    5   circuit.initialize(input_quantum_state, q)
```

Set up a two-qubit quantum circuit with two classical registers on lines 2–4. Initialize the circuit on line 5 with the initialize() method that takes in two arguments: the initial quantum state vector and the quantum register array q.

You can check that the circuit is indeed initialized with this quantum state by looking at its Statevector:

```
backend = Aer.get_backend('statevector_simulator')
job = execute(circuit, backend)
result = job.result()
statevector = result.get_statevector(decimals=3)
print(statevector)
```

Running these lines returns the following array:

```
[0.   +0.j 0.866+0.j 0.   +0.j 0.5  +0.j]
```

This array corresponds to the quantum state vector $|\varphi_0\rangle$.

Gates from Matrices

In Chapter 7, Small Step for Man—Single Qubit Programs, on page 173, you learned that when quantum states are represented by vectors, the operation of a gate can be modeled by matrices. Using Qiskit you can go the other way. When designing quantum algorithms, you know the way you want to manipulate quantum states. With Qiskit, you can define the corresponding matrix, and the system generates the implied circuit internally. Think of this feature as a many-qubits Universal gate.

The matrix you define must be unitary, as explained in Can the Quantum Gate Matrix Be Anything?, on page 187.

To use these user-defined matrices in your code, do the following:

Import the Operator Library: To use your matrix as a gate in your code, import the library shown in the highlighted line in the following:

```
import numpy as np
import math
from qiskit import(
QuantumCircuit,
QuantumRegister,
ClassicalRegister,
execute,
Aer)
from qiskit.visualization import plot_histogram
➤ from qiskit.quantum_info.operators import Operator
```

Define the Gate Matrix: The matrix is defined as a standard Python list of lists: each row of the matrix is a list. For example, consider the 4×4 matrix for a two-qubit gate defined as follows:

$$
\begin{vmatrix}
\dfrac{\sqrt{3}}{2} & 0 & \dfrac{1}{2} & 0 \\[2mm]
0 & \dfrac{\sqrt{3}}{2} & 0 & \dfrac{1}{2} \\[2mm]
\dfrac{1}{2}i & 0 & -\dfrac{\sqrt{3}}{2}i & 0 \\[2mm]
0 & \dfrac{1}{2}i & 0 & -\dfrac{\sqrt{3}}{2}i
\end{vmatrix}
$$

This matrix is represented as a list of lists and passed in as the argument to the Operator() method, shown as follows:

```
my_gate_2 = Operator([
    [math.sqrt(3)/2, 0, 1/2, 0],
    [0, math.sqrt(3)/2, 0, 1/2],
    [1/2*complex(0,1), 0, -math.sqrt(3)/2*complex(0,1),0],
    [0,1/2*complex(0,1),0, -math.sqrt(3)/2*complex(0,1)]
])
```

Define Matrices Using IBM's Convention for Writing Quantum States

When specifying the matrix for the gate in Qiskit, define the matrix using IBM's convention for writing the quantum state with the q[0] qubit in the least significant place or in the rightmost spot. For example, $|q_0 q_1\rangle = |01\rangle$ would actually be written as $|q_1 q_0\rangle = |10\rangle$ when specifying the matrix in Qiskit. To put it another way, the second column, say, in a 2 × 2 matrix for a two-qubit gate will still correspond to the $|01\rangle$ state but is defined as $|q_1 q_0\rangle$. So when working out the matrix, make sure you're correctly lining up the quantum states in your circuit so that the state in qubit q[0] is in the rightmost spot, and so on.

Before using this gate in your code, it's a good idea to check whether it's unitary by calling the is_unitary() method, as follows:

```
# Check unitary
print('Operatator is unitary:', my_gate_2.is_unitary())
```

If it's not unitary, fix the matrix; otherwise, you'll get errors when trying to run your program.

Using the Matrix in a Circuit: To use this matrix in a circuit, use the append() on the circuit object passing in the matrix as the first argument and the array of qubits the gate acts on in your circuit as the second argument, shown here:

```
circuit.append(my_gate_2, [0,1])
```

In this case, the first qubit that the two-qubit gate acts on is q[0] and the second is q[1].

Qiskit offers a rich set of functions for matrix operations, such as computing their tensor products. You can find more information here.[15]

Circuit Metrics

Qiskit's circuit object has several attributes and properties that give you information and metrics about your circuit.[16] We'll use the following circuit as a reference:

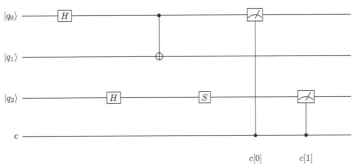

Here's the Qiskit code to set up this circuit:

```
«Import Qiskt, math, NumPy libraries»
circuit = QuantumCircuit(3,2)
circuit.h([0,2])
circuit.s(2)
circuit.cx(0,1)
circuit.measure([0,2],[0,1])
```

Following is a list of some of this circuit's metrics (all metrics are either attributes or methods of the circuit object):

Number of Quantum Registers

To get the number of quantum registers, look at the qregs attribute:

```
circuit.qregs
```

For the previous circuit, this number is the following:

```
[QuantumRegister(3, 'q')]
```

The first argument is the number of quantum registers.

---

15. https://qiskit.org/documentation/tutorials/circuits_advanced/2_operators_overview.html#Combining-Operators
16. https://qiskit.org/documentation/apidoc/circuit.html?highlight=quantum%20circuit%20depth#supplementary-information

You can also directly get the number of qubits with the n_qubits attribute:

```
circuit.n_qubits
```

Number of Classical Registers

To get the number of classical registers, look at the cregs attribute:

```
circuit.cregs
```

For the previous circuit, this number is the following:

```
[ClassicalRegister(2, 'c')]
```

Width or the Number of Quantum and Classical Bits

The width of a quantum circuit refers to the number of quantum bits as well as the number of classical bits making up the classical register. To get this count, use the width() method:

```
circuit.width()
```

Having three qubits and a two-bit classical register, the width of this circuit is 5.

Number of Gates by Type

Qiskit can also tally up the number of gates of each type in a circuit by using the count_ops() method, or the number of operations on qubits by the gates:

```
circuit.count_ops()
```

For the previous circuit, this works out to the following:

```
OrderedDict([('h', 2), ('measure', 2), ('s', 1), ('cx', 1)])
```

You get an ordered dictionary in which each element's key is the gate and value is the number of gates of that type. For example, the first element, ('h',2) indicates that the previous circuit has two H gates.

Number of Operations

To get a count of the total number of operations on qubits by all gates in the circuit, use the size():

```
circuit.size()
```

For the previous circuit, the there are six operations: two for the H gates, two for the Measure, one for the S, and one for the CNOT gate. Notice that even though the CNOT gate acts on two qubits, it's counted as a single operation, as it operates on them as a unit.

Depth or the Number of Simultaneous Operations

Generally speaking, a vertical slice through any circuit shows you the gates that can operate simultaneously on the qubits. Consequently, the number of these vertical slices translates to the amount of time a quantum program takes to run. The number of vertical slices, or layers, is called the depth of the quantum circuit.

Consider, again the quantum circuit shown earlier but, this time, with dotted boxes around the gates, representing the vertical slices, as shown in the following circuit:

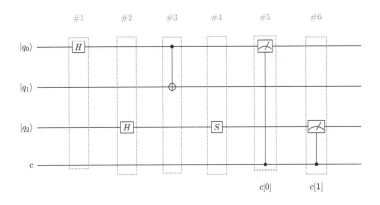

Looking at these vertical slices, it seems that it has six layers. But you can "squeeze" some layers together, making the gates in them operate on the qubits at the same time without affecting the overall working of the circuit. That is, the circuit shown previously can be squeezed to that shown in the following figure:

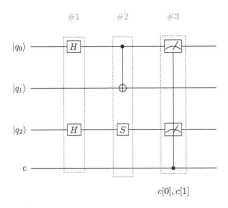

This circuit has only three layers.

Qiskit can figure this out for your circuit by using the depth() method, as stated here:

```
circuit.depth()
```

Number of Independent Sets of Qubits

The quantum circuit shown in the beginning of this section has three qubits—that is, its mega-qubit will have three cells in each qubelet combination. But, while the first two qubits, q[0] and q[1], are tightly coupled, or entangled, by the CNOT gate, the third qubit, q[2], is on its own. In other words, from a computational standpoint, you could technically first run the circuit with only the first two qubits and then combine the result with that of the run from the circuit with the third qubit. That is, this circuit has two independent sets of qubits: (q[0],q[1]), and (q[2]).

Using the num_unitary_factors() method, Qiskit will return the number of independent sets of qubits:

```
circuit.num_unitary_factors()
```

More Commands

We've just mentioned a tiny fraction of Qiskit's vast and rich features. Its documentation is comprehensive and easy to explore. By poking around, you'll come across other features that may interest you, such as displaying the outputs of several runs side by side,[17] showing the qubit on the Bloch sphere,[18] and seeing amplitudes in 3D.[19] Qiskit also lets you simulate the decoherence, or noise, of actual quantum computers in your simulations.[20]

Amazon, Google, and Microsoft's Quantum Computers

The quantum concepts and circuits you've seen in this book are portable—there's nothing unique to IBM's Quantum Computer—and you can program them on the quantum computers from other vendors. In the next section, we point out the ones from Amazon, Google, and Microsoft, where you can run these circuits.

---

17. https://qiskit.org/documentation/tutorials/circuits/2_plotting_data_in_qiskit.html#Options-when-plotting-a-histogram

18. https://qiskit.org/documentation/tutorials/circuits/2_plotting_data_in_qiskit.html#Plot-Bloch-Vector

19. https://qiskit.org/documentation/tutorials/circuits/2_plotting_data_in_qiskit.html#Plot-State

20. https://qiskit.org/documentation/tutorials/simulators/3_building_noise_models.html

Amazon's Braket

Amazon's quantum computing initiative is called Braket.[21] Like IBM's Qiskit, you write Python programs for your quantum circuits in Jupyter Notebooks. The programming methodology, too, is similar to Qiskit.[22]

Amazon lets you run your programs on quantum hardware from several vendors.[23]

Google's Cirq

Google's quantum computer library is Cirq.[24] Although it's a Python-based framework to program quantum circuits, Cirq uses a slightly different methodology to model circuits, driven by the way their quantum processor is built to be noise tolerant. Specifically, the two main concepts[25] are:

Moments: Moments are groups of gates that act on qubits at the same time. Make a vertical slice through the circuit and group all the gates in each slice as a Moment.

Initializing Qubits: Google's quantum computer lets you position your qubits on a 2D grid so that you can keep your qubits far enough away to reduce decoherence or interference.

Consider again the entanglement circuit shown in the following figure:

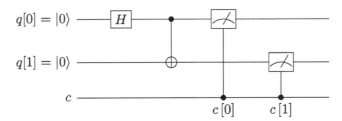

To run this circuit on Cirq, first download and install Cirq for your machine.[26] Then open a new Python3 Jupyter Notebook and enter the following code, splitting it across as many cells as you'd like:

---

21. https://aws.amazon.com/braket/
22. https://aws.amazon.com/blogs/aws/amazon-braket-get-started-with-quantum-computing/
23. https://aws.amazon.com/braket/hardware-providers/
24. https://cirq.readthedocs.io/
25. https://cirq.readthedocs.io/en/latest/circuits.html
26. https://cirq.readthedocs.io/en/latest/install.html

```
① import cirq
   from cirq.ops import CNOT, H
② q = [cirq.GridQubit(i, 0) for i in range(2)]
③ circuit = cirq.Circuit()
   circuit.append([H(q[0]),CNOT(q[0], q[1])])

   # Measure Gates
④ circuit.append(cirq.measure(*q, key='m'))

   print(circuit)

   # Get a simulator to execute the circuit
⑤ simulator = cirq.Simulator()
   # Simulate the circuit several times
   result = simulator.run(circuit, repetitions=5)

   # Print the results
⑥ print("Results:")
   print(result)

   # Show as histogram
   print("\nMeasurements:")
   print(result.histogram(key="m"))
```

❶ Import the cirq library.

Also, import the gates you'll use in the circuit from the cirq.ops library. This will let you refer to the gates as, say, H and CNOT, instead of cirq.H and cirq.CNOT, respectively.

❷ The big difference with other vendors is how Google's Cirq lets you place qubits on a 2D grid. Here, we define an array, q, that holds the coordinates of the qubits.

❸ Declare the circuit object and use the append() to add gates to the circuit. The gates are added in accordance with a policy[27] that dictates the Moments—that is, which operate simultaneously on the qubits. We're inserting the gates in the same order we would for circuits on IBM's Quantum Computer.

❹ When passing in an array of qubits to the Measure gate, use the asterisk. If you wanted to put the Measure gate on a specific qubit, for instance the first qubit, pass in q[0].

❺ Declare the Simulator and run the circuit on it. The number of shots is set by the repetitions parameter in the argument.

---

27. https://cirq.readthedocs.io/en/stable/circuits.html#insertstrategies

❻ The run() method returns an array in which each element is a string of the states recorded by the Measure gates associated with the corresponding index. This is the array for this program:

```
m=11110, 11110
```

By lining up the two elements in this array, you'll see that in these five shots, the qubits collapse to either 11 or 00, just as when this circuit was executed on the IBM Quantum Computer.

The histogram() method tallies up the corresponding states and presents the counts of each state. The recorded state is reported in decimal form. So, the 11 state in binary is 3 in decimals:

```
Counter({3: 4, 0: 1})
```

The state 3, or 11, is seen four times, and the state 0, or 00, is seen once.

Cirq also allows you to import the quantum circuits built using drag-and-drop on IBM's Quantum Computer Console. That is, it imports the code written in QASM.[28] To use this feature, you need to first install Python Lex-Yacc (ply) library using pip install ply==x.y, where x.y is the latest version number. (To find the latest stable version, go here.[29])

For example, import the previous circuit's program written in QASM, as stated here:

```
import cirq
from cirq.contrib.qasm_import import circuit_from_qasm

circuit = circuit_from_qasm("""
OPENQASM 2.0;
include "qelib1.inc";

qreg q[2];
creg c[2];

h q[0];
cx q[0],q[1];

measure q[0] -> c[0];
measure q[1] -> c[1];
    """)
print(circuit)
```

---

28. https://cirq.readthedocs.io/en/stable/circuits.html#importing-cirq-circuit-from-qasm-format

29. https://www.dabeaz.com/ply/

```
# Get a simulator to execute the circuit
simulator = cirq.Simulator()
# Simulate the circuit several times
result = simulator.run(circuit, repetitions=10)
# Print the results
print("Results:")
print(result)
```

Using the circuit object's circuit_from_qasm() method, pass in the entire QASM code as a string. Note the escaped double quotes surrounding the code to handle double quotes in the QASM code. Once the circuit is set up, the rest of the code follows the same pattern you saw in the previous code listing.

Cirq, like Qiskit, offers a vast and deep set of ways to set up and solve quantum circuits on a real quantum computer. My intention here was just to show you that quantum effects are language and vendor neutral—the same quantum circuit can be programmed on quantum computers built by different organizations. That is, while the specific quantum program may differ when you write for one quantum computer versus another, you'll still design the quantum algorithms regardless of which hardware you end up running them on.

Microsoft's Q#

Microsoft's quantum initiative[30] is integrated with Azure Cloud Service[31] and introduced a new language, Q#, to program quantum circuits.[32] Although not Python but more along the lines of C#, you can program the same quantum circuits you've worked with in this book.

Bottom Line

Although the state of the art of quantum computers is not on par with that of classical computers, quantum computers have already taken root in the computing landscape. As engineers in many organizations worldwide work on the problem of decoherence—making quantum computers less susceptible to noise—the primary challenge for their uptake will shift to programming them. As you've seen in this book, quantum computing introduces an entirely new paradigm for designing algorithms. Thus, learning these new concepts and getting familiar with thinking in "quantum" terms will set you up for unleashing the tremendous power of quantum computers.

---

30. https://www.microsoft.com/en-us/quantum/
31. https://azure.microsoft.com/en-us/services/quantum/
32. https://www.microsoft.com/en-us/quantum/development-kit

Try Your Hand

Solutions to these exercises are given in Where to Go from Here Solutions, on page 527.

1. Consider the U_F block used in Deutsch's circuit shown in the following circuit:

    $$|x\rangle \ \underline{\quad}\ \boxed{U_F}\ \underline{\quad}\ |x\rangle$$
    $$|y\rangle \ \underline{\quad}\ \phantom{\boxed{U_F}}\ \underline{\quad}\ |y\rangle \oplus F(\,|x\rangle\,)$$

    Suppose the function $F(\,|x\rangle\,)$ is constant that always returns a $|1\rangle$.

    a. Write the truth table for U_F.

    b. Draw Deutsch's circuit with gates that represent U_F.

    c. Write a Qiskit program to simulate this circuit using a single shot. What state is recorded by the Measure gate that collapses the $|x\rangle$ qubit?

    d. Write a Cirq program to simulate this circuit using a single shot. Place the qubits diagonally across.

    e. Does the quantum circuit simulated on IBM's Quantum Computer behave as the one simulated on Google's Quantum Computer?

2. This exercise is similar to the previous one but uses a balanced function, $F(\,|x\rangle\,)$, defined as follows:

    $$F(\,|0\rangle\,) \ = \ |1\rangle$$
    $$F(\,|1\rangle\,) \ = \ |0\rangle$$

    a. Write the truth table for U_F.

    b. Draw Deutsch's circuit with gates that represent U_F. (Hint: use a combination of CNOT and X gates.)

    c. Write a Qiskit program to simulate this circuit using a single shot. What state is recorded by the Measure gate that collapses the $|x\rangle$ qubit?

    d. Write a Cirq program to simulate this circuit using a single shot. Place the qubits 2 units apart one below the other.

    e. Does the quantum circuit simulated on IBM's Quantum Computer behave as the one simulated on Google's Quantum Computer?

3. In this exercise you'll write a Qiskit program to implement Deutsch-Jozsa's algorithm for a two-qubit function, $F(|x_0\rangle, |x_1\rangle)$, defined as follows:

$|x_0\rangle$	$|x_1\rangle$	$F(|x_0\rangle, |x_1\rangle)$
$|0\rangle$	$|0\rangle$	$|0\rangle$
$|0\rangle$	$|1\rangle$	$|0\rangle$
$|1\rangle$	$|0\rangle$	$|1\rangle$
$|1\rangle$	$|1\rangle$	$|1\rangle$

a. Function F is what type: constant or balanced? Using a classical algorithm, how many samples of F do you need to classify its type?

b. Draw the U_F block that is embedded in the Deutsch-Jozsa algorithm.

c. Write the truth table for U_F.

d. Draw the quantum circuit for the Deutsch-Jozsa algorithm, embedding the U_F block from the previous part.

e. Calculate the matrix A_{U_F} for the U_F block, corresponding to the truth table you computed in the previous part. Use the IBM convention to write the matrix.

f. Write a quantum program for this circuit using Qiskit. Use the Operator() method to specify the matrix for the U_F block. Set the program to run just one shot. Report the result as an array.

g. Does the output match the type of the function you deduced in the first part?

4. In each of the cases below, identify the correct Qiskit statements to set up the respective gates:

a.
$$|0\rangle^{\otimes 3} \quad —\!/^{3}\!— \boxed{H^{\otimes 3}} —$$

i.
```
circuit = QuantumCircuit(3,3)
circuit.h(range(3))
```

ii.
```
circuit = QuantumCircuit(3,3)
circuit.h(3)
```

iii.
```
circuit = QuantumCircuit(3,3)
circuit.h(0,1,2)
```

iv.
```
circuit = QuantumCircuit(3,3)
circuit.h(range(2))
```

b.

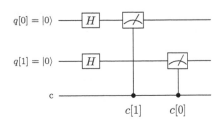

i.   `circuit = QuantumCircuit(2,2)`
     `circuit.h(range(2))`
     `circuit.measure(range(2),range(2))`

ii.   `circuit = QuantumCircuit(2,2)`
     `circuit.h(2)`
     `circuit.measure(2,2)`

iii. `circuit = QuantumCircuit(2,2)`
     `circuit.h(range(2))`
     `circuit.measure(1,0)`

iv.   `circuit = QuantumCircuit(2,2)`
     `circuit.h(range(2))`
     `circuit.measure(range(2),[1,0])`

5. Consider a quantum gate G that acts on the $|0\rangle$ and $|1\rangle$ qubits as follows:

$$|0\rangle \longmapsto \frac{\sqrt{3}}{2}|0\rangle + \frac{i}{2}|1\rangle$$
$$|1\rangle \longmapsto \frac{1}{2}|0\rangle - i\frac{\sqrt{3}}{2}|1\rangle$$

a. Which description best fits this gate?

   i.   Splitter.

   ii. Rotates pentagon $|0\rangle$ qubelets.

   iii. Rotates triangle $|1\rangle$ qubelets.

   iv. Toggles qubelets. That is, a pentagon $|0\rangle$ qubelet is switched to a triangle $|1\rangle$ qubelet, and vice versa.

   v. Only splits a qubit when it acts on the $|1\rangle$ state.

   vi. Splitter and rotates triangle $|1\rangle$ qubelets.

b. When this gate acts on a $|0\rangle$ qubit, are the triangle $|1\rangle$ qubelets rotated? If so, by how much? What's the probability that the $|1\rangle$ qubit collapses to $|1\rangle$?

c. When this gate acts on a $|1\rangle$ qubit, are the triangle $|1\rangle$ qubelets rotated? If so, by how much? What's the probability that the $|1\rangle$ qubit collapses to $|1\rangle$?

d. Write a matrix A_G that describes the behavior of this gate.

e. Is this matrix unitary? Use Qiskit's Operator class's is_unitary() to check.

Use Qiskit's Operator class to convert this matrix into a gate you can use in a circuit.

f. Write a Qiskit program to insert this gate in the following circuit:

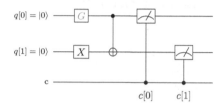

g. Run this circuit on the simulator and write the output states as an array.

h. Other than using Qiskit's Operator class to define this gate, is there any other way you could have defined this gate?

6. Consider the following circuit in which the first two qubits are initialized to the quantum state $|\varphi_0\rangle$:

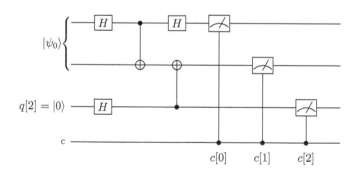

The quantum state $|\varphi_0\rangle$ is:

$$|\varphi_0\rangle \;=\; |00\rangle \,-\, 2\,|01\rangle \,+\, 3\,|10\rangle \,-\, i\,|11\rangle$$

a. Is $|\varphi_0\rangle$ a valid quantum state? If not, how can you make it valid?

b. Write a Qiskit program that initializes the circuit with the quantum state you determined in the previous part.

c. How many independent sets of qubits does this circuit have?

d. Run this quantum circuit on the simulator. Write the output as an array.

7. List the quantum effects you've learned in this book.

Mathematical Review

Understanding quantum computing requires some complex mathematical and computer science concepts. We've tried to make the book as readable as possible and present the concepts with explanation and models, rather than relying directly on the math. Some of these concepts are simply unavoidable. If you haven't heard of—or need a refresher on—logic gates and Boolean algebra, or vectors and matrices, you'll find a crash course in this appendix. This appendix isn't a substitute for a full course on these topics, however. For some good and accessible resources, see here.[1,2]

Classical Logic Gates and Circuits

In conventional computers, all information and data are stored as bits that are either a 1 (true) or 0 (false) state. Bits are switched from one state to another by devices called *gates*[3] that turn designated bits, called the *output bits*, to 1s or 0s, depending on the states of other bits, called the *input bits*. For instance, the following figure shows an AND gate that has 2 input bits and 1 output bit:

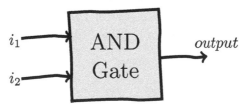

1. Complex numbers: https://en.wikipedia.org/wiki/Complex_number, https://en.wikipedia.org/wiki/Complex_conjugate and https://en.wikipedia.org/wiki/Euler%27s_formula#Applications_in_complex_number_theory.
2. Trigonometric identities: https://en.wikipedia.org/wiki/List_of_trigonometric_identities
3. https://en.wikipedia.org/wiki/Logic_gate

The outputs for all possible combinations of inputs to a gate is encapsulated as a *truth table*.

The truth table for the AND gate, whose single output bit is a 1 if and only if all its input bits are 1 is:

Input 1	Input 2	Output
0	0	0
0	1	0
1	0	0
1	1	1

Others, such as the OR gate, turn a single output bit to 1 if at least one of the input bits is 1. All the possible cases for a two-input OR gate are listed in the following truth table:

Input 1	Input 2	Output
0	0	0
0	1	1
1	0	1
1	1	1

Still others, like the NOT gate, toggle the input bit: it sets the output bit to 1 if the input bit is 0, and the output to 0 if the input is 1. The truth table for the single-input NOT gate is:

Input	Output
0	1
1	0

Although gates manipulate bits, they give rise to the standard programming statements. For example, the last row of the truth table for the AND gate expresses an if-then statement (in a C-based language such as C#):

```
if (inputA == 1) && (inputB == 1) then {
   output = 1
}
```

Thus, gates are just commonplace programming statements in disguise.

A gate by itself does a simple job; it's the collection of these simple gates that, when properly coupled, forms a program of instructions that orchestrates the switching of bits to successfully undertake complicated tasks.

Although each gate does a simple job, the entire circuit can make complex decisions. The collection of gates that make logic decisions by applying bit-level operations can be represented in the language of electronic circuits, called *logic circuit diagrams*.

Boolean Logic Expressions

The following is a list of frequently used Boolean algebraic expressions:

Boolean Expression	Comments
$a \wedge 0 = 0$	
$a \wedge 1 = a$	
$a \vee 0 = a$	
$a \vee 1 = 1$	
$\neg \neg a = a$	Double Negation
$a \wedge b = b \wedge a$	Commutativity of $\wedge$
$a \vee b = b \vee a$	Commutativity of $\vee$
$a \vee (b \vee c) = (a \vee b) \vee c$	Associativity
$a \wedge (b \wedge c) = (a \wedge b) \wedge c$	Associativity
$a \wedge (b \vee c) = (a \wedge b) \vee (a \wedge c)$	Distributivity
$a \vee (b \wedge c) = (a \vee b) \wedge (a \vee c)$	Distributivity
$\neg (a \wedge b) = (\neg a) \vee (\neg b)$	De Morgan's Law
$\neg (a \vee b) = (\neg a) \wedge (\neg b)$	De Morgan's Law
$x \oplus y = x \wedge (\neg y) \vee (\neg x) \wedge y$	Exclusive OR

The symbols $a, b, c, \cdots$ represent either TRUE or FALSE, classical binary states 1 and 0, quantum states $|1\rangle$ and $|0\rangle$, or *logical propositions* (Boolean expressions that evaluate to TRUE/FALSE, 1/0, or $|1\rangle$/$|0\rangle$). Using these equations, you can reformulate any Boolean expression so that it uses only NOT, AND, and OR gates.

You can prove each equation by writing the truth tables for both sides of the equation and verifying that they are the same. (See Section 7.1.1 of *Knuth [Knu11]*.) For example, we'll prove one of De Morgan's Laws by writing the truth tables for both sides of the following Boolean expression:

$$\neg (a \wedge b) = (\neg a) \vee (\neg b)$$

In the table, the truth values for the left-hand side are listed in column 6 and those for the right-hand side are in column 7, the last column:

a	b	$\neg a$	$\neg b$	$a \wedge b$	$\neg (a \wedge b)$	$(\neg a) \vee (\neg b)$
0	0	1	1	0	1	1
0	1	1	0	0	1	1
1	0	0	1	0	1	1
1	1	0	0	1	0	0

The truth values in columns 6 and 7 are identical, thus proving that the left-hand side and right-hand side Boolean expressions evaluate to the same value for all combinations of a and b.

Working with Matrices and Vectors

In quantum mechanics, we frequently multiply matrices as well as matrices with vectors. As shown in *"Fundamental Theorem of Linear Algebra"* [Str93], although the mechanics of these types of multiplications may seem arbitrary, they offer a point of view that gives us a way to represent the operation of gates on quantum states. (For a lucid description of linear algebra in a practical setting, especially the discussion relating to the columns of a matrix, which is of the most interest to us, see *Foundations of Network Optimization and Games* [FB16].)

A *matrix* is an array of numbers arranged as follows:

$$\begin{bmatrix} 1 & 0 \\ -1 & -1 \end{bmatrix}$$

In this matrix, the numbers are organized in two rows and two columns. Although in quantum computing we'll deal with square matrices in which the number of rows are the same as that for columns, here we'll work with rectangular matrices, where the number of rows differs from that for columns, to emphasize that there's nothing special about square matrices in this regard.

It'll be more instructive to talk about matrices whose elements are represented symbolically, as shown here:

$$A = \begin{bmatrix} a_{11} & a_{12} & \cdots & a_{1N} \\ a_{21} & a_{22} & \cdots & a_{2N} \\ \vdots & & & \vdots \\ a_{M1} & a_{M2} & \cdots & a_{MN} \end{bmatrix}$$

(The "⋯" is just a shortcut to indicate that the matrix contains other elements or numbers that are labeled in the same way.) The *elements*, or numbers, a_{mn}, where $m \in 1, 2, \cdots, M$ and $n \in 1, 2, \cdots, N$, of the matrix are laid out in an array of M rows and N columns. The first subscript m is the index of the row, and the second subscript n is the index of the column in the array. Thus, the element a_{12} refers to the number in the first row and second column of the matrix. The number of rows and columns of the array are the dimensions of the matrix, which we'll write as $M \times N$.

A *vector* x is a matrix with just one column:

$$x = \begin{pmatrix} x_1 \\ x_2 \\ \vdots \\ x_N \end{pmatrix}$$

This vector has N rows or elements and is an $N \times 1$ vector.

Multiplying the $M \times N$ matrix A with the $N \times 1$ vector x, we get:

$$Ax = \begin{bmatrix} a_{11} & a_{12} & \cdots & a_{1N} \\ a_{21} & a_{22} & \cdots & a_{2N} \\ \vdots & & & \vdots \\ a_{M1} & a_{M2} & \cdots & a_{MN} \end{bmatrix} \begin{pmatrix} x_1 \\ x_2 \\ \vdots \\ x_N \end{pmatrix}$$

The product will be an $M \times 1$ vector of M elements, as shown here:

$$Ax = \begin{bmatrix} a_{11}x_1 + a_{12}x_2 + \cdots + a_{1N}x_N \\ a_{21}x_1 + a_{22}x_2 + \cdots + a_{2N}x_N \\ \vdots \\ a_{M1}x_1 + a_{M2}x_2 + \cdots + a_{MN}x_N \end{bmatrix}$$

Each element in this vector is obtained by multiplying term-by-term the i-th row with the elements of the vector x. Thus, for the second element in this vector, we multiplied each term in the second row with the corresponding elements in the x vector. (Because each term in a row of the matrix A is multiplied by the corresponding element in the vector x, the number of columns in the matrix A has to equal the number of elements of the vector x.)

Key Step

The critical step is to group the terms associated with each x_n, $n \in 1, 2, \cdots, N$ as a sum of vectors, as follows:

$$Ax = \begin{bmatrix} a_{11}x_1 + a_{12}x_2 + \cdots + a_{1N}x_N \\ a_{21}x_1 + a_{22}x_2 + \cdots + a_{2N}x_N \\ \vdots \\ a_{M1}x_1 + a_{M2}x_2 + \cdots + a_{MN}x_N \end{bmatrix} = \begin{pmatrix} a_{11} \\ a_{21} \\ \vdots \\ a_{M1} \end{pmatrix} x_1 + \begin{pmatrix} a_{12} \\ a_{22} \\ \vdots \\ a_{M2} \end{pmatrix} x_2 + \cdots + \begin{pmatrix} a_{1N} \\ a_{2N} \\ \vdots \\ a_{MN} \end{pmatrix} x_N$$

Each column of the matrix is multiplied by the corresponding element of the vector x. In other words, vectors can be interpreted as a way of extracting just the column we want from a matrix.

To see how vectors act like column selectors, consider the following $N \times 1$ vector whose second element is a 1, and the others are 0:

$$x = \begin{pmatrix} 0 \\ 1 \\ 0 \\ \vdots \\ 0 \end{pmatrix}$$

Substituting this vector in the previous equation, we get:

$$\begin{pmatrix} a_{11} \\ a_{21} \\ \vdots \\ a_{M1} \end{pmatrix} 0 + \begin{pmatrix} a_{12} \\ a_{22} \\ \vdots \\ a_{M2} \end{pmatrix} 1 + \cdots + \begin{pmatrix} a_{1N} \\ a_{2N} \\ \vdots \\ a_{MN} \end{pmatrix} 0 = \begin{pmatrix} a_{12} \\ a_{22} \\ \vdots \\ a_{M2} \end{pmatrix}$$

That is, only the second column is multiplied by 1, the other columns are multiplied by 0. In other words, we have effectively pulled out the second column of the matrix A.

Multiplying Matrices

The idea of using vectors as selectors can be applied to multiplying matrices as well:

- Treat the second matrix as a collection of columns or vectors.
- Then, obtain each column of the product by multiplying the first matrix by the corresponding column of the second matrix.

For example, suppose you're multiplying the following matrices:

$$\begin{bmatrix} 1 & 0 \\ -1 & 2 \end{bmatrix}\begin{bmatrix} 3 & 5 \\ 4 & 6 \end{bmatrix}$$

Think of the second matrix as a collection of the following columns or vectors:

$$\begin{pmatrix} 3 \\ 4 \end{pmatrix}, \begin{pmatrix} 5 \\ 6 \end{pmatrix}$$

The first column of the product is:

$$\begin{bmatrix} 1 & 0 \\ -1 & 2 \end{bmatrix}\begin{pmatrix} 3 \\ 4 \end{pmatrix} = 3 \cdot \begin{pmatrix} 1 \\ -1 \end{pmatrix} + 4 \cdot \begin{pmatrix} 0 \\ 2 \end{pmatrix} = \begin{pmatrix} 3+0 \\ -3+8 \end{pmatrix} = \begin{pmatrix} 3 \\ 5 \end{pmatrix}$$

The second column of the product is:

$$\begin{bmatrix} 1 & 0 \\ -1 & 2 \end{bmatrix}\begin{pmatrix} 5 \\ 6 \end{pmatrix} = 5 \cdot \begin{pmatrix} 1 \\ -1 \end{pmatrix} + 6 \cdot \begin{pmatrix} 0 \\ 2 \end{pmatrix} = \begin{pmatrix} 5+0 \\ -5+12 \end{pmatrix} = \begin{pmatrix} 5 \\ 7 \end{pmatrix}$$

To get the product of the matrices, put the two columns together:

$$\begin{bmatrix} 1 & 0 \\ -1 & 2 \end{bmatrix}\begin{bmatrix} 3 & 5 \\ 4 & 6 \end{bmatrix} = \begin{bmatrix} 3 & 5 \\ 5 & 7 \end{bmatrix}$$

If you're not in the business of multiplying matrices, the method described here may be at odds with the traditional way in which each element of the product matrix is calculated by doing an element-by-element multiplication of each row of the first matrix by each column of the second matrix and then summing each individual multiplication. The method described in this section moves the focus from individual elements and puts the emphasis on columns, a view that mathematicians prefer, as it gives a physical interpretation instead of merely a bunch of calculations. You'll find this meaning of the vector for the qubits as a column selector more fitting when modeling quantum gates and analyzing quantum circuits.

Using a Computer Algebra System for Multiplying Matrices and Vectors

When analyzing and building algorithms for quantum computers, you'll multiply matrices and vectors. To avoid tediously multiplying these by hand, especially as the number of matrices and their sizes gets large, you can use an online mathematical system such as Sage Mathematical Software System[a] or SageMath. SageMath has a web-based interface called SageMathCell[b] which lets you perform quick calculations by directly entering your equations on a web page.

In computer algebra systems, matrices are defined as an array of arrays. That is, the matrix is an array whose elements are arrays themselves. Each array element corresponds to a row of the matrix. For example, consider the 3×4 matrix here:

$$A = \begin{bmatrix} 1 & 2 & 0 & -3 \\ 4 & -5 & 1 & 2 \\ 2 & 6 & 7 & 9 \end{bmatrix}$$

To enter this matrix in SageMathCell, define an array in which each element is another array, one for each of the three rows as follows:

$$A = \text{matrix}\,([[1, 2, 0, -3], [4, -5, 1, 2], [2, 6, 7, 9]])$$

The function matrix() then converts the array of arrays to a matrix for the computer algebra system.

Likewise, consider the following vector:

$$\begin{pmatrix} 2 \\ 0 \\ 1 \\ 0 \end{pmatrix}$$

You would enter this vector in SageMathCell as follows:

$$x = \text{vector}\,([2, 0, 1, 0])$$

The function vector() converts this array into a vector for the computer algebra system.

To multiply the matrix A with the vector x, you enter $A * x$. (Note that you must use the $*$ operator to indicate multiplication.) SageMathCell then returns the vector $(2, 9, 11)$.

Several other functions, such as inverting matrices, are available. Check out the quick-reference wiki for a list of the commonly used functions.[c]

---

a. https://www.sagemath.org
b. https://sagecell.sagemath.org/
c. https://wiki.sagemath.org/quickref

From Qubelets to the Bloch Sphere

The Bloch sphere is a geometrical device to plot quantum states. Historically, it's always been closely associated with quantum bits. In fact, several quantum gates derive their names from how they move quantum states around the sphere. But when using quantum computers to solve hard problems that require multiple qubits, using the Bloch sphere to visualize how the qubits interact with each other and figuring out where to introduce quantum effects can be frustrating.

The Qubelets Model on page 20 is an alternative to toying with the Bloch sphere. But to use it confidently, it's important to show that the two are equivalent.

In Chapter 6, Designer Genes—Custom Quantum States, on page 141, we used the Bloch sphere without explaining where it comes from, so this is supplementary information for those who want to know the details.

Deriving the Bloch sphere entails a Rube Goldberg-esque chain of mathematical ideas from trigonometry, complex numbers, and Euler's formula to work out how the orientations of the pentagon $|0\rangle$ and triangle $|1\rangle$ qubelets accurately describe quantum states of the qubit.

Visualizing the Qubit in 3D Space

To understand the roots of the Bloch sphere and how it relates to qubelets, we'll work with the following qubit:

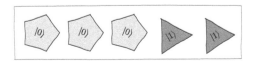

This qubit has three pentagon $|0\rangle$ qubelets, each rotated 20° clockwise, and two triangle $|1\rangle$ qubelets, each rotated 30° anticlockwise.

To draw the qubit in 3D space, we could use the standard Cartesian or rectilinear coordinate system that measures displacement along three orthogonal axes. But in situations dealing with angles, mathematicians find it more convenient to use polar coordinates.[1]

Start out with the array of pentagon $|0\rangle$ qubelets in the quantum state lying along the X-axis as shown here:

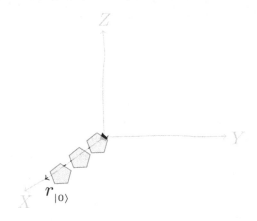

The length, $r_{|0\rangle}$, of this array is the amplitude associated with the pentagon $|0\rangle$ qubelets. In this example, with three pentagon $|0\rangle$ and two triangle $|1\rangle$ qubelets, the length is $\dfrac{3}{\sqrt{3^2 + 2^2}} = \dfrac{3}{\sqrt{13}}$.

Swing the pentagon $|0\rangle$ qubelets within the XY-plane by an angle α equal to the orientation of the pentagon $|0\rangle$ qubelets, as in the following figure:

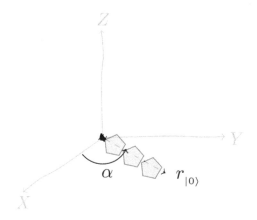

---

1.   https://en.wikipedia.org/wiki/Polar_coordinate_system#Complex_numbers

The projections of these pentagon $|0\rangle$ qubelets along the X and Y axes, respectively, are as follows:

$$\text{Along the X-axis:} \quad = \quad r_{|0\rangle}\cos\alpha$$
$$\text{Along the Y-axis:} \quad = \quad r_{|0\rangle}\sin\alpha$$

Using Euler's formula,[2,3] we write these projections in a single equation as:

$$r_{|0\rangle}(\cos\alpha + i\sin\alpha) = r_{|0\rangle}e^{i\alpha}$$

In this equation, i is the complex or imaginary number $\sqrt{-1}$.

Next, pull the triangle $|1\rangle$ qubelets up (or down) so that the tip of the topmost triangle makes an angle, β, with the Z-axis, as shown here:

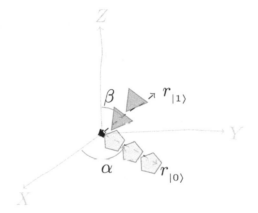

The orientation of the triangle $|1\rangle$ qubelets determines the angle, β, with the Z-axis. The length, $r_{|1\rangle}$, of this array of qubelets is the amplitude associated with the triangle $|1\rangle$ qubelets. In this example, the length is $\dfrac{2}{\sqrt{3^2+2^2}} = \dfrac{2}{\sqrt{13}}$.

The projections along a set of orthogonal axes or planes are as follows:

$$\text{Along the Z-axis:} \quad = \quad r_{|1\rangle}\cos\beta$$
$$\text{Along the XY-plane:} \quad = \quad r_{|1\rangle}\sin\beta$$

Once again, using Euler's formula, we write these projections in a single equation as:

$$r_{|1\rangle}(\cos\beta + i\sin\beta) = r_{|1\rangle}e^{i\beta}$$

2.   https://en.wikipedia.org/wiki/Euler%27s_formula#Applications_in_complex_number_theory
3.   https://www.youtube.com/watch?v=v0YEaeICIKY

The following figure shows how the qubit will end up oriented in 3D space:

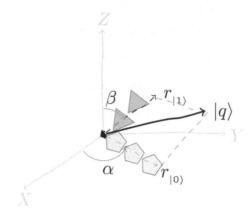

The thick arrow represents the resulting quantum state $|q\rangle$.

Writing the Quantum State Using Polar Coordinates

The quantum state resulting from arbitrary rotations of the pentagon $|0\rangle$ and triangle $|1\rangle$ qubelets can, thus, be written by combining the previous equations for each respective rotation as follows:

$$r_{|0\rangle} e^{i\alpha} |0\rangle + r_{|1\rangle} e^{i\beta} |1\rangle$$

In the example, the pentagon $|0\rangle$ qubelets are rotated 20°, so θ is $20\pi/180 = \pi/9$ radians. Likewise, the triangle $|1\rangle$ qubelets are turned 30°, or β is $30\pi/180 = \pi/6$ radians. Thus, the quantum state is:

$$\frac{3}{13} e^{\frac{i\pi}{9}} |0\rangle + \frac{2}{13} e^{\frac{i\pi}{6}} |1\rangle$$

Although the quantum state is defined using complex numbers, there's nothing imaginary about them: quantum computing works in the physical realm, albeit at tiny scales. The complex numbers are a mathematical artifact that give us a way to express 3D rotations of qubits.

Quantum State in a Transformed Space

The general quantum state with complex numbers written in the previous equation is expressed with four real parameters: $r_{|0\rangle}$, α, $r_{|1\rangle}$, and β.

Next, we'll go through the following sequence of mathematical transformations to rewrite the quantum state with four parameters to a form with two:

- Focus on the measurable aspect of a quantum state to write the quantum state using three parameters.

- Constrain the probabilities of the qubit collapsing to sum to 1, forcing the qubit to lie on a sphere.

- This leads to a transformed space where the quantum state is expressed with two real parameters.

While working through these mathematical operations, we'll switch between different coordinate systems to make the rationale behind the calculations clearer. In practice, though, when you're designing quantum algorithms, you'll rarely need to context-switch so frequently. But you'll often see parts of this analysis in the literature, so it's handy to have it in the back of your mind.

Focus on the Measurable Aspects of a Quantum State

The quantum state of a qubit can only be surmised. The moment we attempt to inspect it, the qubit will collapse to one of the two classical states. We'll use this fact to trim the number of parameters needed to specify a quantum state.

The only measurable quantities are the probabilities of the qubit collapsing to $|0\rangle$ or $|1\rangle$, or the squares of the respective amplitudes of $|0\rangle$ and $|1\rangle$:

$$\text{Probability of collapsing to } |0\rangle = \left| r_{|0\rangle} e^{i\alpha} \right|^2$$

$$\text{Probability of collapsing to } |1\rangle = \left| r_{|1\rangle} e^{i\beta} \right|^2$$

When calculating the magnitude of a complex number, $a + i\,b$, we have to use its *complex conjugate*[4] in which the imaginary part is opposite in sign from the original complex number, $a - i\,b$. When you multiply both, you get:

$$(a + i\,b)(a - i\,b) = a^2 - i^2 b^2 = a^2 + b^2$$

Hence, the right-hand side is a sum of two squares and can never be negative. Thus, multiplying a complex number by its conjugate is a measure of its magnitude.

The complex conjugate of the complex number $e^{ix} = \cos x + i \sin x$ is $\left(e^{ix}\right)^*$ and is written as follows:

$$\left(e^{ix}\right)^* = \cos x - i \sin x = e^{-ix}$$

---

4.   https://en.wikipedia.org/wiki/Complex_conjugate

The asterisk, *, indicates that the sign of the imaginary part of the number in parenthesis is flipped.

To calculate the probability of the qubit collapsing to $|0\rangle$, we multiply the amplitude of $|0\rangle$ by its complex conjugate as follows:

$$| r_{|0\rangle} e^{i\alpha}|^2 = r_{|0\rangle} e^{i\alpha} \times r_{|0\rangle}(e^{i\alpha})^* = r_{|0\rangle}^2 \times e^{i\alpha} e^{-i\alpha} = r_{|0\rangle}^2$$

Likewise, the probability of the qubit collapsing to $|1\rangle$ is:

$$| r_{|1\rangle} e^{i\beta}|^2 = r_{|1\rangle} e^{i\beta} \times r_{|1\rangle}(e^{i\beta})^* = r_{|1\rangle}^2 \times e^{i\beta} e^{-i\beta} = r_{|1\rangle}^2$$

Both these probabilities are independent of the angles α and β. Simply put, these angles don't affect the likelihoods of the qubit collapsing to $|0\rangle$ or $|1\rangle$, the only observable measurement we can make.

Consequently, we can multiply each amplitude term in the equation for the complex quantum state without altering the probabilities. Specifically, we'll multiply by $e^{-i\alpha}$ and simplify the equation for the quantum state as follows:

$$r_{|0\rangle} e^{i\alpha} e^{-i\alpha} |0\rangle + r_{|1\rangle} e^{i\beta} e^{-i\alpha} |1\rangle = r_{|0\rangle} |0\rangle + r_{|1\rangle} e^{i(\beta-\alpha)} |1\rangle$$

As a result, the quantum state can be written using three real parameters: $r_{|0\rangle}$, $r_{|1\rangle}$, and φ, where $\varphi = \beta - \alpha$.

In the example, φ is $\pi/6 - \pi/9 = \pi/18$ radians (or $10°$). So, the quantum state now works out to:

$$\frac{3}{\sqrt{13}} |0\rangle + \frac{2}{\sqrt{13}} e^{\frac{i\pi}{18}} |1\rangle$$

For all intents and purposes, this quantum state is identical to the one specified earlier with four real parameters since both states correspond to the classical states 0 and 1 with the same probabilities.

Constrain Qubit Collapsing Probabilities

Recognizing that the only thing that matters is what can be measured, we reduced the number of parameters to define a quantum state from four to three. We now take it one step further by constraining the probabilities to add up to 1. Recall that the quantum state defined with three parameters is:

$$r_{|0\rangle} |0\rangle + r_{|1\rangle} e^{i\varphi} |1\rangle$$

The amplitude of $|1\rangle$ is:

$$r_{|1\rangle} e^{i\varphi}$$

This amplitude is written in polar coordinates and represents a point, say, (u, v), which can also be stated as $(u + i\,v)$. Thus, the quantum state is:

$$r_{|0\rangle}\,|0\rangle + (u + i\,v)\,|1\rangle$$

For a legal quantum state, the probabilities, or the sum of the squares of its amplitudes, must add up to 1. Thus,

$$
\begin{aligned}
1 &= |\,r_{|0\rangle}|^2 + |\,u + i\,v|^2 \\
&= r_{|0\rangle}^2 + (u + i\,v)(u + i\,v)^* \\
&= r_{|0\rangle}^2 + (u + i\,v)(u - i\,v) \\
&= r_{|0\rangle}^2 + u^2 + v^2
\end{aligned}
$$

The final equation represents a unit sphere in a different Cartesian coordinate system (W, U, V), where we've renamed $r_{|0\rangle}$ to W without any loss of generality. That is, in this new or transformed space, the qubit is represented as an arrow from the origin to the surface of the unit sphere, as shown in the following figure:

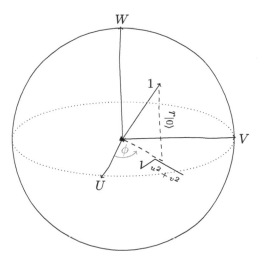

The angle φ is the *difference* (in radians) between the rotations of the pentagon $|0\rangle$ and the triangle $|1\rangle$ qubelets.

So in this transformed space, recall that the quantum state of the qubit containing the three pentagon $|0\rangle$ qubelets rotated 30° and the two triangle $|1\rangle$ qubelets rotated 20° is as shown here:

$$\frac{3}{\sqrt{13}} |0\rangle + \frac{2}{\sqrt{13}} e^{\frac{i\pi}{18}} |1\rangle$$

So the quantum state in the transformed space looks like this:

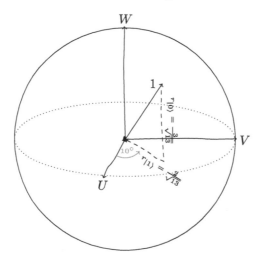

Sphere Leads to Two Parameters

We've established that in a transformed coordinate system, the tip of the qubit arrow can't float anywhere in 3D space—it's constrained to lie on a unit sphere in the Cartesian coordinate system (W, U, V). The quantum state in this new space is, thus, written as:

$$w |0\rangle + (u + i\, v) |1\rangle$$

Since the tip of the qubit arrow is on a unit sphere, we use spherical coordinates[5] to represent its orientation, or its quantum state.

The spherical coordinate system is essentially the polar coordinates upgraded for 3D space: the Cartesian coordinates (W, U, V) are related to the spherical coordinates (r, θ, φ), as shown in the figure on page 407.

---

5. https://en.wikipedia.org/wiki/Spherical_coordinate_system#Cartesian_coordinates

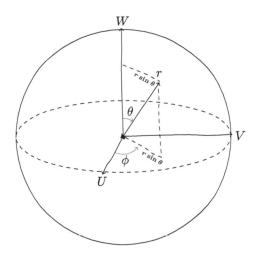

The projection of the solid arrow on the W-axis is $r\cos\theta$ and in the UV-plane is $r\sin\theta$. Resolving the latter along the U and V axes, respectively, and noting that the radius r is constrained to 1, we get the following equations that relate the spherical coordinates to the Cartesian coordinates:

$$
\begin{aligned}
u &= \sin\theta\cos\varphi \\
v &= \sin\theta\sin\varphi \\
w &= \cos\theta
\end{aligned}
$$

The component, w, of the unit radius along the vertical W-axis is $r_{|0\rangle}$, which in turn is $\cos\theta$ and $u^2 + v^2 = r_{|1\rangle}^2$.

Using theses spherical coordinates, we can write the quantum state as:

$$
\begin{aligned}
\psi &= w|0\rangle + (u + i\,v)|1\rangle \\
&= \cos\theta|0\rangle + \sin\theta\,(\cos\varphi + i\sin\varphi)|1\rangle \\
&= \cos\theta|0\rangle + e^{i\varphi}\sin\theta|1\rangle
\end{aligned}
$$

(The last equation is simplified using Euler's formula.)

This equation for the quantum state only has two parameters: the angles φ and θ. It's in this space that the quantum state can be represented with two parameters even though the actual qubit is oriented in 3D space.

Recall that the angle φ is the difference between β, the rotation of the triangle $|1\rangle$ qubelets, and α, the rotation of the pentagon $|0\rangle$ qubelets. Thus, for a qubit whose quantum state has three pentagon $|0\rangle$ qubelets rotated 20° and two triangle $|1\rangle$ qubelets rotated 30°, the angle φ is:

$$
\varphi = \frac{\pi}{18}\ \text{radians}
$$

And we can compute the angle θ as follows:

$$\cos\theta \ = \ \frac{3}{\sqrt{13}}$$

$$\theta \ = \ \cos^{-1}\frac{3}{\sqrt{13}}$$

$$= \ 0.588 \ \text{radians}$$

Or, φ is $10°$ and θ is $33.69°$.

From Sphere to Hemisphere: The True Space

Although we've found a form in which the quantum state is specified with two parameters, there's one more aspect to discuss before we can use quantum states defined in this way in our programs.

Imagine the sphere to be a globe and consider a quantum state that is pointing from its center to New York. A state that is opposite to it will point about midway between the western tip of Australia and the South Pole. Mathematically, though, we first reflect the quantum state through the plane of the equator so that the reflected state now points to the tip of Chile, as shown in the following figure:

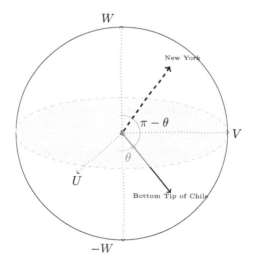

The angle this state makes with the W-axis is $\pi - \theta$ radians.

Then we spin this reflected quantum state by π radians or $180°$ about the W-axis so that it's directly opposite the state pointing to New York.

Thus, for this *opposite* quantum state, ψ', we replace θ by $\pi - \theta$ and φ by $\pi + \varphi$ in the equation for the quantum state, as shown here:

$$\begin{aligned} \psi' &= \cos(\pi - \theta)\,|0\rangle + e^{i(\pi+\varphi)}\sin(\pi - \theta)\,|1\rangle \\ &= -\cos\theta\,|0\rangle - e^{i\varphi}\sin\theta\,|1\rangle \\ &= -\psi \end{aligned}$$

The equation for the quantum state can be simplified because $\cos(\pi - \theta) = -\cos\theta$ and $\sin(\pi - \theta) = \sin\theta$. And, using Euler's formula, $e^{i(\pi+\varphi)} = e^{i\pi}e^{i\varphi}$ can be written as $e^{i\varphi}(\cos\pi + i\sin\pi)$. And, since $\sin\pi = 0$,

$$e^{i\pi}e^{i\varphi} = -e^{i\varphi}$$

Thus, the amplitudes for the quantum state in the bottom half of the sphere differ from those in the top half of the sphere in sign only. As we square the amplitudes to obtain the probabilities of collapsing to the two classical states, respectively, the quantum states in the bottom half will be indistinguishable from those in the top half.

Let's work out the values of the angles φ and θ that give the quantum states $\psi_0 = |0\rangle$ and $\psi_1 = |1\rangle$. Setting $\theta = 0$, and noting that $\cos 0 = 1$ and $\sin 0 = 0$, we get:

$$\psi_0 = |0\rangle + e^{i\varphi} \cdot 0 \cdot |1\rangle = |0\rangle$$

Similarly, setting $\theta = \frac{\pi}{2}$ radians, or 90°, and $\varphi = 0$, and noting that $\cos\frac{\pi}{2} = 0$ and $\sin\frac{\pi}{2} = 1$, the resulting quantum state is:

$$\psi_1 = 0 \cdot |0\rangle + e^{i\varphi}|1\rangle = e^{i\varphi}|1\rangle$$

The angle φ has no discernible effect on which state the quantum state collapses to—it always collapses to $|1\rangle$ no matter what the value of φ is, as shown in this equation:

$$\text{Probability of collapsing to } |1\rangle = \left| e^{i\varphi} \right|^2 = e^{i\varphi}e^{-i\varphi} = 1$$

(Note that when squaring a complex number, we multiply by its complex conjugate.)

But, different values of φ trace out quantum states on the equator.

Thus, we get all quantum states for the qubit as θ varies from 0 to $\frac{\pi}{2}$ radians, or 90°. In effect, every quantum state of the qubit lands on the top half of the unit sphere—the bottom hemisphere isn't needed.

We don't, however, live on half an earth or play tennis with half a ball. We find it more convenient to think of the entire sphere instead of just a hemisphere. So we map the hemisphere onto a full sphere by multiplying the angle each point makes with the W-axis by 2. That is, define an angle θ' such that $\theta' = 2\theta$ or $\theta = \frac{\theta'}{2}$. With this substitution, we can write the quantum state with the new angle, θ', as follows:

$$\psi = \cos\frac{\theta'}{2}\,|0\rangle + e^{i\varphi}\sin\frac{\theta'}{2}\,|1\rangle$$

The points on this unit sphere, called the Bloch sphere, then correspond to the different states of the qubit.

There are two points on the Bloch sphere, corresponding to the $|0\rangle$ and $|1\rangle$ quantum states, respectively, that you should know. The first point is when $\theta = 0$ and $\varphi = 0$ radians; its quantum state is:

$$\psi = \cos\frac{0}{2}\,|0\rangle + e^{i0}\sin\frac{0}{2}\,|1\rangle = |0\rangle$$

And for the second point, when $\theta = \pi$ radians, or 180°, and $\varphi = 0$, the quantum state is:

$$\psi = \cos\frac{\pi}{2}\,|0\rangle + e^{i0}\sin\frac{\pi}{2}\,|1\rangle = |1\rangle$$

That is, the $|0\rangle$ quantum state points straight up while the $|1\rangle$ quantum state is directed vertically down, as shown in the following figure:

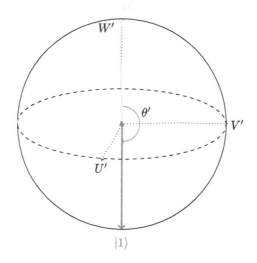

We've labeled the axes using (U', V', W') to emphasize that these quantum states are in the transformed space. You can, of course, relabel these axes to the more conventional (X, Y, Z) coordinate system. For now, though, we'll retain the (U', V', W') system to emphasize that the Bloch sphere is in a different coordinate system than the one of our everyday experience. (For more details on the Bloch sphere, see Section 1.3.3 of *Explorations in Quantum Computing* [Will1].)

Note a few points in the previous picture:

- The latitudes are measured from the north pole towards the equator, unlike those on a globe. So, the north pole is at the 0° latitude. These latitudes are associated with the angle θ' that measures how much the magnitude $|r_{|0\rangle}|$ swings away from the W'-axis.

- All quantum states on a given latitude differ only in $e^{i\varphi}$, where φ is the difference between the rotations of the triangle $|1\rangle$ qubelets and the pentagon $|0\rangle$ qubelets. Since $|e^{i\varphi}|^2 = e^{i\varphi}e^{-i\varphi} = 1$, the probabilities of all quantum states on the same latitude collapsing to $|0\rangle$ or $|1\rangle$ are the same.

- The longitudes measure the angle φ that's swept by the magnitude $|r_{|1\rangle}|$ in the plane of the equator. This angle is the difference between the rotations of the pentagon $|0\rangle$ and triangle $|1\rangle$ qubelets.

- Since we're working with a unit sphere using spherical coordinates, we only need the angles φ and θ' to plot a quantum state. Thus, we don't need the standard Cartesian coordinate axes.

When writing quantum programs, you'll refer to a quantum state using two parameters, θ and φ, that define a point on the surface of the Bloch sphere. So while you won't need to derive its equation, recalling how these parameters relate to a quantum state is helpful when manipulating them in your programs. Thus, in the table on page 412, we summarize the key steps, starting from a general quantum state in four parameters and paring it down to two:

Going forward, we'll find it more convenient to relabel θ' to θ, but it'll still represent the tilt from the vertical on the Bloch sphere. So the quantum state $|\psi\rangle$ will be written as:

$$|\psi_0\rangle = \cos\frac{\theta}{2}|0\rangle + e^{i\varphi}\sin\frac{\theta}{2}|1\rangle$$

Comments	Quantum State
Each qubelet type, the pentagon $|0\rangle$ qubelet and triangle $|1\rangle$ qubelet, is independently expressed in polar coordinates.	$re^{i\gamma}$, where $r \in \{r_{|0\rangle}, r_{|1\rangle}\}$ and $\gamma \in \{\alpha, \beta\}$ are the radius and angle of rotations of the pentagon $|0\rangle$ and triangle $|1\rangle$ qubelets, respectively.
Quantum state with four parameters.	$r_{|0\rangle}e^{i\alpha}|0\rangle + r_{|1\rangle}e^{i\beta}|1\rangle$
Only probabilities, which are the squares of the respective amplitudes, can be directly observed.	$\left|re^{i\gamma}\right|^2 = r^2$ That is, $e^{i\gamma}$ doesn't affect the probability.
Thus, multiplying each term by $e^{i\alpha}$ won't change the probability of the qubit collapsing to $|0\rangle$ and $|1\rangle$ from this quantum state.	$r_{|0\rangle}|0\rangle + r_{|1\rangle}e^{i(\beta-\alpha)}|1\rangle$ Quantum state using three parameters, $r_{|0\rangle}$, $r_{|1\rangle}$, and $e^{i\varphi}$, where $\varphi = \beta - \alpha$.
The amplitude of $r_{|1\rangle}$ is a polar coordinate in a 2D system. By treating $r_{|0\rangle}$ as a third coordinate and recognizing that the sum of the squares of the amplitudes is the probability of the qubit collapsing to $|0\rangle$ or $|1\rangle$, we see that their sum must add up to 1. Thus, the quantum states lie on a unit sphere.	$\left|r_{|0\rangle}\right|^2 + \left|r_{|1\rangle}e^{i(\beta-\alpha)}\right|^2 = 1$
Points in the lower hemisphere map to points in the upper hemisphere, so we just need half the unit sphere to map all quantum states of a qubit.	
But since it's easier to picture a full sphere, we double every angle that a point on the upper hemisphere makes with the vertical axis and, hence, blow it up to a full unit sphere called the *Bloch sphere*. The equation for the quantum state can be written with two parameters.	$\cos\dfrac{\theta}{2}|0\rangle + e^{i\varphi}\sin\dfrac{\theta}{2}|1\rangle$
On the Bloch sphere, the $|0\rangle$ quantum state is at the north pole and the $|1\rangle$ quantum state is at the south pole.	

Equivalence of Qubelets and Bloch Sphere

Consider a qubit containing three pentagon $|0\rangle$ qubelets rotated 30° clockwise and two triangle $|1\rangle$ qubelets rotated 20° anticlockwise, as shown below:

The corresponding angles in radians on the Bloch sphere are:

$$\varphi = \frac{30 - (-20)}{180} = \frac{5\pi}{18} \text{ radians}$$
$$\theta = 2 \times 0.588 = 1.176 \text{ radians}$$

Or, θ is 67.38° and φ is 50° as shown below:

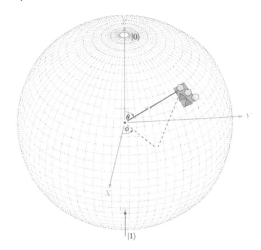

The three pentagon $|0\rangle$ qubelets rotated 20° clockwise and the two triangle $|0\rangle$ qubelets rotated 30° anticlockwise fall on upper hemisphere of the Bloch sphere on the 67.38° latitude and the 50° longitude. (Even though, we've shown the qubelets as a patch, in reality, the quantum state is a point on the surface of the Bloch sphere.)

Since this quantum state is in the upper hemisphere, but not too far from the equator, it has a tendency to collapse more often to $|0\rangle$ than $|1\rangle$. We expect this tendency since the number of pentagon $|0\rangle$ qubelets is just a shade more than the triangle $|1\rangle$ ones.

Thus, a qubit's quantum state depicted using pentagon $|0\rangle$ and triangle $|1\rangle$ qubelets maps to points on the Bloch sphere.

Quantum Mechanics with Qubelets

Quantum computing is rooted in and matured under the umbrella of quantum mechanics: the one can't be divorced from the other. The quantum concepts that drive quantum computers, such as collapsing qubits, canceling qubelets, and splitting and inverting them, are derived from the laws of quantum mechanics. In this section, you'll see the close connections between quantum computing and quantum mechanics. In particular, you'll learn to explain quintessential quantum effects using the Qubelets Model on page 20.

Unlike Einstein's special theory of relativity, which changed our perception of space and time with the publication of a single masterpiece, or later his general theory. which also burst upon the scene and fixed a gap in our understanding of the cosmos, quantum mechanics grew out of attempts to explain what started out as commonplace experiments and then meandered its way to a coherent theory. One after another, experiments that hardly bore the hallmarks of disproving conventional wisdom failed when scientists tweaked them. Compared with the hunt for the Higgs-Boson,[1] a subatomic particle that's responsible for mass in the universe, which involved multi-year efforts, cost several million dollars, and included hundreds of scientists around the globe, these humdrum experiments were like a middle school football team that somehow ended up in the Super Bowl. Yet they racked up deviations from expected behavior that could no longer be dismissed as minor aberrations. Physicists were forced to abandon classical theory and develop new ways to describe how our world works.

We'll examine one such experiment and show its close relationship with quantum computing.

---

1. https://home.cern/science/physics/higgs-boson

Mach-Zehnder Interferometer

The Mach-Zehnder interferometer[2] is a light beam splitting apparatus that's frequently used to demonstrate quantum effects. It's easy to set up and easy to explain the experimental thesis. But what actually gets observed doesn't conform to classical analysis.

In this experiment, start by shining a laser beam toward a beam splitter as shown here:

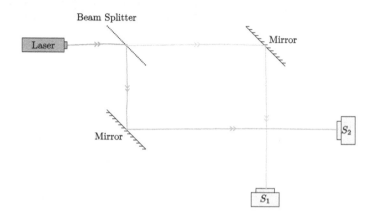

The beam splitter reflects part of the beam, or light wave, which heads toward the mirror on the bottom left of the figure, and transmits the other part, which is directed towards the mirror shown on the top right. (We've implicitly assumed that the beam splitter reflects as much as it transmits. But this assumption isn't germane to the discussion that follows. Beam splitters that are biased more toward one or the other way of changing the path of the light wave work equally well for the experiment we're about to outline.) The beam that's reflected off the top mirror, the *top path*, lights up sensor S_1. Similarly, the beam that bounces off the bottom mirror, the *bottom path*, lights up sensor S_2.

Next, introduce a second beam splitter that recombines the beam from the top and bottom path. According to classical theory, the beams should light up both sensors, as shown in the figure on page 417.

---

2.   https://www.youtube.com/watch?v=CR-eOhdxbes

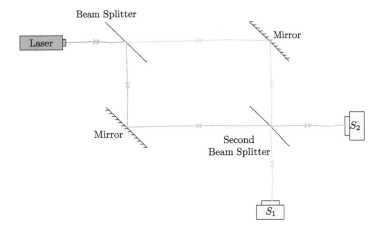

But what physicists saw was that only sensor S_1 got lit—sensor S_2 remained dark. That is, the beams followed the paths as shown as shown in the next figure:

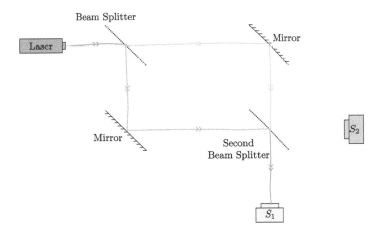

At first scientists argued that the crests of the light wave that moves along the bottom path and is transmitted through the second beam splitter are directly opposed to the troughs of the light wave on the top path that is reflected from the second splitter. As a result, the two light beams headed toward the right sensor, S_2, cancel each other out due to *destructive interference* and, hence, the sensor remains unlit.

Continue to reduce the intensity of the laser so that it emits fewer and fewer photons. Each time, sensor S_2 remains dark. Eventually, we'll reach a point where the laser emits only a single photon.

Single Photon Beam

At this stage, in keeping with classical theory, when it reaches the second beam splitter, it would continue on either of the following two paths:

- Reflected toward sensor S_1 at the bottom.
- Transmitted toward sensor S_2 to the right.

For example, if the photon is reflected toward sensor S_1, then the single photon follows the dotted path, as shown here:

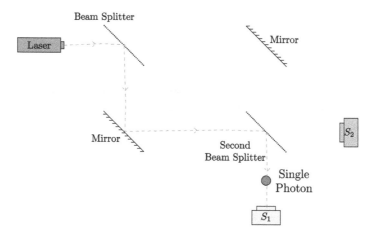

Likewise, if the photon is transmitted by the second beam splitter, it would hit sensor S_2, as shown in the next figure:

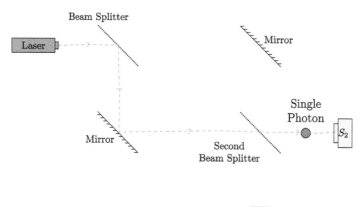

The situation with the photon following the top path after being transmitted by the top beam splitter is analogous. When the photon is also transmitted from the second beam splitter, it'll reach the bottom sensor, S_1, as follows:

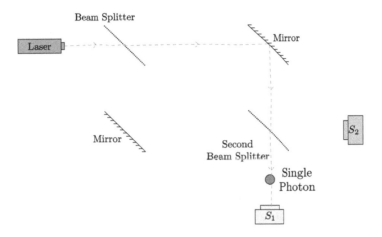

And when it's reflected from the bottom beam splitter, it'll head to sensor S_2 on the right, as shown in the next figure:

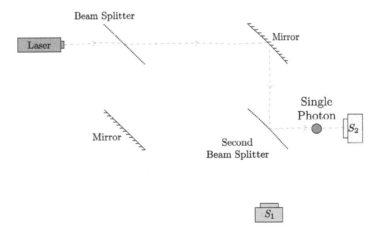

Thus, every time the laser shoots a single photon, unlike the case with multiple photons, either sensor gets randomly lit. In practice, that's not what happens. The photon only ever reaches S_1, which can't be explained by classical mechanics.

In the next section, we'll describe how the Qubelets Model on page 20 resolves this dilemma and correctly show that, even with single photons, only sensor S_1 is lit while sensor S_2 always remains dark.

Single Photon Interference

The breakdown of classical theory to explain experiments such as the Mach-Zehnder interferometer with single photons paved the way for quantum mechanics. In this section, we'll work with qubelets to explain the observed results. Although qubelets are fictional constructs, they nonetheless help us apply the laws of quantum mechanics correctly.

Specifically, we'll start by modeling a photon as a $|0\rangle$ qubit containing a pentagon $|0\rangle$ qubelet, as shown here:

When this photon-qubit reaches the beam splitter, the pentagon $|0\rangle$ qubelet is split into another pentagon $|0\rangle$ qubelet and a triangle $|1\rangle$ qubelet, just like when it's acted on by an H gate, as described in Putting Qubits in Blended States, on page 82:

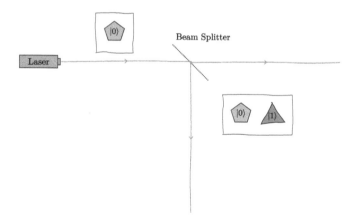

Thus far you've seen new concepts such as qubelets but nothing that jars common sense for which quantum mechanics is so notorious. This view of a logical universe is about to change. All along we've assumed that qubelets can't be isolated from the qubit. But now we'll direct the pentagon $|0\rangle$ qubelet to follow the bottom path and the triangle $|1\rangle$ qubelet to the top path, as shown in the figure on page 421.

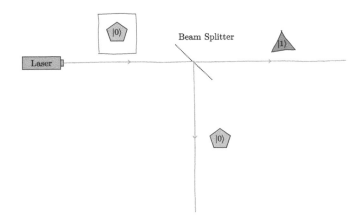

That is, the reflected qubelet is the same type as the incident one, and the transmitted one is of the other type. Thus, the pentagon $|0\rangle$ qubelet is reflected off the beam splitter and the triangle $|1\rangle$ qubelet is transmitted.

It may seem that we're breaking up the qubit and violating the no-separating-the-qubelet-from-qubit restriction we've imposed on it. But, in accordance with quantum mechanics, both paths are actually part of the same system—they're not distinct as we've drawn them. If this notion is confusing, remember that, in reality, the only thing we know for sure is when the photon is detected by the sensors, S_1 or S_2: for all we know, the photon could have circled Mars after leaving the laser before reaching one of the sensors. The classical alternative of considering separate paths and assuming destructive interferences is a bigger headache as it violates the conservation of energy principle—where does the energy of canceled waves go? Thus, physicists have grudgingly accepted the quantum mechanical way of explaining the world, as bizarre as it may appear, so as long as the predictions from the theory matches the observed results.

The pentagon $|0\rangle$ and triangle $|1\rangle$ qubelets after the beam splitter aren't enclosed in a box but are left "floating" to indicate that they're part of the same state and not two photon-qubits.

Thus, we let the pentagon $|0\rangle$ qubelet follow the bottom path to the second beam splitter and the triangle $|1\rangle$ qubelet the top path to the second splitter. The second beam splitter also splits the qubelets just like an H gate, as shown in the figure on page 422.

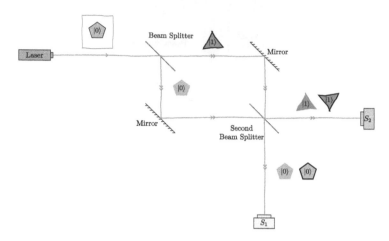

The qubelets drawn without a border are split from the pentagon $|0\rangle$ qubelet traveling along the bottom path, while the qubelets with a border are from the triangle $|1\rangle$ qubelet along the top path.

The pentagon $|0\rangle$ qubelet along the bottom path is split into a pentagon $|0\rangle$ qubelet and reflected toward the bottom sensor, S_1, and a triangle $|1\rangle$ qubelet which is transmitted through the beam splitter toward sensor S_2.

Likewise, the triangle $|1\rangle$ qubelet traveling on the top path is split into a pentagon $|0\rangle$ qubelet that is transmitted toward the bottom sensor, S_1, and an *inverted* triangle $|1\rangle$ qubelet that is headed toward sensor S_2 on the right.

The two pentagon $|0\rangle$ qubelets moving toward the bottom sensor, S_1, are, in effect, a single qubelet. When this qubelet reaches sensor S_1, it'll light it. (Don't assume that the the $|0\rangle$ state is an "off" state and the detector won't activate. The $|0\rangle$ is just an arbitrary label and indicates the presense of a qubelet.)

The non-inverted and inverted triangle $|1\rangle$ qubelets headed toward sensor S_2 cancel each other out. In this case, no qubelet is directed toward sensor S_2. Hence, it always remains dark, as observed in the experiment, and it is never lit in some cases as classical theory would suggest. It's as if the single photon is interfering with itself, a conclusion that's absurd in classical physics.

Note that we began by assuming that the photon is like a $|0\rangle$ qubit. We could equally well have started with a $|1\rangle$ qubit or even a qubit in a blended state and still would have ended showing that it's only sensor S_1 that lights up in every instance. It doesn't matter whether a pentagon $|0\rangle$ or a triangle $|1\rangle$ qubelet reaches the sensor. Either type will activate it. The only time a sensor is not lit is when no qubelet hits it, either because they've all canceled out or because none went toward it.

This analysis with qubelets, which were used to model quantum computing, demonstrates the close relationship with quantum mechanics even though at times it may seem that the world of atoms and photons is far removed from the 1s and 0s of the digital world.

Analysis Is Heuristic

 The material in this section is not rigorous. It's just a heuristic way to give you a taste for the weirdness of quantum mechanics. Don't go waving this to your physics professors. But, by all means, use it to help you understand your homework problems and to frame your answers. I've successfully used this approach to solve many problems from graduate-level texts in quantum mechanics.

Solutions to Exercises

This appendix contains the solutions to all the Try Your Hand exercises in the book.

Quantum Bits Solutions

Solutions for the exercises in Try Your Hand, on page 39.

1. a. Since it's only the ratio of pentagon $|0\rangle$ qubelets to triangle $|1\rangle$ qubelets that matter, we can halve the qubelets of each type, as shown here:

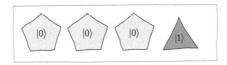

   b. i.   False. This qubit has both pentagon $|0\rangle$ and triangle $|1\rangle$ qubelets. Thus, when it's measured, any of these types of qubelets can be randomly selected. Hence, it could collapse to either of the $|0\rangle$ or $|1\rangle$ idealized states.

   ii. True. Since the ratio of pentagon $|0\rangle$ qubelets to triangle $|1\rangle$ qubelets is 3 : 1, we expect to see the pentagon $|0\rangle$ qubelets 3 times more than the triangle $|1\rangle$ qubelets. Hence, we'll see the corresponding binary state 0 times as often as the 0 state.

   iii. False. Once a qubit is measured by selecting a qubelet from its quantum state, the rest of the qubelets vanish.

   iv. False. Once a qubit is measured by selecting a qubelet from its quantum state, the rest of the qubelets vanish. Thus, if it's measured again, the same qubelet is selected again. Thus, it'll never collapse to a different idealized quantum state.

2. Not much—all you can say is that the qubit had at least one triangle $|1\rangle$ qubelet in its quantum state.

3. $|0\rangle$ is a qubit and 0 is one of the classical binary states. The $|0\rangle$ qubit can be nudged to other blended states while the 0 bit can only be switched to the 1 bit.

4. The Measure would record the classical state 1. That is,

$$|1\rangle \rightarrow 1$$

5. No. The Measure gate records only the specific idealized state the qubit collapses to when it was probed. So, conceivably, if the quantum circuit was run again, the qubit that the Measure gate is inspecting can collapse to another idealized state. But in each case, only a single value will be recorded by the Measure gate in the classical register.

Quantum Logic Gates Solutions

Solutions for the exercises in Try Your Hand, on page 70.

1. The code for the quantum circuit is:

```
Measuring_Two_Qubits_on_a_Real_Computer.qasm
qreg q[5];
creg c[5];

measure q[0] -> c[0];
measure q[2] -> c[2];
```

a. The concatenated string of measured states is 00000.

b. Output on a simulator will look like this:

The output on a simulator is exact: only the 00000 state is seen.

c. Output on a real quantum computer will look something like the output shown on page 427.

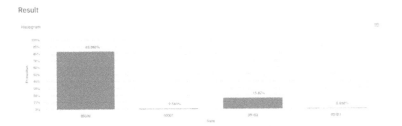

We see that the 00000 state is observed most often. But other states such as 00100 are also seen, albeit with tiny probabilities. (Your output may differ, but the 00000 will appear most often.)

2. a. NOT_NOT_Measure.qasm

```
qreg q[1];
creg c[1];

x q[0];
x q[0];
measure q[0] -> c[0];
```

b. Yes, the state at point A is blended.

c. The state at point A is $|0\rangle$.

d. No, you can't directly observe the state at point A. We surmise that it's a $|0\rangle$ quantum state. But the moment we try and confirm our guess, the quantum state will collapse into one of the idealized quantum states, $|0\rangle$ or $|1\rangle$.

So if we can't physically verify a quantum state, how can we be sure whether our conjecture of the quantum state is correct? This inability to physically confirm our suspicions is one of the ironies of quantum mechanics. But as long as the consequences of our theories lead to things we can predict and physically examine, we should be content with the models devised to explain the behavior of subatomic particles.

e. The Measure gate collapses the qubit at point A and records the corresponding binary value as 0, a classical binary state.

f. Output A. The measured value recorded in the classical register, 0, is shown at the base of the blue bar. The height of the blue bar is 1.000, indicating that the 0 state will always be recorded, at least in the simulator.

3. The quantum circuit is shown here:

$q[0] = |0\rangle$ ———$\boxed{X}$———$\boxed{\measuredangle}$———$\boxed{X}$———

c ——————————————————

$c[0]$

4. The circuit to initialize a qubit to $|1\rangle$ is shown here:

$q[0] = |0\rangle$ ——————$\boxed{X}$—————— $|1\rangle$

c ————————————————

The corresponding code is:

```
x q[0];
```

5. The Measure gate has been placed incorrectly. Hence, it's an invalid circuit and no code can be written.

6. a. The quantum circuit is obtained by switching the $|0\rangle$ state to a $|1\rangle$ before feeding it to the CNOT gate's control, as shown here:

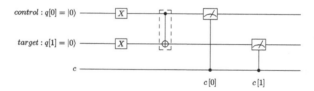

b. The quantum program is:

```
CNOT_Gate_Triggered_on_0.qasm
qreg q[2];
creg c[2];

x q[0];
x q[1];
cx q[0],q[1];
measure q[0] -> c[0];
measure q[1] -> c[1];
```

c. The values in the classical registers when the program terminates are:

$$c[0] = 1$$
$$c[1] = 0$$

7. a. The quantum program is:

```
CNOT_Control_on_1.qasm
qreg q[2];
creg c[2];

x q[0];
x q[1];
cx q[1],q[0];
measure q[0] -> c[1];
measure q[1] -> c[0];
```

b. The values in the classical registers are:

$$c[0] = 1$$
$$c[1] = 0$$

8. a. The quantum states $|a\rangle$, $|b\rangle$, $|c\rangle$, $|d\rangle$, $|e\rangle$, and $|f\rangle$ for different values of $|x\rangle$ and $|y\rangle$ are shown in the following table:

$|x\rangle$	$|y\rangle$	$|a\rangle$	$|b\rangle$	$|c\rangle$	$|d\rangle$	$|e\rangle$	$|f\rangle$
$|0\rangle$	$|0\rangle$	$|0\rangle$	$|0\rangle$	$|0\rangle$	$|0\rangle$	$|0\rangle$	$|0\rangle$
$|0\rangle$	$|1\rangle$	$|0\rangle$	$|1\rangle$	$|1\rangle$	$|1\rangle$	$|1\rangle$	$|0\rangle$
$|1\rangle$	$|0\rangle$	$|1\rangle$	$|1\rangle$	$|0\rangle$	$|1\rangle$	$|0\rangle$	$|1\rangle$
$|1\rangle$	$|1\rangle$	$|1\rangle$	$|0\rangle$	$|1\rangle$	$|0\rangle$	$|1\rangle$	$|1\rangle$

Notice that in each case, the quantum states in $|e\rangle$ and $|f\rangle$ are swapped from those of $|x\rangle$ and $|y\rangle$.

b. The quantum program is:

```
SWAP_Gate.qasm
qreg q[2];
creg c[2];

x q[0];
cx q[0],q[1];
cx q[1],q[0];
cx q[0],q[1];
measure q[0] -> c[0];
measure q[1] -> c[1];
```

The highlighted section is the SWAP gate made up three CNOT gates.

i. The concatenated value is c[1]c[0] = 10.

9. a. The quantum circuit to copy a $|1\rangle$ qubit is:

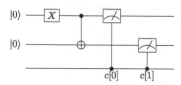

b. The corresponding quantum program is:

Fan_Out_Circuit.qasm
```
qreg q[2];
creg c[2];

x q[0];
cx q[0],q[1];
measure q[0] -> c[0];
measure q[1] -> c[1];
```

10. In the OR gate configuration on page 59, the target qubit fed to the CCNOT gate is $|1\rangle$. Thus, its value after the CCNOT operation is:
$$|1\rangle \oplus (\ulcorner |a\rangle \wedge \ulcorner |b\rangle)$$

Using De Morgan's law, this expression can be rewritten as:
$$|1\rangle \oplus \ulcorner (|a\rangle \vee |b\rangle)$$

Applying the expansion for the exclusive-OR operation:
$$|1\rangle \wedge \neg \ulcorner (|a\rangle \vee |b\rangle) \vee |0\rangle \wedge \textit{lnot}(|a\rangle \vee |b\rangle)$$

This simplifies to:
$$(|a\rangle \vee |b\rangle) \vee |0\rangle$$

The $|0\rangle$ is redundant as it doesn't affect the logical truth of the expression and can be dropped, giving the OR operation:
$$|a\rangle \vee |b\rangle$$

11. a. The quantum circuit is:

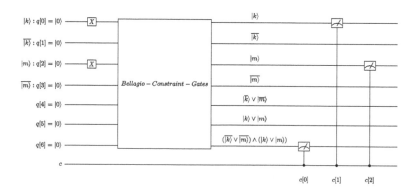

b. The program is:

```
Bellagio_Constraints_k_1_m_1.qasm
OPENQASM 2.0;
include "qelib1.inc";

qreg q[7];
creg c[3];
x q[0];
x q[2];
cx q[0],q[1];
x q[1];
cx q[2],q[3];
x q[3];
x q[1];
x q[3];
x q[4];
ccx q[1],q[3],q[4];
x q[1];
x q[3];
x q[0];
x q[2];
x q[5];
ccx q[0],q[2],q[5];
x q[0];
x q[2];
ccx q[4],q[5],q[6];
measure q[6] -> c[0];
measure q[0] -> c[1];
measure q[2] -> c[2];
```

The highlighted lines set $|k\rangle = |1\rangle$ and $|m\rangle = |1\rangle$.

c. When you run this program on a simulator, the concatenated string of the values in the classical register on termination is 110. This corresponds to the following truth values:

$$\text{Bellagio Constraint truth value} \quad c[0] = 0$$
$$k: \quad c[1] = 1$$
$$m: \quad c[2] = 1$$

d. The value recorded in c[0] is 0, which indicates that the truth value of the Bellagio Constraint is false. Thus, the condition represented by $|k\rangle = |1\rangle$ (Keller performing at Bellagio on Day 1) and $|m\rangle = |1\rangle$ (Maher performing at Bellagio on Day 1) clearly doesn't lead to a valid schedule.

12. a. The logic expression preventing scheduling conflicts at Aladdin is:

$$(\,|k\rangle \ \vee \ |\overline{n}\rangle \,) \wedge (\,|\overline{k}\rangle \ \vee \ |n\rangle \,) = |1\rangle$$

b. The quantum circuit for the logic expression for preventing conflicts for Aladdin is:

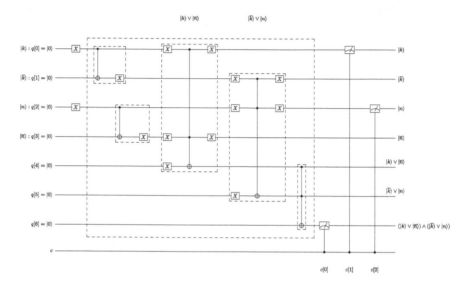

The classical register c[0] records the truth value of the Aladdin Constraint, c[1] records the state of the value representing Kimmel, and c[2] records the state of the value representing Noah.

c. The quantum program is:

```
Aladdin_Constraints_k_1_n_1.qasm
OPENQASM 2.0;
include "qelib1.inc";

qreg q[7];
creg c[3];

x q[0];
x q[2];
cx q[0],q[1];
x q[1];
cx q[2],q[3];
x q[3];
x q[0];
x q[3];
x q[4];
```

```
ccx q[0],q[3],q[4];
x q[0];
x q[3];
x q[1];
x q[2];
x q[5];
ccx q[1],q[2],q[5];
x q[1];
x q[2];
ccx q[4],q[5],q[6];
measure q[6] -> c[0];
measure q[0] -> c[1];
measure q[2] -> c[2];
```

d. Yes, as seen by the state recorded in c[0], the values for $|k\rangle$ and $|n\rangle$ correspond to a valid schedule. Noah performs on the first day and Kimmel performs on the second.

13. a. The logic expression preventing scheduling conflicts at Caesars is:

$$(|m\rangle \lor |n\rangle) \land (|\overline{m}\rangle \lor |\overline{n}\rangle) = |1\rangle$$

b. The quantum circuit for the logic expression for preventing conflicts for Caesars is:

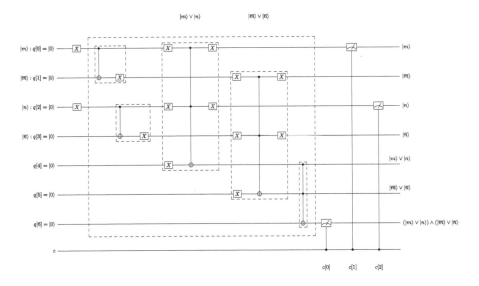

The classical register c[0] records the truth value of the Caesars Constraint, c[1] records the state of the value representing Maher, and c[2] records the state of the value representing Noah.

c. The quantum program is:

```
Caesars_Constraints_m_1_n_1.qasm
OPENQASM 2.0;
include "qelib1.inc";

qreg q[7];
creg c[3];

x q[0];
x q[2];
cx q[0],q[1];
x q[1];
cx q[2],q[3];
x q[3];
x q[0];
x q[2];
x q[4];
ccx q[0],q[2],q[4];
x q[0];
x q[2];
x q[1];
x q[3];
x q[5];
ccx q[1],q[3],q[5];
x q[1];
x q[3];
ccx q[4],q[5],q[6];
measure q[6] -> c[0];
measure q[0] -> c[1];
measure q[2] -> c[2];
```

d. The state recorded in c[0] is $|0\rangle$. Thus, the initial quantum states of $|1\rangle$ and $|1\rangle$ for the variables $|m\rangle$ and $|n\rangle$, representing when Maher and Noah, respectively, perform at Caesars don't give a valid schedule.

e. By experimenting with different initial quantum states for $|m\rangle$ and $|n\rangle$, you'll find that you get a valid schedule when $|m\rangle$ is $|0\rangle$ and $|n\rangle$ is $|1\rangle$. These values imply that Maher performs at Caesars on Day 1 and Noah on Day 2.

Quantum Superposition Solutions

Solutions for the exercises in Try Your Hand, on page 101.

1. The operation of the NOT gate on the $|0\rangle$ qubit in terms of qubelets looks like the figure on page 435.

2. a. The inverted triangle $|1\rangle$ qubelet will become an inverted pentagon $|0\rangle$ qubelet after it's been operated on by a NOT gate:

   b. The inverted pentagon $|0\rangle$ qubelet would collapse to $|0\rangle$, and the corresponding binary value, 0, is recorded in the classical register.

3. a. The $|0\rangle$ qubit after it's been operated on by the X and H gates, respectively, will have the following qubelets:

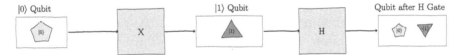

   The $|0\rangle$ qubit on the left, containing a pentagon $|0\rangle$ qubelet, is operated on by the NOT gate. This puts the qubit in the $|1\rangle$ quantum state containing a triangle $|1\rangle$ qubelet, as shown in the middle qubit. The middle qubit, in turn, is operated on by the H gate, which splits its triangle $|1\rangle$ qubelet into a pentagon $|0\rangle$ qubelet and an inverted triangle $|1\rangle$ qubelet.

   b. The qubelets in the qubit are:

   In this case, the $|0\rangle$ qubit on the left is first operated on by the H gate. This splits its pentagon $|0\rangle$ qubelet into a pentagon $|0\rangle$ qubelet and a triangle $|1\rangle$ qubelet. The X gate then switches each qubelet in the middle qubit and puts the qubit in the quantum state shown on the right.

   c. No. Even though the orientation of the triangle qubelets in the qubits are different in the two circuits, when each qubit is measured, there's no statistical difference between the outputs of both circuits.

4. a. The simplified qubit is obtained by halving the number of pentagon
        $|0\rangle$ and triangle $|1\rangle$ qubelets, as shown here:

The probabilities of picking a pentagon $|0\rangle$ qubelet or a triangle $|1\rangle$
qubelet remain the same.

   b. Two of the pentagon $|0\rangle$ qubelets and the triangle $|1\rangle$ qubelets cancel
       out. Further, the qubit with the remaining two pentagon $|0\rangle$ qubelets
       is equivalent to a qubit with a single pentagon $|0\rangle$ qubelet, as shown
       in the following figure:

5. The inverted triangle qubelets don't affect the probability of collapsing to
    the binary states. The likelihood of the qubit collapsing to $|0\rangle$ versus $|1\rangle$
    is based on the ratio of the number of pentagon $|0\rangle$ qubelets versus that
    of the triangle $|1\rangle$ qubelets:

    Number of pentagon $|0\rangle$ qubelets : Number of triangle $|1\rangle$ qubelets $= 4 : 6 = 2 : 3$

    So, the qubit is 1.5 times more likely to collapse to the $|1\rangle$ state than the
    $|0\rangle$ state, which intuitively matches our expectations since the qubit has
    more triangle $|1\rangle$ qubelets.

6. In the left qubit, all three triangle $|1\rangle$ qubelets are effectively a single tri-
    angle $|1\rangle$ qubelet. And in the right qubit, the triangle $|1\rangle$ qubelets cancel
    out. So, the quantum operation takes a $|1\rangle$ qubit and modifies it to a single
    inverted pentagon $|0\rangle$ qubelet, as shown here:

Thus, the following is a possible sequence of quantum operations to apply
on the qubit to transform its state on the left to the one on the right:

   • Invert the triangle $|1\rangle$ qubelet.
   • Apply the NOT gate to switch the inverted triangle $|1\rangle$ qubelet to an
     inverted pentagon $|0\rangle$ qubelet.

In Pauli-Z (Z) Gate, on page 109, you'll learn how to invert triangle |1⟩ qubelets in a quantum program.

7. a. To simulate a coin toss on a quantum computer, we just need to have an H gate operate on a |0⟩ qubit as shown in the following quantum circuit:

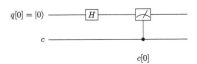

Here's the code:

```
Coin_Toss.qasm
qreg q[1];
creg c[1];

h q[0];
measure q[0] -> c[0];
```

b. Since we're only interested in a single coin toss at a time, we specify just a single shot run.

8. The qubelet diagram for back-to-back H gates being applied to |1⟩ follows:

When the middle qubit is operated on by the second H gate, the inverted triangle |1⟩ qubelet is split into an inverted pentagon |0⟩ qubelet and an *inverted* inverted triangle |1⟩ qubelet. The *inverted* inverted triangle |1⟩ qubelet is just a triangle |1⟩ qubelet that goes back to the non-inverted orientation.

The non-inverted and inverted pentagon |0⟩ qubelets will cancel, leaving the two non-inverted triangle |1⟩ qubelets. The latter is equivalent to a triangle |1⟩ qubelet. Thus, the quantum state of the qubit after it's operated on by both H gates is |1⟩. If this state is measured, the |1⟩ qubit will, of course, collapse to |1⟩ and the binary state 1 will be recorded in the classical register.

9. a. Two back-to-back H gates return the qubit to its original state, |0⟩. The third H gate operates on this |0⟩ qubit and puts it into the blended state shown here:

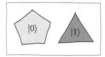

If this qubit is measured, it would collapse to the idealized states, |0⟩ or |1⟩, with equal probability.

b. The quantum program for three back-to-back H gates acting on q[0] is as follows:

```
H_H_H_Measure.qasm
qreg q[1];
creg c[1];

h q[0];
h q[0];
h q[0];
measure q[0] -> c[0];
```

c. The output of this quantum circuit is shown here:

Three back-to-back H gates are equivalent to a single H gate.

10. One way to cancel out the pentagon |0⟩ qubelet is to first pass it to the H gate. The H gate acts on the qubelets in the left qubit as follows:

• Splits the inverted pentagon |0⟩ qubelet to another inverted pentagon |0⟩ qubelet and an *inverted* triangle |1⟩ qubelet. (The triangle |1⟩ is inverted because the pentagon |0⟩ qubelet it acts on is also inverted. The H gate doesn't invert qubelets when acting on a |0⟩ qubit.)

• Splits the inverted triangle |1⟩ qubelet to an inverted pentagon |0⟩ qubelet and a *non-inverted* triangle |1⟩ qubelet. (The triangle |1⟩ is non-inverted because the triangle |1⟩ qubelet it acts on is inverted. The H gate inverts the triangle |1⟩ qubelet when acting on a |1⟩ qubit.)

Thus, when the H gate acts on the blended qubit, it puts the blended qubit on the left to the state on the right, shown as follows:

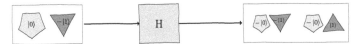

The non-inverted and inverted triangle $|1\rangle$ qubelets on the right qubit cancel each other out, leaving a single inverted pentagon $|0\rangle$ qubelet in its quantum state.

Next, apply a NOT (X) gate to switch the inverted pentagon $|0\rangle$ qubelet to an inverted triangle $|1\rangle$ qubelet, as shown here:

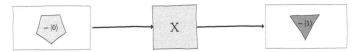

Thus, the required sequence of quantum gates you'd use to take the original blended state to one with an inverted triangle $|1\rangle$ qubelet is an H gate followed by an X gate.

11. The transformed qubit is the following:

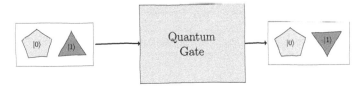

12. The inversions don't affect the probabilities of picking the qubelet combinations. Thus, the $|00\rangle$ qubelet combination has a greater probability of being selected. Hence, the 00 state is the most likely state that's recorded in the classical register.

13. Each qubelet combination is formed by taking a qubelet from each of the three qubits in turn. This gives $2 \times 2 \times 2 = 2^3 = 8$ qubelet combinations in the mega-qubit, as shown in the next figure:

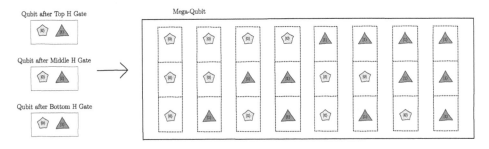

14. a. The triangle $|1\rangle$ qubelet in the top qubit pairs up with the qubelets in the bottom qubit forming the mega-qubit with the two qubelet combinations, shown in the following figure:

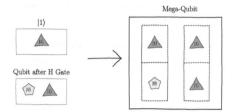

The top qubelet corresponds to the qubit in q[0] and the bottom qubelet to the qubit in q[1]. We represent these combinations by writing the top qubelet followed by the bottom qubelet. So the left qubelet combination is $|10\rangle$ and the right combination is $|11\rangle$.

b. In this circuit, the top qubelet in each combination is a triangle $|1\rangle$ qubelet. This triangle $|1\rangle$ qubelet is fed to the control bit of the CNOT gate. Thus, the qubit passed to the target of the CNOT gate is switched, as shown in the following figure:

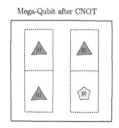

The $|10\rangle$ becomes $|11\rangle$, and the $|11\rangle$ combination turns into $|10\rangle$.

c. When the mega-qubit is measured, the following two classical states are recorded in the c[1]c[0] elements of the classical register:

State	Probability
11	$\frac{1}{2}$
01	$\frac{1}{2}$

Note that the elements in the classical register are written as c[1]c[0]—in reverse order of how the qubits were written earlier.

d. If the bottom qubit collapses to $|0\rangle$, then the right qubelet combination in the mega-qubit was selected. Thus, the top qubit will collapse to $|1\rangle$.

e. The code is as follows:

```
CNOT_with_H_on_Target.qasm
qreg q[2];
creg c[2];

x q[0];
h q[1];
cx q[0],q[1];
measure q[0] -> c[0];
measure q[1] -> c[1];
```

And this is the output:

The states shown at the bottom of the two blue bars represent the string c[1]c[0]—in which the state of the bottom qubit is associated with the first character and the state of the top qubit is the second character. Thus, these states match those on the mega-qubit.

15. a. Place the H gates on the q[0] and q[2] qubits, representing $|k\rangle$ and $|n\rangle$, respectively, as shown here:

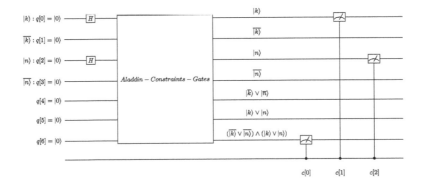

b. The code to place the H gates in this circuit is at the beginning, right after you declare the quantum and classical arrays:

```
Aladdin_Constraints_k_h_n_h.qasm
qreg q[7];
creg c[3];

h q[0];
h q[2];
```

And the output is as follows:

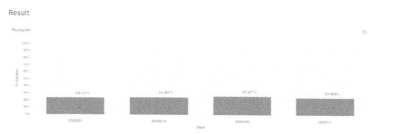

Note that even though we measured three qubits, since the circuit has seven qubits, the state at the bottom of each bar is a string of length 7. We're only interested in the states corresponding to the three positions from the right where the Measure gates record the collapses of the three qubits in the circuit.

We see four states in the output with equal probability. This circuit doesn't yet collapse with a large likelihood to a state that satisfies the constraints.

16. This is the corresponding quantum circuit:

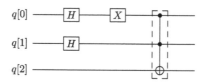

Quantum Tagging and Entangling Solutions

Solutions for the exercises in Try Your Hand, on page 136.

1. a. The quantum circuit that mimics the Z gate but inverts the $|0\rangle$ qubit while leaving the $|1\rangle$ qubit alone is shown here:

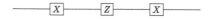

b. i. The qubelets at various stages when the circuit is initialized with a $|0\rangle$ qubit is shown in the following figure:

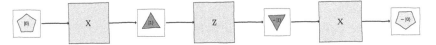

The first X gate switches the $|0\rangle$ qubit to a $|1\rangle$ qubit containing a triangle $|1\rangle$ qubelet. The Z gate inverts this triangle $|1\rangle$ qubelet, and the right X gate switches this inverted triangle $|1\rangle$ to an inverted pentagon $|0\rangle$ qubelet. As a result, the entire circuit inverts a $|0\rangle$ qubit.

ii. The qubelets at various stages when the circuit is initialized with a $|1\rangle$ qubit is shown next:

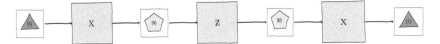

The first X gate switches the $|1\rangle$ qubit to a $|0\rangle$ qubit holding a pentagon $|0\rangle$ qubelet. The Z gate leaves this qubelet alone. The X gate on the right then switches this pentagon $|0\rangle$ qubelet to a triangle $|1\rangle$ qubelet. Effectively, the entire circuit leaves the $|1\rangle$ qubit unmodified.

2. a. The following is the code for this circuit:

```
Line 1  x q[1];
     2  h q[1];
     3  cx q[0],q[1];
     4  h q[1];
     5  x q[1];
```

b. The H and CNOT gates implement the CZ gate, as shown in the dashed box in the following figure:

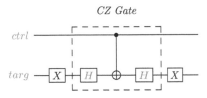

Lines 2–4 in the program in the previous part implement the CZ gate.

This circuit behaves like a CZ gate except that it inverts pentagon $|0\rangle$ qubelets on the target when its control is $|1\rangle$. (The CZ inverts triangle $|1\rangle$ qubelets when its control is $|1\rangle$.)

3. a. The code for the circuit is listed here:

```
// AND Gate
ccx q[0],q[1],p[0];
  ccx q[2],p[0],p[1];
    ccx q[3],p[1],p[2];
      cx p[2],p[3];
    ccx q[3],p[1],p[2];
  ccx q[2],p[0],p[1];
ccx q[0],q[1],p[0];
```

b. The complete code, including initializing qubits $|q_0\rangle - |q_3\rangle$ to $|1\rangle$ as well as the Measure gates is listed next:

```
Line 1  // Initialize 2 Quantum Registers, q and p, and Classical Register
        qreg q[4];
        qreg p[4];
        creg c[5];
5
        // Initialize q[0]-q[3] to |1>
        x q[0];
        x q[1];
        x q[2];
10      x q[3];

        // AND Gate
        ccx q[0],q[1],p[0];
          ccx q[2],p[0],p[1];
15          ccx q[3],p[1],p[2];
              cx p[2],p[3];
            ccx q[3],p[1],p[2];
          ccx q[2],p[0],p[1];
        ccx q[0],q[1],p[0];
20
        // Collapse Qubit and Measure their States
        measure q[0] -> c[0];
        measure q[1] -> c[1];
        measure q[2] -> c[2];
25      measure q[3] -> c[3];
        measure p[3] -> c[4];
```

The qubits are initialized on lines 7–10, and the Measure gates are declared on lines 22–26.

The c[4] register records the collapsed value of the $|p_3\rangle$ qubit, which will be 1 as qubits $|q_0\rangle - |q_3\rangle$ are $|1\rangle$.

4. a. The missing qubelets are shown with a thicker outline in the figure below:

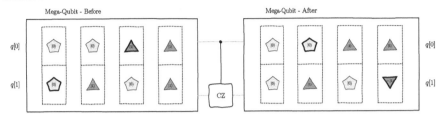

b. The qubits are not entangled. The state of either qubit can't be deduced by knowing the state of the other.

5. a. The mega-qubit is shown in the following figure:

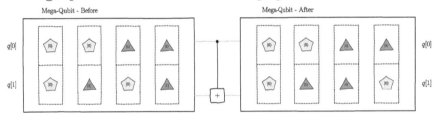

b. Looking at the mega-qubit after the application of the H gates, we see each qubit can collapse to both the 0 and 1 states independent of the collapsed state of the other qubit. That is, neither qubit is forced to collapse to any state by the other. Thus, the qubits are not entangled.

c. The quantum program for this circuit is listed here:

```
H_on_Control_and_Target_of_CNOT.qasm
qreg q[2];
creg c[2];

h q[0];
h q[1];
cx q[0],q[1];
measure q[0] -> c[0];
measure q[1] -> c[1];
```

The output of this program is shown in the following figure:

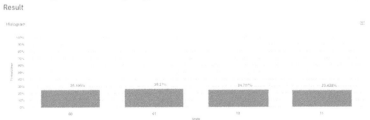

The output shows that the qubits in this circuit collapse roughly equally to all four states. Thus, no particular state is favored, as would be the case if the qubits were entangled.

6. a. Since none of the qubits are split, each qubit is in a single state determined by the quantum logic gates. Thus, the mega-qubit will have only one qubelet combination, as shown in the following figure:

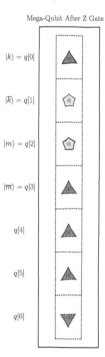

Mega-Qubit After Z Gate

The qubelet in the bottom cell, corresponding to q[6], indicates that all constraints are met. Thus, the Z gate inverts its triangle $|1\rangle$ qubelet by 180° or a half turn.

b. The quantum program is listed as follows:

```
Bellagio_Constraints_k_1_m_0_with_Z_Gate.qasm
Line 1   // Initialize Quantum and Classical Registers
    -    qreg q[7];
    -    creg c[3];
    -
    5    // Set k to |1>
    -    x q[0];
    -
    -    // Bellagio Constraints
    -    cx q[2],q[3];
   10    x q[4];
    -    x q[5];
```

```
     cx q[0],q[1];
     x q[3];
     x q[0];
15   x q[1];
     x q[3];
     x q[1];
     ccx q[1],q[3],q[4];
     x q[1];
20   x q[2];
     x q[3];
     ccx q[0],q[2],q[5];
     x q[0];
     x q[2];
25   ccx q[4],q[5],q[6]; // if q[6] = |1>, all constraints are met
     // End of Bellagio Constraints

     // Rotate q[6]'s triangle |1> qubelet by 180 degrees
     z q[6];
30
     // Collapse and Measure Qubits
     measure q[0] -> c[0]; // k
     measure q[2] -> c[1]; // m
     measure q[6] -> c[2]; // c[2] = 1 indicates all constraints ok
```

On line 6, an X gate sets $|k\rangle$ to $|1\rangle$. The Bellagio Constraints are specified on lines 9–25. The CCNOT gate whose target qubit q[6] switches to $|1\rangle$ if both the constraints are met is declared on line 25. The Z gate on line 29 inverts the triangle $|1\rangle$ qubelet by a half turn. Finally, the Measure gates are declared on lines 32–34. If all constraints are met, c[2] logs a 1.

c. When you run this program on the IBM Quantum Computer's simulator, it'll return a result as shown in the following chart:

The label at the bottom of the bar is 101. Noting that the IBM Quantum Computer reverses the order of the bits, this string represents the bits in the classical register as shown in the table on page 448.

Classical Register	Qubit Measured	Value Logged
c[0]	$q[0] = \lvert k \rangle$	1
c[1]	$q[2] = \lvert m \rangle$	0
c[2]	$q[6]$	1

Since c[2] is 1, the values of $\lvert k \rangle = \lvert 1 \rangle$ and $\lvert m \rangle = \lvert 0 \rangle$ satisfy the Boolean logic expressions.

d. The code with the disentangling gates is listed as follows:

Bellagio_Constraints_k_1_m_0_with_Z_Gate_Disentangling.qasm

```
// Initialize Quantum and Classical Registers
qreg q[7];
creg c[3];

// Set k to |1>
x q[0];

// Bellagio Constraints
cx q[2],q[3];
x q[4];
x q[5];
cx q[0],q[1];
x q[3];
x q[0];
x q[1];
x q[3];
x q[1];
ccx q[1],q[3],q[4];
x q[1];
x q[2];
x q[3];
ccx q[0],q[2],q[5];
x q[0];
x q[2];
ccx q[4],q[5],q[6];
x q[0];
x q[2];
// End of Bellagio Constraints

z q[6];

// Disentangle the Bellagio Constraints
ccx q[4],q[5],q[6];
ccx q[0],q[2],q[5];
x q[0];
x q[1];
x q[2];
x q[3];
x q[5];
```

```
40  ccx q[1],q[3],q[4];
    x q[1];
    x q[3];
    x q[4];
    x q[1];
45  x q[3];
    cx q[0],q[1];
    cx q[2],q[3];

    // Collapse and Measure Qubits
50  measure q[0] -> c[0]; //k
    measure q[2] -> c[1]; // m
    measure q[6] -> c[2]; // c[2] = 1 indicates all constraints ok
```

The Bellagio Constraints are disentangled on lines 33–47. The Z gate on line 30 isn't part of the disentangling gates.

e. When you run this program on the IBM Quantum Computer simulator, your output will be as shown in the following chart:

This time the label at the bottom of the bar is 001. As in the earlier part of this exercise, this string corresponds to the following values in the classical register:

Classical Register	Qubit Measured	Value Logged
c[0]	$q[0] = |k\rangle$	1
c[1]	$q[2] = |m\rangle$	0
c[2]	$q[6]$	0

That is, the value logged in the classical register c[2] is 0 despite all the constraints being met. The reason why a 0 is recorded is that by adding the disentangling gates, q[6] is restored to its original $|0\rangle$ value.

Importantly, although you can't see it in the output, the pentagon $|0\rangle$ qubelet in qubit q[6] is really inverted, or rotated by a half turn, by the Z gate, whose action isn't reversed. In Chapter 10, Quantum Search, on page 295, you'll learn ways to introduce quantum effects in your code to exploit this rotation of the pentagon $|0\rangle$ qubelet to find optimal solutions.

Custom Quantum States Solutions

Quantum States, Amplitudes, and Probabilities Solutions

Solutions for the exercises in Try Your Hand, on page 149.

1. a. The qubit has five inverted pentagon $|0\rangle$ pentagon and three inverted triangle $|1\rangle$ qubelets. Thus, its quantum state is:

$$-\frac{5}{\sqrt{5^2+3^2}}\,|0\rangle - \frac{3}{\sqrt{5^2+3^2}}\,|0\rangle$$

$$= -\frac{5}{5.8309}\,|0\rangle - \frac{3}{5.8309}\,|1\rangle$$

$$= -0.8575\,|0\rangle - 0.5145\,|1\rangle$$

   b.

$$\text{Probability of collapsing to } |0\rangle = \left(\frac{5}{\sqrt{5^2+3^2}}\right)^2 = 0.7353$$

$$\text{Probability of collapsing to } |1\rangle = \left(\frac{3}{\sqrt{5^2+3^2}}\right)^2 = 0.2647$$

As a check, the sum of these probabilities add up to 1:

$$0.7353 + 0.2647 = 1$$

2. a. For $|\psi\rangle$ to be a valid quantum state, the squares of the amplitudes sum up to 1:

$$\left(\frac{-0.35}{N}\right)^2 + \left(\frac{0.28}{N}\right)^2 = 1$$

Thus,

$$N = \sqrt{0.35^2 + 0.28^2}$$

The quantum state $|\psi\rangle$ is:

$$|\psi\rangle = \frac{-0.35}{\sqrt{0.35^2+0.28^2}}\,|0\rangle + \frac{0.28}{\sqrt{0.35^2+0.28^2}}\,|1\rangle = \frac{-0.35}{0.4482}\,|0\rangle + \frac{0.28}{0.4482}\,|1\rangle$$

   b. For the quantum state $|\psi\rangle$, the amplitudes are:

$$\omega_0 = \frac{-0.35}{0.4482}$$

$$\omega_1 = \frac{0.28}{0.4482}$$

The absolute ratio of the amplitudes are:

$$\frac{|\omega_0|}{|\omega_1|} = \frac{0.35}{0.28}$$

This simplies to:

$$\frac{0.35}{0.28} = 1.25$$

$$= \frac{125}{100}$$

$$= \frac{5}{4}$$

Since the amplitude of $|0\rangle$ in the quantum state is negative, this qubit has five inverted pentagon $|0\rangle$ and four triangle $|1\rangle$ qubelets:

3. For a valid quantum state, the sum of the squares of the amplitudes must add up to 1.

In this case, the amplitudes are:

$$\omega_0 = 0.2523$$
$$\omega_1 = -0.7517$$

The squares of the amplitudes, the probabilities of collapsing to 0 and 1, are:

$$\omega_0^2 = 0.2523^2 = 0.064$$
$$\omega_1^2 = (-0.7517)^2 = 0.5651$$

Since the sum of the probabilities $0.064 + 0.5651$ doesn't equal 1, the given expression doesn't represent a valid quantum state.

4. a. The amplitude ω_1 is determined by the following steps:

$$(-0.4472)^2 + \omega_1^2 = 1$$
$$\omega_1^2 = 1 - (-0.4472)^2 = 0.8000$$
$$\omega_1 = \sqrt{0.8000}$$
$$\omega_1 = 0.8944$$

b. To calculate the number of pentagon $|0\rangle$ and triangle $|1\rangle$ qubelets, we first calculate the absolute ratio of the amplitudes:

$$\frac{|\omega_0|}{|\omega_1|} = \frac{0.4472}{0.8944} = 0.5 = \frac{1}{2}$$

That is, the qubit will hold one pentagon $|0\rangle$ qubelet and two triangle $|1\rangle$ qubelets. Because the sign of ω_1 is negative, the pentagon $|0\rangle$ qubelet will be inverted, as shown here:

5. If the qubit contains no triangle $|1\rangle$ qubelets, then $\omega_1 = 0$. Thus, the qubit can only collapse to 0. As a result, the probability of selecting the pentagon $|0\rangle$ qubelet is 1. The pentagon $|0\rangle$ qubelet, however, could be inverted. So, $\omega_0 = \pm 1$.

6. a. The following figure shows the qubelets after each gate:

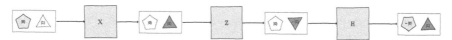

b. The quantum states after each gate operates on the qubit are shown next:

   After X Gate

   $$|1\rangle$$

   After Z Gate

   $$-|1\rangle$$

   After H Gate

   After the H gate operates on the qubit, the qubit contains one inverted pentagon $|0\rangle$ qubelet and one triangle $|1\rangle$ qubelet. Thus, the amplitudes are:

   $$\omega_0 = -\frac{1}{\sqrt{1^2+1^2}} = -\frac{1}{\sqrt{2}}$$
   $$\omega_1 = \frac{1}{\sqrt{1^2+1^2}} = \frac{1}{\sqrt{2}}$$

   The quantum state is:

   $$-\frac{1}{\sqrt{2}}|0\rangle + \frac{1}{\sqrt{2}}|1\rangle$$

c. The probabilities of collapsing to $|0\rangle$ and $|1\rangle$, respectively, are:

   $$\text{Probability of collapsing to } |0\rangle = \omega_0^2 = \left(-\frac{1}{\sqrt{2}}\right)^2 = \frac{1}{2}$$
   $$\text{Probability of collapsing to } |1\rangle = \omega_1^2 = \left(\frac{1}{\sqrt{2}}\right)^2 = \frac{1}{2}$$

d. The quantum program for the previous circuit is as follows:

```
0_X_Z_H_Measure.qasm
qreg q[1];
creg c[1];

x q[0];
z q[0];
h q[0];
measure q[0] -> c[0];
```

e. The output of the quantum program is the following:

Result

The probabilities of the qubit collapsing to $|0\rangle$ and $|1\rangle$ are each 0.5 or 50%. Thus, the probabilities of seeing the classical states 0 and 1 are also 0.5 or 50%. These match the probabilities computed earlier from the final quantum state.

Rotating Qubelets Through Any Angle Solutions

Solutions for the exercises in Try Your Hand, on page 156.

1. a. Since the quantum state is specified using two pentagon $|0\rangle$ and six triangle $|1\rangle$ qubelets, it'll have a greater probability to collapse to 1 than 0. Thus, it'll be in the *lower* hemisphere where the south pole is the quantum state $|1\rangle$.

    b. Since the triangle $|1\rangle$ qubelets are 3 times more than the pentagon $|0\rangle$ qubelets, the quantum state leans more toward $|1\rangle$ than $|0\rangle$. Thus, it'll be closer to the south pole than the equator.

2. This qubit has roughly the same number of pentagon $|0\rangle$ and triangle $|1\rangle$ qubelets. So its quantum state will be around the equator on the Bloch sphere, which corresponds most closely to patch *A*. Patch *B* is associated with a state that would have far more pentagon $|0\rangle$ qubelets than triangle $|1\rangle$ qubelets, while patch *C* would have more triangle $|1\rangle$ than pentagon $|0\rangle$ qubelets.

3. The quantum state represented by the patch favors the $|1\rangle$ state and, thus, the second qubit best matches it. The first qubit's quantum state falls in the upper hemisphere and leans toward collapsing to 0. The last qubit's quantum state falls exactly on the south pole.

4. a. The equation for the quantum state, $|\psi\rangle$, of a qubit is:

$$|\psi\rangle = \cos\frac{\theta}{2}|0\rangle + e^{i\varphi}\sin\frac{\theta}{2}|1\rangle$$

The angle that the magnitude $|r_{|0\rangle}|$ makes with the vertical W-axis is θ, and the angle that the magnitude $|r_{|1\rangle}|$ sweeps out in the equatorial plane is φ. This angle is the difference between the rotations of the triangle $|1\rangle$ and pentagon $|0\rangle$ qubelets.

Since this qubit has just one pentagon $|0\rangle$ and one triangle $|1\rangle$ qubelet, the amplitudes are as follows:

$$\text{Magnitude of amplitude of } |0\rangle = \frac{1}{\sqrt{2}}$$

$$\text{Magnitude of amplitude of } |1\rangle = \frac{1}{\sqrt{2}}$$

Thus,

$$\cos\frac{\theta}{2} = \frac{1}{\sqrt{2}}$$
$$= \cos\frac{\pi}{4}$$
$$= \cos\frac{\frac{\pi}{2}}{2}$$
$$\text{Thus, } \theta = \frac{\pi}{2}$$

That is, this quantum state lies at 90°, or on the equator.

The pentagon $|0\rangle$ qubelet is rotated 90° anticlockwise, and the triangle $|1\rangle$ qubelet is turned 90° clockwise. Thus, the difference in their rotations is $90 - (-90) = 180°$. Hence, the quantum state is:

$$\frac{1}{\sqrt{2}}|0\rangle + e^{i\pi}\frac{1}{\sqrt{2}}|1\rangle$$

Noting that $e^{i\pi} = \cos\pi + i\sin\pi$, and that $\cos\pi = -1$ and $\sin\pi = 0$, the quantum state of this qubit is:

$$\frac{1}{\sqrt{2}}|0\rangle - \frac{1}{\sqrt{2}}|1\rangle$$

b. The quantum state is identical to a |1⟩ qubit split by an H gate.

In both cases, the difference in angles between the triangle |1⟩ qubelets and pentagon |0⟩ qubelets is 180° or π radians.

This example underscores the criteria that it's only the difference in angles between the pentagon |0⟩ and triangle |1⟩ qubelets that matters and not their individual orientations.

c. The difference in rotation angles between the pentagon |0⟩ qubelets and triangle |1⟩ qubelets is 225 − 45 = 180°. Thus, its state would be *identical* to the original qubit.

Universal Gates Solutions

Solutions for the exercises in Try Your Hand, on page 169.

1. a. The quantum program for this circuit is as follows:

```
0_X_U2_Phi_0_Lambda_180_H_Measure.qasm
Line 1  qreg q[1];
     2  creg c[1];
     3
     4  x q[0];
     5  u2(0,pi) q[0];
     6  h q[0];
     7  measure q[0] -> c[0];
```

The U2 gate acts on a |1⟩ qubit. Thus, on line 4 we need to declare a NOT (X) gate to switch the q[0] qubit from its initial |0⟩ state to the required |1⟩ state.

b. The output for this circuit is shown here:

Result

The value recorded in the classical register is always 1 suggesting that the q[0] qubit consistently collapses to |1⟩). This circuit mimics back-to-back H gates.

c. When you run this circuit, you get an output that is similar to the following:

Result

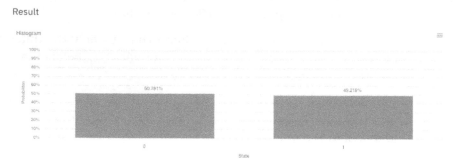

This output shows that the classical register records 0 and 1 each approximately half the time, suggesting that the q[0] qubit collapses to |0⟩ and |1⟩ with the same frequency. In other words, gates in this sequence don't neutralize each other as the back-to-back H gates would.

The qubit doesn't go back to its original state because the $U2$ $(\pi/2, \pi)$ gate doesn't produce qubelets that cancel out when acted on by the H gate like the $U2$ $(0, \pi)$ gate does.

2. a. No. Having the qubit acted on by another H gate wouldn't help since back-to-back H gates don't affect the qubit. It's as if the H gates were not there at all, effectively resetting the circuit, and the qubit is only operated on by the $U3$ $(\pi/3, \pi/6, 0)$ gate.

b. i. The quantum program is listed here:

```
0_U3_Theta_60_Phi_30_H_U3_Theta_60_H_Measure.qasm
qreg q[1];
creg c[1];

u3(pi/3,pi/6,0) q[0];
h q[0];
u3(pi/3,0,0) q[0];
h q[0];
measure q[0] -> c[0];
```

The second $U3$ $(\pi/3, 0, 0)$ gate sandwiched between the two H gates is highlighted.

ii. The output of this program will be similar to the figure on page 457.

Result

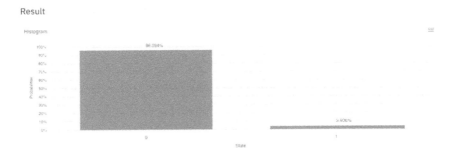

The probability of the q[0] qubit collapsing to $|0\rangle$ has improved so that the frequency of seeing 0 recorded in the classical register is roughly 96%.

3. a. The equation for the quantum state is:

$$|\psi\rangle = \cos\frac{\theta}{2}|0\rangle + e^{i\varphi}\sin\frac{\theta}{2}|1\rangle$$

The angle θ is the tilt from the vertical or Z-axis and the angle φ is the difference in the rotation angles between the triangle $|1\rangle$ and pentagon $|0\rangle$ qubelets.

The right qubit has one pentagon $|0\rangle$ qubelet and two triangle $|1\rangle$ qubelets. Thus, the amplitude of the pentagon $|0\rangle$ qubelet is:

$$\text{Amplitude of } |0\rangle = \cos\frac{\theta}{2} = \frac{1}{\sqrt{1^2 + 2^2}} = \frac{1}{\sqrt{5}}$$

From $\cos\theta/2$, $\sin\theta/2$ is calculated using Euler's formula:

$$\sin^2\frac{\theta}{2} = 1 - \cos^2\frac{\theta}{2}$$

$$= 1 - \left(\frac{1}{\sqrt{5}}\right)^2$$

$$= \frac{4}{5}$$

$$\sin\frac{\theta}{2} = \frac{2}{\sqrt{5}}$$

Thus, the angle $\theta/2$ is:

$$\frac{\theta}{2} = \arccos\frac{1}{\sqrt{5}} = 1.1071 \text{ radians}$$

And θ is 2.2142 radians or 126.86°.

The triangle $|1\rangle$ qubelets are rotated 30° anticlockwise. So the angle φ is:

$$|\psi\rangle = \frac{\pi}{6} \text{ radians}$$

Angles are measured positively in the anticlockwise direction.[1] So 30° anticlockwise is a positive angle.

Thus,

$$e^{i\frac{\pi}{6}} = \cos\frac{\pi}{6} + i\sin\frac{\pi}{6}$$
$$= \frac{\sqrt{3}}{2} + i\frac{1}{2}$$

The quantum state for the right qubit is:

$$|\psi\rangle = \frac{1}{\sqrt{5}}|0\rangle + \left(\frac{\sqrt{3}}{2} + i\frac{1}{2}\right)\frac{2}{\sqrt{5}}|1\rangle$$
$$= \frac{1}{\sqrt{5}}|0\rangle + \left(\frac{\sqrt{3}}{\sqrt{5}} + i\frac{1}{\sqrt{5}}\right)|1\rangle$$

b. Since the angle θ is greater than $\pi/2$ radians or 90°, this quantum state falls in the lower half of the Bloch sphere, as shown in the following figure:

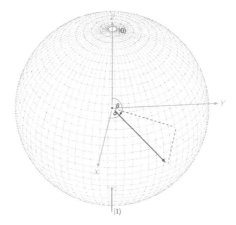

You could also have deduced that the quantum state falls in the bottom hemisphere since the qubit has more triangle $|1\rangle$ qubelets than pentagon $|0\rangle$ qubelets and would, thus, lie closer to the $|1\rangle$ state than the $|0\rangle$ state.

---

1. https://en.wikipedia.org/wiki/Angle#Positive_and_negative_angles

c. Calculate the probabilities by multiplying each amplitude by its complex conjugate, respectively. The probability of the right qubit collapsing to $|0\rangle$ is:

$$\text{Probability of collapsing to } |0\rangle = \left(\frac{1}{\sqrt{5}}\right)^2$$

$$= \frac{1}{5}$$

Similarly, the probability of this qubit collapsing to $|1\rangle$ is:

$$\text{Probability of collapsing to } |1\rangle = \left(\frac{\sqrt{3}}{\sqrt{5}} + i\frac{1}{\sqrt{5}}\right)\left(\frac{\sqrt{3}}{\sqrt{5}} - i\frac{1}{\sqrt{5}}\right)$$

$$= \left(\frac{3}{5} + \frac{1}{5}\right)$$

$$= \frac{4}{5}$$

d. The quantum circuit that puts a $|0\rangle$ into the state computed in the previous exercise is:

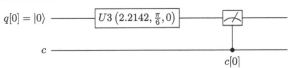

e. The quantum program, excluding the header, is listed here:

```
One_Pentagon_2_Triangles_30_Degrees.qasm
qreg q[1];
creg c[1];
u3(2.2142,pi/6,0) q[0];
measure q[0] -> c[0];
```

The U3 Universal gate is highlighted and declared with $\theta = 2.2142$ radians (corresponding to $126.87°$), $\varphi = \pi/6$, and $\lambda = 0$.

f. The output after running this program is shown in the following figure:

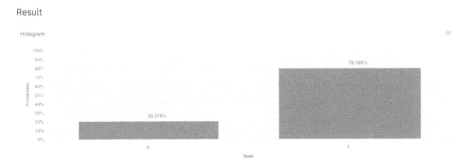

The probabilities of collapsing to 0 and 1 matches the earlier calculations.

Single Qubit Programs Solutions

Quantum Gates as Matrices Solutions

Solutions for the exercises in Try Your Hand, on page 183.

1. a. The amplitude $\omega_0 = 0.7071$. Thus, the probability of the qubit collapsing to 0 is $\omega_0^2 = 0.7071^2 = 0.4999$.

    The amplitude $\omega_1 = -0.2929$. So the probability of the qubit collapsing to 1 is $\omega_1^2 = (-0.2929)^2 = 0.0858$.

    The sum of these probabilities is $0.4999 + 0.0858 = 0.5857$. Since the sum is less than 1, the vector doesn't represent a valid quantum state.

    b. The amplitude $\omega_0 = -0.8062$. Thus, the probability of the qubit collapsing to 0 is $\omega_0^2 = (-0.8062)^2 = 0.6499$.

    The amplitude $\omega_1 = -0.5916$. So the probability of the qubit collapsing to 1 is $\omega_1^2 = (-0.5916)^2 = 0.3499$.

    The sum of these probabilities is $0.6499 + 0.3499 = 0.9998$. Since the sum is, for all intents and purposes, 1, the vector represents a valid quantum state.

2. a. The qubelets before and after the Z gate are shown here:

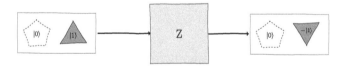

    The Z gate inverts only the triangle $|1\rangle$ qubelet.

    b. The left qubelet only has a triangle $|1\rangle$ qubelet. Thus, $\omega_1 = 1$. And the quantum state of the qubit before the Z gate acts on it is:

$$\begin{pmatrix} 0 \\ 1 \end{pmatrix}$$

    After the Z gate acts on the qubit, the triangle $|1\rangle$ qubelet is inverted. So $\omega_1 = -1$. And the quantum state after the Z gate acts on it is:

$$\begin{pmatrix} 0 \\ -1 \end{pmatrix}$$

3. a. The qubelets before and after the H gate acts on the qubit is shown in the following figure:

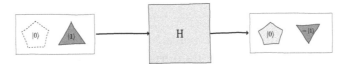

The H gate splits the triangle $|1\rangle$ qubelet into a pentagon $|0\rangle$ qubelet and an inverted triangle $|1\rangle$ qubelet.

b. The left qubelet only has a triangle $|1\rangle$ qubelet. Thus, $\omega_1 = 1$. And the quantum state of the qubit before the H gate acts on it is:

$$\begin{pmatrix} 0 \\ 1 \end{pmatrix}$$

After the H gate acts on the qubit, the triangle $|1\rangle$ qubelet is split into a pentagon $|0\rangle$ qubelet and an inverted triangle $|1\rangle$ qubelet. The amplitudes are:

$$\omega_0 = \frac{1}{\sqrt{1^2 + 1^2}} = \frac{1}{\sqrt{2}}$$

$$\omega_1 = -\frac{1}{\sqrt{1^2 + 1^2}} = -\frac{1}{\sqrt{2}}$$

Wrting the amplitudes in vector form, we get:

$$\begin{pmatrix} \dfrac{1}{\sqrt{2}} \\ -\dfrac{1}{\sqrt{2}} \end{pmatrix}$$

4. a. i. The operation is:

$$A_{NOT}\begin{pmatrix} 1 \\ 0 \end{pmatrix} = \begin{pmatrix} 0 \\ 1 \end{pmatrix}$$

ii. The first column of the A_{NOT} matrix is:

$$A_{NOT} = \begin{bmatrix} 0 & * \\ 1 & * \end{bmatrix}$$

b. i. The operation is:

$$A_{NOT}\begin{pmatrix} 0 \\ 1 \end{pmatrix} = \begin{pmatrix} 1 \\ 0 \end{pmatrix}$$

ii. The complete A_{NOT} matrix is:

$$A_{NOT} = \begin{bmatrix} 0 & 1 \\ 1 & 0 \end{bmatrix}$$

c. i. This qubit has two pentagon $|0\rangle$ qubelets and one inverted triangle $|1\rangle$ qubelet. Thus, its normalized quantum state is:

$$\frac{2}{\sqrt{2^2 + 1^2}}\,|0\rangle \;-\; \frac{1}{\sqrt{2^2 + 1^2}}\,|1\rangle \;=\; 0.8944\,|0\rangle \;-\; 0.4472\,|1\rangle$$

The negative sign for the amplitude associated with $|1\rangle$ indicates that the triangle qubelet is inverted.

The vector for this quantum state is:

$$\frac{1}{\sqrt{2^2 + 1^2}}\begin{pmatrix} 2 \\ -1 \end{pmatrix} \text{ or } \begin{pmatrix} 0.8944 \\ -0.4472 \end{pmatrix}$$

The probabilities of the qubit collapsing to 0 and 1 are:

$$\text{Probability of collapsing to } 0 \;=\; \left(\frac{2}{\sqrt{2^2 + 1^2}}\right)^2 \;=\; \frac{2^2}{2^2 + 1^2} \;=\; 0.8$$

$$\text{Probability of collapsing to } 1 \;=\; \left(-\frac{1}{\sqrt{2^2 + 1^2}}\right)^2 \;=\; \frac{1^2}{2^2 + 1^2} \;=\; 0.2$$

ii. When the NOT gate acts on the qubit with two pentagon $|0\rangle$ qubelets and an inverted triangle $|1\rangle$ qubelet, it switches the two pentagon $|0\rangle$ qubelets to two triangle $|1\rangle$ qubelets, and it switches the inverted triangle $|1\rangle$ qubelet to an inverted pentagon $|0\rangle$ qubelet, as shown in the following figure:

The normalized quantum state of the blended qubit on the right is:

$$-\frac{1}{\sqrt{1^2 + 2^2}}\,|0\rangle \;+\; \frac{2}{\sqrt{1^2 + 2^2}}\,|1\rangle$$

(Note the inverted pentagon $|0\rangle$ qubelet drawn on the right of the right qubit. This placement reflects that the NOT gate switched the inverted triangle $|1\rangle$ qubelet in the left qubit.)

Writing this quantum state in vector form, we get:

$$\frac{1}{\sqrt{5}}\begin{pmatrix} -1 \\ 2 \end{pmatrix}$$

The probabilities of the qubit collapsing to 0 and 1 are:

$$\text{Probability of collapsing to } 0 \;=\; \left(-\frac{1}{\sqrt{5}}\right)^2 \;=\; \frac{1^2}{5} \;=\; 0.2$$

$$\text{Probability of collapsing to } 1 \;=\; \left(\frac{2}{\sqrt{5}}\right)^2 \;=\; \frac{2^2}{5} \;=\; 0.8$$

The probabilities of the qubit collapsing to 0 and 1, respectively, get switched after the NOT gate acts on the qubit. In other words, when a NOT gate acts on a blended qubit, the probabilities of collapsing to the classical states 0 or 1 are switched.

iii. To calculate the quantum state of the qubit after the NOT gate acts on it, multiply the A_{NOT} matrix by the vector for the initial quantum state as follows:

$$A_{NOT}\frac{1}{\sqrt{5}}\begin{pmatrix} 2 \\ -1 \end{pmatrix} = \frac{1}{\sqrt{5}}\begin{bmatrix} 0 & 1 \\ 1 & 0 \end{bmatrix}\begin{pmatrix} 2 \\ -1 \end{pmatrix} = \frac{1}{\sqrt{5}}\begin{pmatrix} -1 \\ 2 \end{pmatrix}$$

This quantum state is identical to the one obtained by analyzing the NOT gate operation using qubelets.

5. a. i. The operation is:

$$A_Z\begin{pmatrix} 1 \\ 0 \end{pmatrix} = \begin{pmatrix} 1 \\ 0 \end{pmatrix}$$

   ii. The first column of the A_Z matrix is:

$$A_Z = \begin{bmatrix} 1 & * \\ 0 & * \end{bmatrix}$$

   b. i. The operation is:

$$A_Z\begin{pmatrix} 0 \\ 1 \end{pmatrix} = \begin{pmatrix} 0 \\ -1 \end{pmatrix}$$

   ii. The complete A_Z matrix is:

$$A_Z = \begin{bmatrix} 1 & 0 \\ 0 & -1 \end{bmatrix}$$

c.   i.   This qubit has one pentagon $|0\rangle$ qubelet and two inverted triangle $|1\rangle$ qubelets. Thus, it's normalized quantum state is:

$$\frac{1}{\sqrt{1^2 + 2^2}} |0\rangle - \frac{2}{\sqrt{1^2 + 2^2}} |1\rangle$$

The negative size for the amplitude associated with $|1\rangle$ indicates that the triangle qubelet is inverted.

The vector for this quantum state is:

$$\frac{1}{\sqrt{5}} \begin{pmatrix} 1 \\ -2 \end{pmatrix}$$

ii.   When the Z gate acts on the qubit with one pentagon $|0\rangle$ qubelet and two inverted triangle $|1\rangle$ qubelets, it'll leave the pentagon qubelet alone but will switch the triangle qubelets, as shown in the following figure:

The normalized quantum state of the blended qubit on the right is:

$$\frac{1}{\sqrt{5}} |0\rangle + \frac{2}{\sqrt{5}} |1\rangle$$

Writing this quantum state in vector form, we get:

$$\frac{1}{\sqrt{5}} \begin{pmatrix} 1 \\ 2 \end{pmatrix}$$

iii.   To calculate the quantum state of the qubit after the Z gate acts on it, multiply the A_Z matrix by the vector for the initial quantum state, as follows:

$$A_Z \frac{1}{\sqrt{5}} \begin{pmatrix} 1 \\ -2 \end{pmatrix} = \frac{1}{\sqrt{5}} \begin{bmatrix} 1 & 0 \\ 0 & -1 \end{bmatrix} \begin{pmatrix} 1 \\ -2 \end{pmatrix} = \frac{1}{\sqrt{5}} \begin{pmatrix} 1 \\ 2 \end{pmatrix}$$

This quantum state is identical to the one obtained by analyzing the Z gate operation using qubelets.

Gate Matrix Restrictions Solutions

Solutions for the exercises in Try Your Hand, on page 192.

1. a. To determine the Hermitian matrix, first get its transpose, A_G^T, by switching the matrix's rows and columns:

$$A_G^T = \begin{bmatrix} 1 & i \\ -1 & -i \end{bmatrix}$$

Next, replace each element with its complex conjugate:

$$A_G^\dagger = \begin{bmatrix} 1 & -i \\ -1 & i \end{bmatrix}$$

b. To check if this matrix represents a quantum gate, first calculate the product matrix, $A_G^\dagger A_G$:

$$A_G^\dagger A_G = \begin{bmatrix} 1 & -i \\ -1 & i \end{bmatrix} \begin{bmatrix} 1 & -1 \\ i & -i \end{bmatrix}$$

To multiply these matrices, we'll use the method described in Multiplying Matrices, on page 396. According to this method, we'll get the product matrix by working out each column of the product individually. The first column of the product matrix is:

$$\begin{bmatrix} 1 & -i \\ -1 & i \end{bmatrix} \begin{pmatrix} 1 \\ i \end{pmatrix} = 1 \cdot \begin{pmatrix} 1 \\ -1 \end{pmatrix} + i \cdot \begin{pmatrix} -i \\ i \end{pmatrix} = \begin{pmatrix} 1 - i^2 \\ -1 + i^2 \end{pmatrix} = \begin{pmatrix} 2 \\ -2 \end{pmatrix}$$

The second column of the product is:

$$\begin{bmatrix} 1 & -i \\ -1 & i \end{bmatrix} \begin{pmatrix} -1 \\ -i \end{pmatrix} = -1 \cdot \begin{pmatrix} 1 \\ -1 \end{pmatrix} + -i \cdot \begin{pmatrix} -i \\ i \end{pmatrix} = \begin{pmatrix} -1 + i^2 \\ 1 - i^2 \end{pmatrix} = \begin{pmatrix} -2 \\ 2 \end{pmatrix}$$

Arrange these columns to get the product:

$$A_G^\dagger A_G = \begin{bmatrix} 2 & -2 \\ -2 & 2 \end{bmatrix}$$

Since the product $A_G^\dagger A_G$ isn't the identity matrix, A_G isn't a valid quantum gate matrix.

2. a. To determine the Hermitian matrix, first get its transpose, $A_{S^\dagger}^T$, by switching the matrix's rows and columns:

$$A_{S^\dagger}^T = \begin{bmatrix} 1 & 0 \\ 0 & -i \end{bmatrix}$$

Next, replace each element with its complex conjugate:

$$A^\dagger_{S^\dagger} = \begin{bmatrix} 1 & 0 \\ 0 & i \end{bmatrix}$$

This matrix for the $S^\dagger$ gate is identical to the A_S matrix for the S gate.

b. To see if this matrix represents a quantum gate, first calculate the product matrix, $A^*_{S^\dagger} A_{S^\dagger}$:

$$A^*_{S^\dagger} A_{S^\dagger} = \begin{bmatrix} 1 & 0 \\ 0 & i \end{bmatrix} \begin{bmatrix} 1 & 0 \\ 0 & -i \end{bmatrix}$$

To multiply these matrices, we'll use the method described in Multiplying Matrices, on page 396. According to this method, we'll get the product matrix by working out each column of the product individually. The first column of the product matrix is:

$$\begin{bmatrix} 1 & 0 \\ 0 & i \end{bmatrix}\begin{pmatrix} 1 \\ 0 \end{pmatrix} = 1 \cdot \begin{pmatrix} 1 \\ 0 \end{pmatrix} + 0 \cdot \begin{pmatrix} 0 \\ i \end{pmatrix} = \begin{pmatrix} 1 \\ 0 \end{pmatrix}$$

The second column of the product matrix is:

$$\begin{bmatrix} 1 & 0 \\ 0 & i \end{bmatrix}\begin{pmatrix} 0 \\ -i \end{pmatrix} = 0 \cdot \begin{pmatrix} 1 \\ 0 \end{pmatrix} - i \cdot \begin{pmatrix} 0 \\ i \end{pmatrix} = \begin{pmatrix} 0 \\ -i^2 \end{pmatrix} = \begin{pmatrix} 0 \\ 1 \end{pmatrix}$$

Arrange these columns to get the product:

$$A^*_{S^\dagger} A_{S^\dagger} = \begin{bmatrix} 1 & 0 \\ 0 & 1 \end{bmatrix}$$

Since the product is the identity matrix, it represents a quantum gate. In fact, the $S^\dagger$ gate is one of the predefined gates in the IBM Quantum Computer.

3. a. To determine the Hermitian matrix, first get its transpose, A^T_H, by switching the matrix's rows and columns:

$$A^T_H = \begin{bmatrix} \dfrac{1}{\sqrt{2}} & \dfrac{1}{\sqrt{2}} \\ \dfrac{1}{\sqrt{2}} & -\dfrac{1}{\sqrt{2}} \end{bmatrix}$$

Since each element of the matrix is real, this matrix is the conjugate transpose. In other words,

$$A_H^\dagger = A_H$$

b. To see if this matrix represents a quantum gate, first calculate the product matrix $A_H^\dagger A_H$:

$$A_H^\dagger A_H = \begin{bmatrix} \dfrac{1}{\sqrt{2}} & \dfrac{1}{\sqrt{2}} \\ \dfrac{1}{\sqrt{2}} & -\dfrac{1}{\sqrt{2}} \end{bmatrix} \begin{bmatrix} \dfrac{1}{\sqrt{2}} & \dfrac{1}{\sqrt{2}} \\ \dfrac{1}{\sqrt{2}} & -\dfrac{1}{\sqrt{2}} \end{bmatrix}$$

To multiply these matrices, we'll use the method described in Multiplying Matrices, on page 396. According to this method, we'll get the product matrix by working out each column of the product individually. The first column of the product matrix is:

$$\begin{bmatrix} \dfrac{1}{\sqrt{2}} & \dfrac{1}{\sqrt{2}} \\ \dfrac{1}{\sqrt{2}} & -\dfrac{1}{\sqrt{2}} \end{bmatrix} \begin{pmatrix} \dfrac{1}{\sqrt{2}} \\ \dfrac{1}{\sqrt{2}} \end{pmatrix} = \dfrac{1}{\sqrt{2}} \cdot \begin{pmatrix} \dfrac{1}{\sqrt{2}} \\ \dfrac{1}{\sqrt{2}} \end{pmatrix} + \dfrac{1}{\sqrt{2}} \cdot \begin{pmatrix} \dfrac{1}{\sqrt{2}} \\ -\dfrac{1}{\sqrt{2}} \end{pmatrix} = \begin{pmatrix} \dfrac{1}{2} + \dfrac{1}{2} \\ \dfrac{1}{2} - \dfrac{1}{2} \end{pmatrix} = \begin{pmatrix} 1 \\ 0 \end{pmatrix}$$

The second column of the product matrix is:

$$\begin{bmatrix} \dfrac{1}{\sqrt{2}} & \dfrac{1}{\sqrt{2}} \\ \dfrac{1}{\sqrt{2}} & -\dfrac{1}{\sqrt{2}} \end{bmatrix} \begin{pmatrix} \dfrac{1}{\sqrt{2}} \\ -\dfrac{1}{\sqrt{2}} \end{pmatrix} = \dfrac{1}{\sqrt{2}} \cdot \begin{pmatrix} \dfrac{1}{\sqrt{2}} \\ \dfrac{1}{\sqrt{2}} \end{pmatrix} - \dfrac{1}{\sqrt{2}} \cdot \begin{pmatrix} \dfrac{1}{\sqrt{2}} \\ -\dfrac{1}{\sqrt{2}} \end{pmatrix} = \begin{pmatrix} \dfrac{1}{2} - \dfrac{1}{2} \\ \dfrac{1}{2} + \dfrac{1}{2} \end{pmatrix} = \begin{pmatrix} 0 \\ 1 \end{pmatrix}$$

Arrange these columns to get the product:

$$A_H^\dagger A_H = \begin{bmatrix} 1 & 0 \\ 0 & 1 \end{bmatrix}$$

Since this product is the identity matrix, the A_H matrix represents the H gate.

4. a. To get the A_U matrix for $U3(\pi/3, \pi/2, -\pi/2)$, set $\theta = \pi/3$, $\varphi = \pi/2$, and $\lambda = -\pi/2$:

$$A_U = \begin{bmatrix} \cos\dfrac{\theta}{2} & -e^{i\lambda}\sin\dfrac{\theta}{2} \\ e^{i\varphi}\sin\dfrac{\theta}{2} & e^{i(\lambda+\varphi)}\cos\dfrac{\theta}{2} \end{bmatrix} = \begin{bmatrix} \cos\dfrac{\pi}{3}{2} & -e^{-i\frac{\pi}{2}}\sin\dfrac{\pi}{3}{2} \\ e^{i\frac{\pi}{2}}\sin\dfrac{\pi}{3}{2} & e^{i(\frac{\pi}{2}-\frac{\pi}{2})}\cos\dfrac{\pi}{3}{2} \end{bmatrix}$$

Noting that $\sin\pi/6 = 1/2$, $\cos\pi/6 = \sqrt{3}/2$, the above matrix simplifies to:

$$A_U = \begin{bmatrix} \dfrac{\sqrt{3}}{2} & -e^{-i\frac{\pi}{2}}\dfrac{1}{2} \\ e^{i\frac{\pi}{2}}\dfrac{1}{2} & e^{i(-\frac{\pi}{2}+\frac{\pi}{2})}\dfrac{\sqrt{3}}{2} \end{bmatrix}$$

Using Euler's formula:

$$e^{-i\frac{\pi}{2}} = \cos\frac{\pi}{2} - i\sin\frac{\pi}{2}$$
$$= -i$$

And,

$$e^{i\frac{\pi}{2}} = \cos\frac{\pi}{2} + i\sin\frac{\pi}{2}$$
$$= i$$

Substituting these terms back in the matrix A_U:

$$A_U = \begin{bmatrix} \dfrac{\sqrt{3}}{2} & \dfrac{i}{2} \\ \dfrac{i}{2} & \dfrac{\sqrt{3}}{2} \end{bmatrix}$$

b. To determine the Hermitian matrix, first get its transpose:

$$A_U^T = \begin{bmatrix} \dfrac{\sqrt{3}}{2} & \dfrac{i}{2} \\ \dfrac{i}{2} & \dfrac{\sqrt{3}}{2} \end{bmatrix}$$

Next, replace each element of the matrix with its conjugate:

$$A_U^\dagger = \begin{bmatrix} \dfrac{\sqrt{3}}{2} & -\dfrac{i}{2} \\ -\dfrac{i}{2} & \dfrac{\sqrt{3}}{2} \end{bmatrix}$$

c. To check if the A_U matrix is unitary, first calculate the product matrix $A_U^\dagger A_U$:

$$A_U^\dagger A_U = \begin{bmatrix} \dfrac{\sqrt{3}}{2} & -\dfrac{i}{2} \\ -\dfrac{i}{2} & \dfrac{\sqrt{3}}{2} \end{bmatrix}\begin{bmatrix} \dfrac{\sqrt{3}}{2} & \dfrac{i}{2} \\ \dfrac{i}{2} & \dfrac{\sqrt{3}}{2} \end{bmatrix}$$

To multiply these matrices, we'll use the method described in Multiplying Matrices, on page 396. According to this method, we'll get the product matrix by working out each column of the product individually. The first column of the product matrix is:

$$\begin{bmatrix} \dfrac{\sqrt{3}}{2} & -\dfrac{i}{2} \\ -\dfrac{i}{2} & \dfrac{\sqrt{3}}{2} \end{bmatrix}\begin{pmatrix} \dfrac{\sqrt{3}}{2} \\ \dfrac{i}{2} \end{pmatrix} = \dfrac{\sqrt{3}}{2}\cdot\begin{pmatrix} \dfrac{\sqrt{3}}{2} \\ -\dfrac{i}{2} \end{pmatrix} + \dfrac{i}{2}\cdot\begin{pmatrix} \dfrac{i}{2} \\ \dfrac{\sqrt{3}}{2} \end{pmatrix} = \begin{pmatrix} \dfrac{3}{4} - \dfrac{i^2}{4} \\ -\dfrac{\sqrt{3}\,i}{2\,2} + \dfrac{i\sqrt{3}}{2\,2} \end{pmatrix} = \begin{pmatrix} 1 \\ 0 \end{pmatrix}$$

The second column of the product matrix is:

$$\begin{bmatrix} \dfrac{\sqrt{3}}{2} & -\dfrac{i}{2} \\ -\dfrac{i}{2} & \dfrac{\sqrt{3}}{2} \end{bmatrix}\begin{pmatrix} \dfrac{i}{2} \\ \dfrac{\sqrt{3}}{2} \end{pmatrix} = \dfrac{i}{2}\cdot\begin{pmatrix} \dfrac{\sqrt{3}}{2} \\ -\dfrac{i}{2} \end{pmatrix} + \dfrac{\sqrt{3}}{2}\cdot\begin{pmatrix} -\dfrac{i}{2} \\ \dfrac{\sqrt{3}}{2} \end{pmatrix} = \begin{pmatrix} \dfrac{i\sqrt{3}}{2\,2} - \dfrac{\sqrt{3}\,i}{2\,2} \\ -\dfrac{i^2}{2} + \dfrac{3}{4} \end{pmatrix} = \begin{pmatrix} 0 \\ 1 \end{pmatrix}$$

Arrange these columns to get the product:

$$A_U^\dagger A_U = \begin{bmatrix} 1 & 0 \\ 0 & 1 \end{bmatrix}$$

Since the product is the identity matrix, matrix A_U is unitary.

d. To determine the parameters for the Universal gate, $U3(\theta, \varphi, \lambda)$, associated with $A_U^\dagger$, equate the $U3(\theta, \varphi, \lambda)$ matrix with that of $A_U^\dagger$:

$$\begin{bmatrix} \cos\dfrac{\theta}{2} & -e^{i\lambda}\sin\dfrac{\theta}{2} \\ e^{i\varphi}\sin\dfrac{\theta}{2} & e^{i(\lambda+\varphi)}\cos\dfrac{\theta}{2} \end{bmatrix} = \begin{bmatrix} \dfrac{\sqrt{3}}{2} & -\dfrac{i}{2} \\ -\dfrac{i}{2} & \dfrac{\sqrt{3}}{2} \end{bmatrix}$$

The idea in these types of matrix equations is to compare the respective elements in the matrix on the left to the one on the right. Start with the element on the right that has the fewest parameters. Thus, looking at the top left element from both matrices:

$$\cos\frac{\theta}{2} = \frac{\sqrt{3}}{2}$$

$$\frac{\theta}{2} = \cos^{-1}\frac{\sqrt{3}}{2}$$

$$= \frac{\pi}{6}$$

$$\theta = \frac{\pi}{3}$$

Next, equate the bottom left (second row, first column) elements in both matrices:

$$e^{i\varphi}\sin\frac{\theta}{2} = -\frac{i}{2}$$

$$e^{i\varphi}\sin\frac{\pi}{6} = -\frac{i}{2}$$

$$e^{i\varphi}\frac{1}{2} = -\frac{i}{2}$$

$$e^{i\varphi} = -i$$

$$\cos\varphi + i\sin\varphi = -i$$

Since the imaginary part on the right is –1, the imaginary part on the left, $\sin\varphi$, must also be –1. The smallest such angle is 270° or:

$$\varphi = \frac{3\pi}{2}$$

This value also makes the real part, $\cos\varphi = 0$.

Finally, to compute λ, compare the top right (first row, second column) terms from both matrices:

$$-e^{i\lambda}\sin\frac{\theta}{2} = -\frac{i}{2}$$

$$-e^{i\lambda}\sin\frac{\pi}{6} = -\frac{i}{2}$$

$$-e^{i\lambda}\frac{1}{2} = -\frac{i}{2}$$

$$e^{i\lambda} = i$$

$$\cos\lambda + i\sin\lambda = i$$

Since the real part on the right is 0, the real part on the left, $\cos\lambda$, is also 0:

$$\cos\lambda = 0$$

$$\lambda = \cos^{-1}0$$

$$\lambda = \frac{\pi}{2}$$

A quick check confirms that this value of λ makes the imaginary part on the right, $\sin\lambda = \sin\pi/2$, equal to 1 as required.

Note that we only needed three of the four element comparisons to get the three parameters for the $U3(\theta, \varphi, \lambda)$ gate. You can verify, though, that these three values correctly equate to the fourth element on the bottom right of the right matrix stated earlier.

The Universal gate that implements the $A_U^\dagger$ matrix is $U3^\dagger(\pi/3, 3\pi/2, \pi/2)$.

e. i. To compute the quantum state when the $U3(\pi/3, 3\pi/2, \pi/2)$ gate acts on the $|0\rangle$ qubit, calculate the following:

$$A_U\begin{pmatrix}1\\0\end{pmatrix} = \begin{bmatrix}\frac{\sqrt{3}}{2} & \frac{i}{2}\\ \frac{i}{2} & \frac{\sqrt{3}}{2}\end{bmatrix}\begin{pmatrix}1\\0\end{pmatrix}$$

$$= \begin{pmatrix}\frac{\sqrt{3}}{2}\\ \frac{i}{2}\end{pmatrix}$$

Or, writing the quantum state as an equation:

$$\frac{\sqrt{3}}{2}|0\rangle - \frac{i}{2}|1\rangle$$

ii. To compute the probabilities of the qubit collapsing to the idealized states, take the squares of the amplitudes but use the conjugate complexes, as explained in Measuring Magnitudes of Complex Numbers, on page 167:

$$\text{Probability of collapsing to } |0\rangle = \frac{\sqrt{3}}{2}\frac{\sqrt{3}}{2}$$

$$= \frac{3}{4}$$

And,

$$\text{Probability of collapsing to } |1\rangle = \frac{i}{2}\frac{-i}{2}$$

$$= \frac{-i^2}{4} = \frac{1}{4}$$

iii. The quantum program is listed here:

```
0_U3_60_90_270_Measure.qasm
qreg q[1];
creg c[1];

u3(pi/3,pi/2,-pi/2) q[0];
measure q[0] -> c[0];
```

iv. The output of this program is shown in the following figure:

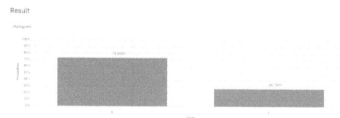

Yes, the likelihoods of finding 0 or 1 in the classical registers is roughly 75% or 25%, respectively. These match the probabilities of the q[0] qubit collapsing to $|0\rangle$ or $|1\rangle$, respectively, as calculated earlier.

f. i. The quantum program for the circuit with back-to-back Universal gates is listed here:

```
Back_to_Back_U3_Gates.qasm
Line 1  qreg q[1];
2  creg c[1];
3
4  u3(pi/3,pi/2,-pi/2) q[0];
5  u3(pi/3,3*pi/2,pi/2) q[0];
6  measure q[0] -> c[0];
```

The $U3(\pi/3, 3\pi/2, \pi/2)$ gate is declared on line 5.

ii. The output of this program is shown in the following figure:

The $U3(\pi/3, 3\pi/2, \pi/2)$ gate restores the quantum state of the q[0] back to $|0\rangle$. In other words, since this gate is the Hermitian matrix of the $U3(\pi/3, \pi/2, -\pi/2)$ gate, it *reverses* the action on the qubit and puts it back to the original state before these gates acted on it. Thus, the concept of back-to-back gates defined by matrices that are Hermitians of each other is similar to what you saw earlier in Back-to-Back H Gates: The First Hint of Taming Randomness, on page 88.

g. i. The quantum program for this circuit is as follows:

```
0_U3_U3_Measure.qasm
qreg q[1];
creg c[1];
u3(pi/3,pi/2,-pi/2) q[0];
u3(pi/3,pi/4,-pi/2) q[0];
measure q[0] -> c[0];
```

ii. The output of this program is shown here:

In this case, the q[0] qubit isn't restored to its original $|0\rangle$ state as in the previous part. Both U3 gates have the same $\theta = \pi/2$, which determines the numbers of pentagon $|0\rangle$ and triangle $|1\rangle$ qubelets in the quantum state, and the same $\lambda = \pi/2$. But they have different values for the second parameter, φ, which measures the relative difference between the orientations of the pentagon $|0\rangle$ and triangle $|1\rangle$ qubelets. Because the second U3 gate's φ angle doesn't exactly "twist back" the effect of the first gate on the qubelets, the quantum state isn't restored. Hence, the qubit doesn't go back to $|0\rangle$ after the second U3 gate and remains in a blended state. When this blended qubit is measured, it collapses to either $|0\rangle$ or $|1\rangle$. As a result, the classical register records both the 0 and 1 states.

5. Let ψ_{Before} be the quantum state of the qubit before it's acted on by the $S^\dagger$ gate. Then, the following matrix equation defines how the $S^\dagger$ gates modifies this quantum state:

$$A_{S^\dagger}\psi_{Before} = \begin{pmatrix} \dfrac{1}{\sqrt{2}} \\ -\dfrac{1}{\sqrt{2}}i \end{pmatrix}$$

To get ψ_{Before}, pre-multiply both sides by the $A_{S^\dagger}$ matrix's Hermitian, $A_{S^\dagger}^\dagger$:

$$\left(A_{S^\dagger}^\dagger A_{S^\dagger}\right)\psi_{Before} = A_{S^\dagger}^\dagger \begin{pmatrix} \dfrac{1}{\sqrt{2}} \\ -\dfrac{1}{\sqrt{2}}i \end{pmatrix}$$

Note that $A_{S^\dagger}^\dagger = A_S$. Thus, $A_{S^\dagger}^\dagger A_{S^\dagger} = I$, the identity matrix. As a result, the left-hand side simplifies to ψ_{Before}. After substituting A_S for $A_{S^\dagger}^\dagger$ on the right-hand side, the above equation reduces to:

$$\psi_{Before} = \begin{bmatrix} 1 & 0 \\ 0 & i \end{bmatrix} \begin{pmatrix} \dfrac{1}{\sqrt{2}} \\ -\dfrac{1}{\sqrt{2}}i \end{pmatrix} = \begin{pmatrix} \dfrac{1}{\sqrt{2}} \\ -i^2\dfrac{1}{\sqrt{2}} \end{pmatrix} = \begin{pmatrix} \dfrac{1}{\sqrt{2}} \\ \dfrac{1}{\sqrt{2}} \end{pmatrix}$$

Thus, the original quantum state before the $S^\dagger$ gate operates on it is:

$$\psi_{Before} = \begin{pmatrix} \dfrac{1}{\sqrt{2}} \\ \dfrac{1}{\sqrt{2}} \end{pmatrix}$$

Analyzing Quantum Gate Matrices Solutions

Solutions for the exercises in Try Your Hand, on page 200.

1. a. The equation for the given quantum state, ψ, is:

$$\psi = \frac{1}{\sqrt{2}} |0\rangle + i\frac{1}{\sqrt{2}} |1\rangle$$

Compare this equation with that of the general quantum state:

$$\cos\frac{\theta}{2} |0\rangle + e^{i\varphi}\sin\frac{\theta}{2} |1\rangle$$

The $e^{i\varphi}$ term injects the complex number into the equation for the state. To determine the value of φ, relate the corresponding terms in the general equation with that of the given quantum state ψ:

$$e^{i\varphi} = \cos\varphi + i\sin\varphi = i$$

The real term, $\cos\varphi$, must be 0 since the right-hand side is a pure complex number:

$$\varphi = \cos^{-1}0$$
$$= \frac{\pi}{2}$$

Further, $i\sin\varphi = i\sin\pi/2 = i$ confirms that the calculations for φ are right. Thus, the angle φ, the relative difference between the orientations of the pentagon $|0\rangle$ and triangle $|1\rangle$ qubelets, is 90°.

To calculate θ, the angle which the quantum state vector leans away from the vertical on the Bloch sphere, compare the amplitudes for $|0\rangle$ and $|1\rangle$ in the general equation for the quantum state with that for ψ:

$$\text{Amplitude for } |0\rangle = \cos\frac{\theta}{2} = \frac{1}{\sqrt{2}}$$
$$\text{Amplitude for } |1\rangle = e^{i\varphi}\sin\frac{\theta}{2} = i\frac{1}{\sqrt{2}}$$

Calculate θ from the amplitude for $|0\rangle$ as follows:

$$\frac{\theta}{2} = \cos^{-1}\frac{1}{\sqrt{2}}$$
$$= \frac{\pi}{4}$$
$$\theta = 2 \times \frac{\pi}{4}$$
$$= \frac{\pi}{2}$$

Setting $\theta = \pi/2$ in the amplitude for $|1\rangle$, $i\sin\theta/2$, gives $i/\sqrt{2}$, validating that our calculations are correct.

Thus, the parameters for the $U3(\theta, \varphi, \lambda)$ gate are:

$$\theta = \frac{\pi}{2}$$
$$\varphi = \frac{\pi}{2}$$
$$\lambda = 0$$

Since we are working on $|0\rangle$, we only need to look at the first column of the gate matrix for U3 which doesn't rely on λ. So, any value of λ can be used as it'll not affect the behavior of the gate on $|0\rangle$.

Recall from Number of Qubelets Define the Amplitudes, on page 145, the number of pentagon $|0\rangle$ and triangle $|1\rangle$ qubelets in the qubit are related as follows:

$$\text{Number of pentagon } |0\rangle \text{ qubelets : Number of triangle } |1\rangle \text{ qubelets} = \cos\frac{\theta}{2} : \sin\frac{\theta}{2}$$
$$= \frac{1}{\sqrt{2}} : \frac{1}{\sqrt{2}}$$
$$= 1 : 1$$

These parameters for the $U3(\theta, \varphi, \lambda)$ gate puts the $|0\rangle$ qubit in the quantum state ψ having an equal number of pentagon $|0\rangle$ and triangle $|1\rangle$ qubelets, with the triangle $|1\rangle$ qubelets rotated 90° anticlockwise, as shown in the following figure:

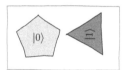

This quantum state is identical to the one worked out in the previous section using the qubelets approach.

The probabilities of the qubit collapsing to $|0\rangle$ or $|1\rangle$, respectively, is the "square" of the amplitudes:

$$\text{Probability of qubit collapsing to } |0\rangle = \left(\frac{1}{\sqrt{2}}\right)^2 = \frac{1}{2}$$
$$\text{Probability of qubit collapsing to } |1\rangle = \frac{i}{\sqrt{2}} \frac{-i}{\sqrt{2}}$$
$$= -i^2 \frac{1}{2}$$
$$= \frac{1}{2}$$

Notice that to compute the probability of collapsing to $|1\rangle$, the amplitude is a complex number, so we multiply by its complex conjugate.

b. The quantum circuit is shown here:

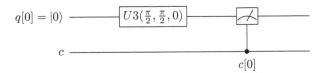

The quantum program is the following:

U3_90_90_0_Measure.qasm

```
qreg q[1];
creg c[1];

u3(pi/2,pi/2,0) q[0];
measure q[0] -> c[0];
```

The output of this program is shown in the following figure:

The classical registers won't log the angles of the pentagon $|0\rangle$ and triangle $|1\rangle$ qubelets. But the classical states recorded match the probabilities of the qubit collapsing to $|0\rangle$ or $|1\rangle$, respectively, calculated in the previous part.

c. The quantum program is as follows:

U3_90_90_0_S_Measure.qasm

```
qreg q[1];
creg c[1];

u3(pi/2,pi/2,0) q[0];
s q[0];
measure q[0] -> c[0];
```

The output of this program is shown on page 478.

Since the S gate only rotates the pentagon $|1\rangle$ qubelets but doesn't split any qubelets, the relative number of pentagon $|0\rangle$ and $|1\rangle$ qubelets remains the same. Consequently, the probabilities of the qubit collapsing to $|0\rangle$ or $|1\rangle$ don't change and, hence, the classical states recorded

Result

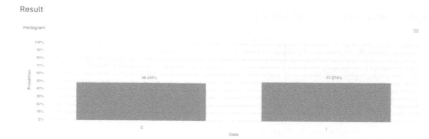

in the classical registers will also be similar to what was recorded in the previous part.

d. No, you can't confirm whether the pentagon $|1\rangle$ qubelets are rotated since the gates didn't change the relative number of pentagon $|0\rangle$ and triangle $|1\rangle$ qubelets. (In later sections you'll learn to write programs that validate the qubelet rotations.)

2. The vector for the general quantum state ψ is:

$$\psi = \begin{pmatrix} \cos\dfrac{\theta}{2} \\ e^{i\varphi}\sin\dfrac{\theta}{2} \end{pmatrix}$$

The φ parameter, which measures the relative difference in orientations between the pentagon $|0\rangle$ and the triangle $|1\rangle$ qubelets, is associated with the triangle $|1\rangle$ qubelets. Thus, turning both qubelets by the same angle doesn't change the quantum state. Redraw the qubit on the right so that the pentagon $|0\rangle$ qubelet is rotated back to the non-rotated state by turning both qubelets 90° clockwise, as shown in the following figure:

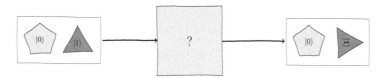

The required gate leaves the pentagon $|0\rangle$ qubelet alone. Thus, the top left element of the gate's matrix must be 1:

$$\begin{bmatrix} 1 & * \\ * & * \end{bmatrix}$$

The * indicates that those corresponding terms aren't yet known.

This gate doesn't take a qubelet of one type and change it to the other type by splitting or switching the qubelet. As a result, the non-diagonal terms in the gate's matrix are 0:

$$\begin{bmatrix} 1 & 0 \\ 0 & * \end{bmatrix}$$

(If the gate were to split qubelets, for example, then the non-diagonal terms would be nonzero.)

The triangle $|1\rangle$ qubelet is rotated 90° clockwise. This rotation is governed by the following equation:

$$e^{i\varphi} = \cos \varphi + i \sin \varphi$$

Substitute $-\pi/2$ for φ (the sign is negative because the rotation is clockwise):

$$e^{-i\frac{pi}{2}} = \cos\frac{\pi}{2} - i \sin \frac{\pi}{2}$$
$$= -i$$

Thus, the gate matrix is:

$$\begin{bmatrix} 1 & 0 \\ 0 & -i \times \text{something} \end{bmatrix}$$

Since this matrix must be Hermitian for a quantum gate, you can confirm that *something* is 1. Hence, this matrix matches that of the $S^\dagger$ gate.

Although this problem is ostensibly about rotating a pentagon $|0\rangle$ qubelet, it's actually equivalent to rotating the triangle $|1\rangle$ qubelet.

Solutions: Quantum Gates and How to Use Them

Solutions for the exercises in Try Your Hand, on page 216.

1. a. False. The Y gate switches and rotates qubelets. That is, when it acts on, say, a triangle $|1\rangle$ qubelet, it'll switch it to a pentagon $|0\rangle$ qubelet and rotate it. But it won't split qubelets. Hence, it doesn't take an idealized quantum state and put it in a blended state.

    b. False. Both the $S^\dagger$ and T gates leave the $|0\rangle$ qubelets alone but rotate the triangle $|1\rangle$ qubelets. So they'll have no effect on the $|0\rangle$ qubit but will rotate the triangle $|1\rangle$ qubelets in the $|1\rangle$ qubit.

c. True. The S gate rotates the triangle $|1\rangle$ qubelets 90°, or a quarter turn *anticlockwise*. The $T^\dagger$ gate rotates the triangle $|1\rangle$ qubelets 45°, or a one-eighth turn *clockwise*. Both leave the pentagon $|0\rangle$ qubelets alone. Thus, two $T^\dagger$ gates rotate the triangle $|1\rangle$ qubelets by 90°, or a quarter turn clockwise, reversing the action of the S gate.

d. True. The S gate rotates the triangle $|1\rangle$ qubelets 90°, or a quarter turn anticlockwise. The T gate rotates the triangle $|1\rangle$ qubelets by 45°, or a one-eighth turn anticlockwise. Thus, when both gates operate on the triangle $|1\rangle$ qubelets, the total rotation is 90 + 45 = 135° anticlockwise.

e. True. The $R_x(\theta)$ gate splits qubelets like the H gate, although asymmetrically. Nonetheless, it puts an idealized qubit, $|0\rangle$ or $|1\rangle$, into a blended state.

2. a. The quantum state after the Y gate acts on the $|0\rangle$ qubit is shown in the following figure:

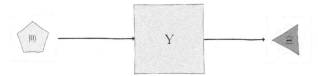

b. If the NOT (X) gate were to act on the $|0\rangle$ qubit, the pentagon $|0\rangle$ qubit would be switched to a triangle $|1\rangle$ qubit but wouldn't be rotated, as shown in the next figure:

c. Regardless of how the triangle $|1\rangle$ qubelet is rotated, it'll always collapse to the idealized $|1\rangle$ qubit, which logs a 1 in the classical register. Thus, in both cases, the outputs will be identical.

3. As each gate acts on the $|0\rangle$ qubit, it affects the qubelets as follows:

First X Gate

Switches the $|0\rangle$ qubit to $|1\rangle$. The qubit will contain only a triangle $|1\rangle$ qubelet.

T Gate

Rotates the triangle |1⟩ qubelet by 45°, or a one-eighth turn anticlockwise.

Second X Gate

Switches the |1⟩ qubit to |0⟩. The 45°-rotated triangle |1⟩ qubelet is switched to a 45°-rotated pentagon |0⟩ qubelet.

The action of these three gates is summarized in the following figure:

Thus, this circuit rotates the pentagon |0⟩ qubelet.

4. a. The program for this circuit is as follows:

```
0_H_SDag_H_Measure.qasm
qreg q[1];
creg c[1];

h q[0];
sdg q[0];
h q[0];
measure q[0] -> c[0];
```

b. The output of this program is shown in the following figure:

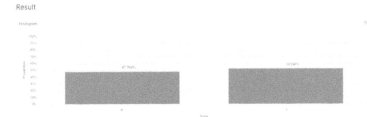

The output shows a 0 or 1 logged in the classical register with about the same probabilities. This distribution indicates that the q[0] qubit collapses about equally to the idealized qubits, |0⟩ or |1⟩. This suggests that the q[0] qubit was in a blended state before it was collapsed by the Measure gate. Had the second H gate reversed the effect of the first H gate, the q[0] qubit would be put back to |0⟩.

The reason why the second H gate, despite being its own adjoint, doesn't reverse the effect of the first H gate on the qubit is that the $S^\dagger$ gate spins the triangle |1⟩ qubelets by –90°, or a quarter turn clockwise. As a direct result of this extra rotation, the triangle |1⟩ qubelets are no longer aligned with the pentagon $|0\rangle$ qubelets, as shown in the following figure:

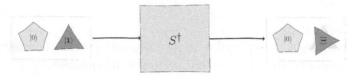

When the right qubit gets split by the second H gate, the triangle $|1\rangle$ qubelets can't cancel out, thereby leaving the qubit in a blended state, as shown in the next figure:

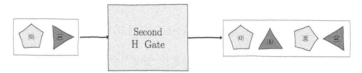

This is the first time you're seeing a quantum state where the qubelets of the same type have different angles. In the next section, you'll learn how to deal with such quantum states. For now, it's enough to recognize that the triangle $|1\rangle$ qubelets can't cancel out to give an idealized state. Thus, the qubit remains in a blended state.

c. The quantum program for this circuit is listed as follows:

```
0_H_SDag_S_H_Measure.qasm
qreg q[1];
creg c[1];

h q[0];
sdg q[0];
s q[0];
h q[0];
measure q[0] -> c[0];
```

This program is the same as that in the previous part other than declaring the S gate as highlighted.

You should get an output for this program that is similar to the one shown on page 483.

This time, the classical register only logs 0, indicating that the second H gate successfully put the q[0] qubit in its original idealized state, $|0\rangle$. The reason for this is that the S gate spun the triangle $|1\rangle$ qubelets back by 90°, or a quarter turn anticlockwise, and aligned them. As a result, the second H gate could cancel out the triangle $|1\rangle$ qubelets from the quantum state.

Result

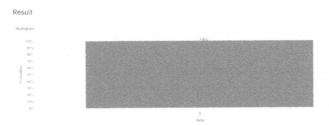

5. a. The code listing for this circuit is as follows:

Rx_60_Gate.qasm
```
qreg q[1];
creg c[1];

rx(pi/3) q[0];
measure q[0] -> c[0];
```

b. The vector for the $|0\rangle$ qubit in q[0] is:

$$|0\rangle \equiv \begin{pmatrix} 1 \\ 0 \end{pmatrix}$$

Thus, the quantum state $|\psi\rangle$ after the $R_x(\pi/3)$ acts on the $|0\rangle$ qubit is:

$$|\psi\rangle = A_{R_x}\left(\frac{\pi}{3}\right)\begin{pmatrix} 1 \\ 0 \end{pmatrix}$$

$$= \begin{bmatrix} \cos\dfrac{\frac{\pi}{3}}{2} & -i\sin\dfrac{\frac{\pi}{3}}{2} \\ -i\sin\dfrac{\frac{\pi}{3}}{2} & \cos\dfrac{\frac{\pi}{3}}{2} \end{bmatrix}\begin{pmatrix} 1 \\ 0 \end{pmatrix}$$

$$= \begin{pmatrix} \cos\dfrac{\pi}{6} \\ -i\sin\dfrac{\pi}{6} \end{pmatrix} = \begin{pmatrix} \dfrac{\sqrt{3}}{2} \\ -i\dfrac{1}{2} \end{pmatrix}$$

c. The vector for $|\psi\rangle$ is:

$$|\psi\rangle \equiv \begin{pmatrix} \dfrac{\sqrt{3}}{2} \\ -i\dfrac{1}{2} \end{pmatrix}$$

Thus, the ratio of pentagon $|0\rangle$ to triangle $|1\rangle$ qubelets is $\sqrt{3} : 1$.

d. To get the angles of rotation of the qubelets, compare the vector for $|\psi\rangle$ with that for the general quantum state. Thus, the pentagon $|0\rangle$ qubelets aren't rotated, but the triangle $|1\rangle$ qubelets are rotated by $-90°$, or a quarter turn clockwise.

e. Probability of $|\psi\rangle$ collapsing to the idealized states is the squares of their respective amplitudes. Thus, the probability of $|\psi\rangle$ collapsing to $|0\rangle$ is:

$$\text{Probability of collapsing to } |0\rangle = \left(\frac{\sqrt{3}}{2}\right)^2 = \frac{3}{4}$$

Similarly, the probability of $|\psi\rangle$ collapsing to $|1\rangle$ is:

$$\text{Probability of collapsing to } |1\rangle = \left(-i\frac{1}{2}\right)\left(i\frac{1}{2}\right) = \frac{1}{4}$$

Because the amplitude for $|1\rangle$ is a complex number, we multiply it by its complex conjugate instead of directly squaring it.

f. The output of running this program should be similar to the following figure:

The probabilities of recording the 0 and 1 bits in the classical register, about 75% and 25%, respectively, match those calculated in the previous part.

Sequence of Gates as Matrix Multiplication Solutions

Solutions for the exercises in Try Your Hand, on page 223.

1. a. No. The correct way to multiply the gate matrices is:

$$|\psi\rangle = A_{S^\dagger}A_H|0\rangle$$

The gate matrices are written in the reverse direction from the order in which the gates act on the qubit.

b. Yes. The $T^\dagger$ gate reverses the action of the T gate so, in effect, the qubit isn't affected by those gates. In terms of matrices, the $|\psi\rangle$ state is calculated as follows:

$$|\psi\rangle = A_Y A_{T^\dagger} A_T A_H |0\rangle$$
$$= A_Y A_H |0\rangle$$

Note that $A_{T^\dagger}$ is the Hermitian of A_T. So, $A_{T^\dagger} A_T = 1$, resulting in the simplification of the previous equation.

c. Yes. The Hermitian of the $A_{S^\dagger}$ matrix, $A_{S^\dagger}^\dagger$, is just A_S. So the given matrix multiplication works out as follows:

$$|\psi\rangle = A_{S^\dagger}^\dagger A_H |0\rangle$$
$$= A_S A_H |0\rangle$$

This equation represents the circuit in which the H gate first acts on the $|0\rangle$ qubit followed by the S gate, as shown in the figure for this part.

d. Yes. The S gate rotates the triangle $|1\rangle$ qubelets by a quarter turn anticlockwise. The $T^\dagger$ gate then rotates the triangle $|1\rangle$ qubelets a one-eighth turn clockwise. Thus, the net rotation of the triangle $|1\rangle$ qubelets is a one-eighth turn anticlockwise. This rotation corresponds to just applying the T gate in place of the S and $T^\dagger$ gates.

We can also show this mathematically in terms of matrices. Start with the following equation, which directly uses the gate matrices as the gates appear in the circuit but in the reverse order:

$$|\psi\rangle = A_{T^\dagger} A_S A_H |0\rangle$$

Next, recognize that the A_T matrix is the square root of the A_S matrix. Thus, replace A_S with $A_T A_T$ in the previous equation:

$$|\psi\rangle = A_{T^\dagger} A_S A_H |0\rangle$$
$$= A_{T^\dagger} A_T A_T A_H |0\rangle$$
$$= A_T A_H |0\rangle$$

The last equation was simplified by noticing that $A_{T^\dagger} A_T = 1$.

e. Yes. The matrix multiplications for this sequence of gates to compute the final state $|\psi\rangle$ is:

$$|\psi\rangle = A_H A_Z A_H |0\rangle$$

Writing out the actual gate matrices for the H and Z gates, the previous equation becomes:

$$|\psi\rangle = \begin{bmatrix} \frac{1}{\sqrt{2}} & \frac{1}{\sqrt{2}} \\ \frac{1}{\sqrt{2}} & \frac{-1}{\sqrt{2}} \end{bmatrix} \begin{bmatrix} 1 & 0 \\ 0 & -1 \end{bmatrix} \begin{bmatrix} \frac{1}{\sqrt{2}} & \frac{1}{\sqrt{2}} \\ \frac{1}{\sqrt{2}} & \frac{-1}{\sqrt{2}} \end{bmatrix} |0\rangle$$

$$= \begin{bmatrix} 0 & 1 \\ 1 & 0 \end{bmatrix} |0\rangle$$

The matrix in the previous equation corresponds to the NOT (X) gate. Thus, the final quantum state can be written as:

$$|\psi\rangle = A_X |0\rangle$$

2. a. No. This circuit won't return anything since the qubit isn't collapsed.

To get this circuit to run on a quantum computer, add a classical register and a Measure gate, as shown in the following figure:

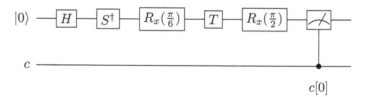

b. The quantum program for the circuit in the previous part is listed here:

```
0_H_SDag_Rx_30_T_Rx_90.qasm
qreg q[1];
creg c[1];

h q[0];
sdg q[0];
rx(pi/6) q[0];
t q[0];
rx(pi/2) q[0];
measure q[0] -> c[0];
```

c. The probabilities of the qubit collapsing to the idealized states are calculated by multiplying the respective amplitudes by their conjugate complexes as follows:

Probability of collapsing to $|0\rangle$

$\begin{aligned} &= (-0.0794593 - i\,0.4330127)(-0.0794593 + i\,0.4330127) \\ &= 0.0794593^2 - i^2\,0.4330127^2 \\ &= 0.0063138 + 0.1875 \\ &= 0.1938138 \end{aligned}$

And,

Probability of collapsing to $|1\rangle$

$\begin{aligned} &= (0.4330127 - i\,0.7865661)(0.4330127 + i\,0.7865661) \\ &= 0.4330127^2 - i^2\,0.7865661^2 \\ &= 0.1875 + 0.6186862 \\ &= 0.8061862 \end{aligned}$

As an additional check, these probabilities add up to 1, indicating that the qubit collapses to either one of these two idealized states.

d. The output of running this program should be similar to the following figure:

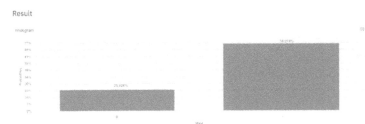

The probabilities of recording 0 and 1 bits in the classical register, about 23% and 76%, respectively, match those calculated in the previous part.

3. a. The quantum state $|\psi\rangle$ is:

$$|\psi\rangle = A_H A_S A_H |0\rangle$$

$$= \begin{bmatrix} \dfrac{1}{\sqrt{2}} & \dfrac{1}{\sqrt{2}} \\ \dfrac{1}{\sqrt{2}} & \dfrac{-1}{\sqrt{2}} \end{bmatrix} \begin{bmatrix} 1 & 0 \\ 0 & i \end{bmatrix} \begin{bmatrix} \dfrac{1}{\sqrt{2}} & \dfrac{1}{\sqrt{2}} \\ \dfrac{1}{\sqrt{2}} & \dfrac{-1}{\sqrt{2}} \end{bmatrix} |0\rangle$$

$$= \begin{bmatrix} 0.5 + i\,0.5 & 0.5 - i\,0.5 \\ 0.5 - i\,0.5 & 0.5 + i\,0.5 \end{bmatrix} \begin{pmatrix} 1 \\ 0 \end{pmatrix}$$

$$= \begin{pmatrix} 0.5 + i\,0.5 \\ 0.5 - i\,0.5 \end{pmatrix}$$

b. The quantum state vector in the Visualizations tab is identical to what's calculated in the previous part.

c. The probabilities of the qubit collapsing to the idealized states are calculated by multiplying the respective amplitudes by their complex conjugates as follows:

$$
\begin{aligned}
\text{Probability of collapsing to } |0\rangle &= (0.5 + i\,0.5)(0.5 - i\,0.5) \\
&= 0.5^2 - i^2\,0.5^2 \\
&= 0.25 + 0.25 \\
&= 0.5
\end{aligned}
$$

And,

$$
\begin{aligned}
\text{Probability of collapsing to } |1\rangle &= (0.5 - i\,0.5)(0.5 + i\,0.5) \\
&= 0.5^2 - i^2\,0.5^2 \\
&= 0.25 + 0.25 \\
&= 0.5
\end{aligned}
$$

d. The code listing for this circuit is the following:

```
0_H_S_H_Measure.qasm
qreg q[1];
creg c[1];

h q[0];
s q[0];
h q[0];
measure q[0] -> c[0];
```

e. The output of running this program should be similar to the following figure:

Result

The probabilities of recording 0 and 1 bits in the classical register, each about 50%, match those calculated in earlier.

Multi-Qubit Programs Solutions

Solutions for the exercises in Try Your Hand, on page 273.

1. a. The amplitude for $|01\rangle$ is the second element of the vector:

$$\omega_{01} = \frac{1}{\sqrt{2}}$$

b. The amplitude for $|00\rangle$ is the first element of the vector:

$$\omega_{00} = \frac{-i}{2}$$

2. No. The columns of a matrix for a quantum gate correspond to the idealized states. The number of idealized states is a power of 2. Since 3 is not a power of 2, a 3×3 matrix can't be a quantum gate matrix.

3. The correct expression is c. This is a single qubit with two pentagon $|0\rangle$ qubelets and a single triangle $|1\rangle$ qubelet rotated a quarter turn anticlockwise. Thus, the correct way to express it is:

$$\frac{2}{\sqrt{2^2+1}} |0\rangle + \frac{i}{\sqrt{2^2+1}} |1\rangle = \frac{2}{\sqrt{5}} |0\rangle + \frac{i}{\sqrt{5}} |1\rangle$$

4. a. Probability of collapsing to each of the four idealized states is calculated in the following table:

Idealized State	Amplitude	Conjugate of Amplitude	Probability of Collapsing
$|00\rangle$	$2/5$	$2/5$	$2/5 \times 2/5 = 4/25$
$|01\rangle$	$4i/5$	$-4i/5$	$4i/5 \times -4i/5 = -16i^2/25 = 16/25$
$|10\rangle$	$-i/5$	$i/5$	$-i/5 \times i/5 = -i^2/25 = 1/25$
$|11\rangle$	$2/5$	$2/5$	$2/5 \times 2/5 = 4/25$

b. For the classical register to record a 1 when you collapse the second qubit means that the quantum state had to collapse to either a $|01\rangle$ or a $|11\rangle$ state. Thus, from the probabilities calculated in the previous part, the probability of logging a 1 is:

$$
\begin{aligned}
\text{Probability of collapsing to 1} &= \text{Probability of collapsing to } |01\rangle + \\
&\quad \text{Probability of collapsing to } |11\rangle \\
&= \frac{16}{25} + \frac{4}{25} \\
&= \frac{20}{25} \\
&= 0.8
\end{aligned}
$$

c. Yes, the quantum state of the system will change.

Since the second qubit collapses to $|1\rangle$, the new state of the system can only have the $|01\rangle$ and $|11\rangle$ states. These must be normalized as follows to get the new state, $|\psi_1\rangle$:

$$|\psi_1\rangle = \frac{\frac{4i}{5}|01\rangle + \frac{2}{5}|11\rangle}{\sqrt{\frac{-4i}{5}\frac{4i}{5} + \frac{2}{5}\frac{2}{5}}}$$

$$= \frac{\frac{4i}{5}|01\rangle + \frac{2}{5}|11\rangle}{\frac{2}{\sqrt{5}}}$$

$$= \frac{\sqrt{5}}{2}\frac{4i}{5}|0\rangle + \frac{\sqrt{5}}{2}\frac{2}{5}|1\rangle$$

$$= \frac{2i}{\sqrt{5}}|0\rangle + \frac{1}{\sqrt{5}}|1\rangle$$

In other words, $|\psi\rangle \neq |\psi_1\rangle$, and the state before and after the measurement of the second qubit are different.

This example shows that the act of measuring a qubit changes the state of the system. This effect, in fact, is a key defining feature of quantum mechanics and underpins Heisenberg's uncertainty principle.[2]

Thus, if you arbitrarily place Measure gates in your code to help you see whether it's behaving as expected, you'll end up actually destroying the effect you're trying to see.

5. This matrix describes a quantum operation that is like a *Controlled* $S^\dagger$ gate as shown by the following circuit:

When the control qubit is $|0\rangle$, any pentagon $|0\rangle$ qubelets in the target qubit's state are left alone but the triangle $|1\rangle$ qubelets are given a quarter turn clockwise.

6. a. Since this gate works on three qubits, its gate matrix's dimensions will be 8×8.

b. The quantum states on the bottom two qubits are swapped only when $|\psi_0\rangle$ is $|1\rangle$. That is,

$$|1\psi_1\psi_2\rangle \mapsto |1\psi_2\psi_1\rangle$$

---

2. https://en.wikipedia.org/wiki/Uncertainty_principle

Specifically, only the following states are affected by this gate:

$$|101\rangle \mapsto |110\rangle$$
$$|110\rangle \mapsto |101\rangle$$

Even though the control qubit is $|1\rangle$ in $|100\rangle$ and $|111\rangle$, swapping the second and third states doesn't change the overall quantum state. For all other cases, the control qubit is $|0\rangle$, and hence, the gate doesn't modify any of those states. Thus, the gate matrix is:

$$\begin{bmatrix} 1 & 0 & 0 & 0 & 0 & 0 & 0 & 0 \\ 0 & 1 & 0 & 0 & 0 & 0 & 0 & 0 \\ 0 & 0 & 1 & 0 & 0 & 0 & 0 & 0 \\ 0 & 0 & 0 & 1 & 0 & 0 & 0 & 0 \\ 0 & 0 & 0 & 0 & 1 & 0 & 0 & 0 \\ 0 & 0 & 0 & 0 & 0 & 0 & 1 & 0 \\ 0 & 0 & 0 & 0 & 0 & 1 & 0 & 0 \\ 0 & 0 & 0 & 0 & 0 & 0 & 0 & 1 \end{bmatrix}$$

7. a. Since this circuit has two qubits, it'll have a 4×4 gate matrix. To obtain the gate matrix, recall that the H gate splits the $|0\rangle$ and $|1\rangle$ qubits as follows:

$$H|0\rangle = \frac{1}{\sqrt{2}}(|0\rangle + |1\rangle)$$
$$H|1\rangle = \frac{1}{\sqrt{2}}(|0\rangle - |1\rangle)$$

In these equations, $H|0\rangle$ and $H|1\rangle$ are the actions of the H gate on the $|0\rangle$ and $|1\rangle$ qubits, respectively.

Now, work out what this circuit does to each of the four idealized states, $|00\rangle$, $|10\rangle$, $|10\rangle$, and $|11\rangle$:

$|00\rangle$ *Idealized State:*
Both the top and bottom H gates split the $|0\rangle$ qubit.

Thus, the mega-qubit formed by this idealized state is:

$$H|0\rangle \otimes H|0\rangle = \frac{1}{\sqrt{2}}(|0\rangle + |1\rangle) \otimes \frac{1}{\sqrt{2}}(|0\rangle + |1\rangle)$$
$$= \frac{1}{2}(|00\rangle + |01\rangle + |10\rangle + |11\rangle)$$

This state corresponds to the following vector:

$$\frac{1}{2}\begin{pmatrix} 1 \\ 1 \\ 1 \\ 1 \end{pmatrix}$$

$|01\rangle$ *Idealized State:*

The top H gate splits the $|0\rangle$ qubit, and the bottom H gate splits the $|1\rangle$ qubit.

Thus, the mega-qubit formed by this idealized state is:

$$\begin{aligned} H|0\rangle \otimes H|1\rangle &= \frac{1}{\sqrt{2}}(\,|0\rangle + |1\rangle\,) \otimes \frac{1}{\sqrt{2}}(\,|0\rangle - |1\rangle\,) \\ &= \frac{1}{2}(\,|00\rangle - |01\rangle + |10\rangle - |11\rangle\,) \end{aligned}$$

This state corresponds to the following vector:

$$\frac{1}{2}\begin{pmatrix} 1 \\ -1 \\ 1 \\ -1 \end{pmatrix}$$

$|10\rangle$ *Idealized State:*

The top H gate splits the $|1\rangle$ qubit, and the bottom H gate splits the $|0\rangle$ qubit.

Thus, the mega-qubit formed by this idealized state is:

$$\begin{aligned} H|1\rangle \otimes H|0\rangle &= \frac{1}{\sqrt{2}}(\,|0\rangle - |1\rangle\,) \otimes \frac{1}{\sqrt{2}}(\,|0\rangle + |1\rangle\,) \\ &= \frac{1}{2}(\,|00\rangle + |01\rangle - |10\rangle - |11\rangle\,) \end{aligned}$$

This state corresponds to the following vector:

$$\frac{1}{2}\begin{pmatrix} 1 \\ 1 \\ -1 \\ -1 \end{pmatrix}$$

$|11\rangle$ *Idealized State:*

Both the top and bottom H gates split the $|1\rangle$ qubit.

Thus, the mega-qubit formed by this idealized state is:

$$H|1\rangle \otimes H|1\rangle = \frac{1}{\sqrt{2}}(|0\rangle - |1\rangle) \otimes \frac{1}{\sqrt{2}}(|0\rangle - |1\rangle)$$

$$= \frac{1}{2}(|00\rangle - |01\rangle - |10\rangle + |11\rangle)$$

This state corresponds to the following vector:

$$\frac{1}{2}\begin{pmatrix} 1 \\ -1 \\ -1 \\ 1 \end{pmatrix}$$

The previous four vectors correspond to the columns of the matrix representing this circuit:

$$\frac{1}{2}\begin{bmatrix} 1 & 1 & 1 & 1 \\ 1 & -1 & 1 & -1 \\ 1 & 1 & -1 & -1 \\ 1 & -1 & -1 & 1 \end{bmatrix}$$

b. While the S gate rotates triangle $|1\rangle$ qubelets a quarter turn anticlockwise, the $S^\dagger$ gate rotates the triangle $|1\rangle$ qubelets *clockwise*. Both gates leave pentagon $|0\rangle$ qubelets alone.

Thus, to obtain the gate matrix for the given circuit, replace i with $-i$:

$$A_{S^\dagger} = \begin{bmatrix} 1 & 0 & 0 & 0 \\ 0 & -i & 0 & 0 \\ 0 & 0 & 1 & 0 \\ 0 & 0 & 0 & -i \end{bmatrix}$$

8. a. To calculate the matrix for this circuit, start by breaking it up as shown in the following figure:

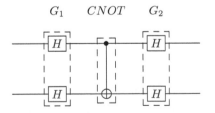

Then the matrix A for the entire circuit is calculated as follows:

$$A = A_{G_2} \times A_{CNOT} \times A_{G_1}$$

A_{CNOT} is the matrix for the CNOT gate. A_{G_1} and A_{G_2} are the matrices for the part of the circuit where each qubit is operated on by an H gate, respectively.

The matrix for the CNOT gate is:

$$A_{CNOT} = \begin{bmatrix} 1 & 0 & 0 & 0 \\ 0 & 1 & 0 & 0 \\ 0 & 0 & 0 & 1 \\ 0 & 0 & 1 & 0 \end{bmatrix}$$

The A_{G_1} and A_{G_2} matrices were obtained in the previous part. That is,

$$A_{G_1} = A_{G_2} = \frac{1}{2}\begin{bmatrix} 1 & 1 & 1 & 1 \\ 1 & -1 & 1 & -1 \\ 1 & 1 & -1 & -1 \\ 1 & -1 & -1 & 1 \end{bmatrix}$$

Thus, the matrix A for the entire circuit is:

$$A = A_{G_2} \times A_{CNOT} \times A_{G_1}$$

$$= \frac{1}{2}\begin{bmatrix} 1 & 1 & 1 & 1 \\ 1 & -1 & 1 & -1 \\ 1 & 1 & -1 & -1 \\ 1 & -1 & -1 & 1 \end{bmatrix} \times \begin{bmatrix} 1 & 0 & 0 & 0 \\ 0 & 1 & 0 & 0 \\ 0 & 0 & 0 & 1 \\ 0 & 0 & 1 & 0 \end{bmatrix} \times \frac{1}{2}\begin{bmatrix} 1 & 1 & 1 & 1 \\ 1 & -1 & 1 & -1 \\ 1 & 1 & -1 & -1 \\ 1 & -1 & -1 & 1 \end{bmatrix}$$

$$= \begin{bmatrix} 1 & 0 & 0 & 0 \\ 0 & 0 & 0 & 1 \\ 0 & 0 & 1 & 0 \\ 0 & 1 & 0 & 0 \end{bmatrix}$$

This circuit, then, modifies the idealized states as follows:

$$\begin{aligned} |00\rangle &\mapsto |00\rangle \\ |01\rangle &\mapsto |11\rangle \\ |10\rangle &\mapsto |10\rangle \\ |11\rangle &\mapsto |01\rangle \end{aligned}$$

It leaves the $|00\rangle$ and $|10\rangle$ states alone but affects the $|01\rangle$ and $|11\rangle$ states. Specifically, when the second qubit is $|1\rangle$, it switches the first qubit.

This circuit acts like an *upside down* CNOT gate where the first qubit is the target and the second qubit is the control, as shown here:

b. To calculate the matrix for this circuit, start by breaking it up as shown in the following figure:

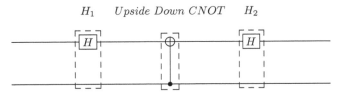

H_1 *Upside Down CNOT* H_2

Thus, the matrix A for the entire circuit can be calculated as follows:

$$A = A_{H_2} \times A_\chi \times A_{H_1}$$

A_χ is the matrix for the upside down CNOT gate calculated in the previous part:

$$A_\chi = \begin{bmatrix} 1 & 0 & 0 & 0 \\ 0 & 0 & 0 & 1 \\ 0 & 0 & 1 & 0 \\ 0 & 1 & 0 & 0 \end{bmatrix}$$

The A_{H_1} and A_{H_2} are the matrices for the pass-through H gate. This matrix was calculated in Working with Blended States: Mega-Qubit as a Tensor, on page 248:

$$A_{H_1} = A_{H_2} = \frac{1}{\sqrt{2}} \begin{bmatrix} 1 & 0 & 1 & 0 \\ 0 & 1 & 0 & 1 \\ 1 & 0 & -1 & 0 \\ 0 & 1 & 0 & -1 \end{bmatrix}$$

Thus, the matrix A for the entire circuit is:

$$A = A_{H_2} \times A_\chi \times A_{H_1}$$

$$= \frac{1}{\sqrt{2}} \begin{bmatrix} 1 & 0 & 1 & 0 \\ 0 & 1 & 0 & 1 \\ 1 & 0 & -1 & 0 \\ 0 & 1 & 0 & -1 \end{bmatrix} \times \begin{bmatrix} 1 & 0 & 0 & 0 \\ 0 & 0 & 0 & 1 \\ 0 & 0 & 1 & 0 \\ 0 & 1 & 0 & 0 \end{bmatrix} \times \frac{1}{\sqrt{2}} \begin{bmatrix} 1 & 0 & 1 & 0 \\ 0 & 1 & 0 & 1 \\ 1 & 0 & -1 & 0 \\ 0 & 1 & 0 & -1 \end{bmatrix}$$

$$= \begin{bmatrix} 1 & 0 & 0 & 0 \\ 0 & 1 & 0 & 0 \\ 0 & 0 & 1 & 0 \\ 0 & 0 & 0 & -1 \end{bmatrix}$$

This is the matrix for the Control Z gate shown in the following figure:

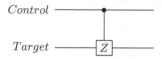

This gate leaves the $|00\rangle$, $|01\rangle$, and $|10\rangle$ alone but inverts the triangle $|1\rangle$ qubelets in the target qubit if the control qubit is $|1\rangle$. That is:

$$|11\rangle \mapsto - |11\rangle$$

9. a. The triangle $|1\rangle$ qubelet in the bottom cell of the qubelet combination on the left is rotated 90° anticlockwise but non-inverted in the bottom cell of that on the right. That is, the bottom triangle $|1\rangle$ qubelet on the left is rotated 90° clockwise on the right. So for the qubelet combination on the right to have the same quantum state as that on the left, the top triangle $|1\rangle$ qubelet in the right combination must be rotated 90° anticlockwise, as shown in the following figure:

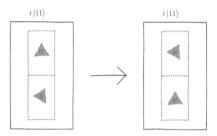

b. The triangle $|1\rangle$ qubelet in the bottom cell of the qubelet combination on the left is inverted but non-inverted in the bottom cell of that on the right. So that the right combination has the same quantum state as that on the left, the triangle $|1\rangle$ qubelet in the top cell of the left combination is given a 180° rotation, as shown in the following figure:

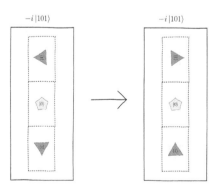

10. a. Expand the tensor product to get the quantum state as follows:

$$|1\rangle \otimes |0\rangle \otimes |1\rangle \otimes |1\rangle \otimes |0\rangle = |10110\rangle$$

This corresponds to a quantum state vector having $2^5 = 32$ elements. All the elements are 0 except its twenty-third element which is 1.

The associated mega-qubit is:

Mega-Qubit for $|10110\rangle$

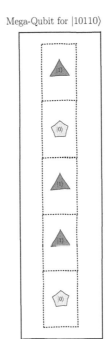

The mega-qubit contains just a single qubelet combination. Thus, even an idealized state can be expressed as a tensor product.

b. Expand the tensor product to get the quantum state, as follows:

$$\frac{1}{\sqrt{2}}(|0\rangle + i|1\rangle) \otimes |0\rangle = \frac{1}{\sqrt{2}}(|00\rangle + i|10\rangle)$$

This corresponds to the following vector:

$$\frac{1}{\sqrt{2}}\begin{pmatrix} 1 \\ 0 \\ i \\ 0 \end{pmatrix}$$

The associated mega-qubit is shown in the figure on page 498.

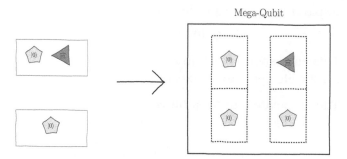

The triangle $|1\rangle$ qubelet in the second qubelet combination is rotated 90° due to the amplitude of $|10\rangle$ being i.

c. Expand the tensor product to get the quantum state as follows:

$$\frac{1}{\sqrt{2}}(|0\rangle - i|1\rangle) \otimes \frac{1}{\sqrt{2}}(|0\rangle + i|1\rangle) = \frac{1}{\sqrt{2}}|0\rangle\frac{1}{\sqrt{2}}(|0\rangle + i|1\rangle) - \frac{i}{\sqrt{2}}|1\rangle\frac{1}{\sqrt{2}}(|0\rangle + i|1\rangle)$$

$$= \frac{1}{2}|00\rangle + \frac{i}{2}|01\rangle - \frac{i}{2}|10\rangle + \frac{1}{2}|11\rangle$$

This corresponds to the following vector:

$$\frac{1}{2}\begin{pmatrix} 1 \\ i \\ -i \\ 1 \end{pmatrix}$$

The associated mega-qubit is the following:

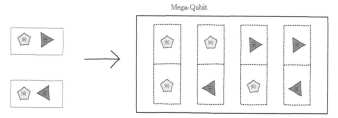

The anticlockwise quarter-turn triangle $|1\rangle$ qubelet in the second qubelet combination contributes $e^{i\pi/2} = i$ to its amplitude coefficent. That is, $\omega_{01} = i$. Likewise, the clockwise quarter-turn triangle $|1\rangle$ qubelet in the third qubelet combination contributes $e^{-i\pi/2} = -i$ to its amplitude coefficient. That is, $\omega_{10} = -i$.

In the last qubelet combination, top triangle $|1\rangle$ qubelet contributes $e^{-i\pi/2} = -i$ and the bottom triangle $|1\rangle$ qubelet contributes $e^{i\pi/2} = i$. That is, the overall amplitude coefficient is the product of these terms: $-i \times i = -i^2 = 1$. In other words, the fourth qubelet combination is equivalent to one where both triangle $|1\rangle$ qubelets are not rotated. You can also see this by giving both qubelets the same rotation but in opposite directions so that any sign changes are canceled out: rotate the top triangle $|1\rangle$ qubelet a quarter turn anticlockwise and the bottom triangle $|1\rangle$ qubelet a quarter turn clockwise.

Thus, the mega-qubit can also be drawn as in the following figure:

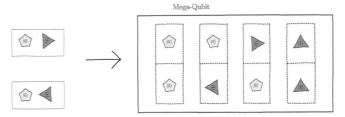

In this figure, the fourth qubelet combination has non-rotated triangle $|1\rangle$ qubelets.

d. The H gate splits the $|0\rangle$ qubit, and the X gate switches the $|1\rangle$ qubit as follows::

$$H|0\rangle = \frac{1}{\sqrt{2}}(|0\rangle + |1\rangle)$$
$$X|1\rangle = |0\rangle$$

Thus, the given tensor product is:

$$|1\rangle \otimes X|1\rangle \otimes H|0\rangle = |1\rangle \otimes |0\rangle \otimes \frac{1}{\sqrt{2}}(|0\rangle + |1\rangle)$$

Expand this tensor product to get the quantum state as follows:

$$|1\rangle \otimes |0\rangle \otimes \frac{1}{\sqrt{2}}(|0\rangle + |1\rangle) = |10\rangle \otimes \frac{1}{\sqrt{2}}(|0\rangle + |1\rangle)$$
$$= \frac{1}{\sqrt{2}}|100\rangle + \frac{1}{\sqrt{2}}|101\rangle$$

This corresponds to the following vector:

$$\frac{1}{\sqrt{2}}\begin{vmatrix} 0 \\ 0 \\ 0 \\ 0 \\ 1 \\ 1 \\ 0 \\ 0 \end{vmatrix}$$

This 8×1 vector has a 1 in the fifth and sixth positions, and 0 elsewhere.

The associated mega-qubit is:

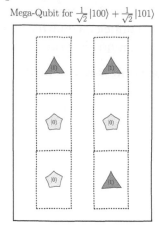

Mega-Qubit for $\frac{1}{\sqrt{2}}|100\rangle + \frac{1}{\sqrt{2}}|101\rangle$

11. a. To see whether the two qubits are entangled, try factoring the quantum state as follows:

$$
\begin{aligned}
|\psi\rangle &= \frac{3}{10}|00\rangle + \frac{1}{10}|01\rangle - \frac{9}{10}|10\rangle - \frac{3}{10}|11\rangle \\
&= \frac{1}{\sqrt{10}}\left(\frac{3}{\sqrt{10}}|00\rangle + \frac{1}{\sqrt{10}}|01\rangle\right) - \frac{3}{\sqrt{10}}\left(\frac{3}{\sqrt{10}}|10\rangle + \frac{1}{\sqrt{10}}|11\rangle\right) \\
&= \frac{1}{\sqrt{10}}|0\rangle\left(\frac{3}{\sqrt{10}}|0\rangle + \frac{1}{\sqrt{10}}|1\rangle\right) - \frac{3}{\sqrt{10}}|1\rangle\left(\frac{3}{\sqrt{10}}|0\rangle + \frac{1}{\sqrt{10}}|1\rangle\right) \\
&= \left(\frac{1}{\sqrt{10}}|0\rangle - \frac{3}{\sqrt{10}}|1\rangle\right) \otimes \left(\frac{3}{\sqrt{10}}|0\rangle + \frac{1}{\sqrt{10}}|1\rangle\right)
\end{aligned}
$$

This quantum state can be factored as the tensor product of two quantum states. Hence, the qubits are not entangled.

b. The given quantum state can't be factored as a product of tensor products. Hence, the qubits are entangled.

You can also directly see this from the quantum state itself. If the first qubit collapses to, say, $|0\rangle$, then the quantum state has collapsed to $|01\rangle$. Thus, the second qubit is forced to collapse to $|1\rangle$. An analogous result holds if the first qubit collapses to $|1\rangle$. Furthermore, you'll see the same behavior had you collapsed the second qubit before the first.

12. To identify the three missing qubelets, first expand the tensor product of the three qubits to obtain the quantum state of the mega-qubit, as follows:

$$
\begin{aligned}
\frac{1}{\sqrt{2}}(|0\rangle + i|1\rangle) \otimes \frac{1}{\sqrt{2}}(|0\rangle + |1\rangle) \otimes \frac{1}{\sqrt{2}}(|0\rangle - |1\rangle) &= \frac{1}{2}(|00\rangle + |01\rangle + i|10\rangle + i|11\rangle) \otimes \frac{1}{\sqrt{2}}(|0\rangle - |1\rangle) \\
&= \frac{1}{2\sqrt{2}}(|000\rangle - |001\rangle + |010\rangle - |011\rangle + \\
&\quad i|100\rangle - i|101\rangle + i|110\rangle - i|111\rangle)
\end{aligned}
$$

The missing qubelet is in the bottom cell of the fourth qubelet combination which corresponds to the $-|011\rangle$ term in the quantum state specified in the above equation. This combination is formed by taking the pentagon $|0\rangle$ qubelet from the top qubit, the triangle $|1\rangle$ qubelet from the middle qubit, and the inverted triangle $|1\rangle$ qubit from the bottom qubit. The inverted qubelet gives the negative sign associated with this combination. Thus, the first missing qubelet is an inverted triangle $|1\rangle$ qubelet.

The missing qubelet is in the top cell of the sixth qubelet combination, which corresponds to the $-i|101\rangle$ term in the quantum state specified in the equation for this exercise. This combination is formed by taking the 90°-rotated triangle $|1\rangle$ qubelet in the first qubit, the pentagon $|0\rangle$ qubelet from the middle qubit, and the inverted triangle $|1\rangle$ qubelet from the bottom qubit. The inverted qubelet gives the negative sign and the 90°-rotated top qubelet gives the complex number i associated with this combination. Thus, the second missing qubelet is a triangle $|1\rangle$ qubelet rotated a quarter turn anticlockwise.

The missing qubelet is in the top cell of the last qubelet combination, which corresponds to the $-i|111\rangle$ term in the quantum state specified in this equation. This combination is formed by taking the the 90°-rotated triangle $|1\rangle$ qubelet in the first qubit, the triangle $|1\rangle$ qubelet from the middle qubit, and the inverted triangle $|1\rangle$ qubelet from the bottom qubit. The inverted qubelet gives the negative sign and the 90°-rotated top qubelet gives the complex number i associated with this combination. Thus, this qubelet combination should be drawn as in the following figure:

$-i|111\rangle$

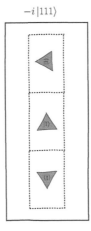

But the qubelet combination shown in the given mega-qubit has an unrotated triangle $|1\rangle$ qubelet in the middle and bottom cells. Hence, we need to bring the qubelet combination shown in the previous figure to the desired form by rotating qubelets without modifying the combination's quantum state. Specifically, invert the bottom triangle $|1\rangle$ qubelet so it's unrotated, while simultaneously rotating the top qubelet 180° so the top triangle $|1\rangle$ qubelet is now rotated a quarter turn clockwise, as shown in the following figure:

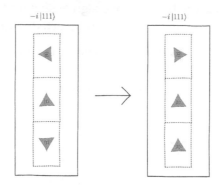

The quantum state of the qubelet combination on the right is still $-i\,|111\rangle$. (The faded qubelets in the top and bottom cells indicate the original position of those qubelets, respectively.)

The final mega-qubit is shown in the following figure:

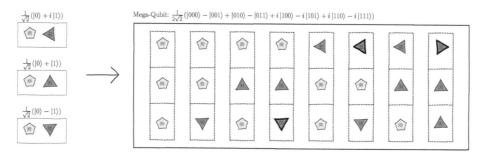

13. a. This mega-qubit can collapse in the following four ways:

Collapsed Quantum State	Probability	State Logged in Classical register
$|00\rangle$	$\frac{1}{4}$	00
$i\,|01\rangle$	$\frac{1}{4}$	01
$|10\rangle$	$\frac{1}{4}$	10
$i\,|11\rangle$	$\frac{1}{4}$	11

Notice that no rotation information is recorded in the classical register.

b. Since the probability of each collapsed state is $1/4$, the magnitude of each amplitude is the square root of $1/4$. Thus, the quantum state for the mega-qubit is:

$$|\psi\rangle = |\psi_0\psi_1\rangle = \frac{1}{2}|00\rangle + \frac{i}{2}|01\rangle + \frac{1}{2}|10\rangle + \frac{i}{2}|11\rangle$$

c. To write the quantum state as a tensor product, factor the previous equation as follows:

$$\begin{aligned}
|\psi\rangle = |\psi_0\psi_1\rangle &= \frac{1}{2}|00\rangle + \frac{i}{2}|01\rangle + \frac{1}{2}|10\rangle + \frac{i}{2}|11\rangle \\
&= \frac{1}{2}|0\rangle\,(\,|0\rangle + i|1\rangle\,) + \frac{1}{2}|1\rangle\,(\,|0\rangle + i|1\rangle\,) \\
&= \frac{1}{\sqrt{2}}(\,|0\rangle + |1\rangle\,) \otimes \frac{1}{\sqrt{2}}(\,|0\rangle + i|1\rangle\,) \\
&= |\psi_0\rangle \otimes |\psi_1\rangle
\end{aligned}$$

d. The tensor product obtained in the previous part can be drawn as shown in the following figure:

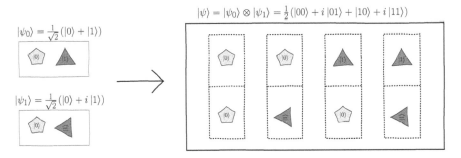

The top qubit on the left, $|\psi_0\rangle$, can be obtained by splitting $|0\rangle$ using an H gate.

The bottom qubit on the left, $|\psi_1\rangle$, has a 90°-rotated triangle $|1\rangle$ qubelet. Hence, after splitting $|0\rangle$ with an H gate, use an S gate to give the triangle $|1\rangle$ qubelet a quarter turn anticlockwise.

The quantum circuit to create this mega-qubit is shown in the following figure:

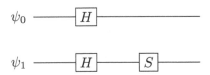

14. No. Once you teleport $|\psi_1\rangle$, the $|keep\rangle$ and $|send\rangle$ qubits collapse and are no longer entangled. Furthermore, they are physically distant from each other. Thus, this circuit can no longer teleport any more quantum states—teleporting circuits are *single-use* circuits. Once they're done teleporting, the qubits are no longer useful. If you want to teleport another state, you need another pair of $|keep\rangle$ and $|send\rangle$ qubits.

15. When the $|\psi_0\rangle$ and $|keep\rangle$ qubits collapse, the $|send\rangle$ qubit is:

$$|send\rangle = \frac{1}{\sqrt{2}}|0\rangle - \frac{i}{\sqrt{2}}|1\rangle$$

The $|send\rangle$ qubit will have one pentagon $|0\rangle$ qubelet and a triangle $|1\rangle$ qubelet that is rotated a quarter turn clockwise.

Since $|\psi_0\, keep\rangle = |10\rangle$, you'll need to apply a Z gate to the $|send\rangle$ qubit to obtain the state that will be teleported.

The Z gate doesn't affect the pentagon $|0\rangle$ gate but turns the triangle $|1\rangle$ qubelet $180°$ so that it ends up rotated a quarter turn anticlockwise. Thus, the state that is teleported is:

$$\frac{1}{\sqrt{2}}|0\rangle + \frac{i}{\sqrt{2}}|1\rangle$$

16. Yes, the circuit can be used to teleport a quantum state.

The Entangler and Loader blocks, together with the $|keep\rangle$, $|send\rangle$, and the quantum state to be teleported, $|\psi_0\rangle$, are labeled as shown in the following circuit:

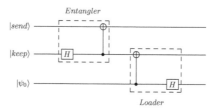

Quantum Cryptography Solutions

Solutions for the exercises in Try Your Hand, on page 291.

1. a. i. False. 0000000 is just the initializing string for the quantum circuit.

    ii. False. The secret key can't be determined at this stage.

    iii. False. The random key is explicitly set by Alice before putting the qubits in a blended state.

iv. True. The random key is the value of the qubits before applying the H gates that put them in a blended state.

v. False. The secret key can't be determined at this stage.

b. Bob's circuit is shown in the following figure:

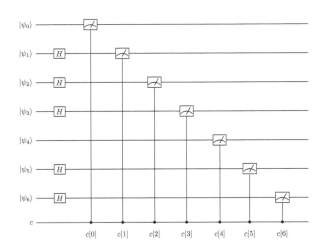

c. Over the classical channel, Alice and Bob declare the qubits on which each used the H gates. So, Alice would say qubits 1, 3, 4, 6, and 7. And, Bob would say qubits 2, 3, 4, 6, and 7.

If both report $|\psi_6\rangle = |1\rangle$, then they know they have a safe channel.

d. Since the seventh qubit was used to establish an enhanced level of trust, it's not used in the secret key.

Each then derives the secret key individually, as follows:

- Alice uses the third, fourth, and sixth bits from the random string she generated: 101.

- Bob measures the values in the classical registers $c[2]$, $c[3]$, and $c[5]$, corresponding to measuring the third, fourth, and sixth qubits. He, too, would come up with 101 for the secret key.

2. a. The quantum circuit is shown in the figure on page 506.

b. The random string generated by your machine is 1010101110.

c. Both your machine and the Pragamatic Bookshelf website apply H gates on qubits 1, 4, and 7. Thus, the secret key derived by each is

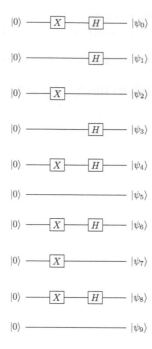

101, the values recorded in the classical registers when $|\psi_0\rangle$, $|\psi_3\rangle$, and $|\psi_6\rangle$ collapse.

3. The BB84 mechanism is based on using consecutive gates such that the second gate reverses the effect of the first. Thus, if the sender uses the S gate to rotate qubits by a quarter turn anticlockwise, the receiver must use the $S^\dagger$ to rotate the qubits by a quarter turn clockwise.

4. a. Only the third state, 11100111, may be observed. The others don't correspond to any qubelet combination in the mega-qubit.

   b. To get the states that the receiver may observe, apply the H gate on qubits 1, 2, 4, and 6 and then expand the resulting tensor product as follows:

$$H|1\rangle \otimes H|1\rangle \otimes |1\rangle \otimes H|0\rangle \otimes |0\rangle \otimes H|1\rangle \otimes |1\rangle \otimes |1\rangle$$
$$= \tfrac{1}{\sqrt{2}}(|0\rangle - |1\rangle)\otimes\tfrac{1}{\sqrt{2}}(|0\rangle - |1\rangle)\otimes|1\rangle \otimes\tfrac{1}{\sqrt{2}}(|0\rangle + |1\rangle)\otimes|0\rangle \otimes\tfrac{1}{\sqrt{2}}(|0\rangle - |1\rangle)\otimes|1\rangle \otimes|1\rangle$$
$$= \tfrac{1}{4}(|00\rangle - |01\rangle - |10\rangle + |11\rangle)\otimes(|10\rangle + |11\rangle)\otimes(|00\rangle - |01\rangle)\otimes|11\rangle$$
$$= \tfrac{1}{4}(|0010\rangle + |0011\rangle - |0110\rangle - |0111\rangle - |1010\rangle - |1011\rangle + |1110\rangle + |1111\rangle)\otimes(|0011\rangle - |0111\rangle)$$
$$= \tfrac{1}{4}(|00100011\rangle - |00100111\rangle + |00110011\rangle - |00110111\rangle - |01100011\rangle + |01100111\rangle - |01110011\rangle + |01110111\rangle$$
$$- |10100011\rangle + |10100111\rangle - |10110011\rangle + |10110111\rangle + |11100011\rangle - |11100111\rangle + |11110011\rangle - |11110111\rangle)$$

Thus, the possible states are any one of the sixteen individual terms in the previous equation.

c. i. When qubit 1 is used to establish an enhanced level of trust, both the sender and receiver must agree on its state. So, the probabilities of both of them agreeing to $|0\rangle$ or $|1\rangle$ are as follows:

Qubit 1 Collapsing to $|0\rangle$:

Qubit 1 will collapse to $|0\rangle$ in the following 8 out of 16 cases:

$$|00100011\rangle$$
$$-|00100111\rangle$$
$$|00110011\rangle$$
$$-|00110111\rangle$$
$$-|01100011\rangle$$
$$|01100111\rangle$$
$$-|01110011\rangle$$
$$|01110111\rangle$$

Qubit 1 Collapsing to $|1\rangle$:

Qubit 1 will collapse to $|1\rangle$ in the following 8 out of 16 cases:

$$-|10100011\rangle$$
$$|10100111\rangle$$
$$-|10110011\rangle$$
$$|10110111\rangle$$
$$|11100011\rangle$$
$$-|11100111\rangle$$
$$|11110011\rangle$$
$$-|11110111\rangle$$

Thus, there is equal probability of the sender's and receiver's qubits matching when the receiver gets the hacked message. In other words, the probability of detecting an interceptor is 0.5.

ii. When qubits 1 and 2 are used to establish an enhanced level of trust, the sender and receiver must agree on both their states. So the probabilities of them agreeing to $|00\rangle$, $|01\rangle$, $|10\rangle$, or $|11\rangle$ are as follows:

Qubits 1 and 2 Collapsing to $|00\rangle$:

Qubits 1 and 2 will collapse to $|00\rangle$ in the following 4 out of 16 cases:

$$|00100011\rangle$$
$$-|00100111\rangle$$
$$|00110011\rangle$$
$$-|00110111\rangle$$

Qubits 1 and 2 Collapsing to $|01\rangle$:

Qubits 1 and 2 will collapse to $|01\rangle$ in the following 4 out of 16 cases:

$$- |01100011\rangle$$
$$|01100111\rangle$$
$$- |01110011\rangle$$
$$|01110111\rangle$$

Qubits 1 and 2 Collapsing to $|10\rangle$:

Qubits 1 and 2 will collapse to $|10\rangle$ in the following 4 out of 16 cases:

$$- |10100011\rangle$$
$$|10100111\rangle$$
$$- |10110011\rangle$$
$$|10110111\rangle$$

Qubits 1 and 2 Collapsing to $|11\rangle$:

Qubits 1 and 2 will collapse to $|11\rangle$ in the following 4 out of 16 cases:

$$|11100011\rangle$$
$$- |11100111\rangle$$
$$|11110011\rangle$$
$$- |11110111\rangle$$

Thus, the probability of the sender's and receiver's states matching is 4/16 or 0.25 when the receiver gets the hacked message. In other words, the probability of the sender and receiver having mismatched two qubits is 0.75. Thus, the probability that an interceptor is detected is 75%.

iii. When qubits 1, 2, and 4 are used to establish an enhanced level of trust, the sender and receiver must agree on all three states. So, the the probabilities of them agreeing to $|000\rangle$, $|001\rangle$, $|010\rangle$, $|011\rangle$, $|100\rangle$, $|101\rangle$, $|101\rangle$, and $|111\rangle$ are as follows:

Qubits 1, 2, and 4 Collapsing to $|000\rangle$:

Qubits 1, 2, and 4 will collapse to $|000\rangle$ in the following 2 out of 16 cases:

$$|00100011\rangle$$
$$- |00100111\rangle$$

Qubits 1, 2, and 4 Collapsing to $|001\rangle$*:*

Qubits 1, 2, and 4 will collapse to $|001\rangle$ in the following 2 out of the 16 cases:

$$|00110011\rangle$$
$$- |00110111\rangle$$

Qubits 1, 2, and 4 Collapsing to $|010\rangle$*:*

Qubits 1, 2, and 4 will collapse to $|010\rangle$ in the following 2 out of 16 cases:

$$- |01100011\rangle$$
$$|01100111\rangle$$

Qubits 1, 2, and 4 Collapsing to $|011\rangle$*:*

Qubits 1, 2, and 4 will collapse to $|011\rangle$ in the following 2 out of 16 cases:

$$- |011100111\rangle$$
$$|01110111\rangle$$

Qubits 1, 2, and 4 Collapsing to $|100\rangle$*:*

Qubits 1, 2, and 4 will collapse to $|100\rangle$ in the following 2 out of 16 cases:

$$- |10100011\rangle$$
$$|10100111\rangle$$

Qubits 1, 2, and 4 Collapsing to $|101\rangle$*:*

Qubits 1, 2, and 4 will collapse to $|101\rangle$ in the following 2 out of 16 cases:

$$- |10110011\rangle$$
$$|10110111\rangle$$

Qubits 1, 2, and 4 Collapsing to $|111\rangle$*:*

Qubits 1, 2, and 4 will collapse to $|111\rangle$ in the following 2 out of 16 cases:

$$|11110011\rangle$$
$$- |11110111\rangle$$

Thus, the probability of the sender's and receiver's states matching is 2/16 or 0.125 when the receiver gets the hacked message. In other words, the probability of the sender and receiver having mismatched three qubits is 0.875. Thus, the probability that an interceptor is detected is 87.5%.

Thus, with increasing number of qubits to match, the probability of detecting an interceptor increases. And with a sufficiently large number of qubits, the chances of an interceptor lurking undetected are virtually nil.

Quantum Search Solutions

Solutions for the exercises in Try Your Hand, on page 332.

1. a. In all qubelet combinations except for the second from right, the pentagon $|0\rangle$ and triangle $|1\rangle$ qubelets aren't inverted. In the second from right column, the pentagon $|0\rangle$ in the bottom cell is inverted while the qubelets in the top two are not. The relative difference in the orientations is 180° Thus, the mega-qubit is:

    $$|000\rangle + |001\rangle + |010\rangle + |011\rangle + |100\rangle - |110\rangle + |111\rangle$$

    The tagged state is the qubelet combination second from right that has an inverted pentagon $|0\rangle$ qubelet in the bottom cell. This column corresponds to the quantum state $|110\rangle$.

    b. Except for the qubelet combination that is second from left, in all other combinations, both the pentagon $|0\rangle$ and triangle $|1\rangle$ qubelets are either both not inverted or both inverted. In other words, there's no relative difference between the pentagon $|0\rangle$ and triangle $|1\rangle$ qubelets. In the second column, the pentagon $|0\rangle$ qubelet isn't inverted while the triangle $|1\rangle$ is, so the relative difference between them is 180°. Thus, the mega-qubit is:

    $$|00\rangle - |01\rangle + |10\rangle + |11\rangle$$

    The tagged state is $|01\rangle$, which is the qubelet combination second from left.

    c. Even though the pentagon $|0\rangle$ and triangle $|1\rangle$ qubelets in the first, second, and fourth columns are inverted, there's no relative difference between them. Likewise, both types of qubelets are also aligned in the same direction in the third column. Thus, there's no relative difference between the pentagon $|0\rangle$ and triangle $|1\rangle$ qubelets in each qubelet combination. As a result, the mega-qubit is:

    $$|00\rangle + |01\rangle + |10\rangle + |11\rangle$$

    All four idealized states have the same sign. Hence, no quantum state is tagged.

d. Even though both the pentagon $|0\rangle$ and triangle $|1\rangle$ qubelets in the first column are inverted, there's no relative difference between their orientations. In the other three qubelet combinations, one qubelet type is inverted and the other isn't. Thus, the relative difference in their orientations is 180°, making their amplitudes negative. The mega-qubit is:

$$|00\rangle - |01\rangle - |10\rangle - |11\rangle$$

The first qubelet combination, $|00\rangle$, has a different sign than the others. So it's the one that is tagged.

2. a. The actions of the gates are briefly specified, as follows:

X Gate

The X gate toggles the qubelets: a pentagon $|0\rangle$ is switched to a triangle $|1\rangle$ qubelet and a triangle $|1\rangle$ qubelet is switched to a pentagon $|0\rangle$ qubelet. (See NOT (X) Gate, on page 205.)

S Gate

The S gate rotates the triangle $|1\rangle$ qubelets a quarter turn anticlockwise but leaves the pentagon $|0\rangle$ qubelets alone. (See S Gate, on page 208.)

$S^\dagger$ Gate

The $S^\dagger$ gate rotates the triangle $|1\rangle$ qubelets a quarter turn clockwise but leaves the pentagon $|0\rangle$ qubelets alone. (See S-Dagger Gate, on page 208.)

b. The mega-qubit after the $S^\dagger$ gate acts on the bottom qubit is:

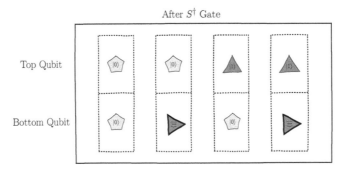

The triangle $|1\rangle$ qubelets in the bottom cell of the second and fourth qubelet combinations are rotated a quarter turn clockwise.

The quantum state is:

$$\frac{1}{2}|00\rangle - \frac{i}{2}|01\rangle + \frac{1}{2}|10\rangle - \frac{i}{2}|11\rangle$$

c. If the control qubit of the CZ gate, the top one in this circuit, is a triangle $|1\rangle$ qubelet, then it'll rotate the triangle $|1\rangle$ qubelet in the target qubit, the bottom qubit, by half a turn. In all other cases, the qubelets are left alone.

Since the top qubit in the fourth colum is a triangle $|1\rangle$, the bottom qubit is rotated by a half turn from its previous orientation. Thus, the bottom triangle $|1\rangle$ qubelet in the fourth column is now a quarter turn anticlockwise from the non-rotated position. Thus, the mega-qubit after the CZ gate acts on the qubits is shown in the following figure:

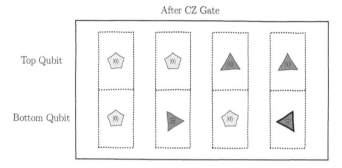

After CZ Gate

The quantum state of the mega-qubit at this stage is:

$$\frac{1}{2}|00\rangle - \frac{i}{2}|01\rangle + \frac{1}{2}|10\rangle + \frac{i}{2}|11\rangle$$

d. To tag the $|01\rangle$ quantum state, the bottom triangle $|1\rangle$ qubelets in the second and fourth columns must rotate by a *quarter turn clockwise*. This will make the bottom triangle $|1\rangle$ qubelet inverted, or rotated by a half turn, and will return the bottom $|1\rangle$ triangle qubelet in the fourth column to its original non-rotated position, as shown in the following figure:

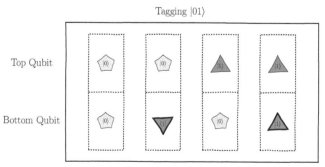

Tagging $|01\rangle$

The quantum gate that rotates triangle $|1\rangle$ qubelets a *quarter turn clockwise* while leaving the pentagon $|0\rangle$ qubelets alone is the $S^\dagger$ gate. This gate must be applied to the bottom qubit after the CZ gate, as shown in the following circuit:

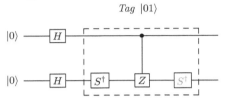

Notice that even though you're restoring the bottom triangle $|1\rangle$ qubelet to its original position, you need to use an $S^\dagger$ gate again, and not the S gate, to reverse the operation of the $S^\dagger$ gate.

The quantum state of the mega-qubit is:

$$\frac{1}{2}|00\rangle - \frac{i}{2}|01\rangle + \frac{1}{2}|10\rangle + \frac{1}{2}|11\rangle$$

e. Before writing the program, draw the the complete circuit to eliminate the non-tagged states, as shown in the following figure:

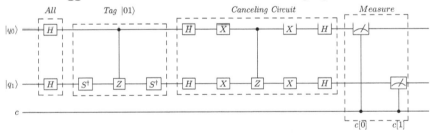

The quantum program for this circuit is listed here:

```
Grover_Complete_Circuit_2_Qubits_Using_SDag_for_Tagging.qasm
// Initialize Quantum and Classical Registers
qreg q[2];
creg c[2];

// Generate All Combinations
h q[0];
h q[1];

// Tag |01>
sdg q[1];
h q[1];
cx q[0],q[1];
id q[0]; // Dummy gate for visually lining up circuit
h q[1];
id q[0]; // Dummy gate for visually lining up circuit
sdg q[1];
```

```
// Canceling Circuit
h q[0];
h q[1];
x q[0];
x q[1];
h q[1];
cx q[0],q[1];
id q[0]; // Dummy gate for visually lining up circuit
h q[1];
x q[1];
x q[0];
h q[1];
h q[0];

// Collapse Qubits
measure q[0] -> c[0];
measure q[1] -> c[1];
```

When you run this program on a real quantum computer, you should get an output similar to that shown in the following figure:

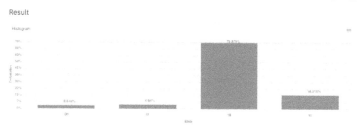

The bar with the 10 label is the tallest, indicating that this circuit collapses to $|q_0\rangle = |0\rangle$ and $|q_1\rangle = |1\rangle$ most often. (On the IBM Quantum Computer, $|q_0\rangle$ is reported as the rightmost bit and $|q_1\rangle$ is to the left of $|q_0\rangle$.) Thus, this program collapses to the tagged state $|01\rangle$ most frequently, confirming that the program works as designed.

f.   The two morals are:

- You may be tempted to think that since you're restoring most of the qubelet combinations back to their original states, the gate after the CZ gate should be the one that reverses the action of the gate before the CZ gate. That is, you may think to apply the S gate to reverse the action of the $S^\dagger$ on the bottom qubit. As the analysis shows, however, that's not the case. The moral: don't blindly apply the back-to-back-gates-to-restore-state quantum concept.

- Compare this circuit with that shown in Tagging the Best, on page 299, in which the $S^\dagger$ gates are replaced by X gates. The circuit with X gates tags $|10\rangle$, not $|01\rangle$, even though both circuits have the same topology. The moral: don't rush to design. Carefully analyze how gates rotate qubelets.

3. To compute the A_{H_3} matrix for three stacked H gates, you have to compute how it acts on the 2^3, or the 8, idealized states by taking the appropriate tensor products as follows:

$|000\rangle$ *Idealized State:*

$$
\begin{aligned}
H|0\rangle \otimes H|0\rangle \otimes H|0\rangle &= \tfrac{1}{\sqrt{2}}(|0\rangle + |1\rangle) \otimes \tfrac{1}{\sqrt{2}}(|0\rangle + |1\rangle) \otimes \tfrac{1}{\sqrt{2}}(|0\rangle + |1\rangle) \\
&= \tfrac{1}{2}(|00\rangle + |01\rangle + |10\rangle + |11\rangle) \otimes \tfrac{1}{\sqrt{2}}(|0\rangle + |1\rangle) \\
&= \tfrac{1}{2\sqrt{2}}(|000\rangle + |010\rangle + |100\rangle + |110\rangle + |001\rangle + |011\rangle + |101\rangle + |111\rangle)
\end{aligned}
$$

When represented as a vector, this state is the first column of A_{H_3}:

$$
\begin{pmatrix}
1 \\
1 \\
1 \\
1 \\
1 \\
1 \\
1 \\
1
\end{pmatrix}
$$

$|001\rangle$ *Idealized State:*

$$
\begin{aligned}
H|0\rangle \otimes H|0\rangle \otimes H|1\rangle &= \tfrac{1}{\sqrt{2}}(|0\rangle + |1\rangle) \otimes \tfrac{1}{\sqrt{2}}(|0\rangle + |1\rangle) \otimes \tfrac{1}{\sqrt{2}}(|0\rangle - |1\rangle) \\
&= \tfrac{1}{2}(|00\rangle + |01\rangle + |10\rangle + |11\rangle) \otimes \tfrac{1}{\sqrt{2}}(|0\rangle - |1\rangle) \\
&= \tfrac{1}{2\sqrt{2}}(|000\rangle + |010\rangle + |100\rangle + |110\rangle - |001\rangle - |011\rangle - |101\rangle - |111\rangle)
\end{aligned}
$$

When represented as a vector, this state is the second column of A_{H_3}:

$$
\begin{pmatrix}
1 \\
-1 \\
1 \\
-1 \\
1 \\
-1 \\
1 \\
-1
\end{pmatrix}
$$

$|010\rangle$ *Idealized State:*

$$H|0\rangle \otimes H|1\rangle \otimes H|0\rangle = \frac{1}{\sqrt{2}}(|0\rangle + |1\rangle) \otimes \frac{1}{\sqrt{2}}(|0\rangle - |1\rangle) \otimes \frac{1}{\sqrt{2}}(|0\rangle + |1\rangle)$$

$$= \frac{1}{2}(|00\rangle - |01\rangle + |10\rangle - |11\rangle) \otimes \frac{1}{\sqrt{2}}(|0\rangle + |1\rangle)$$

$$= \frac{1}{2\sqrt{2}}(|000\rangle - |010\rangle + |100\rangle - |110\rangle + |001\rangle - |011\rangle + |101\rangle - |111\rangle)$$

When represented as a vector, this state is the third column of A_{H_3}:

$$\begin{pmatrix} 1 \\ 1 \\ -1 \\ -1 \\ 1 \\ 1 \\ -1 \\ -1 \end{pmatrix}$$

$|011\rangle$ *Idealized State:*

$$H|0\rangle \otimes H|1\rangle \otimes H|1\rangle = \frac{1}{\sqrt{2}}(|0\rangle + |1\rangle) \otimes \frac{1}{\sqrt{2}}(|0\rangle - |1\rangle) \otimes \frac{1}{\sqrt{2}}(|0\rangle - |1\rangle)$$

$$= \frac{1}{2}(|00\rangle - |01\rangle + |10\rangle - |11\rangle) \otimes \frac{1}{\sqrt{2}}(|0\rangle - |1\rangle)$$

$$= \frac{1}{2\sqrt{2}}(|000\rangle - |010\rangle + |100\rangle - |110\rangle - |001\rangle + |011\rangle - |101\rangle + |111\rangle)$$

When represented as a vector, this state is the fourth column of A_{H_3}:

$$\begin{pmatrix} 1 \\ -1 \\ -1 \\ 1 \\ 1 \\ -1 \\ -1 \\ 1 \end{pmatrix}$$

$|100\rangle$ *Idealized State:*

$$H|1\rangle \otimes H|0\rangle \otimes H|0\rangle = \frac{1}{\sqrt{2}}(|0\rangle - |1\rangle) \otimes \frac{1}{\sqrt{2}}(|0\rangle + |1\rangle) \otimes \frac{1}{\sqrt{2}}(|0\rangle + |1\rangle)$$

$$= \frac{1}{2}(|00\rangle + |01\rangle - |10\rangle - |11\rangle) \otimes \frac{1}{\sqrt{2}}(|0\rangle + |1\rangle)$$

$$= \frac{1}{2\sqrt{2}}(|000\rangle + |010\rangle - |100\rangle - |110\rangle + |001\rangle + |011\rangle - |101\rangle - |111\rangle)$$

When represented as a vector, this state is the fifth column of A_{H_3}:

$$\begin{pmatrix} 1 \\ 1 \\ 1 \\ 1 \\ -1 \\ -1 \\ -1 \\ -1 \end{pmatrix}$$

$|101\rangle$ *Idealized State:*

$$\begin{aligned}
H|1\rangle \otimes H|0\rangle \otimes H|1\rangle &= \tfrac{1}{\sqrt{2}}(\,|0\rangle - |1\rangle\,) \otimes \tfrac{1}{\sqrt{2}}(\,|0\rangle + |1\rangle\,) \otimes \tfrac{1}{\sqrt{2}}(\,|0\rangle - |1\rangle\,) \\
&= \tfrac{1}{2}(\,|00\rangle + |01\rangle - |10\rangle - |11\rangle\,) \otimes \tfrac{1}{\sqrt{2}}(\,|0\rangle - |1\rangle\,) \\
&= \tfrac{1}{2\sqrt{2}}(\,|000\rangle + |010\rangle - |100\rangle - |110\rangle - |001\rangle - |011\rangle + |101\rangle + |111\rangle\,)
\end{aligned}$$

When represented as a vector, this state is the sixth column of A_{H_3}:

$$\begin{pmatrix} 1 \\ -1 \\ 1 \\ -1 \\ -1 \\ 1 \\ -1 \\ 1 \end{pmatrix}$$

$|110\rangle$ *Idealized State:*

$$\begin{aligned}
H|1\rangle \otimes H|1\rangle \otimes H|0\rangle &= \tfrac{1}{\sqrt{2}}(\,|0\rangle - |1\rangle\,) \otimes \tfrac{1}{\sqrt{2}}(\,|0\rangle - |1\rangle\,) \otimes \tfrac{1}{\sqrt{2}}(\,|0\rangle + |1\rangle\,) \\
&= \tfrac{1}{2}(\,|00\rangle - |01\rangle - |10\rangle + |11\rangle\,) \otimes \tfrac{1}{\sqrt{2}}(\,|0\rangle + |1\rangle\,) \\
&= \tfrac{1}{2\sqrt{2}}(\,|000\rangle - |010\rangle - |100\rangle + |110\rangle + |001\rangle - |011\rangle - |101\rangle + |111\rangle\,)
\end{aligned}$$

When represented as a vector, this state is the seventh column of A_{H_3}:

$$\begin{pmatrix} 1 \\ 1 \\ -1 \\ -1 \\ -1 \\ -1 \\ 1 \\ 1 \end{pmatrix}$$

$|111\rangle$ *Idealized State:*

$$H|1\rangle \otimes H|1\rangle \otimes H|1\rangle = \frac{1}{\sqrt{2}}(|0\rangle - |1\rangle) \otimes \frac{1}{\sqrt{2}}(|0\rangle - |1\rangle) \otimes \frac{1}{\sqrt{2}}(|0\rangle - |1\rangle)$$

$$= \frac{1}{2}(|00\rangle - |01\rangle - |10\rangle + |11\rangle) \otimes \frac{1}{\sqrt{2}}(|0\rangle - |1\rangle)$$

$$= \frac{1}{2\sqrt{2}}(|000\rangle - |010\rangle - |100\rangle + |110\rangle - |001\rangle + |011\rangle + |101\rangle - |111\rangle)$$

When represented as a vector, this state is the eighth column of A_{H_3}:

$$\begin{pmatrix} 1 \\ -1 \\ -1 \\ -1 \\ 1 \\ 1 \\ 1 \\ -1 \end{pmatrix}$$

Note that in each of these equations, $H|0\rangle$ and $H|1\rangle$ are as follows:

$$H|0\rangle = \frac{1}{\sqrt{2}}(|0\rangle + |1\rangle)$$

$$H|1\rangle = \frac{1}{\sqrt{2}}(|0\rangle - |1\rangle)$$

The matrix A_{H_3} made up of these columns is:

$$\begin{vmatrix} 1 & 1 & 1 & 1 & 1 & 1 & 1 & 1 \\ 1 & -1 & 1 & -1 & 1 & -1 & 1 & -1 \\ 1 & 1 & -1 & -1 & 1 & 1 & -1 & -1 \\ 1 & -1 & -1 & 1 & 1 & -1 & -1 & -1 \\ 1 & 1 & 1 & 1 & -1 & -1 & -1 & 1 \\ 1 & -1 & 1 & -1 & -1 & 1 & -1 & 1 \\ 1 & 1 & -1 & -1 & -1 & -1 & 1 & 1 \\ 1 & -1 & -1 & 1 & -1 & 1 & 1 & -1 \end{vmatrix}$$

As with the A_{H_2}, the only column that is symmetric is the first one associated with $|000\rangle$.

4. a.   The $|01\rangle$ state is tagged.

To check the tagged state on the IBM Quantum Computer, drag and drop the circuit's gates on the Console and then go to the Statevector section. You should see the chart on page 519.

Statevector

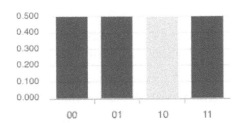

The lighter colored bar, second from right, is labeled 10. Since the IBM Quantum Computer reports states in the reverse order from the way we write it, the 10 state actually corresponds to 01.

b. The quantum state $|\varphi_{01}\rangle$ is:

$$|\varphi_{01}\rangle = \frac{1}{2}\begin{pmatrix} 1 \\ -1 \\ 1 \\ 1 \end{pmatrix}$$

c. To see how the Canceling Circuit removes the non-tagged quantum states, multiply its matrix $A_{Canceling}$ with the vector $|\psi_{01}\rangle$ for the tagged state:

$$A_{Canceling} \times |\psi_{01}\rangle = \frac{1}{2}\begin{bmatrix} 1 & -1 & -1 & -1 \\ -1 & 1 & -1 & -1 \\ -1 & -1 & 1 & -1 \\ -1 & -1 & -1 & 1 \end{bmatrix} \times \frac{1}{2}\begin{pmatrix} 1 \\ -1 \\ 1 \\ 1 \end{pmatrix}$$

$$= \frac{1}{4}\begin{pmatrix} 1 \\ -1 \\ -1 \\ -1 \end{pmatrix} - \frac{1}{4}\begin{pmatrix} -1 \\ 1 \\ -1 \\ -1 \end{pmatrix} + \frac{1}{4}\begin{pmatrix} -1 \\ -1 \\ 1 \\ -1 \end{pmatrix} + \frac{1}{4}\begin{pmatrix} -1 \\ -1 \\ -1 \\ 1 \end{pmatrix}$$

$$= \frac{1}{4}\begin{pmatrix} 1+1-1-1 \\ -1-1-1-1 \\ -1+1+1-1 \\ -1+1-1+1 \end{pmatrix}$$

$$= \begin{pmatrix} 0 \\ -1 \\ 0 \\ 0 \end{pmatrix}$$

That is,

$$A_{Canceling} \times |\varphi_{01}\rangle = -|01\rangle$$

Thus, the Canceling Circuit removes the non-tagged states from the quantum state. When this state collapses, 01 will be recorded in the classical registers.

d. The overall circuit with the Canceling Circuit appended to the Tagging Circuit is shown in the following figure:

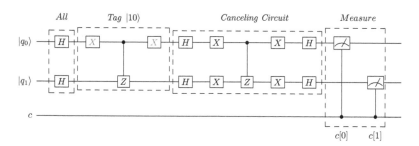

The code associated with this circuit is listed here:

Grover_01_Circuit.qasm

```
Line 1  // Initialize Quantum and Classical Registers
        qreg q[2];
        creg c[2];

     5  // Generate All Combinations
        h q[0];
        h q[1];

        // Tag |01>
    10  x q[0];
        // Control-Z gate
        h q[1];
        cx q[0],q[1];
        h q[1];
    15  // End of Control-Z gate
        x q[0];

        // Canceling Circuit
        h q[0];
    20  h q[1];
        x q[0];
        x q[1];
        // Control-Z gate
        h q[1];
    25  cx q[0],q[1];
        h q[1];
```

```
      // End of Control-Z gate
      x q[0];
      x q[1];
30    h q[0];
      h q[1];
      // End of Canceling Circuit

      // Collapse Qubits
35    measure q[0] -> c[0];
      measure q[1] -> c[1];
```

As described in Putting the Quantum Effects Together, on page 313, lines 12–14 and 24–26 implement the CZ gates in the Tagging and Canceling circuits, respectively.

e. When you run your program on a real quantum computer, the output will be similar to the following figure:

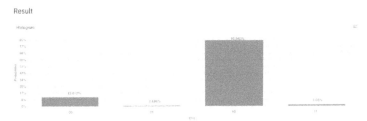

The bars represent the probability that each state is recorded in the classical registers. The third bar, labeled 10 at the bottom, is the tallest bar. Since the IBM Quantum Computer reverses the order of the states from the way we write it, this state actually corresponds to 01. In other words, this circuit eliminates or cancels out the non-tagged states, leaving only the 01 state.

5. a. Each iteration of Grover's Algorithm consists of a Tagging Circuit followed by a Canceling Circuit, not a single Tagging Circuit sitting in front of a sequence of Canceling Circuits.

   b. Within each Tagging Circuit and Canceling Circuit, sets of gates are mirrored. But each iteration is always a Tagging Circuit followed by a Canceling Circuit.

   c. The All Combinations set of gates is only applied once at the beginning of the algorithm to put the qubits in superposition. Each iteration just includes the Tagging Circuit followed by a Canceling Circuit.

6. a. The various sections of the circuit are annotated in the following figure:

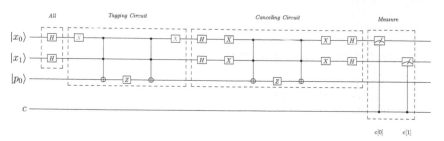

b. The tagged state is $|01\rangle$.

c. The code for the circuit is listed here:

```
Grover_Fundamental_Circuit_2_Qubits.qasm
// Initialize Quantum and Classical Registers
qreg q[3];
creg c[2];

// Generate All Combinations
h q[0];
h q[1];

// Tag |01>
x q[0];
ccx q[0],q[1],q[2];
z q[2];
ccx q[0],q[1],q[2];
x q[0];
id q[1]; // Dummy gate to visually line gates

// Canceling Circuit
h q[0];
h q[1];
x q[0];
x q[1];
ccx q[0],q[1],q[2];
z q[2];
ccx q[0],q[1],q[2];
x q[0];
x q[1];
h q[0];
h q[1];

// Collaspe Qubits
measure q[0] -> c[0];
measure q[1] -> c[1];
```

d. Since you used a simulator, the qubits will collapse to an exact result, as shown in the figure on page 523.

Result

The solitary state is labeled 10. Because the IBM Quantum Computer reverses the order of the states, the collapsed state actually corresponds to 01, which matches the tagged state identified earlier.

7. a. To tag $|1011\rangle$, place the X gates on the $|x_1\rangle$ qubit, as shown in the following circuit:

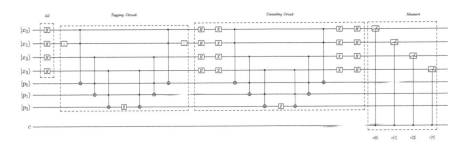

b. The code for the circuit with the X gates inserted to tag $|1011\rangle$ is listed here:

```
Grover_Fundamental_Circuit_4_Qubits_1_Iteration.qasm
// Initialize Quantum and Classical Registers
qreg q[7];
creg c[4];

// Generate All Combinations
h q[0];
h q[1];
h q[2];
h q[3];

// Tag |1011>
x q[1]; // X Gate on |x_1>
ccx q[0],q[1],q[4];
ccx q[2],q[4],q[5];
ccx q[3],q[5],q[6];
z q[6];
ccx q[3],q[5],q[6];
ccx q[2],q[4],q[5];
ccx q[0],q[1],q[4];
x q[1]; // X Gate on |x_1>
```

```
// Canceling Circuit
h q[0];
h q[1];
h q[2];
h q[3];
x q[0];
x q[2];
x q[3];
x q[1];
ccx q[0],q[1],q[4];
ccx q[2],q[4],q[5];
ccx q[3],q[5],q[6];
z q[6];
ccx q[3],q[5],q[6];
ccx q[2],q[4],q[5];
ccx q[0],q[1],q[4];
x q[0];
x q[1];
x q[2];
x q[3];
h q[0];
h q[1];
h q[2];
h q[3];

// Collapse Qubits
measure q[0] -> c[0];
measure q[1] -> c[1];
measure q[2] -> c[2];
measure q[3] -> c[3];
```

c. When you run this program on the IBM Quantum Computer Simulator, you'll get an output similar to the one in the following figure:

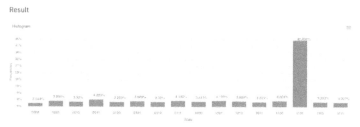

The tallest bar is easily recognizable—the one labeled 1101. Since the IBM Quantum Computer reverses the order of the states, this bar actually corresponds to 1011, matching the tagged state.

The qubits collapse to this state in roughly 46% of the shots.

d. Since this circuit has four independent qubits, you should run $O(\sqrt{4})$, or 2 iterations.

e. The modified code with two iterations is listed here:

```
Grover_Fundamental_Circuit_4_Qubits_2_Iterations.qasm
// Initialized Quantum and Classical Registers
qreg q[7];
creg c[4];

// Generate All 2^4=16 Combinations
h q[0];
h q[1];
h q[2];
h q[3];

//// ITERATION 1
// Tag |1011>
x q[1]; // X Gate on |x_1> to tag |1011>
ccx q[0],q[1],q[4];
ccx q[2],q[4],q[5];
ccx q[3],q[5],q[6];
z q[6];
ccx q[3],q[5],q[6];
ccx q[2],q[4],q[5];
ccx q[0],q[1],q[4];
x q[1];

// Canceling Circuit
h q[0];
h q[1];
h q[2];
h q[3];
x q[0];
x q[2];
x q[3];
x q[1];
ccx q[0],q[1],q[4];
ccx q[2],q[4],q[5];
ccx q[3],q[5],q[6];
z q[6];
ccx q[3],q[5],q[6];
ccx q[2],q[4],q[5];
ccx q[0],q[1],q[4];
x q[0];
x q[1];
x q[2];
x q[3];
h q[0];
h q[1];
h q[2];
h q[3];
```

```
//// ITERATION 2
// Tagging Circuit
x q[1];
ccx q[0],q[1],q[4];
ccx q[2],q[4],q[5];
ccx q[3],q[5],q[6];
z q[6];
ccx q[3],q[5],q[6];
ccx q[2],q[4],q[5];
ccx q[0],q[1],q[4];
x q[1];

// Canceling Circuit
h q[0];
h q[1];
h q[2];
h q[3];
x q[1];
x q[2];
x q[3];
x q[0];
ccx q[0],q[1],q[4];
ccx q[2],q[4],q[5];
ccx q[3],q[5],q[6];
z q[6];
ccx q[3],q[5],q[6];
ccx q[2],q[4],q[5];
ccx q[0],q[1],q[4];
x q[0];
x q[1];
x q[2];
x q[3];
h q[0];
h q[1];
h q[2];
h q[3];

// Collapse Qubits
measure q[0] -> c[0];
measure q[1] -> c[1];
measure q[2] -> c[2];
measure q[3] -> c[3];
```

f. When you run your code with two iterations of the Tagging and Can-
    celing circuits, you'll get an output that'll be similar to the one shown
    in the figure on page 527.

    The tallest bar again is the one labeled 1101. Thus, with two iterations,
    the collapsing of the qubits to the tagged state has surged to about
    91%—roughly nine out of ten shots.

Result

Where to Go from Here Solutions

Solutions for the exercises in Try Your Hand, on page 385.

1. a. The truth table for the constant function $F(|x\rangle) = |1\rangle$ is:

$|x\rangle$	$|y\rangle$	$F(|x\rangle)$	$|y\rangle \oplus F(|x\rangle)$
$|0\rangle$	$|0\rangle$	$|1\rangle$	$|1\rangle$
$|0\rangle$	$|1\rangle$	$|1\rangle$	$|0\rangle$
$|1\rangle$	$|0\rangle$	$|1\rangle$	$|1\rangle$
$|1\rangle$	$|1\rangle$	$|1\rangle$	$|0\rangle$

b. From the truth table in the previous part, when the bottom qubit $|y\rangle$ is $|0\rangle$, the state $|y\rangle \oplus F(|x\rangle)$ is $|1\rangle$, and vice versa. In other words, the U_F block is a pass-through for the top qubit and acts like a NOT (X) gate for the bottom qubit. The resulting Deutsch circuit is shown in the following figure:

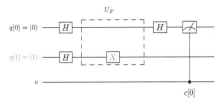

c. The Qiskit program for this circuit is listed below:

```
Line 1  # import Qiskit and other libraries
        import numpy as np
        import math
        from qiskit import(
     5  QuantumCircuit,
        QuantumRegister,
        ClassicalRegister,
        execute,
        Aer)
    10  from qiskit.visualization import plot_histogram
```

```
     # Set up circuit with 2 qubits and 1 classical register
     circuit = QuantumCircuit(2,1)
     circuit.x(1)
15   circuit.h(range(2))
     circuit.x(1)
     circuit.h(0)
     circuit.measure(0,0) # Measure gate on top qubit
     circuit.draw(output='mpl')
20
     # Get Backend and run circuit
     backend = Aer.get_backend('qasm_simulator')
     job = execute( circuit, backend, shots=1 )

25   # plot results
     hist = job.result().get_counts()
     plot_histogram( hist )
```

Note the NOT (X) gate on line 14 to set the bottom qubit to |1⟩ before splitting it by the H gate.

On line 23 the number of shots is set to 1.

After running this program, the Measure gate on the top qubit records a 0 in the classical register indicating that the function $F(\,|x⟩\,,\,|y⟩\,)$ is constant.

d. The Cirq program for this circuit is listed here:

```
Line 1  # Import Cirq libraries
        import cirq
        from cirq.ops import H, X

5       # Declare the qubits - place diagonally: q[0] at (0,0), q[1] at (1,1)
        q = [cirq.GridQubit(i, i) for i in range(2)]

        # Set up Circuit
        circuit = cirq.Circuit()
10      circuit.append([X(q[1]),H(q[0]), H(q[1]), X(q[1]), H(q[0])])
        circuit.append(cirq.measure(q[0], key='m'))

        print(circuit)

15      # Get a simulator to execute the circuit
        simulator = cirq.Simulator()
        # Simulate the circuit several times
        result = simulator.run(circuit, repetitions=1)
        # Print the results
20      print("Results:")
        print(result)
```

On line 6, declare the qubits and place them diagonally at (0,0) and (1,1) on the grid.

On line 18, the number of shots is set to 1.

After running this program, you'll find that the Measure gate on the top qubit records a 0, indicating that the function is constant.

e. Both circuits return identical results when run on the IBM and Google Quantum Computers, respectively. In each case, just a single shot confirms that the function is constant.

2. a. The truth table for the balanced function $F(|x\rangle)$ is:

$|x\rangle$	$|y\rangle$	$F(|x\rangle)$	$|y\rangle \oplus F(|x\rangle)$
$|0\rangle$	$|0\rangle$	$|1\rangle$	$|1\rangle$
$|0\rangle$	$|1\rangle$	$|1\rangle$	$|0\rangle$
$|1\rangle$	$|0\rangle$	$|0\rangle$	$|0\rangle$
$|1\rangle$	$|1\rangle$	$|0\rangle$	$|1\rangle$

b. To figure out the U_F block for this balanced function, first work out the matrix based on the truth table you determined in the previous part.

The state of the qubits on the left of the U_F, $|x\rangle$ and $|y\rangle$, map to those on the right, $|x\rangle$ and $|y\rangle \oplus F(|x\rangle)$), as follows:

$$|00\rangle \mapsto |01\rangle$$
$$|01\rangle \mapsto |00\rangle$$
$$|10\rangle \mapsto |11\rangle$$
$$|11\rangle \mapsto |11\rangle$$

In other words, the matrix A_{U_F} for U_F is:

$$A_{U_F} = \begin{bmatrix} 0 & 1 & 0 & 0 \\ 1 & 0 & 0 & 0 \\ 0 & 0 & 1 & 0 \\ 0 & 0 & 0 & 1 \end{bmatrix}$$

With a little bit of experimentation, you'll come up with the arrangement of the CNOT and NOT (X) gates, as shown in the following figure:

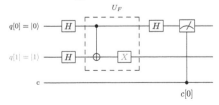

c. The Qiskit program for this circuit is listed here.

```
Line 1  # import Qiskit and other libraries
    -   import numpy as np
    -   import math
    -   from qiskit import(
    5   QuantumCircuit,
    -   QuantumRegister,
    -   ClassicalRegister,
    -   execute,
    -   Aer)
    10  from qiskit.visualization import plot_histogram

    -   # Set up circuit with 2 qubits and 1 classical register
    -   circuit = QuantumCircuit(2,1)
    -   circuit.x(1)
    15  circuit.h(range(2))
    -   circuit.cx(0,1)
    -   circuit.x(1)
    -   circuit.h(0)
    -   circuit.measure(0,0) # Measure gate on top qubit
    20  circuit.draw(output='mpl')

    -   # Get Backend and run circuit
    -   backend = Aer.get_backend('qasm_simulator')
    -   job = execute( circuit, backend, shots=1 )
    25
    -   # plot results
    -   hist = job.result().get_counts()
    -   plot_histogram( hist )
```

The bottom qubit is initialized to $|1\rangle$ by the X gate on line 14.

On line 24 the number of shots is set to 1.

After running this program, the Measure gate on the top qubit records a 1 in the classical register, indicating that the function $F(|x\rangle, |y\rangle)$ is balanced.

d. The Cirq program for this circuit is listed below:

```
Line 1  # Import Cirq Libraries
    -   import cirq
    -   from cirq.ops import CNOT, H, X

    5   # Declare qubits-place one below the other: q[0] at (0,0) & q[1] at (1,0)
    -   q = [cirq.GridQubit(i, 0) for i in range(2)]

    -   # Set up Circuit
    -   circuit = cirq.Circuit()
    10  circuit.append([X(q[1]),H(q[0]), H(q[1]),
    -       CNOT(q[0],q[1]), X(q[1]), H(q[0])])
```

```
    circuit.append(cirq.measure(q[0], key='m'))

    print(circuit)
15
    # Get a simulator to execute the circuit
    simulator = cirq.Simulator()
    # Simulate the circuit several times
    result = simulator.run(circuit, repetitions=1)
20  # Print the results
    print("Results:")
    print(result)
```

On line 6, declare the qubits and place them one below the other at (0,0) and (1,0) on the grid.

On line 19 the number of shots is set to 1.

After running this program, you'll find that the Measure gate on the top qubit records a 1, indicating that the function is balanced.

e.   Both circuits return identical results when run on the IBM and Google Quantum Computers, respectively. In each case, just a single shot confirms that the function is balanced.

3. a.   Since for half the input states, the function returns $|0\rangle$ and for the other half returns $|1\rangle$, the function F is balanced. You would need to sample F three times to establish its type.

    b.   The U_F block is shown in the following figure:

    c.   The truth table for U_F is as follows:

$|x_1\rangle$	$|x_2\rangle$	$|y\rangle$	$F(|x_0\rangle, |x_1\rangle)$	$|y\rangle \oplus F(|x_0\rangle, |x_1\rangle)$
$|0\rangle$	$|0\rangle$	$|0\rangle$	$|0\rangle$	$|0\rangle$
$|0\rangle$	$|0\rangle$	$|1\rangle$	$|0\rangle$	$|1\rangle$
$|0\rangle$	$|1\rangle$	$|0\rangle$	$|0\rangle$	$|0\rangle$
$|0\rangle$	$|1\rangle$	$|1\rangle$	$|0\rangle$	$|1\rangle$
$|1\rangle$	$|0\rangle$	$|0\rangle$	$|1\rangle$	$|1\rangle$
$|1\rangle$	$|0\rangle$	$|1\rangle$	$|1\rangle$	$|0\rangle$
$|1\rangle$	$|1\rangle$	$|0\rangle$	$|1\rangle$	$|1\rangle$
$|1\rangle$	$|1\rangle$	$|1\rangle$	$|1\rangle$	$|0\rangle$

d. The quantum circuit for the Deutsch-Jozsa algorithm to test the type of a two-qubit function is shown in the following figure:

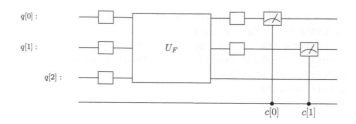

$q[0]$:

$q[1]$:

$q[2]$:

U_F

$c[0]$ $c[1]$

e. To figure out the matrix A_{U_F} for this truth table, work out the quantum state vector for each of the idealized states, but label the states in the IBM convention. That is, write the quantum state as a concatenated string of the states in the quantum registers $q[2]q[1]q[0]$:

Idealized state $|yx_1x_0\rangle = |000\rangle$:
   The output quantum state is $|000\rangle$. In vector form:

$$\begin{vmatrix} 1 \\ 0 \\ 0 \\ 0 \\ 0 \\ 0 \\ 0 \\ 0 \end{vmatrix}$$

   This vector is the first column of A_{U_F}.

Idealized state $|yx_1x_0\rangle = |001\rangle$:
   The output quantum state is $|101\rangle$. In vector form:

$$\begin{vmatrix} 0 \\ 0 \\ 0 \\ 0 \\ 0 \\ 1 \\ 0 \\ 0 \end{vmatrix}$$

   This vector is the second column of A_{U_F}.

Idealized state $|yx_1x_0\rangle = |010\rangle$:

The output quantum state is $|010\rangle$. In vector form:

$$\begin{pmatrix} 0 \\ 0 \\ 1 \\ 0 \\ 0 \\ 0 \\ 0 \\ 0 \end{pmatrix}$$

This vector is the third column of A_{U_F}.

Idealized state $|yx_1x_0\rangle = |011\rangle$:

The output quantum state is $|111\rangle$. In vector form:

$$\begin{pmatrix} 0 \\ 0 \\ 0 \\ 0 \\ 0 \\ 0 \\ 0 \\ 1 \end{pmatrix}$$

This vector is the fourth column of A_{U_F}.

Idealized state $|yx_1x_0\rangle = |100\rangle$:

The output quantum state is $|100\rangle$. In vector form:

$$\begin{pmatrix} 0 \\ 0 \\ 0 \\ 0 \\ 1 \\ 0 \\ 0 \\ 0 \end{pmatrix}$$

This vector is the fifth column of A_{U_F}.

Idealized state $|yx_1x_0\rangle = |101\rangle$:
The output quantum state is $|001\rangle$. In vector form:

$$\begin{vmatrix} 0 \\ 1 \\ 0 \\ 0 \\ 0 \\ 0 \\ 0 \\ 0 \end{vmatrix}$$

This vector is the sixth column of A_{U_F}.

Idealized state $|yx_1x_0\rangle = |110\rangle$:
The output quantum state is $|110\rangle$. In vector form:

$$\begin{vmatrix} 0 \\ 0 \\ 0 \\ 0 \\ 0 \\ 0 \\ 1 \\ 0 \end{vmatrix}$$

This vector is the seventh column of A_{U_F}.

Idealized state $|yx_1x_0\rangle = |111\rangle$:
The output quantum state is $|011\rangle$. In vector form:

$$\begin{vmatrix} 0 \\ 0 \\ 0 \\ 1 \\ 0 \\ 0 \\ 0 \\ 0 \end{vmatrix}$$

This vector is the eighth column of A_{U_F}.

Thus, the matrix A_{U_F} is:

$$A_{U_F} = \begin{bmatrix} 1 & 0 & 0 & 0 & 0 & 0 & 0 & 0 \\ 0 & 0 & 0 & 0 & 0 & 1 & 0 & 0 \\ 0 & 0 & 1 & 0 & 0 & 0 & 0 & 0 \\ 0 & 0 & 0 & 0 & 0 & 0 & 0 & 1 \\ 0 & 0 & 0 & 0 & 1 & 0 & 0 & 0 \\ 0 & 1 & 0 & 0 & 0 & 0 & 0 & 0 \\ 0 & 0 & 0 & 0 & 0 & 0 & 1 & 0 \\ 0 & 0 & 0 & 1 & 0 & 0 & 0 & 0 \end{bmatrix}$$

f.   The quantum program using Qiskit is listed here:

```
Line 1  import numpy as np
        import math
        from qiskit import(
        QuantumCircuit,
     5  QuantumRegister,
        ClassicalRegister,
        execute,
        Aer)
        from qiskit.visualization import plot_histogram
    10  from qiskit.quantum_info.operators import Operator


        U_F = Operator([
            [1,0,0,0,0,0,0,0],
    15      [0,0,0,0,0,1,0,0],
            [0,0,1,0,0,0,0,0],
            [0,0,0,0,0,0,0,1],
            [0,0,0,0,1,0,0,0],
            [0,1,0,0,0,0,0,0],
    20      [0,0,0,0,0,0,1,0],
            [0,0,0,1,0,0,0,0]
        ])



    25  # Check unitary
        print('Operatator is unitary:', U_F.is_unitary())

        circuit = QuantumCircuit(3,2)
        circuit.x(2)
    30  circuit.h(range(3))
        circuit.append(U_F,[0,1,2])
        circuit.h(range(2))
        circuit.measure([0,1],[0,1])

    35  circuit.draw(output='mpl')
```

```
     # Use simulator to run the circuit
     backend = Aer.get_backend('qasm_simulator')
     # Define the run parameters and execute
40   job = execute( circuit, backend, shots=1 )
     # Tally the results
     collapsed_states_array = job.result().get_counts()
     print(collapsed_states_array)
```

The matrix A_{U_F} is defined on lines 13–22 using Operator(). (To use this method, you have to first import it on line 10.) Set up the circuit on lines 28–33. The "gate" corresponding to the matrix A_{U_F} is appended to the circuit on line 31. On line 38 select the simulator to run this program. And on line 40, specify to run only once. Get the collapsed state on line 42.

g. The output of this program is:

```
{'01': 1}
```

Since the output state isn't 00, indicating that the function is not constant, it, therefore, must be balanced.

4. a. The first choice correctly assigns H gates to all three qubits.

The second choice, circuit.h(3), throws an error as the system will try to assign an H on q[3], which is out of range. The circuit was initialized with three qubits: q[0], q[1], and q[2].

The third choice, circuit.h(0,1,2), has three arguments. The h() method only allows a single argument: either the index of the qubit on which to place the H gate, or an array of qubits on which the H gates are placed.

The fourth choice, h.(range(2)), will assign H gates to only the first and second qubits, not all three.

b. The last choice correctly assigns H gates on both qubits and places the Measure gates on the qubits.

The first choice, circuit.measure(range(2),range(2)), works out to circuit.measure([0,1],[0,1]). That is, the Measure gate on the first qubit records the collapsed state in c[0], the first classical register, and the Measure on the second qubit records it in c[1]. The given circuit has it the other way around: the collapse of the first qubit is recorded in c[1], the second classical register, and the collapse of the second qubit is recorded in c[0], the first classical register.

The second choice throws an out-of-range error as the assignments of both the H gate and Measure gates use indices that are outside the range declared.

The third choice only assigns a single Measure gate that records the collapse of the second qubit in the first classical register. The circuit has two Measure gates.

5. a. This gate splits and rotates the triangle $|1\rangle$ qubelets. So the last description best describes the gate.

    b. Yes. The amplitude includes the complex number i, which indicates that the triangle $|1\rangle$ qubelets are rotated 90° anticlockwise. (See Rotating Qubelets Through Any Angle, on page 150, for the definition of the quantum state.)

    The probability that the $|0\rangle$ qubit collapses to $|1\rangle$ is calculated as shown below:

    $$\text{Probability of collapsing to } |1\rangle = \frac{i}{2} \times \frac{-i}{2}$$
    $$= \frac{1}{4}$$

    c. Yes. The amplitude includes the complex number $-i$, which indicates that the triangle $|1\rangle$ qubelets are rotated 90° clockwise. (See Rotating Qubelets Through Any Angle, on page 150, for the definition of the quantum state.)

    The probability that the $|0\rangle$ qubit collapses to $|1\rangle$ is calculated as shown below:

    $$\text{Probability of collapsing to } |1\rangle = i\frac{\sqrt{3}}{2} \times -i\frac{\sqrt{3}}{2}$$
    $$= \frac{3}{4}$$

    Notice that when working with complex numbers, "squaring the amplitude" is replaced by multiplying it with its complex conjugate.

    d. When this gate acts on the $|0\rangle$ qubit, the quantum state written as a vector is:

    $$|0\rangle \overset{G}{\mapsto} \begin{pmatrix} \frac{\sqrt{3}}{2} \\ \frac{i}{2} \end{pmatrix}$$

    This vector becomes the first column of the gate's matrix A_G.

When this gate acts on the $|1\rangle$ qubit, the quantum state written as a vector is:

$$|1\rangle \overset{G}{\longmapsto} \begin{pmatrix} \dfrac{1}{2} \\ -i\dfrac{\sqrt{3}}{2} \end{pmatrix}$$

This vector becomes the second column of the gate's matrix A_G.

Thus, the matrix A_G for this gate is:

$$A_G = \begin{bmatrix} \dfrac{\sqrt{3}}{2} & \dfrac{1}{2} \\ \dfrac{i}{2} & -i\dfrac{\sqrt{3}}{2} \end{bmatrix}$$

e. To check whether the A_G matrix is unitary, write a program using Qiskit as follows:

```
import numpy as np
import math
from qiskit import(
QuantumCircuit,
QuantumRegister,
ClassicalRegister,
execute,
Aer)
from qiskit.visualization import plot_histogram
from qiskit.quantum_info.operators import Operator

A_G = [
    [math.sqrt(3)/2, 1/2*complex(0,1)],
    [1/2, -math.sqrt(3)/2*complex(0,1)]
]

gate_G = Operator(A_G)

print('Operatator is unitary:', gate_G.is_unitary())
```

On line 10, import the Operator library. Define the A_G matrix on line 12. To make this matrix a quantum gate, pass it in an argument to the Operator object on line 17. And then, on line 19, check whether the A_G matrix is unitary.

Running this code will return True, indicating that the A_G matrix is unitary and can be safely used as a gate in a quantum circuit.

f. Add the following lines to the program in the previous part to set up
    the circuit and run it on the simulator:

```
Line 1  # Set up circuit
2       circuit = QuantumCircuit(2, 2)
3       circuit.append(gate_G, [0],)
4       circuit.x(1)
5       circuit.cx(0,1)
6       circuit.measure([0,1], [0,1])
7
8       circuit.draw(output='mpl')
```

On line 2, declare a circuit having two qubits and two classical registers. Then, on line 3 insert the G gate you just defined, followed by
the rest of the gates that make up the circuit.

g. To run the circuit on the simulator, append the following lines to the
    Qiskit code in the previous part:

```
Line 1  # Select Simulator
2       backend = Aer.get_backend('qasm_simulator')
3
4       # Define the run parameters and execute
5       job = execute( circuit, backend, shots=1024 )
6
7       # Tally the results
8       collapsed_states_array = job.result().get_counts()
9       print(collapsed_states_array)
```

On lines 2–9, set the program to run on a simulator and print the
results as an array.

After you run this circuit on the simulator, the two qubits will collapse
roughly into the following two states:

```
{'10': 763, '01': 261}
```

In fact, these qubits are entangled. If you see 1 in c[0], you're guaranteed to see 0 in the other classical register, and vice versa. As the
counts over the 1024 repetitions show, you'll see 0 in c[0] about three
times as often you'll see 1. (Remember that the order of the classical
registers in IBM's Quantum Computer is reversed from the way we've
labeled them. That is, the right-most bit corresponds to c[0].)

h. Yes, you could have defined the matrix as a U3 Universal gate.

6. a. No. The sum of probabilities of collapsing to the four idealized states is:

$$1^2 + (-2)^2 + 3^2 + -i \times i = 15 \neq 1$$

Since this sum doesn't add up to 1, the quantum state $|\varphi_0\rangle$ is not valid.

To make this quantum state valid, normalize it as follows:

$$|\varphi_0\rangle = \frac{1}{\sqrt{15}}|00\rangle - \frac{2}{\sqrt{15}}|01\rangle + \frac{3}{\sqrt{15}}|10\rangle - \frac{i}{\sqrt{15}}|11\rangle$$

b. The Qiskit program that initializes the circuit with $|\varphi_0\rangle$ is listed here:

```
Line 1  import numpy as np
     -  import math
     -  from qiskit import(
     -  QuantumCircuit,
     5  QuantumRegister,
     -  ClassicalRegister,
     -  execute,
     -  Aer)
     -  from qiskit.visualization import plot_histogram
    10  from qiskit.quantum_info.operators import Operator

     -  input_quantum_state = [ 1/math.sqrt(15),
     -                          -2/math.sqrt(15),
     -                          3/math.sqrt(15),
    15                          -complex(0,1)/math.sqrt(15)
     -                        ]

     -  # Define circuit with 3 qubits and 3 classical registers
     -  q = QuantumRegister(3)
    20  c = ClassicalRegister(3)
     -  circuit = QuantumCircuit(q,c)
     -  circuit.initialize(input_quantum_state, [q[0],q[1]])

     -  circuit.h([q[0],q[2]])
    25  circuit.cx(0,1)
     -  circuit.h(0)
     -  circuit.cx(2,1)
     -  circuit.measure(q, c)

    30  circuit.draw(output='mpl')
```

The quantum state $|\varphi_0\rangle$ is defined on line 12. On line 22 the circuit is initialized with the quantum state $|\varphi_0\rangle$. The gates are declared on lines 24–28.

c. To determine the number of independent states, use the num_unitary_factors() of the circuit object:

```
circuit.num_unitary_factors()
```

Since, the two CNOT gates entangle all three qubits, there's only a single independent set of qubits.

d. To run the circuit on the simulator, append the following lines to the Qiskit code in the previous part:

```
backend = Aer.get_backend('qasm_simulator')

# Define the run parameters and execute
job = execute( circuit, backend, shots=1024 )

# Tally the results
collapsed_states_array = job.result().get_counts()
print(collapsed_states_array)
```

The output of this circuit reported as an array will be similar to the following:

```
{'001': 158, '111': 147, '101': 5, '000': 28, '100': 308, '011': 7,
'110': 36, '010': 335}
```

You can also plot these states as a histogram with the following line:

```
plot_histogram( collapsed_states_array )
```

7. The list of quantum effects includes the following:

- Superposition.
- Rotating pentagon $|0\rangle$ and triangle $|1\rangle$ qubelets.
- Canceling qubelet combinations.
- Entangling qubelets.
- Back-to-back H gates for restoring states.

Bibliography

[Col09]   Transnational College of LEX. *What is Quantum Mechanics? A Physics Adventure*. Language Research Foundation, Cambridge, MA, second edition, 2009.

[FB16]   Terry L. Friesz and David Bernstein. *Foundations of Network Optimization and Games*. Springer, New York, NY, 2016.

[Knu11]   Donald E. Knuth. *The Art of Computer Programming, Volume 4A: Combinatorial Algorithms, Part 1*. Addison-Wesley, Boston, MA, second edition, 2011.

[Mer07]   N. David Mermin. *Quantum Computer Science: An Introduction*. Cambridge University Press, Cambridge, UK, 2007.

[Str93]   Gilbert Strang. The Fundamental Theorem of Linear Algebra. *The American Mathematical Monthly*. 1993.

[WG59]   Eugene P. Wigner and J. J. Griffin. *Group Theory and its Application to the Quantum Mechanics of Atomic Spectra*. Academic Press, Cambridge, MA, 1959.

[Wil11]   Colin P. Williams. *Explorations in Quantum Computing*. Springer, New York, NY, 2011.

[WR14]   Hermann Weyl and H. P. Robertson. *The Theory of Groups and Quantum Mechanics*. Martino Fine Books, Eastford, CT, 2014.

Index

Thank you!

How did you enjoy this book? Please let us know. Take a moment and email us at support@pragprog.com with your feedback. Tell us your story and you could win free ebooks. Please use the subject line "Book Feedback."

Ready for your next great Pragmatic Bookshelf book? Come on over to https://pragprog.com and use the coupon code BUYANOTHER2020 to save 30% on your next ebook.

Void where prohibited, restricted, or otherwise unwelcome. Do not use ebooks near water. If rash persists, see a doctor. Doesn't apply to *The Pragmatic Programmer* ebook because it's older than the Pragmatic Bookshelf itself. Side effects may include increased knowledge and skill, increased marketability, and deep satisfaction. Increase dosage regularly.

And thank you for your continued support,

Andy Hunt, Publisher

A Common-Sense Guide to Data Structures and Algorithms, Second Edition

If you thought that data structures and algorithms were all just theory, you're missing out on what they can do for your code. Learn to use Big O Notation to make your code run faster by orders of magnitude. Choose from data structures such as hash tables, trees, and graphs to increase your code's efficiency exponentially. With simple language and clear diagrams, this book makes this complex topic accessible, no matter your background. This new edition features practice exercises in every chapter, and new chapters on topics such as dynamic programming and heaps and tries. Get the hands-on info you need to master data structures and algorithms for your day-to-day work.

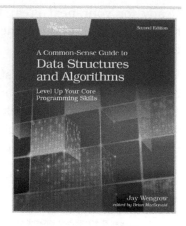

Jay Wengrow
(506 pages) ISBN: 9781680507225. $45.95
https://pragprog.com/book/jwdsal2

Build Location-Based Projects for iOS

Coding is awesome. So is being outside. With location-based iOS apps, you can combine the two for an enhanced outdoor experience. Use Swift to create your own apps that use GPS data, read sensor data from your iPhone, draw on maps, automate with geofences, and store augmented reality world maps. You'll have a great time without even noticing that you're learning. And even better, each of the projects is designed to be extended and eventually submitted to the App Store. Explore, share, and have fun.

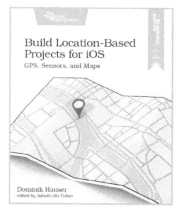

Dominik Hauser
(154 pages) ISBN: 9781680507812. $26.95
https://pragprog.com/book/dhios

iOS Unit Testing by Example

Fearlessly change the design of your iOS code with solid unit tests. Use Xcode's built-in test framework XCTest and Swift to get rapid feedback on all your code — including legacy code. Learn the tricks and techniques of testing all iOS code, especially view controllers (UIViewControllers), which are critical to iOS apps. Learn to isolate and replace dependencies in legacy code written without tests. Practice safe refactoring that makes these tests possible, and watch all your changes get verified quickly and automatically. Make even the boldest code changes with complete confidence.

Jon Reid
(358 pages) ISBN: 9781680506815. $47.95
https://pragprog.com/book/jrlegios

Become an Effective Software Engineering Manager

Software startups make global headlines every day. As technology companies succeed and grow, so do their engineering departments. In your career, you'll may suddenly get the opportunity to lead teams: to become a manager. But this is often uncharted territory. How do you decide whether this career move is right for you? And if you do, what do you need to learn to succeed? Where do you start? How do you know that you're doing it right? What does "it" even mean? And isn't management a dirty word? This book will share the secrets you need to know to manage engineers successfully.

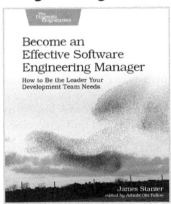

James Stanier
(396 pages) ISBN: 9781680507249. $45.95
https://pragprog.com/book/jsengman

Build Websites with Hugo

Rediscover how fun web development can be with Hugo, the static site generator and web framework that lets you build content sites quickly, using the skills you already have. Design layouts with HTML and share common components across pages. Create Markdown templates that let you create new content quickly. Consume and generate JSON, enhance layouts with logic, and generate a site that works on any platform with no runtime dependencies or database. Hugo gives you everything you need to build your next content site and have fun doing it.

Brian P. Hogan
(154 pages) ISBN: 9781680507263. $26.95
https://pragprog.com/book/bhhugo

Practical Microservices

MVC and CRUD make software easier to write, but harder to change. Microservice-based architectures can help even the smallest of projects remain agile in the long term, but most tutorials meander in theory or completely miss the point of what it means to be microservice based. Roll up your sleeves with real projects and learn the most important concepts of evented architectures. You'll have your own deployable, testable project and a direction for where to go next.

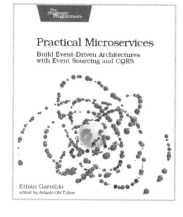

Ethan Garofolo
(290 pages) ISBN: 9781680506457. $45.95
https://pragprog.com/book/egmicro

Real-Time Phoenix

Give users the real-time experience they expect, by using Elixir and Phoenix Channels to build applications that instantly react to changes and reflect the application's true state. Learn how Elixir and Phoenix make it easy and enjoyable to create real-time applications that scale to a large number of users. Apply system design and development best practices to create applications that are easy to maintain. Gain confidence by learning how to break your applications before your users do. Deploy applications with minimized resource use and maximized performance.

Stephen Bussey
(326 pages) ISBN: 9781680507195. $45.95
https://pragprog.com/book/sbsockets

Programming Machine Learning

You've decided to tackle machine learning — because you're job hunting, embarking on a new project, or just think self-driving cars are cool. But where to start? It's easy to be intimidated, even as a software developer. The good news is that it doesn't have to be that hard. Master machine learning by writing code one line at a time, from simple learning programs all the way to a true deep learning system. Tackle the hard topics by breaking them down so they're easier to understand, and build your confidence by getting your hands dirty.

Paolo Perrotta
(340 pages) ISBN: 9781680506600. $47.95
https://pragprog.com/book/pplearn

The Pragmatic Bookshelf

The Pragmatic Bookshelf features books written by professional developers for professional developers. The titles continue the well-known Pragmatic Programmer style and continue to garner awards and rave reviews. As development gets more and more difficult, the Pragmatic Programmers will be there with more titles and products to help you stay on top of your game.

Visit Us Online

This Book's Home Page
https://pragprog.com/book/nmquantum
Source code from this book, errata, and other resources. Come give us feedback, too!

Keep Up to Date
https://pragprog.com
Join our announcement mailing list (low volume) or follow us on twitter @pragprog for new titles, sales, coupons, hot tips, and more.

New and Noteworthy
https://pragprog.com/news
Check out the latest pragmatic developments, new titles and other offerings.

Save on the ebook

Save on the ebook versions of this title. Owning the paper version of this book entitles you to purchase the electronic versions at a terrific discount.

PDFs are great for carrying around on your laptop—they are hyperlinked, have color, and are fully searchable. Most titles are also available for the iPhone and iPod touch, Amazon Kindle, and other popular e-book readers.

Send a copy of your receipt to support@pragprog.com and we'll provide you with a discount coupon.

Contact Us

Online Orders:	*https://pragprog.com/catalog*
Customer Service:	*support@pragprog.com*
International Rights:	*translations@pragprog.com*
Academic Use:	*academic@pragprog.com*
Write for Us:	*http://write-for-us.pragprog.com*
Or Call:	+1 800-699-7764